HOW TO REASSESS YOUR CHESS 4TH EDITION

HOW TO REASSESS YOUR CHESS 4TH EDITION

CHESS MASTERY THROUGH CHESS IMBALANCES

COMPLETELY REWRITTEN

INTERNATIONAL MASTER

JEREMY SILMAN

SILES PRESS   LOS ANGELES

First Edition

10 9 8 7 6 5 4 3 2

Library of Congress Cataloging-in-Publication Data

Silman, Jeremy.

How to reassess your chess : chess mastery through chess imbalances /
by Jeremy Silman. -- 4th ed.

p. cm.

Includes bibliographical references and index.

ISBN 978-1-890085-13-1 (alk. paper)

1. Chess. I. Title.

GV1449.5.S553 2010

794.1'2--dc22   2010042391

ISBN 978-1-890085-14-8 (cloth)

Distributed in Europe by New In Chess
www.newinchess.com

Cover design and photography by Wade Lageose for Lageose Design

SILES PRESS

3624 Shannon Road
Los Angeles, CA 90027

The first edition of How to Reassess Your Chess *was dedicated to Mr. Steven Christopher, who encouraged me to share my teaching ideas with the chess public. It seems only fitting that this final edition should also bear this extremely kind man's name.*

Contents

Preface

It's hard to believe, but *How to Reassess Your Chess* first hit the scene more than twenty years ago! As time went by, my ideas changed, expanded, and matured, and I improved each subsequent edition with new material that reflected this shift in perspective. This growing process continued and it became clear to me that a vast overhaul in my chess teaching philosophy necessitated a final edition. Those that enjoyed past editions will discover that I literally wrote this fourth edition from scratch—all new examples, all new prose, highlighted by lots of humor and some very original ways of presenting the material.

One thing was true of all the earlier editions: none were computer checked since powerful chess engines weren't readily available. However, now we're in a different age, and since the advent of computers in every household allows players of any rating to find the flaws in my (and others) analysis, I made a point of putting every position in this edition though a detailed analytical check by both Rybka 3 and Fritz 12. Though I concentrated on concepts over soulless analysis because I thought too many variations can drown out a book's message, there were times when I gave lines that I felt highlighted the point I was trying to make, or presented a detailed analysis that simply was so bizarre or exciting that I didn't have the heart not to include it in the festivities.

This fourth edition is the result of a lifetime of chess coaching and tournament competition. I've removed the extraneous elements from previous editions since I wanted to stay "on point" as much as possible. In fact, I tossed out anything and everything that I felt distracted from the book's real purpose: mastering the imbalances and allowing them to guide you to the correct plans and moves in most positions. On top of that, I also integrated quite a bit of chess psychology into the lessons—you'll find that many of these ideas have never been seen in any chess book before.

More than two decades after I wrote the first edition of *How to Reassess Your Chess*, I still get many kind letters from all over the globe. This new edition will please those that wanted more "Reassess" material, and it will also introduce a whole new generation to a system that makes chess far easier to grasp and thus far easier to enjoy.

It's always been my passion to help people who feel chess mastery is somehow beyond them to undergo a paradigm shift in their chess consciousness. *How to Reassess Your Chess, 4th Edition* was written to elicit that kind of experience. If it helps you, the reader, to grasp facets of chess that were previously invisible, then the years I spent writing this book will be very well spent.

Jeremy Silman
Los Angeles, CA

Acknowledgements

I would like to thank all my students, who, over the years, have given me permission to use their games as instructive templates. In particular, I must give Pam Ruggiero (aka girl-brain) a full salute for sending me dozens of her games, some of which showed a high level of chess understanding, and others which illustrated weaknesses that most amateur players also share (thereby making these examples invaluable).

A debt of gratitude is also owed to both *New In Chess*, which allowed me to use various quotes from their wonderful magazine, and www.chess.com, that let me reprint some of the articles I wrote for them.

I must give some love to my "posse"—Dr. Manuel Monasterio and the inimitable Vance Aandahl, Grandmasters Yasser Seirawan and Joel Benjamin, and International Masters John Watson, John Donaldson, Dr. Anthony Saidy, and Jack Peters. All of them helped with alternative piece names, analysis, and/or the sharing of general ideas that ultimately enriched the book.

Finally, I want to give a hearty thank you to Edward Winter, who offered important feedback on all things Capablanca, and International Master Elliott Winslow, who was happily retired from all chess-related things, only to be dragged screaming back into the fold when I nagged him, again and again, to put his life on hold and proof this book. Realizing that he had to shut me up or go insane, he ultimately complied.

Introduction

How to Reassess Your Chess is all about turning you, the chess student/lover of the game, into a player with superb positional understanding and skills. You may ask, "Why do I need another instructive chess book?" The answer is: Look at your rating. Look at your playing strength. Do you feel like you have superb positional skills? If not, wouldn't you like to have them?

As a chess teacher and, more importantly, as a student of the game that personally ran into many hard-to-scale learning plateaus, I fully understand the frustration chess fans experience when they find themselves frozen at a particular skill level. It's my belief that every player needs a firm chess foundation to reach his potential, and the lack of such a foundation more or less forestalls any real hope of attaining the chess heights most players dream of.

How to Reassess Your Chess, 4th Edition was designed for players in the 1400 to 2100 range. A close study of its contents will imbue the serious student with a rock solid positional chess foundation, an appreciation of planning plus an understanding of how to make logical plans based on the needs of the position, and surprising insights into previously ignored areas of chess psychology. By employing new ways of presenting concepts and games, and by making the book feel both personal and fun to read, I've done everything possible to ensure that studying becomes a joy and that the material presented—often viewed as too complex for the masses—will suddenly make sense and, as a result, be remarkably easy to retain.

Ideally, this fourth edition should be read from beginning to end. However, two indexes add to the ways the book can be read. One acts as both a games' index and a list-of-players' index, and can be used to find all the games in the book by a favorite player or, at a glance, just see who played whom. The other index is about chess concepts, and can prove to be a very useful study tool—for example, if you wish to study isolated pawns, just look that up in the index and go to each listed page. This lets you make a detailed examination of any particular concept that interests you.

A word about the examples: you'll notice that I've used games by grandmasters and also games by amateurs! I've used new games, and I've also used games from the seventeenth century! I made use of blitz games from the Internet, and even used the blitz players' online names. I have a simple philosophy: if a position or game is instructive, it's important. I don't care if Kasparov played it, or if it's beginner vs. beginner. In fact, lower rated games and/or blitz games often feature the kind of errors real players make, and this makes the example far more personal for a large range of readers.

To top it all off, I didn't shy away from employing humor if I felt it added to the lesson being taught, or improved the book's overall readability. Who said that it's not possible to study chess, learn advanced concepts, and laugh at the same time? I tell stories in the book that push home a point and also entertain. I used online handles because they are colorful and add to the example's fun-quotient. Why shouldn't chess study be fun?

I honestly believe that a thorough study of this book will take you on an enlightening journey that, ultimately, will shatter your old chess misconceptions and drag you laughing into a Golden Age of chess understanding and chess enjoyment.

Part One / The Concept of Imbalances

Contents

Imbalances
Learning the ABCs

"A sound plan makes us all heroes, the absence of a plan, idiots."
—G.M. Kotov, quoting a mysterious "chess sage."

At some time or other every tournament player learns a few opening lines, some tactical ideas, the most basic mating patterns, and a few elementary endgames. As he gets better and more experienced, he significantly adds to this knowledge. However, the one thing that just about everybody has problems with is planning. From class "E" (under 1200) to Master, I get blank stares when asking what plan they had in mind in a particular position. Usually their choice of a plan (if they have any plan at all) is based on emotional rather than chess-specific considerations. By emotional, I mean that the typical player does what he *feels* like doing rather than what the board is *telling* him to do. This somewhat cryptic sentence leads us to the following extremely important concept: **If you want to be successful, you have to base your moves and plans on the specific imbalance-oriented criteria that exist in the given position, not on your mood, tastes, and/or fears!**

Literally every non-master's games are filled with examples of "imbalance avoidance." Beginners, of course, simply don't know what imbalances are. Most experienced players have heard the term and perhaps have even tried to make use of them from time to time; however, once the rush of battle takes over, isolated moves and raw aggression (or terror, if you find yourself defending) push any and all thoughts of imbalances out the door. In this case, chess becomes an empty move-by-move, threat-by-threat (either making them or responding to them) affair.

What is this mysterious allusion to the chessboard's desires (i.e., doing what the chessboard wants you to do)? What are these "imbalance-oriented criteria" that we are going to have to become aware of, and how do we master their use? What, exactly, is a plan? To answer these questions, the first thing we have to do is understand that **an imbalance is any significant difference in the two respective positions**.

This sounds rather vacuous. How can such a simplistic thing be important? The answer is that it's far from simplistic, and that this easy-to-grasp concept allows any player from 1400 on up to understand most positions in a basic but logical fashion. In other words, where a position may have looked much too complex to fathom, the imbalances deconstruct it in a way that makes it user friendly.

Here's a simple example: if one side has more queenside space while the other side is staring at his opponent's weak pawn, those are the imbalances that delineate the moves and plans that both players would follow. In effect, the imbalances act as a roadmap that shows each side what to do.

The following list of the imbalances will be discussed all through this book:

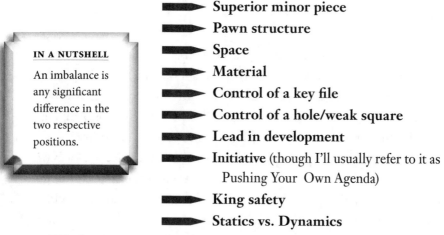

IN A NUTSHELL

An imbalance is any significant difference in the two respective positions.

- ➤ **Superior minor piece**
- ➤ **Pawn structure**
- ➤ **Space**
- ➤ **Material**
- ➤ **Control of a key file**
- ➤ **Control of a hole/weak square**
- ➤ **Lead in development**
- ➤ **Initiative** (though I'll usually refer to it as Pushing Your Own Agenda)
- ➤ **King safety**
- ➤ **Statics vs. Dynamics**

Whole sections are devoted to each imbalance on this list, but first let's take a quick, at times exaggerated, look at all of them. My immediate goal is to give you a feel for what imbalances are. My ultimate goal is to train your mind to embrace "Imbalance Consciousness"—a state where the use of imbalances becomes a natural and often unconscious process.

Superior Minor Piece — Bishops vs. Knights

Diagram 1

White to move

Compare white's Bishop, which is eyeing two position-penetrating diagonals, and black's slacker Knight, and you'll immediately know which minor piece is winning this battle. When we add other imbalances into the equation—White has an advantage in both central and queenside space, a target on a7 (which can be gobbled up by Ra1-b1-b7), and chances to mate (after Bc3 followed by Qd4) black's vulnerable King—one could understand if Black chose this moment to resign.

Diagram 2

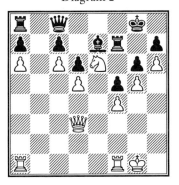

White to move

Black's Bishop, which is caged and useless, is no match for white's Knight, which is the ruler of the known universe. Combined with other favorable white imbalances—central, queenside, and kingside space, control of the hole on e6, and (after Ra1-b1-b7) pressure against a7 and c7—Black would be well advised to resign as quickly as possible.

Pawn Structure—Weak Pawns, Passed Pawns, etc.

Diagram 3

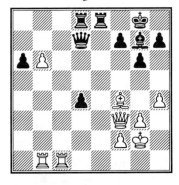

White to move

Black is a pawn up and he has two passed pawns to white's one passer. Yet, Black can resign! The reason? White's passed pawn is further advanced and all his pieces are working with the pawn to make sure it scores a touchdown on b8: **1.b7** (Threatening to win a whole Rook with 2.b8=Q.) **1...Rb8 2.Bxb8 Rxb8 3.Qc6 Qd8** (No better is 3...Qxc6+ 4.Rxc6 Be5 5.Rc8+ Kg7 6.f4 Bd6 7.Rxb8 Bxb8 8.Ra1 d3 9.Kf3 stopping any d-pawn nonsense and intending Rxa6 followed by Ra8) **4.Qc8 Be5 5.Qxd8+ Rxd8 6.Rc8**, 1-0.

Diagram 4

White to move

Black has a weak, isolated pawn on e6. Naturally, White dedicated his game plan to going after it. Thus far, white's Queen and Rooks are piling on the pressure but, since chess is a team game, he's not done yet! **1.Bh3** (A fourth white piece enters the assault against e6) **1...Nd8 2.Ng5** (The entrance of this fifth white piece into the battle for e6 dooms black's pawn.) **2...Bb8?** (This allows a trick that makes black's game even worse) **3.f5! gxf5 4. Bxf5** and e6 will still fall, but now black's King is sitting in "open air" (another imbalance White can use!).

Space—The Annexation of Territory

Diagram 5

White to move

A nightmare for Black, who is so cramped that he's gasping for air! White has claimed an appreciable advantage in space in virtually every sector. Note how black's lack of wiggle room leaves his pieces in a tight little box, while white's are happy free range pieces. In such positions the side with this much extra space will almost certainly win if he can find a way to break into enemy territory. Here White, who enjoys a wealth of riches, can accomplish this by preparing a queenside entry via c4-c5, or a kingside slaughter via g4-g5 (both pawn advances dare to demand even *more* space!). Thus, logical moves would be 1.c5, 1.g5, 1.Rcg1, or 1.Rh1.

Material — The Philosophy of Greed

Diagram 6

White to move

White is solid, but Black seems to have a nice, active position. If black's c-pawn was on c6 he wouldn't have any problems at all, but it's still on c7 and that gives White the chance to embrace his inner greed and claim a material imbalance: **1.Bxb7!** (Taking this pawn does a number of useful things: It gives White "endgame odds"—annoying for Black since the more pieces the materially challenged side trades, the closer to a pawn up endgame victory White gets; it creates a hole on c6 which allows White to grab control of the central light squares along the h1-a8 diagonal; it places great psychological pressure on Black who now has to get something going in an effort to justify the lost pawn.) **1...Kh8** (Black would love to take advantage of the errant white Bishop, but nothing works: 1...c6 2.Qc4+ picks up the c6-pawn; 1...Bg4 2.Qc4+ [2.f3 is also strong] 2...Kh8 3.Bc6 [3.Rd4 is a nice alternative] 3...Qf5 4.Rd2 intending f2-f4 when Black doesn't have enough compensation for the lost pawn.) and now White is very much on top after both **2.Bg2** (A "reset" that can be played if White suddenly freaks out a bit and decides that his Bishop is too far from home.) and **2.Qc4**, making new light-squared inroads.

Control of a Key File — Roads for Rooks

Diagram 7

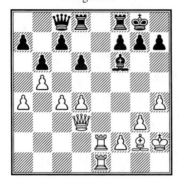

White to move

White is doubled on the e-file (important since it's the only open file on the board), he has more central and queenside space, and his Bishop is the master of the light-squares along the h1-a8 diagonal. Nevertheless, a lot of material has already been exchanged and the presence of Bishops of opposite colors leads one to believe that Black will be able to hold on. On top of all that, Black intends to swap Rooks along the e-file with ...Rde8. Fortunately for White, there's no need to worry since he has **1.Bc6!** (1...Qg4 2.Re4), permanently laying claim to the e-file. Now Black has no active plan and he can only sit back and passively wait, hoping that White won't be able to figure out a way to break through. In the position after 1.Bc6, both sides are playing for two possible results: Black will either lose or draw, and White will either win or draw. Obviously, nobody would want to be in black's shoes.

Control of a Hole/Weak Square — Homes for Horses

Diagram 8

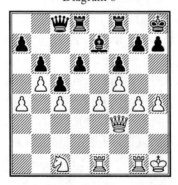

White to Move

White enjoys extra space all over the board, but this battle is clearly about the minor pieces: Both have fallen on hard times—black's Bishop is living in the dirt with no hope of improving its lot, while white's Knight dreams of a better home than the hovel on c1. However, unlike the poor Bishop, the Knight doesn't have to stay in the gutter. Two squares (the mansion on d5 and the mega-mansion on e6) beckon, and all White has to do is figure out how to get his horse there. Once you know your destination/goal, it's easy to find the path to it: **1.Nd3** (1.Ne2 is also good) followed by 2.Nf4 and 3.Ne6. Once the Knight reaches its dream square, a well-timed g4-g5 advance will finish Black off.

Lead in Development — You're Outnumbered!

A lead in development is a very dangerous thing, and the developmentally challenged side should do his best to keep things closed until his King gets safely castled and his other pieces find their way into the fray (thereby catching up in development and allowing a fight of equal armies).

Opening gambits are based on creating the imbalance of material vs. development, and they can give the attacker some quick wins if the opponent foolishly allows the position to open up.

1.e4 c5 2.d4 cxd4 3.c3 dxc3 4.Nxc3 Nc6 5.Nf3 d6 6.Bc4

White has three pieces out to black's one—on top of this, white's other pieces can be developed far faster than black's. It's clear that the second player has to be careful!

6...Nf6?!

The more prudent 6...e6 and 6...a6 are fine.

7.e5!

Diagram 9

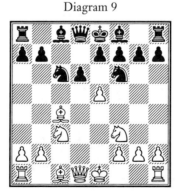

White offers a second pawn so he can rip open the central lines and gobble up the juicy King-treat on e8.

7...dxe5

Foolishly doing exactly what White wanted him to do. Though 7...Nxe5??
8.Nxe5 dxe5 9.Bxf7+ allows White to pick up the black Queen, 7...Ng4! refuses
to let White completely rip the position open.

8.Qxd8+ Nxd8?

8...Kxd8 is a better try.

9. Nb5 Kd7??

It's still a fight after 9...Rb8.

10.Nxe5+ Ke8 11.Nc7 mate.

Initiative — Calling the Shots

I consider the initiative to be a physical manifestation of a psychological
battle—both sides champion their view of things in the hope that the opponent
will have to eventually forgo his own plans and react to yours. Thus, I usually
refer to it as "Pushing Your Own Agenda" (presented in Part Four, Macho
Chess), since that clarifies what the initiative is and, at the same time, it tells
you how to get it!

Diagram 10

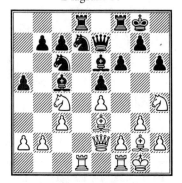

Black to move

White has just played 1.Nh4, intending 2.Ng6 (and, once g6 is covered, an
eventual Nf5). Other than this obvious threat, White would like to swing his
other Knight over to e3 and, from there, to d5. On the other hand, Black would
like to take advantage of the somewhat loose Knight on c4 and the undefended
pawn on a2.

Black can stop the Ng6 threat by 1...Kh7 but, by making a purely defensive
move, White gets the opportunity to continue to push his agenda by 2.Bxc5
Qxc5 (2...Nxc5 3.Ne3 idea Nd5) 3.Ne3 Nb6 (3...Bxa2?? 4.Bh3 and Black

is suddenly dead meat!) 4.Nd5! Bxd5 (4...Nxd5?? 5.exd5 Bxd5 6.Bxd5 Rxd5 7.Qe4+) 5.exd5 Ne7 6.Qe4+ Kh8 7.c4 and White has managed to create some interesting complications.

PHILOSOPHY

The initiative is a physical manifestation of a psychological battle.

Instead of handing White the initiative in this manner, Black should answer **1.Nh4** with **1...Qf7!** when Ng6 is stopped and c4 is under attack (it defends and pushes black's agenda at the same time!). Now the e3-square isn't available for White, but a Knight retreat hangs a2. Suddenly, Black is the one dictating the direction of the game and White has to scramble to keep his position together. His choices are all unappetizing:

- 2.Rxd7 fails to 2...Rxd7 3.Bxc5 Bxc4 4.Qg4 Bxf1 5.Bxf1 (5.Bxf8 Bxg2) 5...Rfd8 and Black is two Exchanges up!

- 2.Bxc5 Bxc4.

- 2.Rd5!? (an imaginative try to infuse some energy into his position and regain the initiative—White is hoping for 2...Bxd5 3.exd5 Ne7 4.Nxa5 Bxe3 5.fxe3 Nxd5 6.Nf5) 2...b6! ending the nonsense and leaving White in a quandary.

- 2.b3 Bxc4 3.bxc4 Bxe3 4.fxe3 and White is left with an exceptionally ugly pawn formation.

King Safety—Dragging Down the Enemy Monarch

Diagram 11

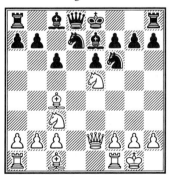

White to move

This isn't a book about attack, but I felt that King safety should be stressed since it's a major factor (imbalance) in many games. In particular, this book will point to an uncastled King as something that should usually be avoided like the plague. In the diagrammed position, White has sacrificed a pawn but enjoys a lead in development and a safe King. Black's King, though, is still in the center and White punishes it before it can get castled.

1.Nxf7! Kxf7 (Better is 1...Qc7 but there's really no reason for Black to continue the game after 2.Nxh8) **2.Qxe6+ Kg6 3.Bd3+ Kh5 4.Qh3** mate.

The focus in this book won't be on attacking techniques, but rather on recognizing the dangers of a central King—this will allow you to punish this transgression when it occurs in your games, and to avoid falling victim to this "illness" yourself.

Statics vs. Dynamics—The Battle Between Short Term and Long Term Imbalances

Statics and dynamics occur in every phase of the game. In general, a dynamic plus is something that needs to be used in a reasonably quick manner—either to score a knockout, or to create a long lasting static advantage of your own. A static imbalance gives its owner something that will be around for a long time—it can be part of an opening system (thus appearing in the first ten moves), cause both sides to march to a particular tune in the middlegame, and still be influencing play right into the endgame.

Diagram 12

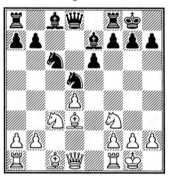

White to move

White has an isolated d-pawn. Black views the pawn as a static weakness: quite a few of his pieces can gang up on it, and the fine d5-square is also a feather in black's cap. White views the pawn as a dynamic strength: it gains central space, controls the two important squares on c5 and e5, and allows White (whose extra space makes his pieces more active than their black counterparts) to build up a nasty kingside attack in many lines. Countless world-class players have championed both sides of this position.

Planning – Creating Your Own Future

In the third edition of *How To Reassess Your Chess*, I gave a thinking technique that I had personally found useful over the years. I felt it might prove equally useful for higher-level amateurs who had been struggling to create logical plans. However, the passage of time (which always brings new experience and insight) drastically changed my view about the practicality of *any* complex system of planning. My change of heart came about when I corresponded with students and lovers of chess from all over the world who were obsessed with finding plans (or were simply trying to grasp what a plan really was), and as a result hadn't fully integrated the imbalances into their play. By breaking imbalances and plans into two separate things, I had inadvertently caused many hard working students of the game to lose sight of the one goal I had intended to push: **master the imbalances**.

Though I no longer have faith in convoluted planning systems, I *have* retained the firm belief that fully understanding the imbalances is 100% attainable for players 1400 and up. Note the word "understanding." This book trains you to recognize the imbalances in any board situation, to understand what each imbalance offers, and to know how to make use of it or diffuse it, depending on which side of the imbalance you are sitting on.

Once you gain this knowledge and integrate it into your play, you'll find that something surprising happens: the imbalances alone will often "tell" you what to do (or, at the very least, give you a firm push in the right direction)! Thus, if you possess a dynamic advantage you will know that your move needs to be dynamic in nature—a quiet positional move most likely won't address the needs of the position. If your opponent has a glaringly weak pawn on an open file, you will know that at some point you will most likely want to go after it by placing your Rooks on that file. If you have a huge advantage in space, you will think twice before trading a bunch of pieces and alleviating some of his cramp.

You can call this adherence to the dictates of the imbalances a plan, or simply a logical move or series of moves. The name isn't important—mastering the imbalances *is* important and makes all this other stuff possible.

Need proof? Go back and look at our first twelve examples. These are illustrations of the imbalances and how to use them, but in every case the imbalances presented simple but effective plans (a series of moves—be it two or four or eight or more—that logically makes use of your positive imbalances is indeed a plan).

Let's take a look at some games where imbalance-basics and impressive plans join together as one.

> **IN A NUTSHELL**
>
> The imbalances alone will lead you to the right move(s) in most positions, or even help you create a detailed plan.

V. Topalov - K. Sasikiran, Sofia 2007

1.d4 Nf6 2.c4 e6 3.Nc3 Bb4 4.e3 b6 5.Bd3 Bb7 6.Nf3 0–0 7.0–0 d5 8.a3 Bd6 9.cxd5 exd5 10.b4 Nbd7 11.b5 Ne4 12.Bb2 Re8 13.a4 Re6 14.Ne2 a5

Diagram 13

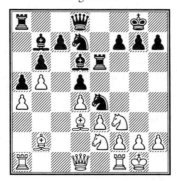

White to move

Once you've read this book and fully integrated all its lessons, a glance will give you the following information:

- White has an advantage in queenside space.

- Black has a potentially weak pawn on c7.

- If Black pushes the c7-pawn to c6 or c5, bxc6 will leave Black with a weak pawn on b6 and a hole on b5.

- Black's d5-pawn is weak since it can't be defended by another pawn.

- Black's only source of counterplay is on the kingside—his d6-Bishop, e6-Rook, e4-Knight, and Queen are all eyeing that area.

- Black's b7-Bishop, which is defending d5, is playing a purely defensive role.

- Black's dark-squared Bishop is giving firm support to the c7-pawn while also playing a key role in any kingside attack that he might drum up.

- White's b2-Bishop is inactive.

Armed with this imbalance breakdown, it might strike you that exchanging white's worst piece for one of black's best would be a great idea. And so, with no calculation, planning, or further rumination, White could confidently play the move Topalov himself chose.

15.Ba3!

White forces the exchange of his worst piece for the critically important Bishop on d6.

15...Rc8 16.Bxd6 cxd6

Of course, 16...Rxd6 was possible, but then c7 would be a permanent source of concern. After 16...cxd6, that's no longer the case. In addition, the e5-square is also covered (ending all Nf3-e5-c6 ideas). Of course, 16...cxd6 comes with its own baggage: the d5-pawn is weak and will need babysitting for the rest of the game.

17.Rc1 Ndf6 18.h3

Diagram 14

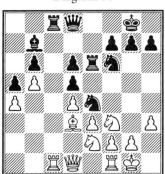

Topalov (*New In Chess* 4, 2007) now said: "As you can see, all this is not about concrete lines, but about clear positional weaknesses. I knew that it didn't matter how long it would take me, but in the end all the Rooks would be exchanged, further highlighting his structural problems."

Topalov, one of the greatest attacking players in the world, is making it clear that his course in this game isn't dependent on his personal tastes (i.e., attack), but rather on the dictates of the board (a quiet buildup in accordance with the imbalances).

18...Re7 19.Qb3 h6 20.Rxc8 Qxc8 21.Rc1 Rc7 22.Rxc7 Qxc7 23.Qc2

Topalov had this to say in regard to the position that would result after the exchange of Queens: "I can chase away the Knight on e4, transfer my Bishop to b3 and sooner or later I will exert pressure with two pieces on d5 and push my kingside pawns."

Okay, there's no getting around it—this is clearly a plan! But did he use any strange "system" to create it? No, this too is based on the imbalances: he will chase away black's advanced Knight by f2-f3 (Knights need advanced squares to be effective—thus he intends to turn a good enemy piece into a passive one), he'll aim his pieces against the weakness on d5, and then he'll gain space on the kingside by advancing his pawns there (which would give him yet another positive imbalance to work with).

23...Qe7 24.Qc1

White's Queen already controls the c-file, but now it also defends e3. This shows white's intention to chase black's one active piece away with an eventual f2-f3 (when the e3-pawn will be happy to have some support).

24...g6 25.Nh2 Kg7 26.h4

This gains kingside space, deprives the e4-Knight of the g5-square, and threatens to win by f3.

26...Ne8 27.f3 N4f6 28.Nf1 h5 29.Nf4 Nd7

29...Nc7 followed by ...Ne6 was a better setup.

30.Qe1 Nf8 31.Qg3 Kh6 32.Nxh5!?

32.Kf2 followed by Nf1-d2-b1-c3 would have continued the grind and maintained the pressure. However, Topalov decides to up the ante in his opponent's time pressure. Can Black find all the right defensive moves with his clock rapidly ticking down to nothing?

The rest of the game, which has nothing to do with our theme, is given with minimum comments:

32...gxh5 (32...Kxh5?? 33.Qf4 wins outright) **33.Qg8 f5** (The only move) **34.Ng3 Ng7 35.Bxf5 Ng6 36.Bxg6 Kxg6 37.Nxh5! Qxe3+ 38.Kh2 Qe7??** (Black cracks in time trouble and plays the losing move. Correct was 38...Qxd4 when a draw would be the most likely outcome) **39.Nf4+ Kf6 40.g4 Qf7 41.Qd8+ Qe7 42.Qg8 Qf7 43.Qd8+ Qe7 44.Qxe7+** (44.Qxb6 was even stronger) **44...Kxe7 45.Kg3 Ne6 46.Nxe6 Kxe6 47.f4 Bc8 48.f5+ Kf7 49.h5 Bd7 50.h6 Kg8 51.Kf4 Be8 52.Kg5 Kf7 53.h7 Kg7 54.h8=Q+ Kxh8 55.Kf6 Bxb5 56. Ke7 Bd3 57.f6 Bg6 58.f7 Bxf7 59.Kxf7**, 1-0.

Here's another example of a player finding a logical (and in this case deadly) sequence of moves by the simple act of trying to enhance an already existing imbalance.

Diagram 15

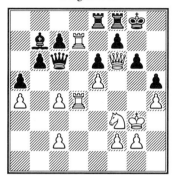

N. Short - J. Timman, Tilburg 1991
White to move

It's clear that White is in complete control of this position—he owns the d-file (thus turning black's Rooks into passive spectators) and his Queen is firmly ensconced on one of black's weakened kingside dark squares. On the other hand, Black can hardly make a move, which means that White doesn't have to fear any incoming fire. If you were to agonize over a plan without consulting the imbalances, you might become frustrated. However, if you merely asked, "I own the kingside dark squares. What other pieces can penetrate on them?" then you would be faced with a limited amount of options:

> 1.Ng5 is the obvious candidate—it leaps to a dark square and threatens to chop on f7. Unfortunately, 1...Qxg2+ would put a damper on white's celebrations.

> 1.Rf4 takes up residence on f4 and intends to follow up with Rxf7, but 1...Qxd7 would be embarrassing.

> And this leaves only one other white piece that can drive down the dark-square highway—white's King! But now we suddenly run into our beginner training/conditioning, which tells us to keep the King at home until an endgame is reached. And it's this very fact that makes this game so charming!

1.Kf4!

This move shocks many players, but if you had a Bishop on d2 would you hesitate to play Bh6, which forces mate? Of course not! Then, if it's safe, why not use the King in the same way?

1...Bc8 2.Kg5, 1-0. The threat of Kh6 followed by mate on g7 ends the game. For example, 2...Kh7 3.Qxg6+ (or 3.Rxf7+ Rxf7 4.Qxf7+ Kh8 5.Kh6 when white's King finishes up its journey with deadly effect) 3...Kh8 4.Qh6+ Kg8 5.Kf6 and mate follows white's total domination of the kingside dark squares.

> **PHILOSOPHY**
>
> Imbalances are the doorway to planning.

So was Short's play a plan, or an illustration of the power of "Imbalance Consciousness?" Call it anything you like, but pay attention to the thing that allowed you to find the solution: the imbalances!

Let's take a moment off from our look at heady concepts and strange new philosophies and have a bit of fun. We're going to look at a game through the eyes of three kinds of players. One (Mr. Metallic) shows us a person who dreams of thinking like a machine. The second is a guy (Mr. Pink) who knows nothing of imbalances, but seeks to live and die by the "Chess is about material and threats" mind-stream. Our third (Mr. Orange) is an imbalance aficionado. The first two will team up and take White, the third will handle the Black pieces. Note that the White players will be better at calculation, while Black will have a superior knowledge of opening theory.

Mr. Metallic and Mr. Pink vs. Mr. Orange, Fantasyland 2009

Mr. Metallic: Any reasonable move leaves us 0.12 to 0.18 ahead. I'll go for that 0.18 figure!

Mr. Pink: I want to play 1.e4. Does this hang anything? No. So far so good! Are we threatening anything after 1.e4? Not yet, but once we get our Bishop and Queen out, we'll shred the sucker! Okay, 1.e4 is good!

1.e4

Mr. Orange: They gained central space, freed their light-squared Bishop and Queen, and took control over the d5-square. 1.e4 is obviously a good move, but my very strange looking opponents seem to be aggressive sorts so I'll throw a bit of violence back at them and see how they react.

1...d5

Mr. Metallic: Ah, an inferior reply. Now we're 0.37 up! Victory is almost ours!

Mr. Pink: Danger! Danger! Our e-pawn is hanging! Danger! We must take his pawn and, when he recaptures, we'll bring a new attacking piece out and attack his Queen at the same time! Oh yeah, this is going to be good.

2.exd5

Mr. Orange: They played the best reply. I'll develop a piece and take back on d5 with my Knight. I've looked this line over a bit and it's interesting—especially if they don't know what they are doing!

2...Nf6

Mr. Metallic: I think we can win material! By definition, I will eat everything that's offered.

Mr. Pink: He didn't allow 2...Qxd5 3.Nc3 when we're attacking his Queen. He would be dead meat then. Now I think we can win a pawn with 3.c4. True, in that case he can attack our Queen with 3...Bg4 but we could attack him right back with 4.f3. Am I good or what?

3.c4

Mr. Orange: The vacant look in their eyes tells me that they don't have a clue. Of course, I can't be sure of that. Perhaps they intend to answer my 3...c6 with 4.d4 when we will transpose into the Panov-Botvinnik Variation of the Caro-Kann. Since I'm mainly a Caro player, I don't mind this at all.

3...c6

Mr. Metallic: He's giving us a pawn! We'll have at least a 0.26 plus.

Mr. Pink: We can chop on c6 when we're a solid pawn up. What if we take by 4.dxc6 and he attacks us with 4...Bg4? We can still attack him back with 5.f3, but ... I see something that's really cool: 5.cxb7!! Bxd1 6.bxa8=Q and it's over! I'm a genius!

4.dxc6

Mr. Orange: Wow! I didn't think they would go for that. I'm now a pawn down but after I recapture with my Knight I'll have a lead in development (which gives me a dynamic plus and chances for attack), control of the hole on d4 (a long-term static advantage), and pressure against white's backward d-pawn (another long-term static plus).

4...Nxc6

Diagram 16

Mr. Metallic: A pity! The other recapture gave us at least a 0.72 advantage. Now he has some play, but a pawn is a pawn, so we should be happy.

Mr. Pink: So we're already a pawn up. Does he have any threats? Just …Bg4, but we can answer it with Nf3 or Be2 or f3 or just about anything. All we need to do now is get our guys out, castle, and our extra pawn will win in the endgame—isn't that what the grandmasters always do?

5.Nc3

Mr. Orange: I own d4, but I would like to increase my control over that square again. I also need to develop my dark-squared Bishop and castle. 5…e5 seems to address all these issues. Of course, …e5 does weaken the d5-square, but he's so far behind in development that there's no way for him to take advantage of d5 for a long time to come.

5…e5

Mr. Metallic: 0.09. We're still in charge and we're still a pawn ahead.

Mr. Pink: He intends to answer 6.Nf3 with 6…e4, attacking our Knight. Fortunately, we should play 6.d3 when his pawn advance is stopped. Then we can follow with Nf3, Be2, 0-0, and we're on our way to glory.

6.d3

Mr. Orange: Okay, I have all sorts of good positional options and I'm a bit confused. 6…Bb4 and 6…Bc5 both look promising, though I don't really want to chop on c3 (after 6…Bb4) since after bxc3 he would suddenly cover the d4-hole. I'll try 6…Bf5 since that targets his weakness on d3 while also preparing the well-timed dynamic thrust …e5-e4 if the situation calls for it. 6…Bf5 also gives me …Qd7 followed by …0-0-0 when I'm really piling up on d3!

6…Bf5

Mr. Metallic: 0.26 up and an extra pawn—it still looks nice for us.

Mr. Pink: Can we make any threats? 7.Qf3 hits his Bishop but 7…Nd4 defends it, attacks our Queen, and threatens …Nc2+. No, we can't do that! We'll just continue our plan—develop, castle, and slide into a pawn up endgame victory. After 7.Nf3 we don't have to worry about 7…e4 since he would be helping us reach that pawn up endgame.

7.Nf3

Mr. Orange: It's hard to go wrong here. I can play 7…Qd7 followed by 8…0-0-0 and snip off d3, but that gives him time to castle. I really like the fact that his King is sitting in the middle, so I'll play more aggressively. 7…Bb4 is very tempting since it makes …e5-e4 even stronger. But 7…e4 also looks good, and it forces him to take a path of my choosing. There's just one problem: what happens after 7…e4 8.Nh4? How about 8…Bg4 9.f3 exf3 10.Nxf3 Bc5 and if I can castle, his Swiss cheese position should allow me to wipe him out.

7...e4

Mr. Metallic: White remains 0.17 ahead with 8.Nh4. Let's do it! Besides, I think we're doing well after 8.Nh4 Bg4 9.f3 exf3 10.Nxf3 Bc5 11.Qe2+!

Mr. Pink: 8.Nh4 does attack his Bishop, but after 8...Bg4 he just attacks us back. Besides, aren't Knights on the rim supposed to be grim? Or was that dim? Well, in any event I don't like it at all. And your 8.Nh4 Bg4 9.f3 exf3 10.Nxf3 Bc5 11.Qe2+ runs into 11...Kd7! when his threat of ...Re8 scares me to death. Let's just take on e4 and go into a pawn up endgame.

Mr. Metallic: But, I see lots of other variations after 11...Kd7. Let me show you!

Mr. Pink: No. We're playing 8.dxe4 and that's that.

8.dxe4

Mr. Orange: I can take on e4 or take on d1. Both look good since any opening of the position has to favor my lead in development. I'll take on e4 and see if he wants to capture on d8 and bring my Rook into play.

8...Nxe4

Mr. Metallic: Let's play 9.Be3 Bb4 10.Qb3 Qf6 11.Rc1 Bh3 12.Qc2 Bf5 13.Bd3 Nxc3 14.bxc3 Qxc3+ 15.Qxc3 Bxd3 16.Nd4 0–0–0 17.Nxc6 Bxc3+ 18.Rxc3 bxc6 19.f3 (19.Bxa7 Rhe8+ 20.Be3 Re4 21.Kd2 Bxc4+ is 0.00) 19...Rd7 20.Kf2, 0.22 up for us!

Mr. Pink: Say what? I didn't understand any of those moves. It all looks insane. Who would play a move like 11...Bh3, and even if the line you gave did occur, the opposite colored Bishops make it a dead draw. You're starting to freak me out, Mr. Metallic! Instead of that garbage, let's just play 9.Be2 and try to castle!

9.Be2

Mr. Orange: He's going to castle. I have to play with as much energy as possible or he'll get his house in order. 9...Bb4, developing with threats, has to be right since 10.Qb3 runs into 10...Nc5.

9...Bb4

Diagram 17

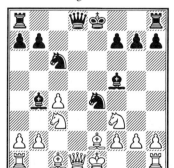

Mr. Metallic: 10.Qb3 Nc5 11.Qd1 Bxc3+ 12.bxc3 Qxd1+ (12...Qa5!?) 13.Bxd1 0–0–0 is -0.34 so we can't do that! We have to play 10.Bd2.

Mr. Pink: Why would we move our Queen to b3 and then back to d1? You're spouting gibberish! 10.Bd2 is clearly the way to go.

10.Bd2

Mr. Orange: He threatens to trade a lot of stuff off so I'll capture on d2 and leave him in a nasty pin.

10...Nxd2. We'll end our three-way battle here. After **11.Nxd2** (11.Qxd2 Qxd2+ 12.Nxd2 Nd4 13.Bd1 0–0–0 14.0–0 Rhe8 is miserable for White since all his pieces are bad, and ...Bd3 is a strong threat. However, 14.Nf1! is a better defense.) **11...Nd4 12.Rc1** (12.0–0 Bc2 13.Qe1 0–0 and white's in bad shape) **12...0–0 13.Nf1** (13.0–0 loses the Exchange to 13...Nxe2+ 14.Qxe2 Bd3) **13...Qg5** (13...Qb6 might have been best) **14.Ne3 Rad8 15.h4**, we find that we were following the game B. Savchenko - K. Asrian, Moscow 2007. Now **15...Qf6** was very strong: **16.0–0** (16.Nd5 Rxd5 17.cxd5 Re8) **16...Nxe2+ 17.Qxe2 Bd3** winning material.

What was the point of this example? These color-coded players are representations of three real human types:

Mr. Metallic

In an age where every serious player has a powerful chess engine, I've watched a chess pandemic appear that's unlike anything that's ever been seen before: While following live grandmaster games, the masses of chess fans all suffer from a shared chess psychosis—they think they know exactly what's going on. Topalov plays some extremely complex move and thousands write in eerie unison, "Topalov is 1.02 up! He's going to win!"

They are parroting their engine's assessment, but they seem to mistake it for their own. They stare at their machine's rapid-fire burst of moves, but do they understand why it's recommending them? One might think that a chess player would see beyond the illusion and not confuse his own strengths with those of his computer. Sadly, this is often not the case. And this same "illness" carries over to postal chess and analysis.

Of course, once these computer-enhanced fans take part in an over-the-board tournament, their false reality quickly crashes and burns. But they can also be brought down to Earth by a few words from a good chess teacher. All he needs to ask (once an interesting position appears) is, "What's going on here?" And suddenly an honest student will realize that he's deceived himself! Since he hasn't mastered the imbalances, he can't answer the question in any deep and penetrating manner. And telling the teacher that so-and-so is 0.43 ahead borders on the insane. A chess engine can be very useful, but it can also turn into a crutch that actually prevents you from improving.

Mr. Metallic was created to show how nobody thinks like a computer, nor would we want to. Chess is a game rich in emotion, art, the rush of competition, and the joy of creation. Streams of variations and displayed numbers (0.21) turn a warm, extremely human game into something cold and unknowable.

Mr. Pink

When you don't have a grasp of the imbalances, you're left with absolutely nothing, or (as in the case of Mr. Pink) with caveman basics like attack, defend, threats, and calculation. These are good things—everyone needs them. But is this simplistic ABC approach all you want for yourself?

Mr. Orange

Though Mr. Orange couldn't calculate quite as deeply as his opponents, he saw far more than either of his foes. The imbalances gave him a well-rounded positional education that offered him a solid understanding of both quiet static positions and sharper dynamic ones.

Go back and look at all the comments. It's clear that Mr. Orange was the only one that had any idea about the position's secrets and ultimate worth. Now we turn to you, the reader of this book. You might not calculate very well, or you might calculate better than Mr. Orange (it's always a good thing if you have the ability to calculate quickly and deeply, but knowledge of the imbalances will often get you by even if your absolute limit is a two-or-three move sequence), but wouldn't you rather be in Mr. Orange's shoes? If so, you're on your way to acquiring the knowledge that most players (for reasons that elude me) simply don't have.

> **PHILOSOPHY**
>
> A chess engine can be very useful, but it can also turn into a crutch that actually prevents you from improving.

Talk to the Board and It Will Talk to You

Everyone has some sort of internal dialogue when it's their turn to move. Most players stare blankly at the board and think, "I go there and he goes there and I go there and he goes there!" It's pure calculation, usually based on fear, aggression, or simply the desire to find something—*anything*—that seems reasonable. However, if I stopped you from calculating and asked, "Can you verbally break this position down for me?" the odds are that your answer wouldn't be lecture-worthy. Make no mistake about this: at any given moment, you should be able to lecture other players about the pros and cons of any position you reach! And, if you can't put your thumb on the pulse of the position, if you don't know what both sides need to accomplish, then how are you going to find the right move? It's like asking for driving directions to an unknown place.

This is why most players feel lost at sea. They feel they don't know what's going on, and so try to patch up the cracks by looking for threats and/or looking for ways to create them. They know something's wrong—something's missing. But they don't know what to do about it, and this creates a feeling of powerlessness. Trust me when I tell you that it doesn't have to be this way.

It's time to get a bit crazy—once you master the imbalances (and if you read this book from beginning to end, you *will* master the imbalances!), it will be time to get up close and personal with the board. In general, you can figure out a good deal about any position by doing the following:

First up is the *Armageddon Discourse*:

Make sure you are aware of any crude threats by the opponent, and also do a quick search for any basic tactical themes that might be present. This is usually done subconsciously by players 1800 and up. However, if you are lower rated, are prone to blunders, or feel that you have serious tactical issues, then it's a good idea to take a few moments to get on top of this stuff.

Once you've made sure that Thor's hammer isn't going to descend on your head, it's time for loftier considerations.

➤ Ascertain the imbalances for both sides.

➤ Then ask the board (in an internal dialogue), "What move or series of moves tries to take advantage of these factors?"

Pretty simple!

Let me stress once again that you should *not* be after plans per se (don't allow yourself to get distracted by the "P" word), but rather moves that cater to the imbalances. As we've seen, when you do this, plans often seem to materialize by themselves.

Let's see how the imbalances can dictate the course that both players take in a game.

G. Kamsky - V. Topalov, Sofia 2009

1.e4 c6 2.d4 d5 3.e5 Bf5 4.Nf3 e6 5.Be2 c5 6.Be3 cxd4 7.Nxd4 Ne7 8.Nd2 Nbc6 9.N2f3 Bg4 10.0–0 Bxf3 11.Nxf3 g6

Diagram 18

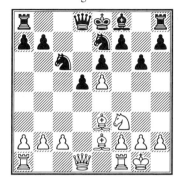

White dialogue: "He's going to play …Bg7 and tie me down to the defense of the e5-pawn. My main plusses are the hole on f6 that his …g6 created, a lead in development, and his central King. So I have to get something going before he rectifies those problems with the simple …Bg7 and …0-0.

"12.Bg5, eyeing f6, doesn't accomplish anything after 12…Bg7 since 13.Bf6? Bxf6 14.exf6 Ng8 wins my pawn. That leaves me with 12.Qd2 followed by 13.Bh6 (the trade of dark-squared Bishops might highlight the weakness of f6 and also leave his King a bit loose), or 12.c4, trying to rip open the position.

"12.Qd2 Bg7 13.Bh6 Bxh6 14.Qxh6 Nf5 15.Qd2 Nh4 isn't much, so I'll give 12.c4 a go and try and generate some action before his King gets castled."

12.c4

Black dialogue: "This move, which tries to open up the position, makes a lot of sense. However, if he captures on d5 my Knight will find a great home there (and there is a Bishop vs. Knight battle, so I want my Knights to be as well-placed as possible). Since none of this worries me, I'll continue with my intended …Bg7 and force his hand. Of course, he can chop on d5 and stop me from castling with Bc5, but what if I simply step back with …Bf8? My King would be quite happy on g7, and I can't be worse with a Knight sitting on that magnificent d5-square."

12…Bg7

White dialogue: "He's about to castle, so I have to follow through with 13.cxd5."

13.cxd5 Nxd5

Black dialogue: "I can't be worse with a Knight like this!"

14.Bc5

Black dialogue: "Of course, my King's in the center so I'm not going to do anything crazy like 14…Nxe5?? 15.Nxe5 Bxe5 16.Bb5+ and I would have to resign. However, I have no problem whatsoever with the exchange or dark-squared Bishops."

14...Bf8

White dialogue: "I'm not going to take on f8 since that would help him get his King to g7. Instead I'll try 15.Qc1 intending to take on f8 followed by Qh6+."

15.Qc1

Black dialogue: "An interesting move. He intends to chop on f8 and then, after ...Kxf8, stop my planned ...Kg7 with Qh6+. I'm also not high on 15...Bxc5 16.Qxc5 Rc8 17.Rac1. It's not the end of the world, but he's managed to stop me from getting my King to safety. Why give him anything? Seems to me that the problem with 15.Qc1 is that he's sticking his Queen on a file that my Rook can occupy. Yes, after 15...Rc8 16.Bxf8 I have a little tactic."

15...Rc8 16.Bxf8 Nd4

White dialogue: "Well, what can you do? When a guy plays well, he plays well. He didn't let me achieve any of my goals."

17.Qd1 Nxe2+ 18.Qxe2 Kxf8 19.Rac1 Kg7

White dialogue: "Okay, I have absolutely nothing. Time to tighten up and make a draw."

Indeed, the game ended in a draw in 43 moves. Note how all the ruminations were centered on the imbalances, and all the variations were also dedicated to the imbalances. This kind of logical breakdown of a position works for grand-masters and it will work for you too!

Our next example demonstrates how basic imbalance dialogue can even help solve double-edged, complicated positions.

Diagram 19

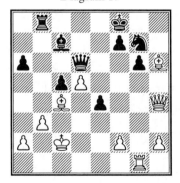

L.V. Nisipeanu - V. Milov, Warsaw 2005
White to move

The position is quite sharp. White could focus on thoughts of the potentially weak pawns on a6, c5, e4, f2, and h2, but he knows from experience that such a dynamic position calls for a dynamic solution (we will discuss Statics vs. Dynamics in Part Six). Several things must have caught white's eye: the Knight is pinned, if the Bishop wasn't on h6, Qh8+ would win, if Qf6 was possible, that would win the Knight, and if d5-d6 could be played, that would open the a2-g8 diagonal for white's light-squared Bishop—a fact that might well increase the power of an attack against black's King.

If we look for a move that addresses all these factors, it would be 1.Bf4, but that loses to 1...Qxf4 2.Qh8+ Ke7 3.Qxg7 Qxf2+. So Bf4 would be ideal *if* it couldn't be taken. Many players would just give up on it and play something like 1.Bg5, which also embraces some of the points we discussed—1...Kg8 allows White to unleash the passed d-pawn by 2.Be7, and 1...Qxh2 loses outright to 2.Qxh2 Bxh2 3.Rh1 when a retreat by black's Bishop allows a landing on h8. Thus, after 1.Bg5 Black pretty much has to block the h-file with 1...Nh5 when 2.Qxe4 is obviously good for White, but one gets the impression that he should have been able to do much better.

In the game, White knew that Bf4 was ideal but not immediately possible, but instead of saying, "I can't", he went out of his way to find a move that would make Bf4 a reality.

1.Rg4!

Winning. 2.Bf4 is threatened and Black has no good way to deal with it.

1...Qxh2

Discouraged, Black goes down right away. However, there wasn't a defense: 1...Qb6 loses to both 2.d6 Qxd6 (2...Bxd6 3.Qf6) 3.Bf4 and 2.Rxe4 Kg8 3.d6 Qxd6 4.Bf4. Perhaps 1...Kg8 was best, but then 2.Bf4 Qd7 3.Bxc7 Qxc7 4.Rxg6 is pretty grim.

2.Qf6, 1-0. Black had no desire to see 2...Be5 3.Bxg7+ or 2...Qxh6 3.d6. There will be much more on this kind of "I want to do it and I *will* find a way!" mentality in Part Four, Psychological Meanderings.

You now know what an imbalance is. You know that imbalances can help you figure out what's going on in most positions. And you know that achieving a firm understanding of each individual imbalance will catapult you past the players that you considered to be your equals. If you're ready to dedicate yourself to the study of this book, if you're ready to immerse yourself in new and illuminating concepts, then head for the next chapter and begin an exciting new journey of chess discovery.

Summary

- Imbalances Breakdown

    - **Superior minor piece**
    - **Pawn structure**
    - **Space**
    - **Material**
    - **Control of a key file**
    - **Control of a hole/weak square**
    - **Lead in development**
    - **Initiative** (though I'll usually refer to it as Pushing Your Own Agenda)
    - **King safety**
    - **Statics vs. Dynamics**

- An imbalance is any significant difference in the two respective positions.

- If you want to be successful, you have to base your moves and plans on the specific imbalance-oriented criteria that exist in the given position, not on your mood, tastes, and/or fears!

- Imbalances act as a roadmap that shows each side what to do.

- Imbalance Consciousness is a state where the use of imbalances becomes a natural and often unconscious process.

- Imbalances are the doorway to planning.

- The imbalances alone will lead you to the right move(s) in most positions, or even help you create a detailed plan.

- The initiative is a physical manifestation of a psychological battle—both sides champion their view of things in the hope that the opponent will have to eventually forgo his own plans and react to yours. Thus, I usually refer to it as Pushing Your Own Agenda.

- A chess engine can be very useful, but it can also turn into a crutch that actually prevents you from improving.

- The Armageddon Discourse is a basic thinking stage where you look for traps, threats, and tactical themes. This is usually done subconsciously by players 1800 and up. However, if you are lower rated, are prone to blunders, or feel that you have serious tactical issues, then it's a good idea to take a few moments to get on top of this stuff.

Part Two / Minor Pieces

Contents

Knights
Psychopaths of the Chessboard!

At times, Knights—also known as nerts, neons, jumpers, octopus, squid, and horses—are very much like clowns. They leap over other pieces, they prance about in a strange drunken gait, their movements make them seem almost alien compared to the other chessmen, and they can even make us laugh when we see a Knight do an octopus imitation by forking the whole royal family and estate (attacking King, Queen, and both country homes/Rooks all at once). However, as any clown-wise child will tell you, there is also something scary about them. They seem docile, but behind the facade and horse-like grin is a psychopath, and nothing is safe.

Diagram 20

Black to move

I was watching a student of mine play random 1-minute games on the ICC (Internet Chess Club) and expected him (he was Black) to resign here. Instead, I was witness to something that seemed more like a tragicomedy (or an episode of the Simpsons) than a chess game:

63...Nf2 64.Be2 Nxg4 65.a6

"Okay" I thought, "it's over. Time for Black to give up." Of course, I couldn't have guessed that black's Knight was really some sort of ravenous demon in disguise, ready to go on a binge and devour everything in sight.

65...Ne5 66.a7 Nc6+

DOH!

67.Kc5 Nxa7 68.Kb6 Nc8+ 69.Kc7 Ne7 70.b4 Nd5+

DOH!

71.Kd6 Nxb4 72.Kc5 Nc2 73.Kc4 Kg3 74.Kc3 Kf2 75.Bc4 Ne1 76.Kd4 Nf3+ 77.Ke4 Nd2+

DOH!

78.Kd4 Nxc4, 0-1. An epic tragedy for White, but Black had to be rather pleased with himself!

I can imagine many of you telling me, "Who cares? White went crazy and gave everything away. Surely a really good player wouldn't fall victim to such foolishness?"

One would think so, but let's take a look at a game of the 15th World Chess Champion, Vishy Anand. You'd consider him a "really good player," wouldn't you?

V. Anand - V. Ivanchuk, World Blitz Moscow 2007

1.e4 c5 2.Nf3 e6 3.d4 cxd4 4.Nxd4 a6 5.Bd3 Bc5 6.Nb3 Ba7 7.Qe2 Nc6 8.Be3 d6 9.N1d2 Nf6 10.f4 0-0 11.Bxa7 Rxa7 12.g4 b5 13.0-0-0 Rc7 14.Rhg1 Qe7 15.Kb1 Nd7 16.g5 Bb7 17.Rg3 Nb4 18.Rh3 g6 19.Qg4 Rfc8 20.Qh4 Nf8 21.a3 Nxd3 22.cxd3 h5 23.gxh6 Qxh4 24.Rxh4 Nh7 25.Nd4 Nf6 26.N2f3 Re8 27.Ng5 e5 28.fxe5 dxe5

Diagram 21

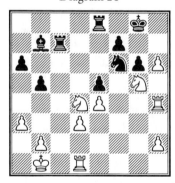

White to move

This was the final game of the event, and would determine who would earn the title of World Blitz Champion. In other words, they had to play quickly but it was serious business! Anand had outplayed his opponent and now had a forced win.

29.Ndf3??

The god of Knights wasn't kind to Anand in this game. He missed 29.h7+ Kg7 (29...Kh8 30.Rf1 is easy) 30.Nde6+! (It's always a scary thing when animals attack.) 30...fxe6 31.Nxe6+ Kh8 (31...Rxe6 allows 32.h8=Q+) 32.Nxc7. This would have been rather nice, but having overlooked the possibility and granting Black a reprieve, the lone enemy Knight suddenly takes matters into its own hands/hoofs.

29...Nh5! 30.Rg1?

Missing his last chance to keep a slight pull: 30.d4 exd4 (Much too risky is 30...f6? 31.dxe5 fxg5 32.Nxg5 Kh8 33.Rd6) 31.e5 Bxf3 32.Nxf3 Kh7 33.Rhxd4 Kxh6 34.Rd6.

30...Kh8

White threatened Rxh5, creating a nasty discovered check down the g-file.

31.Nh3

Anand's once mighty Knights go into full retreat mode.

31...Bc8 32.Nf2 Nf4

A nice square, but who would guess that this lone, unassuming Knight would go on a tear and win the game all by itself in just a few more moves?

33.Nxe5??

This Knight gets uppity and destroys the f4-Knight's defender.

33...Ne2

Argh! Suddenly the e5-Knight and the g1-Rook are both hanging at the same time.

34.Re1 Nd4

Black's Knight shows no mercy. Now e5 is still hanging, so White moves it to safety. To be fair, White no longer had a satisfactory reply—the black Knight had already injected its venom into the white position and, as everyone knows, there is no antidote for a horse bite.

35.Neg4

35.Nfg4 Bxg4 36.Nxg6+ fxg6 37.Rxg4 Kh7 was a better shot, but also pretty depressing.

35...Nf3

Diagram 22

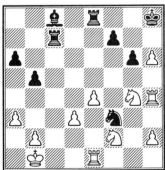

DOH! Yes, it even happens to World Champions. Both Rooks are forked, and there's nothing that can be done about it!

36.Nf6 Rd8

Moving his Rook to safety. The black fork against e1 and h4 isn't going away.

37.Nd5 Rb7, 0-1. White will now lose a full Rook. If I was Ivanchuk, I would have taken that Knight home, framed it, and placed it on the wall so I could give it a loving look every day for the rest of my life.

These two games have a moral: Knights are very tricky pieces and are fully capable of inflicting untold damage on the enemy position. In fact, if you come across some book that's trying to convince you that Bishops are a tad more valuable, spit on it and remember what happened to poor Anand!

> **RULE**
>
> There's a reason why many amateurs fear Knights—they are very tricky and deserve your full respect!

Now that I've trained you to see Knights as the fearsome creatures they really are, let's deconstruct them and see what makes them tick and what makes them sick (and, since Bishops and Knights are always at each other's throats, we'll do an occasional comparison between the two):

- Knights are minor pieces (along with Bishops), and are generally given a point-count value of 3 (the same as Bishops).

- Minor pieces are an imbalance unto themselves; knowing how to use them properly gives you a huge advantage over the competition.

- Knights are the best blockaders of enemy passed pawns. The reason for this is simple: Unlike other pieces, a Knight that's sitting in front of an enemy pawn isn't losing any of its mobility. Advantage Knight! See diagram 23 for an illustration.

- Knights are short-range pieces. Unlike Bishops, which can slide the length of the board in a single move, Knights are more "restrained". Advantage Bishop! See diagram 24 for an illustration.

- Knights can jump over other pieces. There isn't anything else that can do this (Okay, my cat can do it, but he doesn't count!). Advantage Knight!

- Knights have the potential to attack or defend anything on any colored square—it might take several moves, but eventually they will get there. Bishops are always stuck on one color. Advantage Knight!

➤ Knights do quite well in closed positions because, unlike Bishops, pawns can't block them. Advantage Knight! See diagram 25 for an illustration.

➤ Knights crave advanced support points (i.e., a safe square that can't easily be challenged by a hostile pawn). Since they are short-range pieces, having access to such a square is a huge part of proper Knight strategy.

➤ Knights gain in strength as they move further up the board. As a rule of thumb:

- A Knight stuck on the 1st or 2nd ranks is a defensive piece and is inferior to a healthy Bishop (a diseased Bishop is quite another matter).

- A Knight on the 3rd rank is a flexible workhorse and can be used for defense or attack at a moment's notice. A Knight on the 3rd often has serious central influence. See diagram 26 for an illustration.

- A Knight on a 4th rank support point is a very strong, flexible piece. You can count on it to ably perform both defensive and offensive duties. See diagram 27 for an illustration.

- A Knight on a 5th rank support point can be a beautiful thing to behold. It's a potent offensive weapon and is usually superior to a Bishop. See diagram 28 for an illustration.

- A Knight on a 6th rank support point can make children weep and women cry for joy. Here a Knight transforms from horse to Octopus, its many appendages spiking out in all directions and claiming enemy territory as its own. Such a Knight is, at times, stronger than a Rook. See diagram 29 for an illustration.

- A Knight on the 7th and 8th ranks gives us a case of diminishing returns. Once past the 6th, it no longer controls as many squares since its reach runs out of board. Usually a Knight on such an advanced rank is performing some sort of tactical or search and destroy operation.

Diagram 23

White to move

Knight as ultimate blockader

This position is a graphic illustration of the difference between a blockading Knight and a blockading Bishop. White's Knight is firmly blocking the passed f-pawn, but it's still a potent attacker thanks to its ability to jump over other pieces. In this case both e6 and g6 are under the gun. In comparison, the Bishop is purely defensive. Since white's King is free to roam (and black's clearly isn't), the game is easily won: **1.Kb4 Be8 2.Ka5 Ke7 3.Kb6 Kd7 4.Kb7** followed by c6 when it's all over.

Diagram 24

The Bishop is the King of distance

It will take the Knight a minimum of four moves to attack the distant pawn on a6 (for example, Ng4, Ne5, Nd3, Nc5). However, the Bishop needs just one move to threaten that pawn (Be2 or Bb7).

Diagram 25

Black to move

Knights are masters of closed positions

Knights can attack both light and dark squares

White's Knight threatens to go to d3 and then chop on c5. Black's Bishop is very unhappy in this closed position and can't do anything to prevent this, which means he's dead lost. If Black gets desperate and gives the horrible **1...a5 2.Nd3 a4 3.bxa4 Bd7** a go, then **4.Nxc5** (yes, 4.a5 is also game over) captures the pawn (which stood on a dark square), hits the enemy Bishop (on a light square), and defends the a4-pawn (also on a light square) all at the same time.

Diagram 26

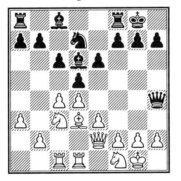

White to move

Knights on the 1st and 3rd ranks

Black has two Bishops, but White has a lead in development and more central space. The Knight on f1 is giving h2 firm support (It's hardly a world beater on that square, but it's serving an important defensive function), while the Knight on c3 puts pressure on d5 and gives support to **1.e4**, which adds to white's space and increases the pressure against d5.

Diagram 27

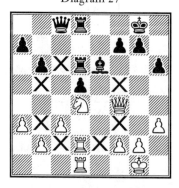

Knight on the 4th rank

The white Knight is an imposing piece. Aside from defending several squares on the 2nd and 3rd ranks, Black must constantly worry about it leaping to b5, c6, e6, or f5. On top of all that, the Knight is firmly blocking black's isolated d-pawn and, if it so chooses, can step back and take part in a direct assault against d5 via Ne2, Rd4, Qd2, and Nf4 with enormous pressure against black's position.

Diagram 28

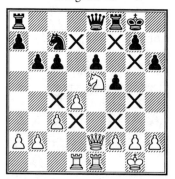

Knight on the 5th rank

White's dynamic Knight is running rings around black's defensive steed. The e5-Knight is on a permanent support point and is eyeing c6, d7, f7 and g6—all spots deep in enemy territory. Note that black's Knight can't make a home on d5 since c3-c4 would chase it away.

Diagram 29

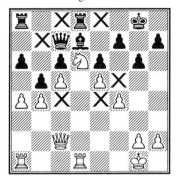

Knight on the 6th rank

This position is completely hopeless for Black. White's Knight is a monster, while black's Bishop is pathetic. Note that the Knight is battering away at several squares deep in black's camp. Though it's clear that it would control less squares on the 7th or 8th ranks, the Knight might leap there if it led to material gain or achieved some other kind of dynamic function.

White has a couple of devastating plans here. One is Ra3 followed by Rda1, Qa2, axb5, and then a decisive penetration down the a-file. Another idea is Ne4-f6 (a new 6th rank post!), Rd6, etc.

Because Knights are short-range pieces, you need to calmly march them to the desired post. This might take two or three moves, but it's something that needs to be done. Some players have a problem with this because they think it takes too much time, and it is indeed a bad idea if pieces are whizzing back and forth in some form of tactical mortal combat where time is more important than life itself. However, most positions don't exist in this state of frenzy, and building up your game (developing, creating a nice pawn center, putting pressure to bear against weak enemy pawns, etc.) is usually the way to go.

Diagram 30

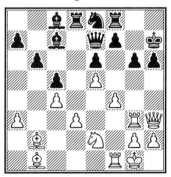

I. Nepomniachtchi - S. Brynell, Wijk aan Zee C 2007
White to move

White clearly has a nice attacking position, while Black doesn't seem to have anything going for him at all (where is his counterplay?). In the actual game, White got a little excited and tried for instant gratification with 1.Bc1 (threatening 2.f5) 1...Rh8 2.Rg4 but after 2...Ng7 Black was holding tight. Instead, he should have improved the position of his Knight, which isn't helping its teammates on e2. Where should this Knight go? How about e4? That looks like a very nice support point, and from that square it lashes out at d6, f6, and g5 (then any move by the e8-Knight would be crushed by Nf6+). Since we know that the Knight's position should be improved, and since we know that e4 is the Promised Land, the only question that remains is "how do we get it there?" The answer doesn't call for any calculation at all: 1.Nc3 with Ne4 to follow. For those wondering what happens if Black whacks the Knight off after **1.Nc3 Bb7 2.Ne4 Bxe4 3.dxe4 Rg8**, Black would find himself under serious kingside pressure after **4.f5** (made possible by the d3-pawn being moved to e4).

Each piece you own should be treated with parental care. If your Bishop is hitting a brick wall, find (or create) a diagonal for the poor thing! If your Knight is sitting around like a couch potato, drag it to an embattled sector and put the lazy thing to work!

1.e4 e6 2.d4 d5 3.Nc3 Nf6 4.e5 Nfd7 5.f4 c5 6.Nf3 Nc6 7.Be3 a6 8.a3 cxd4 9.Nxd4 Bc5 10.Be2 0–0 11.Qd2 Qc7 12.Bf3 Nxd4 13.Bxd4 Nb6 14.Ne2 Bxd4 15.Qxd4 Bd7 16.b3 Bb5 17.Nc3 Rfc8 18.Nxb5 axb5 19.Be2

Diagram 31

V. Topalov - V. Ivanchuk, MTel 2008
Black to move

This position is better for Black, but that assessment might prove somewhat surprising for those players who noticed the active Bishop on e2, the weak doubled-isolated pawn on b5, and white's central and kingside space advantage. However, Black's not without his own perks. After all, he does have a queenside spatial plus and white's pawns on a3 and c2 are both weak and under pressure.

So why doesn't the black position inspire confidence? The Knight! It's horrible, and the superiority of white's Bishop doesn't seem in question. A look at that Knight might well make us accept this point of view; after all, the Knight's forcing its Queen to do babysitting duty. And where is the thing going to go? Both a4 and c4 are poison, and blah, that blasted stupid Knight blah, rave, finger wagging, blah! I added the "blahs" since anyone can whine about a problem, but few actually do anything to rectify the situation. It's clear that the Knight is a goat, but if you're Black, then it's *your* goat and it's *your* responsibility to improve its lot.

A solution can be found only when you make the psychological transition from "I'm doomed!" to "I *must* fix this!" And sure enough, knowing that the Knight has no future on b6 (mixed with a positive mental outlook) makes the solution rather easy to find!

19...Nd7!

The only Knight-move that doesn't give away a piece! Now the Knight is no longer being eyed by the white Queen, and this means that black's lady is suddenly free to feast! 20...Qxc2 is threatened, and 20.Bxb5?? loses immediately to 20...Qa5+ winning the undefended Bishop.

20.Ra2

Ugly, but 20.Bd3 Nc5 21.Be2 (21.0-0 Nxd3 22.cxd3 Qc3 leaves White with the impossible task of having to defend the pawns on d3, b3, and a3) 21...Na6! (Suddenly the Knight is dancing all over the place!) 22.Bd3 Qa5+ 23.Ke2 (23.b4? Nxb4!) 23...Nc5 24.Ra2 (24.b4 Qa4 25.Rhc1 Nxd3 26.cxd3 Rc2+) 24...Nxd3 25.cxd3 Rc3 26.b4 Qc7 leaves no doubt about black's superiority.

20...Nb8!

The once-shunned Knight is heading for c6 where it will kick white's Queen and simultaneously create tactical tricks based on ...Nb4 (the a3-pawn is pinned).

21.0–0 Nc6 22.Qd2

Keeping an eye on the b4-square since 22.Qd3 loses instantly to 22...Nb4.

22...Qb6+!

An important nuance that pushes the enemy King into a corner. This means that back rank mate threats appear in some later lines, and in many endgames the King is no longer close to the center.

23.Kh1 Qa5! 24.Qxa5 Rxa5 and now threats like ...Nb4, ...Nd4, and ...Rca8
(all aimed at slapping the vulnerable pawns on a3 and c2) leave Black with all

the chances. The rest of the game was marred by time trouble, but the right guy won in the end: **25.Raa1 Rca8 26.Rad1 Rxa3 27.Bxb5 Nb4 28.c4 R8a5 29.f5 exf5 30.g4 Rxb3 31.gxf5 Re3 32.Rb1 Nd3 33.e6 d4 34.Be8 Nc5 35.Bxf7+ Kf8 36.f6 gxf6 37.Rxf6 Ke7 38.Rh6 d3 39.Rxh7 d2 40.Rg1 Re1 41.Bh5+ Kxe6 42.Rg7 Ne4 43.Rg6+ Ke5**, 0-1. I was looking at this game with a friend of mine (an IM) and, at this point, he blurted out, "Whose minor piece is better now? Huh? Whose?" The Knight, which once sat on the pathetic b6-square, has made a remarkable metamorphosis.

> **PHILOSOPHY**
>
> If one of your minor pieces isn't earning its keep, put the lazy thing to work! In the case of a Knight, wishful thinking won't get it to that dream post—it's up to you figure out a way to get it there.

You should now know Knight-basics, and you should be aware that if your Knight isn't taking part in the battle, you have to somehow *make* it take part! This isn't easy, but it all starts from the awareness that, 1) There's a problem; and 2) Once you address the problem, you must *insist* on solving it.

We're talking about mixing knowledge, a sharp awareness of the imbalances, and willpower to raise your game to a higher level. Our next example (diagram 32) is a nice demonstration of this process: knowledge tells you that Knights are strong on advanced squares (the 5th and 6th ranks being the most desirable). Awareness leads you to the fact that c6 would be a hole if Black no longer had his light-squared Bishop to defend it, and that a Knight on f5 would also be a feather in your cap. Willpower is the thing that allows you to *insist* on turning these elements into some form of positive reality.

M. Roiz - C. Balogh, Heraklion 2007

1.Nf3 Nf6 2.g3 d5 3.Bg2 e6 4.0–0 Nbd7 5.d3 b6 6.c4 Bb7 7.cxd5 exd5 8.Nc3 Be7 9.e4! dxe4 10.dxe4 Nc5

Diagram 32

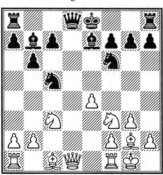

White to move

White has a central pawn majority and the e-pawn gives him a central space advantage. Black's King isn't castled yet, which gives White some options that a castled King wouldn't offer him (for example, Black won't want to start a fight until he gets his King to safety). Earlier I mentioned the potential hole on c6 and the nice outpost on f5. With all this information in mind, white's next move should make perfect sense.

11.Nd4!

White instantly targets both c6 and f5.

11...0–0

11...Nfxe4? is suicide since this capture opens a road right to the uncastled black King: 12.Nxe4 Bxe4 (12...Nxe4 13.Re1) 13.Bxe4 Nxe4 14.Re1 Nf6 15.Qe2 and the game is already over.

12.e5! Bxg2

Perhaps Black should have considered 12...Nd5 though White would then have a few ways to a comfortable edge. The simplest: 13.Nc6 Bxc6 (13...Nxc3?? 14.Nxd8 Nxd1 15.Nxb7 wins) 14.Nxd5 when 14...Bxd5 (14...Bb5!? 15.Re1 Rc8 16.Qg4) 15.Bxd5 gives White two active Bishops in an open position.

Now, after 12...Bxg2, White gains access to the c6-square.

13.Kxg2 Nd5 14.Nc6

A Godzilla of Knights!

14...Nxc3 15.bxc3 Qe8 16.Qd5

The c6-Knight paralyzes Black's whole army. He's far from dead, but such an unpleasant defensive task is not easy to deal with and Black fell apart very quickly: **16...Kh8?** (He could keep his disadvantage to a minimum with 16...Na4 17.Bd2 Bc5) **17.Ba3 f5 18.f4 Rg8 19.Rad1 Bf8 20.Nd8!** (A Knight on the 8th! The critters rarely get that far and it's usually no big deal if they do, but here the double threat of 21.Nf7+ and 21.Qxa8 wins on the spot.) **20...Rxd8 21.Qxd8 Qa4 22.Bxc5 Bxc5 23.Qd2 Qe4+ 24.Rf3**, 1-0.

So far we've seen how a Knight should be used, but how does one combat the nasty creatures? To do so, you'll need to know the following formula:

> **REMEMBER**
>
> Chess mastery is a mixture of knowledge, awareness, and willpower.

Anti-Knight Strategy: Knights lose a lot of their pop if you can take away (or deprive them of access to) all their advanced support points.

Diagram 33

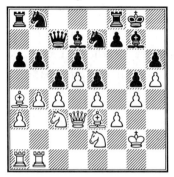

J. Silman - F.R. (1539), Los Angeles training game 2004
White to move

I used this position quite often during lessons with various students, explaining the problems Black faces, letting the student try the White side against me, and then me playing it against the student.

One key point is the two holes on f5 and f4. White would love to eventually post a Knight on f5 while Black wouldn't mind smashing a Knight onto f4. While White has no problem reaching f5 (from e3 or g3), Black can't get to f4 since both e6 and g6 (the black Knight's jump-off points) are poison. Of course, White doesn't have to be in a rush to play Ng3-f5 since that would allow Black to swap it off. Due to this, White will only go there when he can stay—for example, in many endgames where various pieces have been traded, a Knight landing safely on f5 might win one of the pawns on d6 and h6 or, at the very least, force Black to assign those pawns a defender.

> **RULE**
> A hole isn't a problem if the enemy pieces can't reach it.

Other problems Black faces in diagram 33: His dark-squared Bishop is an ugly, ineffective piece. Black has less space in virtually every sector of the board. The only area that can be opened and allow major piece penetration is the queenside, and it's clear that White already has all the play there.

Note that White moved his "bad" Bishop to a4 to get it outside the pawn chain. This means that the Bishop will be active on this square or will be exchanged for black's light-squared Bishop—a Bishop that is one of the defenders of f5.

1.Rb3

Since White isn't worried about ...cxb4, he decides to retain the pawn tension and triple on the b-file before opening it.

1...Bxa4

1...cxb4 2.axb4 (2.Rxb4 is also good) 2...Rc8 3.c5 bxc5 (3...b5 4.Bxb5) 4.bxc5 and White is winning since 4...dxc5 5.d6 c4 6.dxc7 cxd3 7.cxb8=Q leaves White a piece ahead.

2.Nxa4 Nd7 3.Rab1 Rab8 4.R1b2 Rfe8

White is also winning after 4...Rfc8 5.Qb1 cxb4 6.Rxb4 a5 7.Bxb6 Nxb6 8.Rxb6 Rxb6 9.Nxb6, while 4...b5 5.bxc5 bxa4 6.Rxb8 Nxb8 7.cxd6 Qxd6 8.c5 Qd7 9.Qb1 Qd8 10.Rb7 leaves Black hopelessly placed (the g7-Bishop is particularly pathetic).

5.Qb1

A heavy piece setup known as *Alekhine's Gun*. Now White is ready to pull the trigger with bxc5.

5...Bf8 6.bxc5 bxc5 7.Rb7 Rxb7 8.Rxb7 Qa5 9.Qc2 Nb8?

Missing white's reply, but on 9...Qd8 both 10.Qb3 and 10.Bd2 leave Black with trouble finding a useful move.

10.Rb6 Nd7 11.Bd2, 1-0.

Everyone has things they like or love in life, from food to cars to travel locations. And though all of our likes obviously have much to commend them, they also have some dubious characteristics too. The hot fudge sundae that makes your taste buds scream in bliss—it also carries about two million calories. My wife's favorite old (but classic!) MG sports car—it's fun to drive but tends to catch on fire from time to time for no reason in particular. Scuba diving off the Australian coast—it's a rush, but great whites seem to view it as a fast food restaurant.

What does this have to do with Knights? This may shock you, but the mighty steeds you've been studying in this chapter also have their own downside (other than being short range pieces, which we've already addressed): they can be dominated! The most humiliating form of Knight domination is caused by its mortal enemy, the Bishop.

Diagram 34

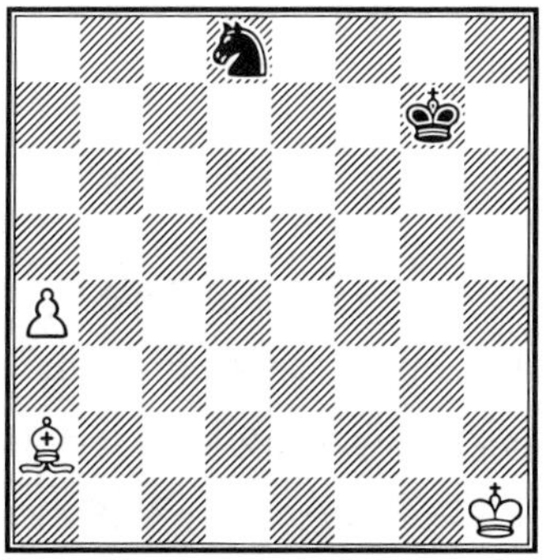

White to move

White's only hope of winning the game is to promote his pawn. This doesn't seem likely because 1.a5 Nc6 2.a6 Kf6 3.Bd5 Na7 stops the pawn in its tracks. Okay, that Knight is clearly an enemy of the state, so why not put it in prison?

1.Bd5!

The Knight is completely dominated. The b7- c6- and e6-squares are off limits, while 1...Nf7 2.Bxf7 promotes the pawn.

1...Kf6

The King tries to come to the rescue.

2.a5 Ke5

2...Ne6 3.Bxe6 (and not 3.a6?? Nc7, =) 3...Kxe6 4.a6 Kd6 5.a7 and it's over.

3.a6! Kxd5 4.a7 and a new Queen will be born.

Another form of Knight domination is the dreaded "entombed piece." This is a situation where a Knight (or Bishop!) is stuck in a cage of pawns.

Diagram 35

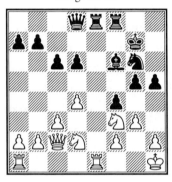

Black to move

1...g4

This creates an obvious attack on the f3-Knight. That should be easy to deal with, but it turns out to be a clean winner for Black.

2.Ng1

Since e5 and g5 are off limits, that only leaves this retreat to g1 or the material losing hop to h4: 2.Nh4 Bxh4 3.gxh4 Qxh4 with an extra pawn and a strong attack.

2....f3! and the tomb has been shut and sealed. Now the Knight can't ever safely move again, while its King is also in the same tiny cell. Black is now, in effect, a piece up (in fact, two pieces up since the white King is sharing the same fate as the horse) and should easily win the game.

In the last example we saw a Knight locked into a tomb by enemy pawns. It's even worse if the Knight's own pawns trap it!

Diagram 36

White to move

The position in diagram 36 is nothing ~~sort~~ *short* of comic. The pawns on f2 and g3 are acting like traitors and have turned the poor Knight into a nonentity! Though a piece for a pawn ahead, White might as well resign:

1.Kc1 Kd3 2.Kd1 c2+ 3.Kc1 Ke2 4.Kxc2 Kf1 5.Kd3 (Trying to keep black's King on h1 and h2 also fails: 5.Kd2 Kg2 6.Ke1 Kxh1 7.Kf1 Kh2 8.Ke1 Kg2 9.Kd2 Kxf2) **5...Kg2 6.Ke4 Kxh1 7.Kf4 Kg2 8.Kxg4 Kxf2 9.Kh4 Ke2 10.g4 f2 11.g5 f1=Q**, 0-1.

The most common kind of Knight domination (though not nearly as apocalyptic as the previous two) is caused by those annoying enemy pawns, which can take control of key jump off points and/or landing strips (open squares) and leave the Knight with nowhere to go and nothing to do.

A. Galkin - E. Romanov, 60th Russian Chmp 2007

1.e4 e5 2.Nf3 Nc6 3.Bb5 a6 4.Ba4 Nf6 5.0–0 Be7 6.Re1 b5 7.Bb3 d6 8.c3 0–0 9.h3 Na5 10.Bc2 c5 11.d4 Qc7 12.Nbd2 cxd4 13.cxd4 Nc6 14.a3 Bd7 15.d5 Na5 16.Nf1 Nh5 17.b3 Rfc8 18.Ne3 g6 19.Bd2 Bd8 20.Kh2 Qb8 21.g3 Bb6 22.Bd3 Rc7 23.Rb1 Qf8 24.Rf1 Rac8 25.Qe2 Nb7

Diagram 37

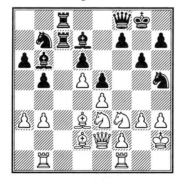

White to move

Black's h5-Knight was hoping to set up shop on f4, but white's g2-g3 left it stymied—if it wants to get back in the game, it has to retreat. However, the other black Knight on b7 has high hopes of living large on c5. Once there, if White chases it with the b-pawn the Knight could chop on d3 or leap onto a4. Once again, a little pawn will dominate a big, powerful horse via **26.b4!** when the once hopeful b7-Knight has no future at all on the queenside (in fact, it eventually migrated to the kingside by ...Nb7-d8, ...f7-f6, and ...Nf7). As you can see, using pawns to limit the activity of enemy Knights is a very important strategic idea—get used to employing it and watch the opponent's Knights whither and die!

Finally it's time to address my favorite Knight maneuver: the artistic but poisonous step-back boogie!

J. Silman - M. Montchalin, Richland 1985

1.d4 Nf6 2.Nf3 c5 3.d5 d6 4.Nc3 g6 5.e4 Bg7 6.Bb5+ Nbd7 7.a4 0–0 8.0–0 a6 9.Be2 b6 10.Re1 Ne8 11.Bf4 Qc7 12.Qd2 Ne5 13.Nxe5 dxe5 14.Bh6 Qd6 15.Bxg7 Kxg7

Diagram 38

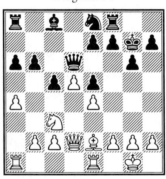

White to move

White notices that potential weaknesses lie on b6, c5, and e5. No, c5 isn't a typo—the seemingly solid c5-pawn can become loose after a well-timed a4-a5 push undermines its defender on b6. Of course, both b6 and e5 might become tender if White could bring pieces to bear on them, but how can this be done?

Let me remind you of our earlier philosophical chess thought: *Chess mastery is a mixture of knowledge, awareness, and willpower.* This is yet another example of that motto. White knows (i.e., has the knowledge based on often-seen patterns) that this kind of pawn structure can lead to difficulties for Black. He's aware that the aforementioned pawns could become weak if there was some way to get his pieces within striking range. And finally, he wants to find a maximum piece setup that will accomplish these goals.

So what pieces in the White army will be able to exert pressure against the designated targets? Clearly the Bishop can't since it's a light-squared Bishop and the pawns lay on dark squares. The Knight, though, would be a tower of strength on c4 where it would kick the enemy Queen and take direct aim at both b6 and e5. White's Queen can also join the party on e3 (hitting c5 in anticipation of the a4-a5 break and also giving e4 some support), while placing it on c3 seems even better since it eyes both c5 and e5. That leaves the a4-pawn with its a4-a5 aspirations and the f2-pawn with its dreams of f2-f4.

So how can White create such a position? This calls for the step-back boogie!

16.Nb1!!

A shocking move that is very anti-intuitive, but also very logical. The Knight returns to its beginning square because it just wasn't happy on c3! Remember that a piece is only happy if it's on a square where it helps with the overall game plan. In this case the c3-Knight might look okay on c3, but it's not addressing all the issues that were discussed earlier. However, wouldn't it be a killer on c4? And suddenly one sees that this odd retreat ties everything together: c3 is now clear for white's Queen while the Knight will head for c4 via a3 or d2.

16...Qf6

This allows White to make his vision a reality. Instead, moves such as 16...Bd7 or 16...Bb7 would limit white's advantage. Another possibility is 16...Nf6 when aside from 17.Qe3, interesting is 17.Na3!? Nxe4 18.Qe3 Nf6 19.Nc4 Nxd5 20.Nxd6 Nxe3 21.Nxc8 Nxc2 22.Nxb6 Ra7 23.a5 with a pleasant edge for White (Black, after he chops one of the Rooks, has a Rook and two pawns for two minor pieces, but the two minors will be very nicely placed while the pawns on a6 and c5 will prove to be extremely weak).

17.Qc3 Nd6 18.Nd2 e6 and now **19.a5!** (instead of my lazy 19.Bf1—I played a4-a5 a move later) would have been thematic, destroying black's queenside pawn chain at the base and gaining a clear advantage.

Summary

> Knights are minor pieces (along with Bishops), and are generally given a point-count value of 3 (the same as Bishops).

> Knights crave advanced support points (i.e., a safe square that can't easily be challenged by a hostile pawn). Since they are short-range pieces, having access to such a square is a huge part of proper Knight strategy.

> Knights gain in strength as they move further up the board. As a rule of thumb:

- A Knight stuck on the 1st or 2nd ranks is a defensive piece and is inferior to a healthy Bishop (a diseased Bishop is quite another matter).

- A Knight on the 3rd rank is a flexible workhorse and can be used for defense or attack at a moment's notice. A Knight on the 3rd often has serious central influence.

- A Knight on a 4th rank support point is a very strong, flexible piece. You can count on it to ably perform both defensive and offensive duties.

- A Knight on a 5th rank support point can be a beautiful thing to behold. It's a potent offensive weapon and is usually superior to a Bishop.

- A Knight on a 6th rank support point can make children weep and women cry for joy. Here a Knight transforms from horse to Octopus, its many appendages spiking out in all directions and claiming enemy territory as its own. Such a Knight is, at times, stronger than a Rook.

- A Knight on the 7th and 8th ranks gives us a case of diminishing returns. Once past the 6th, it no longer controls as many squares since its reach runs out of board. Usually a Knight on such an advanced rank is performing some sort of tactical or search and destroy operation.

> Knights are the best blockaders of enemy passed pawns. The reason for this is simple: Unlike other pieces, a Knight that's sitting in front of an enemy pawn isn't losing any of its mobility. Advantage Knight!

➤ Knights are short-range pieces. Unlike Bishops, which can slide the length of the board in a single move, Knights are more "restrained". Advantage Bishop!

➤ Knights can jump over other pieces. There isn't anything else that can do this. Advantage Knight!

➤ Knights have the potential to attack or defend anything on any colored square—it might take several moves, but eventually they will get there. Bishops are always stuck on one color. Advantage Knight!

➤ Knights do quite well in closed positions because, unlike Bishops, pawns can't block them. Advantage Knight!

➤ Because Knights are short-range pieces, you need to calmly march them to the desired post. This might take two or three moves, but it's something that needs to be done.

➤ If you hear a square calling out to your Knight (or see a beckoning glow), do everything in your power to get your horse there (It doesn't matter if you have to move forward, backwards, sideways, or a combination of all these things to reach it.)!

➤ Just because a minor piece is "nicely" developed to the usual respected squares on the 3rd rank doesn't mean it's doing anything from that post. Does it have a future on that square? Is it working with the other pieces towards the fulfillment of some unified plan? If the answer to these questions is "no," then it's important that you find a better home for the horse and then do your utmost to get it there.

Knights — Tests

After thoroughly absorbing the material you've just looked at on Knights, I'm guessing that you can't wait to show your mastery of the beasts. So go ahead and strut your stuff.

The following tests are designed to give you insight into how much you've learned *and* to serve as extra instruction. If you have trouble solving the tests, don't worry—that means we've uncovered something you don't understand, and this allows you to fix things by rereading the previous material or by picking up the bits of knowledge you're missing in the answers that start on page 431.

PART TWO - TEST **1**

Diagram 39

[Level: 1200 - 1600]

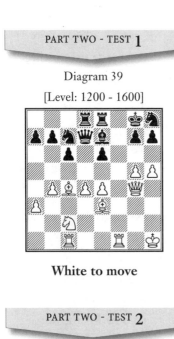

White to move

PART TWO - TEST **3**

Diagram 41

[Level: 2000 - 2200]

Black to move

PART TWO - TEST **2**

Diagram 40

[Level: 1800 - 2000]

Black to move

PART TWO - TEST **4**

Diagram 42

[Level: 1600 - 1800]

White to move

PART TWO - TEST **5**

Diagram 43

[Level: 1900 - 2200]

White to move

PART TWO - TEST **8**

Diagram 46

[Level: 1400 - 1800]

White to move

PART TWO - TEST **6**

Diagram 44

[Level: 1900 - 2200]

White to move

PART TWO - TEST **9**

Diagram 47

[Level: 1800 - 2000]

White to move

PART TWO - TEST **7**

Diagram 45

[Level: 2000 - 2200]

White to move

Bishops
Speed Demons of the Diagonals

While Knights slowly but surely hop and leap to whatever areas of the board they wish to go to, Bishops (Also known in various insane circles as bellhops, bees, and wily angle-sliders. Two Bishops are, on occasion, also referred to as two Jans or, oddly, two Rabbis.) can roar across the length of the board in a single move. It lives for speed, and this little Formula 1 racecar makes anything that dares step onto its diagonal potential road-kill. This means that if those diagonals aren't blocked, the Bishop can be a fierce and highly prized piece.

Bishops have historically been viewed as being either *Good* (the player's center pawns are on the opposite color as his Bishop) or *Bad* (the player's center pawns are on the same color as his Bishop). However, I no longer like these terms, deeming them anti-intuitive and at times confusing. For example, bad Bishops can often be active and, as a result, very strong. Or bad Bishops can also be critically useful defenders. Thus, in this book we'll refer to Bishops as *Active*, *Useful*, or *Tall-Pawns*.

> A Bishop is considered *Active* if it's outside the pawn chain and/or enjoying life on a reasonably clutter-free diagonal.

> A Bishop is considered *Useful* if it's doing an important (defensive or dynamic) task(s). Such a defensive Bishop can be ugly to look at, but its absence would cause your position to undergo serious difficulties.

> A Bishop is said to be a *Tall-Pawn* if it's not serving a useful function and is trapped behind its pawns (thus making it inactive). This kind of Bishop takes on the persona of an overgrown pawn that, sadly, can't turn into a Queen if it reaches the end of the board.

Let's take a deeper look at each of these Bishop-types.

The Active Bishop

Give a Bishop a diagonal that's uncluttered by soda cans, pens, its own pawns or a solid/well-defended wall of enemy pawns (pieces aren't clutter) and we'll consider it to be active. This doesn't mean that an active Bishop can singlehandedly bring down the enemy position or that it will even successfully mesh with the rest of its army. That's up to you and your skills at getting all your bits to work together for a particular goal. But an active Bishop can dash from one sector to another in a flash, so they always need to be respected.

Diagram 48

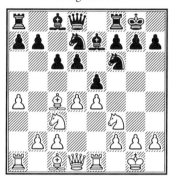

Black to move

White has two active Bishops here—his c4-Bishop eyes the f1-a6 and the a2-g8 diagonals, while his other Bishop patrols the c1-h6 line. Black's light-squared Bishop is also active since it eyes the c8-h3 diagonal (the d7-Knight isn't considered clutter because it can move out of the Bishop's way whenever it wishes to). However, black's e7-Bishop isn't particularly active because it's blocked by the d6-pawn. Of course, it does keep an eye on the shorter d8-h4 diagonal, and it also gives d6 solid support, so it's not close to being a Tall-Pawn. In fact, this Bishop can easily become something special after a …d6-d5 push frees the f8-a3 diagonal, or it can assume diagonal supremacy if White ever captures on e5 (dxe5) since recapturing by …dxe5 would unlock its potential.

This shows us that a Bishop can become active at the drop of a hat, and that innocent looking pawn exchanges (dxe5) can easily turn a dormant enemy piece into an active one.

Why are all the Bishops in diagram 48 at least reasonably active? Because the center is fluid and can open further if pawns are exchanged. However, a couple poor moves can change all this:

1…c5?

I'm sure the e7-Bishop didn't appreciate this move! This unfortunate advance also turns d5 into a gaping hole.

2.d5?

White also seems to be oblivious to the needs of his minor pieces! With one push of the pawn, the d5-hole has been plugged and the c4-Bishop blocked. Talk about self-defeating! Instead, 2.dxe5 Nxe5 3.Nxe5 dxe5 4.Qe2 would leave

Black with that hole on d5, while the e7-Bishop's potential has been greatly reduced. Also note that white's light-squared Bishop is a real fire breather on the a2-g8 diagonal.

In the position from diagram 48, everyone started out with nice Bishops. But more often than not you'll find that your Bishop isn't setting the board on fire.

> **RULE**
>
> Bishops are usually strongest in open positions. The fewer pawns in the way of a Bishop the greater its scope.

> **RULE**
>
> Every time you move a pawn, check to see how it affects the activity of your Bishops! Obviously, turning an open position into a closed one will have a serious effect on these pieces, so train yourself to always take the health and care of your Bishops into account.

What do you do then? Being a fan of the *Wizard of Oz*, I tried closing my eyes, clicking my Birkenstocks together and saying, "There's nothing like an active Bishop. There's nothing like an active Bishop." Sadly, it didn't have the desired effect—when I opened my eyes the Bishop was still sitting there doing nothing. Clearly, inactive Bishops will remain that way unless you do something about it! In other words, if you possess a lazy Bishop that is sitting around daydreaming, you have to find a way to put the thing to work. This mix of Bishop-awareness (knowledge) and willpower can be quite effective.

Diagram 49

MrSchlock (1732) - purplecoyote (1646), Internet 30 minute 2006
White to move

A student of mine was playing White and he couldn't wait to show me this game. When he reached this position he stopped and said, "I have pressure against d6 but it's defended by the Knight and the Rooks will soon come to its defense too. My Bishop isn't doing anything and suddenly I remembered how you constantly yell at me about how I allow my pieces to stay out of play. I got really angry and thought to myself, 'Not this time!'"

1.c5!

Excellent! This is the kind of move that makes teachers proud. Suddenly the slacker on e2 will jump to c4 where it will be incredibly active. We also can't forget that this pawn sacrifice blows open the d-file for the doubled Rooks.

1...dxc5??

This leads to annihilation. He had to try 1...Rad8 2.cxd6 Rxd6 (2...Nxd6 3.Qd4 a6 4.Bc4+ Nxc4 5.Qxd8 Rxd8 6.Rxd8+ Kf7 7.R1d7 is game over) 3.Rxd6 Nxd6 4.Qd4 Nf7 (4...Rd8 5.Bc4+ wins on the spot) 5.Qxa7 and white's extra pawn, combined with black's loose King, should ensure victory: 5...Ne5 (5...Rd8 6.Rxd8+ Nxd8 7.Qd4 h5 8.Qb6 Kg7 9.b4 Qd7 10.a4 Qd2 11.Bf1 is pretty easy since Black is tied down to the defense of d8 and b7. White will end things by pushing his queenside majority and making a crushing passed pawn.) 6.Ba6 (If this tactic wasn't here, then White would play 6.Rd5 with a huge advantage) 6...Rf7 7.Qb8+ Kg7 8.Bxb7 Qc7 9.Qxc7 Rxc7 10.Bd5 Rc2 11.b4 Nd3 12.Bb3 and White is winning.

2.Rd7 Qe8 3.Bc4 Rb8 4.Qf6 b5 5.Be6 White's pieces work together beautifully, and the Bishop has gone from a useless lump of wood on e2 to a slayer of all things on e6. At this point purplecoyote, not wanting blood to gush from the screen, wisely resigned.

Two other things that distinguish an active Bishop is its ability to stop enemy passed pawns from a distance and its use as a "catapult" for its Queen.

Diagram 50

White to move
Ruler of the b1-h7 diagonal

Okay, this is a highly exaggerated situation, but it clearly shows the Bishop stamping the whole b1-h7 diagonal with the brand of its authority. Nothing may safely step there, while in the meantime white's lone pawn, after **1.d6**, will waltz into d8 and make a new Queen.

Diagram 51

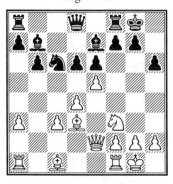

Catapult

White to move

1.Qe4!

A common but important idea. The Queen uses its light-squared Bishop to set up a catapult (usually referred to as a "battery," but that term reminds me of a marital debacle so I try to avoid it) that will throw it deep (and decisively) into the enemy position (in this case, on h7). This is also known as "riding the Bishop's vapors."

1...f5

There's no salvation in 1...g6 2.Bxh6 Nxe5 (Black was lost in any case, but this makes a bad situation worse.) because after 3.Qxb7 Nxd3 4.Qa6 Nb2 5.Bxf8 Bxf8 6.Rfb1 he loses the Knight and leaves White with an extra Rook.

2.exf6 e.p. Rxf6 3.Re1 Na5

There's no real defense. Trying to hold onto e6 falls on its face after 3...Qd7 4.Qh7+ Kf7 5.Bg5! hxg5 (5...Rxf3 6.Bg6+ Kf8 7.Qh8 mate) 6.Nxg5+ Ke8 7.Qg8+ and now 7...Rf8 8.Nxe6 Rxg8 9.Bg6 would make black's toes curl, while 7...Bf8 8.Nxe6 makes the last line look like a mercy killing.

4.Qh7+ Kf7 5.Bg5! and now Black has nothing better than **5...Qg8** (5...hxg5 6.Nxg5+ Ke8 7.Nxe6 Rxe6 8.Qg8+ Kd7 9.Qxe6+ Kc7 10.Qxe7+ offers no hope at all) **6.Bxf6 Qxh7 7.Bxh7 Bxf6 8.Be4** and Black doesn't have enough compensation for the lost Exchange.

The Useful Bishop

Active Bishops are nice, but at times they are merely claiming domination of unimportant real estate. In that case, you have to find (or create) something for them to do. The dream Bishop is both *useful* and *active*—it covers a lot of ground, but it is also serving a very specific (useful) purpose.

Diagram 52

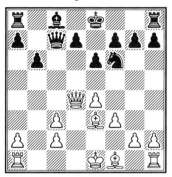

White to move

This is from the game A. Volokitin - Y. Pelletier, Biel 2005 (**1.e4 c5 2.Nf3 e6 3.d4 cxd4 4.Nxd4 Nc6 5.Nc3 Qc7 6.Be3 Nf6 7.Qd2 Bb4 8.f3 Nxd4 9.Qxd4 Bxc3+ 10.bxc3 b6**)

White's dark-squared Bishop is active in that it eyes two diagonals (g1-a7 and c1-h6). However, the g1-a7 diagonal is blocked (the b6-pawn is a rock) and the c1-h6 diagonal has nothing to do with the battle for the central dark squares (the d6-square in particular is screaming for the Bishop's attention). In other words, it's active but not performing a useful function that relates to the other imbalances in the position.

Of course, white's potential dark-square control is offset by the weak pawns on the c-file, so Black has his chances too. Nevertheless, even if the chances are more or less balanced, it's still up to White to pose problems for his opponent by milking his positive imbalances for all they're worth.

After 26 minutes thought, Grandmaster Volokitin played the most principled move.

11.Bc1!

Heading for a3 and, ultimately, d6. Now Black has to be very careful that his King doesn't get stuck in the center.

11...e5!

This fine move stops e4-e5 ideas and also chases the Queen off its powerful central post. Worse were:

11...Qc5? 12.Qxc5 bxc5 13.Ba3 d6 14.0–0–0 Ke7 15.e5 dxe5 16.Bxc5+ Ke8 17.Bb5+ Bd7 18.Rxd7 Nxd7 19.Rd1 Rd8 20.c4, analysis by Volokitin, who says "with the idea of Ba4, Ba3, c5 and c6 and wins."

11...Bb7? 12.Ba3 Rc8 13.c4 Ba6 (or 13...e5 when both 14.Qd6 and 14.Qd2 are strong) 14.e5 Ng8 15.Bd3! Bxc4 16.0-0 Bxd3 17.cxd3 and black's lack of development and central King will leave him with serious long-term difficulties. A sample line: 17...Ne7 18.Rac1 Nc6 (18...Qb8 19.Rxc8+ Qxc8 20.Rc1 Qb7

21.Qg4 Nf5 22.Qe4 Qb8 23.Qc4 and black's problems remain) 19.Qe4 Qd8 20.d4 and Black is left with an unenviable defensive task.

12.Qd2 0–0 13.Ba3 Re8 14.Bb5 and now **14...Re6! 15.c4 Bb7 16.0-0-0** would have led to a more or less equal position. Instead, in the actual game Black played **14...a6** and went down in defeat after **15.Bd6 Qa7 16.Bc4 b5 17.Bb3 Bb7 18.0-0-0 a5 19.a3 Rac8 20.g4 Rc6 21.g5 Nh5 22.Bxe5 Qc5 23.Qxd7 Qxe5 24.Bxf7+ Kf8 25.Bxe8 Rc7 26.Qd8 Qf4+ 27.Kb1 Rc8 28.Qb6**, 1-0.

> **RULE**
>
> While an active Bishop might look good, a useful Bishop trades style for substance and addresses the deeper needs (both dynamic and defensive) of a position.

The useful Bishop can also be purely defensive:

Diagram 53

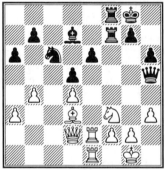

Gamera16 (1827) vs. MrSchlock (1732), Internet 30 minute 2006
White to move

One would think that White should stand better here. His Bishop is far more active than black's silly looking thing, while the e6-pawn (sitting on an open file and facing off to a pair of enemy Rooks!) is weak and the e5-square is a gaping wound in the middle of the board. To top it off, White even has the move!

Yet, things aren't so clear. It turns out that white's d-pawn isn't as safe as one might suppose, while the threat of ...Rxf3, shattering white's King position, is serious and needs to be dealt with. Still, White can avoid that unpleasantness with both 1.Re3 and 1.Ne5. So isn't White better after all?

To find an answer to this, we need to address the Bishops. It turns out that the active white Bishop, with its proud trumpeting over its domination of the b1-h7 diagonal, isn't helping the rest of its forces deal with ...Rxf3, or with the weakness of e5 or its own slightly loose pawn on d4. On the other hand, black's despised mutant on d7 is singlehandedly keeping e6 intact (another way to look at this is that one Bishop is holding off two enemy Rooks!). And, once e6 is no longer in peril, that "inactive" piece can emerge from behind its own lines via ...Bb5 or ...Ba4 or ...Bd7-e8-g6 or ...Bd7-e8-h5 and create its own brand of activity outside its pawn chain.

Let's see how play continued:

1.Ne5

1.Re3 Rxf3! (My student, MrSchlock, missed this idea earlier when he blitzed a move to gain some time on the clock. He insisted that he wouldn't have missed it again.) 2.Rxf3 Rxf3 3.Be2 Rxf2 4.Kxf2 Qh4+ 5.Kg1 Qxd4+ 6.Qxd4 Nxd4 and Black, with two good center pawns for the Exchange, has no reason to be unhappy.

1...Nxe5

Not 1...Nxd4? 2.Bg6 Nxe2+ 3.Rxe2.

2.Rxe5

2.dxe5 makes no sense since it fills the hole on e5, turns the d5-pawn into a passer, and blocks both white Rooks. Remember: you want to make moves that do good things for *your* position, not good things for your opponent's!

2...Qh4 3.R1e2 Qf4 4.R5e3 Qg5 5.g3 Qh5 6.Kh2

In the actual game White set a trap and Black fell right into it: 6.f4 Qxh3?? (Correct was 6...g5 with mutual chances in a complex battle.) 7.Rh2 ("Here I was hit by that 'I'm going to vomit' feeling I always get when I realize I've hung my face."—MrSchlock.) 7...Qg4 8.Rh4, 1-0 since the Queen is lost.

6...e5 7.dxe5

And not 7.Rxe5?? Qxh3+ 8.Kg1 Bg4.

7...Qxh3+ 8.Kg1 d4 9.Re4

9.e6 peters out to equality after 9...dxe3 10.exf7+ Rxf7 11.Rxe3 Bc6 12.Be4 Bxe4 13.Rxe4 Qf5, =.

9...Rf3 10.Bc4+ Kh8 11.Qe1 d3 12.Rd2 Bc6

Diagram 54

Once a useful defender, now black's Bishop has morphed into a fierce attacker!

13.Rh4 Qf5 14.Bxd3 Rxd3 15.Rf4 Qh3 16.Rxf8+ Kh7 17.f3 Rxd2 18.Qxd2 Qxg3+ 19.Qg2 Qe1+, ½-½.

The Tall-Pawn

A Bishop is said to be a *Tall-Pawn* if it's not serving a useful function and is trapped behind its pawns (thus making it inactive). This kind of Bishop takes on the persona of an overgrown pawn and is something you should desperately try and avoid having.

The worst cases of Tall-Pawns occur when a Bishop finds itself entombed. Here's a graphic example:

Diagram 55

Black to move

A true nightmare for White! This kind of Bishop usually loses in the middle-game and the endgame—in both cases, the side with the entombed piece is, in effect, playing with a piece less.

Here black's only concern is getting his King to e2 where it can start vacuuming up all of white's kingside pawns. There is only one way to accomplish this goal.

1...c3!

This turns the a4-pawn into an outside passed pawn. Once white's King is forced to the a-file so it can capture the a-pawn, black's King will have a clear path to e2-nirvana.

2.bxc3+ Kc4 3.Bg1

Or 3.Kb2 a3+ 4.Kxa3 Kxc3 5.Ka4 Kd3 6.Kb4 Ke2 7.Bg1 Kf1, 0-1.

3...a3 4.Bh2 a2 5.Kb2 a1=Q+ 6.Kxa1 Kxc3 7.Kb1 Kd2 8.Bg1 Ke2 9.Kc1 Kf1 10.Kd2 Kxg1 11.Ke3 Kg2 and f2 falls.

Our next example shows the most common kind of entombed Bishop. A student of mine, Daniel S, became a fan of the Botvinnik setup in the English Opening (1.c4 c5 2.g3 g6 3.Bg2 Bg7 4.Nc3 Nc6 5.e4 Nf6 6.d3 0–0 7.Nge2 d6 is just one possible move order). While teaching it to him, I pointed out a typical device that I assured him would occur from time to time. To my surprise, it appeared in many of his blitz games and allowed him to reel in one point after another without a fight.

Diagram 56

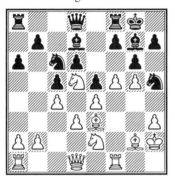

Daniel S (1658) - Gong, ICC 2007

White to move

This one-sided position occurred after Black badly misplayed the opening: **1.c4 Nf6 2.Nc3 g6 3.g3 Bg7 4.Bg2 0–0 5.d3 d6 6.e4 e5 7.Nge2 Bg4 8.h3 Be6 9.0–0 Qd7 10.Kh2 c5 11.f4 Qe8 12.f5 Bd7 13.Be3 a6 14.g4 Nc6 15.g5 Nh5 16.Nd5 Qd8**.

Now (from diagram 56) Daniel played **17.f6**, which forces the Bishop to h8 where it will lay (like someone that's buried alive) for the rest of the game. As mentioned earlier, such a Bishop allows White to confidently play on the kingside, center, or queenside since he will have a piece more taking part in the battle. The finish was a typical bit of blitz brutality: **17...Bh8 18.Bf3 Nf4 19.Bxf4 exf4 20.Nexf4 Ne5 21.Ne7+**, 1-0.

Entombed Bishops are the exception, however. The most common Tall-Pawns are simply Bishops trapped behind (and blocked by) their pawns.

A. Grischuk - C. Bauer, Port Barcares 2005

1.e4 d5 2.exd5 Qxd5 3.Nc3 Qa5 4.d4 Nf6 5.Bd2 c6 6.Bc4 Bf5 7.Nd5 Qd8 8.Nxf6+ gxf6 9.Nf3 e6 10.c3 Nd7 11.Nh4 Bg6 12.Bb3 Nb6 13.Qf3 Be7 14.g3 Qd7 15.0–0 f5

Diagram 57

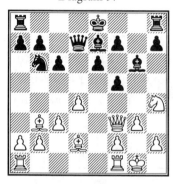

White to move

The problem with black's position is the Bishop on g6 (it really does look like a Tall-Pawn, doesn't it?). This unfortunate piece can't emerge on h5 (white's Queen is keeping that square under wraps), and if it tries to escape to f7 or e8 (via …f7-f6—of course, f7 and e8 don't look so great either) then the e6-pawn will turn into a seriously weak target.

16.Ng2

Stopping …Bxh4, getting ready to hop into f4, and also preparing to torment black's light-squared Bishop by h2-h4-h5.

16…Nd5 17.Nf4 0–0–0 18.Rfe1

The Rook eyes e5 and also serves a prophylactic role: the …f7-f6 push (as unattractive as it might be) is ruled out right away.

18…Nxf4 19.Bxf4 Bd6 20.Bxd6 Qxd6 21.Re5

While black's Bishop is pretending it's a pawn, white's Bishop will serve an active role in the center and on the queenside—it will never have to worry about being challenged by the lump on g6.

White's Re5 not only prepares to double on the e-file (making sure …f7-f6 can't be played), but it also prevents a potential …c6-c5 break. Notice how White isn't in any hurry—his plan is the killing of enemy counterplay first (why let a tied up opponent shed his chains?), and the preparation for his own decisive queenside breakthrough second.

21…Kb8 22.Bc4

This makes way for the advance of his b-pawn.

22…Rhe8

Hoping to play …f7-f6 with …e6-e5 to follow.

23.Rae1!

Access denied! No counterplay allowed!

23...Re7 24.b4

Preparing a queenside pawn storm.

24...Rc7?

Black decides to remain passive, but this leaves him no hope whatsoever of survival. Instead, 24...Rde8 goes all out for ...f7-f6 followed by ...e6-e5. I think he rejected this due to the annoying 25.Qf4! Now (after 25.Qf4) 26.Rxf5 is a threat and stopping it by 25...Rd8 is a return to passivity that ends black's ...f7-f6 hopes. Nevertheless, he needs to activate his pieces, even if it loses a pawn (anything is better than sitting around waiting to die). Thus my recommendation is 24...Rde8 25.Qf4! f6! 26.Rxf5! (Not falling for 26.Rxe6? Qxf4 27.gxf4 Rxe6 28.Rxe6 Rg8 29.Kf1 Bf7 winning the Exchange.) 26...e5 27.dxe5 fxe5 28.Qh6 Rd7 29.Rf3 e4 30.Rfe3 Rf8 when white's a solid pawn ahead (and obviously better), but all of black's pieces are dancing to their own tune (an active army always gives you at least some fighting chances).

25.h4 h5

Diagram 58

A classic Tall-Pawn on g6

26.a4

Missing 26.Bxe6! f4 (26...fxe6 27.Rxe6) 27.Bh3 fxg3 28.Qxg3, winning.

26...Qf8 27.Qf4

This freezes the f5-pawn, takes aim at the enemy King along the h2-b8 diagonal, and denies the black Queen use of h6. The rest of the game was a squash.

27...Rdc8 28.Bf1 Bh7 29.Be2 Bg6 30.Bf3 Ka8 31.b5 Qa3 32.a5 cxb5 33.Rxb5 a6 34.Rxb7 Rxb7 35.Rb1 Qe7 (35...Rcb8 36.Qc7) **36.Rxb7 Qxb7 37.Bxb7+ Kxb7 38.Qd6 Rc6 39.Qb4+ Kc8 40.f4,** 1-0. Even at the end, the black Bishop is still sitting on g6, alone and forgotten.

Clearly, you need to think twice before placing your pawns on the same color as your Bishop! In general, you should only do this if your Bishop can get outside the pawn chain (which would make it active), or if your Bishop is proving useful (most likely as a defender) inside the chain.

Of course, all the knowledge and good intentions in the world won't stop you from ending up with a Tall-Pawn from time to time. If this occurs, you need to:

➤ Get your pawns off the color of your Bishop (unblocking it).

➤ Get your Bishop outside the pawn chain.

➤ Exchange the horrible Bishop for an enemy Bishop or Knight.

The next example (played at a slow time control, so there was plenty of time to think about what was going on) shows both sides ignoring all of these rules. I don't know about Black, but White was familiar with these ideas.

Daniel S (1823) - metapuff (1938), ICC 2007

1.c4 Nf6 2.g3 g6 3.Bg2 Bg7 4.Nc3 0–0 5.e4 d6 6.Nge2 c5 7.0–0 e5 8.d3 Nc6 9.Bg5 Be6 10.Nd5 Bxd5 11.cxd5 Nd4 12.Nxd4 cxd4 13.Qd2 Re8 (the opening was badly played by both sides, so don't pay much attention to it)

Diagram 59

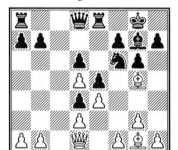

Black was obviously used to people trying to swap their dark-squared Bishop for his and, apparently, he had learned to avoid it with this little Rook move. The idea is that Bh6 can now be met by ...Bh8 when the Rook would no longer be vulnerable to the white Bishop on h6.

To the uninitiated, this might sound quite profound. However, it's also completely wrong! The truth is that, in this particular position, Black should welcome the exchange of dark-squared Bishops with open arms! There are a couple reasons for this, but the most pertinent is that the g7-Bishop is a Tall-Pawn that's trapped behind its chain. Yes, it does defend some squares, but all in all it's a pretty ugly piece. This misconception on black's part rears its head again in a few moves.

> **RULE**
>
> Don't hesitate to exchange your bad pieces for the opponent's good ones!

14.Rac1

White also fails his Bishop exam! His g2-Bishop isn't very happy, so White needs to activate the thing by getting it outside the pawn chain. Thus 14.Bh3 is correct (*Get your Bishop outside the pawn chain!*). This not only stops potential ...Ng4 moves (after White pushes his f-pawn to f4), but it also prevents Black from posting a Rook on the open c-file.

14...Qb6 15.f4

White is only thinking of mate, so less brutal ideas (like getting his Bishop outside the pawn chain with 15.Bh3) are not entering his mind.

15...Nd7

Better was 15...Ng4, heading for e3.

16.f5

16.Bh3 is still screaming for attention.

16...f6 17.Bh6??

Diagram 60

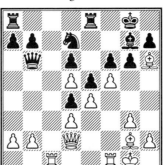

Both sides are getting solid Fs in Bishops 101. White needed to feel his g2-Bishop's pain and play 17.fxg6, unlocking the h3-c8 diagonal. Yes, it sacrifices a piece, but this was now necessary thanks to white's blocking that diagonal with f4-f5 (*Try not to entomb your own Bishop behind its pawn chain!*). It turns out that the capture on g6 is very strong: 17.fxg6 when Black has:

➤ 17...fxg5 18.gxh7+ Kh8 (Trying to hide behind white's pawn. 18...Kxh7 19.Rf7 Qd8 20.Rc7 Qxc7 21.Qxg5 is game over) 19.Rf7 Qd8 20.Bh3 Nc5 21.b4 Na6 22.Bc8!! Rxc8 23.Rxc8 Qxc8 24.Qxg5 is devastating.

➤ 17...hxg6 18.Bh3 is strong.

➤ 17...Qd8 18.gxh7+ Kxh7 19.Bh3 fxg5 20.Rf7 Re7 21.Rxe7 Qxe7 22.Rc7 Rd8 23.Rxb7 with a winning attack for White.

Notice the huge role white's ignored light-squared Bishop plays in all these variations.

17...Bh8??

Poor metapuff is still trying to retain his Tall-Pawn. Instead, 17...g5! 18.Bxg7 Kxg7 shines a very different light on the position. In that case Black wisely got rid of his inactive Bishop while keeping white's f-pawn on f5 (thereby turning the g2-Bishop into a Tall-Pawn). The resulting situation is very comfortable for Black, who has a safe King and enjoys a Knight in a closed position versus an inactive white Bishop.

18.fxg6

Suddenly White wakes up and smells the stagnating Bishops!

18...hxg6 19.Bh3

19.h4 followed by 20.Bh3 is probably even more accurate. Nevertheless, 19.Bh3 proved more than adequate to turn the tide permanently in white's favor. The rest of the game is worth looking at just so you can see how strong a Bishop can become if you manage to get it outside the pawn chain: **19...Nc5 20.b4 Na6 21.a3 Nc7 22.Qc2 Re7 23.Qd2 Nb5 24.Be6+ Kh7 25.h4 Nxa3 26.Kg2 Nb5 27.Rh1 Nc3 28.Rcf1 Qxb4 29.h5 g5 30.Bxg5 fxg5 31.Qxg5 Rg7 32.Qf5+ Kh6 33.Qf6+ Kh7 34.Bf5+ Kg8 35.Qe6+ Rf7 36.Bh7+ Kxh7 37.Qxf7+** (37.Rxf7+ mates) **37...Bg7 38.h6 Qb2+ 39.Rf2 Qxf2+ 40.Kxf2 Nxe4+ 41.Kg2**, 1-0.

This just goes to show that knowing strategic concepts in a theoretical sense is one thing, while being able to actually notice it and put it to use in a real battle situation is quite another. And make no mistake about it—this inability to turn knowledge into practical application goes right up the rating ladder. One student (during our first lesson), rated 2150 FIDE, got angry when I began to talk about the proper use of minor pieces. He said, "I already know all that stuff!" Yet, as we went through his games, he would fail to implement any of it. Instead of treating his minor pieces right, he constantly got sidetracked by "more important" thoughts (material, attack, etc.). Naturally, when he lost to superior players, he rarely understood what went wrong.

To cure this illness, you need to:

➤ Learn the basic ideas and concepts given in this book

➤ Reinforce the information by constant repetition.

➤ Try to solve as many chess problems as possible that are devoted to imbalances.

➤ Go through your own games and make a serious effort to spot where you could have improved the "life" of your minor pieces.

Bishops of Opposite Colors

We've all heard of the strange goings on in relation to *Bishops of opposite colors*. Aren't those things supposed to make endgames unwinnable even if you're a gazillion pawns down? Are we supposed to court them or avoid them? Is it true that the Apocalypse is upon us if Bishops of opposite colors appear on every board, at the same time, in the same round, of the same grandmaster tournament? I run into questions like this all the time!

Of course, Bishops of opposite colors is merely a Bishop vs. Bishop battle. Yet, it's a strange battle that resembles a war between two creatures in different dimensions. Because they will live on different colored diagonals until they are placed in the after-game box, the Bishops can't touch, they can't defend what the other attacks (or attack what the other defends!), and if you place your pawns and/or King on the opposite color of the enemy Bishop, the ghost-Bishop will find that it can't touch anything at all.

Diagram 61

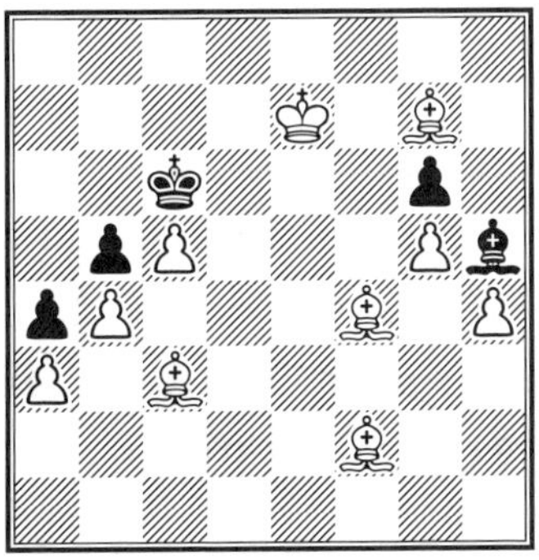

White to move

Okay, this is an insane position! But though it's ridiculous, it does a very good job at showing how absurd a Bishop of opposite colors position can be.

Here White is two pawns and three pieces ahead. Black is passive, and white's King is also far better placed than black's. Yet, the game is a dead draw! How can this be?

The problem for White is that his armada of dark-squared Bishops can't touch a light square if their lives depended on it. This means that the only white unit that can attack the c6-square and the g6-pawn is the King. And, since those two targets are so far apart, white's King can't skip from one to the other in a single move. Thus, Black will always have a "pass" move with his King (...Kc6-d7/d5 and back to c6 over and over) or Bishop (...Bh5-d1-h5-d1, etc), depending on the direction white's King has gone.

Let's look at some moves:

1.Ke6 Bd1 2.Kf7 Bh5

2...Bc2?? loses to 3.h5 gxh5 4.g6 when black's remaining piece will soon have to sacrifice itself on g6 or g8. This tells us that the black Bishop must do two jobs: 1) Defend g6 if it's attacked. 2) Never lose contact with the h5-square. That way h4-h5 can always be met by ...Bxh5 when White fails to get a passed pawn.

3.Bce5 Kd7 4.Bd6 Kc6 5.Kf6 Kd5 6.Ke7

Threatening to take control over c6 by Kd7.

6...Kc6

Now we see that whenever white's King is ready to challenge for the c6-square, black's King must immediately scurry back to c6 and let his light-squared Bishop take over the passing duties.

7.Bc3 Bd1

Black must avoid 7...Kd5?? 8.Kd7 Bg4+ 9.Kc7 when White has gained control over c6, thereby freeing the c5-pawn.

8.Ke6 Bg4+ 9.Kf7 Bh5

9...Bf5?? 10.h5 wins.

10.Kf6 Kd7, ½-½ since White can't make any progress!

It's clear that if we remove three of white's Bishops from diagram 61, we would get a more realistic endgame where White can't win with two healthy extra pawns. And this is where the quasi-truth that "Bishops of opposite colors often allows the defender to draw otherwise lost endgames" comes from. But please note the word "often." Many endgames with Bishops of opposite colors are also won.

Diagram 62

Black to move

This position has the same basic dynamics as found in diagram 61. If White can win the e6-pawn, win the c6-square, or turn his e5-pawn into a passer, the game will be his. If Black can stop White from doing those things, the game will be drawn. In this case the two areas of combat (e6 and c6) are just a step away from each other, so White wins (note that the game would be drawn if black's Bishop stood on a2, b3, c4, or d5).

1...Bf5

No better is 1...Bg8 2.d5+! (The key—Black has to take with the King and give up c6 or take with the pawn and give White a passed e-pawn.) 2...exd5 (2...Kxd5 3.Kd7 Bf7 4.c6 Be8+ 5.Kxe8 Kxc6 6.Ke7 Kd5 7.Kd7) 3.e6 d4 (3...Bh7 4.Kf6) 4.Kf6 d3 5.e7 Kd7 6.c6+ Ke8 7.c7 and a pawn Queens.

2.d5+! exd5

2...Kxd5 gives up control over c6 after 3.Kd7, when 4.c6 will follow.

3.e6 d4 4.Kf7 d3 5.e7 Bd7 6.Bf4, 1-0.

A. Reprintsev - J. Guo, Ottawa 2007

1.e4 c5 2.b3 Nc6 3.Bb2 e5 4.f4 exf4 5.Qf3 Qh4+ 6.g3 fxg3 7.hxg3 Qe7 8.Bc4 Nf6 9.Bxf6 Qxf6 10.Qxf6 gxf6 11.Nc3 Bd6 12.Nge2 Be5 13.0–0–0 d6 14.Nd5 Kd8 15.Rdf1 Be6 16.Nxf6 Ke7 17.Nd5+ Bxd5 18.Bxd5 Raf8 19.c3 Nd8 20.d4 cxd4 21.cxd4 Bg7 22.Kd2 Ne6 23.Kd3 b6 24.Rh5 Bf6 25.Rfh1 h6 26.Rxh6 Rxh6 27.Rxh6 Rh8 28.Rxh8 Bxh8

Diagram 63

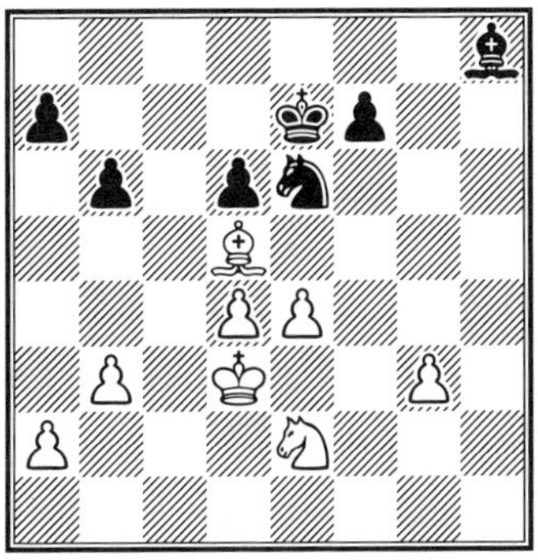

It's clear that Bishops of opposite colors can be a real problem for the superior side. If you have an extra pawn or two and feel that opposite colored Bishops might make the winning process a nightmare, then go out of your way to exchange one of the Bishops. This sounds obvious, but I've seen many players not grab the chance for such a trade and pay for it later in a lost half point.

In diagram 63 White has a solid extra pawn and the superior King (which would love to rush into the enemy position via Kd3-c4-b5-a6). However, the d4-pawn is under pressure and a possible …Nc7 will keep white's King out of b5. Even more bothersome is the presence of Bishops of opposite colors. So, without further ado, he snapped off the Knight and ended the opposite Bishop "threat"!

29.Bxe6! fxe6 30.Nf4

Threatens Ng6+ and also ties the enemy King to the defense of e6.

30…Bg7 31.a4 e5 32.dxe5 dxe5

Not a happy move, but 32…Bxe5 33.Ng6+ followed by 34.Nxe5 leads to a hopelessly lost King and pawn endgame.

33.Nd5+ Kd6 34.Kc4, 1-0. No muss, no fuss. Getting rid of the opposite colored Bishops made the whole winning process smooth and worry free.

Though Bishops of opposite colors do increase the defender's chances of holding an inferior endgame in many cases, the same opposite colored Bishops favors the attacker (in a middlegame or endgame) if more pieces appear on the board.

Diagram 64

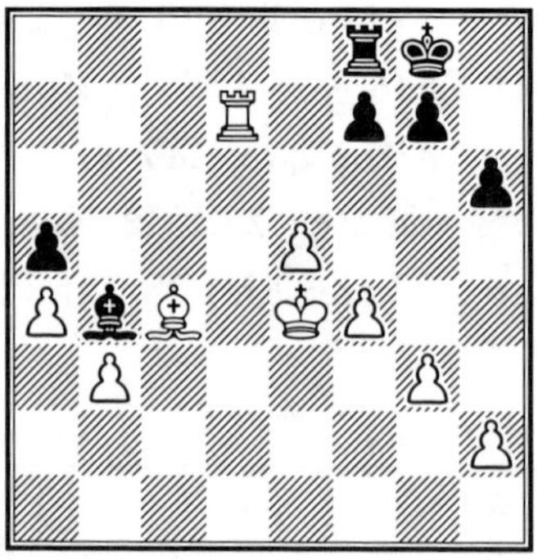

Black to move

White is two pawns up. However, his queenside majority is frozen by black's a-pawn and Bishop. What really makes black's life a living hell is the combination of white's Rook and Bishop hitting f7. This completely immobilizes black's army and leaves him waiting helplessly while White improves his position. The heat against f7, combined with the extra kingside pawn, ensures an easy victory for White.

1…g6 2.g4 Bc3 3.f5 gxf5+ 4.gxf5 Bb4 5.f6 Bc3 6.Kf5

White calmly brings all his pieces to their optimum positions before starting the final assault. When your opponent is helpless, enjoy the luxury of putting every part of your position in perfect order.

6...Bb4

Black's Bishop is forced to keep a permanent eye on b4 since 6...Bb2 allows 7.b4! axb4 8.a5 when the black b-pawn isn't going anywhere (thanks to the opposite Bishops) while white's passed a-pawn will confidently head for a transformative experience on a8.

7.e6 fxe6+ 8.Bxe6+ Kh8 9.Kg6 and Black will soon be mated.

To show you how important the existence of the Rooks was to white's cause, let's look at the same position, sans Rooks.

Diagram 65

Black to move

Now Black's King is free and after **1...Kf8 2.f5 Ke7**, White won't be able to win the game against correct defense (though he would be a fool not to try for a long, long time!).

Summary

> A Bishop is considered *Active* if it's outside the pawn chain and/or enjoying life on a reasonably clutter-free diagonal.

> A Bishop is considered *Useful* if it's doing an important (defensive or dynamic) task(s). Such a defensive Bishop can be ugly to look at, but its absence would cause your position to undergo serious difficulties.

> A Bishop is said to be a *Tall-Pawn* if it's not serving a useful function and is trapped behind its pawns (thus making it inactive). This kind of Bishop takes on the persona of an overgrown pawn that, sadly, can't turn into a Queen if it reaches the end of the board.

> Bishops are usually strongest in open positions. The fewer pawns in the way of a Bishop the greater its scope.

> Every time you move a pawn, check to see how it affects the activity of your Bishops! Obviously, turning an open position into a closed one will have a serious effect on these pieces, so train yourself to always take the health and care of your Bishops into account.

> While an active Bishop might look good, a useful Bishop trades style for substance and addresses the deeper needs (both dynamic and defensive) of a position.

> Always think twice before placing your pawns on the same color as your Bishop! In general, you should only do this if your Bishop can get outside the pawn chain (which would make it active), or if your Bishop is proving useful (most likely as a defender) inside the chain.

> If you have a Tall-Pawn, try to free it by getting the pawns off its color or by getting it outside the pawn chain. Failing those things, you can also try and exchange it for an enemy minor piece (thus following our "trade bad pieces for good ones" rule).

> All the knowledge and good intentions in the world won't stop you from ending up with a Tall-Pawn from time to time. If this occurs, you need to:

  ○ Get your pawns off the color of your Bishop (unblocking it).

  ○ Get your Bishop outside the pawn chain.

  ○ Exchange the horrible Bishop for an enemy Bishop or Knight.

Bishops—Tests

By now you should know how to make a Bishop active, appreciate a Bishop that's a defensive dynamo, and what to do if you end up with a Tall-Pawn. These tests will alert you to what's still hazy, and cement the knowledge that you've gained.

If you have trouble solving the tests, don't worry—that means we've uncovered something you don't understand, and this allows you to fix things by rereading the previous material or by picking up the bits of knowledge you're missing in the answers that start on page 443.

PART TWO - TEST **10**

Diagram 66

[Level: 1600 - 1800]

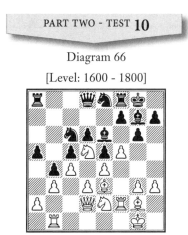

Black to move

PART TWO - TEST **11**

Diagram 67

[Level: 1400 - 1600]

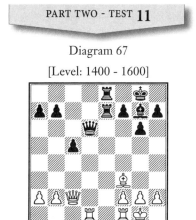

Black to move

What factors combine to give Black a decisive advantage?

PART TWO - TEST **12**

Diagram 68

[Level: 1400 - 1600]

White to move

PART TWO - TEST **13**

Diagram 69

[Level: 1400 - 1600]

White to move

PART TWO - TEST **14**

Diagram 70

[Level: 2100 on up]

White to move

PART TWO - TEST **15**

Diagram 71

[Level: 1400 - 1800]

White to move

PART TWO - TEST **16**

Diagram 72

[Level: 2100 on up]

White to move

Bishops vs. Knights
Grudge Match

Ladies and gentlemen, in this corner we have a Knight—it leaps, it prances, nothing is safe from it, and you never know what the thing will do next! In the other corner we have a Bishop—it enjoys super speed and can go from one edge of the board to the other in a single bound! Are you ready for the brutal battles that occur when one faces the other? Are you ready for the carnage they leave in their wake, and the wailing cries of defeat the losing side makes when his Bishop or Knight fails in this all-minor piece faceoff? Okay, then in that case, let's get ready to rumble!

By now you've learned the ins and outs of both minor pieces. In fact, many of you probably have already picked a favorite. Tigran Petrosian placed Knights on a pedestal, your author also has a deep love of Knights, and most amateurs fear Knights far more than Bishops (Knights are, quite simply, trickier). On the other hand, Fischer was perhaps the greatest aficionado of Bishops ever seen, and the vast majority of grandmasters prefer Bishops to Knights.

Nevertheless, whatever one's bias might be, you have to know how to get the most out of both pieces, and how to pit one against another. Fischer clearly preferred Bishops to Knights, but that didn't stop him from winning a Knight vs. Bishop battle if he felt the position favored the horse. The same can be said for Knight worshippers. If these folk find themselves in a wide-open position, chances are the Bishop will be the minor piece of preference. Ultimately, the real value of the minor pieces depends on the combined imbalances on the board. The position is closed? Knights are often for choice. Are you staring at an endgame with mutual running passed pawns? The Bishop usually wipes the floor with the Knight. And which minor piece would you choose in a position where it's all-important to be able to access both color squares—a Bishop can't do that, so a Knight is the way to go.

This battle of the minor pieces—each possessing different powers—is my favorite in all of chess. If I possess a Knight, I try hard to imprint "Knight characteristics" on the board so that the rapidly approaching battle with the enemy Bishop will favor me. If I have a Bishop, I do everything possible to make the position "Bishop friendly." The ability to create a promising position for your minor piece(s) will set you apart from the other players. In fact, after losing to your superior Knight (or Bishop), your depressed (and clueless!) opponent will often tell you that it was just bad luck that things didn't work out for him!

The following things are critical in all Bishop vs. Knight battles:

▬▶ Be aware that there is, or there is going to be, a Bishop vs. Knight battle!

▬▶ Be aware of *all* the imbalances and how they relate to the minor piece(s) you and your opponent own.

▬▶ Create a board-situation that your minor piece craves!

Feeling the Minor Piece Tension

Our first example shows how an apparently simple position can actually be filled with minor piece tension:

Diagram 73

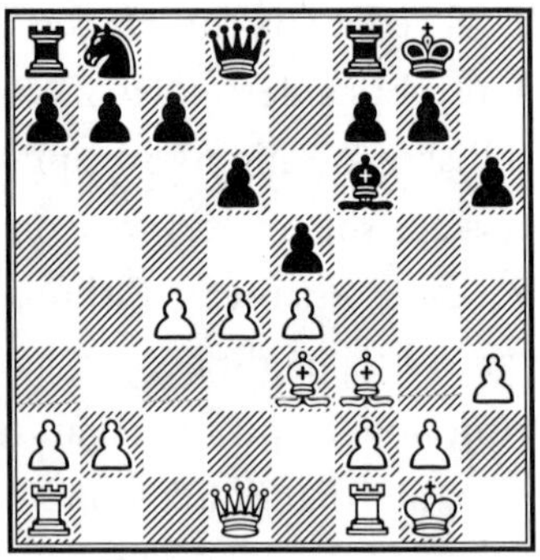

White to move

Please treat the variations in this example as a sort of theatrical drama—it might not be based on reality, but it has a profound effect on the viewer! I'm hoping this game will pass on a sense of urgency—a visual slap in the face that makes you exclaim, "Wow! I didn't realize that a 'boring' minor piece battle was so important, and that it could go back and forth so easily!"

On the surface, things look easy: White has two Bishops and would like to open things up, while Black has a Bishop and Knight and would be happy if he could activate his Bishop and find a nice home for his horse. The main questions here are, should White take on e5, push to d5, or simply ignore the face-off between the d4- and e5-pawns altogether? All these decisions are dependent on how they ultimately affect the state of the minor pieces, but achieving the optimum goals proves far harder than one might suppose.

Let's take a look at these three different options.

Closing the Center

1.d5

This gains space, kills off the black Bishop's hopes for an open a1-h8 diagonal, and deprives the Knight of c6. These things certainly sound great, but it all falls flat after black's thematic reply.

1...Bg5! White suddenly has nothing! Black's move forces the exchange of the dark-squared Bishops. This deprives White of his Bishop pair and (after 2.Bxg5 Qxg5) creates a new minor piece battle of Knight vs. inactive Bishop.

Diagram 74

White to move

Black wins the minor piece battle

> **RULE**
>
> If your opponent has two Bishops, exchange one off and create a more manageable Bishop vs. Bishop or Bishop vs. Knight scenario.

Passing

(diagram 73)

1.Qd2 exd4 2.Bxd4 Bxd4 3.Qxd4 Nc6 4.Qc3 Re8 5.Rfe1 Ne5 6.Be2 Qg5 and Black has no problems: his Knight is a good piece, white's Bishop isn't very impressive, white's central majority isn't going anywhere, and Black enjoys some pressure against e4. If 7.g3?! (Note that 7.c5 dxc5 8.Qxc5?? fails to 8...Nf3+ winning white's Queen) 7...Nd7 (Uncovers the Rook so that e4 is attacked, opens up the e5-square for black's Queen, and also creates the possibility of ...Nc5) 8.Bf3 Qe5 9.Qxe5 Nxe5 10.Be2 Nc6 11.Bg4 Nd4 (There was no hurry for this since 11...Re7 followed by ...Rae8 was also quite good. However, 11...Nd4 shows Black clearly winning the minor piece battle so it's important to highlight.) 12.Rad1 c5 and the Knight has found a permanent home on d4.

Diagram 75

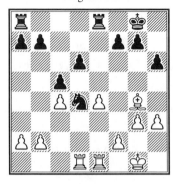

Black's minor piece is a happy camper

Let's Open It Up!

Diagram 73 (repeat)

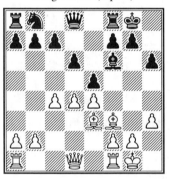

White to move

1.dxe5

The critical try. However, it's not a trivial decision because White has to worry about 1...dxe5, giving his opponent a lock on the d4-square after ...Nc6. Though this sounds impressive for Black, it turns out to be problematic since White gains a bothersome initiative.

1...dxe5 2.Qb3 b6

2...Qc8?? walks head first into 3.Bg4 when white's Bishops have won the day.

3.Rad1 Qe7 4.Bg4 Bg5

Not the only move by any means, but it's certainly the most thematic (trading the horrible Bishop for white's good one makes perfect sense). Naturally, Black would jump at ...Nc6-d4 except that 4...Nc6 allows 5.Rd7.

5.c5!

This not only gives the white Queen active possibilities on the a2-g8 diagonal, but it also allows the light-squared Bishop to be active even if it's driven back (Bg4-e2-c4 is suddenly "on").

5...Bxe3 6.fxe3

White's quite happy with this. His f1-Rook is suddenly king of the f-file and black's dreamed of Knight domination via ...Nb8-c6-d4 is no longer on the table.

6...Kh8

6...Qxc5?? 7.Rxf7 is too strong: 7...Rxf7 8.Rd8+ Qf8 9.Rxf8+ Kxf8 10.Qd5 Nc6 11.Qxc6 and wins.

7.Qc4 g6

Hoping to chase the Bishop away by ...h6-h5.

8.Qc3

Not losing sight of the Bishop versus Knight battle, White takes aim at e5 while also preparing Bg4-e2 when the Bishop can find an active role along the f1-a6 diagonal (most notably leaping to c4 or b5 in many variations).

8.Bc8!? is hard to resist if you see it. Lines like 8...Rxc8 9.Rxf7 Qe8 (9...Qxc5?? 10.Qe6 mates) 10.Rdf1 give White a fearsome attack. Black can put up a much better defense, but I think the variations after 8.Bc8 are still fun for White. This is an enjoyable line to analyze, but has no place in this book since it takes us far afield from our Bishop vs. Knight theme.

I should add that White has many good moves here. For example, 8.c6 also looks tasty and highlights the sad state of black's Knight.

8...f6

8...Qxc5 9.Qxc5 bxc5 10.Rd5 gives White a huge advantage.

9.Rd5 h5 10.Be2 and it's clear that the Bishop is superior to the Knight.

Diagram 76

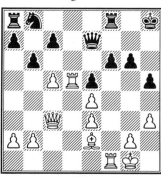

White finally won a minor piece battle

So does this mean that 1.dxe5 is just better for White? Not necessarily! Black lost that battle because he didn't do enough to make his Knight challenge the white Bishops. So let's step back to diagram 73 and show a more principled course for Black:

1.dxe5 dxe5 2.Qb3 Nc6!

This is more like it! Black *insists* on making his Knight an active participant in the game.

3.Qxb7 Nd4

This is how a Knight should be used!

4.Bg4

4.Bxd4 exd4 5.e5 Rb8 is okay for Black.

4...a5 5.Qd5 Qe7 6.c5 Rab8 gives Black good compensation for the sacrificed pawn.

Diagram 77

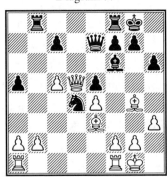

Black's Knight is strutting its stuff

I should add that after 1.dxe5 Black isn't forced to take back with his pawn. Here's a final minor piece battle from the position in diagram 73:

1.dxe5 Bxe5 2.c5

White opens things up as much as possible. Instead, 2.Bg4 Nc6 3.f4 Bxb2 (3...Bf6 4.Qd2 Re8 5.Bf3 gives White an edge, thanks to his center and two nice Bishops) 4.Rb1 Bf6 is okay for Black after 5.Rxb7 Na5 6.Rb4 c5 7.Ra4 Qc7 8.Bf3 Nc6.

2...Nc6 3.cxd6 Qxd6 4.Qxd6 Bxd6 5.Rfd1 Rfd8 6.Be2 Be5 7.Rab1 Bd4

7...g5!, which fights for the dark squares and prevents f2-f4, is far more combative.

8.Bf4 Be5 9.Bxe5 Nxe5 10.f4 and here white's central majority and active Bishop grants him the more pleasant position (though black's Knight is still hoping to make an impact with ...Nc6-d4 at some point).

We've seen the minor piece battle swing back and forth in these lines. Clearly, the Bishop versus Knight faceoff is important and calls for energetic and pointed play if you wish to see your minor piece reign supreme.

The Two Bishops

Now let's settle down a bit and take a look at some basic situations. First on our agenda is the extremely common two Bishops vs. Bishop and Knight battle (I consider this to be an extension of a Bishop vs. Knight situation, though an exchange of Knight for Bishop would turn that into a pure Bishop vs. Bishop fight).

Possessing two Bishops is far better than only having one because the Bishop's main weaknesses—it's inability to control a whole color complex—is cured by the fact that both white and dark diagonals can now be fully patrolled. Of course, if the position is closed and all diagonals are blocked, the Bishops might not be very impressive. But, in general, the Bishop pair is indeed a nice thing to have and needs to be dealt with by the opponent. The simplest way to remove this problem is to exchange one of the enemy Bishops (either by trading your Knight or Bishop for an enemy Bishop), thus creating a far more manageable Bishop vs. Knight or Bishop vs. Bishop situation.

Two Bishops Antidote — Trade One Off

V. Ivanchuk - A. Shirov, Morelia 2008

1.d4 d5 2.c4 c6 3.Nf3 Nf6 4.Nc3 e6 5.Bg5 h6 6.Bxf6 Qxf6 7.e3 Nd7 8.Qd2 g5 9.Bd3 Bg7 10.0–0 0–0 11.Qc2 dxc4 12.Bxc4 c5 13.Rfd1 g4 14.Ne1 cxd4 15.exd4 Nb6 16.Be2 h5 17.Ne4 Qg6 18.Nc3 Qxc2 19.Nxc2 Bd7 20.Rd2 Bh6 21.Ne3 f5 22.g3 f4 23.gxf4 Bxf4 24.Re1 Bc6

Diagram 78

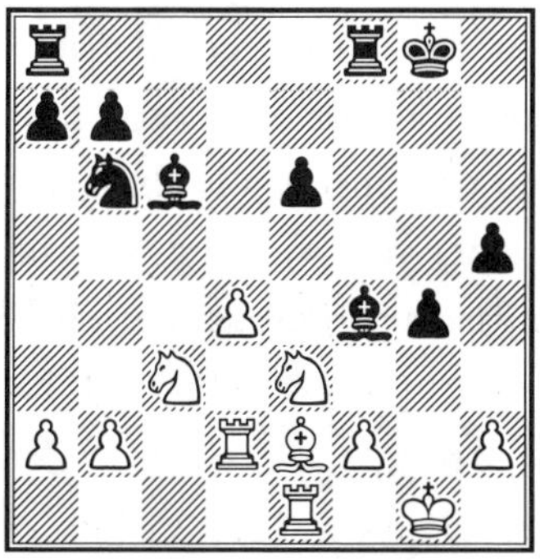

White to move

White seems to be under heavy pressure since black's Bishop pair appears quite fearsome and is clearly better than white's Bishop and Knight. Ivanchuk realizes there's nothing he can do about the guy on f4, but the monster on c6 is quite another matter.

25.Bb5!

White makes use of our anti-Bishop pair formula. A swap of the passive Bishop on e2 for the reaper on c6 takes a lot of the heat off of white's game.

25...Bf3

"No, I don't want to trade."

26.Be2

"I insist!"

26...Bc6 27.Bb5, ½-½.

O. De La Riva Aguado - R. Ponomariov, Pamplona 2005

1.e4 c5 2.Nf3 e6 3.b3 Nf6 4.e5 Nd5 5.Bb2 Nc6 6.g3 g6 7.Na3 Bg7 8.Nc4 0–0 9.Bg2 b6 10.0–0 Ba6 11.d3 Bxc4 12.dxc4 Nde7 13.Qe2 Qc7 14.Rae1 Rad8 15.Bc1 d6 16.exd6 Qxd6 17.Bf4 Qd7 18.Rd1 Qc8 19.h4 Nf5 20.Qe4 Ncd4 21.Nxd4 Nxd4 22.c3 Nf5 23.Qc2

Diagram 79

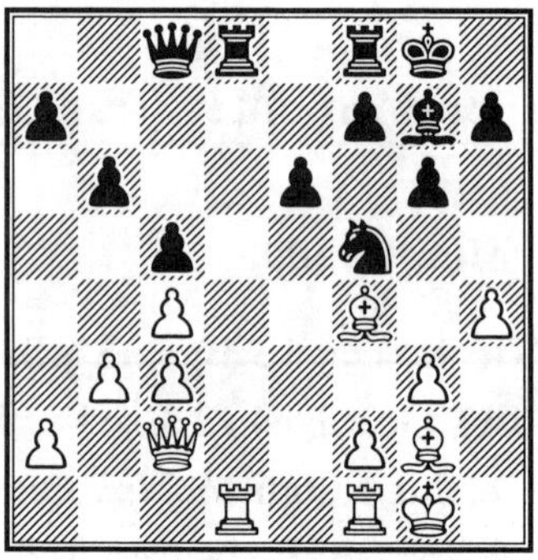

Black to move

White has two Bishops but Black has a central majority of pawns. It's important to note that white's queenside majority, though it controls key squares on d4 and d5, isn't able to expand or transform itself into a passed pawn.

Since Bishops work together very well and control two important diagonals, Black wastes no time in initiating an exchange.

23...Bh6!

There goes white's pair of Bishops!

24. Bxh6 Nxh6

With it's dark-squared brother off the board, the light-squared Bishop will prove to be remarkably ineffective.

From this point on, White can't hope for more than a draw. The Knight will show itself to be far more flexible than the Bishop, and black's central pawn majority will prove hard to contain.

25.Bh3 Kg7

Black's in no hurry, so he uses his King to tighten up the loose dark squares on f6 and h6.

26.Qe2 Qc7 27.Rxd8 Rxd8 28.Rd1 Rxd1+ 29.Qxd1 f5

The rest of the game will be given with minimal comment. In a nutshell, Black slowly but surely repositions his Knight, advances his central and kingside pawns, improves the position of his King, and then shows just how useful the Knight is at both attack and defense.

30.Qd2 Ng8 31.Bg2 Nf6 32.Bf3 e5 33.Kf1 e4 34.Be2 Kf7 35.Ke1 Qe5 36.Qe3 Kg7 37.Kd2 Qd6+ 38.Kc2 Nd7 39.Kc1 Nf8 40.Kc2 Ne6 (Black—who is dreaming of having his pawns act like a tidal wave rushing through white's position—wants to play …h6 followed by …g5 and eventually …f5-f4. The Knight on e6 will defend both the g5- and f4-squares.) **41.Bf1 h6 42.Kc1 g5 43.hxg5 hxg5 44.Kc2 Kf6 45.Kc1 f4 46.gxf4 Qxf4 47.Kd2 Ng7** (The Knight achieved its goals on e6 and now heads to f5 where it will break the block on e3.) **48.Bg2** (48.Bh3 Nf5 49.Bxf5 Qxe3+ 50.Kxe3 Kxf5 is easy for Black) **48…Ke5 49.Bxe4 Qxe4 50.Qxg5+ Nf5** (After showing its attacking powers, the Knight now demonstrates how it can defend its King.) **51.Qd8 Qb7 52.Ke2 Kf4**, 0-1.

Free Range Bishops Are Happier Bishops

Naturally, in many cases the Bishops aren't contained by the pawn structure and can't be removed by an exchange. In that case, they can really show their stuff.

S. Reshevsky - Van den Berg, Amsterdam 1950

1.d4 Nf6 2.c4 e6 3.Nc3 Bb4 4.e3 0–0 5.Ne2 d5 6.a3 Bxc3+ 7.Nxc3 b6 8.b4 c5

Diagram 80

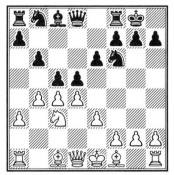

White to move

Black's last move wasn't too bright. White has the two Bishops and Black went out of his way to blast open the center! True, white's King is still in the middle and, at times, opening things up to punish the enemy's King position takes precedence over any gains you give to the Bishop pair. However, in this case Black doesn't get anything going at all, and he'll experience nothing but misery once those diagonals fall into the Bishop's hands.

9.dxc5 bxc5 10.cxd5 cxb4 11.axb4 exd5 12.Be2

White can't be foolish and leave his King in the middle too long. He owns the long-term plusses of two Bishops and a superior pawn structure, so once his King is safe everything should go his way.

12...Nc6 13.b5 Na5 14.Ba3 Re8 15.0–0

Black doesn't have anything that can challenge the might of the dark-squared Bishop.

15...Bf5 16.Bc5 Ne4 17.Bb4 Nxc3 18.Bxc3 Nc4 19.Qd4

Diagram 81

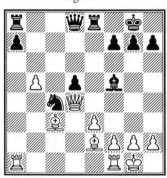

Black's already busted. Both a7 and d5 are weak, and mate is threatened on g7. The c3-Bishop's control over the a1-h8 diagonal is a fearsome thing to behold.

19...Qg5

Black's well aware of his predicament, and he decides to seek kingside coun- terplay. It's not going to work, but he might as well go down fighting.

20.Qxd5

Welcoming the complications that follow. Of course, there was nothing wrong with the prosaic 20.Rxa7 Rxa7 21.Qxa7 Be4 22.g3 when Black has no effective way to continue his attack.

20...Nxe3

His last shot.

21.fxe3 Qxe3+ 22.Kh1 Bg6!

The point of his combination. Naturally, 22...Qxc3 23.Qxf5 Rxe2 24.Qxf7+ Kh8 fails to 25.Qf8+ Rxf8 26.Rxf8 mate.

23.Bh5! Rad8?

Capitulation. Much better was 23...Qxc3 24.Bxg6 hxg6 25.Qxf7+ Kh7 (25...Kh8 26.Ra4 g5 27.Rxa7 Qe5 28.b6 Rab8 29.Qh5+ Kg8 30.h3! Re7 [30...Rxb6? 31.Rxg7+! wins on the spot] 31.Qg6 and White should eventually win) 26.Ra4 g5 27.Qf5+ (27.Rxa7 is also good) 27...Kg8 28.Qd5+ Kh8 29.Qxg5 and White, with his extra pawn, pressure against a7, and threats against the enemy King, can count on victory.

24.Bxg6! Rxd5 25.Bxf7+ Kh8 26.Bxe8 Qxe8 27.Rxa7

The mixture of threats against g7 and back-rank threats leave Black without a defense.

27...Qc8

27...Rg5 (27...Rc5 28.b6 Rxc3 29.b7) 28.Rfa1 wins easily, though 28.b6?? lets Black back in the game after 28...h5 29.b7 Kh7.

28. Rc7!, 1-0. Black has nothing left to play for after 28...Qf5 29.Kg1 or 28...Qb8 29.Rxg7.

Bishops vs. Knights

In our last example, White had the two Bishops but the dark-squared Bishop was the hero since it not only found a home on a very long and clear diagonal, but there was nothing in black's camp that could oppose it. This same idea comes to the fore when contemplating the intricacies of Bishop vs. Knight. If the Knight hasn't found some god-like support point, and if the Bishop finds a clear diagonal, then the Knight will often be at a disadvantage.

The Great Breakout

I. Ivanov - J. Benjamin, Jacksonville 1990

1.c4 g6 2.e4 Bg7 3.d4 d6 4.Nc3 Nf6 5.Be2 0–0 6.Nf3 e5 7.d5 a5 8.0–0 Na6 9.Bg5 h6 10.Bh4 Qe8 11.Ne1 Nc5 12.Bxf6 Bxf6 13.Bg4

Not allowing Black to retain the Bishop pair!

13...Bxg4 14.Qxg4

Diagram 82

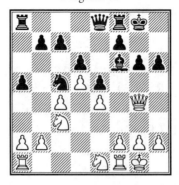

Black to move

Black's worst placed minor piece is the Bishop on f6 (at the moment there can't be any talk of it being superior to a Knight). Since the main imbalance is Bishop vs. Knight, Black immediately goes out of his way to make sure the Bishop is an active participant in the upcoming battle.

14...Bd8!

A very elegant solution to the problem! The Bishop hopes to effectively enter the game along the a7-g1 diagonal via ...c7-c6 followed (ideally) by ...Bb6. Of course, the Bishop might be used to temporarily support d6 by ...Bc7, or hit c3 after ...a4 followed by ...Ba5. All this shows just how flexible the Bishop is on d8.

What's particular instructive about Benjamin's move is that he's not going to move his Bishop to a diagonal that's already open. Instead, he's going to *create* that diagonal!

Note that 14...Bg5 15.Qe2 f5 is playable, though in that case White is a bit better after 16.Nd3 (The side with two Knights usually does well to trade one of them. Knights don't work particularly well together.), when 16...Nxd3 17.Qxd3 f4 (this kind of pawn storm is black's usual plan in such positions) turns the Bishop into a Tall-Pawn, and 16...Nxe4 17.Nxe4 fxe4 18.Qxe4 is very pleasant for the first player—he owns the e4-square, his Knight, in true octopus fashion, influences squares in every direction (e1, c1, b2, b4, c5, e5, f4, f2), and a kingside attack is more or less impossible for Black to achieve while White can easily drum up queenside play with a well-timed c4-c5 push.

> **RULE**
>
> At times there won't be any ready-made diagonals available for your Bishop. If that's the case, see if you can create a useful diagonal for it!

15.Qe2 c6 16.Rd1 Bc7

The Bishop patiently accepts a defensive role, sure that its glory days are yet to come.

17.h4 Qe7 18.g3 Kg7 19.Nf3 a4 20.h5 Ba5

With d6 safe, it's time for the Bishop to shine. The immediate threat is 21...a3.

21.Rc1 Qd7 22.Rfd1 Rae8 23.Kg2 f5

Diagram 83

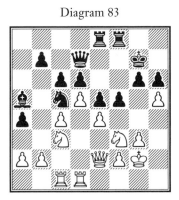

It's clear that Black is doing well. His Knight is better than either of white's, his Bishop is ready to chop on c3 in many lines, while it's also ready to step back to b6 where (combined with the f8-Rook) it will add to the pressure against f2.

24.exf5

Joel Benjamin, in his excellent book *American Grandmaster*, gave the following variations and assessments:

> 24.Nh4 Bxc3 25.Rxc3 Nxe4 26.Nxg6 Nxc3 27.Nxf8 Rxf8 28.bxc3 f4 29.Rd3 Kh8 "with a slight initiative for Black."

> 24.hxg6 Bxc3 25.Rxc3 Nxe4 26.Re3 Nf6 "with some advantage for Black."

24...Rxf5 25.Ne4 Nxe4 26.Qxe4 Ref8 27.Rd3 Rxh5 28.Nh4

28.g4 fails to 28...cxd5 29.cxd5 (29.Rxd5? Rf4 30.Qxf4 exf4 31.gxh5 Qg4+ 32.Kf1 Qxf3) 29...Rf4 30.Qxf4 exf4 31.gxh5 Qg4+ 32.Kf1 Qxh5 33.Rc4 (33.Rcd1 g5) 33...Qf5 34.Rdd4 g5 35.Rxa4 Bb6 36.Rdb4 Qc2 and White's dead.

28...Rxh4! 29.gxh4

29.Qxh4 Qf5 30.Rdd1 Bd8 31.Qh3 Qxf2+ 32.Kh1 Qf3+ 33.Qg2 Qh5+ 34.Qh2 Qg4 35.Rf1 (35.dxc6 Rf5 36.cxb7 Qf3+ 37.Qg2 Rh5+ 38.Kg1 Bb6+ 39.c5 Bxc5+ wins) 35...Rxf1+ 36.Rxf1 Qxc4 37.Qh3 Qxd5+ 38.Kh2 Qd2+ 39.Kh1 Qg5 40.Qe6 Qe7 "and Black wins with his mass of extra pawns."—Benjamin.

The rest of the game was a slaughter:

29...Rf4 30.Qe2 Qf5 31.c5 cxd5 32.cxd6 Bb6 (at last!) **33.Rf1 e4 34.Rg3 d4 35.Qd2 e3 36.Qe1 Qd5+ 37.Kh3 Qe6+** (Both sides were in serious time pressure and were rushing to reach move 40. Naturally, if Benjamin had an extra moment to think he would have played 37...Rxh4+! 38.Kxh4 Qh5 mate!) **38.Kg2 Qd5+ 39.f3 Qxd6**, 0-1. Ivanov lost on time, but his position is completely hopeless.

> **RULE**
>
> Two Knights don't work particularly well together, so exchanging one of them (for an enemy Bishop or Knight) is usually a good idea.

In a way, a Bishop vs. Knight battle is a pretty clear-cut thing. Let's have a look at the basics.

Owner of the Bishop:

▶ Make it as active as possible by placing it on a free diagonal, or *creating* an uncluttered diagonal if one doesn't already exist.

▶ Prove that it's performing a key function and is thus extremely useful.

▶ Steer things into an endgame where the long-range capabilities of the Bishop give it a huge edge over the enemy Knight.

▶ Don't allow the enemy Knight to find its way to an advanced, permanent support point. This calls for *Anti-Knight Strategy*—Do your best to take away all advanced squares from the enemy horse!

Owner of the Knight:

▶ Closing the position is often good for your Knight.

▶ Steer for endgames where all the pawns are on one side of the board. This negates the enemy Bishop's long-range abilities while amplifying the importance of the Knight's ability to attack both white and dark squares.

▶ Do your best to create a permanent advanced home (support point) for your Knight.

▶ If a tasty support point exists but it seems a long way away (and/or very difficult to reach), try hard to find a way to get there! It might take several moves, but that's what moves are for—to place your pieces on their best squares so they can exert maximum effect on the board.

▶ Avoid "Trapped Knight Syndrome"! Many a Knight has been lost when it found itself trapped by the enemy Bishop.

Let's take a look at some of these ideas.

The Incarcerated Knight

Diagram 84

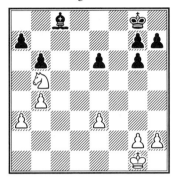

A. Bisguier - R. Fischer, Bled 1961
Black to move

Black's a pawn up but it's doubled, which means he can't force a passed kingside pawn (White just places his pawn on g3 and the enemy pawns can't force their way through). So the real battle (aside from King position, which is always important in the endgame) is going to center on the Bishop vs. Knight imbalance—at the moment the Knight is attacking a7 and also has dreams of cramming itself into d6 via Nd6 followed by e3-e4-e5 when it would be impossible for Black to win since the Knight would be too strong.

Fischer's move immediately addresses these issues.

1...Bd7!

The obvious 1...a6 gives Black absolutely nothing since, thanks to the weakness of b6, White can gain enough time to set up a couple optimum positions: 2.Nd6 Bd7 and now both 3.e4 Bc6 (3...e5 fails to 4.Nc4 Bc6 5.Nxb6 Bxe4 6.Nd7) 4.e5 Bd5 5.g3 Kf8 6.Nc8 (this deprives the Black King use of the b5-square later in the game) 6...b5 7.Kf2 Ke8 8.Ke3 Kd7 9.Nd6 Kc6 10.Kd4 and 3.Kf2 g5 4.Nc4 b5 5.Ne5 Bc8 6.e4 Kf8 7.Ke3 Ke7 8.Kd4 can only make White happy since his Knight has become the dominant piece (while King position is also on white's side). Note that in this last line (after 8.Kd4) the White Knight can swing around to c5 (Ne5-d3-c5) where it completely paralyzes black's position.

2.Nxa7

In the actual game, White avoided taking on a7, but he lost anyway: 2.Nd6 Kf8 3.e4 e5! (e4-e5 couldn't be allowed) 4.Kf2 Bc6 5.Nc4 Bxe4 6.Nxe5 Ke7 7.Nc4 Ke6 8.Ne3 Ke5 9.Ke2 Kd4 10.Kd2 Bc6 11.g3 Bd7 12.Nd1 Ke4 13.Ne3 Kf3 14.Kd3 g5 15.Kd4 Be6 16.Ke5 (16.Kd3 Bh3 followed by ...h5 and ...Kf2-g1xh2 also leads to a black victory) 16...Kxe3 17.Kxe6 Kf3 18.Kf5 Kg2 19.Kxg5 Kxh2 20.g4 b5 21.Kf5 Kg3 22.g5 g6+, 0-1.

2...b5!

Diagram 85

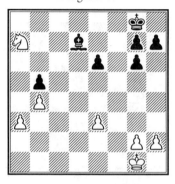

Trapped Knight

Freezing white's queenside pawns and also stopping the eventual extrication maneuver Kg1-f2-e2-d3-c4 followed by Nb5. Now white's Knight is trapped in the Bishop's web and it won't be able to get out.

3.Kf2 Kf7 4.Ke2

4.Kf3 e5 5.Ke4 Ke6 amounts to the same thing.

4...Ke7 5.Kd3 Kd6 6.Kd4 e5+ 7.Ke4 g5 8.h3 Ke6 9.Kd3 Kd5 and black's winning, though a certain amount of subtlety is still called for—interested readers should play around with it and see if they can reel in the victory.

Pawns and Squares Often Determine a Minor Piece's Value

Our next example features two identical positions with one "tiny" difference: the white c-pawn stands on c4 in one and c2 in the other. The difference this makes to the assessment is enormous!

Diagram 86

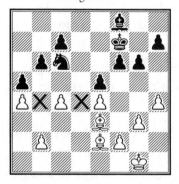

This kind of structure would usually favor Black in every phase of the game— the holes on b4 and d4 make the Knight very valuable, and Black would be delighted to swap dark-squared Bishops, ridding White of his Bishop pair and highlighting the weakness of the dark squares on b4, c5, and d4.

Clearly, the position in diagram 86 is very nice for Black. But what if we make a slight adjustment?

Diagram 87

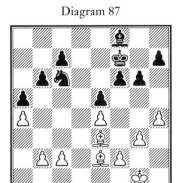

White to move

Here (diagram 87) we have the same position, but this time the c-pawn is on c2. Suddenly White has all the chances since the Knight can be contained by 1.c3. Using your pawn(s) to deprive the enemy Knights of advanced squares is Anti-Knight Strategy. You will be (or should be!) making use of it often, so look at these examples over and over until the Anti-Knight Strategy idea makes perfect sense to you.

Once the concept is burned into your brain, you'll (hopefully!) be less likely to push your pawns forward and blindly give up squares as you do so. Remember: pawns can't move backwards, so every time they advance, potential control of squares is lost. This doesn't mean that you shouldn't march pawns up the board—doing so gains space and often makes the pawn a dynamic part of the proceedings. Just be aware of the downside.

Even the Most Innocent Pawn-Move Can Potentially Weaken a Square

R. Fischer - S. Reshevsky, 2nd Piatigorsky Cup 1966

1.e4 e5 2.Nf3 Nc6 3.Bb5 a6 4.Ba4 Nf6 5.0–0 Be7 6.Re1 b5

This perfectly reasonable move, which gains queenside space and attacks white's Bishop, is the main line of the Ruy Lopez. But as good as it is, it does contain some potential flaws: quite often White will hit it with a2-a4 when a capture on b5 opens the a-file for the a1-Rook and also leaves the b5-pawn a bit loose. The other potential (though rarely seen) flaw is the c5-square—this pawn can't protect it anymore. That leaves the black d-pawn to perform babysitting duty on that square, and if it dares move to d5 later in the game then the c5-square suddenly becomes a gaping hole.

7.Bb3 0–0 8.c3 d6 9.h3 Nd7 10.d4 Nb6 11.Nbd2 exd4 12.cxd4 d5 13.Bc2 Be6 14.e5 Qd7 15.Nb3 Bf5 16.Bg5!

White wants total domination of the c5-square. Since the e7-Bishop was protecting it, White hurries to exchange Bishops and leave c5 bereft of protection.

16...Rfe8 17.Bxe7 Rxe7 18.Rc1 Nb4

Diagram 88

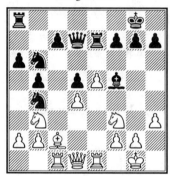

White to move

White has an advantage in space in the center. Black has a majority of queenside pawns, but its crippled since an eventual push to c5 would simply hang material. On the other hand, white's central/kingside pawn majority is still alive and kicking—if those pawns can get moving with f2-f4-f5 then Black might well be overrun. Black's unfortunate condition is caused by the fact that he's saddled with a backward c-pawn and a hole on c5. If he can't find a way to generate some play on his own (very hard to do if your opponent doesn't have any weaknesses to attack), then he'll be in for a long night of suffering.

Note that while c5 is a hole (black's pawns can't cover it), c4 isn't. Why? Because a later b2-b3 will make the c4-square inhospitable to black's pieces.

19.Nc5! Bxc2

Worse is 19...Qc8 20.Bxf5 Qxf5 21.Qb3 Nc6 22.Nxa6 when White has won a pawn.

20.Qd2!

This is what Black missed! White is also better after 20.Rxc2 Qf5 21.Rce2, but 20.Qd2 gains a lot more than Reshevsky intended to give!

20...Qe8 21.Qxb4

Diagram 89

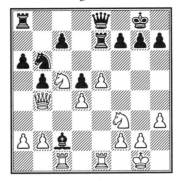

Now we can see the point of white's play: By exchanging his light-squared Bishop (which had no influence on c5) for a Knight (which could eventually challenge that square), White ensures total domination of c5 for the rest of the game. Even if Black manages to exchange his remaining Knight for white's on c5, a Rook will take its place and pour agony down the c-file when White doubles or even triples against c7.

What we are seeing is a strategic exchange of minor pieces that's designed to "win" an advanced square. Since black's Bishop is doomed to remain on light-squares, it will never be able to take part in the battle for c5.

21...a5 22.Qc3 Bg6

22...Bf5 23.Nh4 Bc8 24.f4 would be just as bad—White would enjoy a marked advantage in every sector of the board, while black's Bishop would be a non-entity in the coming battles on the kingside (White dreams of f4-f5-f6 shattering the enemy King's pawn cover) and down the c-file.

23.Nh4

A knight on the rim isn't always grim. This is a good move that frees the f-pawn and also eyes the key f5-square (it's important because White would eventually like to push his f-pawn to f5).

23...Na4 24.Qb3

Fischer doesn't want to give Black even a semblance of counterplay. Indeed, if you can keep your opponent passively placed and waiting for the axe to fall, then it's usually a good idea to do so.

Nevertheless, 24.Nxa4 bxa4 25.Qa3 (and not 25.f4? Be4 when the Bishop is suddenly a great piece) was a strong alternative: 25...Rb8 (This doesn't work. Perhaps 25...c6!? 26.Qxa4 Rb7 27.Nxg6 hxg6 is a better try since threats such as 28...Rxb2 and 28...Rb4 will force White to stay on his toes. Of course, White would have a pronounced advantage, but Black could still put up a fight.) 26.Rc5 Rb4 27.Rxd5 Qa8 (Black appears to have something going here, but it turns out to be an illusion) 28.Rb5! Rxb5 29.Qxe7 Rxb2 (29...c6 30.Nxg6 hxg6 31.e6 fxe6 32.Rxe6 is easy for White, as is 29...Rd5 30.Nxg6 hxg6 31.Qxc7 Rxd4 32.e6) 30.d5 when Nxg6 followed by e6 or d6 (depending on how Black plays) will prove devastating.

24...Nxc5 25.Rxc5 c6 26.Rec1 Re6 27.f4 f5

Extremely ugly (nobody wants to turn their own Bishop into a Tall-Pawn), but 27...Be4 28.f5 Rh6 29.f6! is a crush: 29...Rc8 (29...Rxh4 30. Qg3 wins on the spot) 30.Qg3 (30.Qe3 is also very strong) 30...g6 (30...Bg6 31.Nf5!) 31. Nf3 Rh5 32.Qf4 h6 33.Nd2 and Black's busted.

28.a4

Turning black's queenside into a steaming mess. However 28.Qc2, hitting both c6 and f5, was more straightforward.

28...bxa4

28...b4 29.Qc2 when something in black's position has to give.

29.Qxa4 Rb8 30.Qa3 Qd8 31.Nxg6 hxg6 32.Rxc6 Rxc6 33.Rxc6 Qh4 34.Rxg6?

This has always been accepted as being decisive, but it turns out to be based on a tactical misconception. Correct was 34.Qd6! Rd8 (34...Rxb2 leads to a quick mate: 35.Qe6+ Kh8 36.Rc8+ Kh7 37.Qg8+ Kh6 38.Qh8 mate) 35.Qc7 Kh7 36.e6 defending f4 and winning easily.

34...Kh7

Worse is 34...Qxf4 35.Qe7 Qc1+ 36.Kh2 Qf4+ 37.Rg3 Qh6 38.e6! Rxb2 39.Qf7+ Kh7 40.e7 f4 41.Rxg7+ Qxg7 42.Qh5+ Qh6 43.e8=Q and it's over.

35. Rg5??

Fischer was counting on this to ice the game, but there's a glitch. He had to try his luck in the endgame with 35.Qg3 Qxg3 36.Rxg3 Rxb2 37.Ra3 Rb4 38.Rxa5 Rxd4 39.g3.

Diagram 90

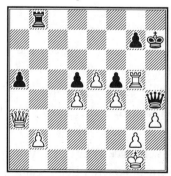

Black to move and draw

35...Rb4??

Both players, and all the annotators until the present, have considered black's position to be resignable. However, he can force a miracle draw by 35...Qxf4! 36.Qe7 Rg8! (and not 36...Qe3+ 37.Kh2 Qf4+ 38.Rg3 which wins for White) 37.Rh5+ Kg6 38.Rh4 Qe3+ 39.Kh2 and now 39...Rh8!! when there's no way to win the game since taking on h8 leads to perpetual check: 40.Rxh8 Qf4+ 41.Kg1 Qc1+, =.

36.Qf3 Kh6 37.g3! Qxh3 38.Qxd5, 1-0. Reshevsky had no need to see 38...Rxb2 39.Qe6+ Kh7 40.Qg6+ Kg8 41.Qxg7 mate.

All Pawns on One Side of the Board = An Octopus' Garden

Diagram 91

Black to move

Though a pawn ahead with tremendous King position, Black can't win. The problem is his Bishop—its long-range powers are useless because all the pawns are on one side of the board. To make matters worse, White has placed his King and pawns on dark squares. This means that black's Bishop can't ever attack them. To draw, all White has to do is move his Bishop randomly around the board until Black finally bows to the inevitable.

Diagram 92

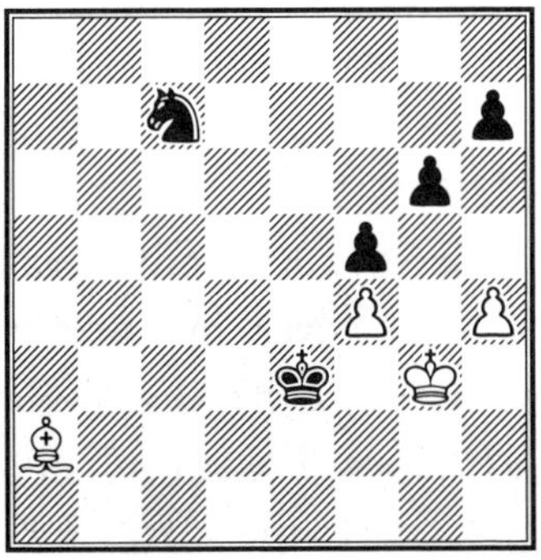

Black to move

This is the same position as the previous diagram, except white's Bishop is better placed and Black has a Knight instead of a Bishop. Now it's a win because the Knight can reach any square. Since nothing is safe from it, in effect the Knight leaves the highly desired "Turbo-Horse" image behind and reaches Octopus levels of influence!

I chose the following variations to illustrate different Octopus-domination scenarios. I wasn't looking for the quickest or most accurate routes, but rather the most visually instructive. Now sit back, relax, and look on in amazement at the clinic the Octopus puts on!

1....Ne8

Heading for d6 or f6 followed by ...Ne4, winning the f4-pawn.

2.h5

Wisely trying to exchange as many pawns as possible. If 2.Bg8 the Octopus would show its defensive powers with 2...Nf6 (A notation change via 2...Of6 crossed my mind!), hitting the Bishop, defending the h7-pawn, and threatening to win the f4-pawn by both ...Ne4+ and ...Nh5+.

2...gxh5 3.Be6

3.Bb3 Ng7 4.Bd1 h6 5.Ba4 h4+ 6.Kxh4 Kxf4 7.Bd1 Ke3

Diagram 93

Access Denied!

(Black's Octopus and h-pawn has formed an invisible shield that deprives the white King entry.) 8.Kh3 f4 9.Kg2 Nf5 (leaping into the battle) 10.Kh3 (No better is 10.Bg4 f3+ 11.Bxf3 Nh4+ 12.Kg3 Nxf3 13.Kg4 Ne5+ 14.Kh5 Nf7 15.Kg6 Kf4 16.Kxf7 h5 and the pawn promotes) 10...f3 11.Bb3 f2 12.Bc4 (12.Kg2 Nh4+ 13.Kf1 Nf3 is game over since the threats of ...Nd2 and ...Nh2 can't be satisfactorily answered) 12...Kd2 13.Kg4 Ng7 (There's the force field again!) 14.Kh3 (14.Ba6 Ke1 followed by ...f1=Q) 14...Ke1 15.Kg2 Nf5 (The Octopus defends one second, attacks the next!) 16.Ba6 Nd4 17.Bf1 Ne2. The hungry Octopus smothers its prey on f1.

3...Nd6

It defends.

4.Bd7 Ne4+

Then attacks.

5.Kh4 Kxf4 6.Be8

6.Kxh5 Nf6+ and the Octopus triumphs again!

6...Ke3 7.Bxh5

7.Kxh5 Nf6+ is yet another fork.

7...f4 8.Bg4 f3 9.Bh3

Or 9.Bxf3 (9.Kh5 Nf6+) 9...Kxf3 10.Kh5 Kg3 11.Kh6 Nf6 12.Kg5 h5 and the pawn promotes.

9...f2 10.Kg4

10.Bf1 Kf3 11.Ba6 (11.Kh5 Ng3+) 11...Ng3 12.Bb7+ (12.Kg5 Ne2 13.Bb7+ Kg3) 12...Ke3 13.Bg2 Ne2 14.Kg4 h5+ 15.Kg5 Nf4 16.Bf1 h4 17.Kxh4 (The pawn eventually has to be taken, which gives Black time to get to his King to e1: 17.Kg4 h3 18.Kg3 h2 19.Kxh2 Kd2 when 20.Kg3 Ke1 21.Bc4 Ne2+ and 20.Bc4 Ne2 21.Kg2 Ke1 are both game enders) 17...Kd2 18.Kg3 Ke1 19.Bc4 Ne2+, 0-1. It's interesting to see how the Octopus consistently blocks the Bishop's diagonals.

10...Ke2 11.Kf4 Nf6 12.Kg5 Nd5 13.Kh6 Nf4 14.Bc8 f1=Q 15.Ba6+ Nd3, 0-1. Once again, the Octopus saves the day by blocking a check to its King. The final position is oddly picturesque.

Mr. Knight Prepares to Take a Journey

M. Matulovic - R. Fischer, Vinkovci 1968

1.e4 c5 2.Nf3 d6 3.d4 cxd4 4.Nxd4 Nf6 5.Nc3 a6 6.g3 e5 7.Nde2 Be7 8.Bg5 Nbd7 9.Bh3 b5 10.a4 b4 11.Nd5 Nxd5 12.Qxd5 Rb8 13.Bxe7 Kxe7 14.Qd2 Nf6 15.Bg2 Bb7 16.Qd3 Qb6 17.0-0 a5 18.Rfd1 Ba6 19.Qd2 Rhc8 20.h3 h5 21.b3 Bxe2 22.Qxe2 Rc3 23.Rd3 Rbc8 24.Rxc3 Rxc3 (threatening 25...Rxg3) **25.Kh2 Qc5 26.Ra2** (26.Rc1 Rxb3). See diagram 94.

White's plight is almost comical. His c-pawn is being assaulted, his pieces are cowering on the second rank, and his Bishop is a Tall-Pawn. Life is far nicer from black's point of view. He's dominating the game, his heavy pieces are mercilessly punishing White, and his Knight will prove to be far stronger that the Bishop. In fact, since c2 is the target, the Knight would like to join in the hunt (always do your best to get all your pieces working for the same goal).

Diagram 94

If you could drop your Knight on a fine support point where it gives a slap to c2, what square would that be? Clearly, the answer is d4, and the road to d4 is ...Nf6-d7-b8-c6-d4 (or, in some cases, ...Nf6-h7-g5-e6-d4). That's a long journey, but white is helpless and the rewards are enormous (if the Knight gets to d4, white's game would do an immediate belly-flop).

26...g6!

The Knight wants to go on a trip, but at the moment it's defending the h5-pawn. After 26...g6, h5 is solidly defended and the horse is ready to head for greener pastures. This push to g6 also sets up a different Knight journey: ...h5-h4 when g4 runs into ...Nf6-h7-g5-e6 and onwards to either d4 or f4. If ...h5-h4 is met by ...gxh4, then ...Nh5-f4 is a nightmare for White.

In every case the Knight has to go on a trip if it wants to reach the really juicy squares, but it's clearly a trip well worth taking!

27.Bf1

White sees the enemy Knight's dance to d4 and realizes that he'll need his Bishop to defend c2 if he wants that pawn to survive. Unfortunately, the Bishop retreat has weakened the e4-pawn.

27...Qd4

Black is suffering from a wealth of riches. Also strong was 27...h4 28.g4 (28. gxh4 Nh5 is another form of "death by Knight") 28...Qd4 29.Bg2 and now ...Nh7-g5-e6 does the trick.

28.f3

Or 28.Bg2 h4 29.g4 Nh7-g5, etc.

28...Re3

28...h4 was also extremely strong. However, Fischer has seen a clear winning sequence and happily goes for it.

29.Qg2

No better is 29.Qf2 when Black has the pleasant choice of 29...Rxe4 or 29...h4 when 30.g4 is ravaged by 30...Nxe4! 31.fxe4 Rxh3+.

29...Qd1 30.Bc4 Qxf3

Material is absorbed and further resistance proved futile: **31.Qxf3 Rxf3 32.Kg2 Re3 33.Bd3 Nxe4 34.Bxe4 Rxe4 35.Kf2 d5 36.Ra1 d4 37.Rd1 Re3 38.h4 Rc3 39.Rd2 Ke6 40.Kg2 f5**, 0-1.

Summary

In a way, a Bishop vs. Knight battle is a pretty clear-cut thing. Here are the basics:

Owner of the Bishop:

➤ Make it as active as possible by placing it on a free diagonal, or *creating* an uncluttered diagonal if one doesn't already exist.

➤ Prove that it's performing a key function and is thus extremely useful.

➤ Steer things into an endgame where the long-range capabilities of the Bishop give it a huge edge over the enemy Knight.

➤ Don't allow the enemy Knight to find its way to an advanced, permanent support point. This calls for *Anti-Knight Strategy*—Do your best to take away all advanced squares from the enemy horse!

Owner of the Knight:

➤ Closing the position is often good for your Knight.

➤ Steer for endgames where all the pawns are on one side of the board. This negates the enemy Bishop's long-range abilities while amplifying the importance of the Knight's ability to attack both white and dark squares.

➤ Do your best to create a permanent advanced home (support point) for your Knight.

➤ If a tasty support point exists but it seems a long way away (and perhaps impossible to reach), try hard to find a way to get there! It might take several moves, but that's what moves are for—to place your pieces on their best squares so they can exert maximum effect on the board.

➤ Avoid "Trapped Knight Syndrome"! Many a Knight has been lost when it found itself trapped by the enemy Bishop.

➤ Anti-Bishop pair formula: In the case of two Bishops vs. a Bishop and Knight, the simplest way to remove the opponent's Bishop pair is to exchange one of the enemy Bishops (either by trading your Knight or Bishop for an enemy Bishop), thus creating a far more manageable Bishop vs. Knight or Bishop vs. Bishop situation.

➤ Two Knights don't work particularly well together, so exchanging one of them (for an enemy Bishop or Knight) is usually a good idea.

Bishops vs. Knights — Tests

You studied Knights, you studied Bishops, and you studied the battle between the two. Now it's time to put your knowledge to the test and see if you can use all that information in a practical manner.

The following tests are designed to give you insight into how much you've learned *and* to serve as extra instruction. If you have trouble solving the tests, don't worry—that means we've uncovered something you don't understand, and this allows you to fix things by rereading the previous material or by picking up the bits of knowledge you're missing in the answers that start on page 455.

PART TWO - TEST **17**

Diagram 95

[Level: 1900 - 2200]

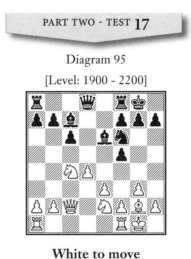

White to move

PART TWO - TEST **18**

Diagram 96

[Level: 2000 on up]

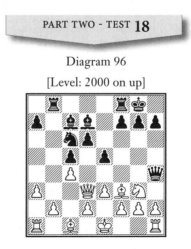

White to move

In this position White tried 15.Bxc6 Bxc6 16.e4, giving Black the two Bishops but closing the game so they would be ineffective. Was this a wise decision?

PART TWO - TEST **19**

Diagram 97

[Level: 1400 - 1800]

White to move

PART TWO - TEST **20**

Diagram 98

[Level: 1400 - 1800]

White to move

PART TWO - TEST **21**

Diagram 99

[Level: 1400 - 1600]

White played **18.Bd3** and a draw was agreed. Was it really equal? Doesn't White enjoy the Bishop pair in an open position?

PART TWO - TEST **22**

Diagram 100

[Level: 2200 on up]

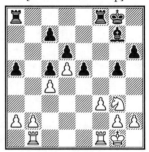

Black to move

PART TWO - TEST **23**

Diagram 101

[Level: 1400 - 1800]

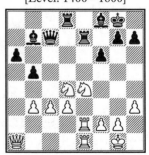

Black to move

PART TWO - TEST **24**

Diagram 102

[Level: 1400 - 1600]

White to move

PART TWO - TEST **25**

Diagram 103

[Level: 1600 - 1800]

Black to move

Assess the position.

PART TWO - TEST **26**

Diagram 104

[Level: 1400 - 2200]

Black to move

Assess the position.

PART TWO - TEST **27**

Diagram 105

[Level: 1400 - 2200]

White to move

Assess the position.

PART TWO - TEST **28**

Diagram 106

[Level: 1400 - 1800]

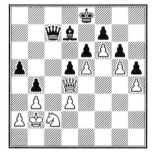

White to move

Whose minor piece is better, and how much better?

Part Three / Rooks

Contents

Rooks
Files, Ranks, and Targets

Creating an Open File

Let's start out with a simple but powerful statement: If you want your Rook(s) to be effective, they need an open file. This seems obvious, but the trick is to *demand* your Rooks get an open file—yet many players merely hope that one will magically materialize and, when it doesn't, wonder why things didn't go their way.

Without an open file, a Bishop or Knight might easily outperform the Rook, leaving it sitting passively behind its pawns while it sadly dreams of unrealized potential. Yes, this is basic, but it's also extremely important and is often neglected by beginners and even tournament players in the "E" (under 1200), "D" (1200 to 1399), "C" (1400 to 1599) and "B" (1600 to 1799) levels. In fact, the battle to energize your Rooks starts right in the opening.

For example, a glance at this poor opening sequence by White will immediately send a message to a trained eye: **1.d4 d5 2.e3 Nf6 3.Nc3**

Diagram 107

The message is that White, most likely, isn't even thinking about the future of his Rooks! In fact, when I teach someone that plays in this type of fashion, I ask him, "What about your Rooks?" Usually the answer I get is something like, "Well, I'm just trying to develop my pieces. I'll deal with the Rooks later." Of course, invariably I find that this kind of player experiences serious problems activating his Rooks, and "later" often never comes.

Returning to that rather innocuous opening sequence (e3 was early—why block your own dark-squared Bishop for no good reason?), we would find that instead of 3.Nc3 (which blocks the c-pawn and leaves the Knight on a square where it won't find much of a life), far better is 3.c4 and only then Nc3. The difference is felt by white's whole army—suddenly the Knight on c3, combined with the pawn on c4, isn't alone in its battle against d5. And, once the Rook moves to c1, a later cxd5 will allow it to exert influence down the c-file. Clearly, pawn tension and pawn breaks are the tools that create open (or half-open) files, and their use goes from the very basic (just seen in diagram 107) to the moderately basic (diagram 108), to solid tournament level (diagram 109), to the downright advanced (diagram 112).

Diagram 108

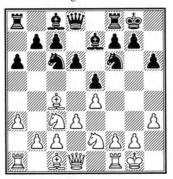

White to move

In this position (diagram 108) black's Rooks don't have many options as far as open files go. However, White's Rooks see happy times ahead by f2-f4 (now or later) gaining kingside space and suddenly making the f1-Rook a participant in the upcoming battle, or by b2-b4 (now or later) fighting for a queenside initiative and striving to get the a1-Rook into the thick of things on that wing.

J. Silman - R. Schain, San Francisco 1977

1.e4 c5 2.Nf3 d6 3.d4 cxd4 4.Nxd4 Nf6 5.Nc3 g6 6.Be3 Bg7 7.h3 Nc6 8.Bc4 0–0 9.Bb3 Bd7 10.0–0 Qc8 11.f4 Rd8 12.Qf3 Nxd4 13.Bxd4 Bc6 14.Rad1 b5

Diagram 109

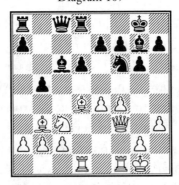

Time to give white's Rooks some love

15.Nd5

This move, which threatens to win by Nxe7+ and also to double black's pawns by Nxf6+, forces Black to capture on d5. However, its real purpose is to create a half-open file for white's Rooks!

15...Nxd5 16.exd5 Bd7 17.Rfe1

Diagram 110

Now we can see the point of white's 15.Nd5—the former e4-pawn has moved off the e-file and onto d5 where it gains space and frees up that file for its Rooks. This allows them to exert tremendous pressure against the e7-pawn.

17...Re8 18.c3 h5

A move based on fear. Black was worried about g2-g4 and makes a move to prevent that advance and also to make f5 accessible to black's Bishop. However, the cure is worse than the disease since now black's kingside is seriously weakened (as shown by the rest of the game).

19.Re3

White intends to double on the e-file and increase his pressure against e7. Chess is easy to play when you have an open road to a glaring weakness (e7). However, the trick isn't in using these things (anyone can do that), it's in *creating* them!

19...Bf5

Calmly following his plan. The alternative, 19...Bxd4 20.Rxd4 Bf5, allows White to make use of the same strong Bishop maneuver that's seen in the game.

20.Bxg7 Kxg7 21.Rde1

Moves don't get more obvious or natural than this! Doubling on the e-file will force two black pieces to play babysitter to the e7-pawn. Note how powerful white's doubled Rooks are in comparison to their passive black counterparts on a8 and e8.

21...Qd7

Black thinks he has everything under control, but white's next move shows that he's badly mistaken.

22.Bd1!

Diagram 111

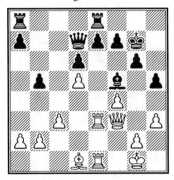

Suddenly black's Bishop is about to be surrounded by g2-g4.

22...Qc7

Stopping g2-g4 by 22...h4 runs into 23.Qf2 when the h4-pawn becomes black's latest "targeted for assassination" unit.

22...a5 23.g4 hxg4 24.hxg4 Bb1 25.f5! gives White a strong attack. For example: 25...Bxa2 26.Rxe7! Rxe7 27.f6+ Kg8 28.Rxe7, or 25...gxf5 26.Qf4 f6 27.g5 Be4 28.gxf6+ exf6 (28...Kxf6 29.Rxe4) 29.Rg3+ and Black can resign.

The rest of the game was pretty straightforward: **23.g4 hxg4 24.hxg4 Bc8 25.f5 f6 26.Kg2 Bb7 27.g5 Qc4 28.Bb3 Qh4 29.Re4 Qh8 30.Rxe7+ Kf8 31.Qe4 Rxe7 32.Qxe7+ Kg8 33.Qxb7** (33.Qe6+ mates. However, I was so happy to snap off his Bishop that I didn't bother looking for anything else.) **33...Rf8 34.Rh1 Qg7 35.Qxg7+ Kxg7 36.gxf6+**, 1-0.

> **RULE**
>
> A half-open file is often used to exert tremendous pressure against weak enemy pawns. In this case "weak" alludes to pawns that can't be protected by other pawns.

P. Negi - A. Beliavsky, Amsterdam 2007

1.e4 e5 2.Nf3 Nc6 3.Bb5 a6 4.Ba4 Nf6 5.0–0 Be7 6.Re1 b5 7.Bb3 d6 8.c3 0–0 9.h3 Bb7 10.d4 Re8 11.Nbd2 Bf8 12.d5 Nb8 13.Nf1 Nbd7 14.Ng3 Nc5 15.Bc2 c6 16.b4 Ncd7 17.dxc6 Bxc6 18.Bb3 Nb6 19.Nh2 a5 20.bxa5 Nc4 21.Bg5 h6 22.Bxf6 Qxf6 23.Ng4 Qd8 24.Ne3 Nxa5 25.Bd5 Rc8 26.Rb1 Bxd5 27.Nxd5 Rc5 28.Qd3 Nc4 29.Nf5 Nb6 30.Nfe3 Nxd5 31.Nxd5 Qa5 32.Re2 Ra8 33.Rb4 Qa6 34.Reb2 g6 35.Qf3 Qc6

Diagram 112

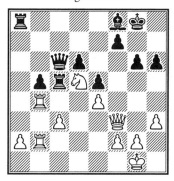

White is obviously better. His huge Knight (compare it to black's horrible Bishop) and pressure against b5 gives him all the chances. He could play the position slowly and torture his opponent, but instead he realized that black's King doesn't have many defenders, and that his own Queen and Knight were putting some heat in that direction. A real attack might easily appear if his Rooks were on an open file and could penetrate into the enemy position. Therefore, why not bust open the b-file?

36.a4!

Forcibly smashing the file open. Similar and also strong was 36.c4! Ra5 (36...bxc4 37.Rb7 wins immediately) 37.a4! (White *insists* that the b-file is cleared!) 37...Rxa4 (37...Rxc4 38.Rxb5 Rxb5 39.axb5 Qb7 40.b6 and the monster passed pawn easily ices the game) 38.Rxa4 bxa4 39.Rb8 Qa6 40.Rd8 Rxd5 41.cxd5 Qb7 42.Qg4 and the threat of Qc8 makes the win easy.

36...Rxa4

36...Ra5 37.c4! transposes into our note to 36.a4.

37.Rxa4 bxa4 38.Rb8

The Rook has burst into black's position and now the combined might of white's Queen, Rook, and Knight (which are all aiming at black's King) promise him a winning attack. His first threat is 39.Ne7+, picking up black's Queen.

38...Qa6 39.Qf6??

A real shame. White could have forced a win by 39.Ne7+ Kg7 40.Nxg6!! Qa7 (40...Rc8 41.Nxe5 dxe5 42.Qg4+ picks up black's Rook) 41.Rxf8 a3 42.Re8 a2 43.Nf8 a1=Q+ 44.Kh2 Qc1 45.Ne6+ fxe6 46.Qf8+ Kg6 47.Rxe6+ Kh7 48.Qf5+ Kh8 49.Qf6+ Qg7 50.Re8+ Kh7 51.Qf5+ Qg6 52.Re7+ Kh8 53.Qf8+ Qg8 54.Qf6+ Qg7 55.Qxg7 mate.

39...Rc8 Suddenly the attack is over and the a-pawn reigns supreme: **40.Nc7 Rxb8 41.Nxa6 Rb1+ 42.Kh2 a3** (Without the help of other pieces, white's

Queen is misplaced on f6. Chess is a team game, and here there's no team to help her out!) **43.Nb4 Rxb4 44.cxb4 a2 45.b5 a1=Q 46.Qd8 Kg7 47.b6 Qb2 48.Qc7 Be7 49.Qxe7 Qxb6 50.f3 Qd4 51.Qd7 Qd2 52.Qd8 h5 53.Qd7 Qf4+ 54.Kh1 Qf6 55.Qc7 g5 56.Qd7 Qe6 57.Qd8 g4 58.hxg4 hxg4 59.Kh2 Qh6+ 60.Kg3 Qf4+ 61.Kf2 Qf6 62.Qd7 Qh4+ 63.Ke2 Qg3 64.fxg4 Qxg2+ 65.Ke3 Qg3+ 66.Ke2 Qf4 67.Qxd6 Qxg4+ 68.Kf2 Qf4+ 69.Kg1 Qg5+ 70.Kf2 Qf6+ 71.Qxf6+ Kxf6 72.Kf3 Kg5 73.Kg3 f6**, 0-1.

Stealing an Open File

As we've seen, a file is a very valuable commodity because it's the road that your Rook (and/or Queen) travels on in order to penetrate into the enemy position. That's why such files are fiercely fought over, with both sides trying hard to make it their own. The most common way of wresting a file from the opponent is to pressure the enemy Rook and give it a simple but painful choice: trade on the file and give it up, or move the Rook away from the file, which also gives it up.

Diagram 113

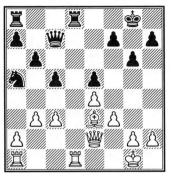

White to move

Black is in serious trouble because his Knight will prove to be much worse than white's Bishop, the dark-squares around his King are weak and easily probed by the Bishop, and White will manage to take over the d-file and use it to penetrate into the enemy position.

1.Bg5!

Announcing that he wants the d-file and that the opposing Rook on d8 must either give it up (by taking on d1), make a feeble attempt to remain on the d-file (by …Rd7 or …Rd6), or run away and bow to white's will.

1…Rd6

The other moves were no better:

➤ 1…Rxd1+ 2.Rxd1 Nc6 3.Rd2! (Avoiding 3.Rd5 Ne7) 3…Re8 4.Qd1 (Doubling on the d-file and laying permanent claim to it) 4…Qc8 (or 4…Nb8 5.Rd6) 5.Rd7 and white's domination is obvious.

➤ 1...Re8 2.Rd5 Nb7 3.Rad1 offers more file domination.

➤ 1...Rf8 2.Qb5! (2.Bf6 is also good) 2...Nc6 (2...a6 3.Qd7) 3.Bf6 Rae8 (3...a6 4.Qd3 followed by Rd2 and Rad1) 4.Rd5 Re6 5.Bh4 with the usual huge advantage.

2.Rxd6 Qxd6 3.Rd1 Qe6 4.Rd5 Nb7 5.Qd2 c4 6.b4 a5 7.Rd7 axb4

Going for broke since 7...Rb8 8.a3 would leave Black bound, helpless, and dead in the water.

8.Rxb7 b3 9.Bh6 and the extra piece and back rank tricks combine to assure White of victory: **9...Qc6** (9...bxa2 10.Qxa2!) **10.Ra7! Rc8 11.Rd7 Qf6 12.axb3 cxb3 13.h3** showing black's helplessness by quietly adding to white's King safety. It's time for Black to resign.

A common situation occurs when both side's Rooks are facing off on a file and, apparently, nobody will ever own it. However, occasionally an odd little Bishop maneuver pops up that temporarily breaks the connection of the opposing Rooks, allowing the stronger side to double or even triple behind it. Then the Bishop can be moved and the prize (the file) taken.

V. Ivanchuk - V. Anand, Linares 2009

1.d4 d5 2.c4 c6 3.Nf3 Nf6 4.Nc3 dxc4 5.a4 Bf5 6.e3 e6 7.Bxc4 Bb4 8.0–0 0–0 9.Qe2 Nbd7 10.e4 Bg6 11.Bd3 Bh5 12.e5 Nd5 13.Nxd5 cxd5 14.Qe3 Re8 15.Ne1 Bg6 16.Bxg6 hxg6 17.Nd3 Qb6 18.Nxb4 Qxb4 19.b3 Rac8 20.Ba3 Qc3 21.Rac1 Qxe3 22.fxe3 f6 23.Bd6 a5

Diagram 114

It seems that a calm state of balance has been created on the c-file—if either player trades Rooks, the other side will recapture and get total control of the file. Thus, in these situations the Rooks usually just stare at each other, refusing to give ground. However, Ivanchuk finds a way to get past all that and claim the c-file for himself.

24.Bc7!

Nice! Now White will play Rc3, Rfc1, and finally move the Bishop back to d6 when the c-file will be his.

24...fxe5 25.dxe5 b6 26.Rc3

And not 26.Rc2 Nxe5 when the Bishop can't take on e5 because the c2-Rook is unprotected. However, after 26.Rc3 Nxe5 no longer works since 27.Bxe5 takes the Knight *and* protects the c3-Rook at the same time!

26...Rf8 27.Rfc1! Rf5 28.g4 Rf7

28...Rg5 leaves the Rook way out of play after 29.h3.

29.Bd6 and Black was in a bad way. Somehow Anand, who was clearly lost, managed to produce a miracle and save the game: **29...Nc5 30.Bxc5 bxc5 31.Rxc5 Rcf8 32.Rxa5 Rf3 33.Ra7 g5 34.Re1 d4 35.exd4 Rxb3 36.Rf1 Rd3 37.Rxf8+ Kxf8 38.a5 Rxd4 39.h3 Kg8 40.a6 Ra4 41.Kf2 Ra5 42.Kf3 Rxe5 43.Re7 Kh7 44.Re8 Ra5 45.Rxe6 Ra3+ 46.Ke4 Rxh3 47.Kd5 Rc3 48.Rb6 g6 49.Kd6 Kh6 50.Rb8 Ra3 51.Ra8 Kg7 52.Kc5 Ra1 53.Kb6 Rb1+ 54.Ka7 Rb4 55.Rb8 Rxg4 56.Rb5 Ra4 57.Rxg5 Rb4 58.Rc5 Kh6 59.Rc6 Kh5 60.Rb6 Rf4 61.Rb5+ g5 62.Kb6 Rf6+ 63.Ka5 Rf7 64.Kb6 Rf6+ 65.Ka5,** ½-½.

Waiting to Pull the File-Opening Trigger

Another interesting situation occurs when a pawn capture can open up a file. In that case, if the side that can initiate the file-opening pawn capture also possesses more space in that area, he can double Rooks behind the pawn and only make use of the pawn trade when the resulting open file will clearly be his.

J. Silman - R. Mcguire, California Chmp 1988

1.d4 Nf6 2.c4 c5 3.d5 e6 4.Nc3 exd5 5.cxd5 d6 6.e4 g6 7.f4 Bg7 8.Bb5+ Nfd7 9.a4 0–0 10.Nf3 Na6 11.0–0 Nc7 12.Bd3 a6 13.f5 Ne5 14.Bf4 Qe7 15.Qd2 Ne8 16.Kh1 b6 17.Rab1 Qc7 18.Nxe5 dxe5 19.Be3 f6 20.g4 g5 21.Rfc1 Nd6 22.b3 Bd7 23.Qe2 a5

Diagram 115

White to move

White has stopped any counterplay that Black might have dreamed of on the queenside, and now he's ready to turn his attention to the other wing.

24.h4 h6

And not 24...gxh4 25.g5 when White gets an immediate attack.

25.Kg2

Preparing to bring the Rooks to the h-file.

25...Kf7 26.Kf3 Rh8 27.Rh1 Rag8 28.Rh2

White has three squares to use on the h-file (h1, h2, and h3) while Black only has two (h7 and h8). This means that White can potentially triple on the h-file while Black can't. Naturally, 28.hxg5? hxg5 would suddenly give Black as many h-file squares as White has.

Clearly, the key to this kind of position is to only capture on g5 (which opens the h-file) when White has maximized the position of his Rooks and Queen.

28....Ke7 29.Rbh1 Kd8 30.Bb5!

With Black tied down by h-file worries, White prepares to penetrate on the opposite wing.

30...Bxb5 31.Nxb5 Nxb5 32.Qxb5 Ke7

32...Kc8 doesn't offer any relief because of 33.b4! axb4 34.a5 and the queenside gets ripped open.

33.Rc1

Also very strong was 33.b4!

33...Kf7 34.d6!

Diagram 116

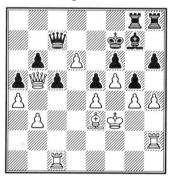

Suddenly White seeks to create (and dominate) a completely different open file! Black's now dead since he must either take the pawn and allow 25.Rd2 with decisive penetration down the newly opened d-file, or run from the pawn, leaving White with the monster on d6.

34...Qd8

34...Qxd6 35.Rd2 was an even quicker win for White.

35.Qc4+

35.Bxc5 (ripping open the c-file!) also does the job, but a player can only make one winning move at a time.

35...Kf8 36.Qe6 h5 37.Bxc5 hxg4+ 38.Kg2 Bh6 39.Bxb6 gxh4 40.Bxd8 h3+ 41.Kf1 Rg7 42.Be7+, 1-0.

This same plan can (and often does) occur on the other wing:

R. Fischer - B. Spassky, Sveti Stefan 1992

1.e4 e5 2.Nf3 Nc6 3.Bb5 a6 4.Ba4 Nf6 5.0–0 Be7 6.Re1 b5 7.Bb3 d6 8.c3 0–0 9.h3 Nb8 10.d4 Nbd7 11.Nbd2 Bb7 12.Bc2 Re8 13.Nf1 Bf8 14.Ng3 g6 15.Bg5 h6 16.Bd2 Bg7 17.a4 c5 18.d5 c4 19.b4 Nh7 20.Be3 h5 21.Qd2 Rf8

Diagram 117

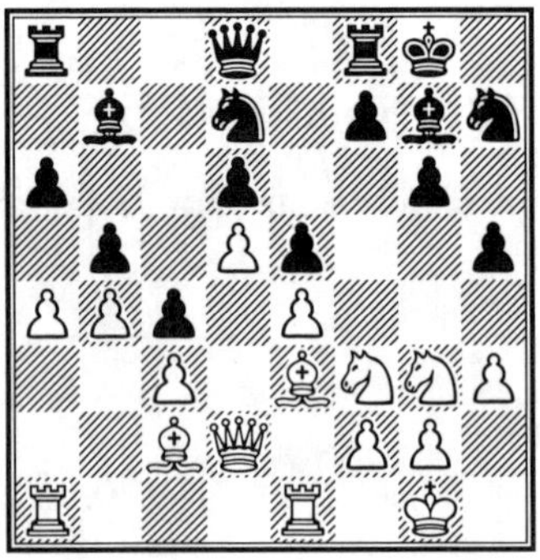

Clearly, 22.axb5? axb5 would lead to a standoff on the a-file (23.Ba7 runs into the annoying 23...Nb6 when ...Nc8 at some point is in the air). But, as in the previous game, why should White be in a hurry to exchange pawns and open the file?

22.Ra3! Ndf6 23.Rea1 Qd7 24.R1a2!

Even better than the 24.axb5 axb5 25.Ba7!? idea, which we saw in diagram 114.

24...Rfc8 25.Qc1 Bf8 26.Qa1

Setting up the legendary Alekhine's Gun (A powerful form of tripling on a file where the Queen places itself behind both its Rooks).

26...Qe8 27.Nf1!!

Very deep. Fischer intends to target the b5-pawn for assassination via a later N1-d2-b1-a3.

27...Be7 28.N1d2 Kg7 29.Nb1 Nxe4!?

Black decides to sacrifice a piece for counterplay rather than sit passively and die in lines like 29...Ng8 30.axb5 axb5 31.Rxa8 Rxa8 32.Rxa8 Qxa8 33.Qxa8 Bxa8 34.Na3 when b5 falls. This variation shows the point of Fischer's 27th move.

The rest of the game, which has nothing to do with our theme, is still extremely interesting: **30.Bxe4 f5 31.Bc2 Bxd5 32.axb5 axb5 33.Ra7 Kf6 34.Nbd2 Rxa7 35.Rxa7 Ra8 36.g4 hxg4 37.hxg4 Rxa7 38.Qxa7 f4 39.Bxf4 exf4 40.Nh4 Bf7 41.Qd4+ Ke6 42.Nf5 Bf8 43.Qxf4 Kd7 44.Nd4 Qe1+ 45.Kg2 Bd5+ 46.Be4 Bxe4+ 47.Nxe4 Be7 48.Nxb5 Nf8 49.Nbxd6 Ne6 50.Qe5**, 1-0.

Control of the 7th or 8th Ranks

The importance of open/half-open files (creating them, fighting to dominate them, penetrating into the enemy position on them, and using them to pressure weak enemy pawns) should be clear by now, but equally important is the enormous power of a Rook on the 7th or 8th rank.

Eighth rank incursions are usually of a tactical or attacking nature, and back rank mates are part of every beginner's tactical training.

Diagram 118

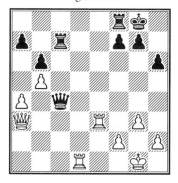

White to move

Black appears to be okay since his pieces are all defended and he's even created luft by ...h7-h6 (that stops all those nasty back rank mates, doesn't it?). However, after **1.Qxf8+!** Black has to resign since 1...Kh7 leaves him a whole Rook down, while **1...Kxf8 2.Rd8** mate is both sudden and brutal.

Our next example addresses another important back rank idea.

W.E. Mason - H. James, New Zealand Chmp 1912

1.e4 c5 2.Nf3 Nc6 3.d4 cxd4 4.Nxd4 d6 5.Be2 g6 6.Be3 Bg7 7.Nc3 Nf6 8.0-0 0-0 9.Qd2 d5 10.Rad1 Nxd4 11.Qxd4 Be6 12.e5 Nd7 13.f4 Nb6

14.Bf3 f6 15.Nxd5 fxe5 16.Qc5 Nxd5 17.Bxd5 Bxd5 18.Rxd5 Qe8 19.fxe5 Rxf1+ 20.Kxf1 Rc8 21.Qd4 Qf7+ 22.Kg1 Rxc2

Diagram 119

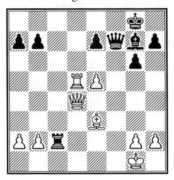

White to move

23.Rd8+ Bf8 24.Bh6, 1-0.

Knowledge of these back rank patterns can lead to some nice creative achievements. Our next game is a good example of this.

J. Pelikan - C. Skalicka, Prague 1939

1.d4 Nf6 2.c4 d6 3.g3 Bf5 4.Bg2 Qc8 5.Nc3 e5 6.e4 Bg4 7.f3 Bd7 8.d5 Be7 9.Be3 c5 10.dxc6 e.p. bxc6 11.Rc1 0–0 12.Nge2 Bh3 13.0–0 Rd8 14.g4 Bxg2 15.Kxg2 Qb7 16.Ng3 g6 17.Rf2 d5 18.cxd5 cxd5 19.exd5 Nxd5 20.Nxd5 Rxd5

Diagram 120

Black's behind in development and his King suffers from some weakened dark-squares. White makes immediate use of these things.

21.Rc8+!

The back rank turns out to be vulnerable.

21...Bf8

A scary move to play (it instantly brings to mind the pattern in diagram 119), but Black didn't like the look of 21...Qxc8 (probably the best try) 22.Qxd5 Nd7 23.Rd2 Nb6 24.Qxe5 with a solid extra pawn, or 21...Kg7 22.Qc1, which is immediately decisive: 22...f6 (22...Nd7 23.Bh6+ Kf6 24.Ne4+ Ke6 25.Rc6+ Bd6 26.Qc4 is a total nightmare) 23.Rc7 Qb4 24.Rd2 Rxd2+ 25.Bxd2 Qd6 26.Ne4 Qe6 27.Rxe7+! Qxe7 28.Bh6+ Kf7 29.Qc4+ Ke8 30.Qg8+ Kd7 31.Bf8 and black's lifespan is nearing its end.

22.Qxd5! Qxd5 23.Rd2 Qb7

23...Qa5 takes us into familiar territory: 24.Bh6 Nd7 25.Rxa8 Qc7 26.Rxd7 Qxd7 27.Rxf8 mate.

24.Rdd8 Nd7 25.Rxa8 Kg7 26.b3 and Black is down material and under tremendous pressure. The end couldn't have been pleasant for the second player: **26...Qc7 27.Ne4 Qc2+ 28.Bf2 Qc7 29.g5! Nb6 30.Bxb6 axb6 31.Rxf8 Qc2+ 32.Kg3 f5 33.Rg8+** (33.Nd6 is even faster) **33...Kf7 34.Raf8+ Ke7 35.Re8+**, 1-0.

As we've seen, a Rook on the 8th rank can lead to all sorts of fun. However, control of the 7th rank is particularly prized because it not only annoys the enemy King, but also targets all the enemy pawns that sit on that rank.

Diagram 121

White to move

Black is a piece ahead, but a series of discovered checks (this kind of position is known as a *windmill*) will divest him of most of his army. The point of this extreme example is to highlight the power of the Rook on the 7th rank, and also how many black goodies are sitting there, waiting to be eaten!

1.Rxd7+ Kg8 2.Rg7+ (Forcing the King back to h8 and thus reloading for another discovered check) **2...Kh8 3.Rxc7+ Kg8 4.Rg7+ Kh8 5.Rxb7+ Kg8 6.Rg7+ Kh8 7.Rxa7+ Kg8** (enough checks, it's time for one final meal) **8.Rxa8**, 1-0.

Okay, that seemed more fantasy than reality, but a Rook on the seventh often wields serious powers, as shown in our next game.

J. Silman - P. Biyiasas, San Francisco 1983

1.d4 d5 2.c4 c6 3.Nc3 Nf6 4.e3 e6 5.Nf3 Nbd7 6.Qc2 Be7 7.b3 0–0 8.Be2 b6 9.0–0 Bb7 10.Bb2 Rc8 11.Rfd1 Qc7 12.e4 dxe4 13.Nxe4 Nxe4 14.Qxe4 Bf6 15.Rd2 c5 16.Qg4 Rfd8 17.Rad1 cxd4 18.Nxd4 Ne5 19.Qg3 Nc6 20.Qxc7 Rxc7

Diagram 122

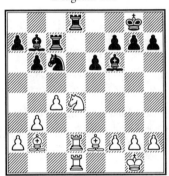

Grandmaster Biyiasas was a fantastic defensive player, so one can understand why he thought he'd be able to hold this "quiet" endgame. However, his position turns out to be far worse than he imagined.

21.Nb5 Rxd2

21...Rcc8 22.Bxf6 gxf6 23.Rxd8+ Nxd8 (23... Rxd8 24.Rxd8+ Nxd8 25.Nxa7 leaves White a solid pawn ahead) and now both 24.Rd7 Bc6 25.Rxa7 Bxb5 26.cxb5 and 24.Nxa7 are winning.

22.Rxd2 Rc8

22...Re7 loses material to both 23.Nxa7 (taking advantage of black's weakened back rank) and 23.Ba3 Re8 24.Rd7.

23.Bxf6 gxf6 24.Rd7

Diagram 123

Suddenly Black is completely lost! The Rook on the 7th rank (which eyes a7, b7 and f7), combined with my queenside majority, superior kingside structure, and active minor pieces will prove to be far more than he can handle.

24...Rb8 25.f4!

Denying black's Knight access to e5.

25...a6 26.Nd6 Nd4 27.Bh5 Bc6 28.Rc7 Rd8 29.Nc8 Be4 30.Nxb6 Bb1

The position after 30...Bg6 31.Bxg6 hxg6 32.Rd7 Rxd7 (or 32...Rb8 33.Rxd4 Rxb6 34.c5 Rc6 35.b4) 34.Nxd7 is an easy win for White, thanks to his three to one queenside pawn majority.

31.Bxf7+ Kf8 32.Bh5

With the removal of the f7-pawn, white's Rook now reigns supreme over the whole 7th rank.

32...Bxa2 33.Rf7+ Kg8 34.Nd7

Playing directly for mate—the 7th rank isn't just a smorgasbord, it's also conducive to several nasty mating patterns.

34...Bb1 35.Nxf6+ Kh8 36.Kf2 Nxb3 37.g4!

Intending f4-f5, blocking out the black Bishop's defense of h7 and forcing mate via Rxh7.

37...Rd2+ 38.Kg3

38.Ke1 was even stronger.

38...Nc5 39.f5 Ne4+ 40.Nxe4 Bxe4 41.fxe6 Rg2+ 42.Kf4 Bc6 43.Rc7 Ba4 44.e7 Rf2+ 45.Kg3 Rf8 (We shared a good laugh, and then I snapped it off!) **46.exf8=R** mate.

As nice as a Rook on the 7th rank might be, two Rooks on the 7th (known as *pigs on the 7th*) are even better! This creates various material winning scenarios, and also sets up many potential mates.

G. Marco - J. Mieses, Monte Carlo 1903

1.e4 c5 2.Nf3 e6 3.d4 cxd4 4.Nxd4 Nf6 5.Nc3 Nc6 6.Ndb5 Bb4 7.a3 Bxc3+ 8.Nxc3 0–0 9.Bd3 d5 10.exd5 exd5 11.0–0 Bg4 12.f3 Bh5 13.Bg5 Qb6+ 14.Kh1 Ne7 15.Re1 Qc5 16.Qd2 Rfe8 17.Bxf6 gxf6 18.Re2 Red8 19.b4 Qc7 20.Nb5 Qd7 21.Nd4 Bg6 22.g4 Kh8 23.Rae1 Nc6 24.Bxg6 fxg6 25.Nxc6 Qxc6 26.Re7 d4 27.Kg2 g5 28.Qd3 f5 29.Qxf5 Qg6 30.Qxg6 hxg6 31.Rxb7 Rdc8 32.Re2 Rc3 33.a4 Rc4 34.a5 a6 35.Kg3 Rd8 36.b5 axb5 37.Rxb5 d3 38.cxd3 Rxd3

Diagram 124

White is two pawns up and should win easily. The point of this example is that it demonstrates, in very simple fashion, just what a pair of pigs can do!

39.Rb7

The threat of 40.Re8 mate forces Black into a defensive posture.

39...Rc8 40.Ree7

The pigs join up on the seventh and prepare to dish out some pain! White could have played 40.a6, but he probably wanted to avoid the complications resulting from 40...Rf8. Of course, that wouldn't have given Black more than a momentary rush: 41.Ra2 Rfxf3+ 42.Kg2 Rf8 43.a7 Rdd8 44.Rab2 Ra8 45.Rb8.

40...Ra3 41.Rh7+ Kg8 42.Rbg7+ Kf8 43.Rf7+ Kg8

Not falling for 43...Ke8 44.Rb7 when the threat of 45.Rh8 mate can only be avoided for a few "I'll give everything away and then get mated anyway" moves.

44.Rfg7+ Kf8 45.Rxg6 Rcc3

More natural is 45...Rxa5, but then 46.Rh8+ Kf7 47.Rxg5! leads to a Rook endgame where White enjoys a three pawn advantage.

46.Rf6+ Kg8 47.Ra7 Rc2 48.Rd6

Threatening mate again and thus forcing his opponent back into a passive stance.

48...Rc8 49.Rdd7 Re8 50.Rg7+ Kh8

A different kind of mate would be seen after 50...Kf8 51.Raf7.

51.Rh7+ Kg8 52.Rag7+ Kf8 53.Rxg5, 1-0.

The pigs on the 7th rank can also serve defensively, giving their owners enough counterplay to hold a position that might otherwise be problematic.

W. Browne - J. Silman, Koltanowski International 1999

1.d4 d5 2.c4 c6 3.Nf3 Nf6 4.Nc3 dxc4 5.a4 Bf5 6.e3 e6 7.Bxc4 Bb4 8.0-0 0-0 9.Qe2 Bg6 10.Ne5 Nbd7 11.Nxg6 hxg6 12.Rd1 Qa5 13.e4 e5 14.d5 Nb6 15.dxc6 bxc6 16.Na2 Nxc4 17.Qxc4 Rab8 18.Nxb4 Qxb4 19.Qxb4 Rxb4 20.f3 c5! 21.Be3 Rxb2 22.Bxc5 Rc8 23.Bxa7 Rcc2 24.Kh1 Rxg2 25.Bg1

Diagram 125

Black has two Rooks on the 7th rank, but their effectiveness seems to be blunted by the Bishop on g1. If Black can't get something going, he'll lose to white's obvious plan of a4-a5-a6-a7, etc. Fortunately, the Rooks don't need to work alone and reinforcements are on the way!

25...Nh5! 26.a5 Ng3+!

Simplest is 26...Rg5! 27.a6 (27.Be3 Rgg2 doesn't get White anywhere since 28.Bg1 Rg5 repeats the position and 28.a6?? loses to 28...Rxh2+ 29.Kg1 Rbg2+ 30.Kf1 Ng3+ 31.Ke1 Re2 mate) 27...Ng3+ 28.hxg3 Rh5+ 29.Bh2 Rhxh2+ 30.Kg1 Rbg2+ with a draw by perpetual check.

27.hxg3 Rxg3

Black is a piece down and is also facing "death by a-pawn", but his control of his 7th rank (and the enemy King's discomfort) is so complete that he'll easily hold the draw.

28.Bc5 Rh3+ 29.Kg1 Rg3+ 30.Kf1 Rxf3+ 31.Ke1 Rh3 32.Bg1 Rg3 33.Bf2 Rh3!

The final point—Black saw (back on the 26th move) that he couldn't play 33...Rf3?? because of 34.Rd2! Rxd2 35.Kxd2 Rxf2+ 36.Kc3 when the a-pawn is supreme.

34.Bg1

Now 34.Kf1 allows 34...Rf3.

34...Rg3 35.Bf2, ½-½.

All this shouldn't give the impression that a Rook on the 7th rank or 8th rank is always advantageous. The following examples should put this in perspective.

Diagram 126

White to move

White has a Rook on the 7th rank, but who cares? There aren't any targets on that rank, and black's King isn't bothered in the least by white's empty 7th rank acquisition.

Though White has the move, he's quite lost (white's pawns on a4 and c4 are ripe and ready for the taking). Thus, control of the seventh and eight ranks is symbolic of what a Rook might accomplish there. If it's not able to "do its stuff", then don't bother moving there in the first place.

Diagram 127

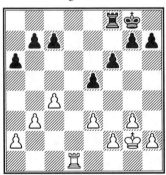

White to move

White controls the only open file, so he has all the chances in this position. After all the hoopla about the 7th rank, we simply have to ask if White should make the leap into d7? If black's Rook stood on e8 instead of f8, then 1.Rd7 would be very strong, but in our actual position the grab for "7th" is misguided since it can be easily challenged.

1.Rd7 Rf7 2.Rd8+ Rf8 and white's not accomplishing anything at all. Since the 7th rank just isn't to be had, White would be well advised to show patience and improve the position of his King with 1.Kf3.

G. Maroczy - A. Burn, Ostend 1905

1.e4 e5 2.Nf3 Nc6 3.Bb5 a6 4.Ba4 Nf6 5.0–0 d6 6.c3 Bd7 7.Re1 g6 8.d4 Bg7 9.Nbd2 0-0 10.Bxc6 Bxc6 11.dxe5 dxe5 12.Nxe5 Bxe4 13.Nxe4 Qxd1 14.Rxd1 Nxe4 15.Nd7 Rfe8 16.Bf4 c6 17.Kf1 Nf6 18.Bg5 Nxd7 19.Rxd7 Re5 20.Be7 Rb5 21.Ba3

Diagram 128

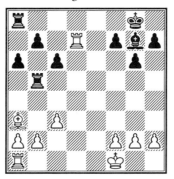

White owns the open d-file, his Rook is proudly sitting on the 7th rank where it attacks b7, and his position seems to be devoid of any weaknesses. Shouldn't White be significantly better here? The answer is rather surprising—White doesn't have more than a small plus. In fact, Maroczy, a magnificent endgame player, wasn't even able to dent black's shell.

21...Bf8

An important move that strives to remove the defender of the b2-pawn.

22.c4 Rb6 23.c5

A draw also results from 23.Bxf8 Kxf8 24.b3 a5 25.Rad1 (25.Re1, threatening to double on the 7th rank, is defanged by 25...Re8, =) 25...a4 26.R1d3 axb3 27.Rxb3 Raa6 28.Rxb7 Rxb7 29.Rxb7 Ra4 30.c5 Ra5 31.a4 Ke8 32.Rc7 Rxc5 33.Ra7 Rc2, =.

23...Rb5 24.Rad1

Far more interesting is 24.Re1 when one can spend many hours delving into the position's hidden treasures. Though an analysis of such an endgame (which often features both sides fighting to get pigs on the seventh) is way outside this book's scope, I recommend that endgame enthusiasts focus on lines such as: 24...b6!? (24...h5!?, 24...Rb8!?, 24...Bxc5!?) 25.cxb6 Bxa3 26.bxa3 Rxb6 27.Ree7 (27.g3! is much tougher, and leads to many intricate variations) and now one simple but fun possibility is 27...Rb1+ 28.Ke2 Rb2+ 29.Ke3 Rxa2 (29...Rf8 is simpler) 30.Rxf7 Re8+ when 31.Kf3 is met by 31...Rf8 and 31.Kd3 is met by 31...Rd8!

I recall a story about a famous grandmaster that wanted to learn the complete truth about a certain endgame position. He got some friends together and they all hunkered down in the grandmaster's apartment for several days, never leaving or seeing the light of day, and living on a diet of pizza, earthworms, and dried paint chips. Their ordeal only ended when the position had been completely deconstructed, rebuilt, and mastered.

Doing a deep analysis (alone or with friends) of any complex position is not only highly enjoyable, but also extremely instructive (though I recommend stocking up on real food and avoiding the earthworms and paint chips). If you have a chess teacher, then all the better! You can turn over your analysis to the chess pro and see how close to reality you were, and then have him show you the things you did wrong and help you fix those weak points. Of course, most people can't afford the time for a seven-day adult slumber chess party (imagine your wife pounding on the door screaming, "Harold! Harold! What about your job Harold? What *are* you doing in there?"). Don't despair! Analyze the position of interest over a several week period, giving it an hour here and an hour there. You'll find the time was well spent!

24...Re8 25.Rd8

It's as if White was saying, "I'm not doing much on the 7th rank, so let's try the 8th!"

25...Rxd8 26.Rxd8 Kg7

Wisely stepping off the back rank. The d8-Rook is almost fully nullified.

27.b4 Be7

And this move, which takes the terror away from checks along the a1-h8 diagonal, leaves White with absolutely nothing. The rest of the game wasn't very interesting: **28.Bb2+ Bf6 29.Bxf6+ Kxf6 30.a3 a5 31.Rd4 axb4 32.axb4 Ke5 33.Rh4 h5 34.Ke2 b6 35.cxb6 Rxb6 36.Kd3 Rb5 37.Re4+ Kd6 38.Rd4+ Ke6 39.Kc4 f6 40.Re4+ Kd6 41.Rf4 Ke6 42.g3 g5 43.Re4+ Kd6 44.Rd4+ Ke7 45.f4 gxf4 46.gxf4 Ke6 47.Re4+ Kd6 48.Rd4+ Ke6 49.Re4+ Kd6 50.Rd4+ Ke6**, ½-½.

Finally, we'll end our theoretical musings on Rooks and the seventh and 8th ranks by offering up this amusing little game:

A. Delchev - H. Nakamura, Mulhouse 2009

1.e4 d6 2.d4 g6 3.Be3 Bg7 4.Nc3 a6 5.f4 b5 6.Bd3 Bb7 7.Nf3 Nd7 8.e5 c5 9.Be4 Qc8 10.Bxb7 Qxb7 11.dxc5 dxe5 12.Qd5 Qxd5 13.Nxd5 Rc8 14.Nb6 Nxb6 15.cxb6 Nf6 16.0–0–0 Ng4 17.b7 Rb8 18.Bb6 f6 19.Rd8+ Kf7 20.Rd7 Bh6 21.g3 exf4 22.Kb1 Ne5 23.Nxe5+ fxe5 24.Ba7 Ke6 25.Rhd1 f3 26.Rc7 e4 27.Rdd7 Rhe8 28.a3 Bg5 29.h4

Diagram 129

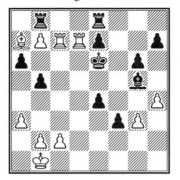

White has been trying to cause havoc on his 7th rank, while also doing his best to make inroads into the eighth so that his b-pawn can promote. On the other hand, Black has held fast, and has also begun his own bid to race the e4- and f3-pawns to his 8th rank and promote them. The goals are clear, though achieving them is going to be based on pure tactics.

This example is raw entertainment, with the rub that it helps solidify the understanding that getting one's heavy pieces (and pawns, since if they get to the eighth they turn into heavy pieces) to those ranks is serious business!

29...e3!

Since black's goal is to get his pawns to the 8th rank, why waste a critical tempo moving the Bishop? In fact, in positions of this nature, time (rushing towards your goal with as much speed as possible) is often more important than material.

Here's an example of the difference one single tempo makes: 29...Bh6?? (Seems logical, but it gives White a critical tempo, which he uses to get his King off the back rank.) 30.Ka2 e3 31.Rxe7+! (31.Bxb8?! Rxb8 32.Rxe7+ Kf5 33.Rc8 Rxb7 34.Rxb7 Kg4 leads to a completely insane position!

Diagram 130

Insanity reigns!

A possible continuation is 35.Rxh7 e2 36.Re7 f2 37.Rxe2 f1=Q 38.Re6 Qf7 39.Rc6 Kxg3 40.Kb1 Kxh4 41.Rxg6 with continuing strangeness in store. This is a major candidate for Larsen's famous, "Long analysis wrong analysis." I'm sure improvements are lurking behind every corner, so happy hunting!) 31...Rxe7 32.Bxb8 f2 33.Rxe7+ Kxe7 34.Bd6+ Ke6 35.b8=Q f1=Q, with a probable draw.

30.Bxb8 f2

White is dead lost because Black has won the pawn race to the 8th rank!

31.Ba7 f1=Q+ (it's a girl!) **32.Ka2 e2**, 0-1. A pity since a truly extraordinary situation could have arisen after 33.b8=Q Rxb8 34.Bxb8 e1=Q (twins!).

Diagram 131

Each side has claimed an advanced rank!

You don't see this every day! White has doubled his Rooks on his 7th rank while Black has doubled his Queens (!) on the 8th rank! The Queens appear to have a bit more punch!

Summary

> If you want your Rook(s) to be effective, they need an open file.

> Without an open file, a Bishop or Knight might easily outperform the Rook, leaving it sitting passively behind its pawns while it sadly dreams of unrealized potential.

> A half-open file is often used to exert tremendous pressure against weak enemy pawns.

> A file is a very valuable commodity because it's the road that your Rook travels on in order to penetrate into the enemy position. That's why such files are often fought over, with both sides trying hard to make it their own.

> The importance of open/half-open files (creating them, fighting to dominate them, penetrating into the enemy position on them,

and using them to pressure weak enemy pawns) should be clear by now, but equally important is the enormous power of a Rook on the seventh or 8th rank.

> 8th rank incursions are usually of a tactical or attacking nature, and back rank mates are part of every beginner's tactical training.

> A Rook on the 8th rank can lead to all sorts of fun. However, control of the 7th rank is particularly prized because it not only annoys the enemy King, but also targets all the enemy pawns that have yet to venture forward.

Rooks — Tests

The humble Rook (also known in some American clubs as an ox) is the master of files and ranks, but do you fully understand your Rook ABCs? These tests will give you an excellent idea about the highs and lows of your Rook IQ.

If you have trouble solving the tests, don't worry—that means we've uncovered something you don't understand, and this allows you to fix things by rereading the previous material or by picking up the bits of knowledge you're missing in the answers that start on page 476.

PART THREE - TEST **1**

Diagram 132

[Level: 1600 - 1800]

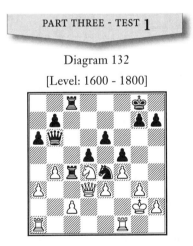

Black to move

PART THREE - TEST 2

Diagram 133

[Level: 1400 - 1600]

White to move

Is 27.Qb3+, 27.Rd1, or 27.g3 correct?

PART THREE - TEST 3

Diagram 134

[Level: 1400 - 2200]

White to move

Is he in any hurry? How do you see this game playing out?

PART THREE - TEST 4

Diagram 135

[Level: 1400 - 1600]

White to move

PART THREE - TEST 5

Diagram 136

[Level: 1400 - 1800]

White to move

PART THREE - TEST 6

Diagram 137

[Level: 1800 - 2200]

White to move

PART THREE - TEST 7

Diagram 138

[Level: 1400 - 1800]

Black to move

White is two pawns down. Is he doomed?

Part Four / Psychological Meanderings

Contents

Material
Fear of Giving Up or Taking Material

Stepping Beyond Fear

Over the years, I've given innumerable lessons and lectures where the sacrifice of material has been addressed. Players of all ratings are, in general, quite comfortable parting with their stuff if a King-hunt and the promise of mate is in the air. However, if material should be sacrificed for positional reasons I've noticed a state of mental "rigor mortis" strike even the hardiest players—they just can't bring themselves to part with a pawn or the Exchange (things you can see, understand, and even feel) if the return is mere positional "compensation" (A term that reminds us of snake-oil; it promises the world, but always remains invisible to the amateur's eye).

I never realized the full extent of this problem until I taught one particular student who loved to launch unsound mating attacks. He'd toss a Bishop in the garbage if it allowed him to give the enemy King a few (more often than not, harmless) checks. I didn't want to fully discourage his aggressive inclinations, but I did want to show him that there are other ways to win a game and that attacks are usually a natural manifestation of various positive imbalances. After quite a few lessons, we finally got around to discussing positional Exchange sacrifices and he fell in love with the idea. Every time I would show him an example, he would say, "Man, I wish I could do that!" I would assure him that the opportunity would arise and, sure enough, his big chance eventually appeared.

In diagram 139 (see next page) it's clear that Black has played very passively, but everything seems to be defended. White, seeing that Black intended to double on the e-file, played **1.Rfe1** and after **1...Rfe8** he followed with 2.Rxe7 and subsequently allowed the exchange of all the Rooks. The resulting position looked (and is) great, but it proved difficult to penetrate and a draw was the eventual result.

I pointed out to White that he could have targeted the two weak pawns on d6 and f6 (before or after the Rook exchanges) via Ne4 with Be1-c3 and Qd2-b2 to follow (mixed with a well-timed h3-h4). This would have left Black in a good deal of pain. However, far more interesting to me was something that most chess masters would do without thinking:

Diagram 139

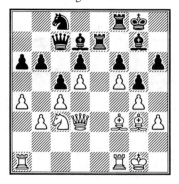

Student (1655) - NN (1627), Los Angeles 2004
White to move

1.Rfe1 Rfe8 2.Re6!!

We had looked at similar "plug" sacrifices in other lessons, so when he noticed this possibility he said, "I saw it, but just couldn't bring myself to give the Rook away. I don't even get a pawn for it, and there's no kingside attack at all! I wanted to do it because of what you showed me in past lessons, but my hand refused to make the move!"

Clearly, the ingrained programming that prevents us from giving away material is extremely strong. As a result, the point of this chapter isn't just to give examples of material sacrifice, but also to help the student break down those walls that prevent him from following his "imbalance training."

Let's start by asking a simple question: "Why is 2.Re6 such a good move?" It's clear that the Rook is a monster on this square, and if it's allowed to remain it not only kills off both black Rooks but it also adds to the pressure against both f6 and d6. But all this won't mean much to the amateur, who will rightly demand to know why the Rook can't be taken. Of course, it *can* be taken, but after 2...Bxe6 3.dxe6 we are left with the following one-sided breakdown of the imbalances:

Diagram 140

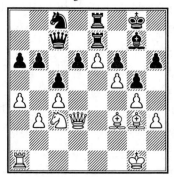

Black to move

Black:

➤ Up a solid Exchange.

White:

➤ More queenside, kingside, and central space.

➤ He possesses two very active Bishops.

➤ The pawn on d6 is very weak.

➤ The pawn on f6 is also vulnerable and can be tortured by Nd5 followed by swinging the Queen and dark-squared Bishop over to the a1-h8 diagonal.

➤ The d5-square is a gaping hole, which can be a home to his Knight or Bishop.

➤ The protected passed pawn on e6 is a monster!

➤ White's minor pieces are extremely active while black's two minor pieces are comically placed.

➤ Black's Rooks don't have any open files and are both dead. In fact, white's minor pieces are far stronger than the enemy Rooks!

What's clear is that White has every advantage in the position, while black's only claim to fame is his material advantage. They need to be weighed against each other, and in this case it's not even close since, on top of everything else (I'll repeat myself here since it's a very important point), the black Rooks (due to their lack of open files) are actually weaker than any one of white's minor pieces!

Nevertheless, the mere fact that Black has a material advantage is more than enough to convince most players to reject the line starting with 2.Re6. It's a pure case of logic vs. unfounded fear. How can a player get beyond this fear? He has to train himself to view each imbalance as something wonderful, and he has to view material as just another imbalance to be collected or rejected, depending on the nature of the individual position.

> **PHILOSOPHY**
>
> In all cases of logic vs. fear, you must learn to embrace logic by reading the board and doing what it tells you to do.

If a player is going to master my concept of "reading the needs of a position by recognizing and trying to make use of all the imbalances" then he must place material gain or sacrifice on that same list. Yes, some imbalances do have a bit more importance than others. However, although material or an insecure King both demand extra attention, you can't place them on a pedestal and lose sight of the big picture.

Diagram 141

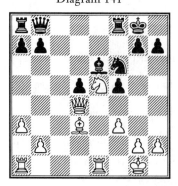

V. Ivanchuk - P. Harikrishna, Merida 2007
Black to move

If I told most non-masters that they could have this position as White, they wouldn't be too pleased. After all, Black seems safe enough, and he's a pawn up and also has the move. Nevertheless, White has his perks too and these must be dispassionately weighed against black's small material plus. Take a moment and see if you can list the imbalances.

Ready? Okay, here's how I see it:

➤ **Black**—One extra pawn. That's it! That's all he has to crow about. Nevertheless, it does carry some weight and forces White to prove sufficient compensation since, if Black can hold things together and manage to make some soothing trades, then he might go on to win an endgame with that "little" extra passed pawn.

➤ **White**—The d3-Bishop is "good" (and active!), while black's Bishop is not only undefended but also playing the role of a defensive pawn. Black's pawns on d5 and f5 are both vulnerable and will need to be carefully defended. White's Knight is a tower of strength while the black steed is a passive defender. White's Queen is far more active than black's. White's control of the open e-file takes aim at the slightly vulnerable e6-Bishop and also the hole on e5.

When you add up these things, it's clear that White has a lot going for him and full compensation for the pawn. In a nutshell, his army is more active than black's, Black has several weak squares in his camp, and White has clear targets (on d5 and f5) to attack while white's position is free from weaknesses. Of course, Black is far from doomed but, using the words of Ivanchuk, "For the central pawn White has a good game and well-placed pieces."

The game continued quietly, with White calmly building up his forces and adding pressure to the enemy targets:

22...Qd6 23.Rac1 Rfe8 24.Rc2 Bd7 25.Rce2

Note that black's a8-Rook is tied down to the defense of a7.

25...a6

25...Qb6?? fails to 26.Qxb6 axb6 27.Nxd7 Rxe2 28.Nxf6+.

26.Nc4!

The Knight heads for e3 where it will take aim at both d5 and f5.

26...Qc6 27.Ne3 Rac8

27...g6 loses to 28.Nxd5! Nxd5 29.Bc4.

28.Nxf5 Bxf5 29.Bxf5 Rxe2 30.Rxe2 Re8 31.Rc2 Qd6 32.g3 g6 33.Bc8 and White, who now has material equality on top of the superior minor piece (the Bishop dominates the Knight), the target on d5, and more activity, eventually won after a long battle.

The student should carefully look over these first two examples again. Clearly, the first one gave White a dominating position, with Black bound and gagged and completely helpless—players 1400 and higher should feel extremely comfortable (even excited!) giving up material for such a one-sided result.

> **PHILOSOPHY**
>
> Learn to treat material gains and losses as you would any other imbalance.

Our second example (Ivanchuk vs. Harikrishna) was altogether different. In that case White had good compensation for the sacrificed pawn, but many players wouldn't feel completely comfortable in white's shoes. This kind of nuanced sacrifice would be more natural for players 2000 and higher. Nevertheless, whether a player is comfortable with something or not, if you read the board and decide that it's the right thing to do based on our battle of imbalances, then you should bravely give it a try; at the very least, when you see such things occur in master games you'll finally understand why it was done and have a greater appreciation for the concept.

Of course, sacrifices do carry some element of risk since if you don't get enough compensation, or don't use that compensation properly, you can easily find yourself down material in some miserable endgame, or wiped out even earlier by the enemy's greater firepower. Naturally, there will be cases where you think a positional sacrifice is called for but misjudge the extent of your compensation and go down in flames. In those instances, you have to dust off your ego, analyze what went wrong, and give it another try if the board begs you to do so.

A good example comes from my own career: I was never comfortable with giving up my Queen for other units. Even if the material I got for my Queen put me ahead, I still didn't like it. This mental block stayed with me right up to the high 2100 level, and it was only after I lost a game due to my inability to swap off my Queen for the opponent's Rook, Bishop, and Knight (obviously this is more than enough for the Queen, but unreasoning fear is often a stronger force than logic and facts) that I decided to put an end to the nonsense once and for all. From that point on I never hesitated

> **PHILOSOPHY**
>
> Don't allow yourself to develop a fear of any aspect of the game! Once that fear becomes a habit, your ability to progress in chess will be severely hampered. Positions with various forms of material inequality are the basis of many cases of psychological chess paralysis.

to enter such situations. At first I wasn't comfortable with this "other stuff for my Queen" idea, but if I felt that I would stand well with a solid position and a Rook, Bishop and pawn for my Queen, I would push fear away and do it! How about three minor pieces for my Queen? No problem! And, slowly but surely, such things became a natural part of my game and fear stopped playing any role in that kind of decision. My philosophy was clear: If you lose you lose, but at least you have the courage to stand up for what you think is right for the position. There's nothing worse than getting pushed off the board and realizing that a lack of self-confidence didn't allow you to even put up a fight!

A sharp Sicilian (**1.e4 c5 2.Nf3 d6 3.d4 cxd4 4.Nxd4 Nf6 5.Nc3 e6 6.Be2 Be7 7.0–0 0–0 8.f4 Nc6 9.Be3 e5 10.Nxc6 bxc6 11.Kh1 exf4 12.Bxf4 Be6 13.Bf3 Qb8 14.b3 Qb4 15.Qd2 Rfd8 16.Rad1 Rac8 17.Qe3 d5 18.Be5 Qa5 19.exd5 Nxd5 20.Nxd5 cxd5 21.Bh5 d4 22.Qe4 g6 23.Bf3 Bf5 24.Qf4 Bg5 25.Qxg5 Qxe5**) led to the following complex position:

Diagram 142

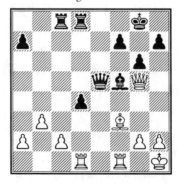

P. Svidler – S. Movsesian, Nanjing 2008
White to move

White's c2-pawn is about to fall and he pretty much has to decide on 26.c4, which leaves Black with a scary looking passed d-pawn and approximately equal chances, or the more macho 26.Bg4, which is the prelude to an Exchange sacrifice. Svidler decided to go for the gusto:

26.Bg4 h6 27.Rxf5 Qg7 28.Qe7?!

This eventually allows Black to gain a bit of time kicking the Queen around. 28.Qh4 was better, with equal chances.

28...gxf5 29.Bxf5

Diagram 143

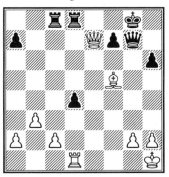

Optically this looks pretty good. White gets a pawn for the Exchange, c2 is well defended, the enemy pawns on a7 and d4 need looking after, and the position of the black King has become a bit drafty.

It's clear that White has real compensation, but there's a problem: White needs to play with energy and try to develop some initiative. If Black can prevent this, and if he can consolidate his position and activate his Rooks, they might end up overpowering the White army. Indeed, after some errors this is exactly what happened:

29...Re8 30.Qd6 Rcd8 31.Qa6 Qg5 32.Bd3 Re7 33.Rf1 Kg7 34.g3 Qd5+ 35.Kg1 Rd6 36.Qc8 Qe6 37.Qb8 Rb6 38.Qd8 Rd6 39.Qb8 Rd5 40.Rf4 Rg5 41.Rf3 Qe5 42.Qd8 h5 43.Rf2 Re6 44.Qd7 Rf6 45.Re2 Qf4 46.Re4??

46.Re8 gave better chances to hold on. After 46.Re4 the game is just over.

46...Qf2+ 47.Kh1 h4, 0-1.

So was Svidler's Exchange sacrifice the wrong thing to do? Will the trauma make him avoid such sacrifices in the future? Not at all! His decision made good sense, but he was outplayed and the game slipped out of his hands. It happens to everyone. I guarantee that he'll be making many more Exchange sacrifices as his career continues.

Only by trying something and getting hands-on experience can you truly understand it. And, even if you courageously go for a "grand scheme" and it all goes to hell, you'll still feel proud of yourself for giving free reign to your creative doppelganger.

Embracing Your Inner Greed

It's clear that giving up material takes courage, but that same courage is often needed to take material.

B. Spassky - R. Fischer, Reykjavik 1972 (13th match game)

1.e4 Nf6 2.e5 Nd5 3.d4 d6 4.Nf3 g6 5.Bc4 Nb6 6.Bb3 Bg7 7.Nbd2 0–0 8.h3 a5 9.a4 dxe5 10.dxe5

Diagram 144

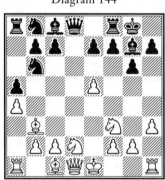

Some people consider this game to be the greatest of all time (though our focus will be on the initial greed, not the later brilliance). In this position Fischer is putting some pressure against the space-gaining e5-pawn (though it's easily defended). Oddly, the most accessible target (remember that something is only weak if you can bring pieces to bear on it) is the pawn on a4 (...Na6-c5 combined with ...Qe8 and, if need be, ...Bd7), but capturing it (which entails a loss of time) will give White definite compensation in the form of central space and development (as Black tosses everything at a4, White will be getting the rest of his army out).

In this example, we aren't looking at the safe consumption of a weak pawn. Instead, we're going to see a player create divergent imbalances (the trade of time/development for material) in an effort to sharpen the play and give himself a shot at victory. Naturally, this approach can lead to joy or despair, depending on whether the bout of greed is positionally and/or tactically justified, and on which player can handle the tension better.

After **10...Na6! 11.O-O Nc5 12.Qe2 Qe8 13.Ne4 Nbxa4 14.Bxa4 Nxa4**
Black has won the pawn and is doing well, but white's kingside space advantage
will allow him to get some play of his own. The rest of the game is an amazing
creative achievement by the 11th World Champion: **15.Re1 Nb6 16.Bd2 a4
17.Bg5 h6 18.Bh4 Bf5 19.g4 Be6 20.Nd4 Bc4 21.Qd2 Qd7 22.Rad1 Rfe8
23.f4 Bd5 24.Nc5 Qc8 25.Qc3 e6 26.Kh2 Nd7 27.Nd3 c5 28.Nb5 Qc6
29.Nd6 Qxd6 30.exd6 Bxc3 31.bxc3 f6 32.g5 hxg5 33.fxg5 f5 34.Bg3 Kf7
35.Ne5+ Nxe5 36.Bxe5 b5 37.Rf1 Rh8 38.Bf6 a3 39.Rf4 a2 40.c4 Bxc4 41.d7
Bd5 42.Kg3 Ra3+ 43.c3 Rha8 44.Rh4 e5 45.Rh7+ Ke6 46.Re7+ Kd6 47.Rxe5
Rxc3+ 48.Kf2 Rc2+ 49.Ke1 Kxd7 50.Rexd5+ Kc6 51.Rd6+ Kb7 52.Rd7+
Ka6 53.R7d2 Rxd2 54.Kxd2 b4 55.h4 Kb5 56.h5 c4 57.Ra1 gxh5 58.g6
h4 59.g7 h3 60.Be7 Rg8 61.Bf8 h2 62.Kc2 Kc6 63.Rd1 b3+ 64.Kc3 h1=Q
65.Rxh1 Kd5 66.Kb2 f4 67.Rd1+ Ke4 68.Rc1 Kd3 69.Rd1+ Ke2 70.Rc1 f3
71.Bc5 Rxg7 72.Rxc4 Rd7 73.Re4+ Kf1 74.Bd4 f2**, 0-1.

So, sometimes going after material entails a certain level of risk—in much
the same way that giving it up might be risky. But more often than not, taking
material is business as usual—*acquiring stuff* is merely the other side of the material coin. In fact, most games are won by eating the opponent's pieces, made
possible by his blunders, or via the slow and steady accumulation of positive
imbalances that ultimately result in material gain (creating weaknesses, freezing
those weaknesses, surrounding them, and finally cashing in).

Diagram 145

J. Birkel - J. Silman, American Open 1993
Black to move

Read this position and you'll quickly realize that Black has the superior pawn
structure and better-placed pieces. His main target is a3, which is attacked by
the a8-Rook, e7-Bishop, and c4-Knight. So black's plan, though unimaginative,
is simple and effective: win the a3-pawn!

16...Qb6!

Offering the exchange of Queens is eminently logical. Why? Because white's Queen is defending a3 while black's Queen isn't (at the moment) part of the a3-battle.

17.Qc3 Ra4

Not the only way—continuing the "exchange threat" by 17...Qa5 was also very strong. However, I wanted to get all my pieces into the party.

18.Nd3 Rfa8 19.Nfe5

19.Nb2 Nxb2 20.Bxb2 held out longer, though White's position would remain thoroughly miserable.

19...Ndxe5 20.Nxe5

Diagram 146

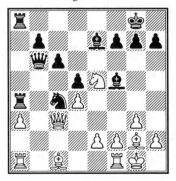

20...Nxe5!

I played 20...Nxa3 (it's strong and to the point), won the pawn, and eventually won the game. However, 20...Nxe5 is even better.

21.dxe5 Bc5

The threat of ...Bd4 is extremely annoying.

22.Qb2

22.e3 d4 is also horrible for White.

22...Qxb2 23.Bxb2 Bxa3 24.Bxa3 Rxa3 and the extra pawn guarantees Black victory since White has absolutely no compensation (no favorable imbalances) for it.

Imbalances vs. Material

The following game—a very complex one—sees Black chatting with two little devils sitting on both shoulders. One devil (the devil of "unbridled sacrifice") tells Black to go for the gusto and sacrifice his Queen. The other devil (the devil of "take it while you can") implores Black to eat a pawn on b2.

H. Uuetoa - A. Mayo, Canada Day Open 1999

1.c4 g6 2.d4 Bg7 3.e4 c5 4.Be3? Qb6 5.Nc3 cxd4 6.Nd5

Diagram 147

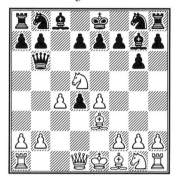

In this sharp position Black can embrace his inner greed by 6...Qxb2 7.Rb1 (7.Nc7+ Kd8 8.Bf4 d3! is very strong. One funny line: 9.Rc1 Bd4 10.Qd2 g5 11.Bg3 Bxf2+!!) 7...Qxa2 8.Ra1 Qb2 9.Rb1 Qa3 10.Nc7+ Kd8 11.Nb5 Qc5 12.Nxd4 Bxd4 (12...Qa5+!?) 13.Bxd4 Qa5+ 14.Ke2 Nf6 and though White has some compensation, he is *two* pawns down.

There is nothing wrong with embracing your inner greed. In fact, taking material and daring your opponent to prove his compensation puts a lot of pressure on him since, to put it in a stark manner, if the sacrifice doesn't work the game is over. The two most famous greed-kings are grandmasters Larry Evans and Victor Korchnoi. These extremely successful players would take whatever was offered and then hang on for dear life!

However, in the position in diagram 147 Black noticed a far more creative (but not necessarily superior) possibility: **6...dxe3!!? 7.Nxb6 exf2+ 8.Kxf2 axb6**

Diagram 148

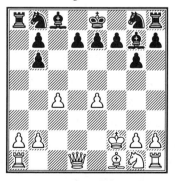

Has Black gone berserk?

That's right. White has a Queen and the move for two minor pieces and a pawn. Yet, White's position is far from easy to handle. Let's have Mr. Mayo himself explain his logic behind the startling 6...dxe3:

"For the queen, Black has an ultra safe King, two minor pieces, an extra pawn, plus almost total dark square control. Also, consider the lovely squares Black gets for his minors—e5, e6, c5, c6 or even d4 beckon piece placement.

"White has a displaced King, development deficit and a horrible light-squared Bishop with no active prospects. He is faced with the immediate loss of two more pawns with ...Bxb2 and so his Queen is confined to defensive duties. One other critical factor to be considered is that White does not have a single effective pawn lever at his disposal. He does not even have the prospect of an active Exchange sacrifice to alter the position (only perhaps passive sacs with Rd5 at some future point)."

In short, black's pieces will be more active than white's, White has no way to break into the enemy position, and Black has various targets (squares and pawns) that he can chew on while the white position is devoid of any plan. It's clear that Mr. Mayo has a very good grasp of the imbalances and how to measure their pros and cons without falling victim to purely material (point count) considerations.

Okay, I can imagine many of you saying, "Nice, but I could never do anything like that."

Why not? Yes, you have to somehow free yourself of the "I can't" mindset, which is also explored in Part Four. But once you notice 6...dxe3, and once you see that you'll be giving up your Queen for two minors and a pawn, don't panic and say, "No way!" Instead calmly look at the imbalances in the resulting position and, if you appreciate what you are getting for the material investment (many positive imbalances for material), why not pull the trigger and do it? In fact, if you really want to improve, you should always jump on such situations (win or lose) so you can expand your chess mind and plant the seeds for future successes.

> **REMEMBER**
>
> If you create "imbalance vision" and make the search for (and understanding of) imbalances an addiction, your playing strength will take a quantum leap forward.

In the game, Mr. Mayo's concept came through with flying colors: **9.Qd2 Nc6 10.Nf3 Nf6 11.Bd3 Ng4+ 12.Ke2 0–0 13.h3 Nge5 14.Nxe5 Nd4+ 15.Kf2 Bxe5 16.Rhf1 d6 17.Kg1 Be6 18.Qb4 Nc6 19.Qb5 Ra5 20.Qb3 Rfa8 21.a3 b5 22.Qc2 bxc4 23.Be2 Bd4+ 24.Kh1 Ne5 25.Rad1 Bc5 26.Rfe1 b5 27.Qc3 Ra4 28.Rf1 b4 29.axb4 Rxb4 30.Ra1 Rab8 31.Ra2 Rb3 32.Qd2 Re3 33.Qc2 c3 34.bxc3 Bxa2 35.Qxa2 Rxc3 36.Bg4 Re3 37.Be6 Rf8 38.Bd5 Kg7 39.Qa6 e6 40.Bxe6 fxe6 41.Rxf8 Kxf8 42.Qc8+ Ke7 43.Qb7+ Nd7 44.Qa8 Re1+ 45.Kh2 Bg1+ 46.Kh1 Bd4+ 47.Kh2 Be5+ 48.g3 Re3**, 0-1.

This was very advanced stuff, but it wasn't about calculation at all. Ultimately it came down to having faith in the power of "lesser" imbalances over material.

And this is a concept that you can (slowly but surely) train into your psyche at almost any rating level.

Our next example shows a pawn sacrifice that directly addresses the imbalances and goals that both sides were trying to achieve. W. Browne - J. Silman, American Open 1998 **1.d4 d5 2.c4 c6 3.Nf3 Nf6 4.Nc3 dxc4 5.a4 Bf5 6.e3 e6 7.Bxc4 Bb4 8.0-0 0-0 9.Qe2 Bg6 10. Ne5 Nbd7 11.Rd1 Nxe5 12.dxe5 Nd7 13.f4 Qc7 14.Na2 Be7 15.e4 Nc5 16.Nc3 Rfd8 17.Rf1 Qd7 18.g4 h6 19.f5 Bh7 20.Be3 Qc7 21.f6 Bf8 22.fxg7 Kxg7 23.g5**

Diagram 149

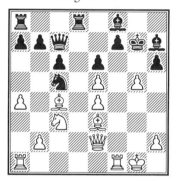

Black to move

This position is an easy read: Black's King is vulnerable and needs to be cared for while white's pawn structure is a mess. Quite simply, Black will have the advantage if he can find a safe haven for his King!

Note how I didn't mention the threat of gxh6+. The reason is that one should have a firm grasp of the imbalances (and the goals that their existence creates) before thinking about threats and replies to them. Now that we know what both sides are trying to achieve (White wants to attack the enemy King, Black wants to find a safe home for it and then punish white's weak central pawns), the correct move for Black will make perfect sense.

23...Bg6!

Played instantly (Browne hoped for 23...hxg5 24.Qh5 when White's pieces are getting uncomfortably close to black's King). However, all of a sudden (after 23...Bg6) black's weak points (f7 is cemented and h5 is no longer a landing space for white's Queen) are solidly defended, and white's position begins to creak and whine.

Why is 23...Bg6 a hard move to find? We've been conditioned to avoid losing material. In this case you are giving up a pawn with check, so the mind automatically screams, "Don't let him take it!" and blinds you to all other possibilities. That's why creating an imbalance-oriented base of knowledge about every position you reach is so important—knowing a position's priorities allows you to step beyond the emotive mind and make decisions where logic, not emotion, rules.

24.gxh6+

24.b4 is answered by 24...Qxe5.

24...Kh7

White's a pawn ahead but the bits on e5, e4, and h6 are like overripe fruit that Black can pick whenever he wants to. Equally important is the black King's new situation—it's found some welcome cover on h7 and the white pawn on h6 actually plays the role of traitor since it's suddenly giving shelter to the opposing King.

I felt very confident here, but both of us now had only 3 minutes to make 16 moves!

25.Bf4 Be7

The critical move (and my original intention) was 25...Rd4! 26.Be3 Rad8! 27.Bxd4 Rxd4 28.Rad1 Rxd1 29.Rxd1 Qxe5 when Black has all the play. But h2-h4-h5 ghosts began to nag at me and, having no time for a deep look, irrationality won out and I decided to stop the h-pawn in its tracks. I passed on 25...Nd7 due to 26.h4.

26.Rf2 Rd4

Going after the e5-pawn by 26...Nd7!? was also tempting, but the clock was ticking and a decision had to be made!

27.Rg2 Rg8 28.Be3

Diagram 150

28...Qxe5?!

I had been dying to sacrifice the Exchange all through this game, and now I jumped at the chance. However, this was not the best moment to do so, and the safer 28...Rd7 would have left Black firmly in charge since 29.Bf4 is strongly met by 29...Bf6!

29.Bxd4 Qxd4+ 30.Kh1, ½-½. I had thought that I stood better here, but a quick look convinced me that things are actually far from clear: 30...Nxe4 (30...Kxh6 with an edge is best, but it didn't occur to me during the game) 31.Bd3 Nxc3 32.Bxg6+ Rxg6 33.bxc3 Qxc3 34.Rf1 Bf6 35.Rxg6 Kxg6. With no time left, neither side wanted to touch this position!

I should point out that offering various material imbalances is a part of many highly respected openings (we'll stress positional sacrifices here, and not attack-based sacs). A few examples:

The Stockholm Variation of the Classical Dragon

1.e4 c5 2.Nf3 d6 3.d4 cxd4 4.Nxd4 Nf6 5.Nc3 g6 6.Be3 Bg7 7.Be2 0–0 8.0–0 Nc6 9.Nb3 Be6 10.f4 Na5 11.f5 Bc4 12.Nxa5 Bxe2 13.Qxe2 Qxa5 14.g4 This position was once thought of as quite dangerous for Black, but when the discovery of **14...Rac8! 15.g5 Rxc3! 16.gxf6 Rxe3 17.Qxe3 Bxf6** hit the streets, the whole line was recognized as innocuous for White.

Diagram 151

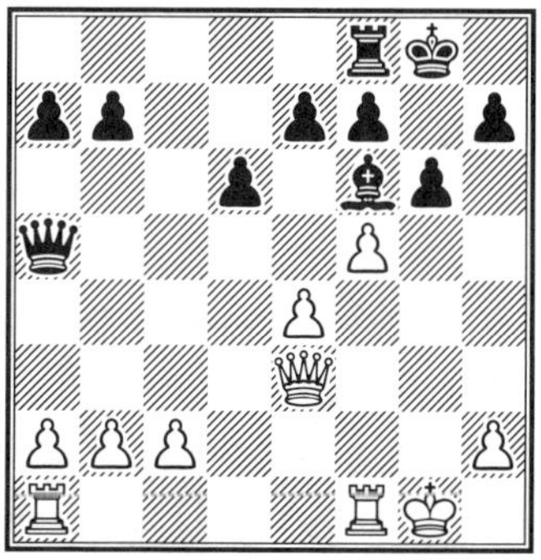

White to move

Why is this acceptable for Black? Aside from the fact that he has a pawn for the Exchange (making the material investment minimal), white's King is also a bit insecure, black's Bishop is not only very active but also serves as a magnificent defender of its own King, and Black enjoys the superior pawn structure.

Another problem for White concerns our eternal search for a plan. White has no play on the queenside or in the center, and aggressive posturing on the kingside will rarely work because the Bishop singlehandedly protects its King (an example of this will be given in the notes that follow). Black, however, can generate queenside play by the advance of his a- and b-pawns (a minority attack) and also place pressure on e4 (...Rc8-c4). All in all, it's thought to be equal but I consider it to be somewhat dreary for White.

The game A. Filipowicz - A. Hollis, Marianske Lazni 1962 continued: **18.c3 Rc8 19.a3 Rc4**

The e4-pawn is now under some heat.

20.Rae1 b5

Starting a classic minority attack. Black intends to move his Queen, play ...a7-a5 and then ...b5-b4 cracking white's queenside pawn structure and leaving him with yet another weakness to guard in that area.

21.Rf3 Qc7 22.fxg6 hxg6 23.Rh3 a5 24.Rf1 Qb7!

24...Qc5, which only offers equality, was played in the actual game.

Diagram 152

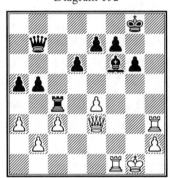

White's attack is an illusion

25.Re1

25.Qh6 looks scary, but Dragon players (and anyone that regularly fianchettos his kingside Bishop) know that it's very hard to mate a King when the defender's uncontested (White doesn't have a dark-squared Bishop to challenge it) dark-squared Bishop defends g7 and h8. After 25...Rxe4! Black laughs at white's so-called attack since 26.Qh7+ Kf8 isn't anything for White, and 26.Rxf6 Rg4+ leaves White having to choose between 27.Rg3 Rxg3+ 28.hxg3 exf6 (two pawns up for Black), and 27.Kf1 Qh1+ with a winning attack for Black!

The immediate 25.Rxf6 might seem to be a better move order, but this also fails: 25...Rxe4! 26.Rxg6+ (26.Qh6 Rg4+) 26...fxg6 27.Qg5 (27.Qh6 Rg4+) 27...Re6 and White's in serious trouble (28.Qh6? Qb6+ wins on the spot).

25...b4 26.axb4 axb4 and White is under severe pressure. His queenside is falling apart and, as we've seen, the attacking leap 27.Qh6 just doesn't get the job done.

Catalan Opening

One would think that many players with White (see diagram 153) would be delighted to achieve such a position by move 13 of the opening (the initial moves are **1.d4 Nf6 2.c4 e6 3.g3 d5 4.Bg2 dxc4 5.Nf3 c5 6.0–0 Nc6 7.Qa4 cxd4 8.Nxd4 Qxd4 9.Bxc6+ Bd7 10.Rd1 Qxd1+ 11.Qxd1 Bxc6 12.Qc2 Be7**

13.Qxc4 0–0). White has a Queen for black's Rook and Bishop, and all of white's pawns are healthy and his King is safe. So, why would anyone in his right mind actually play for this position as Black?

Diagram 153

White to move

Shockingly, world-class grandmaster Ulf Andersson often reached this position, which he considered to be a drawing line. And he proved it over and over by halving the point with many of the world's finest players (Kasparov included!). Why is Black okay here? Quite simply, his position is devoid of weaknesses, he's extremely solid, his c6-Bishop gives him ownership of the light squares, and White found it more or less impossible to tear down black's fortress. In other words, white's only favorable imbalance is his material advantage, and that alone isn't enough to generate any real winning chances.

One sample (the game L. Polugaevsky - U. Andersson, Moscow 1981) is enough to show just how solid black's game is: **14.Nc3 Rfd8 15.Be3 Nd5 16.Nxd5 Bxd5 17.Qg4 Rdc8 18.Bd4 Bf8 19.e4 Bc6 20.h4 Rd8 21.Bc3 Rd3 22.h5 h6 23.Re1 Rad8 24.Kh2 a6 25.Re2 Rd1 26.Re1 R1d3 27.Re2 Bb5 28.Rc2 Ba4 29.b3 Bc6 30.Qf4 Bd6 31.Be5 Bf8 32.Bc3 Bd6**, ¹/₂-¹/₂.

Ruy Lopez, Marshall Attack

Material sacrifices that create a "battle of the imbalances" are commonplace in virtually every opening. An excellent example of this is the highly popular Marshall Attack, which sees Black offering a pawn for a lead in development, active pieces, a slight weakening of the light squares in white's kingside, and good dynamic chances. On the other hand, White has a solid position and an extra pawn.

R. Fischer - B. Spassky, 2nd Piatigorsky Cup 1966

1.e4 e5 2.Nf3 Nc6 3.Bb5 a6 4.Ba4 Nf6 5.0–0 Be7 6.Re1 b5 7.Bb3 0–0 8.c3 d5 9.exd5 Nxd5 10.Nxe5 Nxe5 11.Rxe5 c6

Diagram 154

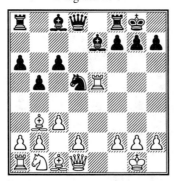

In diagram 154, both sides have put their faith in their respective short and long term imbalances. Black has a lead in development and, at times, scores a brutal knockout. However, even if White nullifies the immediate threats and trades into an endgame, the active black pieces still offer excellent chances for a draw.

12.g3 Nf6 13.d4 Bd6 14.Re1 Bg4 15.Qd3 c5 16.dxc5 Bxc5 17.Qxd8 Raxd8 18.Bf4 h6 19.Na3 g5 20.Be3 Bxe3 21.Rxe3 Rd2 22.Nc2 Re8 23.Rxe8+ Nxe8 24.Ne3 Bf3

Diagram 155

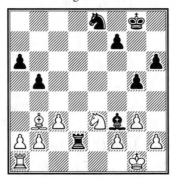

Minus a pawn, but Black has enough compensation

25.Bc2 Nd6 26.b3 Kf8 27.a4 Ne4 28.Bxe4 Bxe4 29.axb5 axb5 30.b4 Rb2 31.g4 Kg7 32.Kf1 Kf6 33.Ra5 Rb1+ 34.Ke2 Rb2+, ¹/₂-¹/₂. White's still a pawn up, but black's still active! The draw is now forced since 35.Kd1 would be dangerous only for White: 35...Bd3 36.Ra6+ Ke5 37.Rxh6 Rxf2 38.h4 Kf4 39.Nd5+ Kxg4.

It's clear that black's compensation for the pawn isn't just a hope and a prayer—it's based on sound positional considerations that last late into the game. One might wonder why everyone wouldn't play a line that gives Black a short-term attack and long-term positional compensation. The answer is that White has many ways to avoid falling victim to a fast mate, and though the resulting positions are often drawn, Black has to suffer a bit—perhaps not the kind of result keen attacking fans would dream of, but fully acceptable as far as theory is concerned.

It must also be admitted that many players with the white pieces aren't too excited by those "pleasant but probably not winning" endgames. These unsatisfied souls constantly seek new ways to stir the pot. One sample: **12.d4 Bd6 13.Re1 Qh4 14.g3 Qh3 15.Re4 g5 16.Qf1** (Avoiding 16.Bxg5?? Qf5—it's not wise to put too many pieces on undefended squares!) **16...Qxf1+ 17.Kxf1 Bf5 18.f3 h6 19.Nd2 Bxe4 20.fxe4** when a major change in the mutual imbalances has occurred!

Diagram 156

White's now down an Exchange, but he has a pawn for it, a nice center, and two Bishops. Full compensation, but the chances are probably more or less balanced.

There's no doubt that material is a major imbalance, with greed winning many games and also losing its share too. If you train yourself to view material as just another (albeit very important) imbalance, you'll open up a whole new level of understanding where sacrificing for tactical or positional compensation is always on the table. On the other hand, bravely taking everything your opponent offers should also be a part of your overall mindset—in either case, the decision depends on a calm assessment of the imbalances that both sides end up with.

Summary

> How can a player get beyond his fear of parting with material? He has to train himself to view each imbalance as something important, and he has to view material as just another imbalance to be collected or rejected, depending on the nature of the individual position.

> If you create "imbalance vision" and make the search for (and understanding of) imbalances an addiction, your playing strength will take a quantum leap forward.

> Embrace your inner greed! Having a material advantage gives you a larger/more powerful army (which can translate to greater force being brought to a key sector of the board) and/or the long-term advantage of "endgame odds" (knowing that most endgames will win for the material up side grants him tremendous flexibility). So by all means, eat everything in your path, as long as you're aware of what (if anything) your opponent is getting in return.

> If you read the board and decide that it's telling you to sacrifice material for a host of positional pluses, don't hesitate to do so! Learning to conquer your chess fears and prejudices is a huge part of improving your overall game.

> Being material ahead usually makes a player feel warm and fuzzy, but it's an imbalance and must be weighed against all the other imbalances. It might offer a decisive plus, or it might pale in comparison to different static or dynamic imbalances (compensation) in any given position.

> Notice how sacrificing material and seeking material gains have been placed together. Both treat material as an imbalance (not something to be feared, avoided, worshipped, or always embraced), and the assessment of either decision (i.e., to take or to sacrifice) has to be based on the other imbalances on the board.

Material — Tests

Of all the test sections in this book, I think this one requires more from the reader than any other. Be very aware that material is the focal point here, and try to be honest *and* fearless about all material (or possible material) imbalances. Afterwards, play over the answers and analysis until you feel that you're comfortable with the strange goings on. Your rally cry must be: "Material is an imbalance and I'm willing to both take it *and* give it up, depending on the nature of the other imbalances." Doing so will help you make the transition from the "material is king" mindset that traps so many in a lifelong rut.

If you have trouble solving the tests, don't worry—that means we've uncovered something you don't understand, and this allows you to fix things by rereading the previous material or by picking up the bits of knowledge you're missing in the answers that start on page 484.

PART FOUR - TEST 1

Diagram 157

[Level: 1800 - 2200]

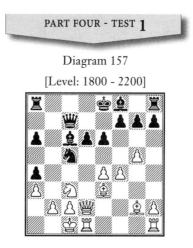

White to move

White has two vastly different philosophical options. What are they?

PART FOUR - TEST **2**

Diagram 158

[Level: 2200 on up]

Black to move

Is 9...Nxg3 worthwhile?

PART FOUR - TEST **3**

Diagram 159

[Level: 1800 - 2200]

Black to move

PART FOUR - TEST **4**

Diagram 160

[Level: 1400 - 1800]

Black to move

PART FOUR - TEST **5**

Diagram 161

[Level: 1800 - 2000]

Black to move

PART FOUR - TEST **6**

Diagram 162

[Level: 1800 - 2200]

Black to move

Is ...Qxh4 wise?

PART FOUR - TEST 7

Diagram 163

[Level: 1400 - 1800]

Black to move

Is taking on e5 wise?

PART FOUR - TEST 9

Diagram 165

[Level: 1800 - 2000]

White to move

Is 14.Rxc6 a good idea?

PART FOUR - TEST 8

Diagram 164

[Level: 1800 - 2200]

Black to move

Is 23...Na4 a good idea?

Mental Breakdown
Overcoming the Trap of "I Can't" and "I Must"

Bowing to Panic

Decades of teaching have shown me that, when I ask my students why they did or didn't play a certain move, I usually get answers like, "I can't do that because…" or "I must play that because…" or "I had to!" or "He has to!"

The highly destructive idea that you *must* do something you *might not wish to do* is so ubiquitous in amateur chess that I would say a player would gain at least a hundred rating points if he managed to rid himself of this one mental/emotional curse.

Let's take a look at the following position for a very basic example of what I'm talking about.

Diagram 166

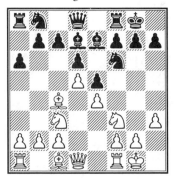

Black to move

I've seen this kind of structure occur in countless amateur games, and far more often than you might imagine, the other side sets up a battery on the h3-pawn via …Bd7 followed by …Qc8. So we'll say Black plays the "subtle" **1…Qc8**. In doing this, Black is more or less yelling his aggressive intent to sacrifice on h3 at his opponent. And, over and over again, I've seen replies like 2.g4?? h5! 3.gxh5 Bxh3 when we've witnessed a self-fulfilling prophecy—white's kingside will be shattered and his worst nightmare will become a reality, or 2.Kh2? when White has prevented …Bxh3 but made a move he really had no intention of playing.

White's reactions were created by panic and, though he wasn't aware of it, he found himself manipulated like a puppet—his opponent (the puppet master) pulls a string and White finds that he no longer is in control of his own actions!

Now we'll go back to **1...Qc8** and see how White *should* have reacted! Let's say White expected 1...b5 when he was going to reply with 2.Bd3, while a quieter move by Black would have seen White respond with 2.a4, nipping black's queenside expansion in the bud. However, after 1...Qc8 appeared on the board White immediately noted the intention of sacrificing on h3. What should White do about this implied threat? The first thing you have to do is train your mind *not* to writhe in terror. Instead, heap scorn on your opponent's idea with a hearty (internal!) "Rubbish!" I'm serious! Whenever you see an enemy threat, your first thought should be "Rubbish!" though even stronger language can be used if you find it sets your thinking processes in the right direction!

> **PHILOSOPHY**
>
> Do you want to be the puppet or the puppet master?

In general, a good player never accepts that an enemy threat will work unless he proves it to himself. In fact, his first impulse when seeing something like ...Qc8 is to break out in laughter or, at the very least, a smirk that says, "You don't expect me to buy into that, do you?" So, if you had intended to play 2.a4 against just about everything but 1...b5, then why not see if you can still play the desired move before looking for something else? The sequence then (physical moves and emotional/intellectual ruminations), will be something like this:

> **RULE**
>
> Every threat should initially be looked at with a derisive attitude.

1...Qc8

White: "What utter Rubbish! Is this guy serious? I want to play 2.a4, and after 2...Bxh3 3.gxh3 Qxh3 something like 4.Nh2 (4.Ng5 is also good) followed by Qf3 seems to do the trick. Then I'm a piece up and should win the game."

2.a4 etc.

As you saw, if Black goes ahead with the intended sacrifice White will have a material advantage and will be well on his way to victory. Thus, stopping a fake threat is akin to stopping your opponent from losing the game! Nobody (beginner or grandmaster) can afford to do that and expect good results.

Of course, you have to prove the threat's ultimate worth before ignoring or preventing it. If it's really dangerous, you just shrug your shoulders and say, "Hard to believe, but it seems to be true!" Then you take a moment out to prevent his idea and continue on with your previous plans as soon as possible.

The keys here are:

➤ Never believe anything your opponent "tells" you. He's not your friend! This "don't believe it until it's proven" attitude is a trained mental state—you are going to have to force yourself to enter that state by using the word "Rubbish" until it all becomes an unconscious process.

- ▶ You're the only advocate for your position. If you don't believe in it, who will?

- ▶ If there's a move you really want to play, stick by it and see if that move will still work in the face of the supposed enemy threat.

- ▶ Train yourself to treat enemy threats with contempt, but don't be foolhardy! Always analyze the ramifications of allowing the threat before ignoring or preventing it.

- ▶ Remember, if you prevent a false threat, *you are actually stopping your opponent from losing the game*! Think about that—games are hard enough to win without you turning traitor and stopping the opponent from committing suicide!

It's My Party and I'll Move What I Want To

Training yourself to play the move you *want* to play, even in the face of a scary (but ultimately bogus) threat, will pay dividends in every kind of position. In a way, this philosophy should be looked upon as you demanding good things for your position—these "good things" won't be given to you, so you have to take them while the taking is good!

1.Nf3 d5 2.d4 Nc6 3.g3 Nf6 4.Bg2 Bf5

Diagram 167

White to move

White's most natural move is 5.0-0, but black's last move not only developed his Bishop but also announced that 5...Nb4 is in the air. "Fear it!" says Black.

And many would do just that, renouncing the intended 5.0-0 for a bit of safety via 5.a3 or 5.c3—surely castling can follow once the danger is gone?

But why should White waste a tempo to avoid the "danger?" I constantly tell my students that, "Every move is like gold. Moves are a very valuable commodity and you don't want to waste them!" So, though both 5.a3 and 5.c3 are playable, are you really getting top value for your gold plated move? Obviously not! Instead, try to make the most valuable move (the move you feel the position really needs) work.

5.0-0!

It's what you *wanted* to do, so *do* it!

5...Nb4 6.c3!?

White can now defend c2 with 6.Na3 (White's most popular choice) or by 6.Ne1. However, 6.c3 demonstrates that black's "threat" of ...Nb4 was certainly nothing to waste a move preventing!

6...Nc2?

Actually 6...Bc2! is best, when 7.Qe1 Nc6 leads to some strange abnormalities (the black Knight didn't accomplish much, and his light-squared Bishop is also oddly placed, but white's Queen is far from ideal on e1), while 7.Qd2 Bxb1 8.a3! Be4 9.axb4 is only slightly better for White.

7.Nh4 Nxa1 8.Nxf5 and Black, whose a1-Knight is trapped on a1 and will certainly die there, is in serious trouble.

So far we've seen that "I can't" gets its power from one side believing his own propaganda ("My move is strong, fear it!") and the other bowing to the opponent's certainty—he tells you (silently … almost psychically) that doing what you want to do is no longer possible because of the threat he just created.

One of the most common situations for brain-melt occurs when one side is quite a bit higher rated than the other. In that case the lower rated player is expecting to lose from move one and, when things get tough, he fully accepts the self-fulfilling prophecy of doom. For example, I once witnessed a game where a grandmaster was playing a 2100 rated opponent. The grandmaster was doing well when he suddenly "hung" a piece. The 2100 looked at it for a long time—to take or not to take? Obviously the grandmaster wouldn't just give a piece away, so it had to be a trap—the grandmaster was clearly saying, "You'll die a horrible death if you dare touch that piece." Eventually the 2100 thought he saw something that might be dangerous and didn't accept the gift. The grandmaster won easily.

After the game the grandmaster asked, "Why didn't you take my piece? I would have resigned if you did!"

Ah, if only Mr. 2100 had screamed (internally) "Rubbish! I'm going to snap that piece off and force him to show me why I can't!"

This story illustrated a one-way delusion—his fear and paranoia combined to create shadows and evil intent that only existed in his own mind. Just as common, though, is a situation where the superior player believes something that's completely wrong but his air of confidence (and those extra rating points!) quickly convinces the lower rated opponent to dance cheek to cheek down delusion lane.

This "propaganda + rating points = mutual delusion" theorem can be seen in our next example.

Diagram 168

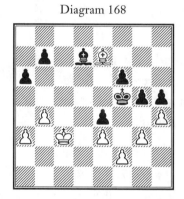

A. Uto (1630) - C. Lamprey (1882), Paris Club Match 2009
White to move

Earlier in the game White had achieved an easily drawn position that was devoid of any danger. However, the higher rated player (Black) outplayed his opponent and achieved some serious-looking kingside threats thanks to his pressure against h4 and his hyperactive King (...Kg4 hitting h4 with a possible ...Kf3 if f2 is left unattended).

Black was suddenly looking extremely confident and White realized that she had screwed things up. Staring in horror at the mess she had made, she forgot about the clock and her flag fell, thus handing Black the victory that he assured her (after the score sheets were signed) would have been his even if the game had continued.

The next day I got a copy of the game, which ended with the following comment by Miss Uto: "My flag fell, but I can't draw this anyway." The higher rated player's "handing down truth" made such a profound impression that she didn't bother challenging his comment and she would have continued to believe it if I didn't immediately e-mail back, "What are you talking about? This is a dead draw. In fact, you should easily draw Kasparov here."

And, finally, she did the right thing and challenged *my* statement. And this leads us to an important rule: Always challenge everything until you have, to the best of your ability, proven or disproven the other person's view. By doing so, you will build correct mental/emotional habits and also learn a lot by forcing yourself to peer as deeply into a situation as you can.

So, how could White have saved the game? Was it really so easy? Yes it was! All she had to do was play the Bishop back and forth to d8 and e7 (tying the black King to the defense of f6) and it would be time to split the point (if Black moved his King back to e6 White would stick the Bishop on d8 and then dance about with her King).

Of course, it's clear that a couple things combined to put White over the edge. The "propaganda + rating points = mutual delusion" theorem was one of the main culprits, but White was also guilty of concentrating on black's threats (a failing we saw in diagram 166) and didn't even consider that she could create her own.

The Eerie Phenomenon of Mutual Delusion

The examples that follow show that delusion and "I can't" (as in Uto's "I can't defend this" and her opponent's "She can't defend this") occur in every possible situation: grandmasters fall victim to it, equally matched players do the same dance of madness, and on and on it goes!

In Kotov's classic book *Think Like a Grandmaster*, he gave an example of this kind of mutual delusion, though in that case he was using it in a discussion about blunders. However, let's look beyond the blunder and try and understand why this particular kind of mistake is made.

Diagram 169

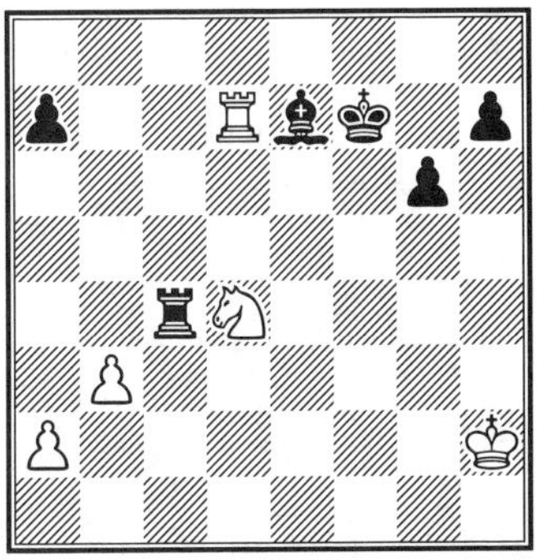

A. Ebralidze - V. Ragozin, Tbilisi 1937
Black to move

Black's a pawn up but his Bishop is pinned, his Rook is under attack, and his a7-pawn is also threatened.

1...Rc7??

In one sense this is the perfect solution! It saves the Rook, defends the a7-pawn, threatens white's Rook, and tries to trade into a winning pawn up Bishop vs. Knight endgame after 2.Rxc7 Bd6+ forking the Rook and King. Nice! The only problem is that after 2.Rxc7 Bd6+ is illegal since the Bishop is pinned! Ragozin had simply forgotten about the pin, but he was 100% sure that if White captured on c7 he would achieve a winning endgame. And, as a result of this *knowing* that 2.Rxc7 was just what he wanted White to do, the illusion wafted across the board to his opponent.

Ebralidze, of course, fully understood his opponent's idea ("He wants me to take it when ...Bd6+ leaves me with a lost endgame.") and thus succumbed to a form of Vulcan mind meld—he saw what Black saw, knew what Black knew, and felt the certainty that Black undoubtedly felt. And so it came to pass that both players were in complete agreement that 2.Rxc7 led to a lost endgame for White. It's interesting to note that a member of the audience became so agitated that Ebralidze wasn't devouring the gift and winning the game that he screamed, "Archil, take his Rook!" Poor Ebralidze, completely immersed in black's reality, gave the fool in the audience an angry glance (No doubt thinking, "I can't take it you idiot! Aren't you even good enough to see such a basic Bishop fork?") and retreated his Rook from d7 to d5. The ultimate irony is that he ended up falling for the very thing he feared most—the Bishop forking his Rook and King: **2.Rd5?? Bf6 3.Nb5 Rc2+ 4.Kg3 a6 5.Rd7+ Ke8 6.Rc7 Be5+, 0-1.**

What we have here isn't a blunder created by flawed calculation—instead it's a picture perfect but extreme case of "falling under the spell" of the opponent's dementia. A kind of mass hallucination!

I loved this story when I first read Kotov's book, but it seemed a bit farfetched to me. But, as fate would have it, I experienced almost the exact same thing while coaching the American junior team with Pal Benko in Szeged, Hungary.

Diagram 170

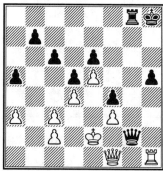

Nguyen Anh Dung - J. Waitzkin, Szeged 1994
White to move

Since coaches were not allowed in the playing hall for fear that they would speak to players, Benko and I were watching from way up above in the balcony. Black has just played his Queen to g2, checking white's King. It's clear that Black has a big advantage and we were sure Josh was going to win this game. After giving the check, he only had five minutes for the next few moves, but surely that would prove to be more than enough?

1.Qf2

We had expected 1.Qxg2 Rxg2+ 2.Kd3 (2.Kd1 puts up a better fight) 2...Rf2 3.Rxh5+ Kg7 4.Rh3 b5 when white's in zugzwang and has to give up material: 5.Rh1 Rxf3+ 6.Kd2 Kg6 and Black should score the full point—7.Rh8 Kf5 8.Rc8 Rf1 9.Rxc6 Ra1 10.Rb6 a4 11.Rxb5 Ke4 12.Rb8 f3 13.Rf8 Rxa3.

However, 1.Qf2 seemed odd. How did we miss it? Then reality hit us both in the face—this simply hangs the h1-Rook! Of course, it was clear that White wasn't aware h1 was floating in the breeze, no doubt feeling that it was defended a moment ago and so "Black still can't take it." Good news for us since now, after the obvious 1...Qxh1, White would resign and we could begin looking at the games of our other players.

But no—instead of snapping off the free Rook (followed by ...Rg2 to boot), Josh sank into deep thought. In fact, he seemed disturbed by 1.Qf2—for some reason he thought this wasn't possible (just like our initial reaction!) and couldn't understand why it was now staring him in the face! One minute ticked by, then two, and it became clear that Josh had bought into white's "he can't take the Rook" (which translates into black's "I can't") delusion.

> **RULE**
>
> Always challenge everything until you have, to the best of your ability, proven or disproven the other person's view.

Naturally we were both freaking out from our perch, and after a third minute passed, Benko started muttering, "Take the Rook! Why isn't he taking the Rook?" I told him to be quiet, but another thirty seconds went by (leaving Josh with just ninety seconds) and Pal, who had lost all control, started raising his voice as he repeated the Rook mantra, "Take the Rook! Why can't he take the Rook?" Of course, the arbiters would not take kindly to the coaches sharing this kind of information, so I quickly grabbed Benko and dragged him away from our scene of anguish. After using up all but a minute (Black was clearly wondering, "How did I miss this defense?"), Josh finally played **1...Qg6** and after **2.Kd2 Qf5 3.Rh4 Rg5 4.Kc1 Qg6 5.Qh2 Kg8** he was once again winning and soon scored the full point: **6.Qd2 Rg2 7.Qd3 Qg5 8.Rh3 h4 9.Kb2 Rg3 10.Rh2 h3 11.c4 dxc4 12.Qxc4 Qf5 13.Qe2 Kf7 14.Qe1 Rg2**, 0-1.

As you can see, if the opponent's delusion can create "I can't" so powerfully that you aren't able to see a one move snatch of a hanging Rook, imagine how easy it is to buy into something believable, like a threat. That's why you have to use the "Rubbish!" prompt when an enemy threat appears. And if the opponent plays a move that you never imagined (e.g. 1.Qf2 in the Waitzkin game), instead of allowing yourself to get confused, seek instant clarity by asking, "How can I punish this?" The logic is clear: if you didn't anticipate his response, then it must be bad and thus deserves to be punished! This is a much healthier mindset than seeing an unexpected move and thinking, "I missed it! I must be doomed!"

Once again, both "Rubbish!" and "How can I punish this?" are positive prompts that set an upbeat tone and allow you to see through the opponent's haze. Start training yourself to use them right away!

When you accept "I can't" into your chess life (okay, you shouldn't accept it into any part of your life, but that's way off topic), you'll find that various missed opportunities litter your games.

Diagram 171

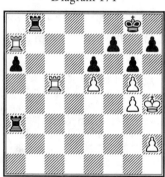

R. Crotto - M. Lazarevic, Rio de Janeiro 1979
White to move

Aside from the fact that black's a pawn up, White also saw that ...R8b3 was coming. Since ...R8b3 followed by ...Rh3 mate seems impossible to stop, Crotto bowed to the god of "I can't" (as in, "I can't do anything about it") and resigned.

However, if you have plenty of time left for thought, why tip your King when you can calmly look at the board for something/anything that might offer some hope? The old saying, "Nobody ever won a game by resigning" is hard to argue with, so why not use that clock time to seek a miracle?

Consider this: if you had a pack of 20 rabid dogs just a minute away from your throat and your only means of "escape" appeared to be leaping several hundred yards onto the jagged rocks below, what would you do? Leap? Lie down and wait to die? Weep until the dogs put you out of your misery? Or, would you use every second of your final bit of time trying your best to figure out some mind-bending way to save your skin?

In chess, you need to put that same emotional burst of energy into hard-to-defend positions as you would a life and death situation. If you think, "I'm doomed" (an offshoot of "I can't"), then you *will* be doomed. Crotto chose the "doom" scenario, but it turns out that salvation was there, just waiting to be discovered: **1.h3! Rbb3**

This is the move that convinced Crotto to give up all hope and resign (it *does* look bad!). Oddly, better is 1...Ra2 2.Rcc7 Rf8 3.Rc6 Ra5 4.Rcxa6 Rxe5, but Black would have little hope of success after 5.Re7 Re4 6.Raa7.

2.Rc8+ Kg7 3.Rg8+! Kxg8 4.Ra8+ Kg7 5.Rg8+! Kxg8, ½-½. A stalemate came to the rescue!

The Curse of "I Can't"

Indiana Jones - girl-brain, ICC clock simul 2008

1.e4 c6 2.d4 d5 3.exd5 cxd5 4.c4 Nf6 5.Nc3 e6 6.Nf3 Bb4 7.cxd5 Nxd5 8.Qc2 Nc6 9.Bd3 Be7 10.a3 Bf6 11.0–0 h6 12.Rd1 0–0 13.Be4 Nce7 14.Qe2 b6 15.Ne5 Bb7 16.Ng4 Nf5 17.Nxd5 Nxd5 18.Bxd5

Diagram 172

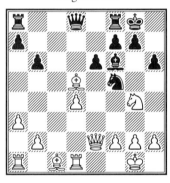

Black to move

Black's clock is ticking away and girl-brain (who was master strength in her prime) has to make a decision: should she recapture on d5 with the pawn or Queen? She knew there was something fishy about 18...exd5, but wasn't 18...Qxd5 19.Nxf6+ even worse since her King would be ripped open? "I can't allow that" immediately shut down all higher brain functions, and she chopped on d5 with the pawn.

18...exd5?

Perhaps part of the fear of opening up her King was caused by her opponent's strength—Israeli grandmaster Ronen Har-Zvi is a very tough customer! However, if you find yourself playing both the board *and* a rating, you're pretty much up the creek. It's interesting to note that chess is very much a caste system. I remember one tournament where I entered an elevator and, as the door closed, some guy squeezed in. He asked if I was Jeremy Silman, I said yes, shook his hand, and said, "It's a pleasure meeting you. What's your name?" His reply stunned me: "Oh, you don't want to know my name, my rating is too low!"

Though this was shocking, I had actually experienced the whole "caste game" earlier in my career. When I was a child and just starting out (with a 1068 rating), players 1400 and above pretty much steered clear of me—I just wasn't strong enough to hang with them. And when I had an expert rating a few years later, I vividly recall watching a couple of strong masters enjoying some five-minute chess in between rounds at a tournament in Salt Lake City. I asked if I could play the winner, and the stronger of the two said, "Sorry, but I only play people that are good!"

Those ratings hold a lot of power in chess, and I think just about every player is vulnerable to "rating fear" (a serious disease that only affects chess addicts). When I was rated in the 1800s, I had a terrible time dealing with those 2000+ gods. As soon as I saw a rating of 2000 or higher I would freeze and lose like a lamb. Finally I had had enough and decided to only look at an opponent's rating *after* the game was over. I implemented this in my very next tournament and was quickly paired with some guy that I wasn't familiar with. I didn't know his rating but, after a dozen moves, came to the conclusion that he was in the 1600–1800 range. I wiped him out and was stunned to discover that he was rated 2182! After that, I lost my fear of experts (2000 to 2199)—it was no longer a matter of numbers; I firmly believed they weren't a threat and that belief propelled me past them.

There's absolutely no doubt that confidence plays a huge role in chess. Those who are paired with a higher rated player and think, "I'm doomed," will find that the evisceration that follows will be quick and quite painful. On the other hand, the guy who revels in the pairing against a higher rated opponent and honestly feels he will crush his egotistical foe usually has quite a few scalps on his wall.

This is why an unproven "I can't" is such a crippling mindset. You are giving power to your own insecurity and to your opponent, and that alone makes you a huge underdog in the coming battle.

If girl-brain hadn't been facing a chess titan, perhaps she would have tried to prove/disprove her initial feeling that 18...Qxd5 (The move Black *wants* to play since the Queen is beautifully placed on d5 and the d4-pawn will prove to be a permanent target—remember, if there's a move you want to play, try hard to make it work!) 19.Nxf6+ gxf6 was too risky. And, in doing so, she might have realized that Black actually has an excellent game. Let's look at a few examples after 20.Qh5 (not good, but it's the kind of thing that would scare an "I can't" addict into not entering this as Black) 20...Kh7 (defending h6 and preparing to make use of the g-file with ...Rg8):

Diagram 173

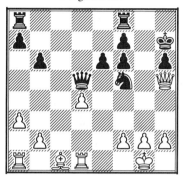

> 21.Bd2 leaves Black with a comfortable edge after 21...Rg8 22.g3 Rg6.

> 21.Be3?? Nxe3! wins a piece and the game (22.Qxd5 Nxd5).

> 21.g3 Ne3 (21...Rad8 is even stronger) 22.Qxd5 Nxd5 with a dream endgame for Black (play against d4 and a super Knight on d5).

> 21.g4?? is white's big try to refute black's setup, but it's powerfully met in many ways: 21...Rg8 (21...Qf3!? and 21...Rad8!? are also very strong) 22.Qxf7+ (loses, but White was already in serious trouble) 22...Rg7 23.Qh5 Qf3 and it's time for White to resign.

As you can see, Black would have had a lot of fun with 18...Qxd5, but she convinced herself that she couldn't do it and thus potential fun turned into misery.

19.Qf3

This forces the win of a pawn (after 19...h5 20.Qxf5 hxg4 21.Qxg4), though Black will (luckily) be able to claim some compensation for it. Nevertheless, Black, who didn't intend to lose material and had lost all confidence in herself, completely fell apart and lost quickly.

In general, an "I can't" moment is rarely based on any profound considerations. You glance at a logical possibility, emotion takes over and screams the "I can't" refrain, and you do something that has little to do with the needs of the position. This happens all the time and the only cure is to *insist* on finding a way to make the desired move work. Don't give up on it unless you've completely proven that it's bad!

Vadim - J. Stein, Los Angeles 2008

1.Nf3 d5 2.d4 Nf6 3.c4 c6 4.Nc3 dxc4 5.a4 Bf5 6.Ne5 e6 7.f3 Bb4 8.e4 Bxe4 9.fxe4 Nxe4 10.Bd2 Qxd4 11.Nxe4 Qxe4+ 12.Qe2 Bxd2+ 13.Kxd2 Qd5+ 14.Kc2 Na6 15.Nxc4 0–0 16.Qe5 f6 17.Qxd5 cxd5 18.Na5 Rfc8+ 19.Kd2 Nc5 20.Ra3 b6 21.Nb3 Ne4+ 22.Ke3

Diagram 174

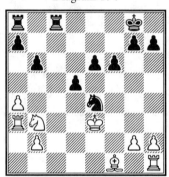

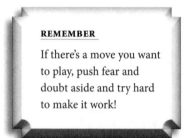

REMEMBER

If there's a move you want to play, push fear and doubt aside and try hard to make it work!

Black to move

Things have gone well for Black in this extremely theoretical variation of the Slav. Here Black played 22...f5?! when after 23.Bd3 his Rooks weren't nearly as active as they could have been after the more natural and far stronger 22...Rc2. During a lesson, I asked Jeremy Stein (who was a strong expert at this time) why he didn't bring his Rook to its 7th rank and he said, "I intended to do that but then I saw 23.Bd3. I realized that I couldn't play 22...Rc2 so I gave 22...f5 a try."

In black's mind, the mere sight of a developing move that simultaneously attacked a Rook caused him to instantly label the move he wanted to play as bad. Instead of analyzing the position after 22...Rc2 23.Bd3 and trying to see what was really going on, he dropped 22...Rc2 like a hot potato. In fact, he tried to put 22...f5 on the board so we could look at the game continuation but I placed the f-pawn back on f6 and said, "Show me why 22...Rc2 23.Bd3 Rxb2 or 23...Rxg2 isn't just very pleasant for you." He quickly agreed that it was far superior to the move played. Then I added, "Jeremy, do you see what's happening here? I'm defending the move you wanted to play. Why didn't you defend it in the game?"

To be fair to Mr. Stein, everyone of every rating falls victim to thoughts like "I can't" and "I have to". The difference is, though grandmasters occasionally cave in to its influence, amateurs are universally enslaved by it! Training oneself to avoid it (at least to some degree) will make an enormous and instantaneous impact on your results and on your general mindset—you'll find yourself pushing your own agenda more and laughing at your opponent's feeble attempts to take you off the proper path.

Our next example shows a World Champion falling victim to this disease.

Diagram 175

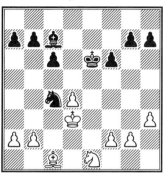

Em. Lasker - M. Euwe, Nottingham 1936
Black to move

Black has a small but permanent edge thanks to his superior pawn structure and total control over the d5-square. Black, whose Knight is under attack, should play the obvious 1...Nb6 followed by 2...Nd5 when White would have to defend for a long time in order to earn a draw. Instead, something strange occurred.

1...Ba5??

Very odd. Black is saying, "You have to move your Knight or take on c4 and allow a trade." Of course, "You have to" drinks from the same cup of laziness as "I can't." Yes, it's possible that White does indeed have to move it (though it wouldn't bother him if he did), but when you have a Knight hanging out to dry (White's itching to play Kxc4) you better be sure "you have to" is 100% accurate!

2.b4!

Euwe must have experienced that "I'm going to throw up" feeling after this appeared on the board and reality came crashing down on his head. Both black pieces are now attacked, so the Bishop has to capture on b4.

2...Bxb4 3.Nc2

The point. By sacrificing the b-pawn, White lured the Bishop to b4 where it would be in striking range of the Knight. After 3.Nc2 Black loses a piece and eventually lost the game.

In general, "I can't" or "He has to/I have to" appears due to:

- Lack of proper concentration.

- Bad mental habits.

- Allowing emotion to override logic.

➤ Not being strong enough to prove whether or not an "I can't" or "He has to" is actually correct.

We all run into situations that are above our level, and there's no shame in that (such moments can act as wonderful learning tools). A lack of concentration can occur due to some outside influence (for example, you were just told that you're going to be audited) or you are just having a "bad hair day." We can't prevent negative biorhythms or some personal Apocalypse from smacking us down from time to time, but we can work on improving concentration, quieting an overly emotional mind, and most definitely fixing mental habits that only lead to anguish.

If you want to defeat "I can't" then you simply must make use of the "Rubbish!" tool. In fact, challenge every quiet command (you saying "I can't", your opponent saying "You have to", etc.) that comes your way. To succeed in this, you have to go over your games from the last several months and look for the moments where things went sour. A computer will help you find those tactical moments, while a teacher will help you with the positional meltdowns. And, in both cases, you'll find that a large percentage of your "slips" were caused by some form of mental surrender. The only way to fix this problem is to be introduced to its existence (which we're doing here), to find instances of it in your own games (thus personalizing it), and then to use the "Rubbish!" tool to train you to stop and challenge every negative thought that your own brain or your opponent tosses your way.

Summary

➤ Whenever you see an enemy threat, your first thought should be "Rubbish!" though even stronger language can be used if you find it sets your thinking processes in the right direction!

➤ In general, a good player never accepts that an enemy threat will work unless he proves it to himself. In fact, his first impulse when seeing a blatant threat like ...Qc8 is to break out in laughter or, at the very least, a smirk that says, "You don't expect me to buy into that, do you?"

➤ If you prevent a false threat, you are (in many cases) actually stopping your opponent from losing the game! Think about that—games are hard enough to win without you turning traitor and stopping the opponent from committing suicide.

➤ Never believe anything your opponent "tells" you. He's not your friend! This "don't believe it until it's proven" attitude is a trained mental state—you are going to have to force yourself to enter that state by using the word "Rubbish" until it all becomes an unconscious process.

➤ You're the only advocate for your position. If you don't believe in it, who will?

➤ If there's a move you really want to play, stick by it and see if that move will still work in the face of the supposed enemy threat.

➤ Train yourself to treat enemy threats with contempt, but don't be foolhardy! Always analyze the ramifications of allowing the threat before ignoring or preventing it.

➤ Every move is like gold. Moves are a very valuable commodity and you don't want to waste them!

➤ Always challenge everything until you have, to the best of your ability, proven or disproven the other person's view. By doing so, you will build correct mental/emotional habits and also learn a lot by forcing yourself to peer as deeply into a situation as you can.

➤ If the opponent plays a move that you never imagined, instead of allowing yourself to get confused, seek instant clarity by asking, "How can I punish this?" The logic is clear: if you didn't anticipate his response, then it must be bad and thus deserves to be punished! This is a much healthier mindset than seeing an unexpected move and thinking, "I missed it! I must be doomed!"

Mental Breakdown — Tests

These problems will test your ability to see beyond chess illusion, and beyond fear. They will also make it clear that we all suffer from the illness of "I can't" and "I must." You are most certainly not alone!

If you have trouble solving the tests, don't worry—that means we've uncovered something you don't understand, and this allows you to fix things by rereading the previous material or by picking up the bits of knowledge you're missing in the answers that start on page 498.

PART FOUR - TEST 10

Diagram 176

[Level: 2000 - 2200]

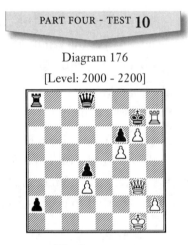

Black to move

What's going on?

PART FOUR - TEST 11

Diagram 177

[Level: 1600 - 2000]

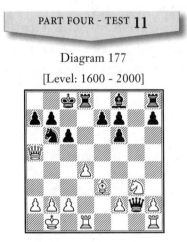

Black to move

The a7-pawn is attacked. What would be the most natural way to defend it? Does the most natural move work, or does White have something up his sleeve?

PART FOUR - TEST **12**

Diagram 178

[Level: 2000 - 2200]

Black to move

PART FOUR - TEST **13**

Diagram 179

[Level: 2000 - 2200]

Black to move

In your head, try and assess the position after 1...Rd5 2.Qb6 cxb5.

PART FOUR - TEST **14**

Diagram 180

[Level: 1400 - 2200]

Black to move

Calculate the following line in your head: 1...Rc2 2.Re2 Rxe2 3.Bxe2 Bc5. Now how would you assess black's winning chances?

PART FOUR - TEST **15**

Diagram 181

[Level: 1900 - 2200]

White to move

You're a piece down. How should White recapture? Analysis isn't necessary!

Macho Chess
The Art of Insistence

Pushing Your Own Agenda

In a way, this is an extension of the "negative" Mental Breakdown chapter. Though we will still be exploring the "I can't" and "rubbish!" mentality, our main focus will be on pushing one's own agenda. Thus, mantras such as "I will find a way!" and "I must!" take precedence here.

While the previous chapter brought the problems of mental domination/supplication to light, and hopefully, made you aware that this is something that affects everyone on some level, this chapter rams home the need for a positive mindset. And, in turn, a positive "I'll do what I want no matter what you say" psychological/emotional state often leads to degrees of mental domination that you might never have thought possible.

Personally, I've had hundreds of games where my opponent begins to react to me. He is usually unaware of his sudden, extremely subtle defensive demeanor, but once I sense this—even though the position is completely equal—I become sure that he's on his way down and that victory will eventually be mine.

Chess writers have traditionally used the word *initiative* when a player is taking control of the game's tempo, but I vastly prefer the psychologically charged mantras I'm using here. One side makes a move that pushes his agenda, the other side reacts, and a note appears that says, "White has now taken the initiative." However, most players don't really understand what that means, and therefore don't know how to make use of it in any practical sense.

> **PHILOSOPHY**
>
> You will gain huge dividends by creating an "I'll do what I want no matter what you say" attitude in chess.

What good is a term, even one that's constantly used, if its real meaning remains a mystery to the vast majority of chess fans? Because of this, I use that term sparingly, and instead tend to explain a situation where one side succeeds in pushing his agenda with words that can be understood, and that teach. And why not—I consider the initiative to be a physical manifestation of a psychological battle; both sides champion their view of things in the hope that the opponent will have to eventually forgo his own plans and react to yours. Make no mistake about it, macho chess—pushing one's own agenda and mantras such as "rubbish", "I will find a way", "I must" and "I'll do what I want no matter what you say"—is all about the initiative, and a player's ability and desire to take iron control over a game!

The following game, played online at a slow time control by Mr. Hubbard (a skilled positional player) and Mr. Abraham (a man who obviously enjoyed a good slugfest), caught my attention in a big way. On move eight White played to make castling difficult for his opponent to achieve. Instead of backing down, Black punched right back, trying to impose his will on White! Though Black was outplayed, we have to salute his "glass overflowing at all times" attitude.

Q. Hubbard (1998) - Abraham (1720), ICC 2005

1.Nf3 Nc6 2.d4 e5 3.dxe5 Qe7 4.g3 Nxe5 5.Bg2 c6 6.0–0 Nf6 7.b3 g6

Diagram 182

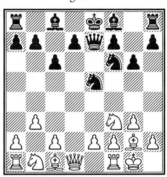

White to move

8.Qd4

White obviously felt that Black, with his King sitting in the center, needed to be punished. Though this isn't by any means the only move, I would never criticize a student for trying to impose his will on the opponent! Of course, both 8.c4 and 8.Bb2 were good alternatives.

Here's a quick look at 8.Bb2 and the kind of slow but effective positional play that might result: 8...Nxf3+ (8...d6 9.Nxe5 dxe5 10.Nd2 with the idea of Nc4 is good for White) 9.exf3! d5 10.Re1 Be6 11.Nc3 Bg7 12.Ne2! (The Knight prepares to maneuver to e6 when black's pawn structure will be permanently inferior to white's) 12...0-0 13.Nd4 Rae8 14.Bh3 Qd6 15.Nxe6 fxe6 16.Be5 and white's control over the e5-square and pressure against e6 guarantee a nice plus.

You don't have to go berserk trying to knock a guy out! Yes, if the opportunity arises, take it, but in most cases calmly pushing your positional/tactical agenda in a logical fashion will get the job done. "Macho chess" should also be logical, imbalance-oriented chess!

8...d6

8...Nxf3+!? was a good alternative.

9.Rd1

9.Nxe5!? was also possible, but 9.Rd1 continues white's efforts to make his opponent bend to his will. Now d6 is under pressure and 9...Bg7 is impossible.

9...Bg7!?

Maybe it's not impossible after all! Black refuses to obey and offers up the d-pawn in an act of commendable defiance. Instead, 9...Nxf3+!? was interesting: 10.Bxf3 Bg7 11.c3 0-0 12.Qxd6 Qxd6 13.Rxd6 Bf5 14.Be3 Rfe8 with compensation for the sacrificed pawn.

10.Nxe5

10.Qxd6?? Qxd6 11.Rxd6 Ne4 would have led to some horrible blow along the a1-h8 diagonal. However, after 10.Nxe5 it's *clear* that Black has two possible moves: 10...dxe5 and 10...Qxe5—White would retain some advantage in both cases.

Diagram 183

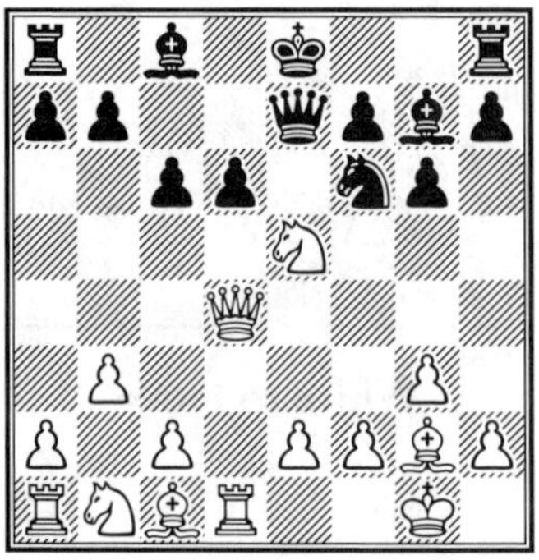

Black to move

10...Nd7!??

I said Black had "two possible moves" and he tossed out a third! The move is a blunder, but I have to admire this guy's spirit! He refuses to be bullied, even if it means committing ritualistic seppuku. "I can't" or "I have to" doesn't exist in Mr. Abraham's vocabulary!

At this point White had to make a big decision: back off and settle for a small plus, or put his brain into hyper-drive and insist on finding something crushing. In the actual game, Mr. Hubbard couldn't deal with the heat down the a1-h8 diagonal—he blinked, unconsciously muttered, "I can't refute your move" and then played 11.c3. There followed 11...Bxe5 (11...dxe5 12.Qe3 0-0 13.Ba3 forces Black to give up the d5-square by 13...c5 when 14.c4 followed by Nc3 is very strong for White) 12.Qd2 Nb6? (The beginning of the end. Best was 12…Nc5, but 12…d5 is inferior: 13.Ba3 Bd6 14.Bxd6 Qxd6 15.c4 or 13…Nc5 14.Bxd5!) 13.Ba3 c5? 14.f4 Bf6 15.Qxd6 Qxe2 16.Bxc5 Bg4 17.Qxf6?! (Far stronger was 17.Bc6+!! bxc6 18.Qxc6+ Bd7 19.Qxf6 Qxd1+ 20.Kf2 Qc2+ 21.Nd2 Qxd2+ 22.Kg1 and it's all over.) 17…Qxd1+ 18.Bf1 Rg8 (18…Kd7 also lost to 19.c4 Rhe8 20.Nc3 Qxa1 21.Qd6+ Kc8 22.Bxb6 axb6 23.Nb5) 19.Qe7 mate.

Though "death by diagonal" seems to be staring you in the face (with all sorts of "I can't and "I must" thoughts zipping through your neurons), White can punish his opponent's hubristic 10…Nd7 only by staring down the barrel of the diagonal gun: **11.Nxc6! Bxd4 12.Nxe7 Bxa1** and, after a few forced moves, we come to a split:

Diagram 184

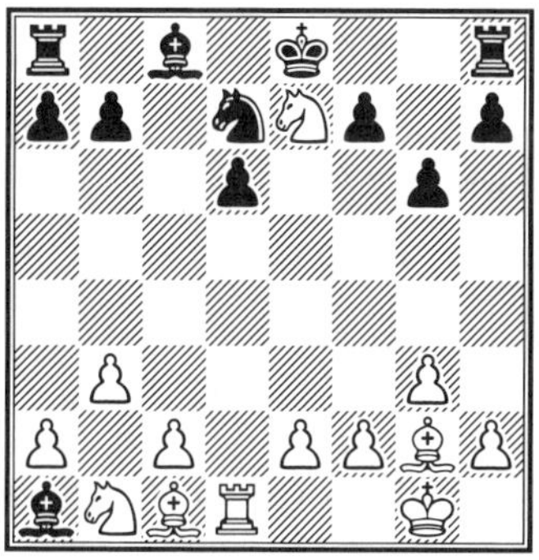

White to move

➤ **13.Nd5 0–0 14.c3 Nb6 15.Nc7 Rb8 16.Bh6 Rd8 17.Bg5** and Black is in serious trouble.

➤ **13.Nxc8! Rxc8 14.Na3!** b6 (14…0–0 15.Bxb7 Rc7 16.Bg2 gives White a winning position—he has two pawns for the Exchange, two powerful Bishops, and pressure against d6) **15.c4 0-0 16.Nb5** and Black is in bad shape.

Finding the refutation to black's outrageous 10…Nd7 called for a certain attitude, the determination of a wronged man, and more than a little courage. If you begin with "I can't" or any kind of fear, then the mental/emotional battle is over before it begins.

Here's a simpler (and amusing!) example of a blitz game where White gives his opponent a tiny push, and Black responds by running him over.

A-meise - Gerard Sorme, ICC 3-0, 2008

1.e4 c5 2.Nf3 Nc6 3.Bb5 e6 4.Bxc6 bxc6 5.0–0 d5 6.d3 Ne7 7.Nc3 Ng6 8.Qe2 Be7 9.Rb1 0–0 10.b3 Ba6 11.Na4 c4!? 12.dxc4 dxc4 13.Rd1?

Diagram 185

Black to move

White should have played 13.Nb2 Qc7 14.Nxc4 Rfd8 15.Bb2 e5 16.Bc3 f6 17.Rfd1 Nf4 and Black's active pieces and two Bishops give him some compensation for the sacrificed pawn.

However, White felt that he might as well attack black's Queen with his Rook and get a "free" move in.

13...cxb3!

Why move the Queen when Black can make his own threats instead?

14.c4?

One can imagine White thinking, "Okay, *now* move your Queen!"

14...Bxc4!

Black's verbal reply would go something like, "Me, move my Queen and do what you want me to do? No way!" With 14...Bxc4, Black still ignores his opponent while feasting on white bits. This is even stronger than 14...bxa2, which was played in the actual game (Black won in 19 moves).

15.Qe1

White: "Okay, now you simply *must* move that Queen!"
Better (but still bad) was 15.Rxd8 Bxe2 16.Rxa8 Rxa8 17.axb3 (17.Rxb3 Bd1) 17...Bd3 18.Ra1 Bxe4 and black's two extra pawns and two Bishops should make the win easy.

15...bxa2!

Black: "Why move my Queen when there are pawns to eat and egos to shred?"

16.Ra1 Qb8 and, with this move, we once again enter the reality where Queens have to move when they are attacked. Sadly for White, it's not a very happy reality at all—he's three pawns down and completely lost.

As is always the case, these ideas affect players of every level. Our next game shows two legends having at it, with the ever-aggressive Marshall asking Capablanca how he intends to defend d3 (a "you have to" moment).

J. Capablanca - F. Marshall, Moscow 1925

1.Nf3 Nf6 2.c4 e6 3.g3 d5 4.b3 c5 5.Bg2 Nc6 6.0–0 Be7 7.d3 0–0 8.Bb2 d4 9.e4 dxe3 e.p. 10.fxe3 Ng4 11.Qe2 Bf6 12.Nc3 Qa5 13.Rac1 Rd8 14.h3 Nge5

Diagram 186

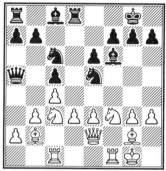

White to move

Will Capablanca obey Marshall and defend d3? Of course not! He didn't become an unbeatable chess machine by hysterically catering to his opponent's whims.

15.Ne4!

Naturally, Capablanca doesn't buy into his opponent's dictates. Instead he ignores the hanging d-pawn and creates his own, far more bloodthirsty, threats. Suddenly Black is facing a fearsome attack against his King!

Also crushing was 15.Nxe5 Bxe5 16.Bxc6 bxc6 17.Rxf7 Kxf7 18.Qh5+ Kg8 19.Qxe5 Rd7 20.Rf1 Qd8 21.Ne4 with an overwhelming position.

15...Qxa2

So what happened if Black chose to make good on his threat and chop on d3? Let's see: 15...Nxd3 (Worse is 15...Nxf3+ 16.Qxf3 Bxb2 17.Qxf7+ Kh8 18.Qf8+ mates) 16.Nxf6+ (Even 16.Bxf6 is strong: 16...Nxc1 17.Rxc1 gxf6 18.Nxf6+ Kf8 19.Qb2 Qc7 20.Nxh7+ Kg8 21.Nf6+ Kf8 22.Ne4 and White is winning) 16...gxf6 17.Bxf6 Nxc1 18.Rxc1 Qc7 19.Ng5! (ignoring the threat against g3!) 19...Qxg3 20.Kh1 and Black won't survive.

16.Nxf6+ gxf6 17.Nxe5 Nxe5

Another depressing line (from black's point of view) is 17...fxe5 18.Qh5 Qxb2 19.Qxf7+ Kh8 20.Be4.

18.Be4!

Diagram 187

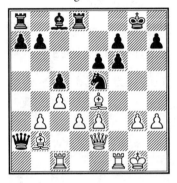

Defending d3 and attacking at the same time. 18.Rxf6 and 18.Ra1 were also very strong.

18...Bd7

18...f5 doesn't offer any hope either: 19.Ra1 Qxb3 20.Bxe5 fxe4 21.Qg4+ Kf8 22.Qg7+ Ke8 23.Qxf7 mate.

19.Ra1 Qxb3 20.Rfb1

Right after the game ended, Capablanca showed that 20.Bxe5 fxe5 21.Qg4+ Kf8 22.Rxf7+ Kxf7 23.Qg5 Rf8 24.Bxh7 Bc6 25.Bg6+ Kg7 26.Bf5+ Kf7 27.Qg6+ Ke7 28.Qxe6+ Kd8 29.Qd6+ Ke8 30.Bg6+ Rf7 31.Rf1 also led to an easy win. However, he pointed out that there was no reason to sacrifice and risk a miscalculation when he can play a crystal clear (and safe) move like 20.Rfb1 and win with no muss and no fuss.

20...Qb4 21.Bxe5 fxe5 22.Rxb4 cxb4 23.Bxb7 Rab8 24.Rxa7 b3 25.Qb2 Ba4 26.Qxe5 Bc6 27.Qg5+ Kf8 28.Bxc6 b2 29.Qe7+, 1-0.

The ability to laugh at your opponent's threats while also seeking the very best for your own position is a huge one. In fact, let's up the voltage a bit and change "seeking" to "insisting"! Most players, when faced with a tough decision, spend a couple minutes looking for the perfect move and then, having failed to find it, play something else that doesn't get the job done. That is *not* insisting!

> **PHILOSOPHY**
>
> If your opponent sends a subliminal "you have to" command, challenge it and let him know that the only agenda that's going to be pushed is yours.

Of course, in many positions several different moves will do, but there usually comes a time when one particular move is needed to win or hold life and limb together. In that case, you *must* find it!

The following example shows just such a case.

Diagram 188

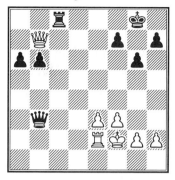

T. Nyback - E. Agrest, Stockholm 2001
Black to move

White's Queen is attacking both the c8-Rook and the a6-pawn. Since losing the Rook would be suicide, losing the a6-pawn appears to be unavoidable. Many players would accept this and most likely draw the game, but the correct mental stance would be to *demand* a solution from yourself—"I *must* defend both units or create play elsewhere that will sidetrack him! I must!"

Once you realize that this is *the* major decision of the game (i.e., you lose back your extra pawn or you retain it), you should be motivated to put every last ounce of energy into finding the solution to your problem. And, if it turns out that there wasn't a solution to be found, or that the answer was beyond your level, don't feel bad—as long as you recognized the moment's importance and tried as hard as you could to solve it, there is no reason not to feel happy with yourself.

In this particular position, Black found the right way to proceed.

1...Qc4!

A nice move that defends a6, defends c8, and also creates a nasty little threat that White completely missed.

2.Qxb6??

White snaps while the snapping is good, but this obvious capture loses immediately. White needed to settle down and process all the things that black's move does. Once he understood that ...Qh4+ was a devastating threat, he would be in the same "must find" situation that Black was a moment before. Then it would be up to White to hunker down and find the best way to put up resistance.

White's assessment of the position's needs is fairly straightforward: ...Qh4+ is a deathblow, and a quiet defensive move like 2.g3 allows Black to consolidate with 2...Rc6 (even better is 2...Qe6 when 3.Qxa6 fails to 3...Qh3) 3.Qb8+ Kg7 4.Qe5+ Rf6. So White needs to avoid the big threat and try and create some counterplay at the same time (since black's two connected passed queenside pawns will kill him if he fails to do so).

If White wants counterplay, he needs to get his Rook into the action. Thus 2.Rd2 (which also gives white's King access to e2 in case of a check on h4) makes a lot of sense. Now 2...Rc6 doesn't have the desired effect: 3.Qb8+ Kg7 4.Qe5+ Rf6 5.Rd6 Qc2+ 6.Kg3 Qf5 7.Qd4 and White is doing very well. So, after 2.Rd2 Qh4+ is still the best move: 3.Ke2 Re8 4.Qxb6 Qxh2 5.Kf2 Qh4+ 6.Ke2 and though Black is obviously better, White is still hanging on and forcing his opponent to work hard for the win.

2...Qh4+, 0-1. Clearly, a "must find the best move" mentality in critical positions is useful both in attack and defense.

At the highest levels of the game, both sides consistently push their own agendas with an unerring singleness of purpose. And, more often than not, when one side "blinks" and accepts that the opponent's ideas are better than his, the blinker quickly finds his position sliding into oblivion.

V. Kramnik - M. Carlsen, Dortmund 2007

1.Nf3 Nf6 2.c4 e6 3.g3 d5 4.d4 Be7 5.Bg2 0–0 6.0–0 dxc4 7.Qc2 a6 8.Qxc4 b5 9.Qc2 Bb7 10.Bd2 Nc6 11.e3 Nb4 12.Bxb4 Bxb4 13.a3 Be7 14.Nbd2 Rc8 15.b4 a5 16.Ne5 Nd5

Diagram 189

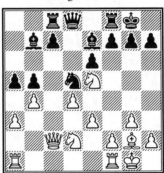

White to move

Black has weaknesses on a5, c5, c6, and c7. However, the pawn on a5 is trying to make a fight of it by threatening b4. Since 17.bxa5? c5 cures Black of his ills, perhaps he's okay after all?

17.Nb3!

Very nice! By depriving Black of his dreamed of ...c7-c5 advance (which would eradicate his weaknesses and free his pieces), White maintains a firm grip on the queenside. White refused to bow to his opponent's will and instead pressed ahead with his own agenda. However, wouldn't most players be transfixed by the loss of the b4-pawn? The only way someone can get beyond the "I can't let him win a pawn" mentality is if they train themselves to see imbalances (like space and control over advanced squares) as being just as important (depending on the position, of course!) as material.

17...axb4 18.Na5 Ba8 19.Nac6

Giving up the b-pawn (whose purpose was to prevent ...c7-c5) has given White the time to get his rather unimposing d2-Knight to the hole on c6. This not only strangles Black and forever stops ...c7-c5 (the work of the noble b4-pawn continues even in death!), but the a-file will soon open, allowing white's Rook to enter hostile territory.

19...Bxc6 20.Nxc6 Qd7 21.Bxd5!

Getting rid of black's one active piece, creating a great Knight vs. inactive Bishop scenario, and further reducing the flexibility of black's pawn structure.

21...exd5

Of course 21...Qxd5?? wasn't possible due to 22.Nxe7+ followed by 23.Nxd5.

22.axb4

Diagram 190

The b4-pawn has reincarnated! Looking at this new situation, we can see that White has retained material equality, kept a firm grasp on c5 and c6, and is ready to penetrate along the a-file. Note the weakness of the b5-pawn, which quickly becomes white's next target.

22...Rfe8

No better is 22...Ra8 23.Ra5 Rxa5 24.bxa5 with a powerful passed pawn.

23.Ra5 Bf8 24.Ne5 Qe6 25.Rxb5 Rb8 26.Rxb8 Rxb8 27.Qxc7 Bd6

27...Rxb4 28.Ra1 leaves Black with serious back rank woes.

28.Qa5 Bxb4

Black could have also resigned after 28...Bxe5 29.dxe5 Qxe5 30.Rd1 Qe4 31.Rxd5 Qb1+ 32.Kg2 Qe4+ 33.Kh3 Qe6+ 34.g4.

29. Rb1 Qd6 30.Qa4, 1-0. There was no reason to play out 30…Bd2 31.Rxb8+ Qxb8 32.Qa2 Bb4 33.Qxd5 with two extra pawns.

Make no mistake about it—this kind of strength of mind isn't just for the elite! You can begin to develop it at any level by training yourself to highlight your position's favorable imbalances while refusing to cave in to your opponent's attempts to turn your head to his way of looking at things. This training can be done by studying grandmaster games and getting a feel for the way the chess gods always stress the positive aspects of their game, and/or you can (and should!) practice this in your own games (tournament or blitz!), making sure that every game you play is a live lesson in positive cues like "Rubbish!" "I must find the best move!" "I will make full use of the positive imbalances in my position!" "It's my party and I'll do what I want to!" and other nuggets of that nature. Yes, it *will* go horribly wrong from time to time, but that's how you learn. When you get nuked (which is inevitable—it happens to everybody), get up, wipe away the radioactive dust, and try again and again and again.

Gerard Sorme (2496) - Haroldo (2397), ICC 3-0.

1.d4 Nf6 2.c4 c5 3.d5 b5 4.cxb5 a6 5.b6 e6 6.Nc3 exd5 7.Nxd5 Nxd5 8.Qxd5 Nc6 9.e4 Be7 10.Bc4 0–0 11.Nf3 Rb8 12.0–0 Rxb6 13.Qh5 d6 14.Ng5 Bxg5 15.Bxg5 Qe8

Diagram 191

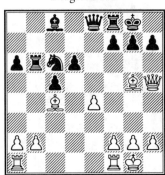

White to move

Even blitz can be a good training ground for mental toughness and pushing your own agenda. In fact, in a quick game a player has to push his agenda on automatic pilot—it has to become as natural as breathing, while reacting eventually becomes something you only do with a very heavy heart.

In diagram 191, Black (who has a good game) threatens both …Qxe4 and …Rxb2. How should White react?

16.Rad1!

The kind of move that's perfect for blitz—good or bad, White is striving to redefine the position on his own terms. Note what is going on: Black was trying to tell White that the loose pawns on b2 and e4 were the factors that really mattered in the position. He wanted White to agree and begin to defend. Instead, White pointed to d6 and insisted that this was more important than b2 and e4. Now it was up to Black to get a grip on the position and find a way to challenge White again.

16...Qxe4??

Black immediately cracks by failing to understand the full import of 16.Rad1. Instead, he could have tested White a bit with 16...Ne5 (16...Be6 17.Bxe6 Qxe6 18.b3 Nd4 19.Rfe1 is about equal) 17.Qe2 Nxc4 18.Qxc4 Be6 when Black has slightly the better of it, but the Bishops of opposite colors and the weakness of d6 prevents him from getting more than that. For example 19.Qc3 Bxa2 20.Rd2 Qe6 (and not 20...Qxe4?? 21.Qa5!) 21.Bf4 (both sides logically build up against the other's weak points) 21...Rfb8 22.Rfd1 and White is fine.

17.Bd3 Bg4

17...g6 18.Bxe4 gxh5 19.Rxd6 Bb7 20.Bf6 is also hopeless for Black.

18.Qh4, 1-0. The fact is, when you keep pushing your stuff, you'll find that most players just won't be able to keep up with you!

Key Positions

We've all seen notes to a game where the annotator says, "This is the key position." But, what exactly *is* a key position? A key position is, in my view, a very personal thing—while one player might see a particular situation as a key position that demands a huge effort to solve, another will see the same position as easy and thus not important at all. A position is only "key" if you sense that the correct move or plan will have a major impact on the game, but the right move or plan isn't clear to you.

Of course, this takes us back to mental toughness and the mindset of insisting on solving an over-the-board problem that you deem important. Semantics isn't important during a heated battle, though understanding the concept of a "key position" can be useful when it's brought up in various books or by other players who are trying to define a position in some way.

Typical examples of situations that could easily be labeled "key" are:

➤ A sharp/tactical position that must be solved or you will be drowned.

➤ A position that you feel should be a win or at least advantageous, but proving that feeling seems far from easy. If your gut tells you there's something nice lurking in the shadows, take the time to find it.

➤ A quiet position that's in need of a plan or (at least) a series of logical moves that address the imbalances. If you don't know what that plan is, if you can't lecture about the imbalances, then *why are you moving?*

Let's look at examples of each of these scenarios.

FIRST—A sharp/tactical position that must be solved or you go under and never come back up:

Diagram 192

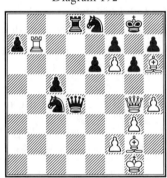

Smallville (H. Nakamura) - Erebuni, ICC 2009
White to move

This occurred in a 3-0 blitz game. Here we have an extremely sharp position. White has two Bishops vs. two Knights and possible tactics against black's King. On the other hand, Black is two pawns ahead, is threatening to exchange Queens (which would end white's attack), and is also threatening to rid himself of that attacking f6-pawn by ...Nxf6 or ...Qxf6.

White must find something special here or he'll lose. For many players, this would be considered a key position since it's do or die—they have to search long and hard for a miracle since anything less is fatal. For Nakamura it's not a key position because the solution was obvious to him (it held no secrets) and was played in an instant:

1.Qxe6!!

Black didn't expect this! Now the tables have completely turned and Erebuni finds himself in his own key position (very few players would be able to easily absorb the nuances of this position)—unfortunately, he has no time! And, with his final seconds ticking away, he must find a defense or lose.

In the actual game he failed to put up any resistance and quickly got mated after 1...Ncd6?? (now it's over) 2.Qe7 Nxb7 3.Qf8 mate. Also unpalatable is 1...Qxf6 2.Qxc4 Qa1+ 3.Kh2 Nd6 4.Qxc5 Nxb7 5.Bxb7 Qd4 6.Qc2 when the two mighty Bishops and the weak dark-squares around black's King leave the second player with an unenviable defensive task.

In a game with a long time control, Black would sit and look for that hidden way out. It might not be there, but then you would almost certainly lose. So, since you have no choice, tell yourself that there *is* a defense and spare no effort in unearthing it! As it turns out, Black has one way and one way only to sure salvation:

1...Ne5! 2.Qe7 Qd1+

An alternative is 2...Qd6, but if ultimately fails: 3.Bd5 Qxe7 4.fxe7 Rxd5 (4...Rd7 5.Rxd7 Nxd7 6.Bc6 Ndf6 7.Bf4 is grim for Black—the two Bishops and the monster passed e-pawn will overwhelm him) 5.Rb8 f6 6.Rxe8+ Kf7 7.Rd8 Nf3+ 8.Kg2 Ne1+ 9.Kf1 Re5 10.e8=Q+ Rxe8 11.Rxe8 Kxe8 12.Kxe1 and White wins.

3.Bf1

3.Kh2?? loses to 3...Ng4+.

3...Nf3+!

Clearly best. Also possible is 3...Qd6, when after 4.Rxa7 c4 5.Qxd6 Nxd6 6.Bf4 black's position is unpleasant but perhaps defensible.

4.Kg2 Nxh4+!

The only move since 4...Ne1+?? 5.Kh3 is game over.

5.gxh4 Qg4+ and Black draws by perpetual check.

SECOND—A position that you feel should be a win or at least advantageous, but proving that feeling seems far from easy. If your gut tells you there's something nice lurking in the shadows, take the time to find it:

Diagram 193

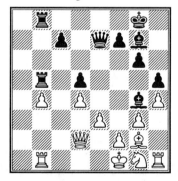

J. Sunye - J. Nunn, Amsterdam 1985

Black to move

White is a pawn up, but it's clear that b4 will fall. Once that happens White will have the better pawn structure but Black will enjoy a safer King, two Bishops, and (thanks to his lead in development) a bothersome initiative.

Because of these facts, Nunn felt that the position should offer him a serious advantage. However, feeling that and proving it are two very different things. For example, Grandmaster Nigel Davies gives the following line: 1...Bf5 2.Rb3 Rxb4 3.Rxb4 Rxb4 4.Bxd5 Rb1+ 5.Kg2 Be4+ 6.Bxe4 Qxe4+ 7.Kh2 "followed by Qe2 when White survives."

So we have a key position—Nunn thinks he's much better, but if he wants to prove it his next move is critical. I have no way of knowing how much time Black took for this decision, but you can be sure he didn't take it lightly and refused to move until he was completely happy with the move he deemed best.

Of course, all that effort doesn't guarantee success, and sometimes you'll find that your position wasn't as good as you had hoped, while other times you'll simply fail to find the right idea. Nevertheless, building this kind of "I must find it!" habit will serve you well in the vast majority of situations.

1...c5!?

Not your everyday move, so this might have been a bit of a shock to White. Black gets rid of his long-term pawn weakness on c7 and also opens the position up for the dark-squared Bishop. All very logical and creative, but this also leaves d5 weak and that plays a big part in white's defensive hopes later in the game. Perhaps it would have been better to retain as much tension as possible by 1...c6 (making sure d5 won't ever be a problem) 2.Bf3 Bf5 3.Rb2 Rxb4 4.Rxb4 Rxb4 5.Kg2 Rc4! 6.Ne2 Rc2 7.Qd1 Bh6 8.Rf1 (8.Re1?? Bxe3!) 8...Kh7 9.Kh1 Qa3 and White's under a lot of pressure.

Whether 1...c5 is best or whether 1...c6 was the move, Nunn's choice sparks the position and forces his opponent to solve difficult problems if he wishes to achieve his best possible result—a draw. Pressure on the opponent and a two-result game (win or draw) is always a good thing!

2.dxc5 Qxc5 3.Bf3

And not 3.bxc5?? Rxb1+ 4.Qe1 Rxe1+ 5.Kxe1 Bc3+ 6.Kf1 Rb1 mate.

3...Rxb4 4.Rxb4 Rxb4 5.Qxd5

There goes d5! Now White is a pawn up but his pieces are still hemmed in and his King is insecure.

5...Rb1+ 6.Kg2 Qc1 7.Kh2?

A mistake. White should have played 7.Qd3! when 7...Bf5 8.e4 Be6 9.Kh2 Rb3 still leaves Black with some pressure, but one would expect that White has sufficient defensive resources to hold the game.

7...Qf1 8.Bg2?

White is definitely losing after this. Like it or not, White had to give up a piece for two pawns by 8.Bxg4 hxg4 9.Qg2 Qa6 10.Nh3 gxh3 11.Kxh3 and then hang on for dear life.

8...Qxf2 9.Nh3

No better is 9.Qe4 Rc1 10.Qf4 Qb2 11.Nf3 Rc2 12.Ne1 Re2 13.Rg1 Be5 and white's stuff will begin to fall.

9...Rxh1+ 10.Kxh1 Bxh3

10...Qxg3 might be even more accurate, but who can argue with something that makes the opponent resign a couple moves later?

11.Bxh3 Qxg3, 0-1.

<u>THIRD</u>—A quiet position that's in need of a plan or (at least) a series of logical moves that address the imbalances. If you don't know what that plan is, if you can't lecture about the imbalances, then *why are you moving*?

Pam Ruggiero (1982) - Neil (2190), U.S. 2007

1.c4 Nf6 2.g3 e6 3.Bg2 d5 4.Nf3 c5 5.cxd5 Nxd5 6.Nc3 Be7 7.0–0 0–0 8.Nxd5 Qxd5 9.d4 Qd8 10.dxc5 Bxc5 11.Bf4 Nc6 12.Qc2 Be7 13.Rfd1 Qb6 14.a3 f6

Diagram 194

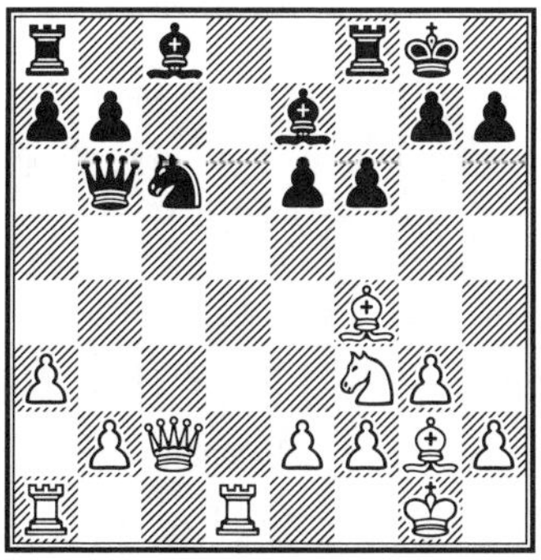

White to move

White has an absolutely wonderful position here—she's ahead in development, her pieces are active, and black's Queen is vulnerable to attack. There's no winning tactic, so White needs to take a long think and find a plan that takes maximum advantage of the positive imbalances that were just mentioned. For Pam, this is indeed a key position, but a titled player probably wouldn't consider it to be very challenging.

In the actual game, Pam played 15.e4—I tend to label this kind of error as a "lazy move" or "soft move." My choice depends on which term will have the greatest effect on the particular student—some demand a no-nonsense approach, while others need a gentle hand. In recent chess literature, some authors have referred to these lack-of-effort mistakes as "half moves"—a politically correct term (both "soft move" and "half move" are good choices if you're teaching children) that lets the reader know that the move doesn't do as much as it should.

But why is 15.e4 a lazy move? Pam knew she had a great position, but she didn't bother taking enough time to really get into its secrets. Instead she felt that gaining space couldn't be bad and then tossed 15.e4 onto the board (which, by the way, blocks the g2-Bishop's diagonal). Now, I'm not just picking on Pam here (who kindly allowed me to use quite a few of her very instructive games)! It's important to shout out that "lazy moves" are played by everyone at every level! Be that as it may, you can do a lot towards lowering the incidents of lazy moves in your own games by catching yourself during key positions or any time you don't know what to do, and demanding the best effort you can possibly give. Then, if you fail to find a good way to handle the position you can still be proud of yourself—you did your best and nobody can ask more of you than that.

Returning to the position in diagram 194, White wants to get as much value for her many positional plusses as possible. Since black's Queen is in the line of fire, White should milk that situation by 15.Be3! when the Queen doesn't have a happy place to move to. Three examples:

➤ 15...Qc7 16.Nd4! (making immediate use of the pin along the c-file) 16...Bd7 17.Qb3 Qb6 (17...Qc8 18.Rac1 a5 19.Bh3 and Black is lost) 18.Qxb6 axb6 19.Nf5 is very strong.

➤ 15...Qa6 16.Ne1! Ne5 (16...e5 17.Be4 f5 18.Bd3 b5 19.Qb3+ wins the b5-pawn) 17.Nd3 Nxd3 (17...Qc4 18.Qc1!—A very accurate move that makes sure the Rooks will protect each other. Also fine is the obvious 18.Rac1, though that gives Black 18...Qxc2 19.Rxc2 Rd8 pinning the Knight to the d1-Rook—18...Qxc1 19.Raxc1 Nxd3 20.Rxd3 a5 21.Bc5 Bxc5 22.Rxc5 and White's Rooks will penetrate into black's position) 18.Rxd3 e5 19.Rc1 Be6 20.Qc7 and White wins material.

➤ 15...Qa5 16.Nd4 Nxd4 17.Rxd4 e5 (17...Rd8 18.b4 Qe5 19.Rxd8+ Bxd8 20.Rd1 and white's pieces are raking black's queenside and both files) 18.Qc4+ Kh8 19.Rd5 (embarrassing black's Queen) 19...Be6 20.Rxa5 Bxc4 21.Bxb7 Rab8 22.Rxa7 Bxe2 23.a4 and the queenside pawns will win the game.

Notice how these lines kept Black under severe pressure, tormented his Queen, and also allowed White to make full use of the open c- and d-files.

The actual game continued: **15.e4? e5 16.Be3 Qc7 17.Rac1 Be6 18.h3?** Another lazy move, and now white's advantage is more or less gone (18.Bf1 followed by Bc4, trading the bad Bishop on g2 for the extremely active enemy Bishop on e6, was a much stronger idea). The further course of the battle had many ebbs and flows, with White once again obtaining a winning position only to blunder and actually lose: **18...Rfd8 19.Bf1 Rxd1 20.Rxd1 Rd8 21.Rd2 Rxd2 22.Nxd2 Qc8 23.Kh2 g6 24.Bc4 Kg7 25.Bxe6 Qxe6 26.Qc4 Qxc4 27.Nxc4 b5 28.Nd2 Kf7 29.Kg2 a5 30.Kf1 Ke6 31.Ke2 Bd6 32.Kd3 h5 33.Bb6 f5 34.Nf3 Kf6 35.Ne1 f4 36.Nf3 g5 37.g4 hxg4 38.hxg4 Be7 39.Ng1 Ke6 40.Ne2 b4 41.a4 Kd6 42.Kc4 Bd8 43.Bxd8 Nxd8 44.Nc1 Nc6 45.Nb3 f3 46.Kb5?** (Both 46.Kd3 followed by Ke3 and Kxf3, or 46.Nc5 would have been extremely good for white) **46...Nd4+ 47.Nxd4 exd4 48.Kc4 Ke5 49.Kd3 b3 50.Kc4 Kxe4 51.Kxb3 Kd3 52.Ka3 Kc2**, 0-1. "Lazy Moves" and "Soft Moves" will be explored in greater detail in the next chapter, Various States of Chess Consciousness.

Summary

- The ability to laugh at your opponent's threats while also seeking the very best for your own position is a huge one.

- You will gain huge dividends by creating an "I'll do what I want no matter what you say" attitude in chess.

- If your opponent sends you a subliminal "you have to" command, challenge it and let him know that the only agenda that's going to be pushed is yours.

- Instead of the word *initiative*, which few really understand, I use terms such as "macho chess", "pushing one's own agenda", "rubbish", "I will find a way", I must", and "I'll do what I want no matter what you say" to illustrate and teach.

- I consider the initiative to be a physical manifestation of a psychological battle; both sides champion their view of things in the hope that the opponent will have to eventually forgo his own plans and react to yours.

- You can train yourself to fully understand and use these concepts by studying grandmaster games and getting a feel for the way the chess gods always stress the positive aspects of their game, and/or you can (and should!) practice this in your own games (tournament or blitz!), making sure that every game you play is a live lesson in positive cues like "Rubbish!" "I must find the best move!" "I will make full use of the positive imbalances in my position!" "I'll do what I want to!" and other nuggets of that nature. Yes, it *will* go horribly wrong from time to time, but that's how you learn. When you get nuked (which is inevitable—it happens to everybody), get up, wipe away the radioactive dust, and try again and again and again.

- A key position is, in my view, a very personal thing—while one player might see a particular situation as a key position that demands a huge effort to solve, another will see the same position as easy and thus not important at all. A position is only "key" if you sense that the correct move or plan will have a major impact on the game, but the right move or plan isn't clear to you.

- The terms, "lazy move", "soft move", and "half move" all describe a move that doesn't do as much as it should.

Macho Chess — Tests

Since my ideas about chess psychology are almost certainly new to you, the chance to test your ability to excise "I can't" and "I have to" from your inner chess dialogue, and to push your own agenda whenever reasonably possible, should prove both interesting and useful.

If you have trouble solving the tests, don't worry—that means we've uncovered something you don't understand, and this allows you to fix things by rereading the previous material or by picking up the bits of knowledge you're missing in the answers that start on page 509.

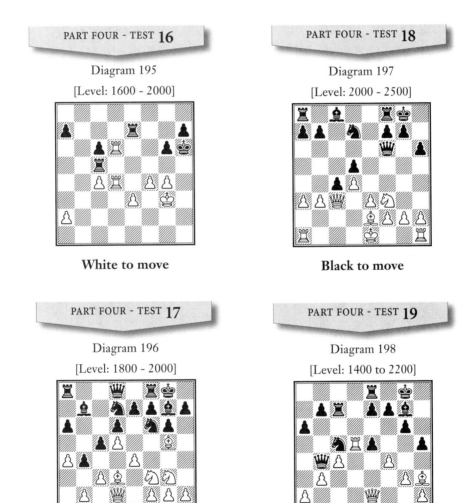

PART FOUR - TEST 16

Diagram 195

[Level: 1600 - 2000]

White to move

PART FOUR - TEST 17

Diagram 196

[Level: 1800 - 2000]

Black to move

PART FOUR - TEST 18

Diagram 197

[Level: 2000 - 2500]

Black to move

PART FOUR - TEST 19

Diagram 198

[Level: 1400 to 2200]

White to move

PART FOUR - TEST 20

Diagram 199

[Level: 1400 - 1800]

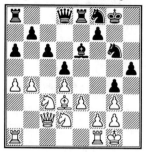

White to move

White's making use of the *minority attack* (queenside play via a b4-b5 advance), but Black put a spanner in the works by starting a scary looking kingside attack (via the threat of ...h5-h4). How can White deal with that threat?

PART FOUR - TEST 22

Diagram 201

[Level: 1400 - 1800]

White to move

How should he defend d4?

PART FOUR - TEST 21

Diagram 200

[Level: 1800 - 2200]

White to move

Black just played ...g6-g5; did that make sense or did he go berserk? How should White respond?

Various States of Chess Consciousness

Once we learn how to move the pieces, the next stage of our chess development is to get stomped by having our chessmen taken one after the other, falling for mates, and various other horrific demises that teach us that the chessboard is a very unforgiving environment. Naturally, the pain of hanging your Queen or falling for tricks creates the desire to stop the bloodbath and protect your army! And with that initial scarring comes a host of psychological chess disorders which ultimately need to be identified and addressed.

Here's a basic example of two players in the 1100 to 1200 rating range and the travails they go through. It was my student's (Teradeath) second lesson. In our first I pointed out that he reacts far too much to his opponent's innuendos. In this game he tried very hard to recognize and fix that failing.

NN - Teradeath (1100), Yahoo Online 2009

1.b3 e5 2.Bb2 Nc6 3.g3 d5 4.Bg2 Nf6 5.d3 Bc5 6.h3?!

Diagram 202

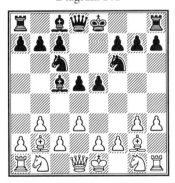

White is the first to crack! He noticed the possibility of …Ng4 and became so worried about a horse stampede around his King that he wasted a tempo to prevent it. Instead he should have gone about his business with 6.Nf3 when 6…Ng4 7.0-0 takes care of the problem while doing something positive that he wanted to do anyway (castling).

I should add that White was probably worried about 6.Nf3 Ng4 7.0-0 Nxf2 8.Rxf2 Bxf2+ 9.Kxf2, but even though point-count will tell us that material is even, the fact is that White is the one who would be happy with that exchange. In the middlegame, two minor pieces usually prove stronger than a Rook and pawn since the Rook won't be doing much until a file opens, and since the extra pawn most likely won't make a huge impact on the early stages of the game. Keep in mind that a Rook is nice, but two minor pieces is a gang!

6...Bb6

Not a terrible move, but quite unnecessary. Is this really the best Black has? Doesn't he have more important things to do with his move? What move would you play if White had no threat (which he doesn't)? The answer is simple: 6...0-0!

Always ask, "What move would I like to play?" Then do your best to make it work.

7.Nf3

Now e5 is threatened and that one tiny threat grabs black's attention and makes him do something he probably didn't want to do.

7...d4?

Of course, if Black had castled then he could defend e5 with the comfortable 7...Re8. However, since that's not possible, the simplest and most positive way to guard the pawn was 7...Qe7 (or 7...Qd6), not fearing 8.Ba3 Bc5.

What's wrong with 7...d4? The first thing is psychological: Black felt compelled to do something he didn't particularly wish to do. Other than that, the move opens the h1-a8 diagonal for white's light-squared Bishop, gives white's Knights access to the c4-square, and blocks black's dark-squared Bishop.

> **REMEMBER**
>
> Before playing a move, always ask, "What wonderful thing does this do for my position?" If you can't answer that question, or if the answer has more negatives than positives, one is left wondering how you can justify playing it.

8.c3

Not horrible, but White isn't aware of the perks this move and the subsequent capture on d4 will give his opponent. This will be discussed over the next few moves.

8...0-0 9.cxd4 Nxd4

Quite reasonable, though Black wasn't aware that 9...exd4 opened the e-file for his Rook (this would allow him to generate pressure against e2 after ...Re8). Amateurs often have serious trouble getting their Rooks into the game during its early stages. However, once they realize that clearing a pawn off a file gives their Rook(s) a highway to travel on, life becomes much easier. This subject is deeply explored in Part Three, Rooks.

10.Nxd4

Wisely avoiding 10.Nxe5? Re8, when White has opened lines to his own King.

10...Bxd4

Still not grasping the significance of a pawn capture on d4. I would prefer 10...exd4 11.Nd2 c6 12.0–0 Re8 when e2 is a permanent target. It's important to get all your pieces into play, and to create long term targets whenever possible!

11.Qc2 c5?

Before looking at the game together, my student gave me a copy of it with full annotations. I was proud of him when I saw the note to his 11th move: "Is this where I cracked? At the time I was thinking, 'I have to!' as in 'I have to protect my c-pawn in case I need to move my Queen.'"

Looking at it now, I see that 11...c5 blocks my Bishop in case I want to get it out of the way, and I can't move my b-pawn because it's pinned. I should have considered just 11...c6, which protects my c-pawn from white's Queen and my b-pawn from white's g2-Bishop."

We had discussed "I can't" in our first lesson, so his noticing it so quickly was a very positive thing (the first step to slowly but surely ironing the problem out is to recognize it). And, of course, he's right on about 11...c6, though White would be okay with 12.Nc3.

12.0–0 Re8 13.Nd2

13.Nc3 was better, when black's dark-squared Bishop is sort of alone on d4.

13...Be6 14.e3?

White didn't notice that this gave up the d-pawn.

14...Bxb2 15.Qxb2 Qxd3 16.Rad1

Diagram 203

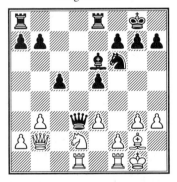

A big moment; how will Black react to the facedown by the d1-Rook?

16...Qg6

Sending the Queen off to the side. This isn't terrible, but it wasn't played for the right reason (his reason was, "Run for your life!"). I would have been much happier if he looked that Rook in the eye and played 16...Rad8!, increasing the tension and asking who is facing down whom. After 16...Rad8 17.Ne4 (Not best, but it will illustrate why Black didn't have to fear the enemy Rook. 17.Bxb7 Bxh3 18.Ne4 was better, though Black has a plus after 18...Qxd1) 17...Qxd1 (It takes a long time for players to get used to giving up their Queen for material equivalents, though the fact is that two Rooks are usually better than a Queen) 18.Nxf6+ gxf6 19.Rxd1 Rxd1+ 20.Kh2 Red8 and white's doomed because of the threat of a Rook coming to d2.

Other good choices were 16...Qa6 and 16...Qb5, holding onto his material plus, but the psychologically powerful 16...Rad8 is a move that would put a huge grin on the face of any teacher.

17.Bxb7 Rad8

Quite good, but a "soft and/or quick move" in that Black hadn't really taken stock of what was going on in the position (as demonstrated by his 18th). 17...Rab8 18.Bg2 c4 getting rid of the weak c-pawn and creating a weakness on b3 would be reasonable—the idea of ridding yourself of weaknesses while simultaneously giving weak points to your opponent is very important but somewhat advanced.

18.Bg2 Rb8?

Black notices the idea of ...c5-c4 and rushes to make use of it. Naturally, he needed to see it a move before by asking (on move 17), "The Rook is going to move, but where would it perform a useful function? I don't want to just move it somewhere, I want to move it where it works with the other pieces and serves a particular purpose."

As it turns out, 16...Qg6 combined with 17...Rad8 was okay if seen in the context of building kingside pressure by 18...Qh5! Then we can see that white's 6.h3 weakened his kingside structure and Black is logically trying to take advantage of it. Here are some illustrative lines that might occur after 18...Qh5. White can try 19.Kh2 or 19.g4:

> 19.Kh2 e4 (19...Ng4+ 20.Kg1 Nf6 21.Kh2 Ng4+ is a draw) 20.Rc1 Ng4+ (moves such as 20...Bg4!?, 20...Rd5!?, and 20...Rd3!? also deserve consideration) 21.Kg1 Ne5 22.Kh2?? (White needed to give up the Exchange by 22.Rxc5! Nf3+ 23.Bxf3 Qxc5 24.Nxe4 with compensation, though White would still have some problems to solve after 24...Qb4) 22...Rxd2! 23.Qxd2 Nf3+ 24.Kh1 (24.Bxf3 Qxh3+ 25.Kg1 exf3 mates) 24...Bxh3 mates.

➤ 19.g4 Qg6 (Mission accomplished! White's kingside is now weaker than ever.) 20.Nc4 Rxd1 21.Rxd1 Bxc4 22.bxc4 h5 23.gxh5 Qxh5 and the vulnerability of white's King will make it hard for him to generate serious winning chances: 24.Rd2 Qf5!? (24...e4!?) 25.Rd6?! (25.Qb5 is better, when 25...Rc8 26.Qb7 Qe6 27.Rb2 e4 28.Rb5 Kh7 seems okay) 25...Ne4 26.Rd1 Ng5 27.Qb5 Re6 shows how quickly storm clouds can appear over white's kingside.

All this analysis is very complicated and advanced, but it's worth checking out so you can get a feel how a ruptured kingside pawn structure can easily give the other side counterplay.

19.Nf3?

It's important to recognize pawn weaknesses and, once you do, to bring your pieces to bear on them. Thus 19.Qa3 (hitting a7 and c5) and 19.Rc1 (hitting c5 and stopping ...c5-c4) should be natural choices that are fully in line with the imbalances.

After 19.Nf3, Black blundered with 19...Bd5?? (allowing 20.Nh4, winning significant amounts of material). Instead, 19...e4 would have granted him the kind of kingside counterplay we saw in the note to black's 18th move.

I can hear many of you saying, "I'm much stronger than those guys! I don't make mistakes like that!" Really? You don't? I beg to differ—everyone under master suffers from the same aberrations as these two players do, though in an increasingly more subtle form as one rises up the rating ladder.

The game we just looked at shows how we're buffeted about the board by the winds of fear (*soft moves* also played a part). We've explored this fear of threats in the previous chapters, Mental Breakdown and Macho Chess, and though we'll continue to see examples of this disease here, it's time to take a serious look at three other psychological disorders:

➤ Lack of Patience

➤ Lazy/Soft Moves

➤ Pay Attention!

Lack of Patience

When you're doing well, it's important to not allow undeserved counterplay. If your advantage is dynamic, then rushing in and clubbing him over and over is often the right thing to do. But if the advantageous imbalances are static (space, superior minor piece, better pawn structure, etc.) then a little patience can go a long way towards making your opponent helpless, which in turn lets you reel in the point without unnecessary adventures.

At times, the decision is about your playing strength and/or comfort level—what can you handle, and what is too hot to handle?

P. Ruggiero - M. Leski, LERA 1990

1.c4 g6 2.Nc3 Bg7 3.g3 Nf6 4.Bg2 0–0 5.Nf3 d6 6.0–0 e5 7.d4 Nbd7 8.e3 c6 9.b3 Re8 10.Ba3 Qa5 11.Qc1 e4 12.Nd2 d5 13.Bd6 Bf8 14.Bxf8 Nxf8 15.f3 exf3 16.Nxf3 dxc4 17.bxc4 Qh5 18.Qd2 Bh3 19.Rae1 Rad8 20.e4 Bxg2 21.Kxg2 c5 22.d5 N8d7 23.Qf4 Qg4 24.e5 Qxf4 25.gxf4 Nh5

Diagram 204

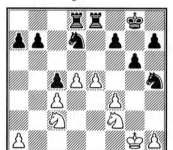

White has outplayed her powerful opponent (an international master!) and has an obvious advantage—the massive center and the extra space that it gives place Black in serious trouble (an advantage in space is fully explored in Part Seven). However, there's a "tiny" problem with the f4- and c4-pawns and with big centers in general: the player with the large center has to defend it—if he can make it indestructible, then the center rules. If the center proves unsustainable, then it will crumble and the opponent's strategy will win out. With this "guard the center" rule in mind, White should look for something that takes care of both vulnerable (c4 and f4) pawns.

Since 26.Ng1 fails to 26...Nb6 (26...f6 first might be even better), White is left with three reasonable moves:

26.Ne2 gums up the white army. Black escapes his difficulties with 26...f6 27.e6 Nb6 28.Rc1 Nxd5! 29.cxd5 Rxd5 30.Nc3 Nxf4+ 31.Kh1 Rd6 32.Ne4 Rdxe6 33.Nxc5 R6e7, =.

26.Nd2 defends both weak spots at the same time and appears to leave White with a clear advantage. Perhaps that's true, but it's not so easy to prove. Since the center is too strong to leave alone (Black either breaks it down or is broken himself), he has to try 26...g5 27.fxg5 Rxe5 and we reach a surprisingly complicated position. A quick glance at a couple lines will show us that any ultimate truth is very hard for a mere mortal to discover: 28.Nf3 (28.Rxe5 Nxe5 29.Rf5 Re8

30.d6 Ng7 31.Rf2 Rd8 33.Nce4 b6, =, or 30.Kh3 Kg7 31.Nb5 Nd3 when Black
is still fighting tooth and nail) 28...Rf5 29.Kh3 f6 (29...Rf4 30.Ne4) 30.Ne4
Re8 31.Nfd2 Rxf1 32.Rxf1 fxg5 33.Kg4 Ng7 34.Rb1 (34. Kxg5 b5 35.cxb5 Re5+
gives counterplay) 34...b6 35.Kxg5 Re5+ 36.Kf4 Rf5+ 37.Ke3 Rh5 and it's still
a bit of a mess, though White will never be in any danger.

In deciding which move to play, Pam didn't trust the contortionist 26.Ne2
and, since she missed the threat of ...Nb6 altogether, she didn't see any reason
to play 26.Nd2. Had she noticed that, I suspect 26.Nd2 would have been chosen.
It looks good, it looks safe, and it would have taken a very strong player to see
that Black actually has ways to rock the boat in that line.

As it turns out, she played a third possibility, **26.Ng5**, and this appears to be
the best move. Nevertheless, she didn't see *why* it was the best move and, as a
result, she would probably have done better with 26.Nd2.

26...Nb6

26...h6 27.Nge4 Nb6 and now 28.Nd2 keeps a safe lock on everything while
28.Nxc5 Nxc4 29.Nxb7 Rb8 30.Nc5 Rec8 31.N5e4 looks strong.

27.Nge4?

Shocked by the fact that she missed the obvious 26...Nb6, she loses her confidence and begins a spiral into oblivion. After the correct 27.f5! Nxc4 28.fxg6
fxg6 29.Nf7 Rb8 30.d6 Black would be toast.

27...Nxc4 28.Nxc5 Rc8

Diagram 205

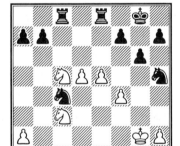

Don't panic!

White's still doing very well, but she didn't anticipate these complications and
soon drowns under them.

29.N5e4

29.N3e4 Red8 30.d6 offered White a safe plus, but White was still off-kilter
about the fact that black's pieces were somehow becoming quite active!

29...f5 30.d6

Rushing headfirst into even more complications. She should have put the brakes on the madness with the solid 30.Ng3 Nf6! (30...Nxg3 31.hxg3 Nd2 32.Rf2 is just good for White) 31.Kh1 (Played to avoid a Knight fork on f3 in the critical line. White must, of course, avoid 31.exf6? Ne3+) 31...Ng4 33.d6 Ngxe5 34.fxe5 Rxe5 35.Rxe5 Nxe5 36.Re1 Nc6 37.Nb5 and Black will be struggling for a long time.

30...Nb6 31.d7 Nxd7 32.Nd6 Rxc3 33.Nxe8 Nc5 34.Rc1

She could have put her fears to rest by 34.Nf6+ Nxf6 35.exf6 Rc2+ 36.Kh1 Kf7 37.Rc1 Rxc1 38.Rxc1 b6 39.Re1! when only White can harbor dreams of victory. Sadly, the world was spinning and clear thought was something to be experienced in a later game. I've been there many times and I'm sure you have too!

34...Nxf4+ 35.Rxf4??

Simply 35.Kh1 was quite safe.

35...Rxc1 36.Nf6+ Kf7, 0-1. A complete meltdown.

It turns out that 26.Ng5, though the best in the position, wasn't the right move for that particular player at that particular time. The less tactical 26.Nd2 would probably have served her better. I know that claiming someone would do better to avoid the best move sounds insane, but if you aren't able to tame the resulting positions then it's best to play something within your personal range. Another way of putting it is this: the best move isn't the best move if you don't know why it's best.

The moral here is: when possible, try to enter lines that you feel you can handle and that suit your personal comfort level, your style, or that particular situation. For example, if I could take a small but solid (and safe!) positional plus vs. grandmaster Shabalov (a man who lives for hyper-complexity) or enter a tactical minefield that might very well offer much more, I would go for the small but solid/safe option unless I was able to convince myself that the complications were definitely good for me, that I had enough time left on the clock to do the position justice, and/or that I could handle it properly without sinking under a maze of variations. On the other hand, if I felt that entering a tactical firestorm was the *only* correct way to handle the position, I would happily enter it—you have to do what the board tells you to do!

> **PHILOSOPHY**
>
> When possible, try to enter lines that you feel you can handle and that suit your personal comfort level, your style, or that particular situation.

On a higher level, patience (and the avoidance of enemy counterplay) is *the* major part of the technical repertoire. This kind of refusal to enter anything that's even remotely risky when possessing a technically winning position (as demonstrated in our next example) is known as *Cat and Mouse*.

St. Novikov - A. Korotylev, 60th Russian Chmp 2007

1.e4 c5 2.Nf3 d6 3.Bb5+ Nc6 4.0-0 Bd7 5.c3 Nf6 6.d4 cxd4 7.cxd4 a6 8.Ba4 b5 9.Bc2 Bg4 10.Be3 e6 11.h3 Bh5 12.Nc3 Be7 13.d5 exd5 14.Nxd5 0-0 15.Nf4 Bxf3 16.Qxf3 Re8 17.Bb3 Rc8 18.Rad1 Ne5 19.Qe2 Ned7 20.f3 Qc7 21.Qf2 Qb8 22.Rd2 Nc5 23.Bd5 Bf8 24.Bd4 Nxd5 25.Nxd5 Nd7 26.Qg3 Rc6 27.Ne3 Qd8 28.Rfd1 Re6 29.Kh1 h6 30.Nd5 Re8 31.a3 Rc8 32.Bc3 Qg5 33.Qf2 Nc5 (33...f5) 34.h4 Qg6 35.Nf4 Qh7 36.Qg3 Nd7 37.h5 Ne5

Diagram 206

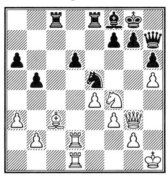

Black has a horrible position—his d-pawn is an obvious target, his Queen is locked away on h7, his pawn-like Bishop is serving a purely defensive function, his King is being eyed by white's Queen, Knight, and Bishop, and White enjoys a space advantage in the center and on the kingside. Worst of all, Black has nothing to attack and no counterplay of any sort—he just has to sit there and wait for the axe to fall.

In such situations, many experienced players begin a game of Cat and Mouse. They go out of their way to avoid any counterplay, and they refuse to activate any enemy piece. Instead they slowly improve their pawns and pieces until everything is optimally placed. And then (and *only* then!) they take aim at some juicy target(s) and enjoy a "snack" (winning a pawn in this fashion adds to the overall advantage and lets the enemy know that he's not only lost in the middlegame, but also in most endgames)—however, the snack won't be eaten if doing so would allow the opponent sudden activity.

This kind of total domination doesn't occur too often, and when it does some players prefer to seek ways to end things a bit faster. But the Cat and Mouse idea makes good sense since it allows the stronger side to keep his opponent completely under his thumb, to avoid any and all tricks, and to pretty much guarantee victory at some point down the road. Also keep in mind that the defending side will be thoroughly miserable throughout this process, and will sometimes just resign so he doesn't have to continue looking at the sickening sight that's in front of him.

38.Rd5

White prepares to improve the position of this Rook. To be quite honest, 38.Rxd6! was stronger, but why trade a Rook for that dead enemy Bishop, and why take any chances whatsoever when you're having such a good time torturing the opponent in slow, delicious fashion? After 38.Rxd6 Bxd6 39.Rxd6 Black would find himself facing some serious threats. Here's an example of what might occur:

➤ 39...f6 40.Rxf6 is awful.

➤ 39...Nc4 (saying, "You must move that Rook!") 40.Nd5 (laughing in black's face by creating the powerful counter-threat of Nf6+) 40...Kh8 (40...Kf8 41.Rg6! fxg6 42.hxg6 would be even more fun for White) 41.Nf6! and Black should resign.

➤ 39...Kh8 40.Bxe5 Rxe5 41.Ng6+ fxg6 (41...Qxg6 42.Qxe5!—even better than 42.hxg6 Rc1+ 43.Kh2 Rh5+, regaining the Queen—42...Qg5 43.Qxg5 hxg5 44.Rxa6 leads to a completely winning endgame for White.) 42.Qxe5 gxh5 43.Rxa6 is hopeless for Black.

➤ 39...Rxc3 40.bxc3 Kh8 41.Nd5 f6 42.Ne7 (There are many ways to win, but this sequence is by far the most attractive!) 42...a5 43.Re6! Ra8 44.Rxe5! fxe5 45.Ng6+ Kg8 46.Qxe5 and the comic position of black's Queen plus the unfortunate threats against black's King would convince most people to immediately give up!

38...Nc4

38...f5? 39.Bxe5 dxe5 40.Ng6 f4 41.Qg4 paints a horrific picture—black's Queen is entombed and white's Rooks will decisively enter the enemy position along the d-file!

39.R1d3 Rc6 40.Rf5 Ne5 41.Nd5 Kh8 42.Rd1

White could have safely won a pawn by 42.Bxe5 Rxe5 43.Rxe5 dxe5 44.Qxe5, but that would have freed black's position a bit and given unnecessary activity to the previously dead black Bishop. A computer, of course, goes crazy over 42.Bxe5, but a real Cat and Mouser would never allow that kind of enemy activity when he can pick off enemy pawns in ways that don't allow anything at all.

42...f6 43.Nb4 Rb6 44.Bd4 Rb7 45.Nxa6

A well-earned meal!

45...Qg8

Diagram 207

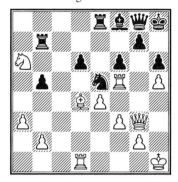

46.Nb4

The Knight is no longer doing anything on a6 and rushes back to the center where it can join the rest of its army. Part of Cat and Mouse is keeping every piece safe, centrally placed, and protected.

46...Qb3 47.Rc1 Rbb8 48.Qe1 Rbc8 49.Qd1

As mentioned earlier, the extra pawn allows White to enter an endgame with full confidence that he'll end up winning.

49...Rxc1 50.Qxc1 Qe6 51.Nd5

Ah, that feels better! Having feasted on the a6-pawn, the Knight has returned to d5 where it holds court over the entire board.

51...Rc8 52.Bc3 Rc5 53.Qd1 Qc8 54.Nf4 Kh7 55.Qb3 Nc4 56.Rd5 Qe8 57.Rxc5 dxc5 58.Qc2

Even stronger was 58.Ng6 Bd6 59.a4 Ne5 60.Qd5. However, white's chosen method is also more than adequate.

58...Kg8 59.Qd3 Bd6

Black should have tried 59...Nb6 60.Ng6 Qd7 but the endgame obviously didn't appeal to him. However, this would have been the wisest course since leaving the Queens on only highlights the black King's vulnerability.

60.Qd5+ Qf7 61.Qa8+ Qf8 62.Qd5+

Perhaps gaining time on the clock and perhaps following the old Cat and Mouse rule that it's better to do a maneuver in several moves instead of one since lengthening the game not only adds to the opponent's misery, but also weakens his attention (which cultivates errors).

62...Qf7 63.Ne6 Be7 64.g4

Black's tied up again, so White takes some time out to defend h5 and improve the position of his King.

64...Ne3 65.Qd7 Kh7 66.Kh2 Kg8 67.Kh3 b4

Black can't stand the humiliation anymore and lashes out. Unfortunately (as is so often the case), this only hastens his demise.

68.axb4 cxb4 69.Bd4 Nc2 70.Bf2

The Knight is suddenly cut off from the rest of its army!

70...b3 71.Qc8+ Kh7 72.Qc4 Kg8 73.Qxb3

Two pawns in the bank and black's still helpless—the end is in sight.

73...Nb4 74.Qc4 Bd6 75.Bg3 Be7

75...Bxg3?? allowed 76.Qc8+ Kh7 77.Nf8+.

76.b3

Not necessary (76.Qc8+ Kh7 77.Nf4 was quicker), but why not defend the Queen and let Black stew in his own juices a bit more?

76...Kh8 77.Qc8+ Kh7 78.Qd7

78.Nf4 with the idea of Ng6 was more to the point, but you can only play one winning move at a time!

78...Kg8 79.Bd6 Bxd6 80.Qxd6, 1-0. Black was probably relieved to end this nightmare.

Lazy/Soft Moves

When I was thirteen and deeply addicted to chess, I hung out with two other chess kids—both were considerably better than me. The oldest and strongest, Peter Wise, kindly looked over my games and gave me advice. One incident always stuck in my mind: I was White and had tossed out about 10 moves of some opening when I played h2-h3. Peter then posed one of the hardest questions anyone had ever asked me—"Why did you play that move?"

I was stumped! Thinking about it, I finally said, "It was my move and I had to do something."

Of course, this sounds incredibly basic, but over the years I've posed this exact question hundreds of times to students during lessons and chess fans that attended my lectures who ranged in rating from 1000 to 2300. And, I often got a similar reply to the one I gave so many decades ago: "I didn't know what to do." "It looked good so I played it." "I was low on time so I played this fast to gain time on the clock." "It threatened his Queen so it had to be good." I say these are similar because in each case the person responding didn't really know what was going on in the position and just did "something," hoping to figure out the truth later in the game.

The fact is, when you're playing a game you should generally be able to lecture on your position at any given time. You might not be right about all the details—in fact, you might be completely off base. But at least, in your mind, you would have a handle on the goings on and, as a result, be able to make moves that conform to that knowledge and certainty. Even a 1200 player can say, "Well, I have an advantage in space so I pushed this pawn in an effort to get more." The pawn push might be good or it might be bad, but at least it would conform to his version of the board's reality.

Naturally, my whole idea of imbalances is designed to give you something to grasp onto. Whether you fully grasp imbalances or have only a faint inkling, recognizing them will give you the guidance everyone needs to make an informed decision (or at least feel confident when playing a move that's completely bonkers—even misguided confidence counts for a lot!).

The point of this section, though, isn't about imbalances per se—it's about a player failing to make use of knowledge he already possesses when pondering a move, or a player being too lazy to even bother making the effort to find something worthwhile.

Once again, the cure for this "it was my move and I had to do something" nightmare starts with an awareness of the problem that the particular position is posing to you. And, when I teach, I go to the next step by telling my students, "Before you make any move, be aware that I'm going to ask you to describe every detail of this position after the game's over, and I'll want you to tell me how the move you played catered to those details." Keep in mind that it doesn't matter if the student gets things right or wrong. What does matter is the effort he makes—it's that effort that trains his mind and ultimately helps him acquire the good chess habits that will serve him for the rest of his life.

Let's take a look at three examples, moving up the rating ladder in each game.

Teradeath (1100) - Khilane08 (1100), Yahoo Online 2009

1.e4 e5 2.Nf3 Qf6

Diagram 208

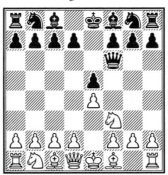

Teradeath wasn't expecting 2...Qf6. Here he needed to ask, "This seems strange. You're not supposed to move your Queen right away because it can be vulnerable to attacks by the other pieces, so how I can take advantage of 2...Qf6?"

That's all it took; he didn't need a deeper understanding of the position than that to come up with a promising move. In the game White gave up on trying to capitalize on his opponent's move and played passively with 3.d3, which frees the c1-Bishop but blocks the other Bishop on f1! Does White really have to punish his light-squared Bishop if he wants to spank ...Qf6? Anyway, Black was so freaked out by the "threat" of Bg5 (a classic "I can't allow it!" moment) that he replied with 3...h6 (ignoring the threat by 3...Nc6 4.Bg5 Qg6 was fully playable) and White suddenly got with the program and continued 4.Nc3 c6 5.d4 with the superior position.

Instead of moving the d-pawn twice, the most obvious move is also the best:

3.Nc3 Nc6

Now 3...c6 4.d4! (This once again makes Bg5 "on" and also initiates quick central play in order to try and punish black's premature Queen move.) 4...exd4 5.Bg5 Qg6 6.Qxd4 leaves White with more central space and a significant advantage in development.

4.Nd5

Hard to resist—White brings his Knight to a nice square and attacks the enemy Queen at the same time. Of course, the quiet 4.Bc4, bringing the Bishop to a very active diagonal, also makes good sense.

4...Qd6

I'm only giving this poor move to show how simple but logical moves like 3.Nc3 can often put so much pressure on an opponent that he can easily make a serious mistake. Instead of 4...Qd6, 4...Qd8 was far safer, though White can be happy with the result of the opening after 5.Bc4 or 5.d4.

5.c4! A move that is purely opportunistic. White wants to overwhelm Black by making use of the tender nature of c7. That requires energy (quiet positional play is no longer called for), so White will do everything in his power to force black's Queen to move away and lose touch with its defense of c7.

Some lines (see diagram 209):

➤ 5...Nb4 6.d4 Nxd5 7.dxe5 Qb4+ 8.Bd2 Qxb2 9.cxd5 Bb4 10.Rc1 and White's advantage is obvious—huge center, space, lead in development, half open file for the Rook, and threat against c7.

➤ 5...Kd8 6.d4 Qg6 (6...Nxd4 7.Nxd4 exd4 8.Bf4 is strong for White) 7.Be2 Qxe4 8.Ng5 Qxg2 9.Bf3 and black's Queen is a goner.

5...Nce7 6.c5! (Forcing black's Queen onto a more vulnerable square) 6...Qxc5 (6...Qc6 7.Bb5! since 7...Qxb5? 8.Nxc7+ picks up the Queen) 7.d4 (Freeing the c1-h6 diagonal for the dark-squared Bishop with gain of time.) 7...exd4 8.b4 and the game is over: 8...Qc6 9.Bb5 Qd6 10.Bf4 Qg6 11.Nxc7+ etc.

5...b6 6.d4 Nf6 (6...exd4? 7.Bf4) 7.c5! bxc5 8.dxe5! (even stronger than 8.dxc5) 8...Nxe5 9.Bf4 Nxd5 (9...Nxf3+ 10.gxf3 Qc6 11.Nxc7+ Kd8 12.Nxa8 Qxa8 13.Qa4) 10.Bxe5 Qb6 11.Qxd5 and White wins.

Diagram 209

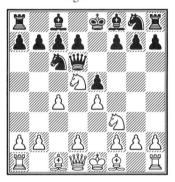

Black to move

This next game features players in the 1600 - 1700 range.

1.c4 Nf6 2.g3 e5 3.Bg2 Nc6 4.Nc3 g6 5.e4 Bc5 (Black, a very aggressive player, intended to fianchetto, but once he saw the hole on d4 he felt compelled to go for more) **6.Nge2 d6 7.h3 Nh5 8.0–0 f5**

Diagram 210

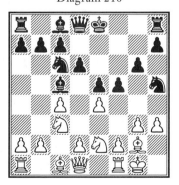

White to move

Black is playing very actively, but one thing isn't kosher in this position: his King is still in the middle. Is it wise to open up the position before you castle?

That alone should excite White and make him dream of ways to completely rip open the center so he can reach the enemy King.

In the game, White played 9.a3 when 9...f4 gives Black serious attacking chances. Clearly, 9.a3 didn't even try to punish Black—it was a lazy move that simply recreated patterns White was familiar with (gaining queenside space with a3 followed by b4). He was playing on autopilot and not even addressing his opponent's moves. If he had stopped and taken stock of the imbalances of this situation (White has a hole on d4 while Black has a kingside space advantage; White's only plus is that centrally placed enemy King), he might have realized that a static plan wasn't the answer and that a dynamic solution was called for (we'll explore the static/dynamic concept in great detail in Part Six, Statics vs. Dynamics). This kind of reasoning takes us to:

9.exf5!

Taking the position in hand and opening up new lines.

9...gxf5

9...Bxf5 loses material to 10.g4 when Black gets some, but not enough, compensation after 10...Bd3 11.gxh5 Qh4 12.Na4.

The problem with 9...gxf5 is that the h5-Knight is suddenly hanging out to dry—nothing is protecting it. White immediately takes tactical advantage of this fact.

10.d4!

Diagram 211

The position has undergone a drastic transformation!

10...exd4

Better is 10...Bb6, but then moves such as 11.b4, 11.Be3, and 11.Nd5 all give White a pronounced advantage.

11.Nxd4!

Giving white's Queen instant access to the d1-h5 diagonal and threatening Qxh5+.

11...Nxg3

Another bloody example is 11...Bxd4 12.Qxh5+ Kf8 13.Bd5 Qd7 14.Bh6+ Bg7 15.Rae1 Ne5 16.f4 and Black can quietly give up.

12.Nxc6 bxc6 13.Bxc6+ Bd7 14.Re1+ Kf8 15.Qd5 and the double threat of 16.Bxa8 and 16.Bh6 mate are more than Black can handle. Clearly, the robotic 9.a3, though a common idea in the English Opening, wasn't right for this particular position. As should be evident, a fresh look can pay huge dividends.

Although these last two examples showed how lazy thinking led to missed dynamic and/or tactical possibilities, the same can be said about positional ideas. In the following game we witness a high-class example of a very astute chess outlook.

J. Rowson - L. Cooper, Walsall 1997

1.c4 b6 2.d4 e6 3.Nc3 Bb7 4.a3 f5 5.d5 Nf6 6.g3 g6 7.Nf3 exd5 8.cxd5 Bg7

Diagram 212

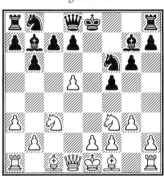

This position features a central space advantage for White, a battle for the important e4-square (Black would like to airlift his b8-Knight there—he usually accomplishes this by ...Na6-c5-e4), some early black pressure along the a1-h8 diagonal, a strong d5-pawn that needs tending else you might drop it, and the fact that White will be better if he can finish development and place his Rooks on c1 and d1. Note that ...d6 for Black is problematic since that would weaken the c6- and e6-squares (White would eye them with Bg2 followed by Nd4).

There's a lot of tension in this seemingly simple position, and the going can get tricky. Most players would toss out 9.Bg2 without thinking, but Rowson didn't fall victim to that kind of soft thinking. Instead he realized that he might be able to make serious gains if he could deprive the b8-Knight access to c5 by making b4 a possibility. Since the immediate 9.b4 fails to 9...Ne4, he came up with:

9.Rb1!

Extremely nice! Now that the Rook is off the a1-h8 diagonal, b2-b4 is suddenly a viable idea. To be honest, I'm not convinced this is actually stronger than 9.Bg2 Na6 10.Bf4, but that doesn't matter—the fact that he kept his hand away from the f1-Bishop and actually thought, "Maybe there's something better. Maybe I can isolate that Knight and deprive him of his usual play." is far more impressive than most combinations.

9...0-0

Black meets an extraordinary idea with a generic reply. Small wonder that he soon finds himself in trouble. Instead, he needed to either fight for the right to employ the usual plan (that b8-Knight *must* find a way to make an imprint on the central battle!), or try and take advantage of the loss of time that 9.Rb1 entailed. Let's give a quick look at both:

9...Na6 10.b4 c5 11.Bg2 (11.dxc6 e.p. dxc6 12.Qb3 Qe7 13.Bg2 might be even stronger) 11...0-0 (11...Qc8 12.Nb5 is good for White, but 11...cxb4 12.axb4 Nc7, putting the despised Knight to work, leads to interesting positions that would be fun to analyze. White appears to have a little something in this line, but I'm not sure how much it really is) 12.0-0 cxb4 13.axb4 Rc8 14.Nb5 Bxd5 15.Bf4 Rc4 16.Bd6 Re8 17.Be5 favors White.

Okay, our all-too-brief look at the thematic 9...Na6 didn't inspire confidence, so let's see if the second option is workable—how can Black try to make something of his lead in development? 9...Qe7! is critical, when White has to be careful about b2, c3, and d5:

Diagram 213

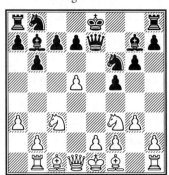

White to move

10.Bg2 Ne4! is comfortable for Black after 11.Bd2 (11.Nxe4 Qxe4 12.Bf4 Qxd5) 11...0-0 12.0-0 Na6 and the Knight is on the way to c5 after all.

Seeking help from my silicon master, Rybka offered up the following insane variation (from diagram 213): 10.Bf4 Ne4 11.Nb5 (11.Nxe4 fxe4 12.d6 cxd6 13.Bxd6 Qe6 14.Ng5 is a whole other world of complications—Black seems to be okay here too) 11...d6 12.Rc1 Na6 13.Nfd4 (It seems to me that, if this brute force idea doesn't work, then White should stay on topic and make sure c5 can't be used by an enemy Knight. Thus 13.b4!? is critical, with 13...0-0 14.Bg2 being a good place to begin another endless analysis for anyone that might be interested) 13...0-0 14.Ne6 Bxb2 (by capturing this pawn, Black ensures that his Knights will have permanent access to the c5-square) 15.Rc2 Bg7 16.f3 Nf6 17.Nexc7 Rad8 18.Nxa6 Nxd5 19.Kf2 Nxf4 20.Rc7 Rd7 21.Rxb7 Rxb7 22.gxf4 Qh4+ 23.Kg2 Qxf4 24.Qd5+ Rbf7 25.Nxd6 Qg5+, draw.

Hopefully this game and illustrative analysis (a true analysis would easily fill several pages) gives you a taste of the psychology and willpower needed in upper level chess: one player comes up with an idea that might allow him to take over the position, and if the other doesn't match him with a bright concept of his own, his game will quickly go downhill.

The actual game (after 9...0-0) continued: **10.Bg2 a5 11.0–0 Na6 12.b4 axb4 13.axb4 c5 14.dxc6 e.p. dxc6 15.Nd4 Qd7 16.Qb3+ Kh8 17.Ne6 Rfe8 18.Nxg7** and White has a clear advantage and eventually won.

Lazy moves often emerge when the hard work in a game is done and you mistakenly think that the rest will play itself. Our next game is a drastic (and painful!) example.

J. Silman - Z. Vranesic, Lone Pine 1975

1.e4 c5 2.c3 e6 3.d4 d5 4.e5 Nc6 5.Nf3 Qb6 6.a3 a5 7.Bd3 Bd7 8.0–0 cxd4 9.cxd4 Nxd4 10.Nxd4 Qxd4 11.Nc3 Qb6 12.Qg4 h5 13.Qf4 a4 14.Be3 Bc5 15.Rac1 Bxe3 16.fxe3 Nh6 17.Kh1 Bc6 18.Qg5 Kd7 19.e4! d4 20.Nd5!! Qd8 (20...exd5 21.e6+ fxe6 22.Qxg7+ Kd6 23.e5 mate) **21.Qxg7 exd5 22.exd5 Bxd5 23.e6+! Bxe6**

Diagram 214

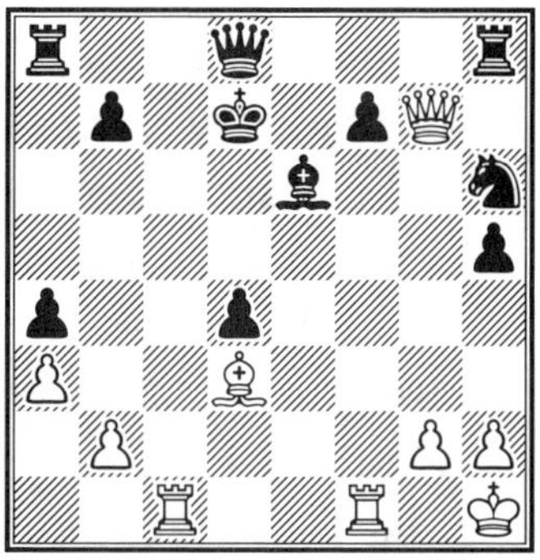

White to move and end his opponent

Here, after finding all the hard moves and achieving a position that Black could resign with a clear conscience, I relaxed and began thinking about the brilliance of my combination. And, while I was busy patting myself on the back, I stopped playing chess.

24.Bb5+?

Amazing. I glanced at this move, saw that it won the Exchange, and just played it without looking for anything better. 24.Qxd4+! Ke7 (24...Ke8 25.Qxh8+ Ke7

26.Qf6+ wins the house) 25.Qb4+ Qd6 26.Rc7+ Bd7 27.Re1+ would have given me the overkill finish that I deserved.

24...Ke7 25.Qf6+ Kf8 26.Qxh8+ Ng8

Obviously, 24.Bb5+ was winning, but it made things harder than they needed to be. Once you take the "lazy train to nowhere," you often find it's shockingly easy to stay on that train until all your good earlier work is undone.

27.Bd3?

27.Rce1 with the threat of Rxe6 was crushing. Other easy winners were 27.Qxh5 and 27.Bc4.

27...Qg5 28.Qxd4 Rd8

Suddenly Black has a bit of activity. His game is still lost, but now White had to put some work into it, which I was clearly not prepared to do.

29.Qb4+ Ne7 30.Bc4

30.Rce1 increases the heat and is still pretty easy.

30... Rd2 31.Qxb7 Nd5

At this point I was extremely upset. I knew I had botched things (though White's still winning) and couldn't get back on track.

32.Qb8+ Kg7 33.Qg3??

33.Rg1 was still winning, but I couldn't bring myself to play such a defensive move. Wasn't I mating him a few moves ago?

Here's what Angus Dunnington (in his book, *Chess Psychology*) had to say about this kind of situation: "When a hitherto sweet-smelling game suddenly turns sour we tend to dwell on where we might have gone wrong, or we simply look down on the area of the board where the opponent has just turned the tables and see only these enemy pieces that have done—or are about to do—the damage."

33...Qxg3 34.hxg3 Ne3 35.Bxe6 Nxf1 36.Rxf1 fxe6 37.Rf4 Rxb2 38.Rxa4 and the game was eventually drawn.

Years later, because of agonizing failures like the one we just saw, I changed my whole mindset. When reaching a position as in diagram 214, I began to take a long time to soak up every juicy bit of goodness it offered. Why rush when I could lick my lips, take a glance at my opponent's red, defeated face, and simply enjoy the moment? Then I would jump back into the position and give myself a small challenge: "How can I execute him in the most effective manner? What's the very best way to mop things up?"

Of course, I still had my share of soft move failures, but my newfound concerted effort to retain focus enabled me to avoid a lot of disasters that my earlier attitude would have created.

Pay Attention!

In my teens and early twenties, one of my biggest failings as a player was the "quick move" (making moves too fast). When it was my turn I'd often just bash a piece on some square (usually planned a few moves before) and expect it to make my opponent swoon. Invariably, the move was either "soft" (not really giving the position what it needed) or a downright blunder. Yet, I wasn't aware of this habit until Dennis Waterman, a very strong master, told me that he'd watched my games for quite a while and noticed that most of my losses were due to this "illness." That one bit of insight made a big difference in my subsequent results, though I continued to suffer the occasional relapse right up to the end of my career.

Here's one of the games Waterman was alluding to.

J. Silman - J. McCormick, Berkeley 1974

1.e4 c5 2.Nf3 d6 3.d4 cxd4 4.Nxd4 Nf6 5.Nc3 Nc6 6.Bg5 e6 7.Qd2 a6 8.0–0–0 Bd7 9.f4 h6 10.Bh4 Rc8 11.Nf3 Qa5 12.Bc4 b5 13.Bb3 b4 14.Bxf6 gxf6 15.Ne2 Qb6 16.f5 Na5 17.Nf4 Nxb3+ 18.axb3 h5 19.Kb1 a5 20.e5 fxe5 21.Nxe5 Bb5 22.Nxf7 Kxf7 23.fxe6+ Ke8 24.Nd5 Qc5 25.Qg5 Qxc2+

Diagram 215

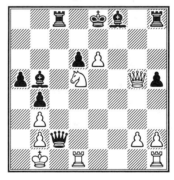

White to move

Here I only had two legal moves, and both seemed more than adequate. So I quickly tossed one out and waited for my opponent to resign.

26.Ka2??

I thought either King move was 1-0 and I didn't take any time to verify this opinion.

26...a4 and suddenly I realized that I'd botched another game since now the b3-pawn is hanging with *check*. A draw was agreed after 26...a4 (27.Nf6+ Kd8

28.Nd5+). Of course, 26.Ka1 (threatening 27.Rc1) would have won on the spot since 26…a4 followed by 27…axb3 would no longer be with check.

Here's one more example of a quick move. Hopefully it will prove scary enough to make you seriously think about sitting on your hands and only moving when you are 100% sure about what's going on and what you want to accomplish. And, of course, make sure the move you intend to play is actually the one your hand is trying to make!

J. Fedorowicz - J. Silman, American Open 1989

1.e4 c5 2.Nf3 Nc6 3.d4 cxd4 4.Nxd4 Nf6 5.Nc3 e5 6.Ndb5 d6 7.Bg5 a6 8.Bxf6 gxf6 9.Na3 b5 10.Nd5 Bg7 11.c3 Ne7 12.Nc2 Nxd5 13.Qxd5 Rb8 14.Ne3 Bh6 15.Qd3 Bxe3 16.Qxe3 Qb6 17.Qf3 Ke7 18.Bd3 Rg8 19.h3 Be6 20.0–0 Rg6 21.Kh2 Rbg8 22.Rg1 Qc6 23.Qe3 f5 24.g3 Rf6 25.exf5 Bxf5 26.Rad1 Bxd3 27.Rxd3 Qc5 28.Qxc5 dxc5 29.Kg2

Diagram 216

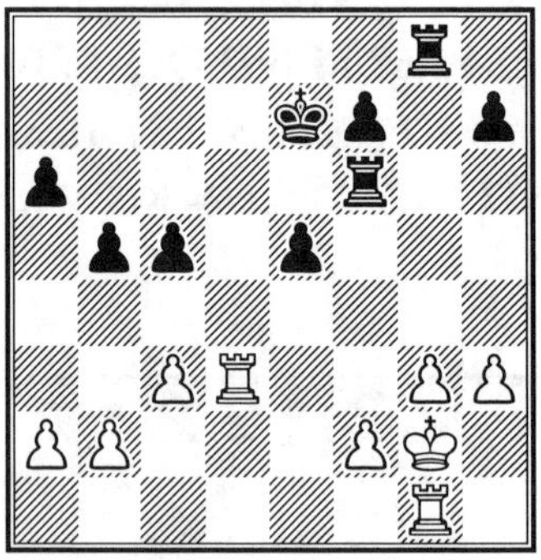

Black to move

I hadn't experienced any serious problems in this game and now intended to play 29…Rd6 when a draw would have followed since 30.Rxd6 (30.Rgd1 Rxd3 31.Rxd3 Ke6) 30…Kxd6 31.Kf3 h5 is completely equal.

However, someone had entered the tournament hall that I wanted to speak to. So, after White played the expected 29.Kg2, I didn't write down his move or even give the position any thought. I just reached out for the f6-Rook, and in true blitz fashion (though I had lots of time left) moved "it" to the d-file.

29…Rd8??

And, as I let this Rook go, it suddenly struck me that I had grabbed the wrong Rook! Fedorowicz gave me a strange look and chopped on d8.

30.Rxd8 Kxd8 31.Rd1+

And, as hysteria, confusion, and self-loathing blasted my mind to bits, the Fed stuck his face in mine and said, "You gotta pay attention!"

Small wonder that I didn't put up any resistance at all and went down quickly: **31...Kc7 32.Rd5 Rd6 33.Rxc5+ Kb6 34.Rxe5 Rd2 35.b4 Rxa2 36.Rf5 Kc6 37.Rxf7 Kd5 38.Rxh7**, 1-0. This one still hurts when I look at it!

For all you blunder prone players out there that move too quickly, memorize/take to heart/obey Grandmaster Fedorowicz's dictate: *You gotta pay attention!*

Naturally, the "pay attention" adage doesn't just protect a player from a wandering hand or an obvious blunder. It also helps you see tricks that might have easily gone unnoticed.

Diagram 217

I. A. Horowitz - M. Pavey, New York 1951
Black to move

Black is an Exchange and two pawns ahead and can win as he pleases. In fact, I can imagine Mr. Pavey feeling rather insulted that White was playing on. Rybka likes 1...Kb6 and 1...Kd6, ending all sane checks and forcing White to self-destruct with 2.Bg2 Qg4+ (forcing the exchange of Queens, which really is game over), or 2.Kg2 Qxg5+ 3.Kh3 Qxh6+, which is downright humiliating.

However, a human tends to like more forcing continuations, so Pavey found something that was both cute and, apparently, devastating.

1...Qxf3+??

Pavey must have expected a handshake at this point. Surely Horowitz would resign now!

2.Qxf3 Ra3

I'm sure Pavey still expected resignation.

3.Kh4!

As I write this, I'm feeling Pavey's pain. Two moves earlier, with so many pieces and pawns on the board, Pavey never imagined that a stalemate would be possible!

3...Rxf3, ½-½. I'm sure this never would have happened if he had known Grandmaster Fedorowicz.

Summary

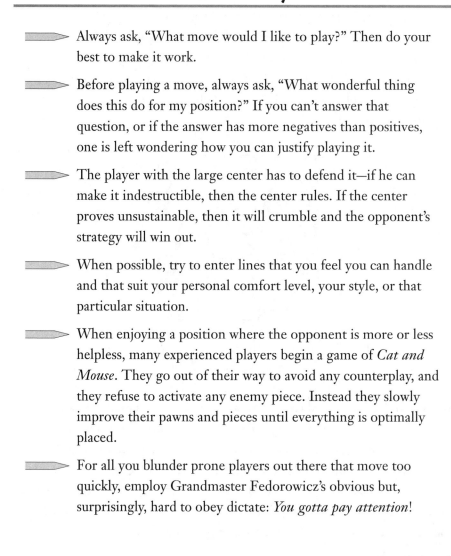

> Always ask, "What move would I like to play?" Then do your best to make it work.

> Before playing a move, always ask, "What wonderful thing does this do for my position?" If you can't answer that question, or if the answer has more negatives than positives, one is left wondering how you can justify playing it.

> The player with the large center has to defend it—if he can make it indestructible, then the center rules. If the center proves unsustainable, then it will crumble and the opponent's strategy will win out.

> When possible, try to enter lines that you feel you can handle and that suit your personal comfort level, your style, or that particular situation.

> When enjoying a position where the opponent is more or less helpless, many experienced players begin a game of *Cat and Mouse*. They go out of their way to avoid any counterplay, and they refuse to activate any enemy piece. Instead they slowly improve their pawns and pieces until everything is optimally placed.

> For all you blunder prone players out there that move too quickly, employ Grandmaster Fedorowicz's obvious but, surprisingly, hard to obey dictate: *You gotta pay attention*!

Various States of Chess Consciousness — Tests

Here you'll be able to test yourself against chess afflictions like Lazy Moves and failure to pay attention. Players in all rating groups can botch a game in the blink of an eye, so let's see if your chess "spider sense" has become a bit more sophisticated in catching these moments.

The following tests are designed to give you insight into how much you've learned *and* to serve as extra instruction. If you have trouble solving the tests, don't worry—that means we've uncovered something you don't understand, and this allows you to fix things by rereading the previous material or by picking up the bits of knowledge you're missing in the answers that start on page 521.

PART FOUR - TEST 23

Diagram 218

[Level: 2200 on up]

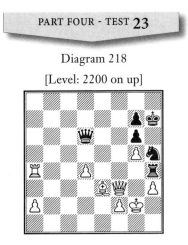

White to move

Is there any difference between Ra8 and Ra7?

PART FOUR - TEST 24

Diagram 219

[Level: 1800 - 2200]

Black to move

PART FOUR - TEST **25**

Diagram 220

[Level: 1800 - 2200]

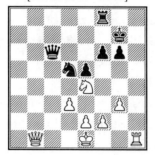

Black to move

PART FOUR - TEST **26**

Diagram 221

[Level: 1400 - 1800]

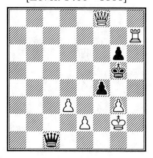

Black to move

One final trick.

Part Five / Target Consciousness

Contents

Introduction

In chess, it's easy to get a bit overwhelmed by all the ABCs that are tossed at the poor student. In particular, memorization-based material is often extremely daunting but also shockingly unrewarding. The most prized lessons in chess are those that train the mind to see things in a completely new way while also planting the seeds for proper mental habits. Here we'll look at *Target Consciousness*, one of the game's most overlooked yet critically important concepts. I try very hard to instill a deep understanding and appreciation of Target Consciousness in all my students (it doesn't matter if they are rated 1200 or 2200). This term helps ram home a form of mental training where the player, in an almost shark-like manner, learns to instantly recognize all potential targets and, once he finds one, to leap on it like a shark rushes to blood.

I created the term when I found students ignoring glaring targets. "Why not make use of that weak square?" I'd ask.

The answer didn't please me. "Square? You're kidding, right? Why bother with a square? It's not like I can capture it and put in the box."

"Okay, why not go after that isolated pawn?" I kept trying!

"I suppose I could, but his King is over *there*!"

I gave it one last go. "Yes, I know where his King is, but it's guarded by his whole army while you don't have more than a couple pieces in that area. His pawn, though, is hanging out to dry."

However, it seemed hopeless. "Yes, I see that the pawn is weak, but his King is over *there*!" Sigh.

As a result of this kind of conversation (repeated with many, many students), I realized that it was my job to make them realize that you can only attack a King if there's reason to do so (*wanting* to attack it isn't a reason!). Thus, I showed an endless cascade of games where grandmasters would dominate a square and/or surround and eventually pick off a pawn and score an easy victory. Once a player is fully convinced that there's a safer, more reliable way to win at chess than unsound King-hunts, the idea of Target Consciousness becomes a passion! And, with that huge shift in general chess consciousness, the player is on his way to becoming a serious threat to anyone.

Of course, at times there won't be any existing targets. In that case you might decide to develop your forces, play for a superior minor piece or more space, nuke the board with a positional sacrifice of some sort, unleash a crazed tactic, try to behead his King (yes, there are many occasions when you *should* go after the enemy King!), or do any number of useful things. But a player that's a Target Consciousness junkie won't only be looking for targets to attack, he'll also be looking for ways to create them! Once he does that, he'll immediately sink his teeth into his new creation and chew the night away.

We'll address three types of targets in this section:

WEAK PAWNS—Perhaps the most common target. If an enemy
           pawn can't be defended by another pawn, then your Target
           Consciousness mindset should make you want to gang up on
           the thing.

WEAK SQUARES—A complex of weak squares allows a Rook to
           smoothly slide down a file (see Part Three: Rooks) and a
           Bishop to do its long-range "dominate the diagonal" dance
           (see Part Two: Minor Pieces). A single weak square, situated
           on the 4th, 5th, or 6th ranks, allows a Knight (or another
           piece) to set up shop close to or deep inside the enemy's camp.
           These things allow your pieces to become stronger than their
           enemy counterparts.

THE KING—If the enemy King is stuck in the center, it might be
           time to put on your executioner's cap and go for it!

Ready to reprogram your brain so that it becomes a lean, mean, Target Consciousness machine? If so, turn the page and let's get this difficult but extremely rewarding process underway!

Weak Pawns
The Sound of Ripe Fruit Falling

Weak pawns appear, in one form or another, far more often than you might suppose. At times the weak pawn offers dynamic compensation—that idea will be explored in Part Six, Statics vs. Dynamics. However, here we'll concentrate on the negative aspect of this kind of pawn and try and instill in the reader an overwhelming desire to go after them like a starving hyena goes after meat.

The Isolated Pawn

An isolated pawn on an open file (of course, an isolated pawn that doesn't stand on an open file usually isn't as big a problem since then the enemy Rooks can't bother it) is subject to attack by just about everything—the attacker's Queen, Rooks, Bishops and Knights can all join in the party. However, the defender's army, if allowed to get active, often gives the pawn's owner quite a bit of compensation. Thus, a general rule is that the side playing against the isolated pawn should strive to exchange as many minor pieces as possible. This limits counterplay and more or less turns the pawn into a pure weakness.

Diagram 222

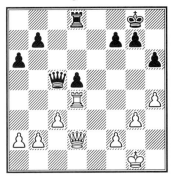

Black to move

Black has an isolated d-pawn but White has created his ideal setup:

➤ No minor pieces—In many situations an isolated pawn can claim active minor pieces as compensation. However, if all the minor pieces are exchanged then that kind of compensation would be impossible and the pawn would be relegated to a pure weakness.

 A Queen and Rook (even better than a Queen and two Rooks, which gives the defender a bit more potential for counterplay) is best since the presence of Queens makes it far too dangerous for the defender's King to come forward and join in the defense of the pawn.

 The Rook blocks the pawn (stopping it from advancing), the Queen is behind it, and this doubling puts maximum pressure against the weakness.

These factors leave Black completely passive, and all he can do is try and hold on. He might draw on occasion (many pawn down Rook endgames occur that can be drawn with perfect play), but it's a miserable defensive chore and most players will crack.

In our present position White threatens to win d5 by making use of the pin along the d-file with c3-c4.

1...b5

For the time being, this prevents the advance of white's c-pawn. White can now make use of two ideas (the particulars of a given position will decide which is superior): he can play to create a new weakness by a2-a4, or he can just go for it by b3 followed by c4.

2.b3

Also possible is 2.a4 bxa4 (2...Qc6 3.axb5 axb5 and now the b3 followed by c4 idea is still very much on the table, while he can also "massage" Black and just torment his weak points by 4.Qd3 which gives attention to both b5 and d5) 3.Rxa4 Rd6 4.Rd4 and White goes right back to his c3-c4 idea.

2...Rc8

Otherwise c3-c4 wins d5.

3.Rxd5 Qxc3 4.Qxc3 Rxc3 5.Rd6 a5 6.Ra6 winning a pawn and, as usual, dooming Black to a lot more suffering.

Diagram 223

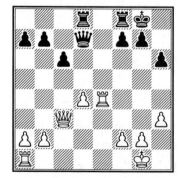

RULE

Trade minor pieces when your opponent has an isolated pawn.

White to move

Of course, the side with the isolated pawn usually strives to retain his minor pieces so he can counterbalance the pawn weakness with dynamic piece play. However, when the minor pieces do get traded, the defender can still avoid a long night of pain by exchanging all the Rooks.

1.Rae1

The threat of 2.Re7 is serious business, and Black has to address it in some way or risk getting into a bit of trouble.

1...Rfe8

1...b6 2.Re7 Qxd4 3.Qxd4 Rxd4 4.Rxa7 can't make Black happy, while 1...Qd5 2.Re7 Rd7 3.Rxd7 Qxd7 4.Qb4 renews the threat of Re7 and once again compels Black to swap the final pair of Rooks with 4...Re8.

2.Rxe8+ Rxe8 3.Rxe8+ Qxe8 and Black has nothing since the Queen and Rook vs. Queen and Rook pin against the d-pawn (as seen in the previous example) no longer exists, while one lone Queen can't pressure the d-pawn enough to inconvenience the defender.

Now that the reader has a basic but highly useful knowledge of how to play against the isolated d-pawn (and how to try and hold on if the isolated pawn goes bad—namely, retain minor pieces and/or exchange all the Rooks), let's see if grandmasters actually make use of these ideas too.

> **RULE**
>
> If you have an isolated pawn and you've failed to generate dynamic compensation for it, it's often a good defensive idea to exchange all the Rooks, which prevents the opponent from placing maximum pressure against your weakness.

A. Fishbein - Y. Shulman, U.S. Chmp 2006

1.e4 e6 2.d4 d5 3.Nd2 c5 4.exd5 exd5 5.Ngf3 Nc6 6.Bb5 Bd6 7.dxc5 Bxc5 8.0–0 Ne7 9.Nb3 Bd6 10.c3 Bg4 11.Be2 0–0 12.Be3 Re8 13.h3 Bh5 14.Re1 Bg6 15.Bd3 Qc7

Diagram 224

This kind of position is often seen in the Tarrasch French. Black accepts an isolated d-pawn but gets free and easy play for his pieces. As you will see, White follows our anti-isolated pawn formula and trades as many minor pieces as possible.

16.Bxg6

That's one!

16...hxg6 17.Qd3 Rad8 18.Nbd4 a6 19.Nxc6

That's another—note that 19...bxc6 isn't possible due to 20.Qxa6.

19...Nxc6 20.Bg5 Be7 21.Bxe7

And there's yet another. Suddenly Black has entered our "doomed to suffer for a long time" scenario.

21...Rxe7 22.Rxe7 Qxe7 23.Re1 Qf6 24.h4

A slip. With 24.Rd1 (preventing the advance of the d-pawn—a critical part of our strategy) White would retain his slight but long-term advantage.

24...Qf5

Black returns the favor. He should have leapt at the chance to play 24...d4.

25.Qe3 Qd7

Preventing white's threatened 26.Qe8+!

26.Rd1

Now the world once again makes sense and White can quietly build up his position at leisure.

26...f6 27.g3 Kf7 28.Kg2

White has improved the position of his King, which is now off the back rank and keeps an eye on the slightly loose light-squares on f3 and h3.

28...Qe6 29.Qb6 Rd7 30.Re1 Qd6 31.Nd4

Diagram 225

Offering to exchange the final minor piece and reach the kind of position we saw in diagram 222. I should add that the Knight is very strong here, so Black is facing a "trade it and reach a miserable position, but leave it be and you might end up suffering in other ways by the Knight's hand" dilemma.

31...Ne5 32.Qb3

Not trading Queens since, as mentioned earlier, that would allow black's King to safely help in defending his pawn: 32.Qxd6 Rxd6 33.Rd1 Rd8 34.Ne2 g5 35.hxg5 fxg5 36.Nd4 Kf6 37.Nc2 Ke6 and black's defensive task is far easier than it was before.

I'll share a tale here. This game was being followed live on a demonstration board (along with four others) in the event's analysis room. Two famous international masters were commenting on it to a large audience and agreed that it should be "drawn at any moment." I was watching from the front row and thought that Black was in for a rough ride—he might draw, but it wouldn't be fun at all! However, I didn't say anything since I felt it would be rude to contradict the speakers, who were exhausted after a long, hard day's work and who had their hands full trying to make sense of this and the other four games as well!

I also think they were influenced by the strength of the player with the Black pieces—they were sure he wouldn't allow himself to get into the kind of trouble we discussed in diagram 222. But no player is infallible, and even grandmasters can (and often do) fall victim to the formulas and setups (no matter how basic you deem them to be) being taught in this book!

32...Nc6 33.Rd1 Ne5

Of course Black avoids 33...Nxd4 34.Rxd4 Qc6 35.Qd1 when we're back to our main "theme" position. The threat of c3-c4 makes life difficult for the second player: 35...Rd8 36.Kg1 (threatening c4, which didn't work right away due to the X-ray from the black Queen to the white King on g2) 36...b5 37.b3 Qxc3 38.Rxd5 Rxd5 39.Qxd5+ Kf8 40.Qa8+ Kf7 41.Qxa6 Qe1+ 42.Kg2 Qe4+ 43.Kh2 Qd4 44.Qb7+ Kg8 45.Kg2 with an extra pawn and excellent winning chances.

34.Qc2 Rd8?

Defending an unpleasant position is never easy, and it only takes one "blink" to see it all go downhill. Perhaps Black should have tried 34...Kg8, though he would still be under a good deal of pressure after 35.Rh1, intending h4-h5.

35.h5! gxh5

35...g5 36.Qh7 Qf8 37.f4 gxf4 38.gxf4 Nc6 39.Qg6+ Kg8 40.Ne6 Qe7 41.h6 and Black is in a very bad way.

36.Qh7 Qf8 37.Qxh5+ Ng6 38.Re1 Qh8 39.Qg4 Rd6 40.Nf5 Rb6

40...Rd8 41.Qb4 is also unpalatable for Black.

41.Nh6+!

Taking advantage of the undefended state of black's Rook.

41...Qxh6

Or 41...gxh6 42.Qd7+ Kg8 43.Qd8+ Kh7 44.Qxb6.

42.Qd7+ Ne7 43.Qxe7+ Kg6 44.Qe8+ Kf5 45.g4+ Kxg4 46.Qe2+ Kf5 47.Qd3+ Kg4 48.Qf3+ Kg5 49.Qe3+ Kg4 50.Qxb6, 1-0.

Though it's usually ideal to retain the Queens (along with a Rook), there are many occasions when the exchange of Queens is perfectly satisfactory, and still ensures that the owner of the isolated pawn will not have an easy life.

C. Sandipan - H. Koneru, Calicut 2003

1.e4 e5 2.Nf3 Nf6 3.Nxe5 d6 4.Nf3 Nxe4 5.Nc3 Nf6 6.d4 Be7 7.Bd3 O-O 8.h3 Na6 9.a3 c5 10.O-O Nc7 11.Re1 Re8 12.Bf4 Ne6 13.Bh2 cxd4 14.Nb5 Qb6 15.Nbxd4 Nxd4 16.Nxd4 Bd7 17.Qd2 Bf8

Diagram 226

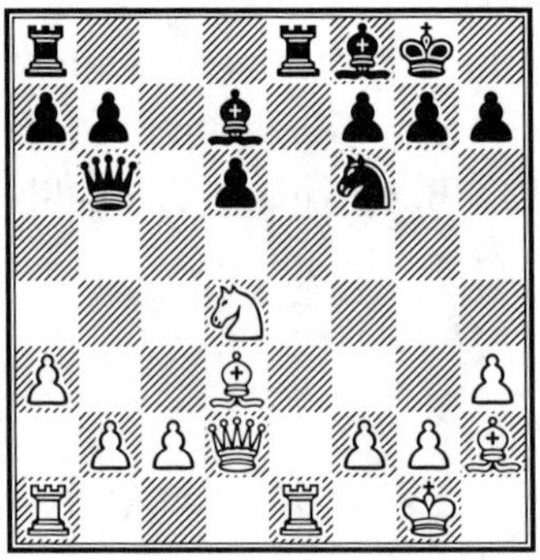

White to move

Black has a rather joyless position—she has an isolated pawn on an open file and can't even boast compensation via active pieces since her whole army looks more than a bit subdued. At the moment, black's most active piece is her Queen, so White trades it off.

18.Qb4 Rxe1+ 19.Rxe1 Nd5

No better is 19...Qxb4 20.axb4 d5 21.c3 when Black remains passive and under pressure.

20.Qxb6 Nxb6

20...axb6 isn't playable due to 21.Be4, winning a pawn: 21...Bc6 (21...Re8 22.Re2 Nc7 23.Bxb7) 22.Nxc6 bxc6 23.c4 etc.

21.b3!

A nice move that takes the a4- and c4-squares away from black's Knight, while also preparing a3-a4, turning the a-pawn into an active participant in the battle.

21...d5 22.a4 Bb4 23.Rd1 g6 24.Bf4 Kf8 25.Ne2

White's plan is simple but effective: he intends to follow up with Be3 (eyeing black's Knight and, if that Knight moves, a7) followed by Nf4 when d5 begins to feel some heat.

25...Be6 26.Be3 Nc8 27.Nf4 Ne7 28.c4!

Diagram 227

Black to move

More usual in this kind of position is B-e2-f3, intensifying the pressure against d5. However, this proves unnecessary since 28.c4! makes use of some tactical nuances to actually force the win of material.

28...Rd8

28...dxc4 fails to 29.Nxe6+ fxe6 30.Bxc4 Kf7 (30...Nf5 14.Bf4) 31.Rd7 when Black is quite lost. Moves such as 28...a6 and 28...b6 are met by the Be2-f3 maneuver.

29.Be4

Stronger is 29.cxd5 Bf5 (29...Nxd5 30.Be4) 30.Bxf5 Nxf5 31.Bxa7 with two extra pawns for White.

29...Bd6

29...b6, ending the threat to a7, makes more sense.

30.Nxd5 and black's isolated pawn has fallen. The rest of the game is off theme: **30...Nxd5 31.cxd5 f5 32.Bf3 Bf7 33.Bxa7 Rc8 34.Bd4 g5 35.Be3 h6 36.Rc1 Rd8 37.Bc5 Ke7 38.Bxd6+ Kxd6 39.b4 Bxd5?? 40.Bxd5**, 1-0.

Thus far we've only looked at isolated d-pawns, but our anti-isolated d-pawn rules also apply to other types of isolated pawns.

Diagram 228

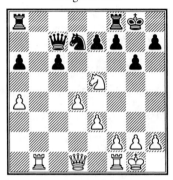

R. Kasimdzhanov - Vallejo Pons, Wijk aan Zee 2009
White to move

Black's pawn on c6 is begging to be attacked by white's heavy pieces, while his other isolated pawn (a6), though not on an open file, also earns a greedy stare from White.

1.Nxd7

Following our rule about exchanging minor pieces. Now the b6- and c5-squares can be safely used by white's Rooks and Queen.

1...Qxd7 2.Qc2 Rab8?

It wasn't wise to leave a6 unattended. More sensible was 2...Rfb8, though black's poor pawn structure would, as usual, leave him with a very unhappy defensive chore.

3.Qc4

Immediately taking aim at black's a-pawn!

3...a5 4.Qc5

He's not giving the poor a5-pawn a break!

4...Qc7 5.Rb5!

This is the kind of unrelenting assault against weak pawns that make Target Consciousness aficionados hyperventilate from pure pleasure.

5...Ra8 6.Qc3

White had many good moves here. Kasimdzhanov's choice makes room on c5 for the b5-Rook.

6...Rfc8 7.Rc5 e6 8.Rc1

Absolutely delicious! Black, who is tied down to a5 and c6, is completely helpless.

Diagram 229

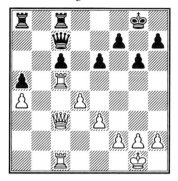

8...Ra6 9.h4

Since Black can only sit around passively and hope his opponent doesn't find a breakthrough, White patiently improves his game before initiating the *coup de grâce*.

9...h5 10.Rb1 Raa8 11.g3 Ra6 12.Kg2

If you have the luxury of endless time, then creating optimal King safety is always a good idea.

12...Qa7

A mistake that hastens the end. More resistance could be had by 12...Rca8, though it's hard to imagine Black actually saving such a miserable position. One possible line (after 12...Rca8): 13.Qc4 Qc8 14.Rbb5 R8a7 15.Qb3 (the way White mixes attacks against a5 and c6 with penetration threats down the b-file is quite picturesque) 15...Ra8 16.Rb7 R6a7 17.Rxa7 Rxa7 18.Qc3 Qd8 19.d5! (19.Rxc6 Qd5+ gives Black more counterplay than he deserves) 19...exd5 20.Rxc6 Ra8 21.Qc5 Rb8 22.Rd6 Qe8 23.Qxd5 and Black will eventually lose (note that 23...Qxa4?? 24.Rxg6+ is an instant winner).

13.Rbb5! Kh7 14.Rxa5 Rxa5 15.Rxa5 Qb7 16.Rc5 and White has an extra pawn and still retains heavy pressure against c6. The rest was easy: **16...Qb1 17.Qc2 Qxc2 18.Rxc2 Ra8 19.Ra2 Kg7 20.a5 Ra6 21.Kf3 Kf6 22.Kf4 Ke7 23.Kg5 e5 24.dxe5 c5 25.Kf4 c4 26.Ke4**, 1-0.

The Backward Pawn

The backward pawn shares many of the same shortcomings as the isolated pawn, and several of the anti-isolated pawn ideas also apply to this weak little critter. Of course, the superior side needs to make sure the backward pawn remains backward, but once this is done then we see old friends like "trade the minor pieces" and "pile up with the Rooks and Queen" rear their effective heads.

L. Ljubojevic - J. Smeets, Amsterdam 2007

1.c4 c6 2.Nf3 d5 3.e3 Nf6 4.b3 Bf5 5.Bb2 Nbd7 6.Be2 h6 7.0–0 e6 8.d4 Bd6 9.Ne5 Qc7 10.f4 Ne4 11.a3 0–0 12.Nxd7 Qxd7 13.Nc3 Qe7 14.Bd3 Nxc3 15.Bxc3 a6 16.c5 Bc7 17.Qc2 Qf6 18.Rae1 Rad8 19.e4 dxe4 20.Bxe4

Diagram 230

RULE

Trade minor pieces when your opponent has a backward pawn.

Black to move

White's backward d4-pawn gains space but, due to the reduced material and absence of the Knights and light-square Bishops (which will soon come off the board), Black enjoys more than enough room to maneuver. Since White has no target to attack, while Black can pound away on d4 with his Rooks, Queen, and dark-squared Bishop, it's clear that black's completely in charge.

20...Rd5

RULE

Place a piece in front of a backward pawn so it can't move forward.

White threatened to rid himself of the backward pawn by 21.d5 so Black freezes it in place. That's a good, thematic thing to do, but I would have preferred the less flashy 20...Bxe4 21.Qxe4 Rd5 with play similar to the actual game. The reason for this will be seen in our next note.

21.b4

White should have given 21.Bxf5 a go since 21...exf5 gives white counterplay down the open e-file, and 21...Rxf5?? 22.d5 Qg6 23.d6 has allowed the weak pawn to turn into a monster passed pawn. Also note that the Bishop, which was such a poor, purely defensive piece, suddenly (after 21...Rxf5?? 22.d5) enjoys a new lease on life with the opening of the a1-h8 diagonal.

After 21.Bxf5 Black would have to play 21...Qxf5 but that allows the exchange of Queens, which in turn lets White safely use his King to give extra support to d4: 21...Qxf5 22.Qxf5 Rxf5 23.g3 Rd8 24.Kg2 Rd7 25.Rf2 Rfd5 26.Rd2 Bd8 27.Re5 Bf6 28.Rxd5 Rxd5 29.Kf3 when White is okay.

21...g6

Both White and Black seem to have decided that Bxf5 isn't anything to worry about (though I feel it's white's best chance), so I won't bring the possibility up again.

> **RULE**
>
> As with an isolated pawn, keeping the Queens on when facing a backward pawn tends to make the defense more difficult.

22.g3 Qg7 23.Qd2 Bxe4 24.Rxe4 Rfd8 25.Rf3 R8d7 26.Kg2 Bd8!

Diagram 231

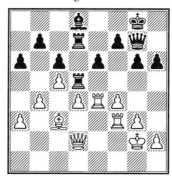

White to move

Black will bring everything possible to bear on the d4 target. Then he'll play a well-timed ...g6-g5 and create a new target. In general, a player can hold when only one point is being attacked. But if you add another weakness to his position then the added defensive burden proves to be too much.

27.Re5 Bf6 28.Rxd5 Rxd5 29.Rd3 Qf8 30.Qe2 Qd8 31.Qe4 Qd7 32.Rd2 Kf8 33.Qe3 Bg7 34.Kf1 g5!

Excellent! Black plays to create a second pawn weakness and/or weaken white's King a bit. White can, of course, chop on g5 (35.fxg5 hxg5) but then the typical isolated pawn "make use of the pin" idea is on the table—White would always have to make sure that ...e6-e5 doesn't do him in.

35.Qe4?

A serious mistake, after which white's position goes from "slightly worse and certainly miserable" to "on the verge of defeat." White should have calmly held on with 35.Kg1 or 35.fxg5.

35...gxf4 36.gxf4

36.Qxf4?? wasn't possible because of 36...Rf5.

36...Rf5?

Missing a tactical shot: 36...e5! wins a pawn since any capture on e5 allows 37...Qh3+, picking up the undefended White Bishop.

37.Ke2 Qd8 and white's position was extremely difficult. The rest of the game featured the black pieces slowly but surely making their way deeper and deeper into the enemy position: **38.Ke3 Qh4 39.Rf2 h5 40.Ke2 Qg4+ 41.Kd3 Bh6 42.Bd2 Qg1 43.Qf3 Qa1 44.Kc4 Bg7 45.Qc3 Qa2+ 46.Kd3 Qb1+ 47.Kc4 Qe4 48.Qe3 Qd5+ 49.Kc3 a5 50.Re2 a4 51.Kd3 Qb3+ 52.Ke4 Rd5 53.Qxb3 Rxd4+ 54. Ke3 axb3 55.Bc3 Rc4 56.Bxg7+ Kxg7 57.Rb2 Rc3+ 58.Kd4 Rc2 59.Rxb3 Rxh2 60.Ke5 Rd2 61.Rg3+ Kf8 62.Ke4 Ke7 63.f5 Re2+ 64.Kf3 Ra2 65.Ke4 Re2+ 66.Kf3 Rc2 67.Rg8 Rc3+ 68.Ke4 Rxa3 69.Rb8 Ra7 70.Ke5 exf5 71.Kxf5 Kd7 72.Rf8 Ra4 73.Rxf7+ Kc8 74.Rh7 Rxb4 75.Rxh5 Kb8 76.Ke5 Rg4 77.Rh8+ Ka7 78.Kd6 Ka6 79.Rh1 Kb5 80.Rb1+ Rb4 81.Rd1 Rb3 82.Rc1 Rh3 83.Rb1+ Kc4 84.Rxb7 Rh6+ 85.Ke5 Kxc5 86.Ke4 Kc4 87.Ke3 Kc3 88.Rc7 Re6+ 89.Kf4 Kc4 90.Kf5 Rh6 91.Ke4 c5 92.Ke3 Rd6 93.Ke2 Kb4 94.Rb7+ Kc3 95.Rb1 Kc2 96.Ra1 Re6+ 97.Kf3 c4,** 0-1.

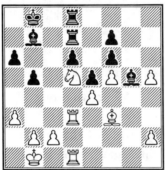

Diagram 232

Z. Andriasian - M. Erdogdu, Kalamaria 2008
White to move

White has a long list of favorable imbalances: He has more central and king-side space, his Knight is better than either enemy Bishop, black's f6-pawn is in need of constant defense, his backward pawn on d6 is under the gun from white's doubled Rooks, and last but certainly not least, he has an extra pawn (though the h5-pawn is a doubled h-pawn, Black must always be on his guard to prevent h5-h6 in a position where the Rooks are exchanged since then it will run for a touchdown).

However, as good as all that is, Black's still (barely) managing to hold things together. And this brings us back to a point I made in our last example, which alluded to the creation of a second weakness: In general, a player can hold when only one point is being attacked. But if you add another weakness to his position then the added defensive burden proves to be too much. This concept is often called *The Principle of Two Weaknesses*.

Clearly, I'm spurring White on to find a way to create one or more new targets in black's camp, which when added to all the rest of white's riches, should prove decisive.

1.a4!

Suddenly black's queenside structure will crumble and turn into targets. The immediate 1.Nb6 Re7 (and not 1...Rc7? 2.Rxd6) 2.a4 (and not 2.Rxd6?? Rxd6 3.Rxd6 Kc7, winning a piece) was also possible.

1...bxa4 2.Nb6 Re7 3.Nxa4

White had quite a few good moves here. Perhaps the best of the lot was 3.c4 Kc7 4.c5 Ree8 5.Rxd6 Rxd6 6.Rxd6 Rd8 7.h4! - Andriasian. White wins since 7...Bxh4 8.Rxd8 Kxd8 9.h6 promote the pawn, while 7...Bf4 allows 8.Rxf6.

3...d5 4.Nc5 d4 5.c3 Rc8 6.cxd4 exd4 7.Nxb7 Rxb7 8.Rxd4 Rb3

8...Rc3 9.Rd8+ Ka7 is possible, when 10.Bh1 Rcb3 11.e5 (bringing the h1-Bishop powerfully into the game) 11...Rxb2+ 12.Ka1 might be best, but most humans would avoid such a complicated line. Instead, simply 10.R8d3 would win in a far less stressful manner.

9.Be2

The advantages created by 1.a4 continue to show themselves. 9.Be2 targets a6 and prepares to bring the Bishop into active play via Bc4-d5.

9...Bf4

9...a5 seems a bit more resilient, though it also would lose to 10.Rd5 a4 11.Ra5 Rb4 12.Rb5+ Rxb5 13.Bxb5 Rh8 14.Be2 when threats such as 15.Rd7 and 15.Rd4 leave Black in a bad way.

After 9...Bf4, the rest of the game featured White training for a speed eating contest as he devoured one weak black pawn after another: **10.Bxa6 Rc6 11.Bc4 Rb4 12.Bxf7 Rc1+ 13.Rxc1 Rxd4 14.Rc4 Rd1+ 15.Ka2 Rd2 16.h3 Rh2 17.Rc3 Rf2 18.Bd5 Ka7**, 1-0.

Doubled Pawns

Most players have a mortal fear of acquiring doubled pawns. However, we'll see in Part Six, Statics vs. Dynamics that they also have their good points (i.e., added control of important squares and space gaining powers). Here we'll concentrate on doubled pawns that are indeed weak—targets to be surrounded and chewed on.

In general, doubled isolated pawns on an open file are every bit as weak as you might imagine them to be (Okay, there *are* quite a few exceptions where the doubled isolated lepers shine—those will also be explored in Part Six, Statics vs. Dynamics):

Diagram 233

The Turkey (1582) - computer, Internet 2008
Black to move

For a short time I taught a young man that only played computers online. He told me that his handle was an abomination of The Turk, a chess-playing automaton that wowed the world when it appeared in 1790.

In one lesson I extolled the virtues of the Maroczy Bind formation and he fell in love with it. Unfortunately his bind turned into a bust and he found himself with a horrible pawn structure and passive pieces. In such positions the superior side usually attacks the more advanced pawn simply because his pieces can reach it. Thus c4 is the target, while c3 is also being eyed by the g7-Bishop.

1...Ba6

Since c4 is the target, Black begins to pile on the pressure by bringing as many pieces as possible to bear on it.

2.f4

This just creates new problems (e4 is weakened), but White was in serious trouble in any case and one can understand his desire to be active.

2...Na5

Simply threatening to snap the c4-pawn off.

3.Rb4 Bh6

Not a "human" looking move, but white's opponent is not human! This powerful move pins the f4-pawn, ties the e3-Bishop down to its defense, and prepares to create new targets in white's camp if allowed.

4.g3 e5!

If you noticed that this creates a backward pawn on d6 and a huge hole on d5, then you deserve a lot of credit—you're training yourself to instantly spot weaknesses over the whole board! However, White's in such a defensive crouch that he's in no position to reach those potential targets. Aside from increasing the pressure against f4, the main purpose of the move is to open the e-file and begin a new attack against e4!

5.Rf1 Rfe8

Not subtle, but strong—it was only now that White realized that he faced some serious nastiness on the e-file.

6.Bd3

In a way this is almost funny—the poor light-squared Bishop is bravely trying to hold up white's whole position by getting off the dangerous e-file, protecting e4, and also protecting c4. Sadly, it's all for naught.

6...exf4 7.Bxf4

White didn't like the look of 7.gxf4, and it turns out that his position would resemble a bug splattered on the windshield of a fast moving car after 7...d5!! (8.e5 fails to 8...Nc6 9.Rbb1 Nxe5—too many weaknesses and too many undefended pieces).

7...Bxf4 8.gxf4 Nb7!

Diagram 234

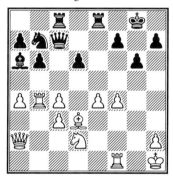

Wow! I didn't see that coming either! The Knight switches to c5 where it will pour pain on e4.

9.Qc2

9.Nb3 seems most natural, but then 9...Nc5 10.Nxc5 dxc5 11.Rb2 Rcd8 12.Bb1 and now a human would probably play 12...f5 (idea 13.exf5 Bb7+ 14.Kg1 Qc6) or 12...Bb7 and expect to win quickly, but my own inhuman helper is excited by 12...Qc6 with the single-minded idea of preying on the myriad weak pawns in white's camp (a4, c4, c3, e4, and f4) via ...f5 or ...Qf6 or ...Qe6 with the unstoppable threat of ...Bxc4.

9...Nc5 10.Kg1 Bb7 11.f5 Qe7 12.Rf3 Nxe4 13.Bxe4 Bxe4 14.Nxe4 Qxe4 15.Qxe4 Rxe4, 0-1. The c4-pawn is finally going to fall. An extremely impressive display of Target Consciousness! I think it's time for all of us to bow to our machine overlords.

Though doubled and/or isolated pawns are usually at their weakest on open files, they can also prove to be problematic even when the Rooks can't reach them.

A.H. Kennedy - E. Loewe, London 1849

1.d4 c6 2.c4 d6 3.e4 e6 4.Bd3 e5 5.d5 Ne7 6.f4 exf4 7.Bxf4 Ng6 8.Bg3 Be7 9.Nf3 Bf6 10.Nc3 Na6 11.Qe2 0–0 12.Rd1 Bg4 13.a3 Be5 14.Qf2 f6 15.Bb1 c5 16.Rd2 Bxc3 17.bxc3 Ne5 18.Qe2

Diagram 235

White's position is a seething wreck. His pieces aren't doing anything, his King is still in the center, his e-pawn is backward on an open file (and it kills its own light-squared Bishop), the c4-pawn is being eyed by the fine Knight on e5, and the pawns on a3 and c3 are both loose. A player schooled in the ways of Target Consciousness would be drooling at this point.

18...Qa5

Simple. The pawns on a3 and c3 are both threatened and material must be lost. Please remember that I realize 18...Qa5 is an obvious move. The move isn't the point here. What I'm after is you training your mind to quickly take note of all possible targets in any and every situation.

19.Rc2 Qxa3 20.0–0 Qa4

Having fed, Black decides to bring his Queen back to base camp before it gets trapped behind enemy lines. This is a very human and reasonable way to play, but a serious look might have convinced Black that his Queen wasn't in danger, which means he could seek more aggressive and productive ideas. This makes good sense here since white's pieces are still rather ineptly placed, black's Queen is still serving a function on a3 by tying white's guys down to the defense of c3, and it never hurts to have a material plus *and* the initiative to boot!

I would prefer 20...Nc7 (the Knight isn't doing anything on a6, so get the poor thing back in the game!) 21.h3 Bh5 (Tempting but wrong would be 21...Nf3+?? 22.gxf3 Bxh3 23.Re1 when d6 is weak and a tactical e4-e5, freeing the b1-Bishop, is also in the air. An example: 23...Ne8 [23...Rfd8 24.Qh2 hits both d6 and h3] 24.Qh2 Bd7 25.e5! dxe5 26.Ra2 Qxc3 27.Bxh7+ and White suddenly has dangerous counterplay) 22.Bh2 a6! when …b7-b5, taking control of the queenside, is suddenly "on." Black would then win most endgames due to his extra pawn, but he's also dominating the middlegame!

After **20…Qa4**, Black went on to win without too much muss or fuss: **21.Bxe5 fxe5 22.Rb2 Qd7 23.Qe3 Bxf3 24.Rxf3 Rxf3 25.gxf3 Rf8 26.Bd3 b6 27.Rg2 Rf4 28.Rg3 Nb8 29.Bf1 Qa4 30.Rg4 Rxg4+ 31.fxg4 Nd7 32.g5 Qd1 33.Qh3 Nf8 34.Kf2 Qd2+ 35.Be2 Qxg5 36.Bg4 Qf4+ 37.Kg1 Qxe4 38.Be6+ Kh8 39.Bf5 Qe1+ 40.Kg2 Qd2+ 41.Kh1 Qe1+ 42.Kg2 Qd2+ 43.Kf1 g6 44.Bd3 Kg7 45.Be2 Qf4+ 46.Ke1 h5 47.Qc8 Qf5 48.Qd8 Qf6 49.Qc8 e4 50.Qc7+ Kh6 51.Qxa7 Qxc3+ 52.Kf2 Qf6+ 53.Ke3 Qd4+ 54.Kf4 g5+ 55.Kg3 Qe3+ 56.Kg2 Qxe2+, 0-1.**

One problem with doubled isolated pawns, even if they aren't on an open file, is that the square in front of them is usually owned by the opponent.

N. Fullbrook - J. Silman, Pacific Southwest Open 1988

1.e4 c5 2.Nf3 Nc6 3.d4 cxd4 4.Nxd4 Nf6 5.Nc3 d6 6.Be3 Ng4 7.Bc4 Nxe3 8.fxe3 Ne5 9.Bb3 g6 10.0–0 Bg7 11.Nd5 0–0 12.Qe1 e6 13.Nf4 Qe7 14.Rd1 Bd7 15.h4 h5 16.c3

Diagram 236

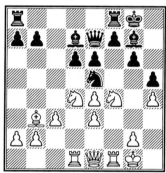

Black has a significant advantage—his Knight is happy on e5 and white's doubled isolated e-pawns can be nibbled on from the sides by moves such as …Ng4 and …Bc6. In other words, they are clearly a static disadvantage. What's even worse is that, while White has nothing on the kingside or in the center (d6 is easily defended, though white's pieces are too inflexible to even make a play for it), Black will take control of the queenside by advancing his a- and b-pawns. This means that Black is both statically and dynamically better.

16…b5 17.Qg3 a5 18.Rd2 a4 19.Bd1 a3

Nothing wrong with 19…Bf6, but I wanted to create another weakness in white's camp (c3) before doing it. The more weaknesses you give your opponent, the merrier the party will be.

20.Bxh5

Desperation. The more "reasonable" 20.b3 leaves c3 very weak (the Rooks will eventually move to the c-file and hunt it down) and also loses the h4-pawn to 20…Bf6.

20…gxh5

According to Rybka, even stronger is 20…Nc4 21.Rdf2 axb2 22.Bxg6 Rxa2. I have no doubt that its right, but I can't criticize myself for gobbling up a free piece!

21.Nxh5 f6 22.b3 Kh7 and White didn't have anywhere near enough compensation for the sacrificed piece. The rest wasn't that difficult: **23.Nf3 Bh6 24.Nf4 Rg8 25.Qh3 Ng4 26.Nd4 Nxe3 27.Qxe3 e5 28.Nf5 Bxf5 29.exf5 Qc7 30.Qe2 Bxf4 31.Qh5+ Bh6 32.g4 Rxg4+ 33.Kh2 Rag8 34.Rf3 Qg7 35.Rxd6 Rg2+ 36.Kh3 Qg3+ 37.Rxg3 R8xg3** mate.

The Irish Pawn Center

English players appear to call tripled pawns the *Irish Pawn Center*. I'm not sure why, though perhaps they are trying to give their Irish "buddies" a jab for fun. For all I know, the Irish call the same center the *English Pawn Center*. Either way, it's more colorful than *Tripled Pawns*.

Having trips is rarely a positive thing. However, as is usual with all weak pawns, squares are controlled and dynamic compensation can, on occasion, be found.

Here we'll address not the "pile up on the poor trips and win them" ideal (it's the same idea that we've seen with other kinds of weak pawns), but another, more subtle, advantage that the Irish Pawn Center bestows on the opponent.

Diagram 237

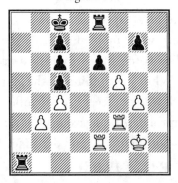

N. Short - I. Sokolov, Wijk aan Zee 2005
White to move

Black's a pawn up but e6 is about to fall, which will create material equality. But is the material (after White takes on e6) *really* equal? It should be obvious that one can attack trips in various ways and demonstrate their vulnerability. But another problem with trips (and it's a big one!) is that a single enemy pawn can freeze the whole Irish Center!

In diagram 237 we see white's two queenside pawns firmly holding black's three in place. Even if the b3-pawn is captured (as eventually occurred in the actual game), the lone c4-pawn keeps the Irish Center in thrall.

1.fxe6 Rd1 2.Rf7 Rd6 3.Rxg7 Rdxe6 4.Rxe6 Rxe6 5.Rf7

So far the play has been pretty straightforward. White intends to get his King into the action so it can help run his g-pawn to g8. Black's pawns (all three of them) don't have any impact at all on the subsequent play.

Note that 5.Rf7 does two things: 1) It stops Black from winning the b3-pawn since 5…Re3 can now be met by 6.Rf3; 2) It will turn the f-file into an impassable barrier for black's King. Thus, the Black monarch won't be able to help fend off the g-pawn's transition to royalty.

5…Kd8 6.Kg3 Re1 7.g5 Rg1+ 8.Kh4 Rh1+ 9.Kg4 Rg1+ 10.Kf5 Rg3 11.g6 Rf3+ 12.Ke6 Re3+ 13.Kf6 Rf3+ 14.Kg7 Rxb3

Black's now a pawn up and even has a 3 to 1 pawn majority on the queenside. As was mentioned earlier though, white's one pawn completely freezes black's three pawns.

Diagram 238

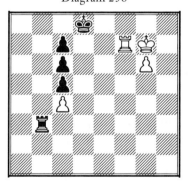

One pawn kills three

15.Kf8 Re3 16.Rf4

No quick moves allowed! It's still not too late to botch it by excitedly pushing the g-pawn, only to discover that you've made a "slight" oversight: 16.g7?? Re8 mate!

After 16.Rf4 Black resigned.

Summary

> How to battle an isolated d-pawn:

○ Trade off all the minor pieces. In many situations an isolated pawn can claim active minor pieces as compensation. However, if all the minor pieces are exchanged then that kind of compensation would be impossible and the pawn would be relegated to a pure weakness.

○ Play for a Queen and Rook vs. Queen and Rook situation (even better than a Queen and two Rooks, which gives the defender a bit more potential for counterplay) since the presence of Queens makes it far too dangerous for the defender's King to come forward and join in the defense of the pawn.

○ A dream setup (with Q and R vs. Q and R): The Rook blocks the isolated d-pawn (stopping it from advancing), and the Queen is behind it.

> Our anti-isolated d-pawn rules also apply to other types of isolated pawns.

> The backward pawn shares many of the same shortcomings as the isolated pawn, and several of the anti-isolated pawn ideas also apply to this weak little critter. Of course, the superior side needs to make sure the backward pawn remains backward, but once this is done then we see old friends like "trade the minor pieces" and "pile up with the Rooks and Queen" rear their effective heads.

> In general, doubled isolated pawns on an open file are usually every bit as weak as you might imagine them to be.

> It should be obvious that one can attack tripled pawns in various ways and demonstrate their vulnerability. But another problem with trips (and it's a big one!) is that a single enemy pawn can freeze all three enemy pawns!

> If you have the luxury of endless time, then creating optimal King safety is always a good idea.

> In general, a player can hold when only one weakness is being attacked. But if you add another weakness to his position,

then the added defensive burden proves to be too much. This concept is often called *The Principle of Two Weaknesses*.

The more weaknesses you give your opponent, the merrier the party will be.

Weak Squares

The idea of a weak square is, for some, an extremely hard concept to fully grasp. While hunting down a weak pawn makes sense in that you can capture it and remove it from the board, a square always remains where it started—it can't be taken, it can't be placed in a box, and it's not something that initially belongs to either player.

One way to look at a weak square is as real estate—you lay claim to it by superior force (money in regard to real estate) and then move one of your guys "in", thus treating it as a home for a Knight or some other piece. Ideally, this "home" will reside close to or inside enemy territory, thus making your piece difficult to dislodge or remove and, as a result, extremely powerful. This kind of weak square is usually (but not always) "claimed" by one of your own pawns, can't be protected by the defender's pawns and, more often than not, is referred to as a "hole."

Diagram 239

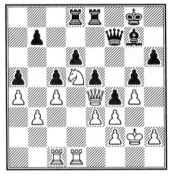

White to move
Find the holes

Aside from the fact that d6-pawn is a weak backward pawn on an open file, there are also a plethora of holes in the position: b6, b5, b4, d5, e4, f5, h5, and h4. Note that d4 isn't a hole because white's pawn on e3 is protecting it (I should add that Black can't reach it with a piece in any case). The listed squares, though, are the ones that completely fit our "hole" criteria:

➤ Though b4 is a hole in white's camp, Black has no way to make use of it. On the other hand, the b5-square/hole fits in nicely with white's designs against the weak pawn on d6—a timely Nd5-c3-b5 followed by doubling or tripling on the d-file will exert maximum pressure against black's poor backward pawn.

➤ The d5-hole has already been claimed by white's Knight, but the Knight is actually blocking its own Rooks' access to d6. Though strong on d5, it would be better served on the e4- and/or f5-holes (or b5, as mentioned in the previous paragraph) where it would join in the battle against d6. The e4-hole is easy to access via Nd5-c3-e4 (once the Queen moves away), but the holes on f5 and h5 are extremely difficult for the horse to reach (black's pawn on f4 keeps the Knight out of its jump-squares on e3 and g3). Thus, though there are quite a few holes, the only ones that can really make a difference in white's plans against d6 are b5 and e4, while the d5-hole might turn into a home for a white Rook.

➤ The b6-square is weak, but it doesn't have anything to do with white's general plan of pressuring the d6-pawn. Just because a piece can live on an advanced square doesn't mean that it should.

Let me stress a point that has been repeatedly made throughout the book: Placing a piece on a square where it doesn't work with the rest of its army is rarely a good idea. Chess is a team game and you want as many pieces as possible to work towards the same goal!

A possible sequence from diagram 239 is: **1.Nc3** (1.Rh1 followed by h4 is another strong idea, but let's keep things simple and within our basic theme) **1...Re6** (Better is the passive 1...Bf8 followed by holding on like grim death as White builds up his army against d6) **2.Rd5 Rf8** (Dreaming of counterplay down the f-file) **3.Rcd1 Qe7 4.Qd3 fxe3 5.fxe3 Qf7 6.Rf1 Rf6 7.Qd1** and the threat of Ne4 is devastating.

Now let's look at a position that seems similar, but is actually a totally different animal.

Diagram 240

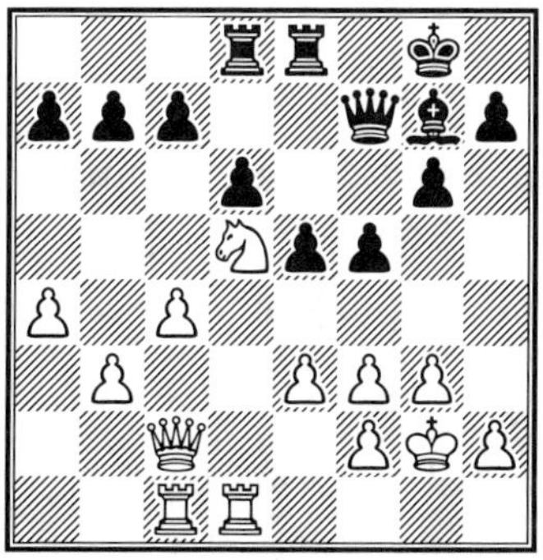

Black to move

All the holes that were so graphically displayed in diagram 239 no longer exist! The b5- and d5-squares can both be made inaccessible to white's pieces by …c7-c6, e4 is now defended by the f5-pawn, and the f5- and h5-squares are firmly defended by the g6-pawn. After **1…e4 2.f4 c6 3.Nc3 Rd7** followed by …Red8, Black is for choice due to his strong Bishop, the fact that white's Knight no longer has any advanced squares to enjoy, and his mobile center which can kick into action at some point via …d6-d5.

More often than not, experienced opponents won't knowingly create a hole in their own position without good reason. Nevertheless, holes *are* often handed to you on a silver platter, but you can only get mileage out of such mistakes if you notice how to create them and make use of the opportunity presented.

Diagram 241

K. Kuenitz (1730) - B. Buggs (1632), Las Vegas 2008
Black to move

White has the better position and Black, an attacking player, decided that, "Enough is enough! It's time to get something going."

1…e5

The best move, and the follow-up presents us with a clear look at the sorry state of amateur square awareness.

2.e4?

A serious mistake that throws away his advantage and hands it to Black! He should have played 2.dxe6 e.p. (creating a hole on d5!) 2…Bxe6 3.e4 (3.Bf2!?) 3…fxe4 (3…Nh6 4.Bf2) 4.Bxe4 and White retains a plus.

2…exf4!

The refutation. In the actual game Black played 2…Nh6? 3.Nf3 Bd7 4.fxe5 dxe5 5.Bf2 Qc8 and now 6.Qb3! (6.Rab1 followed by b2-b4 is also strong) followed by Qa3, piling on the pressure against c5, would have given White a huge advantage.

3.Bxf4 g5! 4.Be3 f4 5.Bf2 Ne5 and Black has suddenly transformed the position and now has a lovely game! His kingside pawn majority promises him good chances against white's King, and the hole on e5 is a marvelous home for black's Knight, which rules the board from its new central perch.

If that seemed a bit complicated for some, let's demonstrate the old "I'm going to make that square mine" mentality with a simpler example.

Diagram 242

Black to move

White's Bishop is a very poor piece, but black's Knight doesn't seem to have an impressive home and f3-f4 might give White a little something on the king-side. However, once you fully embrace your "inner square," the right move will instantly pop into your head.

1...b4!

You guys that live by the "Attack his King or live in shame!" credo and who want to play 1...f5 here, should study this position carefully. After 1...f5 2.f4 black's King has been weakened and, more importantly, the Tall-Pawn on g2 will suddenly leap into action along the soon-to-be-opened h1-a8 diagonal.

> **PHILOSOPHY**
> Fully embrace your "inner square."

2.f4

This move has its problems, but it's the only way to get counterplay (you can't just sit around and wait to die). Even worse is 2.cxb4 Nxb4 3.Qc3 Ra2 when 4.f4 exf4 5.Rxf4 fails to 5...Nd5! 6.exd5 Qe2 and White has to give up.

2...bxc3 3.Qxc3

3.Rf2 exf4 4.gxf4 (4.Rxf4 Nd4 wins since 5.Qxc3 loses immediately to 5...Ne2+) 4...Qxh4 is obviously horrible for White.

3...Ra2 4.fxe5 Qxe5

Diagram 243

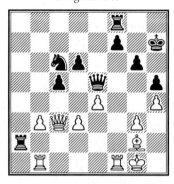

Just four moves after our initial diagram and things have radically changed. Now Black not only has a Rook on the seventh rank, but he is also master of the b4-, d4-, and e5-squares. Combine all that with the awful thing on g2 and it's clear that white's strategically lost.

5.Qc4 Kg7 6.b4 Re2 7.Rf4

And not 7.bxc5?? Qxg3.

7...Nd4 8.Rbf1

Still hoping to stir the pot and create some tactical chances. Simply bad is 8.bxc5 Rc2 9.Qa4 Ne2+ 10.Kh2 Rd2 and the dual threat of 11...Nxf4 and 11...Nc3 wins material and the game.

8...Ne6 9.R4f3 Qb2 10.R3f2 Rxf2 11.Rxf2 Qxb4 12.Qa2 Qd4 13.Bf1 Qe5 14.Kg2 Nd4 and Black is a pawn up and can also claim a far superior minor piece.

Are you getting a feel for this? Do you think you can begin creating weak squares in the enemy camp? If so, you're ready to go a step further—let's take diagram 242 and make a "slight" adjustment.

Diagram 244

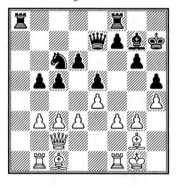

Black to move

I've added a pair of dark-squared Bishops. This means that White can now exchange his dark-squared Bishop for a black Knight once the d4-square is cleared away by ...b5-b4. One should also note that black's Bishop isn't particularly active. Since Black still wants to dominate d4 and should still be dreaming of creating a superior minor piece, the following move makes a lot of sense:

1...Bh6!

There's nothing wrong with the thematic 1...b4, but playing a move like 1...Bh6 shows that you've learned your minor piece lessons (from Part Two) very well. Black offers an exchange of Bishops which would once again lead to a monster Knight (after a subsequent ...b5-b4) vs. a terrible light-squared Bishop situation. It also tries to turn the inactive g7-Bishop into an active participant in the strategic battle that follows.

2.f4

2.Bxh6 Kxh6 3.f4 b4 4.f5 bxc3 5.Qxc3 and now Black can double Rooks on the b-file with 5...Rfb8 followed by 6...Ra8-a7-b7, or give 5...Qf6 a go (we'll discuss the ideas behind this move in our main line). In both cases Black will have all the chances thanks to his superior pawn structure (b3 and d3 are both weak) and far superior minor piece. These favorable imbalances will shine in both the middlegame and the endgame.

Note that 2.Bb2 leaves Black completely in charge after 2...Be3+ 3.Kh2 b4 4.c4 Ra2.

2...b4

Back to our main theme—the creation of holes on b4 and d4!

3.f5 Bxc1 4.Qxc1 bxc3 5.Qxc3 Qf6

An ugly move that's designed to block the f5-pawn's advance to f6 while also preparing to get something started on the g-file.

6.Qd2

6.Qc4 g5! is strong for Black.

6...Rg8 7.fxg6+ Qxg6 8.Qf2

No better is 8.Rf5 Nd4 9.Rg5 Qh6.

8...Qxg3 9.Qxf7+

9.Qxg3 Rxg3 10.Rxf7+ Rg7 offers White a very gloomy endgame.

9...Rg7 10.Qxh5+ Kg8 11.Qf3 Qxh4 and White will be under pressure for a long time to come.

There are many instances where a square isn't weak in the normal sense, but it can still be isolated from the rest of its army and/or claimed by the enemy via the creation of an artificial support point.

Diagram 245

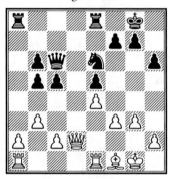

NN (1879) - NN (2118), Los Angeles 2008
Black to move

The d4-square would be a great home for black's Knight if it could stay there. But White appears to have his house in order due to the possibility of making d4 hostile to black's pieces via c2-c3. Thus, at the moment d4 doesn't earn our "hole" label. However, there's more regarding the d4-square than meets the eye.

Other factors in the position: the a2-pawn is vulnerable, the open d-file has yet to be claimed, and a minor piece battle is under way.

1...Nd4

Placing the Knight on a great square and threatening ...Nxf3+. 1...b4 was also good for Black, but why give white's Bishop instant access to c4?

2.Qf2 b4!

"Winning" the d4-square! By stopping c2-c3, Black creates an artificial support point on d4. He also fixes the a2-pawn and turns it into an immobile target.

2...Qf6 3.Kg2 b4 4.Bc4 Red8 5.a4 bxa3 e.p. 6.c3 b5 7.Bd5 Rxd5 8.exd5 Nxb3 9.Ra2 Qd6 10.Rd1 Nd4!! 11.cxd4 exd4 12.Rda1 b4 is a whole other world—though Black is a Rook down, his armada of pawns leave White in serious trouble! This variation is rather fanciful, though, and black's logical choice (2...b4) shows a solid grasp of the position's needs.

3.Bc4

The Bishop's not so bad either, thanks to black's 2...b4. However, as Fischer once said, "You've gotta give squares to get squares." In the present case, the powerful d4-Knight is far superior to the light-squared Bishop.

3...Ra3

Diagram 246

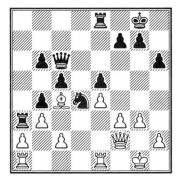

Black continues to demonstrate his understanding of Target Consciousness. He sees that a2 is weak, so he first freezes it in place (known as "fixing a weakness") by making use of the hole on a3, and then he'll prepare to crank up the pressure against a2.

4.Bd5 Qc7 5.Rec1

The idea of 5.Rec1 is to guard the a-pawn laterally by c2-c3. However, the super Knight and the pressure against a2 promises Black a huge strategic advantage. This means that quiet, static play by White will likely prove insufficient. Be it good or bad, I would have tried 5.f4, striving to get counterplay on the kingside.

5...Qa7 6.c3 bxc3 7.Rxc3 Qa5 8.Rcc1 Re7

Admirable singleness of purpose! He intends to bring all the major pieces to the a-file and break the a2-pawn.

9.f4?

Understandable but too late. The passive 9.Rcb1 Ra7 (9...Qc3!?) 10.Rb2 is a tougher defense, though Black retains an obvious advantage.

9...exf4 10.gxf4 Ra7 and a2 fell. Black went on the win the game.

Of course, a weak square isn't just an ideal home for a Knight, other pieces can also find that they are wonderfully placed there.

Diagram 247

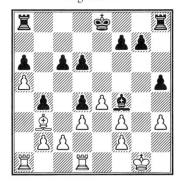

G. Kijk - G. Kaidanov, Norilsk 1987

Black to move

Where is the Black King's best square? The f3-pawn, being doubled, is obviously weak but one might think it's safe enough since it's so deep in white's position while black's Bishop is a dark-squared piece and thus can't attack it. However, f4 would be a lovely square for the King since it's not only advanced but also bashing f3. Thus Black plays to get his King there.

1...Ke7 2.Ra4 Rhb8 3.Bc4 Kf6 4.Kf1 Ra7 5.Re1 Bh6 6.Ke2 Ke5 7.Kf1 Kf4

Diagram 248

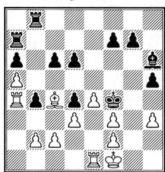

There's little doubt as to which King is the powerhouse and which is the goat. Sometimes a single square, and the desire to reach that square, is all it takes to turn things in your favor.

8.Ke2 Re7! 9.Kf1??

9.Bxa6?? d5 traps the Bishop, but 9.Rg1 d5 10.Bb3 is a better defense, the idea being that 10...f5?? allows 11.Rg6 when White is suddenly doing well. However, instead of blundering by 10...f5, simply 10...Rb5 keeps up the pressure and assures an enduring plus.

9...Kxf3 10.Bxa6 d5 11.exd5 Rxe1+ 12.Kxe1 Re8+ 13.Kf1 Re2 14.Ra1 Rxf2+ 15.Kg1 Rg2+ 16.Kh1 Be3, 0-1 since ...Kg3 followed by ...Rh2 mate is impossible to meet.

Finally, it's not at all uncommon to see positional sacrifices designed to gain control over a complex of squares on a file or diagonal, or a sacrifice that allows the attacker to gain access to a single but very important square.

J. Silman - V. McCambridge, San Francisco 1982

1.d4 Nf6 2.c4 c5 3.d5 e6 4.Nc3 exd5 5.cxd5 d6 6.e4 g6 7.Bf4 a6 8.Nf3 b5 9.Qe2 Nh5 10.Bg5 f6 11.Be3 Bg4 12.h3 Bxf3 13.Qxf3 Nd7 14.g4 Ng7 15.Qg3 Qe7 16.Bg2 0-0-0 17.0-0

White has come out of the opening with an enormous advantage.

17...h5

Diagram 249

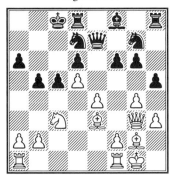

White to move

White enjoys two Bishops and more central space. On top of that, black's pieces aren't well placed, and his King isn't safe on the queenside.

18.b4!

This nice move not only strives to open up black's King, it also aims to take possession of a number of enemy holes. If the c5-pawn captures or moves forward, white's Knight will suddenly have access to the hole on d4. From there, the Knight would eye the deeper holes on c6 and e6.

18...h4

Taking on b4 opens the c-file for white's Rooks and also gives the White Knight access to the d4-square (and from there, c6) after 19.Ne2.

19.Qf3 cxb4 20.Nb1

Heading for d2 and b3, where it will gain access to both a5 and d4.

20...Ne5 21.Qe2 Ne8 22.Bb6 Rd7 23.Nd2 f5 24.f4 Nf7 25.Nb3 Bg7 26.e5!

Diagram 250

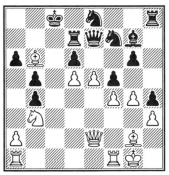

Another nice pawn sacrifice that gives white's Knight access to the c5-square, while also ripping open the g2-Bishop's path along the h1-a8 diagonal.

26...dxe5 27.Rac1+ Nc7 28.Nc5 exf4 29.Qf2 Rxd5 30.Nxa6 Bc3 31.Nxc7 Rd2 32.Qxd2 Bxd2 33.Nd5+ Bxc1 34.Nxe7+, 1-0.

Summary

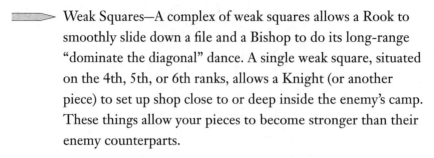 Weak Squares—A complex of weak squares allows a Rook to smoothly slide down a file and a Bishop to do its long-range "dominate the diagonal" dance. A single weak square, situated on the 4th, 5th, or 6th ranks, allows a Knight (or another piece) to set up shop close to or deep inside the enemy's camp. These things allow your pieces to become stronger than their enemy counterparts.

At times a square isn't weak in the normal sense, but it can still be isolated from the rest of its army and/or claimed by the enemy by the creation of an artificial support point.

Let me stress a point that has been repeatedly made throughout the book: Placing a piece on a square where it doesn't work with the rest of its army is rarely a good idea. Chess is a team game and you want as many pieces as possible to work towards the same goal!

Dragging Down the Central Enemy King!

For most amateurs, the enemy King is the main target from the first move onwards. However, viewing chess in that way puts blinders over your eyes that not only hampers you from fully embracing new skills and ideas, but also prevents you from appreciating all the subtle, often extremely beautiful, plans and/or strategies in master chess that often have absolutely nothing to do with an attack against the opposing King.

So far we've seen a quite a few compelling examples of this positional approach in our study of Target Consciousness (squares and weak pawns), and that same strategic view (imbalances) is more or less the subject of this whole book. But now we're going to address when a player *must* push positional niceties out the window and go after the King. It's important to take note of the word "must." By "must," I mean that the imbalances are demanding (or perhaps begging, if you rarely obey the imbalances' voice) that you take this particular course. Thus we won't be exploring gambit openings that lead to kingside attacks. Nor will we be studying how to slowly but surely build up for a kingside or queenside assault (countless other books cover "attacking the King" very well). Instead, we'll look at the single most common example (in amateur chess) of a King begging to die: the uncastled, central King.

Though there are other "must attack" cases, I'm going to concentrate on this one because it's my experience that amateurs tend to leave their King in the center far too long. I see it all the time in scholastic events, and even players as high as 2000 often "forget" to castle. One gentleman I taught with a 1400 rating simply refused to castle, saying that he was sure his castled King would be surrounded in a corner and mated. So he kept his King in the middle and, predictably, got mated there in game after game.

Our basic thesis is this: If your King is safely castled while the opponent's is in the middle of the board, I want you to train your mind to view that central King as a target, and immediately try and ascertain whether there's a way to smite it. At the very least, active play in the center while the enemy's monarch resides there will allow you to make some important gains as he scrambles to get his King to safety.

Here are a few short games by the author that should serve as a warning to those that put off castling, while also showing what one should do if the opponent keeps his King in the center for too long.

J. Silman - Villero, Los Angeles 1990

1.d4 e6 2.c4 Nf6 3.Nc3 Bb4 4.Qc2 b6 5.e4 Bb7 6.Bd3 d5 7.cxd5 exd5 8.e5 Ne4 9.Ne2 Nd7 10.0–0 Bxc3 11.bxc3 Ng5

Diagram 251

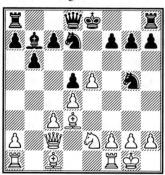

Black, a victim of a botched opening, is already lost: his pieces are inactive, White possesses a huge space advantage in the center, and (I'm sure you were waiting for this!) black's King is still sitting in the middle as if nothing bad could possibly happen to it.

12.Ng3 h5

Black doesn't realize that he can't win a battle if his King is hanging out to dry while white's is safely out of the line of fire on the kingside. Other things being equal, the side with the vulnerable King will always come in second in a head to head clash.

Unfortunately for Black, 12...0–0 13.Bxg5 Qxg5 14.Bxh7+ Kh8 15.f4 is also absolutely awful for him.

13.f4 Ne6

Other moves are also painful:

➤ 13...h4 14.Nf5 Ne6 15.Ba3 (Trapping black's King in the center!) 15...g6 16.Ne3 h3 17.g3 g5 18.f5 Nf4 19.Ng4 (White could take on f4, but 19.Ng4 is far stronger and gives Black no counterplay at all) 19...Nxd3 20.Qxd3 c5 21.e6 Nf6 22.Bxc5!! bxc5 (and not 22...Nxg4 23.Qb5+, mating) 23.Qb5+ Kf8 24.Qxb7 and Black should resign. However, if he likes pain then the following continuation would suit the situation: 24...Qe7 25.Qxa8+ Kg7 26.Qxh8+ (not necessary, but it's clean and easy) 26...Kxh8 27.Nxf6 Qxf6 28.Rae1 Qe7 29.f6 Qf8 30.e7, etc.

➤ 13...Ne4 14.Nxe4 dxe4 15.Bxe4 Bxe4 16.Qxe4 with an extra pawn and an overwhelming position.

14.f5

A classic Pawn Cascade. White's central/kingside pawn majority sweeps everything in its path away.

14...Nef8 15.Qe2

White is dying to crack open some files and diagonals so he can roast the enemy King. 15.Qe2 prepares e5-e6 while also watching the h5-square (it allows him to meet 15...h4 with the very strong 16.Nh5).

15...Qe7

Black dreams of being able to castle queenside. But White has no intention of allowing this to happen!

16.f6!

The storm breaks, white's pieces stream into the enemy position, and the game ends in a river of blood.

16...gxf6 17.Nf5 Qd8

Unfortunate, but 17...Qe6 18.Ng7+ picks up the Queen.

18.Ng7+, 1-0. Not a moment too soon! This way he avoids the humiliation of 18...Ke7 19.exf6+ Kd6 20.Nf5+ Kc6 21.Bb5 mate.

J. Silman - D. Baran (1950), S. California 1994

1.d4 Nf6 2.c4 e5 3.dxe5 Ng4 4.Bf4 g5 5.Bd2 Bg7 6.Nf3 h6? 7.h4 Nxe5 8.Nxe5 Bxe5

Diagram 252

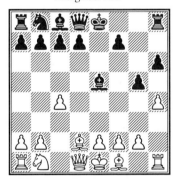

Both Kings are in the center, but while white's King is safely tucked behind its pawns, black's is wide open and, as a result, targeted for death.

9.hxg5 Bxb2?

An act of greed that is far more than his position can handle. He had to try 9...hxg5 10.Rxh8+ Bxh8 11.Qc1! when White is clearly better, but Black can still play a game.

10.Nc3 Bxa1 11.Qxa1

The poor Black King almost looks abandoned! It's now clear that black's dark-squared Bishop was far more important than white's Rook – it was the defender of the dark squares and now, with it gone, the a1-h8 diagonal will act as a road for white's Queen which can leap right into the heart of the enemy position.

11...h5?

Black was horrified by his position and tossed out this feeble move, but he had already fallen off the cliff and nothing would have saved him.

12.Nd5 Rf8 13.Qe5+, 1-0. The King was born on e8 and it died there without ever moving.

H. Lefevre - J. Silman, U.S. Amateur Team West 1990
1.e4 c5 2.b4 cxb4 3.a3 d5 4.exd5 Qxd5 5.Nf3 Bg4 6.axb4 Nc6 7.c3 e5 8.Be2 Bd6 9.Na3 e4 10.Bc4 Qh5 11.Qe2 Nf6 12.Qe3 0–0 13.Nd4

Diagram 253

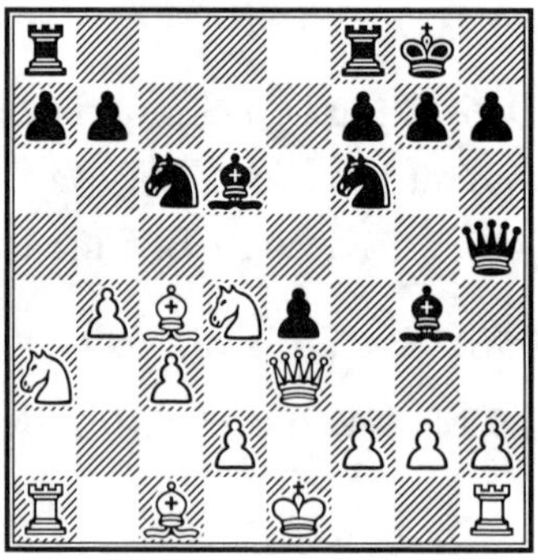

Black to move

The position is a disaster for White – he's way behind in development, black's King is safely tucked away on g8, and white's King is sitting in the middle, uncastled and forlorn. By now the reader should know the drill: 1) Seeing that the enemy King has stayed in the center for too long, immediately get excited and target it for destruction; 2) Don't allow him to castle to safety; 3) Bring as many pieces to the embattled area as possible and prepare some form of decisive penetration; 4) Rip open some lines and go for the throat!

All of this starts with a simple act of recognition: you train yourself to see red when the enemy King is in the middle, you label it as a target, and then you play with as much energy as possible to take advantage of the situation.

13...Ne5

The Knight takes up a strong post and prepares a decisive blow.

14.Be2

It's too late to castle: 14.0-0 Nf3+ 15.Nxf3 Bxf3 (threatening mate on h2) 16.h3 Qg6 (threatening mate on g2) 17.g4 (17.g3 Bxg3) 17...Nxg4 when White will soon be mated.

14...Nd3+!

Opening a center file right to white's King.

15.Bxd3 exd3 16.Qxd3 Rfe8+ 17.Kf1 Bf5!

Any capture on f5 allows 18...Qd1 mate.

18.Qf3 Bd3+, 0-1. Both 19.Qxd3 Qd1 and 19.Kg1 Re1 are mate.

Of course, a central King isn't always a death sentence. For example, if the center is closed, then a longer than usual stay in the middle might be acceptable since the enemy pieces can't get into the offending position. And, at times, players of all levels (even grandmasters) will temporarily put off castling since they feel they can make serious gains with other moves. Sometimes this works, and sometimes the sky falls on their head. Either way, a player who has cultivated Target Consciousness will instantly be aware of the situation and will look hard for a way to punish his opponent's concept. If you can't punish it, then the opponent's idea is playable and you just go ahead with the game in a normal fashion. However, often you *can* punish the central King, and when the King hunt starts, the fun begins.

J. Silman - R. Berube (2260), World Open 1991

1.d4 Nf6 2.c4 e6 3.Nc3 Bb4 4.Qc2 c5 5.dxc5 Nc6 6.Nf3 Bxc5 7.Bg5 Be7 8.e4 Qa5 9.Bd2 Qc7 10.h3 a6 11.Be2 Ne5?

Black was a little worse, but this loses too much time.

12.Nxe5 Qxe5 13.f4 Qd4 14.e5 Ng8 15.0–0–0

Diagram 254

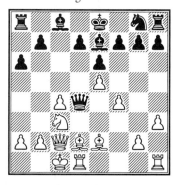

Black to move

White's King is safe and black's is in the center. On top of that, White has a large lead in development and black's Queen is in a vulnerable position. If this kind of position doesn't make you want to claim a pound of your opponent's flesh, then nothing will.

15...f6 16.Kb1 fxe5 17.Bh5+ g6

17...Kf8 18.Ne4 gives White a winning attack.

18.Bxg6+! hxg6 19.Qxg6+ Kd8 20.Nd5!

The point of white's combination – the threat of Ba5+ is decisive.

20...Qxd2

20...Qc5 21.Be3 was also game ending.

21.Rxd2 exd5 22.fxe5 d6 23.Qg7

Black has managed to stave off mate, but the price is a hopeless material disadvantage. Black only lasted a few more moves: **23...Bf5+ 24.Ka1 Kd7 25.Qxh8 Bg6 26.Qg7**, 1-0.

It's clear that going after a central King can pay dividends, but at times the correct path isn't to sound an immediate charge, but to make sure the King remains in the center for as long as possible. The following example is a case in point.

Ed. Lasker - F. Englund, Scheveningen 1913

1.e4 e5 2.Nf3 Nc6 3.Nc3 Nf6 4.Bb5 Nd4 5.Nxe5 Qe7 6.Nf3 Nxe4 7.0–0 Nxc3 8.dxc3 Nxf3+ 9.Qxf3 Qc5 10.Re1+ Be7 11.Bd3

Diagram 255

Black to move

Black is behind in development and his King is in the center. He might be okay if he could castle, but that will prove harder to do than one might imagine. In the present position, 11...0-0 loses a whole piece to 12.Qe4 threatening mate on h7 and Qxe7.

11...d5

On 11...d6, hoping to play ...Be6 and then ...0-0 or ...0-0-0, the simple 12.Qg3 will prove annoying – since black's Queen no longer defends its Bishop, 12...0-0 isn't possible due to 13.Rxe7.

Even stronger than 12.Qg3 is the far more exciting 12.Bh6! gxh6 13.Qf6 0-0 14.Rxe7 and though Black has managed to castle, he's paid too high a price for the privilege.

12.Be3 Qd6

Or 12...Qc6 13.Bd4 Be6 (13...f6 14.Qe3 is really bad!) 14.Bxg7 Rg8 15.Bf6 Bxf6 16.Qxf6 and Black is a pawn down and he *still* can't castle!

13.Bf4 Qf6

13...Qd8 14.Qg3 0-0 15.Bxc7 Qd7 16.Be5 leaves White with an extra pawn and a positional advantage, while 13...Qd7 fails to 14.Qe3 (14.Qh5) 14...Qe6 (14...Qd8 15.Qg3) 15.Qg3 Qf6 16.Bg5 and it's over.

14.Qxd5?!

White gets carried away with dreams of pretty mates. Better was 14.Qe3 Be6 15.Be5 Qh4 16.Bxg7 Rg8 17.Be5 with a very bad position for Black, who is a pawn down and can't castle due to Qxa7.

14...c6?

Missing his chance. He had to try 14...Qxf4 15.Bb5+ c6 (White was clearly smacking his lips at the thought of 15...Kf8?? 16.Qd8+ Bxd8 17.Re8 mate) 16.Bxc6+ bxc6 17.Qxc6+ Kf8 18.Qxa8 Qc7 19.Re4 g6 20.Rae1 Bd8 21.Re8+ Kg7 22.Rxh8 Kxh8 23.Re8+ Kg7 24.Qe4 when White is better, but Black can still put up a long, hard fight.

15.Qe4 Be6 16.Re3

Diagram 256

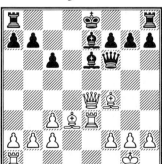

Black's King is still in the center!

There are several more accurate ways to play – 16.Be5 Qg5 17.f4 is one, 16.g3 0-0-0 17.Ba6! is another, and 16.Rad1 is a logical third. However, 16.Re3 isn't bad, and as we'll see, White is once again dreaming of a particular finish, and this time his wish will come true.

16...Bc5

16...0-0-0 17.Ba6! is also quite unpleasant for Black.

17.Be5 Qh6 18.Rg3 Bf8 19.Rd1

Setting up a famous mate. Will Black see it?

19...0–0–0?

Black finally castles, only to be instantly buried. He was lost in any case.

20.Qxc6+! bxc6 21.Ba6 mate.

This example once again confirmed that, while mate is the ideal way to punish a central King, it's usually not so easy to achieve if good defensive skills are demonstrated. However, the attacker is quite happy with any number of concessions (i.e., material or positional advantage) as the defender struggles to get his King to safety.

I'll finish our theoretical discussion of "The central King as a Target" by sharing a tale about Micky Mills, a class "C" player (1500) who, way back in 1974, had a very poor grasp of attacking fundamentals. I was his teacher and, seeing this flaw, recommended that he read *The Art of Attack* by Vukovic.

Some months after my recommendation, Mills was playing in an open tournament (players of every rating were mixed together) that happened to have a brilliancy prize. There were quite a few strong players, including the U.S. Champion John Grefe and many time U.S. Champion Walter Browne, so everyone expected one of the "big guns" to pick up that cash bonus.

Mills was not doing particularly well in the event, and was paired with another "C" player. Nobody paid much attention to the game, but after I got home (with Mills, two Senior Masters [2400], and John Grefe in tow) Micky squealed, "Look at my game! Look at my game! I've played a brilliancy!"

I'm not proud of this, but I have to admit that we all burst into laughter. "Okay," we said in our most sarcastic tone, "show it to us!"

R. Catig (1500) - M. Mills (1500), San Francisco 1974

1.e4 c5 2.Nf3 Nc6 3.d4 cxd4 4.Nxd4 g6 5.Nc3 Bg7 6.Be3 Nf6 7.Be2 0–0 8.Qd2 d5!

So far we were all silent. Black has played the opening well and has no problems.

9.Nxc6

The continuation 9.exd5 Nxd5 10.Nxd5 Nxd4! is very nice for Black: 11.Nxe7+? (11.Bc4 keeps black's edge to a minimum, while 11.Bxd4? Qxd5 12.Bxg7 Qxg2! has led to many Black victories) 11...Qxe7 12.Bxd4 Bxd4 13.Qxd4 Re8 and white's King is trapped in the center.

Diagram 257

White to move suffers from "central King disease".

White's best is to offer a Queen trade by 14.Qe3, but Black (who is after the enemy King) won't accept it: 14...Qb4+ 15.c3 Qa4 16.Qd2 (better is 16.Qd4, though 16...Qa6 17.c4 Bf5 is also miserable for White) 16...Bg4 17.f3 Rad8 and white's position is horrible. A possible continuation: 18.Qg5 Bf5! 19.0-0 h6 20.Qf6 Rd2 21.Bd1 Qf4 22.Bb3 (22.Kh1 Re6 traps white's Queen) 22...Rxg2+! 23.Kxg2 Bh3+ 24.Kxh3 Qxf6 and Black wins.

9...bxc6 10.e5 Ng4

A good response. Also possible is 10...Nd7 11.f4 e6 when the following trap has claimed many victims: 12.Na4? (placing the Knight on an undefended square) 12...Nxe5! 13.fxe5 Qh4+ 14.Bf2 Qxa4.

11.Bxg4 Bxg4 12.h3

Black's also doing well after 12.f4 f6 13.h3 Bc8 14.exf6 Bxf6 15.0–0–0 Qd6.

12...Bf5 13.g4?

Diagram 258

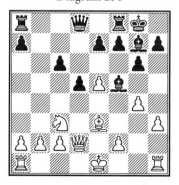

White goes after the bait

Desperate to find something to criticize, we all became hysterical. "You fool!" we howled, "Why did you allow him to attack your Bishop with gain of time?"

"Well," Michael replied coolly, "I was trying to egg him on." This was too much for us. We fell on the floor and laughed uncontrollably. Undaunted, Michael ploughed ahead and simply ignored us.

At this point I must ask the reader if he has noticed the flaws in white's position? One big problem is that e5 is weak and if that pawn vanishes, then the g7-Bishop will rule the a1-h8 diagonal. However, the other problem is the reason this example is being presented here: white's King is still in the center!

13...Be6

We were too busy making fun of Michael to notice 13...Bxe5! 14.Bh6 (14.gxf5 d4) 14...d4! 15.Qe2 (15.Bxf8 dxc3 is grim for White, but 15.Na4 keeps the game going) 15**...**Bf6 16.Bxf8 dxc3 17.b3 Qd2+ 18.Qxd2 cxd2+ 19.Kxd2 Kxf8 20.gxf5 Rd8+ 21.Ke2 Bxa1 22.Rxa1 gxf5 and Black is a pawn up in the endgame.

14.Qd4?

The idea of this move (other than the fact that it defends e5) is to post the Queen on c5—not a bad concept, but it walks into various tactical problems. Far better was 14.f4.

14...f6

A good move that tries to rip open the center and get at the uncastled King, but interesting alternatives existed:

▬▬▶ 14...Qb8 creates a double attack against b2 and e5.

▬▬▶ 14...Rc8!? is a wacky computer move: 15.Qxa7 (15.Na4 Qc7)
15...Bxe5 16.Bh6 d4 17.Rd1 Ra8 18.Qc5 Qc7 19.Bxf8 dxc3
20.Bxe7 cxb2 21.0-0 Bxa2 and White is getting wiped out.

15.f4?

Very poor. White should play 15.exf6 when 15...Bxf6 leaves Black better, but it's still a fight.

15...Qc7

We ribbed Mills for not playing 15...fxe5 16.fxe5 Qc7, which nets a free pawn since 17.Bf4 c5 is crushing. However, the text move also leaves White in a bad way, and might even prove stronger than 15...fxe5.

16.exf6 Bxf6 17.Qc5 Bh4+

More straightforward is 17...d4 18.Bxd4 Qxf4 19.Bxf6 Rxf6 with a winning attack. The path Mills chose is far deeper and far more elegant.

18.Ke2

Other moves:

➤ 18.Kd1 d4! 19.Nb5 Qa5 20.Qxc6 dxe3 21.Qxe6+ Kg7 22.Nc3 Rxf4 wins for Black.

➤ 18.Bf2 Bxf2+ 19.Qxf2 Rxf4 20.Qe3 Bf7 21.0-0-0 e5 has to be winning for Black.

➤ 18.Kd2 d4 wins on the spot (for example, 19.Bxd4 Qxf4+ 20.Be3 Rad8+ 21.Kc1 Qf1+ and mates).

18...Bc8!!

Diagram 259

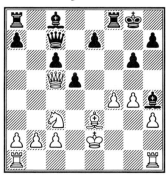

A magnificent move

This first-rate move, which is beyond the powers of the present crop (early 2010) of computers, sets up ...Ba6+ possibilities and also frees the e-pawn, which can now advance to e5 and nuke the center (going after that central enemy King). Michael's earlier moves had not made much of an impression on us, but when we saw this move our pompous smiles began to fade.

19.Nxd5

Very tempting and very greedy, but there really isn't a fully acceptable defense. Other tries:

➤ 19.Kd2 Ba6 (intending both ...d4 and ...Rxf4) 20.Rad1 (20.Kc1!?) and now 20...Rxf4 leads to fascinating tactics, but 20...e5 is simple and probably best: 21.fxe5 d4 22.Bxd4 Rfd8 23.Kc1 Be7 and Black wins a piece.

➤ 19.b4 e5 20.fxe5 Qxe5 looks grim.

➤ 19.Rag1 Ba6+ 20.Kd1 e5 and all I can say is that I wouldn't want to be White.

➤ 19.Kf3 and now both 19...Bb7 (20.Nxd5 Qe5 21.Nc3 Rxf4+) and 19...Ba6 are strong.

19...Ba6+ 20.c4

Black has many possibilities after 20.Kf3, the simplest of which is 20...Qe5 when White has to jettison a piece by 21.Nxe7+ (21.Qxc6 Rac8 is game over) 21...Qxe7 22.Qxe7 Bxe7.

20...Qb7! 21.Nb4 e5!

White's holding on as best he can, but Mills (who appears to be channeling Alekhine) won't stop playing great moves!

At this point we were no longer saying anything. Instead we silently watched the game unfold as Mills made comments like, "His King in the center and I have to get it!" and "I'm busting open the center so that my pieces can penetrate!"

22.Nxa6

Diagram 260

Channeling Alekhine

Other moves were a bit better but still depressing from white's point of view. For example, 22.f5 Be7 23.Qxc6 Bxb4 is an extra piece for Black, 22.a3 exf4 is fun for only one side, and 22.fxe5 Be7 23.Qxc6 Qxb4 gives Black an extra piece and an attack.

22...exf4?

Black learned that he's supposed to open lines in this kind of position and he's making sure he does it! Unfortunately, more direct measures were called for: 22...Qxb2+ 23.Bd2 (23.Kf3 e4+ is horrific) 23...Rxf4! and White is dead lost.

23.Bd4

Worse is 23.Bd2 f3+ 24.Kd1 Qxb2 25.Rc1 Rad8

23...Rae8+?

The most natural move in the world, but it turns out to be inaccurate. Instead, 23...f3+ is quite strong: 24.Kd3 Rad8 25.Nb4 Be7 (the immediate 25...Rxd4+ is also good) 26.Qe5 Rxd4+ 27.Qxd4 Qxb4 28.Qc3 Qc5 29.Kc2 Rf4 30.b4 Qf2+ 31.Kb3 Bf6 32.Raf1 Qe2 33.Qc2 Qe3+ 34.Ka4 f2 gives Black a winning advantage.

24.Kf3??

Kindly allowing a stunning finish. White had to play 24.Kd3 when 24...Qxa6 25.Qxa7 Qxa7 26.Bxa7 f3 27.Bc5 Rf7 28.Rad1 Rd7+ 29.Kc2 Re2+ still leaves White in serious trouble due to the power of the passed f-pawn and the vulnerability of the white King.

After this final mistake by White, Mills really does turn into Alekhine!

24...Re3+!!

Diagram 261

Mills is on fire!

Still clearing lines like a maniac! At this point all of us were exhibiting signs of shock, jaws hanging to the floor.

25.Kg2

After 25.Bxe3 fxe3+ 26.Ke4, Black would be able to choose from a multitude of winning ideas, with 26...Re8+ 27.Kd3 Rd8+ 28.Ke4 Qxb2 being my personal favorite.

25...f3+ 26.Kf1

26.Kg1 Rfe8 27.Bc3 (27.Nb4 Re1+ mates) 27...Rxc3 28.bxc3 (28.Rh2 lasts longer, but the result isn't in doubt after 28...Rce3) 28...Qb2 mates.

26...Rfe8!!

Black now threatens to mate with ...Re1+. Of course, White cannot play 27.Bxe3 due to ...Qxb2.

27.Kg1 Bg3!

Tightening the net around white's King. The Rook is still immune to capture—an incredible situation. Of course, 27...Re1+ also won easily.

28.Rf1 Re1 29.Bc3

29.Be5 Qxb2! creates a geometric oddity!

29...Qxb2!! Now, since 30.Bxb2 Rxf1+ 31.Kxf1 Re1 is mate, White resigned.

Diagram 262

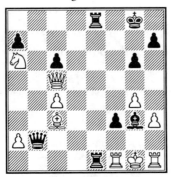

A wonderful finish!

"Who was that masked grandmaster?" Larry Christiansen asked when I showed him the game some months later.

What's of particular interest to me is that Mills didn't offer any variations at all as he was playing through the game (nor was he able to defend his moves with actual variations). Instead, he would explain everything he did by naming a pattern that he learned from the aforementioned Vukovic book. Thus we were pelted by verbal nutshells of wisdom like, "Central King, kill it!" and "Ripping open the center!" and "Maximizing the activity of my pieces!" and "Sacrificing to open lines to his King!" and "It's a double attack!" and "I'm building a mating net!"

Of course, Mills won the brilliancy prize, and none of us could do anything but applaud him. Few players (of any rating) ever create an evergreen such as this, so he can consider himself blessed. It's truly a fantastic creative effort and, perhaps, the greatest game by a non-master of all time!

By fully integrating Target Consciousness into your chess identity, perhaps you'll be able to do something like this too!

Summary

⟶ Our basic thesis is this: If your King is safely castled while the opponent's is in the middle of the board, I want you to train your mind to view that central King as a target, and immediately try and ascertain whether there's a way to smite it. At the very least, active play in the center while the enemy's monarch resides there will allow you to make some important gains as he scrambles to get his King to safety.

⟶ Other things being equal, the side with the vulnerable King will always come in second in a head to head clash.

⟶ By now the reader should know the drill:

○ Seeing that the enemy King has stayed in the center for too long, immediately get excited and target it for destruction;

○ Don't allow him to castle to safety;

○ Bring as many pieces to the embattled area as possible and prepare some form of decisive penetration;

○ Rip open some lines and go for the throat!

Target Consciousness—Tests

The problems here are all about weak pawns, weak squares, and central Kings. You'll have to ascertain which one it is and then decide how to best take advantage of the situation.

The following tests are designed to give you insight into how much you've learned *and* to serve as extra instruction. If you have trouble solving the tests, don't worry—that means we've uncovered something you don't understand, and this allows you to fix things by rereading the previous material or by picking up the bits of knowledge you're missing in the answers that start on page 527.

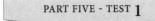

PART FIVE - TEST **1**

Diagram 263
[Level: 1600 - 2199]

White to move

PART FIVE - TEST **2**

Diagram 264
[Level: 1400 - 1600]

White to move

Is c3-c4 a good idea?

PART FIVE - TEST 3

Diagram 265

[Level: 1400 - 1600]

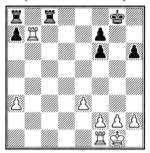

White to move

List black's weaknesses.

PART FIVE - TEST 4

Diagram 266

[Level: 1400 - 1800]

White just played a2-a4. Black won't let White win the b-pawn, so what's the point of a2-a4? Is it any good, or simply a one-move threat?

PART FIVE - TEST 5

Diagram 267

[Level: 1400 - 1800]

Black to move

PART FIVE - TEST 6

Diagram 268

[Level: 1400 - 2000]

Black to move

PART FIVE - TEST 7

Diagram 269

[Level: 1800 - 2000]

Black to move

PART FIVE - TEST 8

Diagram 270

[Level: 1400 - 1600]

White to move

PART FIVE - TEST 9

Diagram 271

[Level: 1400 - 2000]

White to move

Part Six / Statics vs. Dynamics

Contents

Statics vs. Dynamics

Boxer vs. Puncher — A Battle of Opposing Philosophies

I constantly hear amateurs discussing their styles. Usually they love to brag about how attacking is everything to them, while a smaller number pride themselves on a solid grasp of positional concepts. Though there's nothing wrong with enjoying one part of the game over another, if you can't show at least basic skills in both you'll be in for a very rough ride. So a good positional player will find that he's doomed if he doesn't also have a solid grasp of tactics *and* a feel for chess dynamics, while a good tactician will be beaten from pillar to post if he is positionally clueless and/or doesn't know a static plus or minus from a hole in the wall. In other words, personal tastes are wonderful, but at least a modicum of balance is key if you want chess success.

The positional fantasy is to create long-term static problems in the enemy camp (holes, weak pawns, a material deficit, lack of space, etc.) and then "massage" these things while the opponent passively sits around until his position totally collapses into a pile of dust. On the other hand, the tactician dreams of knocking his opponent out with a massive tactical punch, or unleashing a stunning combination that overwhelms his gutted prey. Nice thoughts indeed, and these scenarios do occur quite often at all levels. However, this presupposes that the guy on the other side of the table will stick his chin out to be hit, or that he'll roll into a ball in the face of your positional superiority.

But what if the opponent sees your tactical trick coming? What if he realizes that his game is a positional mess and dares to fight back, refusing to go quietly into that dark night? What if he has some favorable imbalances too, and fully intends to make maximum use of them?

The best chess games are all about the war of ideas, the battle of imbalances, and the face-to-face struggle of one player's will against the other—if you don't have a fighter's mentality, if you wilt in the face of an opponent who grabs the positive features of his position and comes at you again and again as if he was a rabid dog, then you will find that chess success and real chess enjoyment eludes you. A to-the-death battle of mind and knowledge and skill and heart is what makes chess so exhilarating!

And all of this brings us to the enormously important battle of Statics vs. Dynamics—the fight between one side's long-term plusses (we'll concentrate on superior structure here) and the other's short-term, use-them-now-or-die, chances (active pieces, attacking possibilities based on a vulnerable enemy King, or swing-from-the-fence tactics that seemingly appear from nowhere but are actually a logical expression of basic combinative rules).

This chapter is designed to make you aware of the eternal war between a "firm foundation" (positional/static factors) and a "firm fist" (dynamics). It's something you have to take into account when you build your positional dreams or try to create an attack—will the attack fizzle out and leave you a cropper to the opponent's obvious static gains? Will your obvious structural superiority win out or will it fall on its face when the active enemy pieces invade and conquer?

D. Strenzwilk - J. Silman, National Open 1990

1.e4 c5 2.Nf3 Nc6 3.d4 cxd4 4.Nxd4 g6 5.Nc3 Bg7 6.Nb3 Nf6 7.Be2 d6 8.0–0 0–0 9.Kh1 Be6 10.Bg5 h6 11.Bh4 g5 12.Bg3 d5 13.Nc5 dxe4 14.Nxe6 fxe6 15.Bc4 Qc8 16.Bb3 Na5 17.Qe2 Nxb3?!

This capture is a hasty decision that (after 18.axb3) gives the a1-Rook access to the a4-square (why activate an "unemployed" enemy piece?). Better was 17...Qc6, which was more or less equal.

18.axb3 Qc6 19.Ra4 Rfc8 20.Rc4 Qa6

Dangling a carrot before my opponent's "static hungry" eyes. Doesn't this allow White to saddle Black with the worst pawn structure of all time?

21.Rxc8+?

He bows to temptation! Better was 21.Nxe4 (21.Rd1!?) 21...Rxc4 22.bxc4 Nxe4 23.Qxe4 Bxb2 24.Qg6+ Kf8 25.Qxh6+ Bg7 26.Qxg5 Qxc4 when White is a bit better due to black's vulnerable King.

21...Rxc8 22.Qxa6 bxa6 23.Ra1

Diagram 272

Worst pawn structure ever?

Black is a pawn up, but do doubled isolated a-pawns count as full pawns? And what about tripled e-pawns? One can understand white's decision to enter this position—he felt that his structural superiority was so enormous that the position simply had to be better for him. In fact, if one stares at black's pawn structure while refusing to look at anything else, it would be hard not to break out laughing. However, only looking at any position through static-tinted lenses will rarely get the job done.

And this begs a question: What about dynamics? And here we arrive at the flaw in white's thinking—he didn't take his opponent's plusses into account! Let's break things down:

<u>White:</u>

➤ Far superior pawn structure.

➤ Active Rook (which is rightfully targeting black's weak pawns).

<u>Black:</u>

➤ White's King (which is stuffed into a corner and vulnerable to eventual back rank problems) can't take part in the coming battle (it's a liability), while black's King can give support to e7 and e6 via ...Kf7 (it's making itself useful).

➤ Black's Rook is also active, and if white's Knight moves then ...Rxc2 turns the Rook into an all-devouring beast.

➤ The tripled e-pawns aren't as bad as they seem—the e6-pawn in particular supports the d5-square and allows ...Nd5.

➤ Once black's Knight leaps to the wonderful d5-square, it will hammer open the c-file and prove to be far more useful than its white counterpart.

➤ Once black's Knight moves, the g7-Bishop will take immediate aim at white's queenside. Conversely, white's Bishop isn't attacking or defending anything and is swishing thin air along the h2-b8 diagonal.

➤ Black's a pawn up.

To sum up, the real picture is very much in black's favor: it's a battle of white's structural superiority versus black's enormous advantage in dynamics. Note that all of black's pieces are serving an active/dynamic function—his King can defend key points in its camp, while the Rook, Knight, and Bishop will join forces and tear down white's queenside. White's pieces, on the other hand, are all over the place and aren't working together at all.

23...Nd5

Active pieces call for active play! This move immediately optimizes black's minor pieces while also ripping open the c-file so the Rook can join in the party.

24.Rxa6

White starts gorging on the crippled pawns. Alternatives weren't attractive either:

> ➤ 24.Nxd5 exd5 25.c3 and now the calm 25...Rc6 is probably best, though 25...d4 26.cxd4 Bxd4 also leaves Black in complete command of the position.

> ➤ 24.Nxe4 Rxc2 25.h4 gxh4 26.Bxh4 Bd4 27.Rxa6 Kf7 28.Ra4 e5 and black's active pieces rule the roost.

24...Kf7!

Making good use of the King. The e6-pawn is protected, Rxe6 is avoided, and Black is finally ready to hammer away on c3 and/or c2.

25.Rxa7 Bxc3!

Black realizes that it's better to retain his Knight since its ability to attack any square on the board (compared to a Bishop, which is always stuck on one colored complex) will make it a more flexible piece than white's remaining minor. I should add that the Knight covering the c7-square also turns out to be of considerable importance—3...Nxc3? 4.bxc3 Rxc3 allows 5.Rc7.

26.bxc3 Rxc3 27.h4

27.Ra2, though passive, was probably white's best defensive try.

27...Rxc2 28.hxg5 hxg5 29.Kg1 e3

Diagram 273

Revenge of the trips!

The tripled e-pawns show that they also have a dynamic side! Compare them to white's "healthy" pawns, which are sitting around doing nothing.

30.fxe3 Nxe3 31.Bd6

Also depressing was 31.Bf2 Ng4 32.Be1 e5 33.b4 Rc1 34.Kf1 Ne3+ 35.Ke2 Nxg2.

31...Rxg2+ 32.Kh1 Re2 33.Bxe7 Kg6 34.Bc5 g4 35.Bxe3 Rxe3

The rest of the game doesn't need comment—Black plays directly for an easily winning Lucena Position: **36.Rb7 Re2 37.Kg1 Kf5 38.Rf7+ Ke4 39.Rg7 Kf3 40.Rf7+ Kg3 41.Kf1 Rb2 42.Re7 Rxb3 43.Rxe6 Rb1+ 44.Ke2 Kg2 45.Kd2 g3 46.Rg6 Rb8 47.Ke3 Rf8 48.Rg7 Kh2 49.Ke2 g2 50.Rh7+ Kg1 51.Rh6 Re8+ 52.Kd2 Re5 53.Rh8 Kf2 54.Rf8+ Kg3 55.Rg8+ Kf3**, 0-1.

- ▶ In chess, looks don't count for anything. Substance is everything.

- ▶ Always make sure you know what imbalances both you *and* your opponent can make use of.

- ▶ Dynamics can beat statics and statics can beat dynamics. It's up to the player to judge which is of more value in the particular position.

- ▶ Make sure your pieces are working together towards a particular goal.

- ▶ Just because we've been taught that doubled, isolated, and even tripled pawns are bad doesn't necessarily make it so! Don't allow useful guidelines to be turned into gospel.

Statics vs. Dynamics in the Openings

Of course, the battle of Statics vs. Dynamics regularly occurs at the highest level. And it's very common to see the Static vs. Dynamic paradigm created right in the opening.

V. Topalov - L. Aronian, Morelia 2008

1.d4 Nf6 2.c4 e6 3.Nc3 Bb4 4.Nf3 c5 5.g3 cxd4 6.Nxd4 Ne4 7.Qd3 Bxc3+ 8.bxc3 Nc5 9.Qf3 d6 10.Bg2 e5 11.Qe3 0–0 12.Nb3 Qc7 13.Nxc5 dxc5 14.0–0 Nd7

This is a popular line in the Nimzo-Indian. White has the Bishop pair but also has trouble with his pawn structure (the doubled c-pawns are weak). If Black can exchange one of the enemy Bishops or restrain the Bishops' activity in some way, he'll have excellent chances.

Since this is clearly a Dynamic (two active Bishops and a lead in development) vs. Static (superior pawn structure for Black) situation, White has to *insist* that his Bishops somehow reach their full potential.

Diagram 274

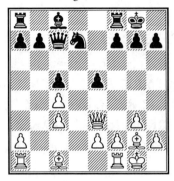

15.f4!

This actually makes white's pawn structure even worse (since he'll soon have an isolated e-pawn to go with his isolated a-pawn and doubled isolated c-pawns), but structure isn't on white's mind—activity is! The advance of the f-pawn intends f4-f5 with chances on the kingside. And, if Black captures on f4 (which he does) then the c1-Bishop will join its light-squared brother on a diagonal superhighway.

15...exf4

To me, this seems like strategic capitulation since White will achieve all his dynamic goals (of course, it takes some powerful chess by Topalov to prove this). In my view, Black should play 15...Re8!?, a move that highlights white's potential problems down the e-file and intends to meet 16.f5 with 16...e4!, blocking the g2-Bishop's diagonal. Note how my recommended response doesn't play into white's hands like 15...exf4 does. Instead it contains the enemy Bishops and hopes to take advantage of white's structural defects. Philosophically (in accordance with my concept of imbalances), 15...Re8 is the way to go, but whether this actually equalizes is up to future analysts. After 15...Re8 16.f5 e4 we reach an important position:

Diagram 275

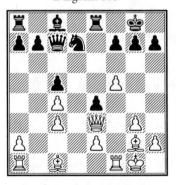

White to move

The critical move is 17.g4 (17.Qf4 Qxf4 [17...Qa5!?] 18.Rxf4 Nf6 19.g4 h6 20.h4 b6 21.g5 [21.Be3 Ba6] 21...Nh5 22.Rxe4 Bxf5 is nothing for White) when Seirawan says, "White wants to play Qe3-h3, Bc1-f4, g4-g5 and to try to deliver mate. I do agree that 15...Re8 makes sense and the question is whether White's 'attack' is really dangerous or not." This uncertainty in the face of two different philosophies is what the Static vs. Dynamic battle is all about!

16.Rxf4

Suddenly the position has become wide open and Black will have serious trouble getting his queenside pieces out. When two vastly different sets of imbalances come head to head, it only takes a blink for one strategy to overrun the other.

16...a5

Black is hoping to get his a8-Rook in the game by ...Ra6.

17.Qe7!

Very nice. Black's Knight is pinned and the threat of Bd5 looms large.

17...Qe5 18.Qxe5 Nxe5 19.Be3 Nd7

A horrible move to make, but there wasn't any other way to defend c5.

20.Re4!

Heading for e7.

20...Ra6 21.Rb1 Rg6 22.Re7 b6 23.Bf4

Diagram 276

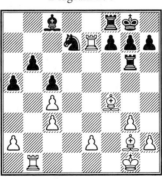

Black to move

White's Bishops are eating up the h2-b8 and h1-a8 diagonals and his Rooks are far superior to black's. Black has completely lost the strategic battle. The rest of the game is an exercise in futility.

23...h5 24.Be4 Re6 25.Rxe6 fxe6 26.Bd6 Rf6 27.Rd1 Kf7 28.Bf4 Kg8 29.Bc7 Rf7 30.Bg6 a4

At first glance this seems surprising, but it turns out that Black loses decisive quantities of material no matter what he tried. For example: 30...Rf8 31.Bd6 Rf6 32.Be8 Rf5 33.Be7 Nf8 (33...Nf6 34.Bxf6 Rxf6 35.Rd8 is also resignable) 34.Rd8 Ba6 35.Bg6 and the position looks more like a teenage slasher film than a chess game.

31.Bxh5 Nf6 32.Bxf7+ Kxf7 33.Bxb6 Ba6 34.Bxc5 e5 35.a3 Bxc4 36.Bb4 e4 37.Kf1, 1-0.

Many structures become raging Static vs. Dynamic battlefields. One of the most interesting (to me) can be seen in the diagram that occurs after the following eight moves: **1.d4 Nf6 2.c4 e6 3.Nc3 Bb4 4.a3 Bxc3+ 5.bxc3 0–0 6.f3 Ne8 7.e4 b6 8.Bd3**

Diagram 277

Black to move

If Black wasn't familiar with the general structure in diagram 277, he might be tempted to follow up with ...Bb7 followed by ...d6 and ...Nd7. However, those "normal" developing moves would demonstrate a complete lack of understanding about the dynamics/statics of the position. The fact is, this kind of structure (which most commonly occurs in the Nimzo-Indian but can also arise from other openings) is seething with mutual bad intent. White claims two Bishops, a huge pawn center, and kingside attacking chances (dynamics). Black targets the c4-pawn for death (going after a static weakness).

Once you realize that c4 is the target, then you will also understand that ...Bb7 can't be right since it has nothing to do with pressuring the c4-pawn. Placing the Knight on d7 is also illogical since it wouldn't be contributing to the "kill c4" plan. However, now that black's goal is clear, his moves should also be clear: 8...Ba6 (hitting c4) 9.Nh3 Nc6 intending ...Na5 (hitting c4 again).

I should also add a bit about the "bizarre" move, 6...Ne8. Why retreat to a seemingly stupid square when there's no need to do so? As it turns out, e8 is a very flexible square for the Knight—it gets out of the way of its f7-pawn, which can now help block a white attack by a well-timed ...f7-f5. In some cases, it can add to its King's defenses by ...g6 and ...Ng7. And it can also join in the group assault of c4 by ...Nd6.

Take a look at the following game where the same basic structure arises and the same plans are employed (hard to believe they knew this stuff 140 years ago!). It's a flawed battle, but serves as an excellent illustration of a cut and thrust Static vs. Dynamic war.

G. Neumann - A. Anderssen, Baden-Baden 1870

1.d4 f5 2.c4 e6 3.Nc3 Nf6 4.e3 Bb4 5.Bd3 Bxc3+ 6.bxc3 c5 7.Ne2 Nc6 8.0-0 b6 9.f3 0-0 10.e4 g6 11.Bh6 Rf7 12.e5 Nh5 13.f4 Ba6 14.Rf3 Na5 15.Qa4 Qc8 16.Ng3 Nxg3

Also possible was 16...Ng7, leaving white's steed on the nowhere-to-go g3-square.

17.Rxg3

Diagram 278

Our classic battle between white's Bishops, dark-square control, and kingside attack (dynamics) versus black's threat to snuff out c4 (statics) is about to begin!

17...cxd4

Rushing to win the c4-pawn, but white's dynamics prove to be of more value. Instead of taking on d4, 17...Qc6 makes a lot of sense: 18.Qxc6 Nxc6 (Also interesting is 18...dxc6 19.d5! Re8! 20.d6 when Black will win c4 [static], but white's control of the kingside dark-squares [dynamic] and his monster pawn on d6 [static/dynamic] leaves him with all the chances) 19.dxc5 (the immediate 19.h4 seems better, and gives White chances for a slight edge) 19...bxc5 20.h4 Rb8 21.h5 Rb2 is okay for Black, who has active play on the queenside (dynamic) and his usual pressure against c4 (static).

18.cxd4 Nxc4 19.Rc1 b5 20.Qd1?

20.Qb4! was correct.

20...Qc6?

20...Qd8, getting the Queen away from the c1-Rook's stare, was more or less equal.

21.h4!

White's kingside chances and his domination of the dark-squares now give him a clear advantage.

21...Kh8 22.h5 Rg8 23.Bxc4 bxc4 24.Rcc3 g5?

White had a strong attack, but this hysterical reaction can't be right.

25.Bxg5 h6 26.Bf6+ Kh7 27.Rg6 Rxf6 28.exf6?

28.Rxg8! Kxg8 29.Rg3+ Kf7 30.exf6 was a simple win.

28...Rxg6 29.hxg6+ Kxg6 30.Rg3+ Kxf6 31.Qh5 Ke7 32.Qxh6 Kd6 33.Qf6 Qd5 34.Kf2 Kc6 35.Qe5 d6 36.Qxd5+ Kxd5 37.Ra3 Bb5 38.Ra5 Kxd4 39.Rxb5 d5 40.Ra5 Kd3 41.Rxa7 d4 42.Rc7 c3 43.a4 Kc2 44.a5 d3 45.a6 d2 46.Rd7 d1=Q 47.Rxd1 Kxd1 48.a7 c2 49.a8=Q c1=Q 50.Qf3+ Kc2 51.Qc6+ Kb1 52.Qxc1+ Kxc1 53.Ke3, 1-0. In this game Black had pressure against the c4-pawn (a static structural plus) and eventually won it (gaining a static material plus). However, white's dynamic imbalances turned out to be more important.

Our next game, played between two of the greatest players of all time, shows black's static (versus white's dynamic) strategy in a better light.

M. Botvinnik - S. Reshevsky, World Chmp Tnmt 1948

1.d4 Nf6 2.c4 e6 3.Nc3 Bb4 4.e3 c5 5.a3 Bxc3+ 6.bxc3 Nc6 7.Bd3 0–0 8.Ne2 b6 9.e4 Ne8 10.Be3 d6 11.0–0 Na5 12.Ng3 Ba6 13.Qe2 Qd7 14.f4

Diagram 279

White has—at least temporarily—managed to hold onto c4, and now he's pursuing his kingside dreams via the threat of f4-f5. However, the aggressive 14.f4 isn't all juicy goodness—the move suffers from a strategic flaw.

14...f5!

Freezing white's f-pawn and thus turning it into a traitor—the white f-pawn now blocks its dark-square Bishop while black's f-pawn makes sure that white's light-squared Bishop and g3-Knight will never be able to use the e4-square. Thus white's minor pieces now find themselves trapped in a sort of cage.

A common (and often strong) maneuver in this kind of position is 14...Qa4, bringing another piece to bear on c4. However, though it succeeds in tearing down c4 (the final realization of his static plan), it also lets White continue with his dynamic kingside plans via 15.f5. This advance gains kingside space, frees the e3-Bishop by opening up the c1-h6 diagonal, and also brings the previously dead f1-Rook into the game. Is rushing to win c4 really worth giving White all of this activity? A possible continuation would then be 15...Bxc4 16.fxe6 and now Black can try:

➤ 16...Bxd3 17.Qxd3 fxe6 18.Rxf8+ Kxf8 19.Nh5 Kg8 20.Rf1 gives White a fierce initiative—note how white's Rook, Bishop, and Knight are far more active than their black counterparts. A taste of what might occur: 20...Qd7 21.Bg5! d5 22.Qf3 Nc7 23.Bh6! and White is winning.

➤ 16...Bxe6 with two tasty choices:

Diagram 280

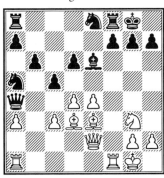

White, a pawn down, must make use of his dynamics

● 17.Bb5 Qb3 18.d5 Bc8 (18...Bg4 19.Qxg4 Qxb5 20.Nf5 Kh8 21.Rf3 gives White a winning attack—not much of a surprise since black's King will soon be surrounded by white's pieces) 19.Bxe8 (Not very intuitive, but since I wasn't able to find a way to get more than a draw by attacking black's Queen, a brute force tactical solution was called for!) 19...Rxe8 20.Rxf7! Qxc3 (20...Kxf7 21.Qh5+ wins on the spot) 21.Rc1 (Also interesting is 21.Raf1 Ba6 22.Qxa6 Qxe3+ 23.Kh1, but why let Black exchange his passive light-squared Bishop for white's attacking unit on e3?) 21...Qe5 22.Rcf1 (threatening death on g7 by Nh5) 22...Bb7 (22...g6 23.Bh6 Bb7 24.Qf3 and the threat of 25.Rf8+ wins on the spot) 23.Nh5 Ba6 24.Qf3! Bxf1 25.Rxg7+ Qxg7 (25...Kh8 26.Qf7 forces mate) 26.Nxg7 Kxg7 27.Qg3+ Kh8 (no better is 27...Kf7 28.Qf4+ Ke7 29.Qf5 Kd8 30.Bg5+) 28.Qxd6 and the combination of white's Queen and Bishop will slaughter black's King on the dark squares.

- 17.d5!? Bd7 18.Qh5 Qb3 (18...Nb3 19.Rae1 [19.Ra2 is also strong, as seen in the analysis of 18...c4] 19...c4 20.Bb1 g6 21.Qh6 Qa5 22.e5 dxe5 23.Bxg6!! hxg6 24.Ne4 Bf5 25.Rxf5! gxf5 26.Qg5+ gives a winning attack, while 18...c4 19.Bb1 Nb3 20.Ra2 g6 21.Qh6 Qa5 22.Raf2 is obviously strong for White) 19.e5 g6 (19...h6 20.Bxh6!) 20.Qh6 Qxc3 (20...dxe5 21.Bxg6!! hxg6 22.Ne4 Bf5 23.Rxf5 gxf5 24.Qg5+ wins) 21.e6! Qxd3 22.exf7+ Rxf7 23.Rxf7 Kxf7 24.Qxh7+ Ng7 25.Rf1+ and White wins.

It's well worth playing over these sharp, fun, tactical variations. It gives the reader a better understanding about the potential of active, unleashed pieces.

> **IN A NUTSHELL**
>
> Statics tend to last longer than dynamics.

Of course, Reshevsky was having none of it! His plan was to snuff out this dynamic potential before finalizing his evil, static designs against c4.

15.Rae1

15.d5, trying to break down f5, seems logical but it fails to 15...fxe4 16.Nxe4 exd5 17.cxd5 Bxd3 18.Qxd3 Qf5 19.c4 Nf6 (Kasparov) 20.Nxf6+ Rxf6 when White no longer has doubled pawns, but c4 is still weak and white's dynamic potential is a thing of the past. In other words, white's dynamic chances have vanished while black's static edge remains. That's one of the nice things about being on the side of statics: they tend to last a long, long time while dynamics are like a flare that burns bright for a few moments before fading into oblivion.

After 20...Rxf6 21.Qxf5 Rxf5 22.Rac1 Re8 23.Bd2 Nb3 leaves Black in charge, while 21.Qc3 Re8 22.Rae1 Re4 is just plain horrible for White.

15...g6

Solidifying f5 and making sure that white's pieces aren't allowed any scope.

16.Rd1

16.d5 Ng7 maintains the block on f5 and doesn't allow white's Bishops any free-ranging diagonals.

16...Qf7

It was still possible for Black to go after c4 with 16...Qa4, while 16...cxd4 17.cxd4 fxe4 18.Nxe4 d5 was also promising. However, it's already been made clear that Reshevsky had no intention of letting white's pieces out of their cage.

17.e5

This turns f5 into a permanent rock and dooms white's pieces to long-term passivity. Like it or not, White had to give 17.d5 Ng7 a try.

17...Rc8

Giving c5 support while also X-raying through to the target on c4.

18.Rfe1

Kasparov, in his excellent *My Great Predecessors, Part IV*, points out that 18.d5 Bb7 19.Bc1 exd5 20.e6 Qf6 21.cxd5 c4 22.Bc2 Nc7 is bad for White because 23.Qf3 fails to 23...Nxe6.

18...dxe5 19.dxe5

Diagram 281

After this, all of white's hopes of dynamic compensation for his static woes go down the drain—he's left with inactive pieces and a miserable defensive chore. It might have been wiser to finally give up the c4-pawn and play for complications via 19.fxe5 cxd4 20.cxd4 Bxc4 21.Bxc4 Nxc4 22.Bh6 Ng7 23.d5 Qd7 24.Qf3. However, Black retains a solid advantage and has a pleasant choice between 24...Rfe8 25.d6 Rc5 (taking aim at a new target on e5) 26.Qf4 Rec8 and 24...exd5 25.e6 Qe7 26.Rxd5 Rfd8.

19...Ng7 20.Nf1 Rfd8 21.Bf2 Nh5!

Nice. This attack against f4 stops White from placing the dark-squared Bishop on h4.

22.Bg3 Qe8

Now that white's forces no longer pose a threat, the Queen heads for the Promised Land on a4 where it will strike at white's weaknesses on a3 and c4.

23.Ne3 Qa4 24.Qa2 Nxg3 25.hxg3 h5!

Black's last two moves have permanently killed white's kingside hopes. Now all Botvinnik can do is hold on tight and hope that Reshevsky can't find a decisive continuation. The rest of the game, though extremely interesting, no longer serves our theme (since it's now Statics vs. nothing), so I'll give it without notes.

26.Be2 Kf7 27.Kf2 Qb3 28.Qxb3 Nxb3 29.Bd3 Ke7 30.Ke2 Na5 31.Rd2 Rc7 32.g4 Rcd7 33.gxf5 gxf5 34.Red1 h4 35.Ke1 Nb3 36.Nd5+ exd5 37.Bxf5 Nxd2 38.Rxd2 dxc4 39.Bxd7 Rxd7 40.Rf2 Ke6 41.Rf3 Rd3 42.Ke2, 0-1.

It's critically important to know if the position demands static or dynamic play from you. At times there might be a choice about which direction you'll take, but more often than not, the writing is on the wall and there's only one correct decision. Ultimately, taking that correct path is dependent on you looking for it in the first place, and a correct reading of the imbalances. Done right, the board will usually scream (quite loudly!) what's expected of you.

A. Volokitin - A. Delchev, Calvia 2004

1.e4 c5 2.Nf3 e6 3.d4 cxd4 4.Nxd4 Nc6 5.Nc3 Qc7 6.Be2 a6 7.0-0 Nf6 8.Kh1 h5 9.Nxc6 bxc6 10.f4 d5 11.exd5 cxd5

Diagram 282

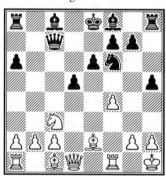

Black has more center pawns, and he has already built a nice space-gaining center—long term, Black will stand well thanks to that center (which is a static plus) and to the pressure against white's queenside pawns that Rooks on the open b- and c-files will create (dynamic pressure against potentially static weaknesses on b2 and c2).

White's plusses are black's lag in development (dynamic) and uncastled King (dynamic). Since development will be nullified once black gets more pieces out, and since his central King can be castled in a couple of moves, White has to realize that what he has is temporary—he must find a way to use these things right away!

12.f5!

Blasting the position open and starting a fight before Black is completely ready to deal with it. Note that this advance will not only create weaknesses in black's position, but it also activates the f1-Rook and opens the diagonal for the c1-Bishop.

12...Bb7 13.fxe6 fxe6 14.Bd3 0–0–0 15.Qe2 Qc6

Diagram 283

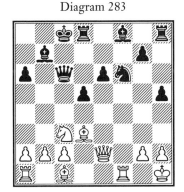

Role reversal

After 15...Qc6 the roles have reversed: White's aggressive opening play has led to a position full of long-term static weaknesses for Black (weak pawns on a6 and e6, a hole on e5), while Black has dynamic chances based on pressure along the h1-a8 diagonal via the b7-Bishop and c6-Queen lineup, and the threat to rip open that diagonal with ...h5-h4-h3.

It should be noted that 15...Ng4 would have failed to 16.Qxe6+ Kb8 17.Bf4 Bd6 18.Qf7! Bxf4 19.Qxf4. Analysis by Volokitin.

16.Bg5 h4 17.Rae1

17.Rxf6!? gxf6 18.Bxf6 might be stronger, though Black is still fighting after 18...Rh6 19.Bxd8 Kxd8.

17...h3

17...Re8 18.Bg6 Re7 19.Rxf6 is winning for White.

18.Qxe6+ Qxe6 19.Rxe6

White, thanks to his "grab the position by the tail" mentality, has bulldozed his way to a clear advantage.

19...Bd6

> **RULE**
>
> A dynamic plus is often cashed in for a longer lasting static plus.

In the actual game, Black erred with 19...d4? (giving white's Knight access to the e4-square). White won as follows: 20.Ne4 hxg2+ 21.Kxg2 Bd6 22.Bxf6 gxf6 23.Rfxf6 Rxh2+ 24.Kg1 Bc7 25.Nd6+ Bxd6 26.Rxd6 Rh1+ 27.Kf2 Rxd6 28.Rxd6 Ra1 29.a3 Ra2 30.Rxd4 Rxb2 31.Rc4+ Kb8 32.Rb4 Rxb4 33.axb4 Kc7 34.Ke3 Kb6 35.c4 Bc6 36.Kd4 Ba4 37.c5+ Kb7 38.Ke5 Bd7 39.Kd6 Bh3 40.Bc4 Ka7 41.Be6 Bg2 42.Kc7 Bf1 43.Bd7 Bg2 44.c6 Bf3 45.Be6! (Not falling for 45.Kd8?? Bxc6 46.Bxc6 a5 47.b5 Kb6, =.) 45...Bg2 46.Kd7 a5 47.c7 Bb7 48.Bd5 Ba6 49.bxa5 Bb5+ 50.Kd8 Ba6 51.Bc6, 1-0.

20.Bxf6 hxg2+ 21.Kxg2 gxf6 22.Rfxf6 Rxh2+ 23.Kg1 Bc7 24.Rf7 Rg8+ 25.Rg6 Rxg6+ 26.Bxg6 Rd2 and Black has "real chances to hold the draw" - Volokitin. Note what occurred in this game: White made use of dynamic plusses to transform the position (against his opponent's will!) into a statically advanta-geous one. Now White was the one with the long-term static plus (an extra pawn) while Black had some com-pensating dynamics in the form of two Bishops and a Rook on the 7th.

> **RULE**
>
> The transformation of one kind of imbalance (static or dynamic) into another kind of imbalance (dynamic or static) is very common.

In most instances the imbalances will clearly point to a dynamic or static course. However, in some cases there is a choice, and the direction you take will then depend on personal preferences, tournament situation, and style.

A. Ramirez - A. Morozevich, Bled 2002

1.e4 e6 2.d4 d5 3.exd5 exd5 4.Nf3 Bd6 5.c4 dxc4 6.Bxc4 Nf6 7.0–0 0–0 8.h3 h6 9.Qc2 Nc6 10.Nc3 Nb4 11.Qb1

Diagram 284

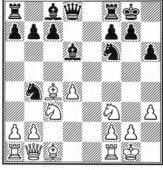

Black must make a big decision

Here we have a fairly common looking isolated d-pawn position (though the position of white's Queen on b1 is odd). In general, this structure immediately tells us that Black will have a long-term static plus (play against the isolated d-pawn and the weakened d5-square) while White will find dynamic compensation in active pieces and chances against the enemy King.

This generic scenario would indeed play out if Black played the natural positional move, 11...c6, giving support to the d5-square and intending to follow up with ...Nbd5. Since normal moves like 12.Re1 Nbd5 13.Ne5 give Black a comfortable game after 13...Be6, White might be tempted to slam down 12.Bxh6!? gxh6 13.Qg6+ Kh8 14.Qxh6+ (14.Bxf7 Nh7 15.Ne5 Bxe5 16.dxe5 Qe7 favors Black since 17.e6? is met by 17...Bxc6! 18.Bxc6 Rf6) 14...Nh7, though it's more or less equal after 15.Ne4 Be7, giving us a nice example of black's static material plus vs. white's dynamic (attacking) chances.

I think most players would toss out 11...c6 if they were sure that 12.Bxh6 wasn't dangerous (and, as the above analysis shows, this would be a fully acceptable decision). But it turns out that Black doesn't have to accept his static role, and can actually change the "personalities" of both sides with a rather surprising (non-dogmatic) move.

11...Be6!

Black accepts a weakening of his structure for iron control over the d5-square and, after 12.Bxe6 fxe6, use of the just-opened f-file. This dynamic, original decision creates a position that very much suits Morozevich's original, active style. Suddenly White (who a moment ago was the active one) has static play against the weakness on e6 while black's active (dynamic) pieces will give him chances of his own.

12.Bxe6 fxe6 13.Re1 Qe8

Not too subtle. Black envisions his Queen leaping to h5 and chomping down on white's King. A more restrained interpretation of black's plan would be 13...Qd7 14.Ne4 Nxe4 15.Qxe4 Rae8 with a solid, completely acceptable position. However, Morozevich most likely wanted to make the game as sharp as possible, thinking

> **IN A NUTSHELL**
>
> Note that White has to be careful not to let Black create (by swapping one of his Knights for a white Knight and his d6-Bishop for the other white Knight) a monster Knight (firmly entrenched on d5) versus an inferior Bishop scenario.

that his fourteen-year-old opponent wouldn't be able to handle the heat.

14.Ne4 Nbd5 15.Nc5 Bxc5 16.dxc5 Nd7 17.Qc2

The critical move was 17.c6, shredding black's pawn structure. After 17...bxc6 18.Nd4?! (18.Qe4 is best, with a small but annoying static edge) 18...Qf7 19.f3 c5 is nothing for White since 20.Nxe6?? Rfe8 is a disaster and 20.Nc6 doesn't give White much of anything.

17...c6

Diagram 285

Black's wonderful Knight on d5 and his control of the half open f-file (which gives him kingside pressure) more than compensate for his small structural problem on e6.

18.Be3

18.Bd2 is a bit more accurate, though White still can't claim any advantage after 18...Qh5 (18...Rxf3? doesn't work due to 19.gxf3 Qh5 20.Qe4 when ...Ne5 is no longer possible) 19.Nd4 Qh4! (Hitting f2 and d4 and forcing White to change plans. Worse is 19...e5 20.Ne2 followed by Ng3-e4 when the Knight has reached its dream square and White stands better) 20.f4 (20. Bc3 Nxc5 21.Nxe6 Nxe6 22.Rxe6 Rae8, =) 20...Nxf4 21.Bxf4 (21.Nf3?? Nxh3+ wins) 21...Rxf4 22.Nxe6 Re8 23.Re2 Rf7 24.Rae1 Nf6, =.

18...Rxf3!

This Exchange sacrifice, combined with his twentieth move, guarantee Black a lasting initiative.

19.gxf3 Qh5 20.Qe4

20.Kg2 Rf8 21.Qe4 Rf6.

20...Ne5!

Black's Knights make a very nice impression.

21.Kg2 Nf6

Worse is 21...Rf8 22.f4.

22.Qf4 Ng6

Black can get a small but safe static edge with 22...Nd3 23.Qg3 Nxe1+ 24.Rxe1 Rf8, but he decided to increase the tension and play for kingside pressure. Indeed, he managed to succeed (after inaccurate play by White) in obtaining a clear advantage, but missed his chances and a draw was the eventual result:

23.Qg3 Nh4+ 24.Kh1 Kh7 25.Bf4 Nxf3 26.Re3 Nd4 27.Re5 Nf5 28.Qg2 Rd8 29.f3 Rd4 30.Bh2 Rh4 31.Rg1 Qf7 32.Rge1 Nd7 33.Rxe6 Nxc5 34.R6e2 Qh5 35.Rg1 Rxh3 36.Re5 Nd3 37.Rxf5 Rxh2+ 38.Qxh2 Qxf5 39.Rg3 Nf4 40.Rg4 g5 41.Qd2 h5 42.Rg3 Kh6 43.Kh2 Qe5 44.Kh1 Ne2 45.Rg2 Ng3+ 46.Kg1 h4 47.Rh2 Nf5 48.Re2 Qf6 49.Re4 c5 50.Kg2 Kh5 51.Qd7 Qxb2+ 52.Kh3 Ng7 53.Qg4+ Kh6 54.f4 Qc3+ 55.Kh2 Qd2+ 56.Kg1 Qc1+ 57.Kh2 Qd2+ 58.Kg1 Qc1+ 59.Kh2 Qd2+, ½-½.

Summary

> This chapter is designed to make you aware of the eternal war between a "firm foundation" (positional/static factors) and a "firm fist" (dynamics).

> Battle of statics vs. dynamics—the fight between one side's long-term plusses and the other's short-term, use-them-now-or-die, chances (active pieces, attacking possibilities based on a vulnerable enemy King, or swing-from-the-fence tactics that seemingly appear from nowhere but are actually a logical expression of basic combinative rules).

> Dynamics can beat statics and statics can beat dynamics. It's up to the player to judge which is of more value in the particular position.

> One of the nice things about being on the side of statics is that they tend to last a long, long time while dynamics are like a flare that burns bright for a few moments before fading into oblivion.

> Conversely, dynamics can sometimes light up the board when you thought you had a static lock!

> It's critically important to know if the position demands static or dynamic play from you.

> At times there might be a choice about which direction (Statics or Dynamics) you'll take, but more often than not, the writing is on the wall and there's only one correct decision.

> A dynamic plus is often cashed in for a longer lasting static plus.

> The transformation of one kind of imbalance (static or dynamic) into another kind of imbalance (dynamic or static) is very common.

Statics vs. Dynamics — Tests

Ready for more Statics vs. Dynamics situations? Think you have the whole concept iced? Well, here's your chance to prove just how well you've groked the Statics vs. Dynamics paradigm.

The following tests are designed to give you insight into how much you've learned *and* to serve as extra instruction. If you have trouble solving the tests, don't worry—that means we've uncovered something you don't understand, and this allows you to fix things by rereading the previous material or by picking up the bits of knowledge you're missing in the answers that start on page 539.

PART SIX - TEST 1

Diagram 286

[Level: 1900 - 2200]

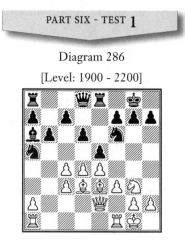

Black to move

Assess this position.

PART SIX - TEST 2

Diagram 287

[Level: 1400 - 2200]

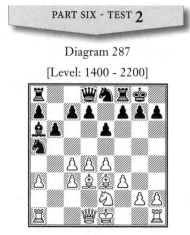

White to move

Assess the position.

PART SIX - TEST 3

Diagram 288

[Level: 2100 on up]

Black to move

You need to see the right move, but also see how to respond to white's best reply.

PART SIX - TEST 4

Diagram 289

[Level: 1800 - 2200]

Black to move

PART SIX - TEST 5

Diagram 290

[Level: 1400 - 1600]

White to move

Assess the position.

PART SIX - TEST 6

Diagram 291

[Level: 1400 - 2200]

White to move

Assess the position.

Part Seven / Space

Contents

Crushing Your Opponent in Space's Embrace

The Great Land Grab

In general, space isn't something amateurs hold in high esteem. Material—yes. Attack—yes. Doubled and/or isolated pawns—yes. All these things are solid—you can capture material, you can win weak pawns, and you can place a huge X on the head of the enemy King and embrace an all-out seek-and-destroy operation against it. But space? Is it really that important?

The answer, of course, is a resounding "Yes!" Ask players who have been squeezed to death by Petrosian, Karpov, or Seirawan—all masters of spatial gains—just how important it is. In fact, an advantage in space is one of *the* most highly prized imbalances among modern grandmasters.

And this pep talk takes us to a short but critical question: "Why?" Let's answer this with a visual image—a large guy staying in an average sized hotel room for twenty-four hours is, more or less, comfortable. But take that same person and cram him into a airplane bathroom and you'll see him falling apart both physically and emotionally—locked into such a small space, you can hardly move, there's nowhere to go, and little can be done.

Now imagine putting your opponent into that same situation on a chessboard. His pieces have little scope. There's no room to maneuver, and his Bishops, Knights, and Rooks tend to get in each other's way. You take your time, improving the position of your pawns and pieces at leisure, watching your opponent's face for signs of impending emotional collapse. He's uncomfortable, helpless, and all he can do is sit there and hope you can't find a way to deliver a deathblow. Who wouldn't feel despair when living out such a scenario?

> **PHILOSOPHY**
>
> All of history's great positional players coveted space because it deprives the opponent of room and dooms his pieces to a life of inactivity. Embracing a love of space is a must for players that want to improve their game.

Our first example, a Karpov masterpiece, illustrates all of this in a clear and impressive manner. Understanding all of this game's nuances isn't important.

What *is* important is to acquire a feel (and respect!) for the power of space and how it's there to be used for players of any level.

A. Karpov - A. Yusupov, Tilburg 1993

1.d4 Nf6 2.c4 e6 3.Nf3 b6 4.g3 Bb7 5.Bg2 Be7 6.Nc3 Ne4 7.Bd2 Bf6 8.Qc2 Nxd2 9.Qxd2 d6 10.d5

Diagram 292

FIRST SPATIAL GAIN: White claims space in the center, and also blocks the b7-Bishop's diagonal.

10...0–0 11.Nd4 e5 12.Nc6 Qd7

12...Nxc6 13.dxc6 gains space and also gives the white pieces access to d5.

13.Nxb8

Strange, isn't it? White's Knight has moved four times so that it could exchange itself for an enemy Knight that has never moved at all! On the surface, such a thing seems nonsensical, but there's a deep positional reason for white Knight's journey to b8: by ridding Black of his last Knight, White intends to create a closed position where Knights are superior to Bishops!

13...Rfxb8 14.h4

SECOND SPATIAL GAIN: This very useful move gains kingside space and also prepares to get the g2-Bishop outside the pawn chain by Bh3. Black will then be in a bit of a quandary: his light-squared Bishop is dead in the water on a6 or b7, but if he allows the exchange of light-squared Bishops by ...Bc8, he will be left with a bad Bishop versus a good enemy Knight.

14...a5 15.a4

IN A NUTSHELL

Black is already doomed to a long, passive, groveling defense. The best result he can realistically hope for is a draw—not a happy prospect for anyone!

Diagram 293

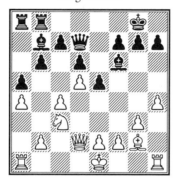

Killing queenside counterplay

Karpov shuts down all of black's queenside possibilities. Note that ...b6-b5 is now impossible, and ...c7-c6 creates (after White captures on c6) pawn weaknesses on b6 and d6 and also hands the d5-square to white's Knight.

Spatial Roundup: White has more space on the queenside, but he also has an obvious advantage in space in the center and on the kingside!

What does this mean for each side's chances? It doesn't bode well for Black! The second player's problem is that he can't initiate active play anywhere on the board. The queenside offers a long-term white plus (thanks to a possible b2-b4 advance), and the other two zones (center and kingside) belong to White thanks to his extra territory in those areas.

15...Rf8 16.e4

THIRD SPATIAL GAIN: This solidifies white's spatial advantage in the center by freezing black's e5-pawn and preventing an eventual ...e5-e4 (which would make the f6-Bishop very active). It also gobbles up a bit more kingside space by grabbing hold of the f5-square.

16...h5 17.0–0–0

Diagram 294

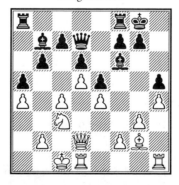

Pawn breaks are lurking

If Black has no way of opening up the queenside, then white's King will feel very safe there. This also allows White to play for line-opening breaks on the kingside, since his own King will be safely entrenched on the other wing.

Now it's time to discuss pawn breaks. In a closed position, pawn breaks are necessary to open lines for attack and to open files so the Rooks can join in the action. Let's look at each side's possibilities:

Black:

▶ An eventual ...g7-g5 destroys black's own kingside pawn protection and is a suicidal idea.

▶ The ...f7-f5 advance is the natural break in such a position (black's c7-d6-e5 pawn chain points to the kingside, which usually means that this is where he wants to play). However, the advance of the f-pawn (after the Bishop moves to d8 or e7 or, after ...g6, to g7) carries some serious baggage here—it further loosens black's kingside pawn cover, it allows White (after exf5) to claim e4 as a home for his Knight, and in many lines it simply helps White penetrate to the black King.

▶ Sacrificing via ...b6-b5 might be good at the right time, but only if a series of tactics somehow justify it. At the moment, and for the next few moves, that will most likely not be the case.

▶ The only break left is ...c7-c6—whether it's good or bad, it probably should be given a try. Better to fight like a cornered badger than to wait around and let the boa swallow you whole. Here's a sample of what could happen: 17...c6 18.dxc6 Qxc6 19.b3 Qc5 20.Kb2 (20.Bf3 Rfd8 21.Bxh5? b5! [See, it can work from time to time!] 22.axb5 [22.cxb5 Bxe4 and 22.Nxb5 Bxe4 both favor Black] 22...a4! 23.Nxa4 Rxa4! 24.bxa4 Bxe4 25.Rhe1 Qxc4+ 26.Kb2 Bf3!! 27.Bxf3? e4+ 28.Ka3 Ra8 29.a5 Bc3 and it's over!) 20...Be7 21.Qe2 Rfd8 22.Rd2 g6 23.g4 (23.f3!? followed by 24.g4 also deserves attention) 23...hxg4 24.Qxg4 Qc8 (24...d5 25.exd5 Qa3+ 26.Kc2 b5 27.axb5 a4 28.Rb1 doesn't quite work!) 25.Qg3 Kg7 26.h5 with a clear advantage to White. As this shows, White retains a clear plus after 17...c6, but things can easily get complicated and White can even fall victim to a crushing attack if he doesn't sense the possible danger.

White:

▶ The b2-b4 break will be huge in an endgame since it will allow White to open queenside lines and penetrate with his

King and Rooks. Black doesn't possess a comparable endgame break.

The c4-c5 break might prove to be a tactical way (in an endgame!) to let white's King into c4 and beyond.

A well-timed f2-f4 is a very important idea. It gains more central and kingside space and will certainly be on white's mind.

A well-timed g3-g4 idea is also in the mix.

It's clear that White has many more breaks than Black does!

17...g6 18.Bh3 Qe7 19.Kc2 Kg7

19...Bg7 leads to a position that's extremely uncomfortable for Black after 20.g4 hxg4 21.Bxg4 f5 22.Bh3 Bc8 23.Rdg1.

20.f3 Rh8 21.Rh2 Ba6 22.Nb5 Raf8

Taking the Knight by 22...Bxb5 would allow White long-term pressure down the c-file after 23.cxb5. White would also retain his kingside chances by eventual f3-f4 and/or g3-g4 advances.

23.Kb1 Qd8 24.Qd3 Be7 25.Re2 Bc8?

This allows the Knight to dominate Black's remaining Bishop. For better for or worse, he had to try 25...Bxb5 26.cxb5 Qe8 followed by ...Bd8.

26.Bxc8 Qxc8 27.Rg1

Diagram 295

A bit of Cat and Mouse

27.f4 was good, but Karpov wasn't in any hurry (why hurry when your opponent is completely helpless?) and decided to enjoy a bit of *Cat and Mouse*. Why do something now when you can make your opponent worry about it, thus leaving him dreading the moment when you finally flick the f-pawn forward?

27...Bd8

27...f5 28.f4 Qd7 (28...fxe4 29.Rxe4 Bf6 30.g4 hxg4 31.fxe5 Bxe5 32.Nd4! Bxd4 [32...Rxh4 33.Ne6+] 33.Qxd4+ Kg8 34.Re6 and it's all over.) 29.Rge1 fxe4 30.Rxe4 Bf6 31.fxe5 Bxe5 32.Nd4 Rf6 33.Ne6+ (probably even stronger than 33.Nc6 followed by 34.Nxe5) 33...Kg8 34.g4 hxg4 (34...Rh7 35.Rg1) 35.Rxg4 Rh6 36.Reg1 and white's advantage is obvious.

28.Na7

28.f4 was still possible, but Karpov decided to let his opponent's suffering linger for as long as possible. Besides, there's no reason to hurry when you can safely improve the position of your pieces before throwing down the final gauntlet.

28...Qh3 29.Qc2 Re8 30.Nc6 Bf6 31.Rf2 Qd7 32.Qe2 Rhf8 33.Rh2 Rh8 34.Qf2 Ref8 35.Rf1

Also strong was 35.g4. As usual, Karpov will bite when he's ready to bite, and not a moment before.

35...Kg8 36.f4

Diagram 296

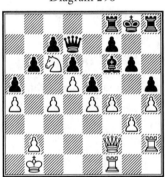

At last!

FOURTH SPATIAL GAIN: Making it clear that White is the absolute master of kingside space.

36...Qg4

Even worse is 36...exf4 37.gxf4 when White will eventually play the crushing "tidal wave" e4-e5.

37.Qf3 Re8

37...Qxf3 38.Rxf3 Re8 39.Rhf2 Rh7 40.f5 g5 41.hxg5 Bxg5 42.f6 h4 43.gxh4 Bf4 (43...Bxh4 44.Rh2 Be1 45.Ne7+) 44.Rg2+ Kh8 45.Rg4 (45.Ne7!?) 45...Rh6 46.Nd4 Rxf6 47.Kc2 Rg8 (47...Rg6 48.Rxg6 fxg6 49.Ne6) 48.Rxg8+ Kxg8 49.Nf5 Kh7 (49...Rg6 50.Ne7+) 50.h5 and Black is doomed—his Rook can't get off of f6 and his King can't approach the h-pawn. White will play to break open the queenside by a properly timed b2-b4 and that will be that.

38.Qxg4 hxg4 39.f5 g5 40.h5

Diagram 297

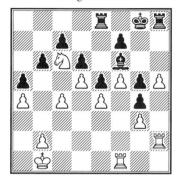

Leaving Black with a Tall-Pawn on f6

Black's Bishop creates an almost comical impression.

40...Ra8 41.Kc2 Kg7 42.Kc3

White finally turns his attention to the queenside, where he'll prepare his thematic b2-b4 break.

42...Ra6 43.Ra1 Rha8 44.b4 Kf8

44...axb4+ 45.Kxb4 Kh7 46.Rha2 Re8 47.Kb3 Raa8 48.Nb4 is lost for Black since he can't prevent Nb4-d3-f2xg4. Then Nf2 followed by g3-g4 will follow, the Knight will return to c6, and an eventual a4-a5 will win the game.

45.b5 R6a7 46.h6 Bh8 47.f6

A little tactic that stops Black from holding tight with ...f7-f6.

47...Bxf6 48.Rf1 Bh8 49.Nxa7 Rxa7 50.Rh5 Ke7 51.Rxg5 Ra8 52.h7 f6 53.Rg8 Rf8 54.c5!

This tactical pawn break is a final, beautiful touch to a wonderfully played game. White's King now decisively penetrates into the enemy position.

54...dxc5 55.Kc4 Kf7 56.d6 cxd6 57.Rxf8+, 1-0 since 57...Kxf8 58.Kd5 with Kc6 and Kxb6 offers no hope at all.

What did we learn from this example? Let's break it down:

➤ A huge advantage in space takes away many enemy options. In fact, if it isn't dealt with properly, the side with less space can easily end up with a passive, cheerless position.

➤ In closed positions, the side with more pawn breaks is the side with the ability to call the shots.

➤ Cat and Mouse is a strategy where your opponent is helpless. In such situations, barring a forced win, it's often good to "Do in twenty what you could do in two." In other words, take your time and let your opponent enjoy the full bouquet of his position's misery.

➤ If you possess an advantage in space, don't forget about the other imbalances. For example, playing for a superior minor piece can be a useful compliment to your territorial gains.

Here's an example where spatial gains push a position already ravaged by positional weaknesses over the brink.

A. Onischuk - J. Peters, Western States Open 2001

1.d4 Nf6 2.c4 g6 3.Nc3 Bg7 4.e4 d6 5.Nf3 0–0 6.Be2 e5 7.Be3 Ng4 8.Bg5 f6 9.Bc1 Nh6 10.dxe5 fxe5 11.c5!

Diagram 298

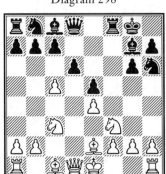

Creating a weakness in the enemy camp

This pawn advance is a thematic, very strong idea in the King's Indian Defense. The move not only vacates the c4-square for white's light-squared Bishop, but it also intends to capture on d6 and leave Black with either an isolated e-pawn (if Black recaptures with the Queen or Knight) or a backward d-pawn (if he recaptures with the c-pawn).

11.c5 nicely illustrates the creation of weak pawns/squares—don't expect them to just magically appear!

11...Nf7

Peters points out that 11...dxc5 leads to a clear white advantage after 12.Bc4+ Kh8 13.Qxd8 Rxd8 14.Bg5 Rf8 (14...Re8 15.Nd5) 15.Nxe5 Bxe5 16.Bxh6 Re8 17.0–0–0.

12. Be3 Nc6 13.0–0 Be6 14.cxd6 cxd6

14...Qxd6 is probably a little better, but White has the superior game (better structure with little to no counterplay for Black) in any case.

15.Qd2 h6 16.Rfd1 Re8 17.Rac1 Re7 18.Nd5 Rd7 19.h3 Kh7 20.Bc4 Qe8

Diagram 299

White to move and gain more space

Black's pawns on d6 and e5 are smothering their own pieces, while white's central forces have an abundance of space. As wonderful as white's position is, the d6-pawn is solidly defended and no instantly decisive blow can be found. Thus, White decides to further constrict black's position by grabbing queenside space too! This will quickly prove to be more than black's already strained defenses can handle.

21.b4!

White demands queenside space!

21...Nfd8

Hastening the end. 21...Qd8 holds out longer, but his passive, structurally/spatially deficient position would remain completely hopeless.

22.b5

More space! More! This obviously strong move was most likely played immediately, which explains how he missed 22.Bxh6! which wins a pawn since 22...Bxd5 (22...Bxh6 23.Nf6+) 23.Bxg7 Bxc4 gets mated: 24.Qh6+ Kg8 25.Qh8+ Kf7 26.Ng5+ Ke7 27.Bf6 mate.

22...Bxd5

22...Qf7 is better. Here's a fanciful variation: 23.Be2 (23.bxc6 bxc6 is still good for White, but 23.Be2 is better) 23...Ne7 (23...Nd4 puts up more resistance) 24.b6 Bxd5 25.exd5 Nf5 26.Qa5! Nxe3 27.fxe3 e4 (27...a6 28.Nd2 is winning) 28.Ng5+!! hxg5 29.Qxa7!! Rxa7 30.bxa7 and a new Queen will be born.

23.exd5 Nb8

23...Ne7 24.b6 e4 25.Nh2 axb6 26.Bb5 is also completely lost.

24.b6 a6 25.Bb3 Qf7 26.Rc8, 1-0. White's central and queenside space advantage, and the difference in piece activity that was a result of it, made his grandmaster strength opponent look like a child. Lack of space has brought many great players to their knees!

In the Onischuk - Peters game, black's pieces were smothered by his lack of space. In a way, I'm reminded of a Volkswagen Bug and how "bug" addicts would cram as many people as possible into that small space (I think the record was 27). Being in the filled up car would be intolerable, but reduce the number to three or four and all would be well.

IN A NUTSHELL

"I got a backward d-pawn and a miserably passive position. At the end, I can barely move."—Peters.

The idea of the spactially challenged side making a few exchanges so that his remaing pieces have room to maneuver is useful in all stages of the game. Here's a typical opening example:

1.d4 Nf6 2.c4 c5 3.d5 e6 4.Nc3 exd5 5.cxd5 d6 6.e4 g6 7.f4 Bg7 8.Bb5+ Nfd7 9.a4 0-0 10.Nf3 Na6 11.0-0 Nb4 12.Re1 a6

Diagram 300

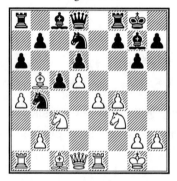

White to move and avoid exchanges

White enjoys much more central space. Note that black's light-squared Bishop is actually in the way of its other pieces. At the moment, white's light-squared Bishop is under attack and has to move. 13.Bc4 has been played from time to time, but 13.Bf1 is recognized as correct. Why? Because 13.Bc4 gives Black time to free his Bishop and trade it off: 13...Nb6 14.Be2 Bg4 when black's forces will have more room to move about (as in I. Watson - J. Nunn, Brighton 1980). On the other hand, 13.Bf1 avoids this: 13...Nf6 14.h3! when Black is forced to continue suffering from a certain amount of claustrophobia.

RULE

It's usually a good idea for the side with more space to avoid unnecessary exchanges.

The idea that the side with more territory should avoid unnecessary exchanges might lead one to believe that space won't be of much use in an endgame since many exchanges would have been made to reach that stage. However, this simply isn't the case.

Diagram 301

V. Kramnik - M. Illescas, Dos Hermanas 1997
White to move

White has an obvious advantage in space and two Bishops. Though the position is rather closed (a situation that usually makes Knights happy), black's horses aren't doing much of anything due to the fact that they don't have access to any advanced support points (d4 can't be reached, and an immediate jump to e5 allows White to chop it off with advantage).

White is clearly better, but it will take time and patience to actually win.

1.Nb1!

A star move. The Knight is heading for c3 where it stops black's planned ...Nc7 followed by ...d6-d5—the white Knight also intends to continue on to a4 where the d7-Knight will be frozen guarding b6.

Some players might ask why this is a big deal, since white's Knight on a4 will be as "frozen" as black's on d7. That's an astute observation, but there's a flaw: once those Knights reach that faceoff position, the d7-Knight will need to be protected from attacks by white's light-squared Bishop. Thus, black's one active plan of ...d6-d5 won't work since exd5 followed by Bh3 forces the win of b6.

What all this means is that Black now finds himself with a situation we've seen before: no space, passive pieces, no play, and little hope.

1...Bb7

1...Ne5 2.Bxe5 dxe5 3.Nc3 Nd6 4.Na4 Nc8 5.Bh3 Kf8 6.f4 exf4 7.gxf4 is a clear advantage for White - Kramnik.

2.f4

Taking more space and also depriving the enemy Knights of the use of the e5-square. As we know from the chapter on Knights, taking away advanced squares from hostile horses is a major part of effective Anti-Knight Strategy.

2...f6 3.Nc3 Kf7 4.Na4! Ke7 5.d4 Kd8

Other moves are even worse:

> 5...cxd4 6.Bxd4 Nc5 7.Bxc5 bxc5 8.e5 Bxg2 9.Kxg2 fxe5
> 10.fxe5 Kd7 11.Kf3 Kc7 12.Kf4 "and the Knight endgame is
> winning for White."—Karpov.

> Kramnik gives 5...Nc7 6.e5 Bxg2 7.exd6+ Kxd6 8.Kxg2, which
> leaves Black in bad shape. He points out that 8...cxd4 leads to
> Armageddon after 9.Ba3+ Nc5 10.Nxb6 e5 11.Na4 Ne6 12.f5.

6.d5

White grabs even more space, and black's prison grows smaller.

6...exd5

6...e5 7.Bh3 Bc8 8.Kf2 (White does want any part of 8.Bxd7 Bxd7 9.Nxb6
Bg4 10.Kf2 Kc7 11.Na4 Bd1 12.Nc3 Bb3—when you have more space, you want
to use it to stamp out enemy counterplay. Here White has clearly failed to do
this!) 8...Kc7 9.Bc1 h6 10.Be6 and Black is still caged and helpless.

7.exd5 Nc7

7...Kc7 8.Bh3 Nf8 9.Kf2—Kramnik.

8.Bh3

Threatening to win the b-pawn by Bxd7.

8...Na8 9.Be6 Nf8 10.f5

Diagram 302

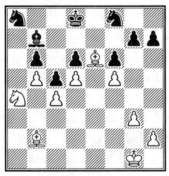

White's enormous spatial plus has taken on epic proportions! In such situations, the victim doesn't know whether to laugh or cry.

10...Bc8 11.Kf2 Bd7 12.g4 Ke7 13.g5

13.h4 was also strong.

13...Nxe6!

Avoiding 13...Be8 14.gxf6+ gxf6 15.Nc3 Nd7 16.Ne4 Ne5 17.Bxe5 when either recapture allows a deadly pawn check.

14.fxe6 Be8 15.gxf6+ gxf6

Black's position is hideous, but the opposite colored Bishops makes winning far from easy.

16.Ke3 Bg6 17.Kd2

Using the King to take care of c4. However, 17.Nc3!? deserved serious consideration.

17...Be4 18.Bc1 Bg2 19.Kc3 Bf1 20.Bh6 Bg2 21.Bf4 Bf1 22.Nb2 Nc7 23.Nd1 Bg2 24.Ne3 Be4 25.Bh6 Ne8 26.Kd2 Nc7 27.Ke2 Ne8 28.Kf2 Nc7

White's been employing the usual Cat and Mouse strategy, hoping to wear down the opponent. Now Kramnik points out that 28...Bb1!? followed by 29...Ba2 was an interesting defensive try.

29.Kg3 Bd3 30.Kg4

Threatening 31.Nf5+ Bxf5 32.Kxf5 with an easy win.

30...Ne8 31.Kf4 Bb1

Diagram 303

White's seemingly endless maneuvering has paid off, and how he has a forced win.

32.Nf5+ Kd8

As usual, taking the Knight doesn't work: 32...Bxf5 33.Kxf5 Nc7 34.Bg7 Ne8 35.Bh8 with a winning zugzwang.

33.Bf8 Bd3 34.Be7+ Kc7 35.Ne3 Kc8 36.Kg4 Kc7 37.Kh5 Ng7+ 38.Kh6 Ne8 39.h4 Kc8 40.h5 Kc7 41.Ng2! Kc8

41...Bxc4 42.Kxh7 Bxd5 43.Nf4 Be4+ 44.Kg8 c4 45.Kf7 c3 46.Kxe8 c2 47.Bd8+ Kb8 48.Ne2 Bf3 49.Nc1 Bxh5+ 50.Ke7 wins—Kramnik.

42.Nf4 Bc2 and now, instead of the mistaken 43.Bxf6? (though White ended up winning anyway), correct was **43.Ng6! hxg6 44.hxg6 f5** (44...Bd3 45.g7 Nxg7 46.Kxg7 Bxc4 47.Bxd6 is easy) **45.g7** (45.Bxd6 also does the job) **45...Nxg7 46.Kxg7 Kc7** (46...Bd3 47.Bxd6 Bxc4 48.Bf4 Bxb5 49.Kf8 is game over) **47.Bd8+! Kxd8 48.Kf8** and White promotes his e-pawn.

Dueling Spatial Plusses

So far we've looked at positions where one side had a monopoly on space. However, far more common are positions where both sides have space in different sectors of the board. For example, in the King's Indian Defense it's common for White to have a huge queenside space advantage (which often allows him to ravage Black on that wing and also to have a marked advantage in most endgames), while Black counters with serious spatial gains on the kingside, which leads to a strong attack against the white King.

1.d4 Nf6 2.c4 g6 3.Nc3 Bg7 4.e4 d6 5.Be2 0–0 6.Nf3 e5 7.0–0 Nc6 8.d5 Ne7

Diagram 304

> **RULE**
>
> In closed positions, you usually want to play where your pawn chain "points".

When playing this variation, both sides pretty much know what's expected of them. The center is closed so play has to be found on the wings. In such positions, you usually want to play on the side where you have more space (of course, there *are* exceptions—don't treat any rule as gospel). Once you determine which side that is, you will try and create weaknesses in the enemy camp, use pawn advances to gain even more territory in your chosen sector, and employ pawn breaks to crack open files for the Rooks so you can use them to penetrate into the hostile position.

The following common sequence shows how each side goes about their business:

9.Ne1

The Knight heads for d3 where it will help make the space gaining (and file opening) c4-c5 push possible. In general, your space lies where your pawn chain points—to add to your space (and rip open files) in that area, you need to push the pawn that's next to your lead pawn. In white's case the lead pawn is d5 and the pawn you want to push (since e4-e5 is impossible) is the c-pawn. In black's case the lead pawn is on e5 and the pawn next to it is the f-pawn. Thus, both sides will make use of a *Pawn Cascade*: White will play c4-c5 (laying claim to the queenside) and Black will play ...f7-f5 (beginning a kingside attack).

> **RULE**
>
> The use of Pawn Cascades allows you to gain extra space and create open files so your Rooks can penetrate into the enemy position.

9...Nd7

Black's Knight gets out of the way of its f-pawn and also eyes the c5-square, temporarily making the c4-c5 push harder to achieve.

10.Nd3

Continuing to prepare the critical c4-c5 push.

10...f5

Black's kingside space advantage is now clear.

11.Bd2

Developing and preparing to bring the a1-Rook to c1 in anticipation of that file opening after c4-c5.

11...Nf6

Black wants to annex even more kingside space with ...f5-f4, but that move doesn't work right away due to 12.Bg4! when the eventual exchange of light-squared Bishops will severely hamper black's kingside attack. 11...Nf6 attacks e4 and forces White to address that threat by either taking on f5 or, more commonly, defending the e-pawn with f2-f3.

12.f3 f4

Now this move works since Bg4 is no longer legal.

13.c5

Both sides achieved their optimum pawn advances.

13...g5

Now the furthest pawn in the chain is f4, so Black wants to push his g-pawn to g4 and open a file right in the face of white's King!

14.cxd6

Opening up the c-file.

14...cxd6 15.Rc1 Ng6 with the beginning of an exciting battle between white's queenside attack and black's kingside attack.

Our next two examples show these ideas at play. For our purpose, a serious analysis isn't called for—I want you to get a visual and visceral feel for this kind of structure, and reams of variations won't be of any help. So sit back and enjoy the intensity of this war of ideas, and pay special attention to both side's adherence to their respective goals. This kind of kingside vs. queenside philosophical argument is always complex and fever-pitched—if you want to play either side, you have to be prepared to experience a heaping dose of gut-wrenching fear!

G. Sosonko - W. Uhlmann, Amsterdam 1975

1.d4 Nf6 2.c4 g6 3.Nc3 Bg7 4.e4 d6 5.Nf3 0–0 6.Be2 e5 7.0–0 Nc6 8.d5 Ne7 9.b4 Nh5 10.g3 f5 11.Nd2 Nf6 12.c5 (A thematic Pawn Cascade, which grabs space, places pressure against d6, and allows White to open the c-file by cxd6 if he feels it's advantageous to do so) **12...f4 13.Nc4 g5** (Preparing his own space gaining Pawn Cascade by ...g5-g4) **14.Ba3 Bh3 15.Re1 Rf7 16.b5 Nc8 17.Bb2 Re7 18.c6 b6 19.a4 Qe8 20.a5 Rb8 21.axb6 axb6 22.Ra3 h5 23.Qd3 Qg6**

Diagram 305

Both sides have completely overrun their respective wings!

24.Rea1 Re8 25.Ra8 Rxa8 26.Rxa8 Rf8 27.Nd2 Bh6 28.Bf1 Bxf1 29.Nxf1 g4 30.gxf4 exf4 31.Qc4 g3 32.hxg3 fxg3 33.fxg3 h4 34.e5 Be3+ 35.Nxe3? (Black was winning in any case, but this move—most likely a product of time pressure—does a swan dive into the lava pit.) **35...Qxg3+ 36.Kh1 Qh3+ 37.Kg1 Qxe3+ 38.Kh1 Qh3+ 39.Kg1** and White resigned without waiting for 39...Ng4, which forces a quick mate. In the end, White still rules the queenside, but his King is dead!

A. Beliavsky - D. Solak, Saint-Vincent 2000

1.d4 Nf6 2.c4 g6 3.Nc3 Bg7 4.e4 d6 5.Nf3 0–0 6.Be2 e5 7.0–0 Nc6 8.d5 Ne7 9.Nd2 Ne8 10.b4 f5 11.c5 Nf6 12.f3 f4 13.Nc4 (A thematic plan. White begins to grind d6.) **13...g5 14.a4 Ng6 15.Ba3 Rf7 16.b5 Ne8 17.a5 Bf8 18.Na4 h5 19.b6**

Diagram 306

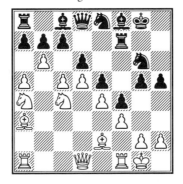

White has nuked the queenside and the game is pretty much over there. Now black's only hope is his attack on the opposite wing—can he strike before he's completely pushed off the board?

19...Bd7 20.bxc7 Qxc7 21.a6 bxa6 22.c6 Bc8 23.Nab2 Rg7 24.Nd3 Nh8 25.Nf2 Nf7 26.h3 Nh6 27.Rb1 Qd8 28.Bb4 Nf6 29.Rb3 a5 30.Bxa5 Qe8 31.c7 Qg6 32.Rb8 (Black is going to suffer catastrophic material losses.) **32...g4** (It's mate or bust! Unfortunately for Black, his position is already too far gone.) **33.hxg4 hxg4 34.Rxa8 Bd7 35.c8=Q Bxc8 36.Rxc8 g3 37.Nh3 Nf7 38.Bb4 Ng5 39.Bxd6 Qh5 40.Bxf8 Nxh3+ 41.gxh3 Qxh3 42.Bxg7+ Kxg7 43.Rc7+ Kg8 44.Rf2 gxf2+ 45.Kxf2 Qh4+ 46.Kg2 Qg3+ 47.Kf1**, 1-0. The checks will soon run out after 47…Qh3+ 48.Ke1.

The idea of playing where your pawn chain points, and of pushing the pawn next to your lead pawn so that more space can be gained and files opened, is an oft-seen theme in several structures. The following game shows the *Pawn-Pointing Rule* and the idea of Pawn Cascades were both understood even in the 1600s!

G. Greco - NN, Europe 1620

1.e4 e6 2.d4 d5 3.e5 c5 4.c3

Diagram 307

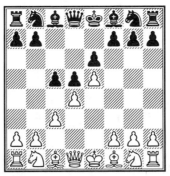

This well-known line in the French Defense features a clear illustration of pawn chains pointing in different directions and how the structure generally dictates the way each side will play. Black's f7-e6-d5 pawn chain points to the queenside while white's b2-c3-d4-e5 chain is taking aim at the kingside. In fully closed positions, this would indicate that Black would eventually attack on the queenside with pawns via ...c5-c4 followed by ...b7-b5-b4 (taking huge amounts of space and opening up files for the Rooks). White's plan would be an eventual f2-f4-f5, trying to crash through on the opposite wing.

However, the French center isn't necessarily doomed to permanent closure, and this means that both sides have other options. In fact, Black usually makes use of a plan based on pressure against d4 via ...Nc6, ...Qb6, and ...Ng8-e7-f5 with a true team effort against white's d-pawn! In this line, ...Bd7 and ...Rc8 also allows Black chances along the c-file once he opens it with ...cxd4. Finally, in many lines Black can strike at e5 too with a well-timed ...f7-f6 punch.

White, of course, enjoys a central space advantage and usually tries to stabilize it with Nf3, Be2, 0-0 and, at times, even Nb1-a3-c2 giving d4 plenty of support! In some cases White can pursue a kingside attack with pieces (Qg4 and/or Bd3) and at other times he can play to occupy d4 with a piece via a well-timed dxc5 following by plonking down a Knight on the newly freed up square.

4...cxd4 5.cxd4 Bb4+ 6.Nc3 Bxc3+ 7.bxc3

Black's last few moves were pretty bad (What did you expect from an unknown foe in 1620?), and his rushed exchanges have turned the potential target on d4 into an unassailable rock. This doesn't mean that Black's devoid of certain positive imbalances and a clear plan: the c3-pawn is backward and can be attacked by placing a Rook (or the Queen) on the half-open c-file. The c4-square is also vulnerable, and can be occupied by an eventual ...Nb8-c6-a5-c4.

Be that as it may, White is much better in this position. He still enjoys a spatial plus in the center and on the kingside. He has two active Bishops—the light-squared Bishop will sit on d3 and send out rays of power along two diagonals (f1-a6 and b1-h7), while the dark-squared Bishop might eventually set up shop on a3 and lay claim to the entire a3-f8 diagonal. And, in case you've forgotten, the f2-f4-f5 Cascade idea is still there, waiting to be utilized.

7...Nc6 8.Bd3

8.Qg4!? was worth considering, forcing Black into unsavory choices such as ...Kf8 or ...g6 (which weakens all the dark-squares). Note that 8.Qg4 Qa5 9.Bd2 would leave Black with the same problem as before.

8...Nge7 9.f4

Dreaming of an eventual f4-f5 Pawn Cascade. Of course, if the f4-f5 advance doesn't occur, then the f4-pawn can actually hurt White by blocking his Bishop's control of the c1-h6 diagonal. Personally, I would have preferred 9.Qg4 Qa5 10.Bd2 0-0 11.Nf3 with a nice attacking position for White.

9...Nf5 10.Nf3 0–0

Allowing White to make his hoped for Cascade a reality. Black had to give 10...h5 a shot (A thematic idea in this kind of position—Black creates an artificial support point on f5 by stopping g2-g4). After 11.0-0 g6 (11...0-0!? is possible, but usually the Rook likes to stay on h8 for defensive reasons) 12.Ng5 (12.Ba3 Ne3) 12...Kf8 13.a4 Kg7 14.Re1 and now the threat of 15.Bxf5 exf5 16.e6 forces Black to play either 14...Re8 (not ideal since the Rook does a good defensive job on h8) or 14...Nce7 (not ideal since this Knight had hoped to jump to a5 and eventually c4). White is better, but black's position isn't easy to crack and, if white's not careful, Black might be able to eventually build up some pressure against c4 and c3.

11.g4 Nh4 12.0–0 Nxf3+ 13.Qxf3 Bd7 14.Qh3 g6

14...h6 15.g5.

15.f5

Diagram 308

The Pawn Cascade overwhelms the black position.

15...exf5 16.gxf5

White also wins with 16.Qh6, threatening both 17.gxf5 and 17.Bg5. However, Greco's move is simpler and quite lethal.

16...gxf5

There's no defense:

➤ 16...Kh8 17.e6 fxe6 18.fxg6 Rxf1+ 19.Kxf1 Qg8 (19...Qf6+ 20.Ke1 Qg7 21.Bh6 Qf6 22.Bg5 Qg7 23.Bf6) 20.Bg5 Rf8+ 21.Kg2 threatens crunchy moves such as 22.Rf1 and 22.Qh4 and gives White an overwhelming attack.

➤ 16...Qa5 17.Qh6 Bxf5 18.Rxf5 Qxc3 19.Rh5! Qxd4+ 20.Kh1 with a mating attack.

➤ 16...Qe7 17.Qh6 Rfc8 18.Ba3 Qxa3 19.fxg6 fxg6 20.Bxg6 Qe7 21.Rf7 Qxf7 22.Bxf7+ Kxf7 23.Qxh7+ Ke8 24.Qh8+ Ke7 25.Qf6+ Ke8 26.Rf1 and mates.

17.Rxf5 Bxf5 18.Bxf5, 1-0. The legendary Greco ate up his overmatched foe.

Fighting Against Space

We've seen the benefits that an advantage in space bestows upon its owner. However, this doesn't mean that the spatially challenged player has to roll over and die. In general, there are four ways to deal with space:

- ➤ Exchange pieces so your limited territory is no longer uncomfortable.

- ➤ Use pawn breaks to crack his seemingly indestructible pawn-façade.

- ➤ Try and prove that your opponent's gain in space has left weak squares in its wake.

- ➤ Treat a space-gaining enemy pawn center as a target!

Exchange Pieces!

We've already discussed piece exchanges as a means of soothing the pain of a constricted position. Here's a basic example:

Diagram 309

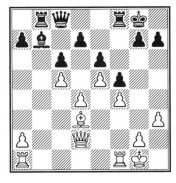

Black to move

White enjoys more central and queenside space, and he also has a very good Bishop while black's is seemingly inactive (of course, if black's a-pawn was on a6 and white's a-pawn on a5 then the black Bishop would be a true Tall-Pawn and white's advantage would be decisive).

Here we'll let a couple rules guide us: "Trade bad minor pieces for good ones", "Get your Bishop outside the pawn chain", and "Exchange pieces when you have less space." With so many rules smacking us in the face, black's move is a no-brainer!

1...Ba6

Activating the Bishop and forcing its exchange.

2.Rfb1 Bxd3 3.Qxd3 Qc7

Intending to trade all the Rooks via ...Rxb1 followed by ...Rb8.

4.Rb3 Rxb3 5.axb3 Rb8

White's remaining Rook is staring at a7, but black's Rook, by snapping at b3, is just as good.

6.Qc3

6.Ra6 Rb4 7.Kh2 Qb7 8.Ra3 a5, =

6...Qb7 7.Ra3

7.Ra4 gives Black all the play after 7...a5! 8.Rxa5 (8.Qxa5 Qxb3 leaves white's King far worse off than black's.) 8...Kf7! (So black's King can defend d7. It turns out that Black will easily regain his pawn since potential targets on b3, d4, and f4 make it impossible for White to hold everything together.) 9.Ra3 Qb4 10.Qxb4 (10.Qb2 Qe1+ 11.Kh2 Qe3 12.b4 [12.g3? Rb4 is just bad for White] 12...Qxf4+ can only favor Black.) 10...Rxb4 and white's once-mighty space advantage no longer counts for anything. After 11.Kf2 Rxd4 White will draw, but Black can play on a bit and let his opponent grovel before making peace.

As you can see, black's game is actually easier to handle since in some lines the white King can find itself in an uncomfortable situation.

7...Kf7

Black's King needs to be able to defend d7 in many lines.

8.Kf2 a6

Though this looks stupid, it's actually quite useful! The idea is that if and when White captures black's a-pawn, the capturing piece would also attack d7 if the pawn stood on a7. Thus, by placing it on a6 Black will gain a tempo since guarding d7 won't be immediately necessary.

9.Qa5

9.g4!? might be white's best, though 9...g6 promises Black a trouble free game.

9...h6 10.Ke3

10.h4!?

10...g5 11.g3

11.fxg5 hxg5 12.Kd2 Qb5 13.Qxb5 Rxb5 14.Kc3 a5 15.Ra2 Kg6 and the Black King has dreams of marching in via ...Kg6-h5-h4-g3!

11...Qb4 12.Qxb4 Rxb4 13.Kd3 a5 14.Kc3 gxf4 15.gxf4

Avoiding 15.Rxa5 fxg3 16.Kxb4 g2 17.Ra1 f4.

15...Rb5 16.Ra1 Kg6 17.Rg1+ Kh5 18.Rg7 Rb7

Diagram 310

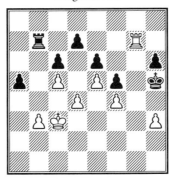

White to move

It looks like Black is making serious headway, but White now uncorks a saving trick.

19.b4!! axb4+ 20.Kb3 Kh4 21.d5! Rb8 22.dxe6 dxe6 23.Rg6 and White's active Rook will earn him a draw.

Use Pawn Breaks!

A pawn break is the weapon of choice when facing an opponent who gleefully marches his pawns forward in an attempt to annex every square on the board. A pawn break either challenges your opponent's advanced structure head on, or maps out its own space in another sector. Here's an easy-to-understand example of how a pawn break works.

Diagram 311

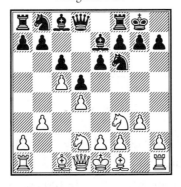

SinEater7 - DLJ, Internet game 2006
Black to move

White, seeing that he could grab queenside space, has just played c4-c5. It turns out that if white's a1-Rook was protected, then this advance would be worthy of at least some consideration. However, the a1-Rook *isn't* protected, and thus the space-gaining advance of the c-pawn is simply a mistake. I'll explain this cryptic comment about the undefended a1-Rook in the note to black's second move.

This kind of error is made all the time on the amateur level, so it's very important for the student to become familiar with the antidote.

1...b6!

This pawn break, which directly challenges the c5-pawn's right to be on that square, refutes white's idea. Now 2.cxb6 is pretty much forced, though both 2...axb6 and 2...Qxb6 give Black a very nice position.

To understand why having to play 2.cxb6 is a slap in the face for White, take a look at the position after 1.c5. Which pawn is more valuable, white's c5-pawn or black's a7-pawn? Clearly, the more central c-pawn is far better than the thing on a7 (in general, center pawns are more valuable than wing pawns). Next, look at the position after 2.cxb6 axb6. In effect, White has exchanged his c-pawn for black's a-pawn! So, by playing 1.c5, White lost a tempo to trade his c-pawn for black's a-pawn, while also opening up a file for the previously "dead" Rook on a8! It's clear that White is a very nice person!

Of course, White didn't play 1.c5 to swap it off for a wing pawn. He intended to keep his c-pawn on c5 by giving it support. Thus he now compounds his problems with the logical but tactically flawed 2.b4.

2.b4? a5!

Diagram 312

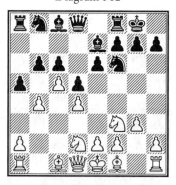

White loses material

Believe it or not, White is actually losing material here! Why? Because his whole queenside structure can't be maintained, and this takes us back to the "undefended a1-Rook" comment. If the a1-Rook was on b1 or if white's Bishop was on b2 (defending the Rook), then 3.a3 would support all the pawns. However, since the Rook isn't defended, 3.a3 fails to 3…axb4 when White can't recapture because of the pin on the a-file.

It's critical that you fully understand why white's game is falling apart, so please explore this position again and again until it all makes perfect sense.

3.Qa4

A noble try, but it's already too late to stop the bleeding. Note that 3.cxb6 axb4 leaves Black a full pawn ahead since the b6-pawn will soon be removed from the board. Also, 3.Ba3 Na6 wins a pawn since it simultaneously attacks both b4 and c5.

3…Ba6

Black is up to the challenge and finds the best move. White still can't avoid losing a pawn.

4.a3

Poor SinEater7 is still dreaming of holding his pawn chain together. Unfortunately, his fantasies are about to come face to face with reality.

4…Bb5! 5.Qb3 axb4 6.Qxb4 bxc5 7.dxc5 Na6 8.Qb2 Nxc5 and white's dead lost—he's a pawn down, his a-pawn is weak, and he is way behind in development.

Now let's take a look at the same general structure, but this time White willingly plays c4-c5, knowing he can't maintain the advanced c-pawn.

A. Kornev - S. Rublevsky, Russia 2007

1.d4 d5 2.c4 c6 3.Nf3 Nf6 4.e3 a6 5.Nc3 e6 6.c5 b6

The thematic pawn break. As in our previous example, 7.b4 fails to 7…a5.

7.cxb6

Diagram 313

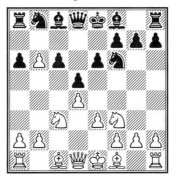

The space-gaining c5-pawn has been forced off its perch, but white's positional idea is crystal clear: he wants to follow up with Na4, Bd2, and Rc1 with control over the hole on c5 and pressure against the backward pawn on c6. Black, of course, doesn't allow this to happen.

7...Nbd7 8.Na4

This position has occurred a lot over the years, but practice has shown that White can't expect to achieve a meaningful advantage.

8...Nxb6 9.Bd2 Nxa4 10.Qxa4 Bd7 11.Ne5 c5

If White had been able to freeze black's c-pawn on c6, then he would have stood better. However, the "weak" pawn is anything but the helpless target White had hoped it would be—instead of letting the pawn sit passively in place, Black challenges for queenside space via a second pawn break.

12.Nxd7 Qxd7 13.Qxd7+ Kxd7 14.dxc5 Bxc5 15.Rc1 Rhc8 16.Bd3, ½-½. Not a very exciting example (to say the least!), but it does illustrate the usefulness of pawn breaks as a means of freeing a position that's somewhat spatially challenged.

So far we've seen pawn breaks with ...b6, ...a5, ...c5, and (in the King's Indian) ...f5 mixed with ...g5-g4. One other major break (White, of course, has his own series of breaks in different positions, but once you master the ideas behind the typical black breaks, the white breaks will be easy to find) is the ...e7-e5 break. Here's a rather frenetic example.

W.G. Hansen - D. Ciric, Politiken Cup 1989

1.e4 c6 2.d4 d5 3.exd5 cxd5 4.c4 Nf6 5.c5

Not a very good move since White is going after space before he's even developed one single piece!

5...e5

Diagram 314

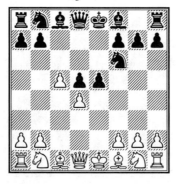

Ripping white's space gaining structure to bits

Black had other reasonable moves (5...b6 is our usual response in this kind of position, while the patient 5...g6 has also been played), but 5...e5 is clearly the most challenging and extreme attempt to refute white's c5-push. This move starts an immediate fight (taking advantage of white's undeveloped army), and instantly attacks the c5-pawn's main defender on d4.

6.dxe5 Ng4

6...Ne4 is also good.

7.Qd4?

White, who wanted to dictate matters with 5.c5, is so taken aback by the turn of events that he immediately makes a serious mistake.

7...Nc6 8.Bb5 Qa5+ 9.Nc3 Qxb5! 10.Nxb5 Nxd4 11.Nxd4 Bxc5 12.Ngf3 Nxe5 13.0–0 0–0, 0-1. Apparently White, who is down a pawn, simply gave up in disgust.

Armed with all these pawn break patterns, let's look at a heavyweight example that mixes them together.

G. Kaidanov - V. Milov, Gibraltar 2007

1.d4 d5 2.c4 c6 3.Nc3 Nf6 4.Nf3 a6 5.c5 Bf5 6.Bf4 e6 7.e3 Nbd7 8.Be2 Be7

Diagram 315

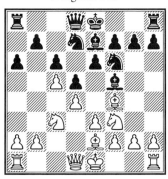

White has an obvious space advantage on the queenside and he also controls more squares (d6 and e5) in the center. If White can maintain his advantage in space while also avoiding unnecessary exchanges *and* not allowing a freeing pawn break (black's potential breaks are ...b7-b6 and ...e6-e5), he'll have a clear advantage.

9.Nd2

Black had intended to play for a soothing exchange of Knights by ...Ne4. White's move (9.Nd2) makes this unpalatable.

9...Bg6 10.Rc1 Qc8 11.a3 0–0 12.g4 Ne8 13.h4 f6 14.h5 Bf7

Black is pinning all his hopes on the second pawn break—...e6-e5.

15.Nf3

Diagram 316

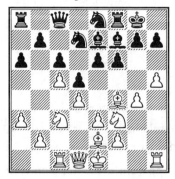

White, by preventing black's hoped for ...e6-e5 push, clearly wants a space advantage on every part of the board! Aside from mere space, the 12.g4/13.h4 pawn-duo intends to sweep Black away on the kingside. The idea is that Black seems devoid of counterplay, which means White will have a free hand on either wing.

However, things aren't that simple. Though black's normal ...b7-b6 break has been rendered innocuous for the moment (opening the c-file so the c1-Rook stares at c6 seems more than a little risky), he's poising himself to smash open the center with the other thematic pawn break, ...e6-e5.

15...Nc7

15...Bd8 followed by ...Bc7 and ...e6-e5 is a logical recommendation by Milov.

16.Na4

Clamping down on the queenside and giving c5 more support (one point of ...e6-e5 is to crack the main defender of c5, so white's 16.Na4 anticipates this).

16...Qd8 17.Bd3 e5

Diagram 317

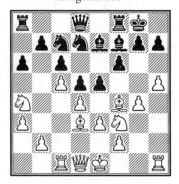

Busting loose

Black refuses to passively sit around and wait for the axe to fall. Instead, thanks to this key break, he sacrifices a pawn so that his pieces jump to life and give him serious counterplay. White might still be better, but things will now become far more complicated—mistakes are frequent visitors when the opponent is suddenly punching back!

18.dxe5 Ne6 19.exf6

19.Qc2!? h6 20.Bf5 is critical, but assessing the wild complications that arise after 20…Nxf4 21.exf4 fxe5 22.fxe5 Bg5 is far from easy. Here's a glance into some of the position's possibilities:

Diagram 318

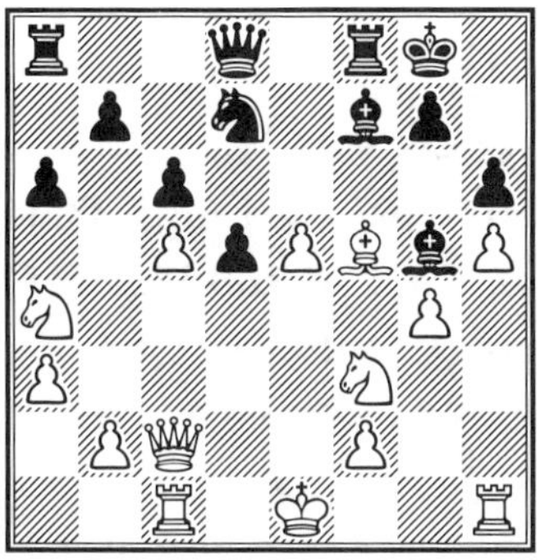

Position after 22…Bg5

White to move

➤ 23.Rd1 Nxe5 24.Nxe5 Qe7 25.0–0 Qxe5 26.Nb6 Rad8 27.Nd7 Rxd7 28.Bxd7 Qe7 29.Bf5 Bf4 30.Rd4 Bb8 31.Rb4 Re8 and the vulnerable dark squares around white's King give Black adequate chances: 32.Rb3 d4 33.Bg6 Bxg6 34.Qxg6 Rd8 35.Qc2 Qh4 36.f3 d3, =.

➤ 23.Nxg5 hxg5 24.Bxd7 Qxd7 25.Nb6 Qxg4 26.Nxa8 Qf3 27.Rh2 Qf4 28.Rg2 Qh4 29.Qd3 Bxh5 30.Qg3 Qe4+ 31.Kf1 Bf3 32.Nb6 (32.Rh2 Qe2+ 33.Kg1 Rf4 when the threat of …Rg4 is nasty) 32…Qe2+ 33.Kg1 Bxg2 34.Qxg2 Rf4 35.Rc3 Qxb2 36.Rg3 Rh4 and White has some annoying problems to solve.

All this gives the impression that Black is okay after 19.Qc2!? h6 20.Bf5 Nxf4 21.exf4 fxe5 22.fxe5 Bg5 23.Nxg5 hxg5, but is that true? Instead of 24.Bxd7, White can do better with 24.h6! Nxe5 25.hxg7 Kxg7 (25…Re8 26.Nb6 Rb8 27.Kf1 Qf6 28.Kg2) 26.Rh7+ Kg8 27.Rh6 with a clear advantage.

19…Nxf6 20.Ne5 Nxf4 21.exf4 Qc7 22.g5 Ne4 and Black has some compensation in the form of white's offside a4-Knight, central King, and time pressure.

Diagram 319

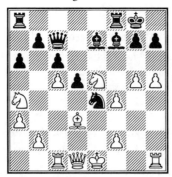

Chaos

In the end, White missed his chances and even went down in defeat: **23.g6 Be8 24.Qg4 Bf6 25.h6 Bxg6 26.Nxg6 hxg6 27.f3 Qa5+ 28.b4 Qxa4 29.Qe6+ Rf7 30.fxe4 Qxa3 31.Rd1 Qb2 32.e5 Qg2 33.h7+ Kh8 34.Qxf7 Qxh1+ 35.Kd2 Qh2+ 36.Kc3 Qa2 37.Qxg6 Rd8 38.Kd4 Qf2+ 39.Kc3 Qa2 40.Bc2 d4+ 41.Kd3 Qa3+ 42.Ke4 Qe3+ 43.Kf5 Qh3+ 44.Ke4 Qe3+ 45.Kf5 Bh4 46.Ke6 Qxf4 47.Qf5 Qh6+ 48.Qg6 Qf4 49.Qf5 Qh6+ 50.Qg6 Qe3 51.Rg1 Bf6 52.Be4 Qb3+ 53.Kf5 Qh3+ 54.Qg4 Qxh7+ 55.Kf4 Qh6+ 56.Kf3 Bxe5 57.Ke2 d3+ 58.Kd1 Kg8 59.Rh1 Qf6 60.Bf5 Bc7 61.Be6+ Kf8 62.Qf5 Qxf5 63.Bxf5 Ke7 64.Rh3 d2 65.Rf3 Rd4 66.Bc8 Bf4 67.Bxb7 Rxb4**, 0-1.

Gains in Space = Potential Weak Squares

Pawns protect squares. This seems obvious, but it's something that needs to be pondered and appreciated since many players forget that as pawns advance, the potential amount of squares they control diminishes. This means that as a player pushes his pawns and gains more and more space with them, he is also potentially leaving weakened squares in their wake.

Diagram 320

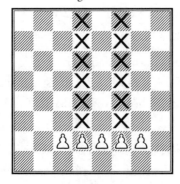

The e2-pawn potentially controls all the squares with Xs. However, if you push it to e3 then it loses contact with d3 and f3. If it moves to e4, it's already lost the potential to control d3, d4, f3, and f4.

In general, the other pawns can take up the slack created by the advance of the e-pawn. For example, pushing the e2-pawn to e4 gives up control over d3, d4, f3, and f4, but the c2-pawn will take over defensive duty for d3 and d4, while the g2-pawn does the same for f3 and f4. However, if White goes for a big pawn center via c2-c4, d2-d4, and e2-e4, pawn control over d3 and d4 is forever lost.

It's these "lost" squares that can (and often do) fall into enemy hands when a player, failing to recognize the pitfalls of indiscriminate pawn advances, grabs too much space for his own good.

I'm going to annotate the following game in a very strange way—variations will be ignored, and commentary as to whether a move is good or bad will also be passed over. Instead, I'll concentrate on three squares (c5, d3, and f4), how white's pawn moves ultimately gave them up, and how black's pieces and pawns are fighting for them.

J. R. Capablanca - R. T. Black, New York 1911

1.e4

The e-pawn has soared past the d3- and f4-squares, leaving only the c2-pawn to care for d3 and the g2-pawn to nurture f4.

1...c5 2.b4 cxb4

One of the guardians of c5 (white's b-pawn) has already fallen.

3.a3 bxa3 4.Bxa3 d6 5.Nf3 Nc6 6.d4 g6 7.h4 Bg4 8.c3

It's not important at the moment, but the d3-square is now permanently bereft of the protection of a white pawn.

8...Bg7 9.Nbd2 Nf6 10.Qb3 Qb6 11.Qa2 Bxf3 12.gxf3

Diagram 321

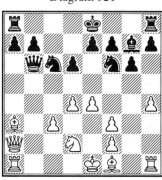

There goes the f4-square! Now both d3 and f4, abandoned by white's pawns, are on their own (it's up to the pieces to defend them, though such strong units are never particularly happy playing the roll of babysitter).

12...Nh5

This Knight shows that it's aware of the f4-square's plight!

13.Nc4 Qc7 14.Bc1

The Bishop promises f4 that it's neither alone nor forgotten.

14...0–0 15.Rb1 Kh8 16.Bh3 b6 17.Bg4 Nf6 18.Ne3 h5 19.Bh3 Na5 20.Bd2 Bh6

Black reminds his opponent that his desire for f4 is still burning bright.

21.Rc1 Kh7 22.c4 Nb7 23.Nf5 Ng8 24.Nxh6 Nxh6 25.Bxh6

The Bishop made a promise to f4 on move 14, but now (for reasons that are hard to fathom) it forgets about its vow and allows itself to be removed from the board.

25...Kxh6 26.Qd2+ Kh7 27.f4 e5

An excellent move. The c5-square was made persona non grata to the b7-Knight by the d4-pawn. So Black wisely removes it.

28.fxe5 dxe5 29.d5 Nc5

Diagram 322

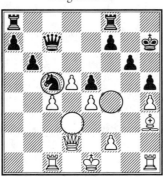

The eagle has landed! The eagle has landed! On top of its domination of c5, the Knight is also eyeing d3 (a square that the c4- and e4-pawns can see in their rearview mirrors, but can never touch). The weakness of our three squares of note (c5, d3, and f4) is beginning to play a key role in the game.

30.Qe2 Qe7 31.Bf5 Kg7 32.Rc3 Rh8 33.Rg3 Rh6 34.Qe3 Qf6 35.Rhg1 Kh7 36.Rg5 gxf5 37.Rxf5 Qe7 38.Qf3 f6 39.Rxh5 Nd3+

Black's Knight wants to singlehandedly taste all three squares. White has to let the Knight have its way, since 40.Qxd3 allows 40...Rxh5.

40.Kd1 Nf4

Completing its journey, the busy jumper beats back white's attack and ends the game.

41.Rxh6+ Kxh6 42.Qg3 Rc8 43.Qc3 Qc5, 0-1. A fitting end—black's Queen also makes use of the hole on c5. Hopefully this game made you more aware of the potential dangers of pushing a pawn!

Of course, pushing your pawns and creating squares that might prove weak later in the game is unavoidable. The key here is awareness—as long as you know the downside of every pawn advance, you'll be able to better judge whether or not such a square will really to be a problem as the game progresses.

I. Skulsky - J. Donaldson, Northwest Futurity 1982

1.d4 Nf6 2.c4 c5 3.d5 e6 4.Nc3 exd5 5.cxd5 d6 6.e4 g6 7.Nf3 Bg7 8.Bb5+ Bd7 9.Bxd7+ Nbxd7 10.Bf4 0–0 11.0–0 Qe7 12.Re1 Ng4 13.Qe2 Nge5 14.Nxe5 Nxe5 15.Bg3 Rae8 16.f4 Nd7 17.Qf3 a6 18.a4 Qd8 19.Re2

Diagram 323

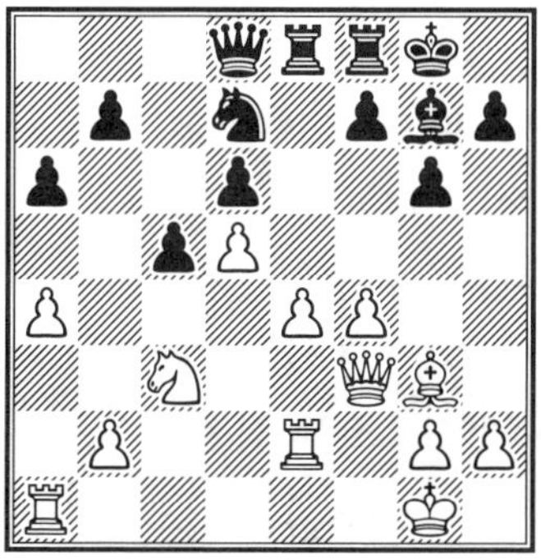

We are looking at a typical Benoni pawn structure. White's central space advantage is obvious, and so is his plan: to advance the e4-pawn to e5 and, perhaps, onwards to e6! At the moment Black has prevented this, but the simple Rae1 will give the e5-push a green light. What can Black do to stop his opponent's idea in its tracks?

19...c4!

Black places his finger on a weakness that White never knew he had—the d3-square! This is a natural result of the c2-c4 and e2-e4 moves, which left d3 without a natural pawn defender. Now ...Nd7-c5-d3 is a real threat, as shown by the following variation: 20.Rd1 Nc5 21.e5 Nd3 22.e6 fxe6 23.dxe6 Qb6+ 24.Kh1 Nxb2 25.Rb1 (25.Nd5 Qc6) 25...Bxc3 26.Qxc3 Nxa4 27.Qa1 Qc6 and White is losing.

20.Bf2

The Bishop steps back and stops …Nc5. However, by doing this he also took the Bishop away from e5, making his own advance harder to achieve.

20…Qa5 21.Rd1 b5

Donaldson gains queenside space and turns his queenside pawns into a mobile, dynamic force.

22.axb5 axb5 23.Ree1?

Black has made visible gains over the last few moves, and 23.Ree1 (which is a form of emotional surrender) allows him to get a firm grip on the initiative. Whether White liked it or not, he had to follow through with his own plan via 23.e5! dxe5 24.f5! b4 25.Ne4 when, for the small price of a pawn, White has created some play of his own!

23…Ra8 24.Rd2 b4 25.Nd1 Rfe8

A good, solid move (very much in the Donaldson "never give the opponent counterplay" style) that continues to deny White his e4-e5 push while also putting a bit of pressure on e4. Another way to handle the position is 25…Nc5 26.Bxc5 Qxc5+ 27.Qf2 Rfc8 28.Qxc5 Rxc5 when White faces some serious problems.

26.Bd4

White was clearly worse, but now he's lost.

26…Bxd4+ 27.Rxd4 Qc5 28.Qf2 Ra1

Black had many good choices. Perhaps the best was 28…c3 29.bxc3 bxc3 30.Re2 Nf6 31.h3 Nxe4! 32.Rdxe4 Rxe4 33.Qxc5 dxc5 34.Rxe4 c2 and it's all over.

29.Kf1 Nf6 30.Qd2 Ng4 31.h3 Ne5!

Diagram 324

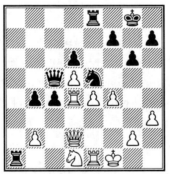

Very nice! White had stopped this Knight from reaching d3 from the c5-square (by 20.Bf2). However, he never imagined that the Knight would find its way into d3 by this route!

32.Qe3 Nd3 33.Rxd3 cxd3 34.Qxc5 dxc5 35.Nf2 Rxe1+ 36.Kxe1 c4 37.Kd2 Rd8 38.Ng4 c3+ 39.bxc3 b3, 0-1 (White lost on time).

A Space-Gaining Pawn Center
Might be a Target

Space is created by the expansion of pawns. If you think of a line of pawns as a fence, you will easily understand the concept of the territory behind your "fence" being yours. In the 1800s and early 1900s, a big pawn center was thought to be advantageous in almost every situation. How could a constricting pawn fence not be good? However, in the 1920s a group of players (Nimzovich, Reti, Alekhine, Bogoljubov, Gruenfeld, and Breyer) turned this "pawn center is good" mentality on its head. These "Hypermoderns" realized that one could allow the opponent to build away like a demented beaver, only to have it placed under pressure from a distance by a combination of pawns and pieces.

One of the most powerful demonstrations of a center being laughed at and treated like a target is the Gruenfeld Defense. Though this new opening first attracted attention in 1922 when Gruenfeld beat Alekhine with it, it was actually first employed way, way back in 1855:

J. Cochrane - Mahescandra, Calcutta 1855

1.d4 Nf6 2.c4 g6 3.Nc3 d5 4.e3 Bg7 5.Nf3 0–0 6.cxd5 Nxd5 7.Be2 Nxc3 8.bxc3 c5 9.0–0 cxd4 10.cxd4 Nc6

Diagram 325

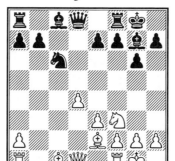

White has a firm pawn center, but it's held at bay by black's pieces, which apply pressure from deep within their own camp.

11.Bb2 Bg4?! (11...Qd5, =) **12.Rc1 Rc8 13.Ba3 Qa5 14.Qb3 Rfe8?? 15.Rc5 Qb6 16.Rb5 Qc7 17.Ng5 Bxe2 18.Nxf7??** (18.Qxf7+ Kh8 19.Ne6 wins on the spot) **18...Na5??** (18...Nd8! 19.Rc5 [19.Nh6+ Kh8; 19.Nd6+ Bc4 20.Nxe8 Qd7] 19...Nxf7 20.Rxc7 Rxc7 21.Re1 Bc4 is clearly better for Black) **19.Nh6+ Kh8 20.Qg8+ Rxg8 21.Nf7** mate. Black had a perfectly acceptable position until the rain of mutual blunders began! Nevertheless, it's a pity nobody noticed this game at that time—it might have completely changed the 19th century's landscape of chess thought.

The Alekhine Defense (1.e4 Nf6) is another Hypermodern opening that was actually toyed with long before Hypermoderns existed! The oldest example I could find was from 1802 (!) in the game Madame de Remusat - Napoleon I, Paris (1.e4 Nf6 2.d3 Nc6 3.f4 e5 4.fxe5 Nxe5 5.Nc3 Nfg4 6.d4 Qh4+ 7.g3 Qf6 8.Nh3 Nf3+ 9.Ke2 Nxd4+ 10.Kd3 Ne5+ 11.Kxd4 Bc5+ 12.Kxc5 Qb6+ 13.Kd5 Qd6, mate). I don't know if Allgaier saw this game, but he analyzed 1.e4 Nf6 in 1819 and decided that it was garbage. This opening wasn't given any respect until Alekhine used it twice in 1921 to score a win and a draw against Saemisch and Steiner—then it was off to the Hypermodern races with various adventurous players goading white's center pawns forward in an attempt to smite them if they dared to go too far!

N. Pegoraro - Henderson, Ischia 1996

1.e4 Nf6 2.e5 Nd5 3.d4 d6 4.c4 Nb6 5.f4 dxe5 6.fxe5 Nc6 7.Be3 Bf5 8.Nc3 e6 9.Nf3 Be7 10.d5

The older main line is 10.Be2 0–0 11.0–0 f6 12.exf6 Bxf6 when black's piece-pressure against the center creates a position with more or less equal chances for both sides. Pegoraro's move avoids the balanced game that 10.Be2 offers and instead tries to use the center pawns to push Black right off the board.

10...exd5 11.cxd5 Nb4

Diagram 326

Suddenly white's pawns have high-stepped into enemy territory and d5 is about to be treated as a foodstuff. White's pawn center looks more imposing than ever, but its imminent demise means that he has to attack with all his might—it's too late to revert back to quiet positional play, now pure dynamics lead the dance!

12.Nd4

Attacking f5 and also defending against ...Nc2+.

12...Bd7

The more natural 12...Bg6 has been shown to lose by force.

13.Qf3

Defending d5 and threatening a2-a3. Now it's black's turn to show some enterprise!

13...c5!

Since ...Nc2+ would follow if the d4-Knight moved, White has no choice by to capture black's c-pawn, thereby destroying what remained of his once-mighty pawn center.

14.dxc6 e.p. bxc6 15.e6

Trying to keep black's King in the center for as long as possible. 15.a3 c5 16.axb4 cxd4 17.Bxd4 0-0 is fine for Black (18.Bd3 Bc6!).

15...fxe6 16.0–0–0

There's not a white center pawn in sight!

16...N6d5 17.a3 Nxc3 18.Nxe6

Diagram 327

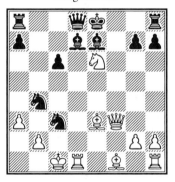

Ah, there's nothing like the smell of napalm splashing over the board! Unfortunately for White, he's the one getting cooked.

18...Nca2+ 19.Kb1 Bxe6 20.Rxd8+ Rxd8 21.axb4 Nxb4 22.Be2 Rf8 23.Qh5+ g6 24.Qe5 Bf5+ 25.Ka1 Rd5 26.Qb8+ Kf7, 0-1. White didn't like what was about to happen to him. After 27.Qxa7 Nc2+ 28.Ka2 Nxe3 White will be behind in material if he doesn't recapture (not to mention lines like 29.Rc1 Rd2 30.Qxe3 Ra8+ 31.Kb3 Rb8+ 32.Kc3 Bb4+ 33.Kc4 Be6+), but 29.Qxe3 Ra5+ 30.Kb3 Rb8+ is no less painful: 31.Kc3 Bf6+ 32.Kd2 Rxb2+ 33.Ke1 Ra1+ 34.Kf2 (34.Bd1 Bg4) 34...Rxh1.

Of course, over the years the strategy behind "center bashing" has deepened—eventually it was understood that, aside from trying to shatter the center and feast on its tattered remains, one could also force the center to advance and make use of the newly weakened squares these advances often create. These same ideas can be used against all sorts of pawn centers, no matter what openings they may arise from. However, let's return to the Gruenfeld Defense for a classic example of a center under siege.

S. Gligoric - V. Smyslov, Kiev 1959

1.d4 Nf6 2.c4 g6 3.Nc3 d5 4.cxd5 Nxd5 5.e4 Nxc3 6.bxc3 Bg7 7.Bc4 c5 8.Ne2 0–0 9.0–0 Nc6 10.Be3 Qc7 11.Rc1 Rd8

Diagram 328

Is white's space gaining center strong or weak?

This position exudes a wonderful sense of balance and teamwork. White has a huge pawn center, but Black is taking aim at it with everything he can muster. Note that he's not just attacking randomly, he's doing his best to beat down d4. This is being carried out by black's dark-squared Bishop, his c-pawn, his Knight, and his d8-Rook—many pieces, one goal!

On the other hand, White wants to make his center indestructible. If he can do that, then he can squeeze his opponent and eventually turn black's helplessness into an attack on the wing, or a breakthrough down the middle. Thus, he is meeting black's aggression against d4 with his own tightening of that pawn—his c-pawn, dark-squared Bishop, Knight, and Queen are all holding life and limb together.

12.h3

The immediate 12.f4 can be met by 12...Bg4, undermining d4. 12.h3 prepares f2-f4 by preventing ...Bg4.

12...b6 13.f4 e6 14.Qe1 Bb7

The Gligoric - Smyslov game is an example of what happens when a central advance creates holes that the opponent can make use of. However, here's another classic game that leads to a different central outcome: 14...Na5 15.Bd3 f5! 16.g4! fxe4 17.Bxe4 Bb7 18.Ng3 Nc4 19.Bxb7 Qxb7 20.Bf2 Qc6 21.Qe2 cxd4 22.cxd4 b5 and white's center had been torn down and Black enjoyed the more pleasant position. However, Spassky (who had White) played extremely well from this point on, while Fischer pushed for a win even after his advantage had vanished and ultimately paid the price: 23.Ne4 Bxd4 24.Ng5 Bxf2+ 25.Rxf2 Rd6 26.Re1 Qb6 27.Ne4 Rd4?! (27...Rc6! left Fischer with all the chances) 28.Nf6+ Kh8 29.Qxe6 Rd6 30.Qe4 Rf8?! (Now White is a bit better) 31.g5 Rd2 32.Rf1 Qc7? 33.Rxd2 Nxd2 34.Qd4 Rd8 35.Nd5+ Kg8 36.Rf2 Nc4 37.Re2 Rd6 38.Re8+ Kf7 39.Rf8+, 1-0, B. Spassky - R. Fischer, Siegen ol 1970.

15.Qf2?

White is just worse after this, so the natural 15.f5 needed to be played. However, Black would have a problem-free game after 15...Na5 16.Bd3 exf5 17.exf5 Re8.

15...Na5 16.Bd3 f5!

Diagram 329

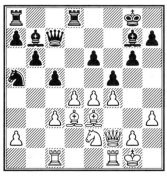

An enormously important move that does many useful things:

 It continues the attack against white's center.

 It blocks the f4-pawn (white's whole attack was based on the f4-f5 advance), which in turn blocks white's dark-squared Bishop, Knight, Queen, and f1-Rook.

 It forces open the h1-a8 diagonal, thereby increasing the activity of the b7-Bishop.

17.e5

17.Ng3 Qd7.

17...c4 18.Bc2 Nc6

Black is better. White's kingside attack has been stifled and his zombie pieces are knocking against their own pawns on c3, d4, and f4 (the c2-Bishop is snuffed by the c4- and f5-pawns). Black, on the other hand, has a mobile queenside pawn majority, a light-squared Bishop that seems more laser beam than chess piece, and a Knight that can set up shop on d5.

19.g4

This loosens up the h1-a8 diagonal and thus puts his own King in jeopardy. However, it was either this attempt at kingside counterplay or passively waiting around to die.

19...Ne7

A good place for the Knight—it keeps an eye on his kingside pawn structure while threatening to leap to d5.

20.Kh2 Qc6

This move speaks for itself—the problem White faces along the h1-a8 diagonal takes on a concrete form.

21.Ng3 b5

Note that Black isn't worried about 22.gxf5 exf5, though this leaves White with two connected passed center pawns. Why wouldn't White be delighted with such a turn of events? The answer is that passed pawns aren't very useful if they can't be pushed, and in this position the d-pawn will be liquefied if it ever dares move to d5. For more on passed pawns, see Part Eight.

22.a4 a6 23.Rb1 Rab8 24.Bd2

Diagram 330

24...bxa4?!

Black opens lines on the queenside, thinking that he is the one that can profit from it. However, white's pieces also gain a bit of activity and, in general, one should not allow the opponent anything if he's bound and helpless. Instead, he should have put this move off for a moment in favor of 24...Ba8! This strange looking retreat actually has a clear-cut point: by getting the Bishop out of the b8-Rook's way, Black threatens 25...bxa4 when, depending on white's 25th move, he has ideas like ...Rb2 (if white's Rook moved off of the b-file) or the Exchange sacrifice with ...Rb3 (as occurred in the actual game). These ideas more or less force 25.axb5 (or 25.gxf5 exf5 26.axb5) when 25...axb5 gives Black two new aims: he can play for an eventual ...b5-b4 push by ...Nd5 (the ...b4 push turns the c4-pawn into a passer and also undermines d4), and/or he can get the Bishop off of a8, follow with ...Ra8, and play for penetration down the a-file.

The rest of the game no longer serves our theme, but is still full of interest: **25.Ra1 Ba8 26.Bxa4 Qc7 27.Ra2 Rb6 28.gxf5 exf5 29.Bc1 Nd5 30.Ne2 a5 31.Bc2 Rb3! 32.Bxb3 cxb3 33.Ra4 Bf8 34.Bb2 Ne3! 35.Rfa1 Nc4 36.Ng3 Be7 37.Nf1 Qc6 38.Rxc4 Qh1+ 39.Kg3 h5**, 0-1. The threat is 40...h4 mate, and any move of white's Queen gives up the key g1- or f3-square, allowing mate in three.

Finally, let's take a look at one more "big center vs. piece pressure" game. This time the center wins!

R. Reti - Em. Lasker, New York 1924

1.Nf3 d5 2.c4 c6 3.b3 Bf5 4.g3 Nf6 5.Bg2 Nbd7 6.Bb2 e6 7.0–0 Bd6 8.d3 0–0 9.Nbd2 e5 10.cxd5 cxd5 11.Rc1

Diagram 331

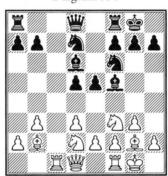

Piece pressure vs. black's space gaining center

Reti prepares his favorite setup: the Rook goes to c2 (making way for the Queen and preparing to double), his Queen to a1 (creating heat along the a1-h8 diagonal), and Rfc1 (taking the c-file). The "attack the center from a distance" strategy works in the Gruenfeld because Black has an open file that allows the Rooks to join directly in the center assault (see diagram 328). However, here that's not the case and quiet play can easily lead to a passive position for White since Black can effortlessly strengthen his center, leaving white's army vainly staring at a brick wall.

Reti's setup is very picturesque, and one can understand his attachment to it, but Lasker shows that it just doesn't hold up against his old school methodology. Thus, White needs to add a bit of spice to it via a well-timed e2-e4 strike. The question is, does this have to be employed now, or will it prove to be even better later (depending on black's reply to 11.Rc1)?

11.Rc1 has been maligned by virtually every annotator—they insist that 11.e4 was the way to go. Perhaps, but I'm not sold on the idea that 11.Rc1 is, by itself, bad. Before exploring the question of the worth of 11.Rc1 by continuing with the actual game, let's glance at 11.e4, a move that declares immediate war on black's center. Black's possible replies:

➤ 11...dxe4 12.Nxe4! (White doesn't get much from 12.dxe4 Be6 when 13.Ng5 is met by 13...Bg4) 12...Bxe4 (12...Bc7 13.Nxf6+ Qxf6 14.Nh4 Be6 15.Rc1 Bb6 16.Bxb7 Rad8 17.Ba3 Rfe8 18.Qe2 and Black doesn't have enough for the lost pawn) 13.dxe4 Nxe4 14.Nh4 Ndf6 and now 15.Re1 Nxf2 (15...Nc5 16.Nf5 is just bad for Black) 16.Kxf2 Qb6+ 17.Kf1 Bb4 gives Black more play than he deserves. Thus, 15.Qe2! is cleaner, when 15...Nc5 16.Nf5 is a pleasure for White.

➤ 11...Be6 12.exd5 Bxd5 13.Nc4 Qb8 14.Re1 Re8 15.Rc1 and White has strong pressure against black's e5-pawn (note the team effort: the b2-Bishop, both Knights, and the e1-Rook all play their part in keeping Black in a defensive posture).

➤ 11...Bg4 12.exd5 Nxd5 13.h3 Bh5 14.Nc4 Qf6 15.Qe2 and, as usual, black's center is under the gun (15...Rfe8 16.Qe4!).

➤ 11...Bg6! It's very hard for White to prove a significant advantage after this calm, logical move.

Diagram 332

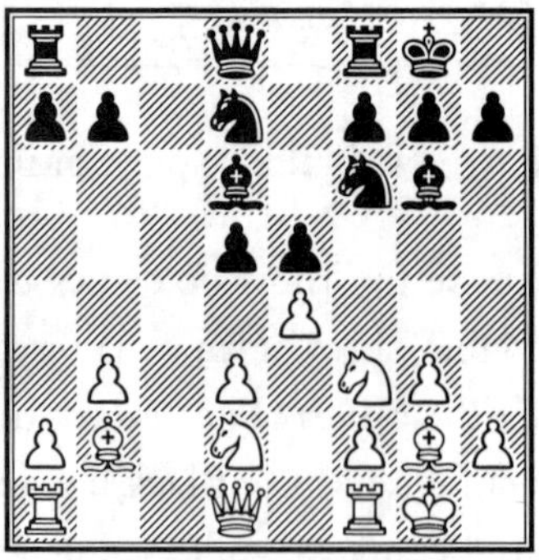

● 12.Qe2 Re8 13.Rfc1 Nc5 14.Nh4 Bh5, =.

- 12.d4 Nxe4 13.Nxe5 (13.dxe5 Be7 14.Nxe4 [14.Rc1 Nec5 with the idea of plopping something onto d3 gives White nothing] 14...dxe4 15.Nd2 Nc5 16.Qe2 Qd3 17.Qxd3 [17.Rae1 Qxe2 18.Rxe2 Bh5! 19.f3 exf3 20.Bxf3 Bxf3 21.Nxf3 Rad8 leaves Black with the better pawn structure] 17...Nxd3 18.Bd4 Rfd8 and Black has no problems) 13...Nxe5 14.dxe5 Bc5 15.Qe2 (15.Nxe4 dxe4 16.Qe1 e3 17.fxe3 Qb6 18.Rd1 Rad8 19.Bd4 Bxd4 20.exd4 [20.Rxd4 Rxd4 21.exd4 Qxd4+ 22.Qf2 Qxe5, =] 20...Bh5! 21.Rd2 Rxd4 22.Rxd4 Qxd4+ 23.Qf2 Qxf2+ 24.Rxf2 b6 25.Rd2 Rc8! 26.Bh3 [26.Rd7 Rc1+, =] 26...Rc1+ 27.Kf2 g5, =) 15...f5 16.exf6 e.p. Nxf6 17.Rad1 (17.Qb5 Qd6) 17...Kh8! 18.Nf3 Ne4 Black has a good, active position.

- 12.exd5!? (Trying to grab the c4-square for the d2-Knight— the goal, as ever, is to place more pressure on black's center and, clearly, a Knight on c4 does that very well) 12...Bxd3 (White is threatening to capture e5, Nc4 is in the air, and black's light-squared Bishop is a bit vulnerable on d3. On the other hand, if Black can protect e5 and get his f- and e-pawns marching up the board together, then he can will be able to generate some serious dynamic possibilities for himself.) 13.Re1 Ng4! (A very combative move that makes way for the advance of the f7-pawn while also eyeing f2. Another possibility is 13...Re8 14.Nc4 Bxc4 15.bxc4 Rc8 16.Rc1 with a slight advantage for White. A fantasy continuation that shows how this position can heat up is 16...Qa5 [16...Qb6!? might be stronger] 17.Bh3! Qxa2 [and here 17...Rc7 seems a solid choice] 18.Re2 Qa6 19.Nxe5 Bxe5 20.Bxe5 Rxc4 21.Ra1 Qb5 22.Rb1 Qc5 23.Bxd7 Nxd7 24.Bd4 Qf8 25.Rxe8 Qxe8 26.Rxb7 and Black's in serious trouble) 14.Ne4 (and not 14.h3?? Nxf2! 15.Kxf2 Bc5+) 14...Bxe4 15.Rxe4 f5 16.Re2 e4 (16...Re8!?) 17.Nd4 Nc5 (Both side's Knights are heading for some juicy squares.) 18.Rc1 Nd3 19.Ne6 Qa5 20.Bxg7 Rf7 21.Bd4 Qxd5 22.Qxd3 Qxe6 23.Qd2 Be5 24.Bxe4 (24.h3 Nf6 25.Bxe5 Qxe5 26.Qh6 Re8 27.Rec2 e3 28.Kh2 exf2 29.Rxf2 Ne4 30.Bxe4 Qxe4 31.Rcc2 is +=. However, 24...Bxd4 seems stronger: 25.hxg4 Qb6 26.Qf4 Raf8 27.gxf5 Rxf5 28.Qg4+ Kh8 29.Bxe4 Rxf2 30.Rxf2 Qf6 31.Rcf1 Bxf2+ 32.Kg2 Qb2 and Black's okay.) 24...fxe4 25.Rxe4 Qf5 26.Rxg4+ Qxg4

27.Bxe5 (One would think White stands much better here, but it turns out to be more illusion than reality.) 27...Rd7 28.Qe3 Re8 29.Kg2 Rd5 30.Qf4 (30.f4 leaves White's King open. Black shouldn't have any problems after 30...Red8) 30...Qxf4 31.Bxf4 Re2 32.Rc8+ Kf7 33.Rc7+ Re7 34.Rc2 Re6 35.h4 Rc6, =.

It seems that 11.e4 didn't offer White anything special. 11.Rc1 though, retains the tension and keeps the e2-e4 push in the ready for a more opportune moment. Nevertheless, 11.e4 is a very important move for our theme. In general, you don't want to wait around while the opponent's center grows more and more stable. You need to attack it with as much energy as possible.

11...Qe7 12.Rc2?!

Reti can't resist the siren call of his favorite setup. However, 12.e4! has more pop than it did on the 11th move because Rc1 turns out to be a far more useful move than ...Qe7 (which runs into some Nf3-h4-f5 tempo losses). Here's a quick sample: 12.e4 Bg6 (12...dxe4 13.dxe4 and now 13...Nxe4?? 14.Nh4 wins, 13...Bxe4?? 14.Nxe4 Nxe4 15.Nh4 Ndf6 16.Qc2 Ng5 17.Nf5 Qe6 18.h4 wins, and 13...Be6 14.Nc4 gives White an edge) 13.Nh4 (13.exd5!? is also very interesting) 13...Bh5 (13...d4 14.Nf5 Bxf5 15.exf5 favors White thanks to his laser light-squared Bishop) 14.Nf5 Qe6 15.Qc2 and White is better.

12...a5

Intending ...a4.

13.a4?

White is caving to his opponent's will. I still think 13.e4!?, going after black's center before it's too late, was worth a shot.

13...h6 14.Qa1

14.e4 Bh7 no longer poses any problems.

14...Rfe8 15.Rfc1

Diagram 333

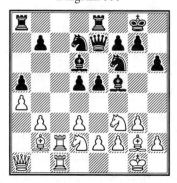

Reti's beloved setup

White finally got the position he wanted, but so did Black! Though White is hitting black's center from a distance and also controls the c-file, all is not well in Boonsville. The problem is that his pawn-strikes against the center no longer work, and he can't up the pressure in any meaningful way. As for the c-file, all the penetration squares are well covered. This means that White has driven down a dead-end street.

15...Bh7 16.Nf1 Nc5! 17.Rxc5!?

White, who realizes that he's been outplayed by Lasker and that things have turned sour, employs an Exchange sacrifice in order to imbalance the position and give himself something to crow about. Defensive moves such as 17.N3d2 and 17.Qa2 are met by 17...Na6 followed by 18...Nb4.

17...Bxc5 18.Nxe5

White's gotten a pawn for the Exchange, his dark-squared Bishop is slicing down the newly opened a1-h8 diagonal, and black's once mighty center has been dismantled. However, black's position is solid, his pieces are well placed, both his Rooks will contribute down the c- and e-files, and he's material ahead. Thus, White doesn't have full compensation for the Exchange.

18...Rac8

18...Bd6, forcing White to loosen up the e-file and the g1-a7 diagonal with 19.f4, was also good.

19.Ne3 Qe6

Defends d5 and stops Bh3.

20.h3 Bd6?

A serious mistake, which suddenly gives White the upper hand! Black had several good moves (The tightening 20...b6, the greedy 20...Bxe3 21.fxe3 Qb6 22.Bd4 Qxb3 23.Rb1 Qc2 24.Rxb7 Qxe2, and 20...h5, which takes the g4-square away from the white Knights). However, best might have been 20...Qd6! when 21.d4 blocks his b2-Bishop and activates black's h7-Bishop, while 21.Kh2 falls victim to 21...Bxe3 22.Rxc8 (22.fxe3 Rxc1 23.Qxc1 Rxe5 leaves Black with an extra piece) 22...Rxc8 23.fxe3 Rc2 and the threats of 24...Rxe2 and 24...Qb6 hitting both b3 and e3 give Black a winning game.

The rest of the game, with minimal notes, shows Reti missing his chance and, once again, getting outplayed by his legendary opponent: **21.Rxc8 Rxc8 22.Nf3?** (22.N5g4!) **22...Be7 23.Nd4 Qd7 24.Kh2 h5 25.Qh1 h4 26.Nxd5 hxg3+ 27.fxg3 Nxd5 28.Bxd5 Bf6 29.Bxb7 Rc5 30.Ba6?** (30.Be4 gave some drawing chances) **30...Bg6 31.Qb7 Qd8** (31...Qd6!) **32.b4 Rc7 33.Qb6 Rd7 34.Qxd8+ Rxd8 35.e3 axb4 36.Kg2 Bxd4 37.exd4 Bf5 38.Bb7 Be6 39.Kf3 Bb3 40.Bc6 Rd6 41.Bb5 Rf6+ 42.Ke3 Re6+ 43.Kf4 Re2 44.Bc1 Rc2 45.Be3 Bd5**, 0-1.

Summary

> Space is created by the expansion of pawns. If you think of a line of pawns as a fence, you will easily understand the concept of the territory behind your "fence" being yours.

> An advantage in space is one of *the* most highly prized imbalances among modern grandmasters.

> A huge advantage in space takes away many enemy options. In fact, if it isn't dealt with properly, the side with less space can easily end up with a passive, cheerless position.

> If you possess an advantage in space, don't forget about the other imbalances. For example, playing for a superior minor piece can be a useful complement to your territorial gains.

> It's usually a good idea for the side with more space to avoid unnecessary exchanges.

> In general, there are four ways to fight against an enemy space advantage:

 ○ Exchange pieces so your limited territory is no longer uncomfortable.

 ○ Use pawn breaks to crack his seemingly indestructible pawn-façade.

 ○ Try and prove that your opponent's gain in space has left weak squares in its wake.

 ○ Treat a space-gaining enemy pawn center as a target!

> Pawns protect squares. This seems obvious, but it's something that needs to be pondered and appreciated since many players forget that as pawns advance, the potential amount of squares they control diminishes. This means that as a player pushes his pawns and gains more and more space with them, he is also potentially leaving weakened squares in their wake.

> Of course, pushing your pawns and creating squares that might prove weak later in the game is unavoidable. The key here is awareness—as long as you know the downside of every pawn advance, you'll be able to better judge whether or not such a square will really to be a problem as the game progresses.

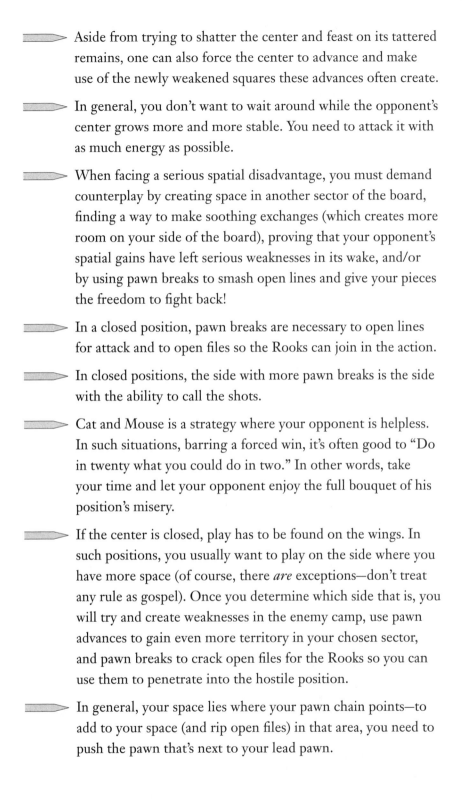

> Aside from trying to shatter the center and feast on its tattered remains, one can also force the center to advance and make use of the newly weakened squares these advances often create.

> In general, you don't want to wait around while the opponent's center grows more and more stable. You need to attack it with as much energy as possible.

> When facing a serious spatial disadvantage, you must demand counterplay by creating space in another sector of the board, finding a way to make soothing exchanges (which creates more room on your side of the board), proving that your opponent's spatial gains have left serious weaknesses in its wake, and/or by using pawn breaks to smash open lines and give your pieces the freedom to fight back!

> In a closed position, pawn breaks are necessary to open lines for attack and to open files so the Rooks can join in the action.

> In closed positions, the side with more pawn breaks is the side with the ability to call the shots.

> Cat and Mouse is a strategy where your opponent is helpless. In such situations, barring a forced win, it's often good to "Do in twenty what you could do in two." In other words, take your time and let your opponent enjoy the full bouquet of his position's misery.

> If the center is closed, play has to be found on the wings. In such positions, you usually want to play on the side where you have more space (of course, there *are* exceptions—don't treat any rule as gospel). Once you determine which side that is, you will try and create weaknesses in the enemy camp, use pawn advances to gain even more territory in your chosen sector, and pawn breaks to crack open files for the Rooks so you can use them to penetrate into the hostile position.

> In general, your space lies where your pawn chain points—to add to your space (and rip open files) in that area, you need to push the pawn that's next to your lead pawn.

Space — Tests

The section on space was enormous, which means there was a lot to absorb. The tests here will give you a good idea as to whether or not you've become an expert on the use and deconstruction of space.

If you have trouble solving the tests, don't worry—that means we've uncovered something you don't understand, and this allows you to fix things by rereading the previous material or by picking up the bits of knowledge you're missing in the answers that start on page 553.

PART SEVEN - TEST 1

Diagram 334

[Level: 1600 - 2200]

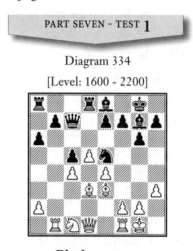

Black to move

In prose, what is this position all about? Also, what kind of moves and themes would be most logical?

PART SEVEN - TEST 2

Diagram 335

[Level: 1400 - 2000]

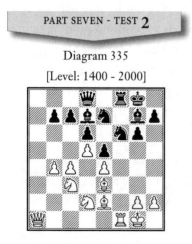

White to move

Assess the position and then find white's best move.

PART SEVEN - TEST 3

Diagram 336

[Level: 1800 - 2100]

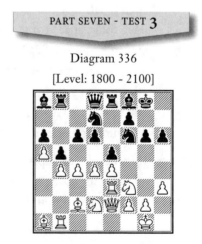

Black to move

What's better, 1...Bg7, 1...exd4, or 1...Nh5?

PART SEVEN - TEST 4

Diagram 337

[Level: 1400 - 1800]

Black to move

Point out the imbalances and then find black's most logical move.

PART SEVEN - TEST 5

Diagram 338

[Level: 1400 - 1800]

Black to move

In this kind of position, three moves should stand out above all the others. What are those three moves, and which one do you think is best?

PART SEVEN - TEST 6

Diagram 339

[Level: 1800 - 2200]

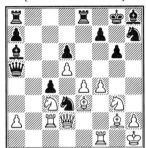

White to move

PART SEVEN - TEST 7

Diagram 340

[Level: 1400]

White to move

Is grabbing space by 1.a5 worth considering?

Part Eight / Passed Pawns

Contents

Baby Queens on the Run

Throughout this book, I've blended most pawn structure themes in with other subjects (weak pawns, space, etc.), but after a lot of thought I decided to give passed pawns their own section. My reasons for doing so:

> ➤ A passed pawn can be a static powerhouse and/or a dynamic game winner. Thus understanding it will also improve your understanding of statics and dynamics.

> ➤ A passed pawn discourse is the ideal training ground for the concept of blockade.

> ➤ A pawn majority's ultimate goal is the creation of a passed pawn. Thus, understanding passed pawns vastly increases your understanding of pawn majorities.

> ➤ A passed pawn, even a protected passed pawn, can often turn out to be a serious disadvantage. This shocking fact alone warrants the creation of this section!

Whether you refer to it as a "passed pawn," a "passer," a "passed banana" (a favorite among players in Denver), a "baby Queen," a "posing Polly" (a passed pawn that just sits there, looking good but doing nothing), or (in the case of a fast-moving passed pawn) a "nimble Louie," this particular kind of pawn has captured the imagination and respect of amateurs everywhere. A protected passed pawn is given even more reverence since nothing can hurt it, and at any moment it might rocket to the eighth rank ("nimble Louie!") and (if the pawn is owned by the opponent) turn into something unpleasant. In this chapter we're going to stare in awe at an unstoppable passer, while also demonstrating how nimble Louie's sprinting abilities can be forestalled by a blockade. Yes, a passed pawn can and often does invade the end zone and make a touchdown, but it can just as easily find itself glued to a square, unable to move or influence the game in any meaningful way.

The material in this section will make your view of passed pawns more realistic, and give you the ability to decide when a passer is gold, and when it's nothing more than gaud.

Creation

The most common way for a passed pawn to be "born" is via a pawn majority. Here's a clear example of a pawn majority's power:

Diagram 341

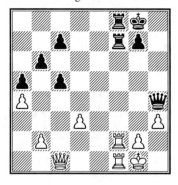

White to move

Black appears to be fine, but he's actually hopelessly lost! Why? Because White has a healthy kingside pawn majority while Black's queenside majority is crippled. Of course, that alone won't be decisive since black's Queen is very actively placed. However, White realizes that he can force the trade of all black's pieces, leaving him with a dead won King and pawn endgame.

1.Rxf7 Rxf7

1...Qd4+ 2.R7f2 leaves White with an extra Rook.

2.Rxf7 Kxf7 3.Qc4+! Qxc4 4.dxc4

Diagram 342

Things are now clear: White can easily make a passed pawn by advancing his kingside pawns, while Black can't create a passer on the other side because his majority is diseased—if Black tries ...c6 followed by ...b5, White responds with b2-b3 when black's hopes are crushed since …b5-b4 is a dead end street, and taking on a4 or c4 also leaves him with nothing after White recaptures.

4…Kf6 5.Kf2 Ke5 6.Ke3

Access denied!

6…Kf5 7.g4+ Kg5 8.Kf3 Kh4

8…c6 9.Kg3 Kf6 10.Kf4 g5+ 11.Kg3 Ke5 12.h4 is a race Black won't even come close to winning.

9.Kg2 c6

9…g5 10.Kh2 c6 11.Kg2 b5 12.axb5 cxb5 13.cxb5 c4 14.b6 c3 15.b7 c2 16.b8=Q c1=Q and now both 17.Qh8 and 17.Qg3 get the job done.

10.Kh2

White's King can endlessly move between h2 and g2 until Black runs out of pawn moves. Then his King will have to leave h4, thereby allowing white's majority to start its march after Kg3, h3-h4, etc.

10…g6 11.Kg2 Kg5

11…g5 leads to the same kind of end as that in the note to black's 9th move.

12.Kg3 Kf6 13.h4 Kg7 14.Kf4 Kf6 15.h5

We finally see the birth of a passed pawn!

15…g5+

It's more or less the same thing after 15…gxh5 16.gxh5 Kg7 17.Kg5.

16.Ke4 Ke6 17.h6 Kf6 18.h7 Kg7 19.Kf5 Kxh7 20.Kxg5 Kg7 21.Kf5 Kf7 22.g5 Kg7 23.g6

White could also win by Ke6 when all of black's queenside pawns will be devoured.

23…Kg8 24.Kf6 Kf8 25.g7+ Kg8 26.Kg6 b5 27.axb5 cxb5 28.cxb5 c4 29.b6 c3 30.b7 c2 31.b8=Q mate.

It's clear that a pawn majority can be a huge static plus since it can sit quietly for ages, apparently doing nothing. Then, in the blink of an eye, it can rush forward and give birth to a Queen. However, a pawn majority can also be a dynamic powerhouse, mixing the creation of a passed pawn with some seriously nasty space gaining boa action.

B. Spassky - L. Aronson, Moscow 1957

1.c4 Nf6 2.d4 e6 3.Nc3 c5 4.d5 exd5 5.cxd5 d6 6.e4 g6 7.f4 Bg7 8.Bd3 0–0 9.Nf3 Na6 10.0–0 Nc7 11.a4 b6 12.Re1 a6 13.Rb1 Rb8 14.Bd2 Re8 15.h3 b5 (It's white's central pawn majority versus black's queenside pawn majority—in general, the center is more important.) **16.axb5 Nxb5 17.Bxb5 axb5 18.b4 Nd7** (18...c4 is possible, but in that case the passed c-pawn would be firmly blockaded by the c3-Knight and, after 19.Ra1, Black would have to worry about an eventual e4-e5 while also facing pressure against b5 via Ra5.) **19.Qc2 Qc7 20.Kh2 Ba6 21.Nd1 Rbc8 22.Rc1 Qb7 23.Qb1 Rc7 24.Ne3 Nf6**

Diagram 343

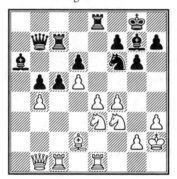

White to move

It's time to kick white's central pawn majority into action.

25.e5! dxe5 26.d6 Rcc8 27.fxe5 Nd7 28.Ng4

Diagram 344

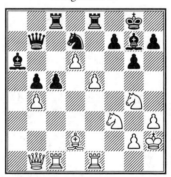

Black's on the run

It's clear that white's space gobbling central pawns (which are forcing the enemy pieces to run for their lives) constitute a clear dynamic advantage, *if* they don't get eaten by black's pieces (note the pressure against e5 by black's e8-Rook, d7-Knight, and g7-Bishop). White's massive buildup of kingside pieces is also more than a bit imposing.

28...Qd5

28...c4 29.Qa1 Qc6 (29...h5 30.Nh6+) 30.Bh6 Bh8 31.Qd4 (powerful centralization) is very much in white's favor, but 28...cxb4!? might have been worth a shot.

29.Rcd1

29.Bh6!? seems more accurate.

29...Qe6

29...Bb7 was probably best.

30.Bh6 Bb7 31.Bxg7 Kxg7 32.Qc1

32.Ng5 Qf5 33.e6 Qxb1 34.Rxb1 fxe6 35.Rf1 was an immediate winner.

32...Bxf3 33.Qh6+ Kh8

33...Kg8 34.Nf6+ Nxf6 35.exf6 Qxf6 36.d7 Bc6 37.Rxe8+ Rxe8 38.dxe8=Q+ Bxe8 39.Qe3 and White wins.

34.Nf6 Nxf6

34...Nf8 was the only way to continue the game, though white's advantage is decisive after 35.Nxe8 Rxe8 36.gxf3.

35.exf6 Qxf6 36.d7

The passed pawn finally moves, and makes a crunching sound as it does so.

36...Bc6? 37.dxe8=Q+, 1-0.

As you can see, a healthy/mobile pawn majority can be both a static and dynamic plus. In the previous example, the opening choice delineated the battle of mutual majorities right off the bat, but at other times it's up to you to decide whether or not you think a pawn majority would be the best way to go.

NN - G. Greco, Europe 1620

1.e4 e6 2.d4 d5 3.e5 c5 4.c3 Nc6 5.Nf3 Bd7 6.Be3 c4 7.b3 b5 8.a4 a6 9.axb5 axb5 10.Rxa8 Qxa8 11.bxc4

Diagram 345

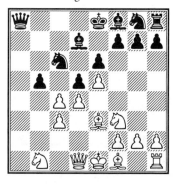

Decision time!

Black has to recapture his pawn on c4. Either choice is playable, but one stands out above the other.

11...dxc4!

Breaking the old "always captures towards the center" rule. This gives Black far more to work with than the pedestrian 11...bxc4. With 11...dxc4, Black creates a nice home on d5 for a Knight, opens up the a8-h1 diagonal for his Queen (and potentially for his light-squared Bishop too), and (most importantly!) creates a queenside majority of pawns. This means that Black, whenever he chooses to do so, can make a passed pawn by ...b5-b4.

12.Be2

12.d5 exd5 13.Qxd5 Qb8 is also fine for Black.

12...Nge7 13.0–0 Nd5 and Black, with his Knight living on the juicy d5-square and his pawn majority ready to make a passed pawn (by ...b5-b4) any time he wants, has an excellent position. The rest of the game (which has many ups and downs) is given without comment: **14.Bd2 Be7 15.Ng5 Bxg5 16.Bxg5 0–0 17.Bf3 Na5 18.Bxd5 Qxd5 19.f4 Bc6 20.Qd2 Nb3 21.Qc2 Nxd4 22.cxd4 Qxd4+ 23.Kh1 Be4 24.Qc3 Qc5 25.Nd2 Bd3 26.Rc1 Rc8 27.Nb3 cxb3 28.Qxc5 Rxc5 29.Rxc5 h6 30.Rc3 b2 31.Rb3 b1=Q+ 32.Rxb1 Bxb1 33.Be7 Kh7 34.g4 Be4+ 35.Kg1 Bf3 36.h3 h5 37.g5 Kg6 38.Kf2 Bd5 39.Ke3 h4 40.Kf2 Kf5 41.Ke3 Bg2 42.Bf8 g6 43.Bb4 Bxh3 44.Be1 Kg4 45.Bd2 Bg2 46.Kf2 h3 47.Bc1 Bd5 48.Kg1 Kg3 49.Be3 h2+ 50.Kf1 h1=Q+, 0-1.**

A Little Help From Its Friends

When reaching an endgame where one side has a passed pawn, we've already seen that a King and pawn endgame is the Promised Land. Other than that, what other piece revels in the ownership of a passed pawn? Let's take a look:

Diagram 346

White to Move

A glance will show that, without help from the King or another pawn, white's b-pawn isn't going anywhere.

Diagram 347

White to move

Same thing here! The b-pawn is blocked and, without help from other members of white's army, there's no way to make black's Knight move off of b5.

Diagram 348

White to move

Even the mighty Rook can't help its passed pawn move down the board on its own!

Diagram 349

White to move

We've finally solved the puzzle! White's Queen can, without help from its compatriots, break the blockade and get the passed pawn in motion: **1.Qa3!** (Making sure that if the Queens are traded, the pawn will be as far away from the enemy King as possible.) **1...Kf8 2.Qa5 Qb8** (Of course 2...Qxa5 3.bxa5 Ke8 4.a6 leads to a quick coronation) **3.b5 Ke8** (Trying to help out, otherwise White powers down the board with b6 and Qa7 when the pawn can't be stopped.) **4.b6 Kd8 5.Qa7 Kc8** (Both 5...Qe5 6.b7 and 5...Qxa7 6.bxa7 are hopeless) **6.Qxf7 Qxb6 7.Qxg6**, 1-0.

> **RULE**
>
> A passed pawn usually shines brightest in King and pawn endgames and Queen endgames since, in this case, the lone enemy Queen can't maintain a blockade on its own.

Since passed pawns are so strong in Queen endgames, their creation allows some seemingly hopeless positions to jump to life.

Diagram 350

White to move

White is four pawns down and doesn't even have a passed pawn! Computers think White is doomed, and who can blame them?

1.b5!

Give me a passed pawn NOW!

1...axb5

1...Qe4 2.b6 Kg7 3.Qc8 doesn't change anything—white's b-pawn is just too fast and Black can't expect more than a perpetual check.

2.Qb6 Qf3 3.a6

Five pawns down, but white's passed pawn is further advanced than black's—that little fact makes all the difference!

3...Qg4+ 4.Kf1 Qc4+ 5.Kg1 Qc1+ 6.Kg2 and White just oozes around the vicinity of h1/h2/g1/g2/f1/f2. If given a free move, White will push the pawn to a7, otherwise it's "Black checks, White moves his King, Black checks, White moves his King" until a draw is agreed.

Passed Pawn Tango

Most amateurs fear passed pawns since they envision such a pawn (both "Nimble Louie" and "baby Queen" would fit here) literally dancing down the file to its ultimate glory. And ... at times that's exactly what happens! Of course, this can only occur if the owner of the pawn controls that big square at the end of the board.

J. Silman - K. Shirazi, Pacific Southwest Open 1988

1.d4 Nf6 2.c4 d6 3.Nc3 Bf5 4.Nf3 g6 5.g3 Bg7 6.Bg2 Ne4 7.Nd5 c5 8.0-0 Nc6 9.dxc5 dxc5 10.Nh4 0-0 11.Nxf5 gxf5 12.g4 e6 13.gxf5 Qh4 14.Qd3 Be5 15.f4 Bd4+ 16.e3 exd5 17.cxd5 Nb4 18.Qxe4 Rae8 19.Qf3 Nc2 20.exd4 Nxa1 (White's pawn structure is worth a second glance!) **21.Qd1 Qf6 22.Bd2** (22.dxc5! is the computer's choice, but 22.Bd2 is also good.) **22...Qxd4+ 23.Kh1 Nc2 24.Rg1 Ne3 25.Qh5 Qxb2 26.Bxe3** (26.Be4+ forced mate: 26...Kh8 27.f6 Rxe4 28.Qh6 Rg8 29.Rxg8+ Kxg8 30.Qg7 mate. However, I was low on time and saw a move I deemed to be a clear winner, so I played it!) **26...Kh8** (26...Rxe3 27.Be4+ Kh8 28.f6 Rxe4 29.Qg5 mates)

Diagram 351

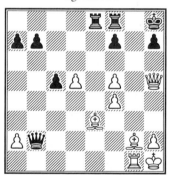

A very complex game has led to this chaotic (but dead won for White) position. One might think that more fireworks are in store, but instead I play to get the passed pawn to its house of worship on d8.

27.Bxc5!

This frees the d4-square, which allows White to create serious threats along the a1-h8 diagonal. But the real idea behind this move is the domination of the d8-square!

27...Rg8 28.Qd1!

This does two things: It threatens Bd4+, and it also backs the d-pawn up for its run to the end of the board.

28...Qg7 29.f6

29.d6 was also very strong, but 29.f6 (which is also crushing) was what I had in mind when I played 27.Bxc5.

29...Qh6 30.Be7

And there it is—the d8-square is white's and Black is helpless against the threat of d5-d6-d7-d8. The rest doesn't need comment: **30...Rc8 31.d6 Rc5 32.Bf3 Rxg1+ 33.Qxg1 Rc8 34.Qg7+ Qxg7 35.fxg7+ Kxg7 36.d7**, 1-0.

The Dynamic Passer

We'll consider two ways a passed pawn can take on a very dynamic stance. One is similar to the Passed Pawn Tango, which we just looked at, and the other is the use of the pawn as an attacking unit.

A. Rubinstein - P. Leonhardt, Prague 1908

1.d4 d5 2.c4 e6 3.Nc3 Nf6 4.Bg5 Be7 5.e3 0-0 6.Nf3 Nbd7 7.Qc2 h6 8.Bh4 c5 9.Rd1 Qa5 10.Nd2 cxd4 11.exd4 e5 12.dxe5 Nxe5 13.Nb3 Qb4 14.Bxf6 Bxf6 15.cxd5 Nc4 16.Bxc4 Qxc4 17.Qe2 Bxc3+ 18.bxc3 Qxc3+ 19.Rd2 Bd7 20.0-0 Rfe8 21.Qd1 Bb5 22.Re1?? (22.Qa1! is just a little better for Black) **22...Rxe1+ 23.Qxe1 Re8 24.Qd1 Ba4??** (Both players missed the surprisingly strong 24...Re4! when the threat of 25...Qe5 wins outright! Note that 24...Re4 25.Nd4 Ba4! is gin.) **25.h3**

Diagram 352

Black to move

White managed to survive some terrible opening play and can now can sit back and celebrate his new lease on life—there are no more serious enemy threats to fear and his passed d-pawn is a definite asset. Surprisingly for a player of Leonhardt's class, Black makes two poor moves in a row, allowing White to take over the game.

25...Bxb3?!

Black should retain this Bishop since it keeps an eye on the d5-pawn's path through d7. With all the minor pieces off, Black can only blockade with a Queen or Rook, and neither of those powerful pieces really wants to be employed as a babysitter. In fact, this mistake allows me to present a highly useful rule [sidebar]:

Better was 25...b6, taking the c5-square away from the Knight. Other moves that could have also been considered were 25...Qb4!? and 25...Re4 26.Re2 Bxb3 27.axb3 Rd4, though the endgame should be drawn after 28.Re8+ Kh7 29.Qb1+ Qd3 (29...g6 30.Re7) 30.Qxd3+ Rxd3 31.Rb8. In all these cases, Black would have retained some slight pressure on white's position.

26.axb3 Rd8?

With his last two moves, Black has allowed White to realize the rule calling for the creation of a Queen and Rook vs. Queen and Rook situation. Much better was 26...Qe5! 27.d6 Qe1+ 28.Qxe1 Rxe1+ 29.Kh2 Re8 when, with the Queens off, black's King can safely enter the fray—if it can reach d7, the black King would not only blockade the pawn, but would also begin the process of attacking and winning it! Of course, White has various tries after 29...Re8 that will try to take advantage of black's present passivity (a well-timed Rd2-c2-c7 is one, while g4, Kg3, and f2-f4-f5 grabs a serious amount of space). But accurate defense should easily give Black the half point.

27.d6 Qc6 28.d7 Kf8 29.Qg4 Qe6 30.Qb4+ Qe7 31.Qc3

Diagram 353

Black is now doomed to eternal passivity. The rest of the game saw White enjoying a good "Cat and Mouse," patiently and relentlessly torturing his opponent until he finally cracked: **31...Qe6 32.Qc5+ Qe7 33.Qc7 b6 34.Kh2 a6**

> **RULE**
>
> The ideal plan for a player with an advanced passed pawn is to exchange all the minor pieces, leaving both sides with a Queen and Rook(s) vs. Queen and Rook(s). This creates possibilities of obtaining the kind of advantageous Queen endgames discussed earlier, and also makes the blockade of the passer uncomfortable. Note that the Queens should be retained, since that piece's power makes the defending King's participation in the defense rather risky.

35.g3 b5 36.b4 f6 37.h4 Kf7 38.h5 Kf8 39.Kg2 Qe4+ 40.Kh2 Qe7 41.Kg1 Qe1+ 42.Kg2 Qe4+ 43.Kh2 Qe7 44.Rd4 Kf7 45.Rd2 Kf8 46.Kg2 Qe4+ 47.Kh2 Qe7 48.Rd6 Kf7 49.Qc6 Qe5 50.Kg2 Ke7 51.Rd3 Kf7 52.Rd2 Ke7 53.Rd3 Kf7 54.Kg1 Qe1+ 55.Kg2 Qe5 56.Rd2 Ke7 57.Rd3 Kf7 58.Kg1 Qe1+ 59.Kg2 Qe5 60.Kg1 Qe1+ 61.Kg2 Qe5 62.Rd2 Ke7 63.f4 Qe6 64.Qc5+ Kf7 65.f5 Qe4+ 66.Kf2 Qe5 67.Qxe5 fxe5 68.Kf3 Ke7 69.Ke4 Rxd7 70.Rxd7+ Kxd7 71.Kxe5 Ke7 72.g4 Kf7 73.Kf4 Kf6 74.g5+ hxg5+ 75.Kg4 Kf7 76.Kxg5 a5 77.bxa5 b4 78.a6 b3 79.a7 b2 80.a8=Q b1=Q 81.Qa7+ Kf8 82.Kg6, 1-0.

Now let's take a look at the passed pawn as an attacking unit. This kind of macho (almost psychotic!) passer has no interest in turning into a Queen. It's proud of what it is, and loudly screams: "I'm coming for you, enemy King, so fear me because I'm going to toss you face down on the board and stomp you to death!"

A. Bisguier - W. Lombardy, New York 1957

1.d4 Nf6 2.Nf3 e6 3.Nbd2 c5 4.e3 d5 5.c3 Nbd7 6.Ne5 Nxe5 7.dxe5 Nd7 8.f4 f6 9.Bd3 g6 10.exf6 Qxf6 11.e4 c4 12.Bc2 Qxf4 13.Nxc4 Qc7 14.Qd4 Rg8 15.exd5 Bg7 16.Qh4 Nf6

Diagram 354

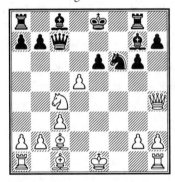

Black—a pawn down and facing a monster attack—is obviously toast, and Bisguier (an attacking genius) mops up his powerful opponent in just a few moves.

17.d6!

The pawn enters the fray! It has no silly dreams of promotion, instead it intends to help the rest of its army hunt down and execute the enemy King. In other words, the pawn is a full-blown attacking piece!

17...Qc6 18.Bg5

Every move is forcing; Black won't be given a chance to even catch his breath.

18...b5

Other replies also meet with a bloody demise:

➤ 18…Rf8 19.0-0 renews the threat to f6 and leaves Black without a defense. One sample: 19…Nh5 20.Be7 Qc5+ (Even more picturesque is 20…Bd7 21.Rxf8+ Bxf8 22.Qg5 Qxc4 23.Qxg6+ hxg6 24.Bxg6 mate! This wouldn't have been possible without the help of the brave little passed pawn.) 21.Kh1 Bd7 22.Bxf8 Bxf8 23.b4 Qb5 24.a4 Qc6 (24…Qd5 25.Rad1) 25.Ne5 Qxd6 (The pawn falls with a smile on its face, happy to have served an important role in its army's conquest of the enemy!) 26.Nxg6 and it is time for Black to give up.

➤ 18…Nd5 19.Qxh7 wins copious amounts of material.

➤ 18…Nh5 19.Bd8 (threatening mate on e7) 19…Bf8 (19…Qd7 20.Ba4 b5 21.Bxb5 Qxb5 22.Qe7 mate) 20.Bc7 Qxg2 21.Rf1 (threatening a couple mates) 21…Bd7 (Stopping Qd8 mate but allowing something else. Moves such as 21...Qxf1+ or even 21..."resigns" were better options.) 22.Rxf8+ Kxf8 23.Qe7 mate. This mate comes courtesy of the d6-pawn, who gave its Queen critical support!

19.Bxf6 Qxc4 20.Bd4

Of course, 20.Qxh7 was also good.

20…Bf8 21.Qxh7, 1-0. Black had no wish to experience 21…e5 (defending the Rook with its Queen) 22.Bxg6+ Kd8 (or 22…Rxg6 23.Qxg6+ Qf7 24.Qxf7+ Kxf7 25.0–0+ Kg8 26.Bxe5 and White, who is an outrageous Exchange and four pawns ahead, should feel a certain degree of confidence.) 23.b3! Qe6 (Alternatives such as 23…Rg7 24.Qh4+ Kd7 25.bxc4 and 23…Qc6 24.Qxg8 only prolong black's pain) 24.Qc7 mate is yet another nod at the power of the d6-pawn.

Three Kinds of Useless Passed Pawns

Though possession of a passed pawn can offer a static promise of endgame "insurance" or a dynamic bonus if it starts rolling down the board, at other times a passed pawn can be completely useless. There are three kinds of useless passed pawns:

➤ There is a life and death struggle going on and the pawn has absolutely nothing to do with it.

➤ Successful blockade relegates it to useless status.

➤ It turns out to be more weakness than strength.

This means that you shouldn't fall in love with a passed pawn without looking at the board and carefully judging its place in the ultimate scheme of things. Let's take a closer look at all three—then you will be able to wisely judge whether or not a passed pawn is right for whatever position you have in front of you.

> **PHILOSOPHY**
>
> Useless Pawn One: Don't hug a pawn if bombs are falling all over the board!

G. Greco - NN, Europe 1620

1.e4 e5 2.f4 exf4 3.Nf3 Ne7 4.h4 h5 5.Bc4 Ng6 6.Ng5 Ne5 7.Bb3 f6 8.Nh3 g5 9.hxg5 fxg5 10.d4 Ng6?! (10...Ng4) **11.g3 fxg3??** (Black is in passed pawn hog heaven, but he's oblivious to the fact that his King is going to die.) **12.Nxg5?** (12.Qf3! was much stronger) **12...g2??** (The final straw—12...Qf6 was forced.)

Diagram 355

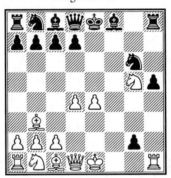

Black, who is a pawn ahead, thinks he can brag about his two kingside passed pawns. Not only that, but the passed g-pawn is also attacking white's Rook and threatens to turn into a Queen. However, all that melodrama is meaningless here, as are both of black's kingside pawns. The only things that matter in this position are development and King safety. Sadly for Black, he's on the loser's end of both.

13.Bf7+ Ke7 14.Rg1 Nh4

One can understand black's feelings—this move protects his Knight and also defends his beloved g-passer!

15.Bxh5 Bg7 16.Qg4 Bxd4

Black is still dreaming of promoting his g-pawn by ...Bxg1, ...Bd4, and ...g1=Q. Well, why not? True, this speeds up his defeat, but he was dead lost in any case.

17.Qxh4 Rxh5 18.Qxh5 Bxg1 19.Qf7+ Kd6 20.Qd5+ Ke7 21.Qe5+ Kf8 22.Qh8+ Ke7 23.Qg7+ Kd6 24.Nf7+, 1-0. Oddly enough, Black still has his g-pawn, and it's still completely useless!

V. Ivanchuk - P. Leko, Mukachevo Match 2007

1.e4 e5 2.Nf3 Nc6 3.Bb5 a6 4.Ba4 Nf6 5.0–0 Be7 6.Bxc6 dxc6 7.Nc3 Nd7 8.d4 exd4 9.Nxd4 0–0 10.Qe2 Ne5 11.Be3 Bd6 12.Rad1 Qh4 13.h3 Re8 14.f4 Ng6 15.e5 Bc5 16.Qf3 Qe7 17.Ne4 Bxd4 18.Bxd4

Diagram 356

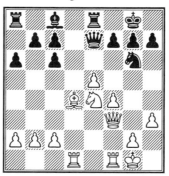

The position looks very promising for White. His pieces are more active than black's and his pawns are healthier and far more dynamic. In fact, an eventual f4-f5 push will not only allow White to strive for a far advanced passed pawn by e5-e6, but it will also create serious kingside angst by the threat of f5-f6.

18...f5!

Black, by force, turns white's central pawn majority into a protected passed e-pawn. But wasn't it the dream of the pawn majority to become a passed pawn? Therefore, does black's 18...f5 make any sense at all? Actually, it does! By giving White a protected passed pawn, he ends all the dynamic potential of white's former pawn majority. Gone is the space guzzling threat of f4-f5, gone is the kingside smash of an eventual f4-f5-f6. All that remains is white's passed e-pawn.

This leaves us with one final question: The e5-pawn *is* a protected passer, so where's the downside? Yes, we're still not clear on whether it will be a "Nimble Louie" or a "Posing Polly", but at the very least it should offer White useful endgame insurance. Or, is there something in this verbal analysis that's missing? I'll answer this in the note to black's 19th move.

19.Ng3

19.Ng5 h6 20.Qh5 Nxf4 21.Rxf4 hxg5 wouldn't make White happy, but what about 19.Nc5, which threatens 20.Nxb7! Bxb7 21.Qb3+? Black can meet this is a couple ways, but one adequate reply is 19...Rb8 20.b4 (20.Qb3+ Qf7 21.Be3 b6 22.Rd2 Qxb3 23.Nxb3 c5, =) 20...b6 21.Nb3 (21.Nd3 Be6 22.Qxc6 Rbd8 23.Be3 Bxa2, =) 21...Qxb4 22.Qxc6 Qe7, =.

19...Be6

> **PHILOSOPHY**
>
> Useless Pawn Two: Blockade can turn a passed pawn into a traitor!

Diagram 357

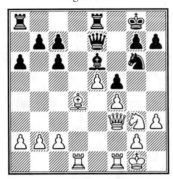

It's official: the e5-pawn is a Posing Polly! But isn't it still useful as endgame insurance? In fact, black's doubled majority *has* to be inferior to the mighty passed pawn! Right? Nope. There are three reasons for this:

- The e5-pawn is acting as a traitor to white's army! That's right, a traitor! First off, it blocks the d4-Bishop. Second, it stops up the e5-square (which white's Bishop and Knight might like to use if it was open). Finally, it blocks the e-file which, in turn, lets Black comfortably stick a minor piece on e6 (White Rooks doubled on the e-file would pressure a piece there, but now e6 is rock solid).

- Black's queenside majority, though devalued due to the doubled c-pawns, is still mobile and active (after an eventual ...b6 followed by ...c5 they will control key squares and gain queenside space). On the other hand, white's e-pawn has no dynamic plusses at all.

- We still have to address where each side will play on. Black's queenside majority (after ...b6 and ...c5) will give him a comfortable game on the queenside. The center, with the exception of the d-file which both sides can make use of, is blocked. The kingside offers White nothing at all.

Once you take all this in, you will come to realize that White has no real advantage.

20.b3 Rad8 21.c4

This prevents ...Bd5 ideas, and also stops Black from eventually trading off a double c-pawn by ...c6-c5-c4xb3.

21...Rd7 22.Rd2 Red8 23.Rfd1 a5 24.Ne2 c5

The d4-square is now off limits to the white army. This means that white's Knight can't influence the blockading e6-square by Nd4. Thus, 24...c5 actually helps protect e6!

25.Be3 Rxd2 26.Rxd2 Rxd2 27.Bxd2 b6 28.Qd3 Qd7 29.Qxd7 Bxd7 30.Nc3 Bc6 31.Kf2

31.Nd5 appears tempting, but after 31...Bxd5 32.cxd5 Kf7 the d5-pawn will be hard to defend. One problem is that the d2-Bishop is tied down to the defense of f4. The other is that ...Ne7 will turn the impressive looking white center into a juicy target. For example: 33.g3 (33.g4 Ne7! and 33.e6+ Ke8 are also bad for White) 33...Ne7 34.d6 cxd6 35.exd6 Nd5 followed by ...Ke6 and ...Kxd6.

31...Kf7 32.g3 Ke6 33.Be3, ½-½. White's pieces have nowhere to go and nothing to do. Couple that with the Bishops of opposite colors and there's no reason either side should continue the game.

Let's take an exaggerated look at the concept of a protected passed pawn being a traitor:

Diagram 358

White to move

White's protected passed pawn is frozen in place by the fine blockading black Knight. What else does White have to crow about? Nothing—the queenside and kingside are locked up and the only open file is, at the moment, controlled by Black. Thus, White doesn't have anything in this position.

However, if we were to remove the traitorous e5-pawn (just take it off and toss it into the box!) then White wins immediately since all his pieces spring to life: his tripled heavy pieces nuke the e-file, his Bishop ravages the a1-h8 diagonal, and his Knight can leap into e5 if the situation demands it.

Sadly for White, the e5-pawn must remain on the board (I suppose you could offer the pawn to your opponent: "I'll give you my e-pawn. Seriously! I'll just take it off the board and hand it to you!"), which means that all of white's pieces are misplaced due to their hitting the e5-brick.

Since Black intends to double up on the d-file, White would be advised to initiate some exchanges and agree to a quick draw after **1.Rd1 Rxd1 2.Qxd1 Rd8 3.Rd3 Rxd3 4.Qxd3 Qd8**, =.

A passed pawn that's in enemy territory (5th rank or beyond) can be very strong, but it can also be very weak because it's stepped a bit beyond the protective embrace of its army! Before pushing your passer that far (or allowing your opponent to push his passed pawn that far!), you have to carefully determine just how secure it is.

Diagram 359

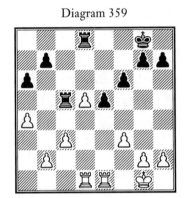

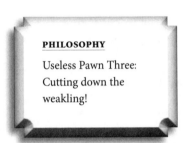

PHILOSOPHY

Useless Pawn Three: Cutting down the weakling!

J. Peters - J. Silman, Los Angeles 1990
White to move

In this game I sacrificed a pawn, knowing that his extra passer was too far and too frail to survive.

1.d6

No better is 1.f4 Rcxd5 2.Rxd5 Rxd5 3.fxe5 fxe5 4.Kf2 Kf7 5.Ke3 Ke6, =. The funny thing is, black's now the one with the passed pawn!

1...Kf7

Black has to be careful since White would be more than happy to return the pawn in a way that allows him to acquire a new set of positive imbalances. Thus 1...Rc6 2.f4 exf4 3.Re7 Rcxd6 4.Rxd6 Rxd6 5.Rxb7 favors White, whose Rook has managed to take up residence on the 7th rank.

2.Rd3

Once again, 2.f4 fails to get anything after 2...Ke6 3.fxe5 fxe5, =.

2...Ke6, ½-½. After 3.Red1 Rd7 4.b4 Rc6 5.a5 Rcxd6 6.Rxd6+ Rxd6 7.Rxd6+ Kxd6 8.c4 f5 the King and pawn endgame is drawn.

At times, though, it's not completely clear whether a far advanced pawn will be strong or weak. Here's a case in point:

NN - G. Greco, Europe 1620

1.e4 c5 2.f4 Nc6 3.Nf3 d6 4.Bc4 Nh6 5.0–0 Bg4 6.c3 e6 7.h3 Bxf3 8.Qxf3 Qd7 9.d3 0–0–0 10.f5 Ne5 11.Qe2 Nxc4 12.Bxh6 Na5 13.b4 Nc6 14.Bd2 exf5 15.exf5 f6 16.b5 Ne7 17.Qe6

Diagram 360

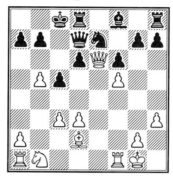

Black to move

The Queen has just leapt to e6 where it flexes its muscles and also dares Black to capture and give White a monster passed pawn on e6. But, would that pawn be a monster on e6, or a goner?

17...Qxe6! 18.fxe6

The pawn is imposing here, but it turns out to be extremely vulnerable.

18...Ng6

Another way is 18...Re8 19.a4 Nd5 20.c4 Nc7.

19.d4 d5 20.Be3 c4 21.Bc1 Re8 22.Re1 Bd6 23.a4 Nf8

The pawn has fallen, leaving Black with an extra pawn and a winning position.
24.Nd2 Nxe6 25.Nf3 g5 26.Nh2 h5 27.a5 Rhg8 28.a6 b6 29.Nf1 f5 30.Ne3 Nc7 31.Rf1 f4 32.Nd1 Ne6 33.Ra2 g4 34.Nf2 f3 35.hxg4 hxg4 36.Nh1, 0-1.
White decided that he didn't want to look at the position after 36...Rh8 37.gxf3 Rh3! 38.fxg4 Reh8.

Blockades

When one speaks of a passed pawn, the chess-trained mind will instantly think, "Blockade!" One can't be mentioned without the other sending a flare up in your brain. Indeed, some blockades turn out to be remarkably powerful, but others don't get the job done.

Failed Blockades

B. Ivkov - I. Platonov, Wijk aan Zee 1970

1.Nf3 c5 2.c4 Nf6 3.Nc3 e6 4.g3 b6 5.Bg2 Bb7 6.0–0 Be7 7.b3 0–0 8.Bb2 d5 9.e3 dxc4 10.bxc4 Nc6 11.Qe2 Nb4 12.Ne1 Bxg2 13.Kxg2 Qd7 14.a3 Nc6 15.Nf3 Rfd8 16.Rfd1 Qb7 17.Kg1 Rd7 18.Rab1 Rad8 19.d3 h6 20.Ne1 Ne8 21.Nb5 Bf6 22.Bxf6 Nxf6 23.Qf3 Qc8 24.Qe2 Ne8 25.Nc3 Nd6 26.Nf3 Qa8 27.d4 Na5 28.Ne5 Rc7 29.d5 f6 30.Ng6 e5

Diagram 361

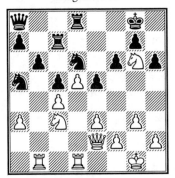

White plays to tear down the blockade

31.Nb5 Nxb5 32.Rxb5 Nb7 33.e4 Nd6 34.Rb3 Kh7 35.Nh4 Qc8 36.Rc1 Re8?

Losing the battle of the blockade! Black, who most likely thought his position was safe enough, needed to take the bull by the horns and make the f5-square hands-off to white's pieces: 36...g6! 37.f4!? (The critical try, but White doesn't have to rush this.) 37...exf4 38.gxf4 Re8 (38...g5 39.fxg5 hxg5 40.Rg3! Re8 41.Rf1! gives White a deadly attack: 41...Nxe4 42.Qh5+ Kg8 43.Nf5 Nxg3 44.Qg6+ Kh8 45.Qxf6+ Kg8 46.Qxg5+ Kh8 47.Qh5+ Kg8 48.hxg3 wins for White) 39.e5 Nf5 40.Nxf5 Qxf5 41.e6 Qxf4 42.Rf1 Qd4+ 43.Re3 intending Rd1 followed by shoving the connected passers down black's throat.

Diagram 362

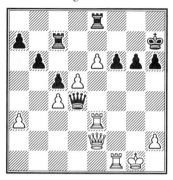

Position after 43.Re3

All thoughts of a blockade have been shattered!

In these lines Black either allowed e4-e5, killing the blockade, or weakened his King so badly that it fell victim to a not-so-subtle slice and dice strategy. Therefore, after 36...g6 37.f4 Black would do better to make sure he keeps a firm grip on e5 (thereby protecting the integrity of the blockade on d6) by 37...Re8! This not only holds the blockade, it also places potential pressure against e4. Again: by not taking on f4 right away, the blockade-destroying e4-e5 is prevented. After 37...Re8 let's look at two white tries:

Diagram 363

Fighting to retain a firm blockade!

38.Re3 seems like a sane alternative, but then 38...exf4 39.gxf4 Rg7! reminds White that his King isn't as safe as he would like it to be. 40.Kh1 (40.e5 g5!) 40...g5 41.Ng2 gxf4 42.Nxf4 Qg4 43.Nh5 Qxe2 44.Rxe2 Rf7 45.Ng3 Re5 and Black has managed to not only retain a blockade on d6, but also on e5 (by freezing e4, ...f6-f5 is a good move in many variations)! Note how the d6-Knight stops the passed d-pawn cold, while also pressuring both c4 and e4.

Diagram 364

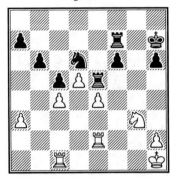

Position after 45...Re5

Black has won the blockade battle

➤ 38.f5 gxf5 39.Qh5 Rg8 40.Nxf5 Nxf5 41.Qxf5+ Qxf5 42.exf5
Rg5 is equal since, though the d6-blockade has been broken,
White must worry about his own weaknesses on c4 and f5.

It's very important to go over these variations slowly and with a lot of attention (in fact, it's not the variations that are important, but rather the concepts
and philosophy they stress)! They (and the whole game) clearly demonstrate
the importance (for both sides!) of fighting tooth and nail over the blockade.
As you will see in the actual game, black's one innocent "blink" was enough to
place him on the road to ruin.

37.Qh5 Qd7 38.Qg6+ Kg8 39.Nf5

The threat of Nxh6+ forces the exchange of black's proud blockading Knight.

39...Nxf5 40.Qxf5 Qxf5 41.exf5 Kf7 42.a4

Diagram 365

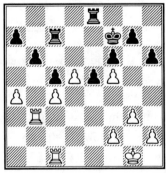

Black's in serious trouble

42...g6

I don't like this move, but the more logical 42...Ke7 (intending to set up a firm blockade on d6 with his King) leads to a completely passive position after 43.a5 Rb8 44.Rcb1 Rcb7 45.f3! Kd6 46.Kf2.

43.fxg6+ Kxg6 44.Kf1 e4 45. Ke2 Kf5 46.Ke3

Black has no counterplay, while White can increase the pressure with a4-a5 on the queenside, and a well-timed f2-f3 on the kingside. The rest of the game, given without notes, is a testament to Ivkov's world-class technique: **46...Rd8 47.Rf1 Re7 48.a5 Rd6 49.Rb5 Rc7 50.f3 exf3 51.Rxf3+ Kg5 52.Kf2 bxa5 53.Ra3 Rb6 54.Raxa5 Rxb5 55.Rxb5 Kf5 56.Kf3 Ke5 57.Ke3 Kd6 58.Kf4 Re7 59.Ra5**, 1-0.

> **PHILOSOPHY**
>
> When a passed pawn exists on the board, a blockade of the pawn is often of critical importance for both sides. Will the defender manage to create a successful blockade? Will the side with the passer managed to prevent it? Games are won and lost on these things, so enter such blockade battles as if your chess life depended on the outcome!

J. Silman - B. Allen, Santa Barbara 1989

1.d4 d5 2.c4 e6 3.Nf3 c6 4.e3 Nf6 5.Nc3 Ne4 6.Bd3 f5 7.0-0 Bd6 8.Ne5 0-0 9.f3 Nxc3 10.bxc3 a6 11.a4 dxc4 12.Bxc4 b5 13.axb5 cxb5 14.Bxb5 Qc7 15.Ba4 Qxc3 16.Bd2 Qc7 17.Rc1 Qe7 18.Nc4 Bc7 19.Qb3 Nd7 20.Bb4 Qh4 21.Bd6 Bxd6 22.Nxd6 Qe7 23.Nxc8 (23.Rc6!) 23...Raxc8 24.Rxc8 Rxc8 25.Qb7 Rd8 26.Qxa6 Nf6 27.Bb3 Nd5 28.e4 Nc7 29.Qc4 fxe4 30.fxe4 Qd6 31.Rc1 Rd7 32.d5 exd5 33.exd5 Ne8 34.Re1

Diagram 366

Black to move

White is a solid passed pawn ahead. However, the fact that there are very few pawns left on the board, plus the possibility of a Knight-blockade on d6, allows Black to put up serious resistance. At the moment White is threatening to take the Knight, and he also intends Re6 followed by piling up his remaining forces against black's King.

34...Nf6?

Folding. Black had to grab the blockade and hope for the best by 34...Qb6+ 35.Kh1 Nd6, but White maintains extremely good winning chances with 36.Qc3 h6 (36...Rb7!?, 36...Rc7!?, 36...Qf2!?) 37.h3 Rc7 38.Qe5 Rc8 39.Ba4.

35.Re6 Qb8 36.h3

36.d6 Kh8 37.h3 was a bit more accurate, but it doesn't have any real effect on the position's landscape.

36...Kh8

There's no longer a way to blockade the pawn since 36...Rd6 37.Qc5 forces the Rook back.

37.d6!

Any thoughts that Black might have had of a successful blockade have just evaporated. The pawn on d6 is far too strong, and now a redirection of white's Queen and Bishop so that they take aim at h7 will bring Black completely to his knees.

37...h6 38.Qd3 Rb7 39.Bc2 Qc8 40.Qf5 Qg8

40...Rb5 was the last chance to put up a fight.

41.d7! Rxd7 42.Rxf6 Rd5

42...Rd8 fails to 43.Rxh6+ gxh6 44.Qf6+ Qg7 45.Qxd8+. The rest of the game doesn't need comment: **43.Qxd5 Qxd5 44.Rf8+ Qg8 45.Rxg8+ Kxg8 46.Kf2 Kf7 47.Ke3 Kf6 48.Ke4 Kg5 49.g3 g6 50.Bd1 Kf6 51.h4 Ke6 52.Bc2 Kf6 53.g4 g5 54.h5**, 1-0.

Successful Blockades

W. Lombardy - R. Fischer, New York 1957

1.d4 Nf6 2.c4 g6 3.Nf3 Bg7 4.g3 0–0 5.Bg2 d6 6.0–0 Nc6 7.d5 Na5
8.Nfd2 c5 9.a3 b6 10.b4 Nb7 11.Bb2 a5 12.b5 e5 13.dxe6 e.p. fxe6 14.e4
e5 15.Nc3 Rb8 16.Nd5 Be6 17.a4 Nd7 18.Ra3 Bh6 19.f4 exf4 20.Nxf4 Bf7
21.Nd5 Bxd5 22.cxd5 Rxf1+ 23.Bxf1 Bg7 24.Bxg7 Kxg7 25.Nc4

Diagram 367

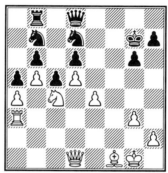

Black to move

A glance might convince some players that White is better—his blockading
Knight eyes b6, d6, and the e5-square, his Bishop might find activity along the
h3-c8 diagonal, and black's b7-Knight seems to be a very sad piece.

25...Ne5!

Black challenges white's blockade while placing his inactive d7-Knight on a
very fine square. Ideally Black would like to follow up with ...Nxc4 followed
by ...Qf6 or ...Qe7, ...Rf8 or ...Re8, and ...Nb7-d8-f7-e5 when the Knight
completely dominates the Bishop.

26.Nxe5

Also possible was 26.Qa1 Qf6!? (26...Qc7!? 27.Rf3 Re8, =) 27.Nxb6 Rf8
28.Ra2 Qf3 29.Bg2 (29.Nc4 Qxf1+ 30.Qxf1 Rxf1+ 31.Kxf1 Nxc4 favors Black)
29...Qe3+ 30.Kh1 Qd4 31.h4 (31.Qxd4 cxd4 followed by ...Nc5 is very much
in black's favor) 31...Rb8 32.Bh3 Qxe4+ 33.Kh2 Qd4, =.

26...dxe5 27.Qg4?!

White fails to respond to the threat of black's blockade with enough energy.
Correct was 27.d6! not allowing black's Knight to sit safely on d6 under cover
of white's self-blocking (traitorous!) d-pawn.

Diagram 368

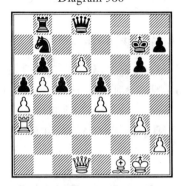

Saying "No!" to the blockade

After 27.d6 Black has two ways to handle the position:

 27...Qxd6 28.Rd3 Qf6 29.Rd7+ Kh8 30.Bc4 (Suddenly white's pieces have sprung to life! His Rook is on the 7th rank and his Bishop is superior to black's Knight. Fortunately, Black can easily equalize by creating threats of perpetual check against the enemy King.) 30...Rd8 31.Qd5 Rf8 32.Qd2 (32.Qxb7 Qf2+ is a draw by perpetual check) 32...Rd8 33.Qd3 (Or 33.Qd5 Rf8 with a draw) 33...Rxd7 34.Qxd7 Qd8 35.Qxb7 Qd4+ 36.Kg2 Qxc4, =.

27...c4!? is a fantastic idea!

Diagram 369

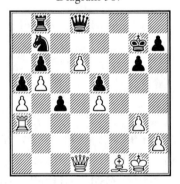

Both players are going berserk!

Both sides are giving away their passed pawns! 27...c4 frees up the c5-square, allowing for ...Nc5 (when the Knight will be extremely strong) or a tactical ...Qc5+. It also deprives white's Rook of the use of the d3-square.

28.Bxc4 (28.d7 Qe7 29.Qd5 [29.Rc3 Rd8 30.Bxc4 Nc5 31.Bd5 Rxd7 with a nice position for Black thanks to his powerful Knight.] 29...Rd8 and Black is better.) 28...Qxd6 29.Qxd6 Nxd6 30.Bd5 Nb7 (Threatening to get the Knight to c5!) 31.Bxb7 Rxb7 32.Rc3 Rd7 33.Rc6 Rd4 34.Rxb6 Rxe4, =.

27...Qe7 28.Rd3 Nd6 29.Qe6 Re8

Diagram 370

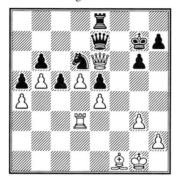

Black has won the battle for the blockade

The beautiful Knight on d6 (a blockading superhero) can't be rousted from its perch, which means that Black has all the chances. Why is that the case? Because the e4-pawn will be under permanent pressure, white's d-pawn isn't going anywhere and is now an official traitor, and black's passed c-pawn (once it gets going) will cause White some serious problems. Note that the Knight also controls the blockading square in front of its c-pawn, meaning that it will be hard for White to stop it once the thing decides to begin its march down the board.

Here's the rest of the game, with only one more note: **30.Bh3 Qc7 31.Qd7+ Qxd7 32.Bxd7 Rd8 33.Bc6 Nxe4 34.Re3 Nd2 35.Re2 Nc4 36.Re4 Nb2 37.Kf2 Nd1+?** (A rare technical mistake from Fischer. Far stronger was 37...Kf6 38.Ke2 c4 with a winning endgame. After 37...Nd1+ Fischer has to win the game all over again.) **38.Ke1 Nc3 39.Rxe5 Nxa4 40.Re7+ Kh6 41.Kd2 c4 42.Re4 Nc5 43.Re7 Na4 44.h4 Rf8 45.d6 c3+ 46.Kc2 Rf2+ 47.Kb3 Rb2+ 48.Kxa4 c2 49.Re1 Rb4+ 50.Ka3 Rb1 51.Be4 Rxe1 52.Bxc2 Re6 53.d7 Rd6,** 0-1. This game's passed pawn and minor piece interplay deserves to be looked at again and again!

Blockade—Caveat (Obicem) Emptor

At this point the hard working student, having read and mastered the material about blockading passed pawns, will studiously follow my advice, triumphantly planting a Knight in front of the enemy passer and celebrating that this unchallengeable blockade will ensure him excellent chances. Then, when he realizes that his position doesn't seem to offer him anything to do, he'll passively sit (cursing my name with every tick of the chess clock) and watch as his Silman-based edifice gets crushed like an eggshell.

Ah, the questions that would follow! "How could this happen?" "Was Silman lying to us all?" "Does Silman even know how to play chess?"

Calm down! Blockading an enemy passed pawn is extremely important, but I left out one small piece of the puzzle: If you don't have some form of active play, then you are doomed to a miserable defensive task that you probably won't recover from.

A. Rubinstein - G. Salwe, Karlsbad 1911

1.e4 e5 2.f4 Bc5 3.Nf3 d6 4.c3 Nc6 5.Bb5 Bd7 6.d4 Bb6 7.fxe5 dxe5 8.d5 Nb8 9.Bd3 Qe7 10.Na3 Nf6 11.Nc4 Ng4 12.Nxb6 axb6 13.h3 Nf6 14.0–0 0–0 15.Bg5 Qd6 16.Qe1 Ne8 17.Be3 f6 18.c4 c5 19.a3 Na6 20.Nh4 Qe7 21.Rc1 Nd6 22.g4 Rac8 23.Nf5 Bxf5 24.gxf5 Nb8 25.a4 Nd7

Diagram 371

White's in charge

Black has firmly and permanently blocked white's passed d-pawn, and his d6-Knight should, according to our discussions about blockade, be viewed as a genuine hero. It all sounds so nice, yet it's all so very, very wrong! The problem is that Black has no counterplay, which means that he has to quietly wait around and hope that White can't find a way to break into his position. Though a passively placed player can draw from time to time, one usually cracks in the face of the opponent's relentless pressure.

26.Rc2 (Since Black can't do anything, White can quietly and safely set up his ideal attacking position before nuking the kingside.) **26...Ra8 27.b3 Rf7 28.Rg2 Kh8 29.Kh2 Nf8 30.Qh4 h6 31.Rfg1 Nh7 32.Rg6 Raf8 33.Qg4 Ng5 34.h4 Qd8** (Giving up, but he was also dead after 34...Nh7 35.Bxh6 Ne8 36.Be3 followed by h4-h5-h6) **35.hxg5 hxg5 36.Kg2 Kg8 37.Rh1 Re8 38.Qh5**, 1-0.

Of course, the same idea of "having no play" needs to be applied to the side with the passed pawn—if the passed pawn is firmly blocked and the blockading side has all the remaining play, then the blockader gets to have all the fun.

J. Smejkal - D. Bronstein, Vitrobud Sandomierz 1976

1.c4 c5 2.Nf3 Nf6 3.Nc3 d5 4.cxd5 Nxd5 5.e3 Nxc3 6.bxc3 g6 7.Be2 Bg7 8.0–0 0–0 9.d4 Nc6 10.Rb1 b6 11.Ba3 Be6 12.Ng5 Bd7 13.d5 Na5 14.c4 h6 15.Nf3 e5 16.e4 f5 17.Nd2 h5 18.Bb2 f4 19.Bc3 Nb7 20.a4 a5 21.Nf3 Re8 22.Qd2 Nd6 23.Qb2 Rb8 24.Bd3

Diagram 372

Black to move

This might seem to be good for White—he has permanent pressure against b6 and e5, and his passed d-pawn, though blockaded, might act as endgame insurance in the future. However, Bronstein had a different way of looking at this position—he realized that, once he gave backup to both b6 and e5, thus making them invulnerable, White would suddenly find himself without any play at all. In that case, a pawn advance on the kingside (where he already holds a clear spatial advantage) would sweep the white King away.

24...Nf7

Taking care of the e5-pawn. For the moment, black's Queen will remain on d8 and defend b6.

25.Qc2 g5 26.Rb2 g4

Black's superiority on the kingside is now obvious.

27.Nd2 Bf8!

This Bishop prepares to become a defensive hero.

28.Rfb1 Bd6 29.Nf1 Bc7

Diagram 373

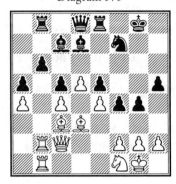

The triumph of black's strategy!

Suddenly both b6 and e5 are rock solid, and White is left wondering what to do. Having achieved his defensive plans, it's now time to go for a kingside knockout.

30.Qd1 Qf6 31.Be2 f3

A logical and strong move, though he could have also considered 31...Ng5!? 32.f3 h4 33.Nd2 g3 when h2-h3 would always be met by the kingside destroying ...Bxh3!

32.d6??

White panics at the sight of his King being swamped by enemy pieces and goes completely berserk! He should have played 32.gxf3 (32.Bd3!?) 32...Ng5 33.Kh1 gxf3 34.Bd3, though it must be admitted that Black retains an extremely strong attack after 34...Kf7 35.Ne3 Rg8.

32...fxe2 33.Qxe2 Nxd6 34.Ng3 Qf7 35.Rd2 Bc6 36.Rbd1 Rbd8 37.Qe3 Qg6, 0-1.

Summary

> A passed pawn can be a static powerhouse and/or a dynamic game winner. Thus understanding it will also improve your understanding of statics and dynamics.

> A passed pawn discourse is the ideal training ground for the concept of blockade.

> A pawn majority's ultimate goal is the creation of a passed pawn—understanding passed pawns vastly increases your understanding of pawn majorities.

> A passed pawn, even a protected passed pawn, can often turn out to be a serious disadvantage.

> A passed pawn usually shines brightest in King and pawn endgames and Queen endgames since, in this case, the lone enemy Queen can't maintain a blockade on its own.

> The ideal plan for a player with an advanced passed pawn is to exchange all the minor pieces, leaving both sides with a Queen and Rook(s) vs. Queen and Rook(s). This makes the blockade of the passer uncomfortable since Queens and Rooks are not ideal blockaders. Note that the Queens should usually be retained since that piece's power makes the defending King's participation in the defense rather risky.

> There are three kinds of useless passed pawns:

  ○ There is a life and death struggle going on and the pawn has absolutely nothing to do with it.

  ○ A successful blockade relegates it to useless status.

  ○ It turns out to be more weakness than strength.

> When a passed pawn exists on the board, a blockade of the pawn is often of critical importance for both sides. Will the defender manage to create a successful blockade? Will the side with the passer managed to prevent it? Games are won and lost on these things, so enter such blockade battles as if your chess life depended on the outcome!

> Blockading an enemy passed pawn is extremely important, but I left out one small piece of the puzzle: If you don't have some form of active play, then you are doomed to a miserable defensive task that you probably won't recover from.

Passed Pawns — Tests

There are a lot of facets to passed pawns—knowing when they are good or bad, knowing how to devalue them or how to turn one into a world beater, knowing which pieces highlight a passed pawn or freeze it into place, knowing if the passer is safe or vulnerable, etc. These problems will give you a heads up as to just how much you've learned about them.

If you have trouble solving the tests, don't worry—that means we've uncovered something you don't understand, and this allows you to fix things by rereading the previous material or by picking up the bits of knowledge you're missing in the answers that start on page 563.

PART EIGHT - TEST **1**

Diagram 374

[Level: 1400 - 1900]

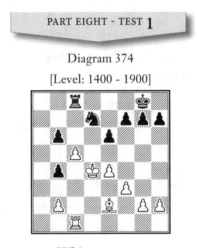

White to move

Is White's c-pawn a goner or a monster?

PART EIGHT - TEST **2**

Diagram 375

[Level: 1800 - 2200]

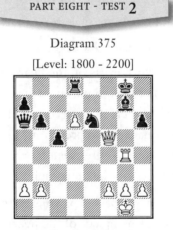

White to move

Who is better, and by how much?

PART EIGHT - TEST **3**

Diagram 376

[Level: 1800 - 2200]

Black to move

PART EIGHT - TEST **4**

Diagram 377

[Level: 2000 - 2200]

White to move

PART EIGHT - TEST **5**

Diagram 378

[Level: 1800 - 2200]

Black to move

PART EIGHT - TEST **6**

Diagram 379

[Level: 1600 - 2000]

White to move

PART EIGHT - TEST **7**

Diagram 380

[Level: 1600 - 2200]

Black just played …c7-c5 and now White has to decide whether to take en passant or to retain his passed pawn and play in another way. How would you describe both choices and the philosophies behind them?

PART EIGHT - TEST **8**

Diagram 381

[Level: 1400 - 1800]

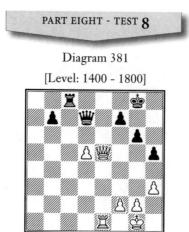

White to move

How large is white's advantage?

PART EIGHT - TEST **9**

Diagram 382

[Level: 1600 - 2100]

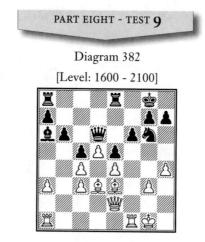

Black to move

Give a verbal breakdown of what's going on, and also look for black's correct initial move.

Part Nine / Other Imbalances

Contents

Imbalances in the Opening

Creating an Opening Repertoire

By far, the most common question I'm asked is, "What openings are best for me and how do I create a proper opening repertoire?" Of course, I warn them about the "spending all your study time memorizing variations rather than learning how to play good chess" syndrome, but then I cave to their query and point out the following critical points which have to be addressed when choosing an opening system that's right for a particular individual:

➤ Choose openings that suit your style/temperament—just because the world's best players use it doesn't mean that it's right for you!

➤ Choose openings that suit both your schedule and memory—if you decide on a mainline Najdorf for Black (**1.e4 c5 2.Nf3 d6 3.d4 cxd4 4.Nxd4 Nf6 5.Nc3 a6**), make sure you have the vast amount of time it takes to look at the endless stream of variations, and make sure you have the ability to memorize all that information. There are many openings that demand far less "theoretical housekeeping" and are far more forgiving of those whose memories have seen better days.

➤ Choose openings that cater to your chess strengths—i.e., if you play closed positions really well, go for systems that tend to lock up the center. If you are a strong positional player but can't always "keep up" in sharp tactical situations, pick lines that avoid chaos. If tactics is what you're all about, make sure your opening choices are conducive to that particular talent.

➤ Choose openings that make you happy—this might sound a tad strange, but if the positions you achieve from your openings don't make you feel excited, happy, or at the very least, deeply satisfied, then why in the world are you using those systems?

➤ Don't choose openings based on the opinion of others, on chess squiggles like += and =, or on computer assessments. Even if a position is thought to be mildly better for the other side, that doesn't mean it's not fully playable—often a player's affinity for a particular position is far more important than its reputation. Basically, if you like it, then play it.

Now, let's come to a FULL STOP!

The above information is for players who want their openings to highlight their existing strengths and, as a result, give them immediate positive results. However, if you are more interested in improving your overall understanding (rather than just gaining a few rating points due to the help of a complementary opening repertoire), then a very different opening philosophy can be implemented:

▶ Choose openings that *don't* suit your style/temperament!

▶ Choose openings that cater to your chess *weaknesses*!

▶ Choose openings that freak you out and leave you feeling vulnerable and insecure!

In other words, this system of thought recommends openings that force you to come face to face with your chess failings so you can patch them up! Thus, if you're starting out and don't feel comfortable attacking the opponent's King, take up crazy gambits that lead to wide open positions and sharp tactics (1.e4 e5 2.d4 exd4 3.c3 dxc3 4.Bc4 is one example). If you are an experienced player (perhaps 1400 - 1900) who has earned his successes by playing solid openings but who fears sharper positions, switch to 1.e4 and dive head first into more fluid situations. If you are a pretty good attacker but hide from positional chess, which you view as dull or alien, throw away your beloved 1.e4 and switch to 1.d4 or even 1.c4 and see how the other half lives. Grandmaster Nick de Firmian, an internationally feared attacking player, did this when he realized that his positional understanding wasn't on the same (extremely high) level as his dynamic skills. He took up 1.d4 for a year and, once he gained the necessary lessons, went back to 1.e4 wiser and stronger than ever.

Be warned! This "bizarro" repertoire is only for brave souls who are extremely dedicated to improving every facet of their game, no matter how much pain and humiliation it takes for them to achieve it (and there *will* be pain and humiliation since you'll suffer many losses as you slowly but surely raise the level of your chess IQ).

Of course, all this (via either philosophical repertoire system) is just the start of creating a very personal, very effective opening repertoire. For example, learning all the basic plans and tactics that usually arise from your openings is also a must. However, even with the addition of the plans and tactics, both philosophical repertoire systems are still missing one final piece of the opening puzzle: Whether your opening is dynamic, static, closed, or open, you need to fully understand the interplay of imbalances that your opening offers.

Integrating Imbalances With Your Opening Choices

Integrating your understanding of imbalances (and, since you've gotten this far in the book, I expect you to have a very healthy grasp of this subject!) into your openings is a virtual must, since most of the time the lines you've memorized will be avoided by opponents who don't know what's going on, and/or don't know what the right moves are. This isn't a big deal for a player who understands the soul of his opening, since he'll immediately realize if his opponent's non-book move does or does not make sense, and what has to be done to punish it or, if the move is fine but new, how to handle the position in a logical manner. Players who only know a bunch of moves won't be able to do this.

One example is the Accelerated Dragon, Maroczy Bind: **1.e4 c5 2.Nf3 Nc6 3.d4 cxd4 4.Nxd4 g6 5.c4**

Diagram 383

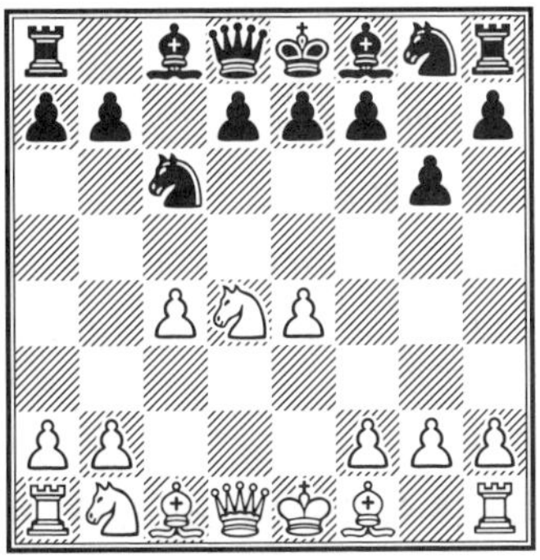

Black to move

As Black, you need to know white's intentions and your general plans, setups, the kinds of endgames that you do and don't want, and the usual imbalances all these things will offer you. Since this isn't an opening book, we'll keep it very simple.

Maroczy Basics:

White's 5.c4 gains central and queenside space, making black's usual pawn-break ideas (...b7-b5 and ...d7-d5) very difficult to achieve. White gets a firm grip on d5 and will usually place a Knight there—if Black plays ...e7-e6, he deprives white's army use of d5 but also leaves the d7-pawn and the d6-square potentially weak.

At times White can simply hunker down with b2-b3 and f2-f3 and hope that his space advantage will suffocate Black. White can also advance his queenside pawns, hoping to overrun that wing, or play f2-f4-f5 and build up a kingside attack.

It's clear that passive play won't hold up in the face of white's space advantage. But what can Black do? There are several plans:

➤ Black can set up shop on the dark squares. There are a few ways to do this, but the most common is to swap the c6-Knight for white's horse on d4, and eventually trade the dark squared Bishops. Then squares such as a5 and/or b4 become livable for black's Queen, and c5 or d4 can be grabbed by black's remaining Knight.

➤ Black can swap off as many minor pieces as possible and leave himself (ideally) with a powerful Knight (on c5 or d4) versus a bad light-square Bishop. This often leads to a favorable endgame for Black.

➤ Black can play for the …b7-b5 pawn break, fighting for queenside domination.

➤ Black can play for the …d7-d5 pawn break, ripping open the center. I said that 5.c4 made these pawn breaks difficult for Black to achieve, but not impossible!

So we've determined that the main imbalances in the Maroczy are space (which brings about pawn breaks, designed to combat white's spatial advantage), possible minor piece plusses, and square control. There's a lot more, of course, but this little bit of knowledge will make an Accelerated Dragon fan's life much easier.

Let's look at a couple of these ideas in action. First up, the …d5 break:

J. Berry - J. Silman, Phoenix 1975

1.c4 c5 2.Nf3 g6 3.d4 cxd4 4.Nxd4 Nc6 5.e4

Transposing back into a Maroczy Bind.

5…Bg7 6.Be3 Nf6 7.Nc3 b6 8.Nc2

Following the old adage that the side with more space should avoid unnecessary exchanges.

8…Bb7 9.Be2 0–0 10.Qd2 d6 11.0–0 Qd7 12.f3 Rfd8 13.Rad1 Rac8 14.Bh6 e6

Diagram 384

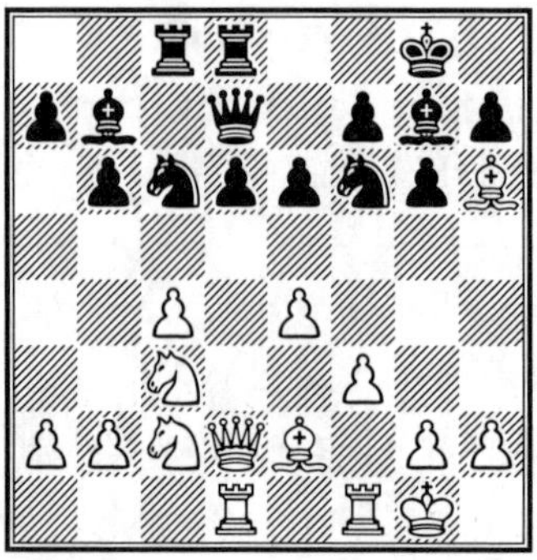

Instead of playing one of the safer systems versus white's Maroczy, I decide that some risks are in order if I want to go all out for a win (thus my choice of 7...b6). With 14...e6 I show my desire to break with a well-timed ...d6-d5 push.

15.Bg5 Ne7

Still aiming for ...d6-d5.

16.Qf4 Ne8 17.Qh4 f6 18.Bc1 Nc7

They call this single-minded determination! For Black, it's ...d6-d5 or bust.

19.Rd3 d5!

Diagram 385

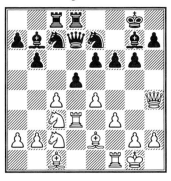

At last! It almost seems like the whole world is concentrating on d5!

20.Rfd1 Qe8

Black has achieved his aim—he's created a sharp game with chances for both sides. Will White be able to handle this change from the usual safe "Maroczy control" to the present knife fight?

21.Ne3

White gets nothing from 21.cxd5 exd5 22.Nd4 dxe4 23.fxe4 Ba6 24.Rh3 h5 with equal chances. Note that 25.g4? f5! is something White should avoid.

21...f5?

It turns out that I was the first to go wrong! I fell in love with the tension and wanted to increase it right away. However, it was far wiser to try 21...Qf7!? if I was determined to ride the tension train, or 21...dxe4! if I just wanted an easy game: 22.Nxe4 Rxd3 23.Bxd3 Bxe4 24.Bxe4 Rd8 with approximately equal chances.

22.cxd5 exd5 23.exf5?

The complex nature of the position (and the ticking of the clock!) is also making it hard for White to find the correct path. He should have played 23.exd5 Nexd5 24.Nexd5 Nxd5 25.Bg5! and black's in trouble.

23...gxf5 24.Nc2 Ng6 25.Qf2 Ne6

Diagram 386

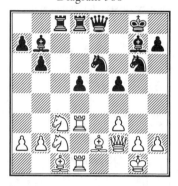

White's bind has been shattered and black's extremely active army gives him the better chances. The rest of the game was marred by mistakes in mutual time pressure: **26.Bf1 d4! 27.Nxd4 Nxd4 28.Rxd4 Rxd4 29.Rxd4 Bxd4 30.Qxd4 Qe5 31.Qd7 Rc7** (31...Qc5+! 32.Kh1 Qf2 33.Qe6+ Kg7 34.Qd7+ Kh8 gives Black a clear advantage) **32.Qd8+ Kg7 33.Bg5 Rf7 34.h4? h6 35.Bd2 Qc5+ 36.Kh2 Qe7?** (36...Bxf3! was the way to go.) **37.Qxe7 Rxe7 38.h5 Ne5?** (38...Rd7! maintained a large plus) **39.Nb5 Bxf3??** (The usual blunder right before the time control. 39...Kf6 or 39...Kh7 was equal) **40.Bc3??** (With no time to think and his flag hanging, he trusted me. 40.Bb4! would have turned the tables.) **40...Bxh5** (Time pressure is over, and so is white's position.) **41.Nd6 Kg6 42.Kg3 Nf7 43.Nc4 Be2**, 0-1.

The next Maroczy example shows three ideas that typically occur in this line—control over the dark squares (c5 and d4 in particular), the creation of a superior minor piece, and the ...b7-b5 pawn break:

E. Formanek - J. Donaldson, Hartz 1987

1.e4 c5 2.Nf3 Nc6 3.d4 cxd4 4.Nxd4 g6 5.c4 Bg7 6.Be3 Nf6 7.Nc3 0–0 8.Be2 d6 9.0–0 Bd7 10.Rc1 Nxd4 11.Bxd4 Bc6 12.f3 a5 13.b3 Nd7

Diagram 387

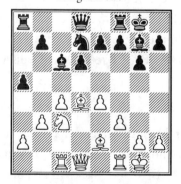

The start of a thematic black plan—he goes out of his way to exchange the dark-squared Bishops so that his other pieces can have free reign on the dark squares.

14.a3 Bxd4+ 15.Qxd4 Nc5

The first sign of possible minor piece problems for White can be seen: black's Knight is better than white's, and his Bishop is also superior to the poor piece on e2.

16.Bd1 e5!

This takes control of the dark squares on d4 and f4, freezes the e4-pawn, and gains space. The potential weakness of the backward d-pawn will never be a factor.

17.Qe3 Ne6

Still working those dark squares! Black's picturesque Knight is now reaching out to c5, d4, f4, and g5.

18.Ne2?!

Passively trying to keep black's Knight out of d4. Note that moves such as 18.Nd5 or 18.Nb5 would both be met by Black snapping it off with his Bishop followed by ...Nd4. The resulting minor piece battle (monster Knight versus poor Bishop) would clearly be in black's favor. In this opening, Black is always looking for ways to create that particular minor piece advantage.

18...b5!

Diagram 388

In the previous game I achieved the ...d5 break, and now we see Black making his dreams of a ...b5 break come true.

19.Bc2 bxc4 20.bxc4 Qc7 21.Rb1 Rab8 22.h3 Rxb1 23.Rxb1 Rb8 24.Rxb8+ Qxb8

The endgame is very much in black's favor (better Knight, better Bishop, and he'll soon develop pressure against c4). The rest is a good illustration of

Mr. Donaldson's excellent technique: **25.Kf1** (25.Qb3 Qa7+ 26.Kf1 Qc5) **25...Kg7 26.Ke1 Nc5 27.Kd2 Qb7 28.Kc1 Qb6 29.Kd2 Bd7 30.Qc3 f6 31.Bd3 Be6 32.Kc2 h5 33.h4 Nd7 34.Kd2 Qc5 35.g3 Nb6 36.Qb3 Nxc4+ 37.Bxc4 Bxc4 38.Qb7+ Bf7 39.Qe7 Qxa3 40.Nc3 Qb2+ 41.Kd3 Qb3 42.Kd2 Qb4 43.Kd3 Qd4+ 44.Kc2 Qf2+ 45.Kc1 Qe3+ 46.Kc2 Qxf3 47.Kd2 Qf2+ 48.Kd1 Qd4+ 49.Kc2 a4**, 0-1.

IM Donaldson has all the Maroczy themes down to a science, but as we saw, just knowing a few setups and being aware of the imbalances generally enables a player to come up with clear, logical, effective plans. Let me repeat: these plans aren't based on emotion or wish fulfillment—they are based on a clear appreciation of the imbalances.

Speaking of wish fulfillment, let's take a look at what can happen when a player decides to do something that suits his style, but doesn't suit the position!

Long ago (in 1834), there were two players (De la Bourdonnais and Mc-Donnell) who ruled the chess landscape with an iron grip. As is often the case, the public wanted to see these chess titans go at each other in a match, and that wish led to a protracted struggle of no less than 85 games, which were played over six matches in the same year! When the smoke cleared, De la Bourdonnais had won a decisive victory which proved that he was—without any doubt—the best player of his day. One reason for this match win was that De la Bourdonnais (described by an English observer of the time as, "a large, slovenly Frenchman who spent most of his time spitting and cursing, and at other times singing and laughing.") played every phase of the game well, while McDonnell (an Irishman who was "quiet and reserved") was pretty much a seek and destroy kind of guy. At the highest levels of any sport, a lack of balance is usually an insurmountable failing, and this match was just another example of that rule in action.

In several games, McDonnell (as Black) played a solid positional reply to 1.d4 (1.d4 d5 2.c4 dxc4) but then—deciding that he could make the opening choice suit his style rather than making moves that were conducive to the opening choice—he lashed out with the hyper-aggressive but ill-advised ...f7-f5 (as early as move 3 and also later), hoping to heat things up. As a result, he was repeatedly slaughtered in various gory ways.

De la Bourdonnais - A. McDonnell, Match 1 Game 8, 1834

1.d4 d5 2.c4 dxc4 3.Nc3 f5?

Diagram 389

Just three moves into the opening and we already get the impression that something odd has occurred. While black's first two moves create the time-honored Queen's Gambit Accepted, his third (a suggestion of Philidor!) is something that rarely (probably never!) appears on a modern chessboard. This leaves us with an obvious question: Is 3...f5 bad, and if so, why? Surely a chess legend like Philidor and an attacking powerhouse like McDonnell saw a lot of good in 3...f5. Can you spot the positive features of black's third move?

The main point of 3...f5 is to fight for control over the important e4-square. Black envisions that, after a further ...Nf6, ...e6, and ...c6, he'll have a firm grip on e4 and, as a result of having stopped White from expanding in the center with e2-e4, he'll also have an unassailable hold on d5. These are noble positional dreams for a guy whose late-night ruminations were usually filled with enemy Kings running for their lives!

However, dreams are one thing and reality is quite another—in this case black's aggressive grab at e4 does more harm than good: ...f5 (a dynamic try for static gold) weakens both e5 and e6, loosens up his King, blocks the c8-Bishop, and weakens the a2-g8 diagonal.

In a way, McDonnell's love affair with ...f5 demonstrates both his strength and his main weakness as a player: acting the role of bully and trying to make everyone believe your flawed vision works against inferior opposition, but when the opponent can see beyond the glitz and show how a move like ...f5 is rotting away the very foundation of your position, it's time to back off and try something less weakening. As we will see, McDonnell refused to accept the truth, and so his stubbornness led to him being pummeled time and again for the same mistake!

This reminds me of amateurs who fall in love with gambits like 1.e4 c5 2.b4 or 1.e4 e5 2.Nf3 d5. They can be very effective against their inferiors and even their peers, so by all means play them if you enjoy this kind of game. But don't embrace delusion and claim that they are good—they most certainly are not! Give it a go if you must, but once someone finally prepares for you in a proper manner and pushes you off the board, accept the writing on the wall and toss the whole mess into the garbage bin.

4.e3

White, who is well aware of the shortcomings of black's 3...f5 idea, realizes that crazy adventures are not called for since he's not developed (don't attack if your pieces aren't ready for action). Thus, he intends to do the following:

▬▶ Develop.

▬▶ Win the c4-pawn before Black tries to defend it via ...c6 followed by ...b5.

▬▶ Dominate the weakened light-squares on the a2-g8 diagonal.

4...e6

Black closes the a2-g8 diagonal (knowing White will capture on c4), gives added support to the d5-square, and frees his f8-Bishop. So far, everything is going according to black's plan.

5.Bxc4

It's hard to resist a move that develops, eats a pawn and takes control over a severely weakened diagonal!

5...c6

Still plodding along with his plan of gaining control over the e4- and d5-squares.

6.Nf3

White wants to get more pieces out before he goes into kill-mode. This move develops, eyes the hole on e5, allows for Ng5 in many variations (targeting e6), and also prepares to castle. Notice how white's moves have been simple, safe, and natural, yet his opponent's position has deteriorated after each one. This is due to the fact that black's 3...f5 created long-term weaknesses that won't be going away any time soon. In other words, if Black manages to hang on in the opening, White will make use of black's structural weaknesses in the middlegame and torture him for a long time to come. And if White sees a chance to nuke his opponent, he'll happily take it.

6...Bd6 7.e4

White, who enjoys a significant lead in development, shows a good sense of timing! Since his King can now castle at the drop of a hat, and since black's King will remain in the center for the foreseeable future, de la Bourdonnais has every right to crack open the center because 0-0 followed by Re1 will quickly follow, while Qb3 is also lurking in the shadows.

7...b5 8.Bb3 a5?

Horrible, but even better tries like 8...fxe4 9.Nxe4 and 8...b4 9.e5 (9.Ne2 fxe4 10.Ng5 also has some serious bite) 9...bxc3 10.exd6 leave Black with a vile position.

9.exf5 exf5 10.0-0

Diagram 390

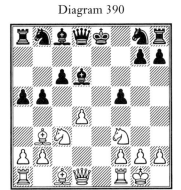

Black's complete lack of development, the open e-file, and the weakness of the a1-g8 diagonal (courtesy of black's 3...f5) promise the second player a painful demise.

10...a4 11.Bxg8 Rxg8 12.Bg5 Qc7 13.Qe2+?!

De la Bourdonnais, who was often playing blitz on the side for money while McDonnell was thinking, tended to move very quickly in these match games (while McDonnell took forever on every move). As a result of this, here he misses a couple of more forcing (and obvious) continuations. Far stronger was 13.Rc1 (Actually, 13.Re1+ Kf7 14.d5! b4 15.dxc6 might get the job done even faster: 15...bxc3? [15...Ra5 16.Nd5] 16.Qd5+ Kg6 17.Re6+ mates) 13...Qb7 14.Re1+ Kf7 15.d5 c5 16.Re6! Bxe6 (16...Ra6 17.Qd3) 17.dxe6+ Kxe6 18.Qd3, intending Re1+, gives White a devastating attack.

13...Kf8??

Black won't recover after this lemon. He had to play 13...Kf7, though white's advantage is obvious after 14.Rfe1.

14.Rfe1 Kf7 15.Rac1

The immediate 15.d5 was also juicy.

15...Qb7 16.d5! h6 17.dxc6 Qa6

Both 17...Qxc6 18.Nxb5 and 17...Nxc6 18.Nxb5 are also hopeless.

18.Nxb5 hxg5 19.Nxd6+

Diagram 391

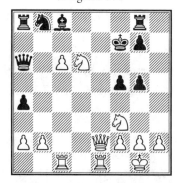

It's a forced mate; so put on your seat belt, cause it's going to be a bumpy ride!

19...Kg6 20.Ne5+ Kf6 21.Qh5 g6 22.Qh7

Faster was 22.Ne8+! Rxe8 23.Qxg6+.

22...Be6 23.Nxg6

Crushing, but 23.Ng4+! fxg4 24.Ne4+ led to a quick mate.

23...Nxc6 24.Rxc6! Qd3

Avoiding 24...Qxc6 25.Rxe6+! Kxe6 26.Qe7+ Kd5 27.Qe5 mate, but allowing an even quicker end.

25.Qe7+

I'm sure McDonnell was thinking, "Beat me already! End my pain!" Black would have gotten his wish if White had played the simple 25.Rxe6+! Kxe6 26.Qf7 mate. On the other hand, the mate White chooses is a lot more fun.

25...Kxg6 26.Rxe6+ Kh5 27.Qh7+ Kg4 28.Rc4+ f4 29.h3+ Qxh3 30.Qxh3 mate. Good times!

After this slaughter, both players seemed to make some much-needed opening adjustments in the QGA (Queen's Gambit Accepted). White switched to 3.e3 (a move that has the modern seal of approval), and Black appeared to give up his dreams of a world where ...f7-f5 is always wonderful.

Nevertheless, though the opening was going through a mutual refinement phase by both players in the next three games (the 10th, 12th, and 15th of Match One), the result was the same: White won them all. McDonnell's handling of the system was getting better and better, but his 0-4 score in the QGA duel had to be hard to swallow. Thus, it wasn't a surprise that emotion took over and he found himself revisiting his beloved ...f7-f5, albeit in an improved fashion.

De la Bourdonnais - A. McDonnell, Match 1 Game 17, 1834

1.d4 d5 2.c4 dxc4 3.e3 e5 4.Bxc4 exd4 5.exd4 Nf6 6.Nc3 Be7 7.Nf3 0-0 8.Be3 c6 9.h3 Nbd7 10.Bb3 Nb6 11.0-0 Nfd5 12.a4 a5 13.Ne5 Be6 14.Bc2 f5

Diagram 392

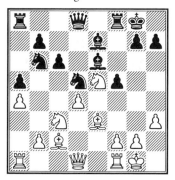

Black has played the opening well and has created a firm hold of the d5-square. Though his 14...f5 wasn't necessarily best, it does have some solid positional perks: it ends white's attacking ambitions along the b1-h7 diagonal and also deprives the White Knight of the e4-square. Unfortunately, Black didn't play ...f5 for these reasons—he played it because he wanted to attack the White King!

15.Qe2 f4?

Horrible! Once again, McDonnell plays a move that suits his tastes, but doesn't suit the position! Hopefully by now, the readers of this book know that you have to play moves that are based on the imbalances and the needs of the given position—in general, you can't do what you want to do, you have to do what the position wants you to do!

Instead of this display of "Chess Tourette Syndrome", the calm 15...Bf6 (intending ...Re8 and ...Nb4) would have promised Black an acceptable game.

16.Bd2 Qe8

Having opened up the b1-h7 diagonal for white's light-squared Bishop, the least Black could have done was to challenge that line with 16...Bf5 when 17.Bb3 Kh8 keeps body and soul together.

17.Rae1

The problems along the e-file are a direct result of the ...f7-f5 advance, since that push instantly weakened the e6- and e5-squares.

White could have tried 17.Ng6 hxg6 18.Qxe6+ Qf7 19.Qxg6 Qxg6 20.Bxg6 Bf6 21.Nxd5 (21.Ne2 seems better) 21...Nxd5 22.Bc3 but he probably didn't like 22...c5 23.dxc5 Nxc3 24.bxc3 Bxc3 when the Bishops of opposite colors give Black serious drawing chances.

17...Bf7?

17...Bf5 still made more sense.

18.Qe4 g6 19.Bxf4 Nxf4 20.Qxf4 Bc4 21.Qh6 Bxf1

Diagram 393

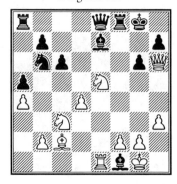

Black now (deservedly so!) gets hit on the head with a hammer.

22.Bxg6! hxg6 23.Nxg6 Nc8

And now De la Bourdonnais demonstrates a forced mate in six.

24.Qh8+ Kf7 25.Qh7+ Kf6 26.Nf4

Threatening Ne4 mate.

26...Bd3 27.Re6+ Kg5 28.Qh6+ Kf5 29.Re5 mate.

Incredibly, next time they engaged in a QGA, McDonnell once again made use of the completely mistaken …f5 followed by …f4, this time getting splattered as soon as the pawn hit the f4-square!

De la Bourdonnais - A. McDonnell, Match 2 Game 6, 1834

1.d4 d5 2.c4 dxc4 3.e3 e5 4.Bxc4 exd4 5.exd4 Nf6 6.Nc3 Be7 7.Nf3 0–0 8.0–0 c6 9.h3 Nbd7 10.Be3 Nb6 11.Bb3 Nfd5 12.Qe2 Kh8 13.Rae1 Bd6 14.Bc2 f5 15.Ne5 f4??

Diagram 394

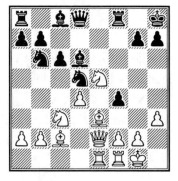

Here we go again!

Apparently McDonnell's love of pain transcended the yearnings of common sense. The idea that one shouldn't increase the activity of the enemy pieces

(...f4 gives the c3-Knight access to e4 and opens up the b1-h7 diagonal for white's light-squared Bishop) doesn't seem like rocket science to me, but perhaps I'm mistaken?

16.Qh5

Splat! McDonnell somehow didn't see this "subtle" move coming—perhaps he had a few too many to drink before the game?

16...Nf6

Also awful is 16...h6 17.Nxd5 Nxd5 18.Qg6 Bf5 19.Bxf5 Rxf5 20.Qxf5 Bxe5 21.Qxe5 fxe3 22.fxe3 and Black should resign.

17.Ng6+ Kg8 18.Bb3+ Nbd5 19.Nxd5 cxd5 20.Bxd5+ Nxd5 21.Qxd5+ Rf7 22.Ne5

Even stronger is 22.Bxf4!

22...Be6 23.Qxe6 Bxe5 24.dxe5 fxe3 25.Rxe3 Qe8 26.Qxe8+ Rxe8 27.f4 and White easily won.

Surely the "Saga of the ...f7-f5-f4 Suicides" finally came to a close? After all, even insects can be trained that fire burns if they stick their mandibles in it over and over again. But no . . . McDonnell chose this moment to dig his heels into the sand and three games followed where this position was reached:

Diagram 395

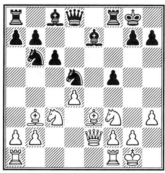

White to move

There followed:

➤ **13.Rae1 f4?? 14.Bxf4 Rxf4 15.Qxe7 Qxe7 16.Rxe7** and White won in Match 2 Game 8.

➤ **13.Rae1 g5?** (A bold new try, preparing ...f5-f4 instead of doing it right away!) **14.Bd2 Bf6 15.Ne5 Qe8 16.f4** (Not bad, but 16.Nxd5 Nxd5 17.Bb4, winning the Exchange, is even better) **16...g4 17.hxg4 fxg4 18.f5** and Black was already losing and indeed went down in flames again in Match 3 Game 3.

➤ **13.Ne5 f4 14.Bd2 g5 15.Rae1 Kg7 16.Nxd5 Nxd5 17.Nxc6!
bxc6 18.Bxd5 Qxd5 19.Qxe7+** (Black's busted again!) **19...Rf7
20.Qb4 Bf5 21.Re5 Qd7 22.d5 cxd5 23.Qd4 Kh6 24.h4 Be6
25.Rfe1 Re8 26.Rxg5 Ref8 27.Qe5 Bg4 28.Rh5+ Bxh5 29.Qg5**
mate, De la Bourdonnais - A. McDonnell, Match 3 Game 5, 1834.

And, mercifully, Black finally got the message and stopped bashing his head against the rotting …f7-f5-f4 wall (once the …f7-f5-f4 nonsense ended, several other QGA games were played with 1.d4 d5 2.c4 dxc4 3.e3, but McDonnell let his f-pawn quietly rest on f7—he even managed to win a couple).

This series of games is the finest example I've ever come across of a gifted attacking player trying, over and over, to create a kingside attack in an opening that simply didn't offer that option! All Black ended up doing was creating self-inflicted weaknesses and, ultimately, finding that his own King was the one getting mated!

The message here should be crystal clear: if you *must* attack, play an opening that gives you a chance to make it a reality. However, even the greatest of attackers can't always get positions that allow them to do their thing. Thus, strive to create some balance in your skill-set. Attack is great, but at least be competent at using the imbalances to surround a weakened pawn, take advantage of weak squares, and all the other wonderful positional things you can do if the situation calls for it.

A. Shirov - E. Bacrot, Bundesliga 2003-04

**1.e4 e5 2.Nf3 Nc6 3.Bb5 a6 4.Ba4 Nf6 5.0–0 Be7 6.Re1 b5 7.Bb3 0–0
8.c3 d5 9.d4 exd4 10.e5 Ne4 11.cxd4 Bg4** (11…Bf5 is a safer choice) **12.Nc3
Bxf3 13.gxf3 Nxc3 14.bxc3** (Hoping for a pawn cascade by f3-f4-f5) **14...f5**
(freezing white's f-pawns—the passed e-pawn isn't, at the moment, a worry for Black) **15.Kh1 Na5 16.Rg1 Qd7 17.Qe2 Qe6 18.Bg5 c6**

Diagram 396

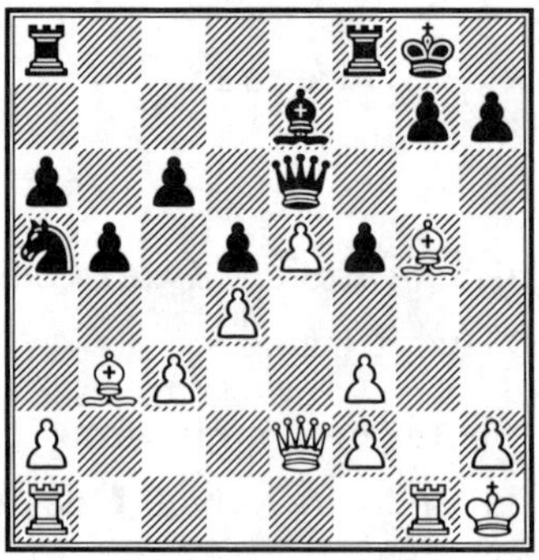

Unlike the games from the De la Bourdonnais - McDonnell match, this position *demands* that White attack on the kingside! Of course, that's good news for Shirov, who is one of the finest attacking players on Earth. However, White would have to go for the kingside attack even if he was the ultra positional Ulf Andersson. At the risk of repeating myself for the thousandth time, you have to do what the position wants you to do!

Of course, Shirov deliberately played this opening variation in the hope of reaching this kind of position—a position that suits his style very well.

Why does White have to attack here? He stands worse on the queenside and the center is more or less locked. That only leaves the kingside, so playing there is a no-brainer. Of course, other "small details" like the e5-pawn influencing the kingside and the open g-file (a road to black's King) only strengthens one's resolve to throw everything you have at the enemy monarch.

19.Bc2

An easy move to make—black's Knight is far away from its beleaguered King while white's light-squared Bishop can join in the kingside festivities from a distance. Thus, why allow Black to swap and deprive the white army of a new recruit?

19...Ra7 20.f4 Kh8 21.Qh5 Ba3

Shirov (in *New In Chess* 4, 2004) points out that 21...Bxg5 22.Rxg5 g6 23.Qh6 Rg7 24.Rag1 Rff7 25.h4 would have also lost.

22.Rg3 Nc4 23.Rag1

White's attacking moves aren't hard to find (chess is much easier to play once you know what your right plan is). Now he has to figure out a way to break through.

23...Qf7 24.Qh4

In most attacking situations, the Queen can be viewed as the "knockout punch." The defender is usually delighted to make the trade, so White wisely avoids it.

24...Nd2 25.Rh3

Not subtle in any way, shape, or form, but highly effective nonetheless!

Diagram 397

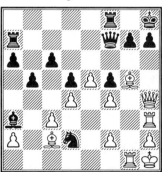

Notice how every White piece is participating in the attack—a real team effort!

25...Qg8 26.f3

Stronger was 26.Bf6 Ne4 27.Bxe4 dxe4 28.Rhg3 (28.c4, uncovering an attack on a3 by the h3-Rook, was also very powerful) 28...Rff7 29.e6 Rxf6 (29...Rfb7 30.Rh3 is hopeless for Black) 30.Qxf6 Qf8 31.Qe5 with an easy win.

26...Nc4 27.Bd3 Nb2 28.Bb1 Nc4 29.Bf6 Nd6

29...Ne3 held out longer.

30.Be7 Rxe7 31.Qxe7, 1-0.

White played for an attacking position (the kind of position that best suited his style) right from the opening, he achieved it, and then he devoted all his energy into making the attack crash through. This blend of opening choice and style, and then opening to middlegame (and, if necessary, to endgame) follow-through (all in perfect balance with your chess strengths and tastes), is extremely important if you want to milk every drop from the openings you employ.

Here's a quick example of such a situation from the positional player's point of view (we seem to have had a tad too many attacks in the preceding examples!). In this game White plays a line that's designed to give him a tiny positional edge based on more space and a queenside pawn majority. White deliberately entered it in the opening (and Black also deliberately allowed it, expecting to draw), turned the slight plus into something more substantial in the Queenless middlegame, and then turned these "tiny" things into victory in the endgame.

J. Silman - Van Buskirk, Santa Barbara 1989

1.d4 e6 2.c4 Nf6 3.Nc3 Bb4 4.Qc2 c5 5.dxc5 O-O 6.a3 Bxc5 7.Nf3 Nc6 8.Bg5 Nd4 9.Nxd4 Bxd4 10.e3 Qa5 11.exd4 Qxg5 12.Qd2 Qxd2+ 13.Kxd2

Diagram 398

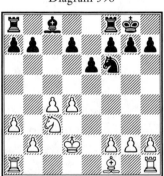

Heaven for me, hell for others

All this is well known theory. White's central and queenside space advantage, and his central King, allows him to look forward to a safe, pleasant grind. This kind of thing would make McDonnell turn over in his grave, but for me it was pure heaven. Clearly, making your openings suit your "chess personality" is extremely important!

13...b6 14.b4 Bb7 15.f3

This little pawn move blunts the action of the b7-Bishop and takes the e4- and g4-squares away from the Black Knight.

15...Rfc8 16.Nb5 Ne8 17.Bd3 Kf8 18.Rhc1 Ke7 19.c5 d6 20.cxb6 axb6 21.Rxc8 Bxc8 22.a4

Diagram 399

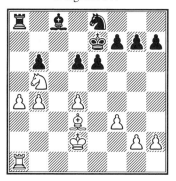

White still enjoys more space and, after a bit of pawn structure tweaking, his queenside majority is about to become a passed pawn.

22...d5 23.a5 h6 24.Kc3 bxa5 25.Rxa5 Rb8 26.Ra7+ Rb7 27.Kb3 Rxa7 28.Nxa7 Bb7 29.b5 Nd6 30.Kb4

The noose tightens—all of white's pieces (King included) are more active than their black counterparts.

30...Kd7 31.Kc5 Ba8

This is one ugly Bishop!

32.b6

My Knight and b-pawn form a wall that prevents the Black King from getting to the queenside. The rest of the game (given without notes) remains true to the opening's vision: **32...Nb7+ 33.Kb4 Nd8 34.Bb5+ Ke7 35.Nc8+ Kf6 36.Nd6 e5 37.Ne8+ Ke7 38.Nxg7 exd4 39.Nf5+ Ke6 40.Nxd4+ Kd6 41.Nf5+ Ke5 42.Nxh6 d4 43.Be8 f5 44.Nf7+ Nxf7 45.Bxf7 Kf4 46.Bc4 Ke3 47.h4**, 1-0.

So far, most of the games have been rather one-sided. At a high level, it's far more common to see one side fight to prove the supremacy of his positive imbalances while the other side does everything possible to prove his own case.

M. Carlsen - J. Nunn, Amsterdam 2006

1.e4 c5 2.Nf3 d6 3.d4 Nf6 4.Nc3 cxd4 5.Nxd4 a6 6.Be3 e5 7.Nf3

White intends to fight for the d5-square with Bc4 and this clumsy looking move helps him do it. The point is that 7...Be6, developing a piece and stopping white's Bc4 in its tracks, runs into 8.Ng5 when Black has to decide whether to let White grab the two Bishops, or to move his Bishop again and allow Bc4.

7...Be7 8.Bc4 0–0 9.0–0 Be6 10.Bb3

White doesn't take on e6 since 10...fxe6 would give firm protection to both d5 and f5.

10...Nc6 11.Qe2 Na5 12.Rfd1 Nxb3 13.cxb3

This clears the c2-square for white's upcoming Knight maneuver.

13...Qe8 14.Ne1

A slice of d5 is still on the menu! The Knight heads for c2-b4 (or in some lines, e3) and ultimately, d5.

14...h6 15.Nc2 Qd7 16.Nb4

Diagram 400

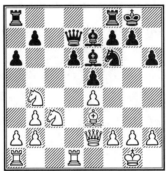

White's opening strategy from move seven on was dedicated to achieving this kind of "give me the d5-square" position. Carlsen now has a slight plus, but black's two Bishops promise him adequate chances.

16...Rfc8 17.f3 Bd8 18.Rd3 a5 19.Nbd5 Nxd5 20.Nxd5 a4 21.bxa4 Rxa4 22.b3 Ra6 23.Rad1 Ra5??

Moves such as 23...f5 and 23...Ba5 would have kept things fairly even. Sadly, 23...Ra5 hangs the d-pawn!

24.Nb6 Bxb6 25.Bxb6 Ra6 26.Rxd6 and White went on the win: **26...Qe7 27.Qb2 Qg5 28.a4 h5 29.a5 h4 30.b4 Raa8 31.Qd2 Qxd2 32.R1xd2 Rc4 33.Bc5 Rc8 34.Rb6 Rc7 35.Kf2 Kh7 36.Bd6 Rd7 37.Ke3 f6 38.Bxe5 fxe5**

39.Rxe6 Rxd2 40.Kxd2 Rxb4 41.Rxe5 Rb2+ 42.Kc3 Rxg2 43.Rh5+ Kg6 44.Rxh4 Ra2 45.Kb4, 1-0.

White succeeded in this game, but black's plusses never had a chance to show their stuff. Small wonder then, that all this was repeated a couple months later!

M. Carlsen - S. Karjakin, Cap d'Agde 2006

1.e4 c5 2.Nf3 d6 3.d4 Nf6 4.Nc3 cxd4 5.Nxd4 a6 6.Be3 e5 7.Nf3 Be7 8.Bc4 0–0 9.0–0 Be6 10.Bb3 Nc6 11.Qe2 Na5 12.Rfd1 Nxb3 13.cxb3 Qe8 14.Ne1

We've been here before, but this time Karjakin stands up for black's two Bishops and dynamic potential. As is so typical of high-class opening battles, they ultimately boil down to a philosophical difference of opinion!

14...Ng4!

Far more dynamic than Nunn's 14...h6.

15.Nc2 f5 16.f3 Nxe3

16...Nf6!? was also interesting.

17.Nxe3 fxe4 18.Nxe4

This looks lovely, but it leaves the road clear for black's d-pawn to eventually advance. More circumspect was 18.fxe4, keeping the d-pawn at bay. There might follow 18...Qg6 19.Ncd5 Bg5 (Karjakin) when black's Bishops are beginning to emerge from hibernation.

18...Rd8 19.Nd5 Qf7 20.Qd3 Bxd5 21.Qxd5 Qxd5 22.Rxd5 Kf7 23.Rad1 Ke6

Diagram 401

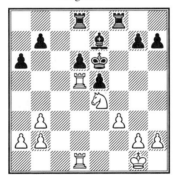

If we assess this position by "what looks good," one would think that White is doing extremely well (after all, his Knight rules on e4 and his Rooks are joining their steed in bashing d6). But if you take a look at the imbalances, you might begin to come to a different conclusion:

> White's doubled queenside pawns leave him half a pawn down (at least until he un-doubles them with b3-b4-b5).

> White's Rooks look great, but they are stuck on the d-file (if the d1-Rook leaves that file, then the d5-Rook will hang, while if the d5-Rook moves, it might allow Black to get his central pawns in motion by ...d6-d5). This means that the c-file is up for grabs, and once a black Rook claims it an incursion to the 7th rank should pay dividends.

> White's Knight is a monster as long as the d-pawn can't advance. But can white's Rooks stay in their present position forever? If not, that d-pawn will move, and that means the once god-like horse will suddenly become inferior to black's Bishop.

Black's position is already a bit more comfortable, though White should certainly hold the draw.

24.b4 Rc8 25.b5

Taking a moment off to keep black's Rook out of c2 doesn't have the desired effect: 25.R1d2 Rc1+ 26.Kf2 Rc4 (threatening both ...Rxb4 and ...Rxe4) 27.Nxd6 Rxb4 28.Ke2? (28.b3) 28...Bg5 and White is suddenly in serious trouble.

25...Rc2 26.bxa6

26.Nxd6!? axb5 (26...Rd8 will transpose to our next note) 27.Nxb5 Rxb2 28.Nc7+ Kf6 29.R5d2 Bc5+ 30.Kf1 Rxd2 31.Rxd2, =.

26...bxa6 27.Ra5?!

Black's d-pawn looks weak, but it will soon become a hero. Thus, he should have taken this final opportunity to chop it off: 27.Nxd6! Rd8 28.Rxe5+! Kxe5 29.Nf7+ Kf6 30.Nxd8 Rxb2 31.a4 Bc5+ 32.Kh1 Ra2 33.a5 Bb4 34.Nc6 Bxa5 35.Nxa5 Rxa5 with a theoretically drawn endgame.

27...Rb8 28.b3 Rb6 29.Kf1 Rbc6 30.h3 h5 31.Rd3 g5 32.Rd2 Rxd2 33.Nxd2 d5 (At last!) **34.Ra4 a5 35.Ke2 Bd8 36.Kd3 Rc1 37.b4 axb4 38.Rxb4 Rg1 39.g4 Rg3 40.Rb8 e4+ 41.Ke2 Rg2+ 42.Kf1 Rxd2 43.Rxd8 hxg4 44.hxg4 exf3 45.Re8+ Kd6 46.Rf8 Rxa2 47.Rf5 Ke6 48.Rxg5 d4 49.Rf5 d3 50.Ke1 Re2+**, 0-1.

REMEMBER

An opening battle between two theoretically astute players ultimately boils down to a philosophical difference of opinion. But if you don't know the philosophy (imbalances & general ideas) behind your opening lines, then all you're left with is random moves.

Let's explore this idea of a philosophical battle in a bit more detail:

V. Ivanchuk - T. Radjabov, Wijk aan Zee 2009

1.d4 Nf6 2.c4 g6 3.Nc3 Bg7 4.e4 d6 5.Be2 0–0 6.Nf3 e5 7.0–0 Nc6 8.d5 Ne7 9.b4 Ne8 10.a4 f5 11.a5

Diagram 402

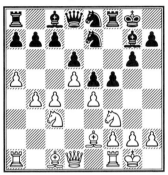

And here grandmaster Radjabov gave us one sentence (from *New In Chess* 2, 2009) that is both simple and profound: "White has gained a lot of space on the queenside, but Black has a lot of play on the kingside."

That's it! This is what everyone needs to be able to do with any and every opening he plays—you need to know what your opening is giving to you, and what it's giving to your opponent.

This kind of thing seems self-evident, but if, after the first 15 moves of your favorite opening, I was to pull you aside and ask you to explain exactly what this line is offering you and what it's offering your opponent, would you be able to instantly lecture me on its basic building blocks? Can you do this with every opening you play? Most players can't, and this is a tragedy since it's so very simple to arm yourself with this oh-so-critical information.

In most cases, these philosophical opening arguments are never resolved if the openings are sound main line systems—both sides have their chances and the player who understands the position better, had a good-biorhythm day, or is simply stronger, usually does quite well. In the case of inferior or experimental openings, there might very well be a resolution with one side permanently being branded as inferior. Here's an example of a well-intentioned positional try for Black achieving good results until a certain something appeared to destroy his fun.

M. Okkes - J. Bosch, Holland 2003

1.e4 c5 2.Nf3 a6

The O'Kelly Variation. The point of this rather rare but interesting variation is seen after 3.d4 cxd4 4.Nxd4 Nf6 5.Nc3 e5! 6.Nf3 Bb4 when Black gets active play.

3.c4

Considered in many sources to be white's best move. The other challenging option is 3.c3.

3...d6 4.d4 Bg4 5.d5

5.dxc5 Bxf3 6.Qxf3 dxc5 and the hole on d4 promises Black his full share of the chances:

- 7.e5 Nc6 8.e6 fxe6 9.Bd3 Nf6 10.Qh3 Nb4 11.Ke2 Qd4 12.Rd1 Nxd3 (12...Rd8!? might be even stronger) 13.Rxd3 Qxc4 14.Nd2 Qg4+ with a material plus for Black in K. Arakhamia - B. Kurajica, Malaga 2001.

- 7.Qb3 Nc6 8.Qxb7? Nb4 9.Na3 Rb8 10.Qa7 Qc8 11.Be3 e6, 0-1, C. Caminade - O. Foisor, Naujac 2002.

- 7.Bd3 Nc6 8.0–0?? Ne5 9.Qg3 Nxd3 10.Rd1 Nxc1 11.Rxd8+ Rxd8 12.Nc3 Rd1+, 0-1, M. Marcetic - S. Maksimovic, SRB ch 2007.

- 7.Be3 Nc6 8.Nc3 e6 9.Be2? (9.Qg3!?) 9...Nd4 10.Bxd4 cxd4 11.Rd1 Qb6 and Black was clearly better in A. Butunoi - A. Ardeleanu, Arad 2006.

5...e5

Black's opening plan is devoted to the creation of a good Knight versus bad Bishop situation. 5...e5 anticipates this by closing the center.

6.Nc3 Nd7 7.Be2 Bxf3 8.Bxf3 g6 9.h4 h5 10.Be2 Bh6

Diagram 403

The point of black's previous play: this move deprives White of the two Bishops and seeks a position where white's light-squared Bishop will be no better than, or even inferior to, a Knight.

11.g3 Kf8

The immediate 11...Bxc1 is also good.

12.Bd3 Kg7, =.

Nothing wrong with that! One can understand why this line became popular, but then something extremely unpleasant appeared.

1.e4 c5 2.Nf3 a6 3.c4 d6 4.d4 Bg4 5.dxc5 Bxf3 6.gxf3! (instead of 6.Qxf3, which we looked at earlier) **6...dxc5**

The alternative is 6...Qa5+ 7.Nc3 Qxc5 (7...dxc5 8.Qb3 Nd7 [8...Qc7? 9.Bf4!] 9.Qxb7 Rb8 10.Qc6 e6 11.Qa4 Qxa4 12.Nxa4 left White a pawn up for nothing in A. Butunoi - N. Yachou, Arad Vados 2007 and in D. Mastrovaskilis - A. Ardeleanu, Dresden 2007) 8.Be3 Qc6 when white's lead in development and two active Bishops justifies the labeling of black's game as "suspect."

7.Qxd8+ Kxd8

Diagram 404

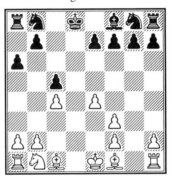

This isn't at all what Black had in mind when he played 4...Bg4—remember that this was supposed to be a quiet positional try based on gaining a superior minor piece. Instead he ended up with a vulnerable King, he's facing two killer enemy Bishops, and White possesses a seriously scary initiative. Black's slightly superior pawn structure and his control of the d4-square (all long term static plusses) can't make up for the listed dynamic defects.

8.Nc3

8.Be3 e5 9.f4 f6 10.Nc3 Nc6 11.0–0–0+ Nd4 12.fxe5 fxe5 13.f4 exf4 14.Bxf4 Ke8 15.Nd5 Rd8 16.Bc7 Rd7 17.Bh3 Rf7 18.Rhf1 Nh6 19.Bc8 and Black was busted in F. Borkowski - A. Nazarov, Katowice 1990.

8...e6 9.Be3 Nf6 10.0–0–0+ Nfd7 11.f4 b6 12.f5 Nc6 13.fxe6 fxe6 14.Bh3 Ke7 15.Bg5+ Nf6 16.e5 Nxe5 17.Rhe1 Nf3 18.Bg2

Even stronger was 18.Bxf6+ (of course, there's also nothing wrong with 18.Rxe6+) 18...gxf6 19.Nd5+ Kf7 20.Bxe6+ Kg6 21.Re3 Bh6 (21...Ng5 22.Rg1) 22.Ne7+ Kh5 (22...Kg7 23.Nf5+) 23.Bf7+ Kg5 24.Bd5 Ne5 25.Rh3 and Black is toast.

18...Nxg5 19.Bxa8 Kf7 20.Bg2 Nh5 21.h4 Nf4 22.hxg5 Nxg2 23.Re4 Be7 24.Rg1, 1-0, R. Fontaine - B. Andonov, French Team Championship 2009.

Most players want an opening repertoire that suits their tastes/style and will hold up as the flow of fashion comes and goes. None of the mainstream openings (Caro-Kann, French Defense, 1.e4 e5, Sicilian, Gruenfeld Defense, King's Indian, Queen's Gambit, English Opening, etc.) will ever be refuted, so if you want to stick with something over a long period of time, go with the oldies but goodies and try and avoid strange gambits or a "too good to be true" flavor of the month. Staying with something allows you to create an intimate knowledge of all its secrets, and you'll find that it will serve you well for a lifetime.

Waylaid into Opening Chaos

Usually you will find yourself in an opening of your choosing (something you've prepared beforehand—though whether that preparation is deep or shallow is up to your strength, experience, and/or work ethic), which means you should already know (to some extent) the main imbalances, ideas, and plans. On the other hand, your opponent might surprise you (for example, with 1.b4 or, as Black, something like 1.e4 e5 2.Nf3 d5) and drag you into something you're clueless about.

In the first case (i.e., you get an opening you're familiar with), you should do fine since, even if your opponent leaves known theory at some point, you'll be able to make moves that are sensible and good (fully in accordance with the imbalances) for the upcoming middlegame. Things get a bit more taxing if you end up in undiscovered country, though if it's some positional line then you should get by fine by simply returning to your "imbalance roots." For example, after 1.b4 you realize that White is gaining queenside space and also intends Bb2. Pretty simple! You can say, "Okay, he took queenside space so I'll take something too—how about central space?" And so 1...e5 makes perfect sense. Then you would continue going for the center (and striving to make your center indestructible) while he would attack your center from the side and try to continue making queenside gains. You wouldn't know any theory about 1.b4, but your approach would ensure a balanced fight.

Harder to deal with is some tactical surprise in the opening. In this case, rational thought (imbalances) might have to take a back seat to raw calculation. However, just because your opponent tries to drag you down the rabbit hole doesn't mean you have to go! The following shows just such a situation.

J. Silman - T. Hanks, National Open 1998

1.d4 g6 2.e4 Bg7 3.Nf3 c6 4.Nc3 d5 5.h3 Nf6 6.e5 Ne4

Diagram 405

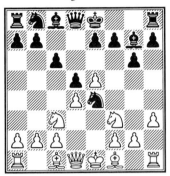

Annoying! I was dimly aware of some analysis covering 7.Nxe4 (which is the only way to actually try and refute 6...Ne4) 7...dxe4 8.Ng5 c5, but I didn't remember any of the details. My opponent had made his first six moves instantly and seemed quite pleased with himself—it was clear that *he* knew exactly what would be going on after the capture on e4!

Though I had no problem fighting players on the stage of their choosing, it had to be "fair" in that I felt I could outplay anyone in a positional fight (as long as we can let those imbalances lead us to the Promised Land, all should be well), while I also was confident of being able to find the right tactics against some garbage opening that begged to be tactically refuted. But this 6...Ne4 was different—the complications were far from clear, and if he was booked to the hilt then I would be a fool to walk into his preparations (in effect, instead of playing Mr. Hanks, I would be playing a team of grandmaster analysts). So, considering all this, my decision was easy to understand:

7.Bd3

Avoiding his tactical preparations and forcing a difficult strategic battle. Now the winner will be the player with the most skills, not the player with the best memory! The philosophy of stepping away from sharp opening surprises with a calming move that keeps the position sane and "imbalance friendly" has served me well on many occasions, and I recommend you make use of it to!

7...Nxc3 8.bxc3 c5 9.0-0 with a slight pull for White.

Though my "don't needlessly leap into the rabbit hole" philosophy showed its worth over the course of my career, there were times when my opponent's "transgression" was so great that I couldn't back down. Here's a case in point:

J. Silman - D. Root, Berkeley 1981

1.d4 d5 2.c4 e5

Just two moves, and Black has managed to push his d- and e-pawns to their 4th rank. Here, answering 2...e5 with a quiet move (3.Nc3, 3.e3, etc.) just won't cut it since black's pawn center and easy development assures him a good game. Would you let Black, after just *two* moves, get away with this affront to all that's sane and right? No! Black has demanded too much too fast, and a guy has to draw a line in the sand at some point!

3.dxe5

I didn't know much Albin Counter Gambit theory (I spent my study time on more mainstream openings), but the die had been cast and I accepted that my dream of a quiet positional struggle wasn't going to come true. Now my mood swung to one of do or die—he would follow with the space-gaining ...d4 and then try and build up an attacking position, and I would welcome the fight by mixing energetic development with raw, overwhelming greed.

3...d4 4.Nf3 Nc6 5.g3 Bg4 6.Bg2 Qd7 7.0–0 h5 8.Qb3 Nge7 9.Bg5 h4

Diagram 406

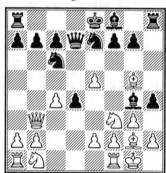

Black's attacking like a madman, but isn't he offering me a *second* pawn? I'm willing to put up with a lot of humiliation for two pawns!

10.Bxh4

I felt like I was at an all-you-can-eat buffet.

10...Ng6 11.Bg5 Rh5 12.Nbd2 Bb4 13.Rfd1

The theme of the game is obvious: he plays some hyper-aggressive move, and I either develop another piece or devour something.

13...f6

Really—you want me to take something else?

14.exf6

Okay, that's *three* pawns. Now show me what you got!

14...0-0-0 15.fxg7

Diagram 407

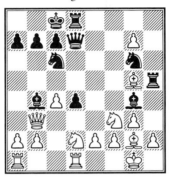

I never realized that chess was such an easy game. Of course, we're still living in the world of imbalances: he's trying to get to my King (for him, it is dynamics or bust) and I'm swallowing down everything that's offered (White is wallowing in the sweet static taste of a huge material advantage).

15...Rg8 16.Ne4 Qxg7 17.h4

A case of too many good choices. 17.Bf6 was probably best, while 17.Nf6 Rxg5 18.Nxg8 was also strong, though a tad complicated. But why risk anything? I decided to lock in the victory by battening down my kingside hatches.

17...Be7 18.Bxe7 Qxe7 19.Nxd4

Four pawns. Lust for material (which offers you something chewy and tangible) is often far more gratifying than attack (which can easily turn out to be pie-in-the-sky).

19...Bd7 20.Qa3

Of course, Black can't afford to trade Queens.

20...Nxd4 21.Rxd4 c5 22.Rd5 (22.Rxd7! was even crisper), 1-0.

Keeping things on the opening paths you are familiar with is a good practical rule of thumb. However, when your opponent butts heads and insists on starting an immediate (but theoretically dubious) knife fight, you often have to get down and dirty and leap into the fray, even if you're not conversant with theory.

Summary

> The imbalances are a critical tool for a proper understanding of any and all opening systems.

> Choose openings that suit your style/temperament—just because the world's best players use it doesn't mean that it's right for you!

> Choose openings that suit both your schedule and memory.

> Choose openings that cater to your chess strengths—i.e., if you play closed positions really well, go for systems that tend to lock up the center. If you are a strong positional player but can't always "keep up" in sharp tactical situations, pick lines that avoid chaos. If tactics is what you're all about, make sure your opening choices are conducive to that particular talent.

> Choose openings that make you happy—this might sound a tad strange, but if the positions you achieve from your openings don't make you feel excited, happy, or at the very least, deeply satisfied, then why in the world are you using those systems?

> Don't choose openings based on the opinion of others, on chess squiggles like += and =, or on computer assessments. Even if a position is thought to be mildly better for the other side, that doesn't mean it's not fully playable. Often a player's affinity for a particular position is far more important than its reputation. Basically, if you like it, then play it.

> If you wish to create a temporary "learning" repertoire based on facing and fixing your weaknesses, then you can consider these three things:

  ○ Choose openings that *don't* suit your style/temperament!

  ○ Choose openings that cater to your chess *weaknesses*!

  ○ Choose openings that freak you out and leave you feeling vulnerable and insecure!

> Whether your opening is dynamic or static, closed or open, you need to fully understand the interplay of imbalances that your opening offers.

> An opening battle between two theoretically astute players ultimately boils down to a philosophical difference of opinion. But if you don't know the philosophy (imbalances and general

ideas) behind your opening lines, then all you're left with is random moves.

> You always need to know what your opening is giving to you, and what it's giving to your opponent.

Imbalances in the Opening – Tests

I'm going to do something different in this group of problems. If a problem presupposes that the position arrives from an opening you know, I'll list the basic imbalance schema (to create an artificial "I know what's going on here!" mindset) and then pose a specific question. If a problem presupposes that the position arrives from an opening you know nothing about, I'll simply give you a specific question.

The following tests are designed to give you insight into how much you've learned *and* to serve as extra instruction. If you have trouble solving the tests, don't worry—that means we've uncovered something you don't understand, and this allows you to fix things by rereading the previous material or by picking up the bits of knowledge you're missing in the answers that start on page 575.

PART NINE - TEST **1**

Diagram 408

[Level: 1900 - 2200]

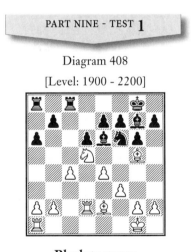

Black to move

White is threatening to win by Nb6 or Nxe7+, while chopping on f6 is also looming. It's clear that white's Knight has to be taken, but with what? Black usually tries to avoid giving up the two Bishops by ...Bxd5 in analogous positions, but taking with the Knight might hang the e7-pawn (which is often indirectly protected, and this might or might not be the case here). What is the right way to capture on d5?

PART NINE - TEST **2**

Diagram 409

[Level: 1600 - 2000]

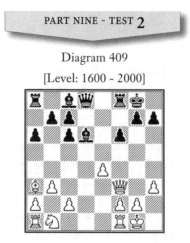

White to move

The Exchange Variation of the Ruy Lopez gives White the superior pawn structure (a healthy pawn majority versus a crippled one), but in return Black gets two Bishops and potential pressure down the e-file against white's e-pawn. In the present situation, Black can also play with the idea of ...f6-f5, opening the position up even further for his Bishops. How should White handle this position?

PART NINE - TEST **3**

Diagram 410

[Level: 1400 - 2000]

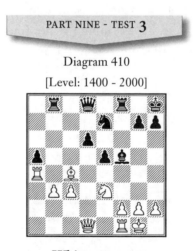

White to move

This is a position from the Sveshnikov Sicilian. Both sides played the opening logically and White has emerged with a small edge. Both sides have active pieces. Black has some pressure against b3 and would love to get his central pawn majority moving by ...d6-d5. Though White has definite designs against a5, his immediate goal is to stop black's dream of ...d6-d5 so that the d-pawn will remain a static weakness instead of a dynamic plus. Once he does that, he can pile up on d6 and place Black permanently on the defensive. What moves best strive to achieve these two goals (i.e., to stop ...d5 and hit d6)?

Diagram 411

[Level: 1400 - 1600]

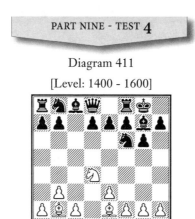

Black to move

White has just played his 7th move and has absolutely nothing. Obviously, it wasn't a very good opening choice. So, what we have here is something White hadn't deeply studied and almost certainly something Black hadn't prepared at all—he was on his own.

What is black's most pronounced favorable imbalance? Once you find that, you'll fully understand and appreciate the moves that follow.

Diagram 412

[Level: 1400 - 1800]

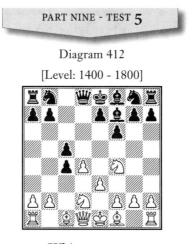

White to move

Yet another "I've never been here before!" kind of position. How would you assess this position? And what specific things in black's position catch your attention?

Mixing Imbalances

Congratulations. You've almost completed a long journey into the exploration, understanding, and use of positional concepts based, of course, on imbalances. To regiment your studies throughout the book, I found it necessary to present the information in the form of individual imbalances. However, the vast majority of games are fought on a battleground composed of many imbalances that, more often than not, are at odds with each other.

The following tests are designed to give you insight into how much you've learned *and* to serve as extra instruction. If you have trouble solving the tests, don't worry—that means we've uncovered something you don't understand, and this allows you to fix things by rereading the previous material or by picking up the bits of knowledge you're missing in the answers that start on page 583.

Mixing Imbalances — Tests

PART NINE - TEST **6**

Diagram 413

[Level: 1400 - 1900]

Black to move

PART NINE - TEST **7**

Diagram 414

[Level: 1800 - 2200]

Black to move

PART NINE - TEST **8**

Diagram 415

[Level: 1800 - 2200]

Black to move

Assess this position.

PART NINE - TEST **9**

Diagram 416

[Level: 1400 - 1800]

Black to move

Assess the position.

PART NINE - TEST **10**

Diagram 417

[Level: 1800 - 2200]

White to move

PART NINE - TEST **11**

Diagram 418

[Level: 1400 - 1800]

White to move

Assess the position.

PART NINE - TEST **12**

Diagram 419

[Level: 1400 - 1800]

Black to move

Assess the position.

PART NINE - TEST 13

Diagram 420

[Level: 1400 - 1800]

White to move

Assess the position and find a move that fits into that assessment.

PART NINE - TEST 14

Diagram 421

[Level: 1600 - 2000]

White has just played Nh4, a move tried in a few games. Why would he play such a move?

PART NINE - TEST 15

Diagram 422

[Level: 1600 - 2000]

White to move

Does Bb2 make any sense?

PART NINE - TEST 16

Diagram 423

[Level: 1600 - 2000]

White to move

Does Nh4 make any sense?

PART NINE - TEST 17

Diagram 424

[Level: 1800 - 2200]

White to move

Does 1.g4 make sense here?

PART NINE - TEST **18**

Diagram 425

[Level: 1600 - 2000]

Black has just played 19...Be6 when there followed 20.Qc2 Nc4 21.Bc1. What do you think of white's last two moves, and how do you assess the position after 21.Bc1?

PART NINE - TEST **19**

Diagram 426

[Level: 1600 - 2100]

Black to move

Black is a piece down but saw that she could regain it by ...Ng3, extricating her Knight and threatening two pieces at once. How would you assess the position after ...Ng3?

PART NINE - TEST **20**

Diagram 427

[Level: 1400 - 2000]

White to move

Here White played 18.Bb1. What's the point of this move?

PART NINE - TEST **21**

Diagram 428

[Level: 1600 - 1800]

White to move

Is 29.Nd5 a good idea?

PART NINE - TEST 22

Diagram 429

[Level: 1400 - 1800]

White to move

PART NINE - TEST 24

Diagram 431

[Level: 1400 - 2000]

White to move

There's a lot going on here. Instead of drowning you in the complications, let's have you search for a single shred of clarity: what is the most important square on the board in this position?

PART NINE - TEST 23

Diagram 430

[Level: 1800 - 2200]

White to move

PART NINE - TEST 25

Diagram 432

[Level: 1400 - 1800]

White to move

Pawn structure tends to dictate the ideas and plans for both sides. What is the structure saying in this position?

Answers to Tests

Answers

Part Two / Minor Pieces — Knights

ANSWER
PART TWO

TEST 1

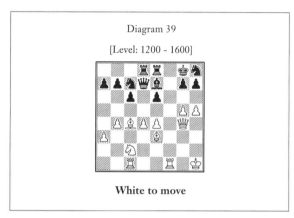

Diagram 39

[Level: 1200 - 1600]

White to move

This position is from a "postal" game on Chessworld.net between 0404it (2150) and RR (unrated), 2008. Both players could use more exciting names, but the position they reached is quite an instructive one. White has more space in every sector of the board. White has two active Bishops. White has an attack against the enemy King. White controls the center. White has the better pawn structure (e6 is weak). Black's Knights play a purely defensive role. These facts tell us that White enjoys an overwhelming position.

> **Explaining the Rating Spread**: The answer is very straightforward and not only entombs the Knight, but also attacks the King. A 1200 might miss the entombed horse, but going after black's King with g6 would certainly prove attractive.

Mr. 0404it finishes the game in exemplary fashion:

1.g6!

White had the choice of several good moves, but this makes (by far!) the nicest impression. If you played this to specifically entomb black's h8-Knight, then give yourself a pat on the back!

1...h6

Playing such a move must feel similar to slicing one's own wrists with a dull blade. However, Black couldn't have been very excited by lines like 1...Bf6 (1...Rf8 is better, but 2.gxh7+ Kxh7 3.Rg1 Rf7 4.Rcf1 Rdf8 5.Bd3 gives White a devastating attack) 2.gxh7 Kxh7 3.e5 Be7 4.Bd3+ Kg8 5.h6 (threatening 6.h7 mate) 5...g6 6.Bxg6 and it's all over.

Diagram 39a

What's that thing on h8?

After 1...h6 we have the honor of being witness to a classic Knight entombment and the coining of a new chess term. From this moment on, an entombed horse on h1, a1, a8, or h8 will be known as a *Vestigial Knight*—it looks like a Knight, it smells like a Knight, but it doesn't move or twitch (even if you poke it) or serve any real function. In effect this means that White is a piece up and can win a middlegame (since he has a larger army to make use of) or an endgame with ease.

2.Ne1!

A lovely move that shows white's class. Seeing that Black is completely helpless, White realizes he's in no hurry to lower the boom and first seeks to improve the position of his lamest piece—the c2-Knight. The concept of calmly bringing all your pieces to their best squares is a very important one, and is often overlooked by the amateur. The following quote by Grandmaster Jesse Kraai (during a lecture in 2008) pushes the point home: "Bad players like to play with their 'pretty' pieces. It is the mark of good players that they won't go on an adventure before they solve the problem of their bad pieces."

2...Rf8 3.Nd3 Rxf1+ 4.Rxf1 Bd6 5.Nc5 Bxc5 6.dxc5

White's advantage has grown since he now has two Bishops vs. a Knight and a thing on h8.

6...Qe7 7.Bf4, 1-0. There's nothing to be done about 8.Bxc7 when e6 falls and the remnants of black's position crashes to the ground.

ANSWER
PART TWO

TEST 2

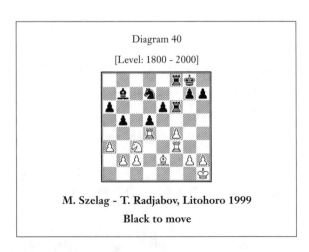

Diagram 40

[Level: 1800 - 2000]

M. Szelag - T. Radjabov, Litohoro 1999
Black to move

1.e4 e6 2.d4 d5 3.Nc3 Nf6 4.e5 Nfd7 5.f4 c5 6.Nf3 a6 7.Be3 Qb6 8.Rb1 Nc6 9.Qd2 Qa7 10.Be2 cxd4 11.Nxd4 Bc5 12.Rd1 0–0 13.0–0 b5 14.Rf3 Bb7 15.Rg3 Rac8 16.a3 Nxd4 17.Bxd4 f6 18.exf6 Rxf6 19.Kh1 Bxd4 20.Qxd4 Qxd4 21.Rxd4 Rcf8 22.Rf3 - Diagram 40

This position might fool some players into thinking that White is okay since black's Bishop is bad and his Knight doesn't appear particularly threatening. And doesn't Black also have the worse pawn structure (three pawn islands to two)?

These pro-white ruminations might appear reasonable, except that they fail to take into account black's pluses and the dynamic possibilities available to him. For instance, Black is placing serious pressure on the f4-pawn and, if either Rook were forced to move away from the pawn's defense, Black would win a pawn and most likely the game with it. Also note that one of black's "despised" extra pawn islands is comprised of powerful center pawns, which gain space and take squares and files away from the enemy pieces. Finally, white's Knight isn't doing anything. It can't safely move forward and it won't be a world-beater if it moves backwards either.

Since white's f-pawn is under pressure, the first thing Black needs to do is ask if he can increase that pressure or chase one of the defenders away. Since going after f4 right away via ...e5 or ...g5 fails to achieve anything of significance (White would capture either pawn), that leaves us looking at the other idea of harassing a defender. At the moment, the f3-Rook is solidly guarded and can't be successfully attacked. The d4-Rook is another matter; it's obvious that the light b7-Bishop can't influence the d4-square, but what about black's Knight? And once you pose that simple question, the correct move is suddenly easy to find.

> **Explaining the Rating Spread**: There seems to be a lot going on, so a Knight retreat to b8 most likely wouldn't occur to anyone under 1800, and could be easily missed by much higher rated players. Nevertheless, I would expect those in the 1800 - 2000 range who have read the earlier material on Knights to come up with the solution.

22...Nb8!

Winning material by force! Who would have guessed that a Knight retreat would have been so powerful?

23.Kg1

The only way to defend the f4-pawn is 23.g3, but that fails badly: 23...e5 24.Rd1 d4 25.Nb1 g5 and white's position has been run over. Notice that that "bad" light-squared Bishop on b7 has suddenly turned into a seek-and-destroy missile.

23...Nc6 24.Rd1 Rxf4 25.Rxf4 Rxf4 26.g3 Rf6 27.Re1 Nd4 28.Bd1 Kf7 and, with a solid extra pawn, Black eventually won.

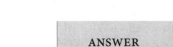

ANSWER
PART TWO

TEST 3

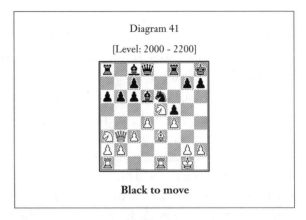

Diagram 41

[Level: 2000 - 2200]

Black to move

A glance would convince many players that Black is in trouble. White has a lead in development, he has more space, he threatens to capture the pawn on c6, and he even has the superior pawn structure! In fact, other than his two rather inactive Bishops, it's hard to see what Black has to crow about.

I featured this position in a lecture I gave that had about 200 spectators (the ratings ranged from beginner to 2200+). I asked the crowd who was better here. The vast majority felt that White had a considerable advantage, while none of the 200 thought that Black had more than equality.

> **Explaining the Rating Spread**: A tough one! I wouldn't be surprised to see some masters missing it. Somehow, it's anti-intuitive to give up the coveted two Bishops and to hand White a protected passed pawn to boot! Nevertheless, as you grow to appreciate a Knight's blockading powers, you will begin to actively strive to create such situations.

1...Bxe5!

Wonderful! Black happily gives away his two Bishops in order to hand White a protected passed pawn! This is either very deep, or very stupid. However, since I gave it an exclamation point, you should probably vote for the former.

Note that 1...Qe8, retaining the two Bishops while also defending c6, is a mistake since 2.Nac4 grants White the advantage for all the reasons mentioned earlier. After 2...Be7, one problem Black will face is his weakness down the e-file, which White can highlight by the simple 3.Re2 followed by Rae1 (3.Nf3 is also excellent).

2.dxe5

Unfortunately, 2.fxe5 fails to 2...f4 3.Bf2 f3 when Black has a strong attack.

2...c5

A very logical move that both denies White use of the d4-square and prepares to place the c8-Bishop on b7 where it will laser its way through white's position.

An interesting alternative is 2...g5, trying to blast open the g-file or, if White takes on g5, hoping to push the f-pawn down white's throat. This demented looking move is fully playable, but Black doesn't need to be in any hurry. He can always come back to this advance of the g-pawn once he tightens up his position and gets his Bishop on its ideal diagonal.

Diagram 41a

A picture perfect blockading Knight

It's time to take a long look at the position after 2...c5. What has Black accomplished? One key point is that the e-file is now closed. White's pawns are also on dark squares—this pawn structure significantly curtails the usefulness of the e3-Bishop. Once black's Bishop reaches b7, the superiority of this Bishop over its e3 counterpart won't be open to question.

All of this should certainly make us feel good about black's prospects, but aren't we forgetting about white's protected passed e-pawn? Not at all! That pawn is closing down the e-file and is firmly blockaded by the e6-Knight. This fine, flexible, square (it allows the Knight to exert influence over c5, d4, f4, and g5) wouldn't be safe if the e-file was open, so some might label the e5-pawn as a traitor!

Simply put, after 2...c5 white's pieces have no penetration points or targets to attack. White also lacks a pawn break. On the other hand, black's pieces will prove to be far more active than white's, and the ...g7-g5 pawn break will hang over the other side like the Sword of Damocles.

3.Rad1

Rooks belong on open files, don't they? White is happy to follow general rules, but he'll soon discover that the d-file is a road to nowhere.

3...Qe8

Quietly moving his Queen to safety while also giving his Knight some support. Other Queen moves like 3...Qe7 and even 3...Qh4 are also good.

4.Nc4 and now Black has to choose between 4...Bb7 (it would be hard to resist placing this Bishop on the tasty a8-h1 diagonal) with ...g7-g5 to follow, and the immediate 4...g5 5.fxg5 f4 with an immediate attack. This attack (now or in another move or two) is completely justified because black's Bishop, f-pawn, kingside Rook, Knight, and Queen would all take part in the festivities.

Those who are dying to get more information on passed pawns and blockading will find it in Part Eight.

ANSWER
PART TWO
TEST 4

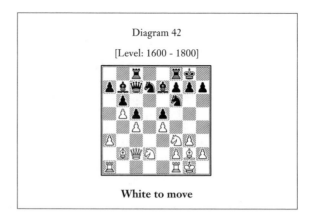

Diagram 42

[Level: 1600 - 1800]

White to move

This is from the game girl-brain - Brooklyn, ICC 2007. White wasn't sure what to do and, accordingly, played a move (1.Bc3?) that actually hindered her proper plan. The key here is being aware of the holes on d4 and d5. Black needs to get a Knight to d4 as quickly as possible, and White needs to get a Knight to d5 at warp speed. Once you realize where your pieces should go, it becomes easy to find the correct moves to make it happen. However, if you are just mindlessly calculating moves with no real plan in mind, then you'll usually play something that has little or nothing to do with the needs of the position.

In the diagram, White would love to play Nd2-b1-c3-d5. However, moving the d2-Knight would result in the loss of the e4-pawn. Thus, defend the pawn!

> **Explaining the Rating Spread**: I would hope that players in the 1400 to 1800 range would recognize a huge hole and try to get their Knight to it. However, in this case e4 is weak, so this process calls for some patience. As a result, I upped the difficulty level to 1600.

1.Rfe1!

Defending e4 and thus freeing the d2-Knight of guard duty.

As mentioned earlier, in the actual game White played the nonsensical 1.Bc3?, taking the c3-square away from the Knight. The continuation (which doesn't boast ideal play for either side) was: 1...Rfd8 2.Rfd1 Ne8 3.Nf1 (Finally noticing that d5 would make a nice home for her Knight! Fortunately, in this case all roads lead to Rome.) 3...f6 4.Ne3 Qb8 5.Nd5 (White's doing well) 5...Bf8 6.Rd2 (6.Bh3 was very strong) 6...Nc7 7.Rad1? (Literally ignoring black's idea—if you refuse to take your opponent's plans into consideration, you are dooming yourself to a lot of pain. Instead of 7.Rad1, simply 7.Bh3, stopping ...Ne6 in its tracks, would have given White a very large advantage.) 7...Ne6 8.Nh4 Nd4 and though White still has a slight plus, black's chances have significantly improved. Also note how useless white's idea of doubling on the d-file has turned out to be.

1...a6 2.a4 axb5 3.axb5 Ra8 4.Rxa8 Rxa8 5.Nb1! followed by Nc3-d5 with a solid plus.

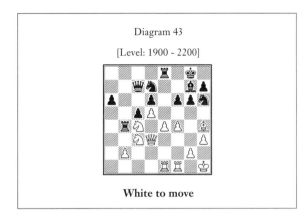

Diagram 43

[Level: 1900 - 2200]

White to move

This position occurred in the game J. Silman - S. Booth, Los Angeles 1987. Both sides have vulnerable queenside pawns (a6 for Black and b2 for White), but white's more active minor pieces and advantage in central space (which leaves Black constantly worrying about both f4-f5 and e4-e5 advances) gives him the better chances. At the moment the pride of white's position is the c4-Knight, but Black would love to exchange it for his far less imposing beast on d7 (via ...Nb6). When you look at the position in this fashion, white's first move shouldn't come as a surprise.

> **Explaining the Rating Spread**: Though you might be getting used to Knight retreats by now, the solution is obscured by central possibilities, and chances to create pressure against a6. Also, White already has a Knight on c4, so why bring the other Knight to bear on that same square? Clearly, there's a lot more going on than a simple Knight retreat, and that's what makes it an advanced problem.

1.Nb1! Nb6

Black would love to play 1...f5, but it fails to 2.exf5 Rxe1 3.Bxe1 Nxf5 4.Bxb4.

2.Nbd2

Mission accomplished, White retains an Octopus on c4. And why is the Octopus so strong on that square? A glance shows that its many arms reach in all directions: of course, it eyes internal squares on a3, d2, and e3, but that's to be expected. It turns into a superhero when one realizes that it defends the pawn on b2, eyes a5 (which can be a jumping off point to c6 via Nc4-a5-c6—this also means that when White starts attacking the a-pawn with Ra1, Black won't want to push the pawn to a5 since that would walk right into the Knight's influence.), eyes b6, puts serious pressure on d6, and also takes a swing at e5 (this prepares for white's thematic e4-e5 push or, if f4-f5 is played, Mr. Octopus keeps the hole on e5 from becoming terminal).

2...Nxc4

This only helps White. Though 2...Qb8 3.Na5! Rxb2 4.Rb1 is seriously annoying, and though 2...f5 3.e5! is even worse, the tight 2...Nf7 would have done more to keep white's advantage within acceptable limits.

3.Nxc4 Nf7 4.Ra1 Qb7?

Things get out of hand after this. He had to try 4...Qe7 when 5.Rfe1 takes the e1-square away from white's Bishop. Then 5...Qd7 followed by ...Qb5 keeps Black in the game.

5.Be1 Rb5 6.Bc3 Qe7 7.Rfe1

Black's now strategically lost. He has no active play, his pieces are passive, his d6-pawn is in need of constant defense, and his a6-pawn is, ultimately, a goner.

Diagram 43a

Worship the Octopus on c4

7...Qb7 8.f5 g5 9.Ra4 Ra8 10.Rea1 Kf8 11.Qb1 Kg8 12.Qa2

It's all over. The rest doesn't need any comment.

12...Qe7 13.Rxa6 Rd8 14.Ra8 Rbb8 15.Rxb8 Rxb8 16.Qa7 Qe8 17.Qc7 Rd8 18.Ra7 h5 19.Qe7 Qxe7 20.Rxe7 Ne5 21.Bxe5 fxe5 22.Rb7 Kf8 23.Kg1 g4 24.hxg4 hxg4 25.Kf2 Bf6 26.Kg3 Be7 27.Kxg4 Kf7 28.Kf3 Ra8 29.Nxd6+, 1-0.

ANSWER
PART TWO

TEST **6**

Diagram 44

[Level: 1900 - 2200]

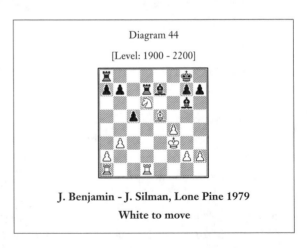

J. Benjamin - J. Silman, Lone Pine 1979
White to move

1.e4 c5 2.Nf3 Nc6 3.b3 e5 4.c3 Nf6 5.Bb5 Be7 6.0–0 0–0 7.d4 exd4 8.e5 Nd5 9.cxd4 cxd4 10.Bb2 Nc7 11.Bxc6 dxc6 (Black's two Bishops give him a comfortable advantage. Unfortunately, Black gets lazy and allows White to slowly but surely steer the game into drawish equality.) **12.Nxd4 c5 13.Nc2 Qxd1 14.Rxd1 Be6 15.Nc3 Rfd8 16.Ne3 f6 17.Ne4 fxe5 18.Bxe5 Nb5 19.f4 Nd4 20.Kf2 Nf5 21.Nxf5 Bxf5 22.Kf3 Rd7? 23.Nd6 Bg6??** (Of course, if Black had seen white's reply, he would have played 23...Bxd6 with a quick draw in view.) - Diagram 44

24.Nc8!

Benjamin, in his excellent book, *American Grandmaster* (Everyman Chess, 2007), writes, "this is not an obvious square for the Knight, but it came to me when I saw 24.Nf5 Bxf5 doesn't work. I heard Silman mutter 'cheap bastard'. I'll assume he meant this in a gracious way—Jeremy and I have since been good friends for years."

I don't remember making that rude mutter (Benjamin couldn't have been more than two years old at the time of this game, so the realization that I was about to lose to a fetus undoubtedly prompted a bout of serious angst.), but I can imagine my horror at seeing the Knight plonk itself down on its 8th rank and instantly turn a position that I'd long deemed to have two possible results (a win for me or a draw) into something far less palatable.

As mentioned earlier, Knights usually don't tread on this rank, but when they do make an effective jump to the 8th there are often tactics at work. In this case the Knight makes use of the single most common tactical building block: an undefended piece (the d7-Rook being the culprit here).

> **Explaining the Rating Spread**: A bit mean of me since I'm sure most of you were looking for positional ways to use the white Knight. Instead I tossed in a tactic, and a surprising one at that (since 8th rank jumps are rare). The calculation itself isn't hard, but noticing it is!

24...Rxd1 25.Nxe7+ Kf7 26.Rxd1 Kxe7 27.g4!

While 24.Nc8 shows a good tactical eye, this pawn move demonstrates excellent technique and a calm desire to milk every last drop of juicy goodness from the position.

27.Bxg7 Bh5+ 28.g4 Bxg4+ 29.Kxg4 Rg8 wouldn't give White anything at all, while the tempting 27.Bd6+ Kf6 28. Bxc5 allows 28...Be8! when Benjamin says, "Black suffers no further damage. With only a one-pawn majority, White will be hard pressed to win."

I had viewed 24.Nc8 as a lucky find, and it was only after the high-class 27.g4 that I realized my young opponent was destined for great things.

27...Rd8 28.Rxd8 Kxd8 29.f5 Bf7 30.Bxg7 and White went on to win.

ANSWER
PART TWO

TEST 7

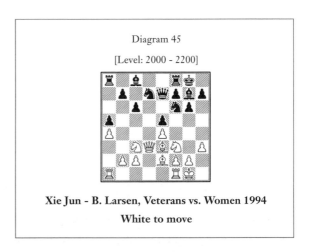

Diagram 45

[Level: 2000 - 2200]

Xie Jun - B. Larsen, Veterans vs. Women 1994

White to move

1.e4 g6 2.d4 Bg7 3.Nc3 c6 4.Nf3 d6 5.h3 Nf6 6.a4 0–0 7.Be3 Nbd7 8.Be2 e5 9.dxe5 dxe5 10.0-0 Qe7 11.Qd3 a5 - Diagram 45

This position is known to be in white's favor thanks to the two holes on b6 and d6. By now, whenever you see a hole I would expect you to ask, "Can I get a Knight there?" And, after some reflection, you might notice that if a Knight could reach c4 then both holes would be accessible. Thus, 12.Nd2 suggests itself. However, one must also take note of what the opponent intends, and this leads us to 12.Nd2 Nc5 (we allowed it!) 13.Qc4 b6 14.Bxc5 bxc5 15.Nb3 Nd7 with ...Ba6 to follow when Black is fine. Clearly, White needs to demonstrate a bit of subtlety (though you can be very proud of yourself if you noticed the Nf3-d2-c4 maneuver).

> **Explaining the Rating Spread**: Noticing the holes on b6 and d6 shows that you know your stuff, but finding a way to make use of these weaknesses by Nf3-d2-c4 takes it to another level. And then we add on yet another nuance by making you hold off on the Knight maneuver in favor of the preventative Qc4. All this makes the solution an "advanced players only" drill!

12.Qc4!

Black's ...Nc5 is prevented

12...Re8 13.Rfd1 h6

13...Qb4!? has also been tried. Gary Lane then gives 14.Ng5 Rf8 15.b3 (I think 15.Qa2!? might offer even more: 15...h6 16.Nf3 Nxe4 17.Nxe4 Qxe4 18.Bd3 Qd5 19.Bc4 Qe4 20.Rd6 Nf6 and now both 21.Bxf7+!? and 21.Bxh6!? are promising) 15...h6 16.Nf3 Qxc4 17.Bxc4 with an edge.

14.Nd2

Intending to move the Queen to b3 and then toss the Knight on c4 when the rabid horse will hit a5, b6, d6, and e5.

14...Nh7

14...Bf8 with the idea of ...Qb4 is also possible.

15.Qb3 Ng5 16.Nc4 Nc5?!

16...Ne6 is better, but 17.Rd2 still leaves White with a small edge.

17.Qa3 Nce6 18.Qxe7 Rxe7 19.Nb6 Rb8 20.Bg4 Re8 21.Bxg5 hxg5

Diagram 45a

White finds another instructive Knight move

22.Nb1!

A very nice move. This Knight didn't have a future on c3 (both b5 and d5 are covered), so it heads to c4 (via a3 or d2) where it will join in the fight for b6 and d6. Also note that the retreat of the Knight makes c2-c3 possible, taking the d4-square away from black's pieces.

The finish is quite nice:

22...Bf8 23.Nd2 Bc5 24.Ndc4 Bxb6 25.Nxb6 Kf8 26.Rd2 Ke7 27.Rad1 Rf8 28.Nxc8+ Rfxc8 29.Rd7+ Kf6 30.Bxe6 fxe6 31.g4!, 1-0. There's no good defense to the threat of R1d3 followed by Rf3 mate.

ANSWER
PART TWO
TEST **8**

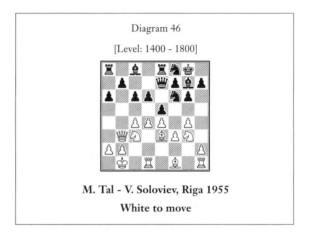

Diagram 46

[Level: 1400 - 1800]

M. Tal - V. Soloviev, Riga 1955

White to move

1.d4 Nf6 2.c4 g6 3.Nc3 Bg7 4.e4 0–0 5.Be3 d6 6.f3 e5 7.Nge2 c6 8.Qb3 Nbd7 9.0–0–0 Qe7 10.Kb1 Re8 11.g4 a6 12.Ng3 Nf8 - Diagram 46

Black just moved his Knight to f8 and clearly intends to play 13…Ne6 when it will be able to leap into d4 or f4.

> **Explaining the Rating Spread**: The right move can be arrived at in different ways. For example, if you simply wanted to gain space, then d5 is it. Or, if you were worried about …exd4, then once again d5 is the move. However, I am hoping that you noticed …Ne6 and played d5 in a deliberate attempt to stuff the enemy Knight!

White now played **13.d5** because he intended to begin an attack by h2-h4-h5 and the center needs to be closed to make this worthwhile—he also wanted to stop the f8-Knight from finding fame and fortune on e6. In other words, he used the advance of his d-pawn to dominate the enemy Knight and force it to remain on a purely defensive square. After **13…N6d7 14.h4** White had a clear advantage and went on to win.

ANSWER
PART TWO

TEST 9

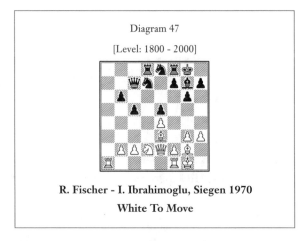

Diagram 47

[Level: 1800 - 2000]

R. Fischer - I. Ibrahimoglu, Siegen 1970

White To Move

1.e4 c6 2.d3 d5 3.Nd2 g6 4.Ngf3 Bg7 5.g3 Nf6 6.Bg2 0–0 7.0–0 Bg4 8.h3 Bxf3 9.Qxf3 Nbd7 10.Qe2 dxe4 11.dxe4 Qc7 12.a4 Rad8 13.Nb3 b6 14.Be3 c5 15.a5 e5 16.Nd2 Ne8 17.axb6 axb6 - Diagram 47

This is very nice for White: he has the two Bishops, the b5 and c4 squares can easily fall into his hands, and d5 is a gaping hole (compare this to d4, a square that is *not* a hole since it can be healed by the simple c2-c3).

> **Explaining the Rating Spread**: Yes, another Knight retreat! I would have made the rating spread lower (since I know you guys are getting used to your horses going backwards), but the fact that the Knight is already eyeing the nice c4-square, and that moves like Qb5 are also very tempting, makes the problem rather difficult.

18.Nb1!

You should be getting used to this idea by now! The Knight heads for c3 where it will eye both b5 and d5.

18...Qb7

On 18...Qc6 19.Nc3 Nc7 20.Ra7 Ra8 White has 21.Nd5! Nxd5 22.exd5 Qd6 23.Rfa1 Rxa7 24.Rxa7 Nf6 25.Qb5! and now 25...Nxd5 26.Rd7 Nc7 27.Rxd6 Nxb5 28.Rxb6 Nd4 29.c3 gives White a winning endgame thanks to the more active Rook, weakness of c5, and the power of white's two raking Bishops.

19.Nc3 and white's position is clearly superior. The rest of the game was a beautiful demonstration of technique by Fischer:

19...Nc7 20.Nb5

20.Rfd1 was also strong (and certainly the most natural looking move), but White decides to swap the Knights and gain entry to b5 for his Queen.

20...Qc6 21.Nxc7 Qxc7 22.Qb5

Black's position is cheerless (two Bishops, pressure down the a-file, pressure against b6, more active pieces). Nobody could resist Fischer in positions of this nature.

22...Ra8 23.c3 Rxa1 24.Rxa1 Rb8 25.Ra6

Things are getting worse for Black with every move.

25...Bf8 26.Bf1

The entry of this Bishop into the battle marks the beginning of the end. Notice how Fischer makes sure every piece is in play.

26...Kg7 27.Qa4 Rb7 28.Bb5

Total domination—every white piece is superior to their black counterparts.

28...Nb8 29.Ra8 Bd6 30.Qd1 Nc6 31.Qd2

I'll let the reader decide for himself whether or not the shocking 31.Bh6+ Kxh6 32.Rg8 does or doesn't work.

31...h5 32.Bh6+ Kh7 33.Bg5 Rb8 34.Rxb8 Nxb8 35.Bf6 Nc6

After 35...Be7 36.Qg5 Bxf6 37.Qxf6 we get a picturesque case of a Bishop dominating a Knight (white's Queen is also dominating the black Queen).

36.Qd5 Na7 37.Be8 Kg8 38.Bxf7+ Qxf7 39.Qxd6, 1-0.

Part Two / Minor Pieces – Bishops

ANSWER
PART TWO

TEST **10**

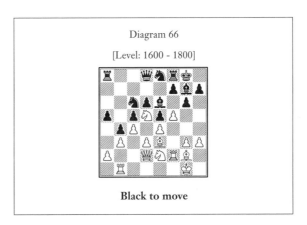

Diagram 66

[Level: 1600 - 1800]

Black to move

Black's in trouble and has to make a painful decision: should he capture on d5 or retreat his light-squared Bishop?

Giving up the Bishop isn't something one would normally want to do—it's not only a useful piece, but after 1...Bxd5 both 2.exd5 (threatening to make use of the e4-square with g4 and Ng3 while also looking forward to an enduring attack against black's King), and 2.cxd5 (intending to continue with the usual kingside attack via Rbf1, g3-g4-g5, etc) favor White. However, like it or not Black *must* play that way!

Why the urgency? Why create a tasty square for white's pieces or leave White with a readymade kingside attack? Why willingly go into an inferior position? The answer is twofold. First, you are *already* in an inferior position—we're seeking damage control, not equality (in other words, you need to be realistic). Second, the retreat leads to a far worse situation!

Explaining the Rating Spread: Though I doubt that everyone would notice the potential strength of capturing away from the center with 1...Bxd5 2.exd5 (though white's kingside attack after 2.cxd5 is pretty obvious), the real question is whether or not a player will see that f5-f6 is doable after 1...Bd7 since a glance would tell Black that his f6-square is adequately covered. This makes the problem more than just a "don't let your Bishop get entombed" walk in the park. I would expect many class "C" players to see the downside of 1...Bxd5, but I would also expect many in that rating group to simply miss the tactics that make f5-f6 gin.

1...Bd7?

Like it or not, 1...Bxd5 followed by 2...Nd4 had to be tried.

2.f6 Bh8

The pawn can't be taken. Both 2...Bxf6?? 3.Nxf6+ Nxf6 4.Bg5 and 2...Nxf6?? 3.Bg5 lead to decisive material loss for Black.

3.Bh6

Winning the Exchange while also intending to follow up with a good, old fashioned entombing. Of course, 3.g4 followed by g5 would be the normal recipe since White would, in effect, be a piece ahead. That alone would be enough to make any sane person chop on d5 via 1...Bxd5 (don't allow your pieces to be entombed!). But why not pick up a Rook and stick the Bishop in a coffin too? Remember that in chess, greed is often a good thing!

I should mention that 3.Bg5 (with the idea of Ne7+) is also extremely strong.

After **3.Bh6** may I dare suggest that 3...Nd4 4.Ne7+ is black's best option? His suffering would end, and the spectators would enjoy a good laugh.

Other moves are just as joyless for Black:

> 3...Nc7 4.Bxf8 Kxf8 5.Nxc7 (5.Qg5 is also strong, but let's stick to our "piece entombed by pawns" theme) 5...Qxc7 6.g4 Kg8 7.g5 and Black should resign—he's literally a Rook down (since the thing on h8 may think it's a Bishop, but we know better).

> 3...Nxf6 4.Bg5 (4.Bxf8 also gets the job done) 4...Nxe4 19.dxe4 f6 20.Raf1 is nightmarish.

> 3...Bxf6 4.Nxf6+ Nxf6 19.Bxf8 Kxf8 20.Raf1 offers Black one of those

"I better resign before anyone sees me playing this position" moments.

ANSWER PART TWO

TEST 11

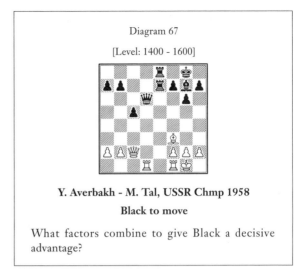

Diagram 67

[Level: 1400 - 1600]

Y. Averbakh - M. Tal, USSR Chmp 1958

Black to move

What factors combine to give Black a decisive advantage?

1.d4 Nf6 2.c4 e6 3.Nc3 c5 4.d5 exd5 5.cxd5 d6 6.e4 g6 7.Be2 Bg7 8.Nf3 0–0 9.0–0 Re8 10.Qc2 Na6 11.Bf4 Nb4 12.Qb1 Nxe4 (Most likely unsound, but quite typical of Tal during that period.) **13.Nxe4 Bf5 14.Nfd2 Nxd5 15.Bxd6?** (15.Bg3 Qe7 16.Bf3 Rad8 17.Re1) **15...Nf6 16.Bf3 Nxe4 17.Nxe4 Bxe4 18.Bxe4 Qxd6 19.Qc2 Re7 20.Bf3 Rae8 21.Rad1** - Diagram 67

Black's a solid pawn up. However, we already know that a one-pawn advantage doesn't guarantee victory when Bishops of opposite colors are on the board. Thus, Black will want to retain as many pieces as possible and show that his Bishop is a strong attacker that can go after things the other Bishop can't defend. To this end, control of d4 is critical since, from there, the Bishop will eye f2 while also blocking off the d-file. Note that the extra pawn allows black's Bishop to safely reside on d4, while white's Bishop doesn't have the same luxury. Ultimately, the extra pawn, superior Bishop, and iron control of the e-file should combine to give Black a winning game.

> **Explaining the Rating Spread**: The material advantage and black's control of the e-file is obvious, so that leaves black's grip on d4 as a major thing to notice. This is fully in a 1400's range.

21...Bd4 22.a4 b6

Black's in no hurry since White can't do anything (he has no targets to attack in black's position and no means to effect any useful penetration) but wait and hope that his opponent doesn't find a way to break through. When your opponent is helpless, it's always a good idea to tighten up your position. 22...b6 takes the pawn away from the white Bishop's stare and also gives extra support to c5.

23.b3 Re5 24.Rd2 h5

This little pawn move is designed to create new weaknesses in white's kingside.

25.Re2

White is trying to trade everything he can in an effort to reach a pure Bishop of opposite colors endgame. Even though he's a pawn down, he would have real chances to hold such a situation.

25...Rxe2 26.Bxe2 h4 27.Kh1

White isn't in any hurry to stop black's h-pawn with 27.h3 since that would leave a severe weakness along the h2-b8 diagonal. Black would try to make decisive use of this with 27...Qf4 and, if allowed, ...Be5.

27...Qf4 28.g3

A weakness has been provoked and white's King will soon find itself facing more than a bit of heat.

28...Qf6 29.Qd1 Rd8

Diagram 67a

Can White handle the heat?

30.Bg4?

White cracks under the pressure. A better defense was 30.Qd3 (hoping to cover the h1-a8 diagonal and also offer an exchange of Queens with Qf3), though White would still face a long, miserable slog. On the other hand, the natural looking 30.Kg2 is simply bad: 30...Bc3 31.Bd3 Qc6+ 32.f3 h3+ 33.Kh1 (33.Kxh3 Qd7+ 34.Kg2 Qxd3) 33...Qd6 34.Be2 Qe7 35.Qc2 Rd2 36.Qxc3 Qxe2 mates.

30...Bxf2! 31.Qe2

Now it's easy. He had to try 31.Qf3 Qxf3+ 32.Bxf3 when white is two pawns down but he can still make use of the opposite colored Bishops to put up a fight.

31...Rd2!

White probably missed this. Now 32.Qxd2 Qc6+ mates.

32.Qe8+ Kg7 33.gxh4 Qd4 34.Bh3 Qd3 35.Bg2 Rd1, 0-1. After 36.Qb5 Rxf1+ 37.Bxf1 Qe4+ 38.Bg2 Qxh4 Black would be two pawns up while also retaining serious play against the vulnerable enemy King.

ANSWER
PART TWO
TEST 12

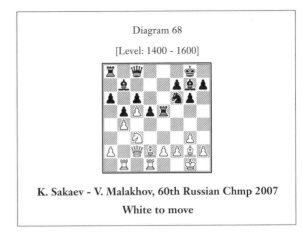

Diagram 68

[Level: 1400 - 1600]

K. Sakaev - V. Malakhov, 60th Russian Chmp 2007

White to move

1.d4 d5 2.c4 c6 3.Nf3 Nf6 4.Nc3 a6 5.c5 Nbd7 6.Bf4 Nh5 7.Bd2 Nhf6 8.Bf4 Nh5 9.Bd2 Nhf6 10.Qc2 g6 11.g3 Bg7 12.Bg2 0–0 13.0–0 b6 14.b4 Bb7 15.Rab1 Re8 16.Rfd1 Qc8 17.Na4 b5 18.Nc3 e5 19.dxe5 Nxe5 20.Nxe5 Rxe5 - Diagram 68

Black is spatially challenged on the queenside, but the most noticeable drawback to his game is the light-squared Bishop which, on b7, is a true Tall-Pawn. White's Bishop on d2 can leap into activity via Bf4, but white's other Bishop seems to be hitting granite on d5. Thus, white's first order of business is to crack open the center and activate the slacker on g2. Remember: More often than not you have to make a Bishop active—you can't count on it to happen by itself!

> **Explaining the Rating Spread**: I know that Bf4 was tempting, but my main concern is that you noticed that your g2-Bishop isn't as active as it could be. If that simple thought crossed your mind, then I'm happy. And if you also decided to do something about the g2-Bishop's plight and decided on e2-e4, then prepare to be worshipped as a chess god.

21.e4 dxe4

Worse is 21...d4 22.Ne2 when the d-pawn will fall.

22.Nxe4 Nxe4 23.Bxe4

Now we can see that e2-e4 had another point too: it opened the d-file for white's d1-Rook and made the hole on d6 accessible to white's pieces.

After 23.Bxe4 white's advantage can't be in doubt: aside from the disparity in the state of both sides' light-squared Bishops, the weakness of the c6-pawn (which will be vulnerable for the rest of the game) means that White has a target and Black doesn't.

23...Qe6 24.Bf3 Qf6 25.Bf4 Re7 26.Rd6

Black's position has noticeably deteriorated. How did this happen? It's clear that White didn't do anything brilliant. In fact, all he did was to activate his Bishop, take aim at a weak pawn, and make use of a hole on an open file. These are things anyone can do! Yet, white's play is bringing a strong grandmaster like Malakhov to his knees!

26...Re6 27.Rxe6 Qxe6 28.Qd2

More simple chess—White claims the d-file.

28...Qf5

Perhaps 28...Re8 was a tad better, though after 29.Rd1 Qc8 (29...Qh3 30.Qd6 leaves Black with nothing better than 30...Qc8. However, notice that 29...Qh3 30.Qd7?? would be unfortunate due to 30...Re1+) 30.Kg2 Black would be doomed to a long, passive, miserable defensive chore.

29.Re1

Greed is good. White grabs both center files. Now every white piece is doing a better job than its black counterpart.

29...Bf8 30.Kg2 a5 31.a3 axb4 32.axb4 h5 33.h4 Qc8 34.Be5 Qd8 35.Qf4

Total domination. The rest of the game illustrates just how horrible black's light-squared Bishop really is.

Diagram 68a

35...Bg7 36.Rd1 Qe7 37.Bxg7 Kxg7 38.Rd6 Re8 39.Qd4+ Qe5 40.Qxe5+ Rxe5 41.Rd7 Ba8 42.Rd8 Bb7 43.Rd7 Ba8 44.Bd1 Re1 45.Bb3 Rb1 46.Rxf7+ Kh6 47.Bc2 Rb2 48.Bd3 Rxb4 49.Rf6 Kg7 50.Rxg6+ Kf7 51.Rg5 Bb7 52.Bg6+ Kf6 53.Bxh5 Rc4 54.Rg6+ Kf5 55.Rg8 Ke5 56.Bf3 Rd4 57.h5, 1-0. Black's light-square Bishop remained pathetic right up to his resignation.

ANSWER
PART TWO

TEST 13

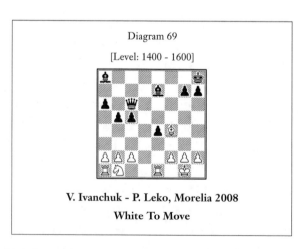

Diagram 69

[Level: 1400 - 1600]

V. Ivanchuk - P. Leko, Morelia 2008

White To Move

1.e4 e5 2.Nf3 Nc6 3.Bb5 a6 4.Ba4 Nf6 5.0–0 Be7 6.Re1 b5 7.Bb3 0–0 8.d4 Nxd4 9.Bxf7+ Rxf7 10.Nxe5 Rf8 11.Qxd4 c5 12.Qd1 Qc7 13.Ng4 Nxg4 14.Qxg4 d5 15.Qh5 dxe4 16.Qd5+ Kh8 17.Qxa8 Bb7 18.Qa7 Ra8 19.Bf4 Qc6 20.Qxa8+ Bxa8 - Diagram 69

White has two Rooks for a Queen, but he's behind in development, black's Bishops seem quite active, and ...e4-e3 (opening up the terrifying h1-a8 diagonal) is in the air. Since white's Rooks should, theoretically, be able to dominate the Queen if he solidifies his position and kills off black's activity, Ivanchuk's move makes a lot of sense.

> **Explaining the Rating Spread**: I think most 1400s would notice the potential danger along the h1-a8 diagonal. And, since this section is all about Bishops, it stands to reason that the answer has something to do with them. Thus, 21.Be3, preventing that diagonal from being opened by ...e4-e3, is something well within a 1400's range.

21.Be3!

This blocks the e-pawn, which in turn makes sure that the h1-a8 diagonal won't become a factor in the subsequent play.

21...Qf6 22.c3 Bd6 23.Nd2 Qe5!

An important maneuver for Black. By forcing g2-g3 (24.Nf1 is possible, but then the Knight would be relegated to passive defense), Black hopes to use his Queen and a8-Bishop to take advantage of the subsequent light-square holes that this pawn advance created.

The battle is very interesting: White is doing his best to block his opponent's light-squared Bishop while Black is doing everything in his power to create new diagonals for it that will ultimately allow game-saving counterplay against the white King.

24.g3 h6 25.a4!

Diagram 69a

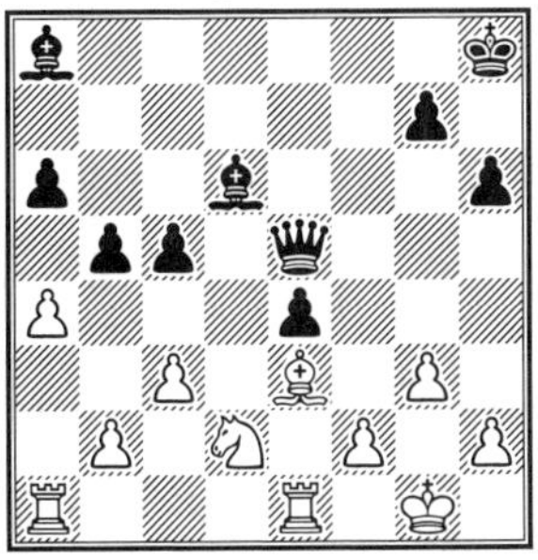

Opening the a-file allows the a1-Rook to become active. Black will be in serious trouble if both Rooks manage to penetrate into the enemy camp. The battle lines are now clearly drawn: what will invade the hostile position first—white's Rooks or black's light-squared Bishop and Queen? The rest of this very complicated game, given with minimal notes, will see both players battling to make their respective goals come true: **25...Bc6** (25...b4?? would be a blunder since it allows White to get rid of one of the enemy Bishops and open new files for his Rooks: 26.Nc4 Qe6 27.Nxd6 Qxd6 28.Red1 Qe7 29.cxb4 cxb4 30.Rac1 and all of white's dreams have been realized.) **26.axb5 axb5 27.Nb3 Bf8 28.Red1 Bd5 29.h4 Kg8** (After 29...Bxb3 30.Rd8 Kg8 31.Raa8 Qf5 Black's tied up, but since 32.Rxf8+ Qxf8 33.Rxf8+ Kxf8 34.Bxc5+ is only a draw, it's not clear if White has any way to make decisive use of the pinned f8-Bishop; Black can easily generate counterplay on the kingside light-square holes. For example: 32.Bf4

[32.Rac8 Be6] 32...Bc4 33.Bd6 Qh3 and suddenly Black is the one in the driver's seat.) **30.Nc1!** (The Knight is heading for f4; if Black can't achieve counterplay against white's weakened kingside light-squares, he's doomed.) **30...g5 31.hxg5 hxg5 32.Ra5 Qc7 33.Ra6** (And not 33.Rxb5? Bc4 when White has nothing better than 34.Rb3, giving up the Exchange.) **33...Qf7 34.Rb6 Be7 35.Rxb5 Be6** (Black's primed and ready to go on the offensive via ...Bh3 followed by ...Qf3, or ...Be6-g4-f3. Things now get very tense.) **36.Rb8+ Kg7 37.Rb7 Kh6** (37...Kg6!? was probably more accurate.) **38.Re1** (It doesn't seem right to take this Rook off the d-file and out of the attack. Instead 38.Ne2 appears stronger. The idea is that 38...Qf3?? fails to 39.Rxe7 Bh3 40.Rd6+ Kh5 41.Nf4+! Kg4 (41...gxf4 42.Re5+) 42.Rg7 and Black is dead. Since this is a book of concept and not endless analysis, I'll leave it to the interested reader to figure out the ultimate worth of 38.Ne2.) **38...Qf6??** (A blunder. Correct was 38...Bh3 [Finally leaping at his light-square chances!] 39.f4 Qh5 40.Re2 Qf3 and Black is okay.) **39.Rb6 Qf5 40.Nb3 Kh5 41.Nd2 Bd7 42.Ra1 Bd8 43.Rb8,** 1-0.

ANSWER
PART TWO

TEST **14**

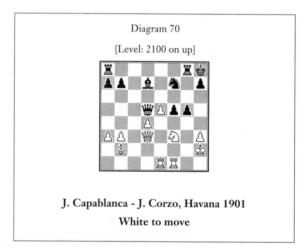

Diagram 70

[Level: 2100 on up]

J. Capablanca - J. Corzo, Havana 1901

White to move

A very famous game. The position is quite interesting. The main features are the opposite colored Bishops, white's two passed center pawns, and black's kingside pawn majority. At the moment white's center pawns are frozen in place. Black's kingside majority is chugging along, but the advances have left various weaknesses in their wake. Most pronounced (at least to my eye) is the sad situation of white's Bishop—the poor thing has been relegated to Tall-Pawn status. As we know, if you have such a Bishop, you need to either get it outside the pawn chain (thus making it active) or get the blocking pawns out of its way. These goals can be actualized by positional or tactical means.

On the other hand, black's Bishop looks very nice! If he is able to create a permanent blockage on both e6 and d5 (for example, his Knight on e6, Queen on d7, and Bishop on d5) then he'll enjoy a significant advantage.

So which Bishop will be the hero? Since it's White to move, it's his job to *insist* that his Bishop rules the day. Because the black King is sitting on the same diagonal as white's Bishop, it's clear that a transformation from Tall-Pawn to monster would occur if those pawns were to suddenly vanish. Capablanca, then only twelve-years old, probably understood all this information in an instant. Then he uncorked one of his most memorable combinations.

> **Explaining the Rating Spread**: If you realized that the Bishop on b2 was a serious problem, and if you noticed the potential along the a1-h8 diagonal, and if you then did everything you could to rectify it, we can say you did very well. The rest of the solution is all about advanced tactics—but tactics that serve to make white's strategic dreams come true.

1.e6!!

The e-pawn sacrifices itself in an effort to clear the central dark squares and activate its Bishop.

Another, far simpler, win was 1.Qc4! Be6 2.Qxd5 Bxd5 3.e6 when black's position falls apart (due, of course, to the opening of the a1-h8 diagonal). For example: 3...Nh6 4.Re5 Rad8 5.e7, 1-0.

1...Bb5

1...Bxe6 loses instantly to 2.Rxe6 when 2...Qxe6 3.d5+ picks up black's Queen.

2.Qxb5!!

Sacrificing the Queen and removing the blockader on d5. This allows the final dark square blockage to be removed.

White doesn't have to play in this manner (but who could resist giving up the Queen?). Just 2.Qd2 does the trick: 2...Nd8 3.Re5 and the a1-h8 once again turns into a fast track freeway for the b2-Bishop.

The point of all these methods (1.e6 or 1.Qc4, 2.Qxb5 or 2.Qd2—two positional methods and two tactical ones) is the same: to bust up black's blockade of the d4-pawn and rip open the a1-h8 diagonal for the b2-Bishop.

2...Qxb5 3.d5+ Rg7 4.exf7 h6

4...Rf8 5.Nxg5 is completely devastating.

Diagram 70a

5.Nd4

A very human move—it feels natural, gains time by hitting the Queen, and also seems (and is) extremely strong. Yet, it's not the most accurate. Instead, the counterintuitive 5.Nh4! (retaining the pin along the a1-h8 diagonal) is the way to go: 5...Kh7

(5...gxh4 6.Rg1) 6.Bxg7 gxh4 7.f8=Q Rxf8 8.Bxf8 Qxd5 9.Rg1 Qd2+ 10.Kh1 Qd3 11.Rg2 Qxh3+ 12.Kg1 and white's two Rooks and Bishop (not to mention the attack against black's King) easily overpowers black's lone Queen.

5...Qxf1

Capablanca's analysis vs. 5...Qd7 goes as follows: 6.Nxf5 Qxf7 7.Bxg7+ Kh7 8.Re7 Qxd5 9.Be5+ Kg6 10.Rg7+ Kh5 11.Ng3+ Kh4 12.Rf4+ gxf4 13.Rg4 mate.

6.Rxf1 Rxf7 7.Rxf5 Rxf5 8.Nxf5+ Kh7 9.Ne7!

Killing the King and also depriving black's Rook access to the c-file.

9...Rf8 10.Kg2 h5 11.d6 g4 12.hxg4 hxg4 13.Be5 Kh6 14.d7 Rd8 15.Ng8+ Rxg8

Even worse is 15...Kg6 16.Nf6 Kf7 17.Bc7.

16.Bf6 White's now a piece up. The rest was easy: **16...Kg6 17.d8=Q Rxd8 18.Bxd8 b5 19.Kf2 Kf5 20.Ke3 Ke5 21.Kd3 Kd5 22.Kc3 g3 23.Bh4 g2 24.Bf2 a5 25.b4 Ke4 26.Bb6 Kd5 27.Kd3 Kc6 28.Bg1 Kd5 29.Bh2 Kc6 30.Kd4 a4 31.Ke5 Kb6 32.Kd5 Ka6 33.Kc5** (Not falling for 33.Kc6?? g1=Q 34.Bxg1 stalemate), 1-0.

ANSWER
PART TWO

TEST **15**

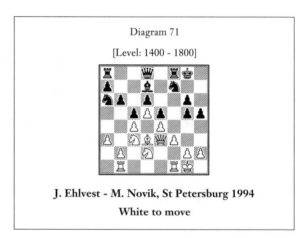

Diagram 71

[Level: 1400 - 1800]

J. Ehlvest - M. Novik, St Petersburg 1994

White to move

This position offers a simple but effective illustration of a time honored rule: Trade your bad pieces for your opponent's good ones!

One glance should convince you that white's Bishop is a Tall-Pawn while black's is actively patrolling two diagonals (e8-a4 and c8-h3). Is there any way for White to exchange these two pieces?

> **Explaining the Rating Spread**: I hope you noticed the plight of your Bishop and, having done that, did your best to make its life easier. Since a detailed study of the section on Bishops would have made you aware of the ways to deal with a Tall-Pawn, I have complete faith that you found the solution. If not, don't despair. Just give that section another read!

1.Bc2!

Preparing to exchange the lousy Bishop for black's active one via Ba4.

1...Qe7

I would have given serious consideration to 1...Qe8, preventing the immediate exchange of Bishops.

2.Ba4 Bxa4 3.Nxa4 Nd8 4.b4 and white's queenside play gave him a marked advantage.

ANSWER
PART TWO

TEST 16

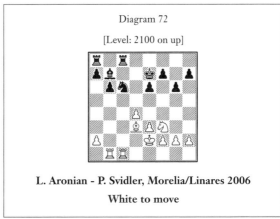

Diagram 72

[Level: 2100 on up]

L. Aronian - P. Svidler, Morelia/Linares 2006

White to move

1.d4 Nf6 2.c4 g6 3.Nc3 d5 4.Bg5 Ne4 5.Bh4 c5 6.cxd5 Nxc3 7.bxc3 Qxd5 8.e3 cxd4 9.Qxd4 Qxd4 10.cxd4 e6 11.Rb1 Be7 12.Bxe7 Kxe7 13.Bd3 Nc6 14.Nf3 b6 15.Ke2 Bb7 16.Rhc1 Rhc8 - Diagram 72

The main imbalance in this position is the battle between white's central pawn majority and black's queenside pawn majority. Many amateurs are programmed to quake in their boots when they realize their opponent has a queenside majority—"Isn't that a big advantage?" they ask. It can be, but center pawns tend to be more valuable in the middlegame and in positions where quite a few pieces still remain on the board. And, as we can readily see, white's center pawns give him a spatial plus (it's nothing huge, but it's something!).

However, there's another battle going on here too: the battle of the Bishops! White has noticed that black's center and kingside pawns are all on light squares. If this were permanent, such a state of affairs would bode well for white's Bishop since the enemy pawns would be potential targets. Thus, White plays to fix the enemy pawns on light squares.

> **Explaining the Rating Spread**: This is all about finding subtle ways to create things that don't yet exist. Very advanced, which explains the rating spread.

17.g4!

Excellent! White intends g4-g5 and there's no convenient way to stop it.

17...h6

Other choices:

> 17...f5 18.gxf5 gxf5 19.Rg1 (Another choice is 19.d5 exd5 20.Rg1 [Much worse is 20.Bxf5 Ba6+] 20...Rg8 21.Nh4 Ne5 22.Nxf5+ Kf6 23.Nd4 Nxd3 24.Kxd3 with a very nice endgame for White) 19...Rg8

20.Rg3 Rxg3 21.hxg3 with a small but pleasant structural edge (three pawn islands to two, and weaknesses on h7, e6, and a hole on e5).

➤ 17...f6 18.g5 f5 19.h4 when White has achieved his aim of fixing black's central and kingside pawns on light squares.

18.h4 Na5

The alternative was 18...Rc7 19.g5 Rac8 (threatening ...Nxd4+. The immediate 19...hxg5 20.hxg5 Rac8 21.Rh1! correctly announces that the h-file is far more important that the c-file) 20.Kd2 and now 20...h5 is a real success for White since black's kingside pawns are permanently stuck on light squares. Instead, 20...hxg5 21.hxg5 Nb4 (21...Na5 22.Ne5 leads to the same kind of positions that occur in the game) 22.Rxc7+ Rxc7 23.Rxb4 Bxf3 24.e4 with a position that's still rather uncomfortable for Black.

19.g5 hxg5 20.hxg5 Rxc1 21.Rxc1 Rc8 22.Rxc8 Bxc8 23.Ne5

Diagram 72a

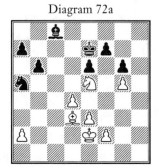

Black was hoping that the exchange of all the Rooks would ease his defensive chore, but the superiority of the white Knight and Bishop over their black counterparts, plus the fact that black's pawns have been stuck on light squares, is a guarantee that Black still has a lot of suffering to go through.

23...Bb7 24.a3 Nc6 25.Ng4

Since black's position is quite passive, White retains the Knights (only to offer the trade at the best possible moment) and proceeds to improve the position of his King and gobble up as much central space with his pawns as possible. There's no hurry, and as I've said before: When you have an opponent passively waiting for his fate, take your time and improve your position as much as possible before undertaking any committal action. This isn't to say that Black is lost here, but his position is far from easy to defend.

25...Nb8 26.Kd2 Bc6 27.Kc3 Nd7 28.f4 a5 29.e4 b5 30.Bc2 f5?

Black cracks. He should have played 30...f6.

31.exf5 exf5 32.Ne5 Nxe5 33.dxe5

Suddenly black's position is hopeless. His kingside pawns are still on light squares, but now White has a protected passed pawn and an easy route into black's position via Kc3-d4-c5.

33...b4+

Material would have been lost anyway after the King made its way to c5.

34.axb4 axb4+ 35.Kxb4 Bd7 36.Bb3 Bc6 37.Kc5 Be8?

This makes it easy for White. Black had to try 37...Bf3, when a theoretical (and complex) position is reached that is supposed to be winning. Of course, this kind of thing is far outside the scope of this book. Suffice it to say that White mixes threats against g6 (Bg8-h7) with a well-timed e5-e6 advance and decisive King breakthroughs to gain the full point. Note that all this is possible because black's pawns are on light squares and thus vulnerable to the enemy Bishop. The plan initiated with g2-g4-g5 has been a resounding success!

38.e6, 1-0. The end might have been 38...Kf8 39.Kd6 Bb5 40.e7+ Ke8 41.Bd5 Ba4 42.Bc4! Bd7 43.Bf7+ and that's all she wrote.

Part Two / Minor Pieces — Bishops vs. Knights

ANSWER
PART TWO
TEST 17

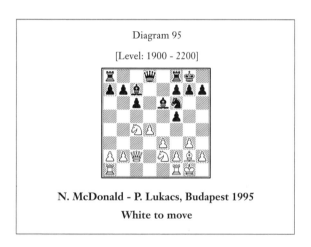

Diagram 95

[Level: 1900 - 2200]

N. McDonald - P. Lukacs, Budapest 1995

White to move

1.d4 Nf6 2.Bg5 d5 3.Bxf6 exf6 4.e3 c6 5.Nd2 Bd6 6.g3 0–0 7.Bg2 f5 8.Ne2 Nd7 9.0–0 Nf6 10.c4 dxc4 11.Nxc4 Bc7 12.Qc2 Be6 - Diagram 95

Black has doubled f-pawns. This isn't the end of the world, but it does make his position rather inflexible. White's pawn on d4 gives him a central and queenside space advantage. In fact, the half open c-file, the c4-Knight, control over c5, and white's light-squared Bishop all make it clear that this is the area where White should try and make some inroads.

Other than pawn structure considerations, the main imbalance is black's two Bishops vs. white's Bishop and Knight. However, the structure plays a role here too since the pawns are severely limiting the Bishops' activity.

So the two main bits of information White needs to concentrate on is:

> Seek queenside play (an eventual minority attack with b2-b4-b5 is in the air).

> Optimize your Knights!

Optimizing the Knights means bringing one or both of them to an advanced post where they can influence the upcoming queenside battle (remember that your whole army has to work for the same goal). Thus, the c5-square suggests itself. Once there it will hit b7 and, if it's chased away by ...b7-b6, the c6-pawn (which will be sitting on an open file) will be quite weak.

Because the pawn structure favors White, and because the Knights are better suited to this structure, White will retain a small but annoying edge for some time to come.

> **Explaining the Rating Spread**: This is far from easy because White not only has to be able to get his Knight to c5, but he also has to be aware of the Minority Attack. On top of that is the question about ...Bxe5 after white's Ne5. In my view, that's too much to take into account for anyone below 1900, but I would love it if lots of readers proved me wrong!

13.Ne5!

Heading for d3 and then to c5. Trying to get the e2-Knight to c5 isn't as effective: 13.Nf4 Bxf4 14.gxf4 Bd5 offers equal chances, while 13.Nc1 Bd5 14.Nd3 Bxg2 15.Kxg2 Qd5+ 16.Kg1 Ne4 is also fine for Black.

Note that 13.Ne5, in comparison to 13.Nc1, takes the Knight off the threatened c4-square. This means that 13.Nc1 allows 13...Bd5 because the f5-pawn can't be taken (the white Queen needs to remain on c2 to defend the c4-Knight), but 13.Ne5 Bd5 isn't playable since 14.Qxf5 picks up a free pawn. Of course, keeping the Knight on e2 has the added benefit that a well-timed Nf4 is still on the table.

13...Nd5

Other choices:

> ■■■■▶ 13...Bxe5 14.dxe5 leads to some surprisingly complex positions that give White a bothersome initiative. A sample: 14...Nd7 (14...Nd5 is possible, but it doesn't put any pressure on e5 and thus gives White a free hand) 15.Qc3 Qb8 (Black's Queen isn't well placed after 15...Qc7 16.f4) 16.f4 f6 17.Nd4 Qe8 18.Rad1 fxe5 19.fxe5 is a little better for White since 19...Nxe5 20.e4 is annoying: 20...fxe4?? 21.Rxf8+ Kxf8 22.Qc5+.

> ■■■■▶ 13...Nd7 when 14.Nd3 and 14.Nxd7 Qxd7 15.Nc1 Bd6 16.Nd3 both leave White with all the play thanks to the factors mentioned earlier. Note that 14.Nxc6 is an interesting but dubious decision due to 14...bxc6 15.Bxc6 Rc8! 16.d5 Be5 (16...Nb8!? 17.Bb7 Bxd5 18.Bxc8 Qxc8 19.Rac1 Na6 also gives Black a small edge) 17.dxe6 Nb8 18.Rad1 Qe7 19.Qxf5 Nxc6 20.exf7+ Qf7 21.Qxf7+ Rxf7 when black's extra piece has to be more important than white's three pawns.

> ■■■■▶ 13...Qe7 14.Nd3 Rad8 15.b4 (15.Nef4 is also good) 15...Bd6 16.Rab1 and, as usual, white's for choice.

14.Nd3 g6 15.Nc5 Bc8 16.Nc3 Nf6 17.b4 With his thematic Minority Attack in motion, White soon took over the queenside and scored an instructive win: **17...a6 18.a4 Bd6 19.b5 axb5 20.axb5 Rxa1 21.Rxa1 Qc7 22.bxc6 bxc6 23.Qa4**

Nd7 24.Na6 Bxa6 25.Qxa6 Nb8 26.Qc4 h5 27.Na4 h4 28.Nc5 hxg3 29.hxg3 Rc8 30.Rb1 Qe7 31.Rb7 Qe8 32.e4 Bxc5 33.dxc5 fxe4 34.Bxe4 (I suspect time trouble was at work here. Simply 34.Bh3 Rd8 35.Rxf7 was decisive) **34...Nd7 35.Ra7 Ne5 36.Qc3 Rd8 37.Rc7 Qe6 38.Kg2 Rd7 39.Rc8+ Kh7 40.Qa1 Rd1 41.Qxd1 Qxc8 42.Qh5+**, 1-0.

ANSWER
PART TWO

TEST 18

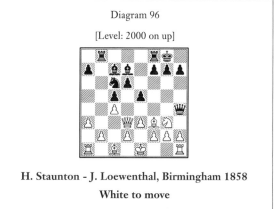

Diagram 96

[Level: 2000 on up]

H. Staunton - J. Loewenthal, Birmingham 1858

White to move

In this position White tried 15.Bxc6 Bxc6 16.e4, giving Black the two Bishops but closing the game so they would be ineffective. Was this a wise decision?

1.c4 e5 2.Nc3 Nf6 3.e3 Bb4 4.Qb3 c5 5.Nd5 Nc6 6.Ne2 d6 7.Ng3 Be6 8.a3 Ba5 9.Qxb7 Bd7 10.Qb3 0–0 11.Nxf6+ Qxf6 12.Be2 Qh4 13.Bf3 Rab8 14.Qd3 Bc7 - Diagram 96

White's a pawn up, but Black has a lead in development and would have enjoyed good compensation after the pedestrian 15.0-0 f5 16.Bd5+ Kh8. However, here Staunton had a sudden inspiration—why not add a superior minor piece to his extra pawn? And so the sequence **15.Bxc6 Bxc6 16.e4** came into existence. This would be great if White had the time to play 0-0, Qe2, d3, and f2-f4. However, Black isn't going to sit back and accept a closed position and inferior Bishops.

> **Explaining the Rating Spread**: Another hard problem. I think players under Expert would have trouble evaluating things. After all, Black's down a pawn and it does indeed look like black's Bishops are dead in the water. To get beyond some easy misconceptions in this position, one needs a solid grasp of Statics vs. Dynamics (explored in detail in Part Six), and an advanced eye for tactics.

16...f5!

This rips open the position and, in doing so, shatters white's illusions. The lesson here is clear: if you are going to give your opponent two Bishops, be absolutely certain that he can't open things up!

Conversely, if you have the two Bishops and they seem dead, *insist* on finding a way to bring them to life! The concept of mental toughness (pushing your own agenda) can be found in Part Four.

17.0–0

This is not what White wanted to play, but he suddenly realized that 17.Nxf5 failed to 17...Bxe4 18.Nxh4 (18.Qg3 Qxg3 19.Nxg3 Bxg2 20.Rg1 Bc6 followed by 21...Rf3 is crushing since finding any reasonable moves for White will prove more than a little difficult) 18...Bxd3 when white's position is hopelessly lost. Notice how black's light-squared Bishop puts the Knight to shame.

Of course, trying to hunker down with 17.f3 loses a piece to 17...f4.

17...fxe4

This simple capture leaves Black with a clear advantage. Material is now even, but all of the black pieces are superior to their white counterparts. Loewenthal managed to eventually win, though he seemed to try hard to botch it:

18.Qc2 Rf4 19.b3 Rbf8 20.Bb2 R8f6 21.Rae1 Rh6 22.h3 Rhf6 (22...e3! with the idea of ...Bxg2 would have been very strong) **23.Re3 Ba5 24.Qd1 Qh6 25.Qe2 Qg6 26.Bc1 Rh4 27.Re1 Rff4 28.Nf1 Rf3 29.Ng3 Rxe3 30.Qxe3 Qf7 31.Re2 Rf4 32.Bb2 Qg6 33.b4 Bb6 34.b5 Bb7 35.Qc3 h5 36.Re3 h4 37.Nh1 Qf7 38.a4 Qc7 39.d3 Ba5 40.Qc2 exd3 41.Qxd3 e4 42.Qd1 Qe7 43.g3 hxg3 44.Rxg3 Rf7 45.Re3 d5 46.cxd5 Qg5+ 47.Ng3 Bxd5 48.Bc1 Qe5 49.Qc2 c4 50.Bb2 Qg5 51.Bd4 Bb6 52.Qd2 Qf4 53.Nh5 c3 54.Bxc3 Qg5+ 55.Ng3 Bxe3 56.Qxe3 Qxe3 57.fxe3 Rf3 58.Be5 Rxe3 59.Nf5 Rd3 60.a5 e3 61.Nd4 Rd1+ 62.Kh2 e2 63.Nxe2 Rd2 64.Bb8 Rxe2+ 65.Kg3 Rb2, 0-1.**

ANSWER
PART TWO

TEST **19**

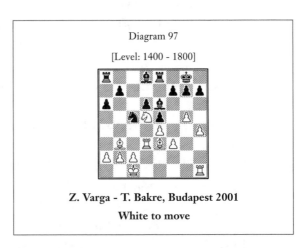

Diagram 97

[Level: 1400 - 1800]

Z. Varga - T. Bakre, Budapest 2001

White to move

1.e4 c5 2.Nf3 d6 3.d4 cxd4 4.Nxd4 Nf6 5.Nc3 Nc6 6.Bg5 a6 7.Qd2 Qb6 8.0–0–0 Nxd4 9.Qxd4 Qxd4 10.Rxd4 e6 11.f3 Bd7 12.Bc4 Bc6 13.Rdd1 Be7 14.Bb3 0–0 15.Rd3 Rfe8 16.Bf4 e5 17.Be3 Bd7 18.g4 Be6 19.g5 Nd7 20.Nd5 Bd8 21.h4 Nc5 - Diagram 97

One might think that the position is all about the weakness of the d6-pawn, but that would be incorrect. Instead, I'm looking for a pure minor piece mentality.

> **Explaining the Rating Spread**: The section is on minor piece battles, so any answer should have something to do with that. And there's no cleaner minor piece battle than a Bishop versus a Knight. I know that this

is something players in the indicated rating spread can fully understand (now, or with a bit more training).

White should play for the superior minor piece (great Knight vs. poor Bishop) by **22.Bxc5 dxc5 23.Ne3 Bxb3**

Swapping a pair of Bishops (thus depriving Black of his 2 Bs) and leaving all the light-squares in the hands of the Knight.

24.axb3

White, who has a flexible Knight (it can leap into c4, d5, f5, or g4 at a moment's notice) and ownership of the open d-file, has a clear advantage. Of course, an advantage doesn't mean you'll win, as evidenced by the remainder of this mistake filled game:

24...f6 25.Rd7

25.Rg1 prevents any counterplay and keeps a firm grip on the game.

25...fxg5

Better was 25...Re7 26.Rhd1 Rxd7 27.Rxd7 fxg5 28.h5! when White—whose Rook and Knight are far superior to their black counterparts—still has a solid plus, even though he's a pawn down.

26.Nf5 Bf6

Diagram 97a

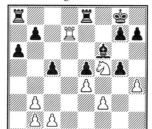

27.Rg1?

Missing 27.hxg5! Bxg5+ 28.f4!! Bxf4+ 29.Kb1 g6 (29...Kh8 30.Rxg7 h6 31.Rxb7 is better, but still very much in white's favor) 30.Rg7+ Kf8 31.Rhxh7 gxf5 32.exf5 with the idea of f6 followed by Rh8 mate.

27...h6 28.Rxb7?

28.hxg5 Bxg5+ 29.Kb1 would have maintained a significant edge.

28...Rab8 29.Rc7 gxh4 30.Nxg7 Bg5+ 31.Kd1

Now white's advantage is gone. However 31.Kb1 Rec8 32.Rd7 Rd8 33.Rxd8+ Rxd8 34.Ne6 Rd2 35.Nxg5 hxg5 36.Rxg5+ Kf7 also petered out to a draw.

31...Red8+ 32.Ke1 h3 33.Ne6 h2 34.Rh1 Rd2 35.Rg7+ Kh8 36.Nxg5??

Losing. He could have drawn by: 36.Rh7+! Kg8 37.Rg7+ and Black has to allow the perpetual check since 37...Kh8 38.Rh7+ Kxh7 39.Nxg5+ Kg6 40.Kxd2 Kxg5 41.Rxh2 is good for White. The rest of the game must have been painful for White.

36...Rxc2 37.Rh7+ Kg8 38.Rxh6 Rc1+ 39.Kf2 Rxh1 40.Rg6+ Kf8 41.Kg2 Rc1 42.Kxh2 Rxb3 43.Rxa6 Rxb2+ 44.Kh3 c4

44...Rh1+ 45.Kg4 Rg2+ 46.Kf5 Rh5 ends things immediately.

45.Kg4 c3 46.Kf5 Rcb1 47.Kf6 Rb6+ 48.Ne6+ Rxe6+, 0-1.

ANSWER
PART TWO

TEST 20

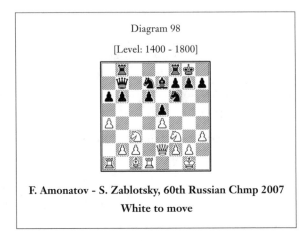

Diagram 98

[Level: 1400 - 1800]

F. Amonatov - S. Zablotsky, 60th Russian Chmp 2007

White to move

1.e4 d6 2.d4 Nf6 3.Nc3 e5 4.Nf3 Nbd7 5.Bc4 Be7 6.0–0 0–0 7.a4 c6 8.Ba2 b6 9.Qe2 a6 10.Rd1 Qc7 11.h3 Rb8 12.d5 cxd5 13.Bxd5 Bb7 14.Bxb7 Qxb7 - Diagram 98

A typical Sicilian structure (but from a Pirc that turned into a Philidor!). Black's d-pawn is backward (but solidly defended) and the d5-square is weak, but he hopes to get counterplay via ...Rfc8 and/or ...b6-b5. However, White has a way to play for the creation of a superior minor piece.

> **Explaining the Rating Spread**: Another problem that will prove to be easy for players in the indicated spread to understand and/or solve. Exchanging pieces and leaving yourself with a minor piece that's superior to your opponent's is a basic but extremely important strategy.

15.Bg5!

White plays directly for a superior Knight vs. Bishop position, which would also create a permanent grip on d5. This move is both thematic and easy to understand: black's Knights are the guardians of d5, while white's Bishop will never be able to directly affect that square. Thus, White wants to swap off both black Knights, leaving him with a dark squared Bishop vs. (ideally) a white Knight lording over the board on d5.

15...Rfc8 16.Bxf6

Not best. Did you notice that white's f3-Knight had nothing to do with the embattled d5-square from f3? It's important to hone your board vision so that you quickly recognize when pieces aren't well placed. One way to tell if a piece isn't carrying its weight is to ask, "Is my piece helping the rest of the army accomplish the main strategic goal?" If it's not doing so, it may very well be a slacker!

Correct was 16.Nh2, which instantly brings this Knight into the d5-equation: it intends to continue to g4 where (after Bxf6, getting rid of one enemy Knight) it can exchange itself for black's remaining horse (creating the hoped for great Knight vs. passive Bishop situation), or it can continue to e3 where it threatens to leap into d5 or f5.

It's important that you appreciate how this maneuver turns a once lazy Knight into an active participant in the battle for d5. Play after 16.Nh2 might continue 16...h6 17.Bxf6 Nxf6 18.Ng4 Nxg4 19.hxg4 Rc5 20.Nd5 Rbc8 21.c3 Bg5 22.g3 when Black has no real counterplay and faces a long, miserable defense due to white's powerful Knight and the long-term weakness of d6. To quote IM Elliott Winslow: "Burn this position into your memory and learn its nuances; it's a bread-and-butter Sicilian-killer."

16...Nxf6 17.Nd5 Nxd5 18.Rxd5 g6?

18...f5! would have kept white's advantage to a bare minimum since 19.c3 Rc5, 19.c4 b5, and 19.Rad1 Qc6 all give Black far more counterplay than he deserved.

19.c3 Rc5 20.Rxc5 bxc5 21.Nd2 Qc6 22.Nc4 and the Knight was ruler of all creation on c4.

Diagram 98a

The finish was remarkably smooth since Black was reduced to sitting back and watching White improve his position bit by bit: **22...Kg7 23.Qc2 Qb7 24.Rb1 Qb3 25.Qxb3 Rxb3 26.Kf1 Kf6 27.Ke2 Ke6 28.Ne3 f5 29.f3 h5 30.Kd3 Bd8 31.Nd5 Rb8 32.b4 cxb4 33.cxb4 Kd7 34.g4 hxg4 35.hxg4 Ke6 36.Rh1 fxg4 37.fxg4**, 1-0. The superiority of the Knight over the Bishop stands out in the final position. Black resigned because he's completely passive and has to wait as White builds up for the decisive blow. One entertaining possibility: 37...Rc8 (37...Bg5 38.Nc7+ followed by 39.Nxa6) 38.Rh6 Kf7 39.Rh7+ Ke6 40.Rg7 g5 (the poor Bishop has now achieved full Tall-Pawn status) 41.b5 (Also good is 41.Ra7) 41...axb5 42.axb5 Rb8 43.b6 Ra8 (43...Bxb6 44.Re7 mate) 44.b7 Rb8 45.Kc4 and Black, who is in zugzwang, has to shed massive amounts of material.

ANSWER
PART TWO
TEST 21

Diagram 99

[Level: 1400 - 1600]

T. Radjabov - V. Anand, Linares 2008

White played **18.Bd3** and a draw was agreed. Was it really equal? Doesn't White enjoy the Bishop pair in an open position?

1.e4 c6 2.d4 d5 3.Nc3 dxe4 4.Nxe4 Bf5 5.Ng3 Bg6 6.Nh3 Nf6 7.Nf4 e5 8.Nxg6 hxg6 9.dxe5 Qa5+ 10.Bd2 Qxe5+ 11.Qe2 Qxe2+ 12.Bxe2 Nbd7 13.0–0 0–0–0 14.Rad1 Nb6 15.Bc1 Bd6 16.Rfe1 Kc7 17.h3 Rhe8 18.Bd3 - Diagram 99

Yes, White might well have an edge if he could retain his Bishops, but there was no way to stop Black from using our basic anti-two Bishops plan of trading off one of the Bs. In this case, Black would achieve it by …Nfd5 followed by …Bf4. Note that preventing this plan with 18.c4 failed tactically to 18…Bxg3 when White has to give up a pawn (19.Rxd8 Bxf2+) since 19.fxg3?? Rxd1 wins a whole piece.

> **Explaining the Rating Spread**: The idea of trading off one of the enemy Bishops if the opponent has two of them is something a 1400 player can understand and use.

After **18.Bd3** play might have continued **18…Nfd5 19.Ne4** (19.c4 Nb4 is annoying since it's impossible for the d3-Bishop to defend itself while also keeping an eye on both c4 and a2) **19…Bf4** and White has absolutely nothing.

ANSWER
PART TWO
TEST 22

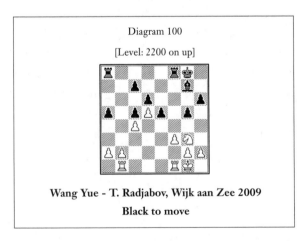

Diagram 100

[Level: 2200 on up]

Wang Yue - T. Radjabov, Wijk aan Zee 2009

Black to move

1.d4 Nf6 2.c4 g6 3.Nc3 Bg7 4.e4 d6 5.Nf3 0–0 6.Be2 e5 7.Be3 Ng4 8.Bg5 f6 9.Bh4 g5 10.Bg3 Nh6 11.d5 Nd7 12.0–0 f5 13.exf5 Nxf5 14.Nd2 Nd4 15.Nde4

h6 16.Bg4 b6 17.f3 Nc5 18.Bxc8 Qxc8 19.Bf2 Qd7 20.Ng3 a5 21.Nce2 Nf5 22.Nxf5 Qxf5 23.Ng3 Qg6 24.Bxc5 bxc5 25.Qb1 Qxb1 26.Raxb1 - Diagram 100

Black will be able to generate serious queenside pressure by ...a5-a4 followed by ...Rf8-b8-b4 placing heavy heat against both c4 and b2. However, the "other" battle is between black's Tall-Pawn and white's Knight, which will feel quite proud of itself after Ne4. Though going right for the queenside by 26...a4 followed by 27...Rfb8 would compensate for the inferior minor piece, Black wisely asked, "Why can't I win both battles?"

> **Explaining the Rating Spread**: I would be happy with any player under 2200 that noticed both the minor piece battle and black's queenside chances. However, actually seeing and having the courage to play black's best move is quite another matter. It's very instructive, but also calls for a lot of vision, courage, and confidence.

26...e4!

Suddenly the Bishop isn't a Tall-Pawn anymore! Turning the dormant Bishop into a serious force is well worth the sacrificed pawn. This kind of thing, and the psychological processes involved in actually playing such a move, will be explored in Part Four, Psychological Meanderings.

27.Nxe4 Bd4+ 28.Kh1 a4

Black has been very methodical: first he activates his Bishop, then he forces white's King to step to the far right of the board (away from the real fight on the queenside!), and finally he begins his assault against white's queenside pawns.

29.h4?

This turns out poorly. Better was 29.Rfc1 Rfb8 30.Nc3, though Black has no problems after 30...Rb4 31.b3 Bxc3 32.Rxc3 Re8 33.Ra1 Re2.

29...gxh4 30.Kh2 Rfb8 31.b3 axb3 32.axb3 Ra2 and black's active pieces gave him all the chances. The rest of the game is a picture perfect case of a Bishop schooling a Knight: **33.Rfd1 Kf7 34.Rd2 Ra3 35.Kh3 Raxb3 36.Rxb3 Rxb3 37.Kxh4 Kg6 38.Rc2 Rb1 39.Ng3 h5 40.f4 Bf6+ 41.Kh3 Rb3 42.Kh2 h4 43.Ne2 Kf5 44.Ra2 Rb4 45.Ra8 Rxc4 46.Re8 Rb4 47.Re6 Rb3 48.g4+ hxg3+ e.p. 49.Nxg3+ Kg4 50.Ne2 Rb2 51.Kg2 Be5 52.Kf2 Bxf4 53.Re7 Kf5 54.Rf7+ Ke5 55.Kf3 Bd2 56.Rxc7 Kxd5 57.Ng3 Rb3+ 58.Kg2 Bf4 59.Ne2 Be5 60.Kf2 Ke4 61.Rh7 Rf3+ 62.Ke1 d5 63.Kd2 d4 64.Rh4+ Kd5**, 0-1.

ANSWER
PART TWO

TEST 23

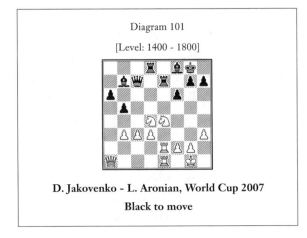

Diagram 101

[Level: 1400 - 1800]

D. Jakovenko - L. Aronian, World Cup 2007

Black to move

1.e4 e5 2.Nf3 Nc6 3.Bb5 a6 4.Ba4 Nf6 5.0–0 Be7 6.Re1 b5 7.Bb3 0–0 8.h3 Bb7 9.d3 d5 10.exd5 Nxd5 11.Nxe5 Nd4 12.Bd2 c5 13.Nc3 Nxb3 14.axb3 Nb4 15.Rc1 f6 16.Nf3 Qc7 17.Ne4 Rfe8 18.Bxb4 cxb4 19.c4 bxc3 e.p. 20.bxc3 Ba3 21.Rc2 Rad8 22.Qa1 Bf8 23.Rce2 Re7 24.Nd4 - Diagram 101

Black is a pawn down but has the two Bishops. Does this offer sufficient compensation for the material deficit? Probably not; let's not forget that white's Knights are very nicely placed, and if they can remain entrenched in the center, will certainly offer White a significant advantage. In other words, don't get fixated on the pawn and neglect the minor piece battle!

> **Explaining the Rating Spread**: I have a lot of faith in 1400 players, so I'm doubling down on them! After reading all the material on Bishops and Knights, I fully expect players in that range to have developed a sharp eye for support points. However, if that concept is still a bit vague, then Part Five (Target Consciousness) will add more than a little clarification.

As we know, it's very important not to allow enemy Knights advanced support points (Anti-Knight Strategy!), so the thematic move is **24...b4!**, weakening white's grasp of d4 and therefore depriving the Knight of a permanent support point there. After **25.c4 Bc8!** Black stops Nf5 and, after more preparatory moves, intends ...f6-f5 depriving the other horse of its central home too! In that case black's chances would be significantly better than they were in the actual game.

It's critical that the student develop this anti-support point mindset! In the game Black played **24...Rde8?!** and after **25.b4!** the d4-Knight was a permanent fixture and, after various ups and downs, White eventually managed to win the game: **25...Kh8 26.Ng3 g6 27.Rxe7 Rxe7 28.Rxe7 Qxe7 29.Qd1 f5 30.Qe2 Kg8 31.Qxe7 Bxe7 32.f4 h5 33.Nge2 Kf7 34.Kf2 Bf6 35.Nf3 Ke6 36.Ned4+ Kd6 37.Ne2 Bd5 38.Ke3 Bd8 39.g3 Bb6+ 40.Nfd4 Bg2 41.c4 bxc4 42.dxc4 Ba7 43.Nc3 Kd7 44.h4 Bf1 45.c5 a5 46.Ncb5 Bxb5 47.Nxb5 Bb8 48.Kd3 axb4 49.Kc4 Ke6 50.Nd4+ Kd7 51.Kxb4** and the rest was easy.

ANSWER
PART TWO

TEST 24

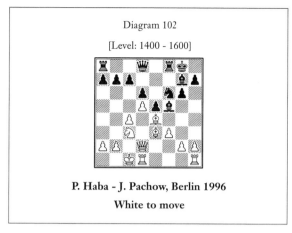

Diagram 102

[Level: 1400 - 1600]

P. Haba - J. Pachow, Berlin 1996
White to move

1.d4 Nf6 2.c4 g6 3.Nc3 Bg7 4.e4 d6 5.f3 0–0 6.Be3 e5 7.d5 Nh5 8.Qd2 f5 9.0–0–0 Nd7 10.Bd3 Ndf6 11.Nge2 fxe4 12.Nxe4 Nxe4 13.Bxe4 Bf5 14.Nc3 Nf6 - Diagram 102

There's a battle raging for the e4-square. White finds a way to win that fight and also to give himself a superior minor piece.

> **Explaining the Rating Spread**: It's no secret that this section is all about Bishops and Knights and all the things that make them tick, so this example's basic battle for a square should be within everyone's reach.

15.Bg5! Bxe4 16.Bxf6!

And not 16.Nxe4? Nxe4! when White didn't win the e4-square after all.

16...Rxf6 17.Nxe4

There's no doubt that the Knight is superior to the Bishop.

17...Rf4 18.Kb1 Qd7 19.c5!

Initiating queenside play. Black now has serious problems: he has less central space, White will generate strong queenside pressure, and black's usual kingside counterplay is nowhere to be found. All this, plus the enormous superiority of the Knight, leaves the second player in bad shape.

19...dxc5 20.Nxc5 Qf5+ 21.Ne4

Not allowing ...Rf4-d4.

21...Bf8 22.Qe2 Bd6 23.Rd3 Rf8 24.Rc1 h6 25.a3

White takes a moment to tend to his King; you never know when a safety square for his majesty will be welcome. Now Black faces a dilemma: he can play passively, hang on and hope for the best (such a strategy rarely meets a happy end), or he can try for kingside counterplay via ...h6-h5 and ...g6-g5-g4. However, this would weaken his own King position and could easily lead to the old "cure is worse than the disease" situation.

25...g5

Black decides to go down swinging.

26.h3 h5 27.g4!

Diagram 102a

As if minor piece and queenside supremacy weren't enough, White now takes over on the kingside! By fixing black's g-pawn on g5, his Queen will be forced to babysit it for a long time to come.

27...hxg4?

This mistake opens the h-file and allows White to grab that too. Nevertheless, the superior 27...Qg6 also left Black with bleak prospects. White would then have to choose between going for the throat with 28.gxh5 Qxh5 29.Rg1 Kh8 30.Rxg5, or keeping everything tight and under control while simultaneously increasing the pressure by 28.Ka2 h4 29.Rb3 b6 30.Rc6.

28.hxg4 Qg6 29.Rh1 Kg7 30.Rh5 The rest couldn't have given Black any pleasure: **30...Be7 31.Rc3 Bd8 32.Rxc7+ Bxc7 33.Rxg5 Bb6 34.Rxg6+ Kxg6 35.Qh2 Rxe4** (35...Rxf3 36.Qh5+ Kg7 37.Ng5 Rf1+ 38.Ka2 Kf6 39.Nh7+) **36.Qh5+ Kg7 37.Qg5+ Kh7 38.Qe7+ Kg8 39.fxe4 Rf1+ 40.Ka2** (White's 25th move is vindicated!) **40...Bd4** and 1-0 without waiting for the reply. 41.d6 Rf2 42.Qxb7 would have left Black feeling embarrassed for playing on.

ANSWER
PART TWO
TEST 25

Diagram 103

[Level: 1600 - 1800]

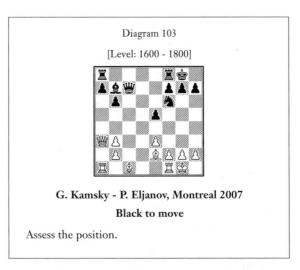

G. Kamsky - P. Eljanov, Montreal 2007

Black to move

Assess the position.

1.d4 Nf6 2.Nf3 d5 3.c4 e6 4.Nc3 Bb4 5.e3 0–0 6.Bd3 c5 7.0–0 dxc4 8.Bxc4 Nbd7 9.Qb3 cxd4 10.Qxb4 dxc3 11.Qxc3 Qc7 12.Qb3 b6 13.Be2 Bb7 14.Nd4 Nc5 15.Qa3 e5 16.Nb3 Nxb3 17.axb3 - Diagram 103

White has two Bishops vs. black's Bishop and Knight. However, at the moment black's Bishop is far stronger than either white Bishop (its control of the a8-h1 diagonal is terrifying), and the Knight also has far more possibilities than the enemy Bishops (it can leap to e4, d5, or even to c5 via d7). Why are the white minor pieces so ineffective? The answer is simple: the c1-Bishop isn't developed and can't seem to find a diagonal to call its own!

> **Explaining the Rating Spread**: I think some players would be misled into favoring White by his pressure against a7 down the a-file, and his two Bishops. Hopefully this problem will make you a bit more sympathetic towards Knights.

The inability of the c1-Bishop to show its stuff leaves Black with a clear advantage. Now let's make a "slight adjustment" in the position: put white's e-pawn on e4, his f-pawn on f3, and his dark-squared Bishop on e3.

Diagram 103a

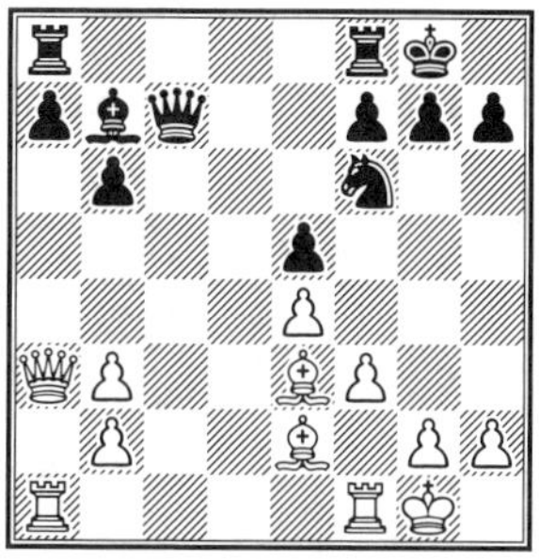

Black to move
Now White is better

Suddenly black's advantage is gone and White is the one who possesses a significant plus. Everything has changed! The Knight can no longer rest on e4 or d5 and the b7-Bishop's diagonal has now been completely shut down. Let's not forget white's problem dark-squared Bishop. It's still a problem, but a problem for Black! Sitting proudly on e3, it radiates power along two diagonals (g1-a7 and c1-h6).

As you can see, simply owning two Bishops and expecting them to win the game for you shows a serious misconception! All the position's details need to be considered before making any kind of assessment.

Returning back to position in the actual game (diagram 103), Black needs to make sure the c1-Bishop remains miserable and, of course, he needs to make sure White can't ever reach the fantasy situation mentioned above.

17...Rfd8

So simple, and so strong. A Rook takes the open file and prevents Bd2.

18.Re1

If 18.b4 then 18...Qc2 is annoying: 19.Bb5 (19.Ba6 Bxa6 20.Qxa6 Rd1 21.Rxd1 Qxd1+ 22.Qf1 Qc2 and White is in bad shape after both 23.h3 h6 24.Kh2 Rc8 and

23.e4 Qxe4 24.Bd2 Nd5 25.Bc3 f6) 19...a6 20.Ba4 Qg6 21.f3 e4! (not allowing the "dream" e3-e4) 22.f4 Rd3 23.Qa2 Rc8 with a winning game.

18...a5

This is a very important, and very effective, move! Now the b3-pawn is fixed in place (since 19.b4 loses immediately to 19...axb4), a7 is no longer under any pressure, and Qb4 is permanently off the table.

19.e4

Sacrificing a pawn to free the c1-Bishop—not an ideal solution, but it was becoming increasingly difficult to find a useful move! On 19.f3 (hoping against hope that he'll be allowed to follow up with e4 and Be3) 19...e4 (Telling White that dreams rarely come true) 20.f4 Qc2! 21.Qe7 (21.Bf1 Rd1! is immediately decisive, and 21.Qa4 Nd5 22.Bd1 Qc7 23.Qxe4 Nb4 24.Qc4 Rac8 and now both 25.Qe2 Qd6 and 25.Qxc7 Rxc7 are both quite grim for White) 21...Rd7 22.Qe5 Qxe2! 23.Rxe2 Rd1+ 24.Kf2 Ng4+ 25.Kg3 Nxe5 26.fxe5 Rc8 27.Rd2 Rg1 White, who is still in a straightjacket, will soon lose material or find himself in a mating net.

19...Bxe4 20.Bg5 h6 21.Rac1 Qb7 22.Bxf6 gxf6 23.Bf1 Rd4

Diagram 103b

White has managed to develop his pieces and even tear apart the enemy King's pawn cover. Unfortunately, Black is a solid pawn ahead, his King is far safer than one might suppose, and his pieces are on good, central squares. White (who is quite desperate) tries to create kingside threats, but it doesn't lead to anything at all. The finish: **24.b4 Rxb4 25.Rc4 Rxc4 26.Bxc4 Kg7 27.h4 Bg6 28.Qg3 h5 29.Rd1 Qc7 30.Be2 Kh7 31.Qf3 Rd8 32.Re1 Rd6 33.b3 Qc5**, 0-1.

ANSWER
PART TWO

TEST 26

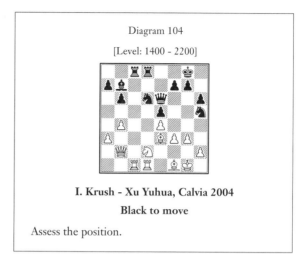

Diagram 104

[Level: 1400 - 2200]

I. Krush - Xu Yuhua, Calvia 2004
Black to move

Assess the position.

**1.d4 Nf6 2.c4 e6 3.Nc3 Bb4 4.Qc2 0–0 5.a3 Bxc3+ 6.Qxc3 b6 7.Bg5 Bb7
8.e3 d6 9.Nf3 Nbd7 10.Nd2 h6 11.Bh4 c5 12.f3 Rc8 13.dxc5 Nxc5 14.b4 Ncd7
15.Qb2 Ne5 16.Be2 Ng6 17.Bf2 d5 18.0–0 e5 19.cxd5 Qxd5 20.Rfd1 Qe6 21.e4
Nf4 22.Bb5 Rfd8 23.Be3 Ne8 24.g3 Nd6 25.Bf1 Nh5 26.Rac1** - Diagram 104

This position is pleasant for White thanks to her pair of Bishops and the misplaced Knight on h5. Neither side has any serious weaknesses though, so there's no need for over-optimism from white's side or panic from black's. In general, there are two ways for the inferior side (in this case, Black) to play in such situations: one is to accept that you're worse and just improve your game bit by bit in an effort to steer the position to eventual equality and a draw. The other is to seek tactical chances, remembering that you can't force such things since overaggressive moves tend to create self-inflicted weaknesses and can make things worse. In the present case Black should carefully weigh both. The thematic "go for it" idea is 26...f5 (trying to get the b7-Bishop into the action), but 27.Rxc8 Rxc8 28.Bh3 Nf6 29.Re1 leaves Black under serious pressure.

> **Explaining the Rating Spread**: Assessments should all be in the "favor-
> able to White because of her two Bishops" box, but after that there's lots
> of nuance and wiggle room.

Since 26...f5 didn't get the job done, Black should tighten up her position first. Perhaps a chance for ...f7-f5 will appear later, perhaps not. But there's no shame in being realistic and accepting that the opponent's two Bishops are better than your Bishop and Knight. Once you make this sober determination, you should seek the usual anti-Bishop pair ideas (try to exchange one of the Bishops), get all your pieces into play, and create a solid "wall" that's devoid of weak points. For example: 26...Nf6 (Don't allow your Knight to rot away on the side of the board!) 27.Rxc8 (27.a4!?) 27...Rxc8 28.Rc1 Rxc1 29.Qxc1 Nfe8 with a solid but slightly inferior game. Okay, you might be scared to death if you were facing Kramnik here, but do you really believe that your non-Kramnik opponent has the technique to eviscerate such a position? After 30.Qc3 (30.Qc2 would stop any ...f5 nonsense—white's better, so why should she allow things to get out of control?) 30...f5! (Black has the usual array of "hold on tight" moves, but this move now seems rather interesting) 31.Bh3 Qf6 32.Qb3+ Kf8 and who knows what might happen?

In the actual game, Black lashed out.

26...g5?!

The idea is to crack e4 with ...g5-g4. However, the poor placement of the h5-Knight and the fear that a further opening up of the position will favor the Bishops (which it usually does!) makes the push of the g-pawn rather dubious.

Again: Unless you're sure that an aggressive/committal idea will bear fruit, don't embark on an adventure that will only add to your defensive chore by creating new weaknesses in your own camp!

27.Nc4 Nxc4 28.Rxd8+ Rxd8 29.Bxc4 Qf6 30.Be2 Rd7 31.Qb3

A nice move that threatens 32.Qa4, simultaneously hitting d7 and a7.

31...a6 32.b5

Diagram 104a

Excellent play by Miss Krush (chess player names don't get any better than Krush)! By freezing the b6-pawn, it becomes a "diagonal casualty"—how can Black guard it after Bf2 followed by Qe3?

32...a5 33.Rd1 Rd6 34.Bf2! g4

At this point, Black has every right to panic!

35.fxg4 Ng7 36.Rxd6 Qxd6 37.Qe3 Qg6 38.Bf3 Ne6 39.Qxb6 Bxe4 40.Be2 Ng5? Anything but this! The resulting endgame offers Black no hope at all. The rest of the game was more execution than battle: **41.Qxg6+ fxg6 42.b6 Bb7 43.Be3 Nf7 44.Bd2 a4 45.Bb5 Kg7 46.Bxa4 Nd6 47.Bb3 g5 48.a4 Kf6 49.a5 e4 50.Bc3+ Ke7 51.Bb4 e3 52.Bc4 Kd7 53.Bxd6 Kxd6 54.Be2 Be4 55.a6 Kc6 56.b7 Kc7 57.Kf1 Kb8 58.Ke1 Bc2 59.Bc4**, 1-0.

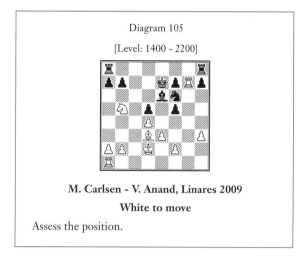

Diagram 105

[Level: 1400 - 2200]

M. Carlsen - V. Anand, Linares 2009

White to move

Assess the position.

1.d4 d5 2.c4 c6 3.Nc3 Nf6 4.e3 e6 5.Nf3 Nbd7 6.Qc2 Bd6 7.g4 Nxg4 8.Rg1 Qf6 9.Rxg4 Qxf3 10.Rxg7 Nf6 11.h3 Qf5 12.Qxf5 exf5 13.cxd5 cxd5 14.Nb5 Bb4+ 15.Bd2 Bxd2+ 16.Kxd2 Ke7 17.Bd3 Be6 - Diagram 105

With the superior pawn structure and active Bishop vs. Tall-Pawn, White has a small but annoying plus.

> **Explaining the Rating Spread**: A basic assessment is pretty straight-forward (thus the 1400 level citation). Deciding that exchanging white's Knight for black's poor Bishop is the way to go isn't straightforward at all (leading us to the 2200 level citation)!

18.Nc7!?

A surprise, but it fits in nicely with our overview of Bishops. Carlsen realizes that the enemy Bishop, though ugly, is actually a good defensive piece (in other words, it's inactive but useful). Due to this, he exchanges the Bishop for the Knight, which will force the King to defend f5.

18...Rag8 19.Nxe6 Kxe6 20.Rxg8 Nxg8

The Knight is heading to e7, where it will defend both d5 and f5. However, 20...Rxg8 21.Rc1 Rg2 22.Ke2 Rh2 was a more active defensive possibility, with good chances to hold the draw.

21.Ke2 Ne7 22.Kf3

The King improves its position and, after some preparation, intends to take up residence on f4 where it will work with the Bishop in pressuring f5.

22...Rc8 23.a4 Rc7 24.a5 h6 25.h4

White is making spatial gains on both wings and is slowly but surely improving the positions of his pieces and pawns. The advance of white's a-pawn means that ...a7-a6 would fix black's queenside pawns on light-squares (this makes them vulnerable in the Bishop versus Knight endgame that can easily occur). If Black tries ...b7-b6 at some point, White can capture and use the a-file for a bothersome Rook penetration. Note that black's Rook can't do anything on the c-file because the Bishop covers c4 and c2, while the b2-pawn covers c3. White's h-pawn will advance to h5 where it keeps the Knight out of g6. That allows white's King to go to f4 without fearing a Knight check.

Once all this is done, White will improve the position of his Rook, mixing threats of taking the c- and g-files with attacking possibilities against the h6-pawn.

I should add that all this is very advanced. Instead of feeling deflated by the complexity of it all, I implore you to watch for two things:

Diagram 105a

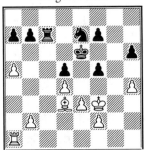

▬▶ Keep your eyes on the Bishop and how it constantly proves itself to be far more flexible than the Knight.

▬▶ Watch how White makes sure all his pieces are ideally placed.

You're looking to absorb patterns here, not to understand reams of analysis or grandmaster level maneuvering!

25...Kf6 26.h5 Nc8 27.Kf4 Nd6 28.Rg1

28.a6!? was also interesting.

28...Rc8 29.f3

Very useful—e4 is taken away from the Knight (Anti-Knight Strategy) and e3-e4 becomes a possibility at the right time. Note that White has no interest in b2-b3 since, aside from being unnecessary (...Nc4 would hang the f5-pawn), it would block the bishop's access to a4 and give the enemy Rook access to c3.

After 29.f3, a near-zugzwang position has occurred: If Black moves his Rook off the c-file White would claim it by Rc1, if Black plays 29...b6, then 30.axb6 axb6 31.Ra1 gives White the a-file, if Black moves his King to e7 then moves such as 30.Bxf5 or 30.Rg7 or 30.Ke5 all become possible, if 29...Rc7 then 30.Rg8 is very strong, and finally, if 29...Ke6 (as played in the game), then 30.Rg7 adds to black's woes. This means that, like it or not, 29...a6! (even though it fixes the queenside pawns on light-squares) needs to be given a shot since White can't maintain the zugzwang—in that case 30.Rg2 Rc1 gives Black counterplay, 30.b3? Rc3 favors Black, and 30.Bb1 Ke6 holds since 31.Rg7 now allows 31...Rc1 with a key tempo on the Bishop.

29...Ke6?

As pointed out in the note to white's 29th move, 29...a6! was correct.

30.Rg7 Rh8

Else White would win the h-pawn via Rh7.

31.Bc2!

The Bishop shows its stuff! Since the f5-pawn is well defended, the Bishop moves to b3 where it will torture d5.

31...Rc8 32.Bb3 Rh8 33.Rg1 Rc8 34.Rg7 Rh8 35.Rg2 Rc8 36.Rg1

Diagram 105b

White has been using zugzwang motifs to improve his position with gain of time. Black's problem is that he can't give White the c-file, but he also can't play a move like ...Rc7 since that would drop h6 to Rg7-h7. This means Black is left going back and forth, hoping White can't find a decisive breakthrough.

36...Ne8

On 36...Nc4 both 37.Bxc4 and 37.e4 would pose Black serious problems. The move Black played allows White to break with e3-e4 (whether of not that wins is another matter), however he wasn't able to stem the tide any longer. For example, 36...a6 would lead to another zugzwang: 37.Rg7 (threatening Rh7) 37...Rh8 38.Rg2 (threatening Rc1) 38...Rc8 39.Rg1 and Black has to either give up the c-file or move his Knight and allow e3-e4.

37.e4

Avoiding the catastrophic 37.Rg8?? Nf6 38.Rxc8 Nxh5 mate.

37...fxe4 38.fxe4 Nf6 39.e5 Ne4

Not 39...Nxh5+?? 40.Ke3 when the Knight is trapped on h5.

The game raged on for quite awhile. Both sides made some serious slips, but ultimately Black went down in defeat. I'll give the rest without commentary, but the battle between the Bishop and Knight continues until one of the pieces finally disappears: **40.Ke3 b6 41.axb6 axb6 42.Kd3 Nf2+ 43.Ke2 Ne4 44.Ke3 f6 45.Rg6 Rc1 46.Rxh6 Rh1 47.Bc2 Rh3+ 48.Kf4 Rh4+ 49.Kf3 Nd2+ 50.Ke2 Rh2+ 51.Kd1 Nc4 52.Rxf6+ Ke7 53.Bg6 Rd2+ 54.Kc1 Rxd4 55.b3 Nxe5 56.Rxb6 Rh4 57.Bf5 Nf3 58.h6 Nd4 59.h7 Nxf5 60.Rb8 Nd4 61.Kb2 Kd6 62.h8=Q Rxh8 63.Rxh8 Kc5 64.Rh5 Nc6 65.Rh4 Nb4 66.Ka3 d4 67.Rh5+ Nd5 68.Kb2 Kc6 69.Ka3 Kc5 70.Rh4 Nb4 71.Rh8 Nc6 72.Rh5+ Kd6 73.b4 d3 74.Rh3 Ne5 75.Kb3 d2 76.Kc2 Nc6 77.Rh4 Kd5** and Black resigned without waiting for the reply.

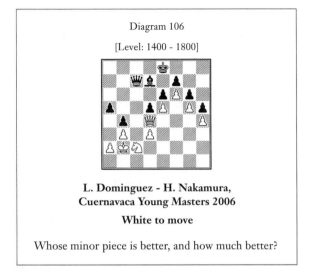

Diagram 106

[Level: 1400 - 1800]

**L. Dominguez - H. Nakamura,
Cuernavaca Young Masters 2006**

White to move

Whose minor piece is better, and how much better?

1.e4 e6 2.d4 d5 3.Nc3 Nf6 4.e5 Nfd7 5.f4 c5 6.Nf3 Nc6 7.Be3 cxd4 8.Nxd4 Bc5 9.Qd2 0–0 10.g3 Nxd4 11.Bxd4 Bxd4 12.Qxd4 Nb8 13.0–0–0 Nc6 14.Qc5 Bd7 15.Kb1 Rc8 16.Qd6 Na5 17.Bd3 Rc6 18.Qa3 a6 19.Ne2 b5 20.Nd4 Rc8 21.Rhe1 Re8 22.Nf3 Qb6 23.Qb4 Nb7 24.g4 Nc5 25.Qd2 b4 26.f5 Nxd3 27.f6 Qc5 28.cxd3 Qf8 29.Nd4 a5 30.Rc1 h6 31.g5 g6 32.h4 h5 33.Rxc8 Rxc8 34.Rc1 Ba4 35.Qe3 Qd8 36.b3 Bd7 37.Rxc8 Qxc8 38.Nc2 Bb5 39.Kc1 Qc3 40.Qd4 Qc7 41.Kd2 Bd7 42.Kc1 Kf8 43.Kb2 Ke8 - Diagram 106

Barring some strange tactical problem, this kind of structure—combined with this specific minor piece battle—is almost always won for the Knight in both middlegames and endgames. There are several reasons why black's game is so miserable:

- The Bishop will be purely defensive since white's pawns will eventually all be on dark squares (meaning that the Bishop can't ever attack them).

- White's enormous kingside space advantage chokes both the black Bishop and King.

- This specific pawn structure allows a particular tactical idea (looked at in the notes) that will always torture Black from beginning to end.

- White's King can step on a dark square and be immune from the Bishop, but black's King can always be kicked about by the nimble Knight.

All in all we're looking at a case of total Knight domination!

Explaining the Rating Spread: I'm hoping everyone appreciated the superiority of the Knight. The real problem was in determining just how much better the Knight really is.

44.a3

First on the agenda is to clear away the b4-pawn. This in turn gives White access to c3 while also preparing a timely b3-b4 push.

44...bxa3+ 45.Nxa3 Kd8 46.Nc2 Kc8 47.Qc3

Exchanging Queens allows the white King to safely advance and strive for deep penetration into the enemy position.

47...Kb7 48.Qxc7+ Kxc7 49.Kc3 Kb6 50.b4

Diagram 106a

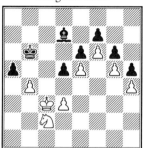

White's King wants to move forward and the a5-pawn was preventing this. Thus the exchange (which will ultimately give white's King access to b4) makes good sense.

50...a4

Everything loses. The most logical moves seem to be 50...axb4+ or 50...Bb5 (both amount to the same thing), but White's King and Knight combine to push black's pieces back and allow a decisive penetration into the heart of black's position: 50...Bb5 51.Nd4 Be8 52.Nb3 axb4+ (52...a4 53.Nc5 and now 53...Bc6 lets White demonstrate the following key tactical idea: 54.Nxe6! fxe6 55.f7 and a new Queen appears. Thus, Black has to meet 53.Nc5 with 53...Kc7 when White picks up the a-pawn by 54.Kb2 Kb6 55.Ka3 Kc7 56.Nxa4) 53.Kxb4 Bb5 54.Nc5 (threatening the decisive 55.Nxe6!) 54...Be8 55.d4 (Black's King must give ground since a Bishop move allows the tactic on e6) 55...Kc6 56.Ka5 Bd7 57.Ka6 Bc8+ (57...Be8 loses quickly to 58.Nb7 followed by 59.Nd6) 58.Ka7 Kc7 59.Ka8 Bd7 60.Na6+ (Once again the Knight lays down the law! The King must accept a game-losing retreat.) 60...Kc8 (Or 60...Kb6 61.Kb8! Kxa6 62.Kc7 Ba4 63.Kd8 Kb5 64.Ke7 Kc4 65.Kxf7 Kxd4 66.Kxe6, 1-0.) 61.Ka7 Kd8 (61...Bc6 62.Kb6 Ba4 63.Nc5 Be8 64.Nb7 with Nd6 to follow) 62.Nc5 Bc8 (62...Kc7 63.Nb7 and the Knight once again decisively lands on d6) 63.Kb6 Bd7 64.Nb7+ Ke8 65.Nd6+ Kf8 66.Kc7 Ba4 67.Kd8 Bc6 68.Nc8 Ba4 69.Nb6 Bb5 70.Nd7+ Kg8 (No better is 70...Bxd7 71.Kxd7 Kg8 72.Ke7 Kh7 73.Kxf7, 1-0) 71.Ke7 Bd3 72.Nc5 (threatens both the Bishop and 72.Nxe6) 72...Bf5 73.Nb7 when 74.Nd6 picks up f7 and ends the game.

It's worth going over this analysis again and again. No, you don't have to memorize anything. But I do want you to see how perky the Knight is, and how it has the ability to attack pawns from a number of angles and also kick black's King out of the white King's way.

51.Nd4

Black's King can't move to b5 and black's Bishop needs to constantly prevent Nxe6.

51...Ka6 52.Kb2 Kb6 53.Ka3 Be8 54.Ne2 Bb5 55.Nc3 d4

More Knight tactics follow 55...Bxd3 56.Nxd5+! Kb5 (56...Kc6 57.Ne7+ Kb5 58.Nc8 followed by Nd6) 57.Nc7+ Kc4 58.Nxe6!, 1-0.

56.Ne2 Bxd3 57.Nxd4 Bc4

57...Bb5 58.Nxe6.

58.Kxa4 Bd5 59.Ne2 Bc6+ 60.Kb3 Bb5 61.Nf4 Be8 62.Kc4 Bb5+ 63.Kd4 Be8 64.Ne2 Bc6

The Knight gets to do the honors after 64...Kb5 65.Nc3+ Kxb4 66.Ne4 when Nd6 ends things quickly.

65.Nc3 Bg2 66.b5, 1-0. There was no reason to continue since 66...Bf3 67.Kc4 Bb7 68.Kb4 Bf3 69.Na4+ Kc7 70.Kc5 would be business as usual for the King and Knight.

Part Three / Rooks

ANSWER
PART THREE

TEST 1

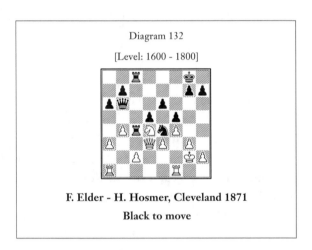

Diagram 132

[Level: 1600 - 1800]

F. Elder - H. Hosmer, Cleveland 1871

Black to move

1.f4 d5 2.Nf3 e6 3.e3 c5 4.Bb5+ Bd7 5.Bxd7+ Nxd7 6.b3 Be7 7.Bb2 Ngf6 8.Nc3 a6 9.0-0 0-0 10.Ne2 Rc8 11.Ng3 c4 12.Qe2 Qc7 13.Kh1 Bd6 14.Rac1 Qa5 15.a3 Qb6 16.Nd4 Nc5 17.b4 Nce4 18.Rf3 c3 19.dxc3 Nxc3 20.Qe1 Nce4 21.Nxe4 Nxe4 22.Rh3 Be7 23.Qe2 f5 24.Rf1 Nf6 25.Rhf3 Ne4 26.Rc1 Bf6 27.Rff1 Nc3 28.Qd3 Ne4 29.Ba1 Bh4 30.g3 Bf6 31.Ne2 Bxa1 32.Rxa1 Rc4 33.Nd4 Rfc8 34.Kg2 - Diagram 132

Black's domination of the c-file and pressure against c2 is obvious. The problem is that white's Knight is firmly guarding the pawn, nullifying the Rooks' efforts. Since your target is c2, and since his Knight is defending that point while your Knight isn't doing anything at all about it, the correct plan should be easy to find.

Explaining the Rating Spread: This is a problem that is solved by pure verbalization; you see your target, you see the defender, and you ask how you can get rid of that piece of glue that's holding his position together. I thought a 1400 might be looking for an aggressive way to break through and thus miss the idea of playing for a simple exchange. But I hope I'm wrong and that every reader 1400 on up found this easy.

34...Nc3!

That's it! Black intends to follow with 35...Nb5 exchanging white's defensive horse. In a sense, you can say that 34...Nc3 attacks c2!

35.Rf2 Nb5 36.Nxb5 Qxb5 and White's in serious trouble. The rest of the game, though far from perfect, ended up with the right side winning: **37.Ra2 d4** (What's the rush? A move like 37...Qa4, which threatens 38...Rxb4, would keep White bound and helpless) **38.exd4 Qd5+ 39.Qf3 Qxf3+ 40.Kxf3 Rxd4 41.Ke3 Re4+ 42.Kd3 Rd8+ 43.Kc3 Kf7 44.Ra1 h6 45.Raf1 g5 46.fxg5 hxg5 47.Rf3 Kf6 48.R1f2 Red4 49.Re3 e5 50.Rfe2 R4d5 51.Kb2 b5 52.Kb3 f4 53.Rf3 g4 54.Rf1 f3 55.h3 Rd1 56.Ref2 Rxf1 57.Rxf1 Kf5**, 0-1.

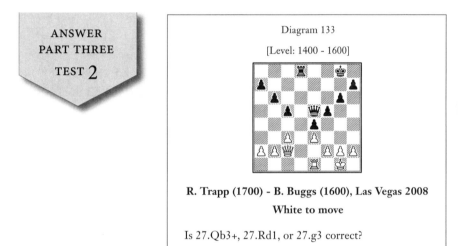

ANSWER
PART THREE

TEST 2

Diagram 133

[Level: 1400 - 1600]

R. Trapp (1700) - B. Buggs (1600), Las Vegas 2008

White to move

Is 27.Qb3+, 27.Rd1, or 27.g3 correct?

There are two things of note here: Black would love to claim permanent ownership of the d-file and there's a hole on d3. Two of the three moves mentioned in the problem don't address these concerns, while one does.

> **Explaining the Rating Spread**: You don't want to give Black the d-file, do you? I'm sure players in the 1400 range will find this an easy exercise.

> 27.g3? allows Black to have his way with the file and with the d3-square. He can grab the file forever with 27...Qd5 or 27...Qd6, he can clamp down on d3 with 27...c4 (followed by 28...Rd3), or he can leap to d3 (27...Rd3) right away.

> 27.Qb3+ sets a devious trap: 27...Qd5?? 28.Rd1! and the game is over since 28...Qxb3 29.Rxd8+ leaves White with an extra Rook. However, a trick isn't any reason to play a move, and after the correct 27...Kg7 28.Rd1 Rd3 black's latched onto d3. Then 29.Rxd3 exd3 gives Black a monster passed pawn.

> 27.Rd1! (the move actually played) denies Black his dreams and equalizes the game, which eventually ended in an uneventful draw.

ANSWER
PART THREE

TEST 3

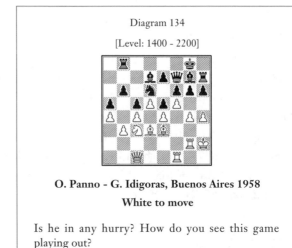

Diagram 134

[Level: 1400 - 2200]

O. Panno - G. Idigoras, Buenos Aires 1958

White to move

Is he in any hurry? How do you see this game playing out?

1.d4 Nf6 2.c4 g6 3.g3 Bg7 4.Bg2 0–0 5.Nc3 d6 6.Nf3 c5 7.d5 Na6 8.0–0 Nc7 9.Bf4 Rb8 10.a4 h6 11.Qc1 Kh7 12.Rd1 b6 13.e4 Nd7 14.h3 a6 15.Bf1 Ne5 16.Nxe5 dxe5 17.Be3 a5 18.f4 f6 19.Kh2 Ne8 20.Bd3 Nd6 21.Rf1 Qd7 22.f5 Qe8 23.b3 Bd7 24.Ra2 Rh8 25.Rg2 Qf7 26.h4 Kg8 27.g4 Rh7 - Diagram 134

Black, who suffers from a lack of space in the center and on the kingside, can't do anything but go back and forth. This means that White can take his time and build up his position in any way he sees fit. White's extra kingside space—plus the fact that his Rooks, Bishops, and Queen are all aimed in that direction—offer him excellent chances of a successful kingside attack. I hope you also noticed black's g7-Bishop, which has earned full Tall-Pawn status! Dare we assign the h7-Rook honorary Tall-Pawn status too?

The question about how you see this game playing out might seem odd, but a trained eye would conclude that Black might very well play …g6-g5 at some point, leading to a well known pawn structure (we addressed it in Part Three, Rooks) with very clear plans to combat it. Huge kudos if you made that connection between one pawn structure and a very possible future one!

In the game, Grandmaster Panno, a wonderful positional player, did his best *Cat and Mouse* imitation, torturing his opponent for a long, long time until he finally put the poor guy out of his misery.

> **Explaining the Rating Spread**: I have full confidence that the 1400 group will recognize that White isn't in any hurry at all. On the other hand, seeing the possible shift of pawn structures is very difficult, and so the spread leapt right up to Master!

28.Rf3 Kh8 29.Qf1 Rg8 30.Rfg3 g5 (Bingo! We arrive at a structure that you should be familiar with!) **31.Rh3 Bf8 32.Qf3 Rgg7 33.Kg1 Kg8 34.Ne2 Rh8 35.Ng3 Rgh7 36.Qd1 Qe8 37.Rhh2 Bg7 38.Ra2** (Toying with the thematic idea of 39.b4 axb4 40.a5, crashing through on the queenside.) **38…Nb7** (Black avoids it!) **39.Nh5 Qb8 40.Rh3 Be8 41.Ng3 Bf8 42.Rah2 Bd7 43.Kf2 Qe8 44.Qh1** (Panno dazzles his opponent with a very mean looking Alekhine's Gun, but black's defenses hold and White has to create a more imaginative piece configuration.) **44...Qf7 45.Be2 Bc8 46.Bf3 Bd7 47.Ne2** (White realizes that it will take a sacrifice to break through black's defenses, and this move is the first step in setting this up. The Knight will move to d3 where it will hit e5. Then the Queen will find its way to h2, his dark-squared Bishop to c3, and finally the Knight will slam onto e5 and crack Black open!) **47...Nd6 48.Nc1 Bc8 49.Nd3 Ba6 50.Kg3 Qg7 51.Kf2 Qf7 52.Qe1 Nb7 53.Qc3 Bg7 54.Kg3 Bf8 55.Rh1 Qe8 56.Qd2 Qf7 57.Qh2** (Mixing duties between pressure down the h-file and a strike on e5.) **57...Nd6 58.Bd2** (Black is being reminded that queenside-shredding sacrifices are still in the air.) **58...Nb7** (Poor Black sees threats coming from every direction. This stops any queenside silliness, just in case! But White has something far more lethal in mind.) **59.Bc3 Qg7 60.Kf2** (White has brilliantly surrounded his opponent and maximized all his possible breaks—his pieces are now perfectly balancing their attention on the queenside, center, and kingside!) **60...Nd6 61.Nxe5** (One can almost imagine a booming sound and smoke rising lazily into the sky.) **61...fxe5 62.Bxe5 Qf7 63.hxg5 Bg7** (63...hxg5 64.Bxh8) **64.g6 Qe8 65.g5**, 1-0. A great performance by Panno!

ANSWER
PART THREE

TEST 4

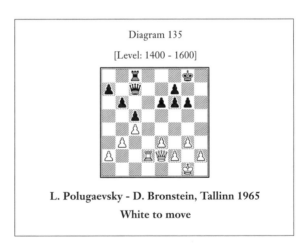

Diagram 135

[Level: 1400 - 1600]

L. Polugaevsky - D. Bronstein, Tallinn 1965

White to move

1.c4 Nf6 2.Nc3 e6 3.Nf3 c5 4.g3 b6 5.Bg2 Bb7 6.b3 Be7 7.Bb2 0-0 8.0-0 d5 9.e3 Nbd7 10.Qe2 Rc8 11.d3 dxc4 12.dxc4 Ne4 13.Nxe4 Bxe4 14.Rfd1 Qc7 15.Ne5 Nxe5 16.Bxe4 Bf6 17.Rd2 Rfd8 18.Rad1 Rxd2 19.Rxd2 Ng6 20.Bxf6 gxf6 21.Bxg6 hxg6 - Diagram 135

Both sides are left with a Queen and Rook, and there's only one fully open file on the board. It's clear that the solution is all about the d-file, and this leaves only one final mystery: will White play 22.Qd3 (taking the file "head first"), or 22.Qd1 (taking the file "feet first")? One of these has to be chosen, or Black will equalize with ...Rd8.

> **Explaining the Rating Spread**: I'm sure players in the 1400 group will wonder why I made this so easy. However, as mentioned above, there's no doubt in my mind that some players will take the "head first" option.

22.Qd1!

Much better than 22.Qd3 since White can always exchange Queens if he wishes to. However, why make that trade when the retention of both heavy pieces can lead to some unpleasant pressure against black's King? Furthermore, if White chose the "head first" option, Black could ignore a Qd7 leap to the seventh rank. But a "feet first" Rd7 leap? That can't be ignored!

22...Qc6 23.Rd7 Rc7 24.Rd6 Qe4 25.Rd8+

And not 25.Rxe6? Qxe6 26.Qd8+ Kg7 27.Qxc7 Qe4, =.

25...Kg7 26.Rb8!

Threatening decisive penetration by Qd8 (after avoiding perpetual checks with h2-h3 or h2-h4). In the actual game, White played the inferior 26.h4 which allowed Black to get back in the game, though Polugaevsky won anyway: 26...Qc6 27.h5 Rc8 28.hxg6 Rxd8 29.Qxd8 Qe4 30.gxf7 Qb1+ 31.Kg2 Qe4+ 32.Kf1 Qb1+ 33.Ke2 Qxa2+ 34.Kf3 Kxf7 35.Qd7+ Kg6 36.Qe8+ Kg7 37.Qa4 Qb1 38.Qxa7+ Kg6 39.Qxb6 Qf5+ 40.Kg2 Qe4+ 41.Kh2 Qc2 42.Qxe6 Qxf2+ 43.Kh3 Qf1+ 44.Kh4 Qh1+ 45.Qh3 Qb1 46.Qg4+ Kh6 47.Qf3 Kg6 48.Kg4 Kg7 49.Qb7+ Kg6 50.Qd5 Qc2 51.Kf4 Qf2+ 52.Qf3 Qb2 53.Qe4+ Kf7 54.Kf5 Qf2+ 55.Qf4 Qc2+ 56.e4, 1-0.

26...Rb7 27.Rc8

Trading Rooks would be crazy since white's is very threatening while black's is out of play. Don't exchange good pieces for bad ones!

27...g5 28.h3 and the threat of 29.Qd8 gives White a decisive advantage.

ANSWER
PART THREE

TEST 5

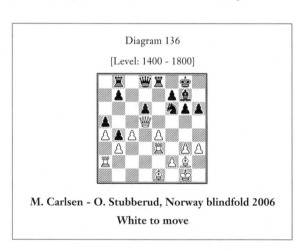

Diagram 136

[Level: 1400 - 1800]

M. Carlsen - O. Stubberud, Norway blindfold 2006

White to move

1.Nf3 Nf6 2.c4 g6 3.d4 Bg7 4.Nc3 0–0 5.g3 d6 6.Bg2 Nbd7 7.0–0 e5 8.h3 a6 9.e4 exd4 10.Nxd4 Re8 11.Re1 Rb8 12.a4 c5 13.Nc2 Ne5 14.b3 h6 15.Bf4 Nh5 16.Bd2 Nd3 17.Re3 Nb4 18.Nxb4 cxb4 19.Nd5 a5 20.Ra2 Be6 21.Be1 Bxd5 22.Qxd5 Nf6 - Diagram 136

White (who was playing 10 simultaneous blindfold games!) has two Bishops (they aren't very active at the moment) and the superior pawn structure—d6 in particular is begging to be attacked. Black would love to defend d6 and get his Knight to c5, where it hits e4 and b3 (tying down various white pieces in the process). Of course, White also has to address the threat to his Queen. Where should it go?

Explaining the Rating Spread: Who doesn't like Alekhine's Gun? I have absolutely no doubt that players of all levels who are familiar with this setup will rush to make it happen.

23.Qd1

This makes good sense and, if you found this move, then I can assume that Alekhine's Gun (looked at in Part Three, Rooks) made an impression on you. The idea is simple: to lead with the Rooks as White triples against d6.

23...Qc7 24.Rd2 Red8?

Embracing pure passivity, which isn't very wise. Far better is 23...Re6 intending to swing the Knight to its ideal home on c5 followed by ...Rbe8, creating maximum heat against e4. White can't allow that to happen, so an interesting battle would ensue where both sides would be fighting hard to get their way: 24.f4! Rbe8 (24...Nd7 25.e5! is a whole other kettle of fish: 25...Nf8 26.Rxd6 [26.Bd5!? Ree8 27.Rf3 dxe5 28.f5 is also interesting] 26...Rxd6 27.exd6 Qb6 28.Bf2 Bd4 29.Qd2 [29.Re2 Bxf2+ 30.Rxf2 Rd8 31.Bd5 Rxd6 32.Kg2 Nd7 and black's Knight finds the c5-square after all, though 33.Qf3 Nc5 34.Re2 still leaves White with an edge] 29...Qxd6 [29...Bxe3 30.Bxe3 is just good for White] 30.Bd5 Qf6 31.Re4 Bxf2+ 32.Qxf2 Nd7 and Black will be okay once his Knight makes one last jump to c5) 25.Bf2 Nxe4 (25...Bf8 is better when White doesn't have more than a slight pull) 26.Bxe4 Rxe4 27.Rxe4 Rxe4 14.Rxd6 and black's position isn't easy.

These lines are very instructive since they demonstrate a proper battle of ideas and imbalances where each side strives to maximize whatever their position offers. Compare that with the move played in the game (24...Red8)—this simply throws up his hands in exasperation and goes into panic mode.

25.Red3 and White is in control of the position (and in control of his opponent's state of mind). The rest featured more passive play by Black, which led to just the result one would expect: **25...Ne8 26.Rd5 b6 27.R2d3 Bf8 28.e5 Be7 29.exd6 Bxd6 30.Bd2 Kh7 31.Bf4**, 1-0.

ANSWER
PART THREE

TEST 6

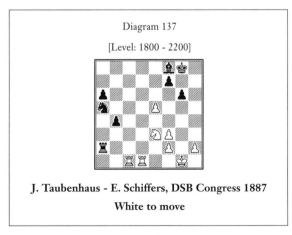

Diagram 137

[Level: 1800 - 2200]

J. Taubenhaus - E. Schiffers, DSB Congress 1887

White to move

1.e4 e5 2.Nf3 Nc6 3.Bb5 a6 4.Ba4 Nf6 5.d3 d6 6.c3 Be7 7.d4 exd4 8.cxd4 0–0 9.Nc3 b5 10.Bc2 Bg4 11.Be3 Bh5 12.0–0 b4 13.Ne2 Bg6 14.Ng3 d5 15.e5 Ne4

16.Rc1 Na5 17.Nxe4 dxe4 18.Nd2 Qd5 19.Qg4 c5 20.Bxe4 Bxe4 21.Nxe4 h5 22.Qf3 Rfd8 23.Nxc5 Qxf3 24.gxf3 Rd5 25.Nd3 Rad8 26.Nf4 Rxd4 27.Bxd4 Rxd4 28.Nxh5 Rd2 29.Ng3 Rxb2 30.Nf5 Bf8 31.Rfd1 g6 32.Ne3 Rxa2 - Diagram 137

White is winning, though black's passed b-pawn might seem a bit scary. In fact, Black is placing all his hopes on that pawn! White could switch to "defend" mode with 33.Ra1 Rxa1 34.Rxa1 but then lines like 34...Nc6 35.Nc4 (or 35.f4 a5 36.Nc4 b3 37.Kg2 Bb4) 35...a5 36.f4 b3 37.Nd2 b2 38.Rb1 Bh6 are, of course, good for White but hardly immediately game ending (Black would continue to twitch and beg for quite a while and, as we all know, a wounded animal/opponent is always dangerous).

Instead of allowing Black to lengthen the game and, perhaps, get lucky, why not make full use of your pair of Rooks? After all, they are both blessed with open files and, it must be admitted that most of black's army is far, far away from its King.

> **Explaining the Rating Spread**: This isn't easy because a lot of players would panic in the face of black's rapidly advancing b-pawn!

33.Rc8

33.Rd8 amounts to the same thing. Also crushing is 33.Rc7 (but not 33.Rd7 since after 33...b3 34.e6 the pawn advance 34...b2 comes with tempo) 33...b3 34.e6! b2 35.e7 Bxe7 36.Rxe7 Ra1 37.Re8+ Kg7 38.Rb8 Nc4 39.Rxb2 Rxd1+ 40.Nxd1 Nxb2 41.Nxb2 and White wins.

So a seventh rank attack gets the job done (not a surprise), but it turns out that an attack along the eighth rank is completely lethal since the combined might of white's Rooks, the e6-pawn, and the Knight will bury black's King.

33...b3

Also hopeless is 33...Kg7 34.Rd7 b3 35.e6 Kf6 36.Rxf8 Kxe6 37.Rfxf7 b2 38.Rfe7+ Kf6 39.Ng4+ Kg5 40.Rd5+ Kh4 (40...Kf4 41.Rf7 mate) 41.Rh7 mate.

34.Rdd8 b2 35.Rxf8+ Kg7 36.Rg8+ Kh6 37.h4!

There were many other ways to win; Taubenhaus not only finds the best move, but also the most exciting!

37...b1=Q+ 38.Kg2 f5

38...Rxf2+ doesn't help: 39.Kxf2 Qb2+ 40.Kg1 Qb1+ 41.Kg2 Qb2+ 42.Kh3 and Black will be mated in several moves.

39.exf6 e.p. g5 40.Rxg5, 1-0. Black had no reason to see 40...Rxf2+ 41.Kxf2 Qb2+ 42.Kg3 Qe5+ 43.Kh3 when Ng4+ will mate in a few moves.

ANSWER
PART THREE
TEST 7

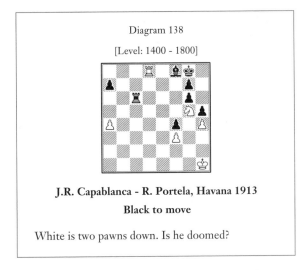

Diagram 138

[Level: 1400 - 1800]

J.R. Capablanca - R. Portela, Havana 1913

Black to move

White is two pawns down. Is he doomed?

Though Black is two pawns ahead, he has no chance of winning this game because of the bind created by white's eighth rank Rook and powerful Knight. Black's King and Bishop are immobilized, and his Rook is stuck on its third rank in an effort to prevent Ne6, which would win the enemy Bishop. The game should be drawn.

> **Explaining the Rating Spread**: Two extra pawns sounds like a lot, but you also have to take the activity of white's pieces into account. I have faith that the 1400 players who are reading this book will realize that winning just isn't in the cards for Black.

1...Ra6 2.Kg2 Rxa4?!

Apparently the mighty Portela isn't interested in drawing with his legendary opponent. It turns out that he had, earlier that year, already drawn a game against Capablanca in a simultaneous exhibition. He played Capablanca again a short time after that—three games at twenty moves per hour—and, though Portela lost the first two (in one he was doing fine but botched it), he seemed to have decided that only a win would do. One can imagine that, at this point, Portela might have thought that he was the superior player and was just unlucky. Thus, he decides to go all out for victory so he can end his series of games against Capablanca with some dignity!

3.Ne6

The Knight takes the first step of what turns out to be a memorable rampage. Believe it or not, it's about to devour the f8-Bishop and the pawns on g6, f4, h5, and g7!

3...Kf7 4.Nxf8 Ke7?

Tempting fate. 4...Ra2+ would have drawn.

5.Ra8 a5??

Playing for the loss, and ultimately getting his wish. 5...Ra2+ had to be tried.

6.Nxg6+ Kd6 7.Rf8 Kd5 8.Nxf4+ Kd4 9.Nxh5 Kc3 10.Kg3 Rc4 11.Nxg7 a4 12.h5 a3 13.h6 a2 14.Ra8, 1-0. No dignity for poor Portela.

Part Four / Psychological Meanderings — Material

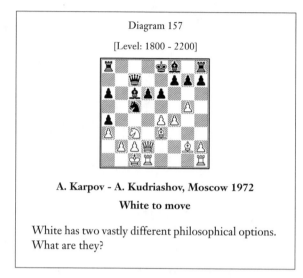

Diagram 157

[Level: 1800 - 2200]

A. Karpov - A. Kudriashov, Moscow 1972

White to move

White has two vastly different philosophical options. What are they?

Black has two problems: His King is in the center and his queenside pawn structure is shattered. On the other hand, Black is hoping to castle and then generate an attack down the b-file by ...Rb8 and ...Qb7.

White must make a big choice: Should he strive to punish black's central King by opening up the center, or should he keep things simple by somehow taking advantage of black's queenside pawn weaknesses (which will eventually lead to the fall of the a4-pawn and, as a result, material gain)?

> **Explaining the Rating Spread**: I think anything that asks for the philosophy behind a position is advanced. And when you mix in two completely different viewpoints, then it's even harder!

1.Bxc5

Karpov rarely chose risky tactical operations over a safe bind and positional suffocation. And, in this case, why should he? 1.Bxc5 adds to black's structural mess and also removes one of the a4-pawn's defenders. Now his plan is simple: exchange all of the defenders of a4 and then win it!

Tactical geniuses and adrenalin junkies might prefer the far sharper 1.f5!? when one possible line (just to give you a taste of what White's after) is 1...Qb7 2.Nd5 Rb8 3.Qc3 exd5 4.exd5 Bd7 5.Bxc5 dxc5 6.Rhe1+ Kd8 7.d6 Qb5 8.f6 g6 9.Re7 with a raging attack. For example, 9...h6 (trying to get his kingside pieces into play) 10.Rxf7 hxg5 11.Qe5 Bh6 12.Rxd7+ Qxd7 13.Bc6 wins.

1...dxc5 2.e5

First one exchange, then another! In the first case White got rid of a dangerous attacking piece and completely destroyed black's pawn structure. Now he's trading off another queenside attacking piece, stripping Black of the two Bishops, and also removing the a4-pawn's main defender. Each exchange is dicing down black's dynamic potential while also highlighting his weaknesses. Finally, note that 2.e5 is fixing the pawn structure (something Knights like) and also giving the Knight access to e4. In other words, he's also setting up a position where the Knight is stronger than the e7-Bishop.

2...Be7

Developing and preparing to castle. However, while the black King scurries to safety, Karpov continues to follow his plan.

3.Bxc6+ Qxc6 4.Qe2

Every move fits seamlessly with the others. White takes aim at a6, eyes a possible Qc4 (hitting a6 and a4 while also blocking the c5-pawn), and also has high hopes for Qe4 since the Queen exchange (which takes away the final defender of a4) leaves Black in a hopeless endgame.

4...c4

On 4...Rb8 White grabs hold of the c4-square by 5.Qc4 when 5...0-0 6.Nxa4 is mission accomplished (White's a solid pawn ahead), and the sharper 5...h6 allows 6.g6! fxg6 7.Rhg1 Kf7 8.Qd3 g5 9.Rdf1 with a strong attack.

4...0-0 allows White to fulfill his plan in a very pure manner: 5.Qe4 Qxe4 6.Nxe4 Rfd8 7.Rxd8+ Rxd8 8.Rd1 Rxd1+ 9.Kxd1 and the a4-pawn is a goner.

With 4...c4 Black stops Qc4 and frees the a3-f8 diagonal for his Bishop.

5.Qe4 By forcing the trade of Queens (notice that his whole plan was based on reducing enemy counterplay through exchanges) White ends Black's dreams of queen-side counterplay once and for all. Not only is black's Queen the "hammer" for his b-file attack, it's also the last remaining piece capable of defending a4. Thus, trading it also leaves a4 defenseless.

5...Rc8

5...Qc8 6.Rd4 followed by 7.Rxc4 is hopeless, but 5...Qxe4 puts up more resistance.

6.Qxc6+ Rxc6 7.Nxa4 White was a pawn up for nothing and went on to win the game.

ANSWER
PART FOUR

TEST *2*

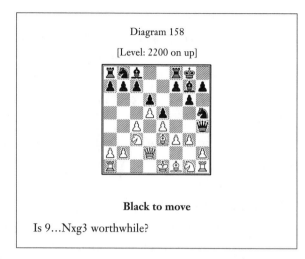

Diagram 158

[Level: 2200 on up]

Black to move

Is 9...Nxg3 worthwhile?

1.d4 Nf6 2.c4 g6 3.Nc3 Bg7 4.e4 d6 5.f3 0–0 6.Be3 e5 7.d5 Nh5 8.Qd2 Qh4+ 9.g3 - Diagram 158

This line of the Samisch King's Indian has had moments of popularity among those who like doing something offbeat, and who love playing positions that offer strange material imbalances. It turns out that taking on g3 is the critical continuation.

> **Explaining the Rating Spread**: If you haven't seen the answer before, then this will prove extremely difficult even for masters, many of whom will feel (with some justification) that it simply can't be sound.

9...Nxg3!? 10.Qf2

Did you stop here after seeing that this move wins material? Did black's next move (11...Nxf1) occur to you, or did the "autopilot brain" dismiss it instantly since it obviously loses the Queen? This is, of course, very advanced and I don't expect you to find this kind of sacrificial sequence (so don't feel bad if you didn't!). However, once you go over all the examples in this section, once you ponder them and begin to view them as imbalance vs. imbalance, then you'll find yourself developing an appreciation and understanding of situations that appear to spit in the face of point count.

Of course, 10.Bf2 is met by 10...Nxf1.

10...Nxf1

Initiating a positional sacrifice of the Queen! I've known several strong players who were very attracted to this idea but didn't really believe in its ultimate soundness. Nevertheless, I suspect there's still a lot to discover in this system and it might well prove to be better than its reputation.

11.Qxh4 Nxe3 12.Qf2 Nxc4

A very interesting position! Black has two Bishops and two pawns for the Queen. That's not a bad material tradeoff for the second player. He also has a solid position with only one potential weakness (c7), and Black knows that even if c7 falls, the time White takes to get it might allow black's army to get frighteningly active. Other than attacking c7, White only has one other plan: pushing the h-pawn to h5 in an effort to frighten black's King.

Diagram 158a

Though white's army doesn't work together very well and doesn't have many options as far as plans are concerned, Black has pawn breaks like ...c7-c6 and ...f7-f5, as well as all sorts of annoying Knight leaps. The dark-squared Bishop can occasionally turn into a beast on the h8-a1 diagonal if, after ...f7-f5, White captures on f5 and allows a later ...e5-e4. But even if this never happens, the Bishop can go to h6 with serious effect.

In general, the position is very difficult for both sides to handle and its study will give you an appreciation as to just how well minor pieces can handle themselves when facing off against a Queen.

Please keep in mind that I'm not trying to convince you to play this variation in your own games. The point is to break the conditioning that's left you with a fear of losing material, and to make you feel more comfortable when material imbalances are created.

Here are two examples of White drowning in the kind of complications that result from this line. Both are filled with serious mistakes, but don't let that blind you to power of the black army once it's unleashed. I purposely didn't add notes. Just sit back and enjoy the carnage:

L. Voloshin - J. Michalek, Plzen 2003

1.d4 Nf6 2.c4 g6 3.Nc3 Bg7 4.e4 O-O 5.Be3 d6 6.f3 e5 7.d5 Nh5 8.Qd2 Qh4+ 9.g3 Nxg3 10.Qf2 Nxf1 11.Qxh4 Nxe3 12.Qf2 Nxc4 13.O-O-O c6 14.Kb1 Bd7 15.Nge2 b5 16.Ng3 b4 17.Nce2 cxd5 18.exd5 f5 19.h4 Na6 20.h5 Nc5 21.hxg6 hxg6 22.Rh4 f4 23.Ne4 Bf5 24.N2g3 fxg3 25.Qxg3 b3 26.axb3 Nxb3 27.Rd3 Rab8 28.Qg2 Nd4 29.Ka1 Rfc8 30.Rh2 Nb3+ 31.Kb1 Ncd2+, 0-1.

T. Studnicka - L. Klima, Pilsen-Lobzy 2003

1.d4 Nf6 2.c4 d6 3.Nc3 g6 4.e4 Bg7 5.f3 O-O 6.Be3 e5 7.d5 Nh5 8.Qd2 Qh4+ 9.g3 Nxg3 10.Qf2 Nxf1 11.Qxh4 Nxe3 12.Qf2 Nxc4 13.Nb5 Na6 14.b3 Nb6 15.Ne2 Bd7 16.Nbc3 f5 17.Qe3 c6 18.O-O-O Rac8 19.Kb1 Rf6 20.h4 Nc5 21.h5 fxe4 22.fxe4 cxd5 23.exd5 Rcf8 24.Rdg1 Rf3 25.Qd2 Bf5+ 26.Kb2 Rd3 27.Qg5 e4 28.hxg6 hxg6 29.Rg3 Nxd5 30.Rxd3 Nxd3+ 31.Ka3 Nxc3 32.Nxc3 Bxc3 33.Qe7 Bb4+ 34.Ka4 Bd7+, 0-1.

ANSWER
PART FOUR

TEST 3

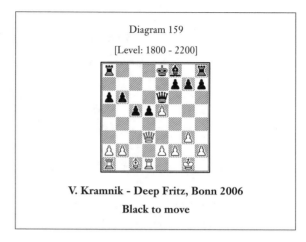

Diagram 159

[Level: 1800 - 2200]

V. Kramnik - Deep Fritz, Bonn 2006

Black to move

1.d4 Nf6 2.c4 e6 3.g3 d5 4.Bg2 dxc4 5.Qa4+ Nbd7 6.Qxc4 a6 7.Qc2 c5 8.Nf3 b6 9.Ne5 Nd5 10.Nc3 Bb7 11.Nxd5 Bxd5 12.Bxd5 exd5 13.O-O Nxe5 14.dxe5 Qc8 15.Rd1 Qe6 16.Qd3 - Diagram 159

Black's King still hasn't castled and his d-pawn is hanging. Since 16...Rd8 fails to 17.Qxa6 and since 16...d4 (which does nothing to address the dangers of his central King) 17.Qe4 Rd8 18.e3 Qd5 19.Qd3 Qxe5 20.Qxa6 Be7 21.Qb5+ Kf8 22.exd4 Rxd4 23.Rxd4 Qxd4 24.Qxb6 Qd1+ 25.Kg2 Qd5+ 26.f3 f6 27.Qb8+ Bd8 28.Be3 Kf7 29.Bf2 Re8 30.Qa7+ Be7 31.Re1 is grim for the second player, one would think that our starting position in diagram 159 is simply bad for Black. However, this isn't the case.

> **Explaining the Rating Spread**: The vast majority of players will think, "My pawn is hanging and I have to do something about it." However, there's no effective way to defend the pawn. Sorry, but this is another tough one!

16...Be7!

So simple, yet so easy to miss! Black's central King is the cause of a lot of his pain, so he hurries to develop, castle, and get his whole army into the battle. Yet in our robotic zeal to protect d5 ("it's threatened, so I should guard it"), it's easy to go into reaction mode and end up in a death spiral.

17.Qxd5 Rd8 18.Qb3

Not falling for 18.Qxe6?? Rxd1+ when Black wins.

18...Rxd1+ 19.Qxd1 0–0 and suddenly Black is the one with a lead in development, more active pieces, a queenside pawn majority, and pressure against White's pawns on a2 and e5. In other words, Black suddenly has quite a few favorable imbalances to play with, along with a safe King. The only thing White can crow about is his extra pawn. The game was eventually drawn: **20.Qb3 c4 21.Qc3 f6 22.b3 Rc8 23.Bb2 b5 24.Qe3 fxe5 25.bxc4 Rxc4 26.Bxe5 h6 27.Rd1 Rc2 28.Qb3 Qxb3 29.axb3 Rxe2 30.Bd6 Bf6 31.Bc5 a5 32.Bd4 Be7 33.Bc3 a4 34.bxa4 bxa4 35.Rd7 Bf8 36.Rd8 Kf7 37.Ra8 a3 38.Rxf8+ Kxf8 39.Bb4+ Kf7 40.Bxa3 Ra2 41.Bc5 g6 42.h4 Kf6 43.Be3 h5 44.Kg2**, ½-½.

ANSWER
PART FOUR

TEST 4

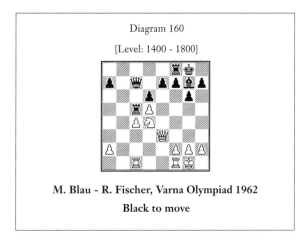

Diagram 160

[Level: 1400 - 1800]

M. Blau - R. Fischer, Varna Olympiad 1962

Black to move

It's clear that the c-pawn is the big target in this position and that Fischer is dying to chop it off. But this isn't a case of embracing one's "inner greed." Instead it's the logical culmination of one player creating weaknesses in the enemy camp, surrounding it/them, and finally feasting as the targets fall.

Clearly, the acquisition of material plays a huge part in chess strategy, but ideally one would like to do so in a controlled manner. Thus, one must take a few things into consideration:

> If too many pawns are exchanged, the side with a pawn less will, in some cases, still get serious drawing chances.

> In one's zeal to win material it's easy to allow unnecessary counterplay. Thus, Black should do his best to avoid giving White more play than he deserves.

> Which minor piece has more impact in the battle along the c-file?

Since 1...Rxc4 fails to 2.Nc6 Rxc1 3.Nxe7+ Kh8 4.Rxc1, black's correct move is self-evident.

> **Explaining the Rating Spread**: Would a 1400 want to prevent Nc6? No doubt about it!

1...Bxd4! 2.Qxd4 Rc8 3.Rc2

On 3.Qe3 (hoping to pick up e7 and a7 for c4 and d5), Black would get his a-pawn off the vulnerable rank by 3...a5. Then the threat of ...Rxc4 is once again "on" since he would be winning two pawns on c4 and d5 for the lone e7-pawn.

3...Rxc4 4.Rxc4 Qxc4 5.Qxa7 Qe4!

This fine centralizing move holds onto e7 (remember to retain as many pawns as you can and optimize your winning chances—the defender in such situations usually tries to exchange as many pawns as possible), stops the counterplay that would result if White were allowed to chop on e7, and prepares a long siege against both a2 and d5. Black still has every intention of winning a pawn, but he'll only take it on his terms!

Diagram 160a

6.h3 Rc4

Intending to resume the hunt against a2 by …Ra4.

7.Rd1 Kg7

It never hurts to improve the position of one's King.

8.Qb7 Qe2

Not only stopping any checks on b2 and eyeing a2, but also pushing white's Rook to a passive square.

9.Rf1 Ra4

So a2 is going to (finally!) fall, after which Black will then turn his guns onto d5.

10.Qb3 Rxa2 11.Qc3+ f6 12.Qe1 Qe5! and Black was a solid pawn up and in complete control. The game concluded as follows: **13.f4 Qxd5 14.Qxe7+ Kh6 15.Qf8+ Kh5 16.g4+ Kh4 17.Qxf6+ Kxh3 18.Qc3+ Kxg4 19.Qc8+ Kh4 20.Qd8+ Kh5**, 0-1.

ANSWER
PART FOUR

TEST **5**

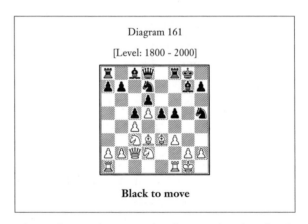

Diagram 161

[Level: 1800 - 2000]

Black to move

A glance gives the impression that White is doing very well. He's ahead in development, he is threatening to capture the pawn on f5, and his King seems safer than black's. And … all this is true! What can Black do to change his apparent inferiority?

The problem is that no "normal" move will stop the pain:

1…Qf6 2.g4! (2.Bxf5!?) 2…e4 3.Be2! (3.Bxe4!? is also interesting) 3…Qg6 (3…exf3 4.Nxf3 Qe7 5.Bg5 Bf6 6.Bxf6 Nhxf6 7.gxf5 also favors White) 4.Kh1 exf3 5.Nxf3 fxg4 6.Bd3 is unpleasant for Black—after all, the better developed side (White) is usually very happy if the position opens up. Note that after 6.Bd3 Qe8 7.Bxh7+ Kh8 8.Ng5 Qxe3? gets mated by 9.Rxf8+ Bxf8 10.Nf7+ Kg7 11.Qg6.

1...f4?? hangs the pawn on h7, but even if that pawn was safe on h6 this push to f4 would still be a mistake since it hands the e4-square to White.

Both 1...Nb8 and 1...Nb6 are typical computer "hold everything together no matter how ugly it is" moves. Yes, they do give f5 some badly needed support, but they aren't fighting for any gains, just survival!

> **Explaining the Rating Spread**: Actually, the correct move would be played by anyone who has been introduced to the idea in the past. It's a very common tactical device in the King's Indian Defense. However, if Black doesn't know it, I would expect it would be fairly hard to find.

1...e4! 2.fxe4 f4 3.Bf2 Ne5 4.Be2 Qg5 5.Nf3 Nxf3+ 6.Bxf3 Be5 (6...Bg4!?) and suddenly Black has much to boast about: his ownership of the e5-square turns any piece that lives there into a monster, the open g-file can easily grant Black an attack once a black Rook makes it way to g8 or g7, White must always be careful not to allow the f4-pawn to step forward to f3 where it might succeed in dismantling the white King, and the extra white pawn on e4 is a traitor since it kills the previously active white Queen and light-squared Bishop, while also depriving the c3-Knight of the use of the e4-square.

Black didn't wait to see if something nice happened to him with a move like 1...Nb8, instead he *made* something nice happen—he created a litany of positive imbalances where none existed before.

In situations of this type (where everything seems to be against you), if a pawn sacrifice like this appears, you have to play it even if it is still a bit better for the opponent (of course, I'm not saying that Black is worse here in any way, shape, or form). Why? Because being a bit worse with *no play* rarely ends well. But being a bit worse (and does anyone really care about "- 0.20" anyway?) with lots of play means that all three possible results are still actively "on."

ANSWER
PART FOUR

TEST 6

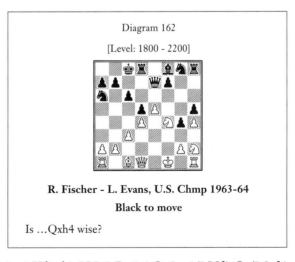

Diagram 162

[Level: 1800 - 2200]

R. Fischer - L. Evans, U.S. Chmp 1963-64

Black to move

Is ...Qxh4 wise?

1.e4 e5 2.f4 exf4 3.Bc4 Qh4+ 4.Kf1 d6 5.Nc3 Be6 6.Qe2 c6 7.Nf3 Qe7 8.d4 Bxc4 9.Qxc4 g5 10.e5 d5 11.Qd3 Na6 12.Ne2 Nb4 13.Qd1 0–0–0 14.c3 Na6 15.h4 g4 16.Nh2 h5 17.Nxf4 - Diagram 162

17...Qxh4?

There are a few reasons why 17...Qxh4 is a very poor move:

▶ The Rook on h1 wasn't in the game, but suddenly it's handed a half-open file. In general, try to avoid making the enemy pieces more active!

▶ The h2-Knight isn't exactly a hero, but after black's h4-capture the Knight soon finds itself doing a praiseworthy job.

▶ Black is suffering from long-term positional pressure along the f-file—the f4-, f5-, and f6-squares are all weak and the f7-pawn can easily become a target. He should be doing his best to develop his remaining forces and shore up the defects in his position. Instead the pawn grab loses time and highlights his problems instead of curing them.

▶ Finally, taking on h4 doesn't even win a pawn! White gets it back in a couple moves and quickly turns an interesting position (after 17.Nxf4) into a positional rout!

Keep in mind, it's okay to snip off a pawn if you're actually winning it and if you aren't giving your opponent too many other imbalances in return. But to waste time, not develop your pieces so they can push your own agenda, and to discover that you didn't even win a pawn after all (which would at least allow you to drown your positional sorrows in material gain) is simply a disaster!

> **Explaining the Rating Spread**: White's reply to the capture on h4 (18.Kg1) is the kind of quiet move that many players miss, and the abundance of ideas in the position makes things hard to assess.

After 17...Qxh4? (Something like 17...Qd7 followed by ...Ne7, ...Kb8, and ...c5 would have been far more constructive.) Fischer made beautiful use of black's many kingside weaknesses:

18.Kg1

This defends h1 and threatens to take advantage of the undefended h8-Rook by Nxg4.

18...Nh6 19.Nf1

Bringing the inactive Knight into play with gain of time and also forcing the win of the h5-pawn.

19...Qe7 20.Nxh5

Not only taking a pawn, but also clamping down on the f6-square.

20...Rg8

This doesn't make a good impression, but black's game was already markedly inferior.

21.Nfg3

The other Knight (which a moment before seemed rather sad on h2) enters the battle and deprives the h6-Knight of f5.

21...Rg6 22.Nf4

Diagram 162a

The g6-Rook is under attack, but suddenly the h6-Knight is also threatened with death since the h1-Rook is hitting it and the c1-Bishop is ready to pounce once the f4-Knight gets out of the way.

22...Rg5

Black didn't have an adequate reply since 22...Rg8 23.Nxd5! Rxd5 24.Bxh6 is also pretty depressing (though better than what happens in the actual game).

23.Be3 Nc7

Going down in flames, but lines like 23...Nf5 24.Nf5 Rxf5 25.Qxg4 Qd7 26.Rh7 and 23...f6 24.Nd3 Rg6 25.Bxh6 Bxh6 26.Nf5 were also hopeless.

24.Qd2 Rg8 25.Nfe2

Winning a full piece. Black could have resigned here but decided to prolong his suffering.

25...f6 26.exf6 Qxf6 27.Bxh6 Bd6 28.Rf1

Making sure that every piece is doing a job.

28...Qe6 29.Bf4

When you're a piece up, swapping off all the opponent's active pieces and ending all counterplay is the usual formula for risk-free success.

29...Rde8 30.Rh6 Bxf4 31.Qxf4 Qe7 32.Rf6 Ne6 33.Qe5 Ng5 34.Qxe7 Rxe7 35.Rf8+ Rxf8 36.Rxf8+, 1-0.

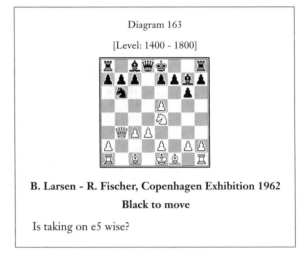

Diagram 163

[Level: 1400 - 1800]

B. Larsen - R. Fischer, Copenhagen Exhibition 1962

Black to move

Is taking on e5 wise?

1.f4 Nf6 2.Nf3 g6 3.d3 d5 4.Nbd2 d4 5.c3 dxc3 6.bxc3 Nd5 7.Qa4+ Nc6 8.Ne5 Bg7 9.Ne4 (It was probably better to try 9.Nxc6 Qd7 10.Bb2 when white's okay) **9...Nb6 10.Qb3 Nxe5 11.fxe5** - Diagram 163

This is a little known exhibition game between the two legendary giants. The initial moves illustrated Larsen's usual originality and Fischer's straightforward and often greedy style.

Black can retain an edge with simple moves such as 11...Be6 or 11...0-0 (better pawn structure, a lead in development, and various weak squares in white's camp. For example, if White defends e5 with d3-d4, then c4-square falls into black's hands after ...Be6). However, Fischer decided that grabbing the e5-pawn was the way to go. He knew White would get some activity for it, but he also judged that ultimately it would dry up and the extra material would then propel him to victory:

> **Explaining the Rating Spread**: I'm hoping that everyone reading this book understands that if you can take something, and you can't see why you shouldn't, then by all means chop away!

11...Bxe5

Fischer carefully judged white's compensation and determined that the material imbalance he was acquiring was worth more than white's initiative.

12.Qb5+ Nd7 13.Bh6 c6 14.Qb3 Nf6 15.Bg7 Rg8 16.Bxf6 exf6 17.d4 f5! 18.Nf2

18.dxe5 fxe4 19.Rd1 Qb6 is obviously very good for Black.

18...Bf4 19.e4 fxe4 20.Bc4 Rg7

Also interesting was 20...Qe7 21.0-0 b5 22.Be2 Be6 23.Qc2 and now both 23...Bf5 and 23...Be3 24.Qxe4 Bd5 retain a solid advantage thanks to the extra material and the positional imbalance of two active Bishops.

After 20...Rg7 the game continued: **21.0-0 b5** (21...Be3!? deserved serious consideration: 22.Rae1 Bxf2+ 23.Rxf2 f5) **22.Nxe4 bxc4 23.Qxc4 Be3+ 24.Kh1 Bf5 25.Qxc6+ Kf8 26.Nd6 Rb8 27.Qc5 Qb6 28.Qe5 Bg5 29.Rae1 Qd8 30.g4 Bf6 31.Qd5 Be7 32.gxf5 Qxd6 33.Qxd6 Bxd6 34.f6 Rg8 35.c4 g5 36.c5 Bf4 37.h4**

Rg6! 38.d5 Rxf6 39.hxg5 Bxg5 40.d6 Rc8 41.Rxf6 Bxf6 42.d7 Rxc5 43.Re8+ Kg7 44.d8=Q Bxd8 45.Rxd8 Rc1+ 46.Kg2 Rc2+ 47.Kg3 Rxa2, 0-1.

ANSWER
PART FOUR
TEST 8

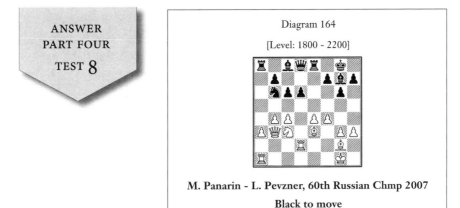

Diagram 164

[Level: 1800 - 2200]

M. Panarin - L. Pevzner, 60th Russian Chmp 2007

Black to move

Is 23...Na4 a good idea?

1.d4 Nf6 2.c4 d6 3.Nc3 Nbd7 4.e4 e5 5.Nf3 Be7 6.Be2 0–0 7.0–0 c6 8.Re1 a6 9.a3 a5 10.b3 Re8 11.Bf1 Bf8 12.g3 exd4 13.Nxd4 g6 14.Bg2 Bg7 15.h3 Nc5 16.Bf4 Nfd7 17.Be3 Ne5 18.Re2 a4 19.f4 Ned7 20.b4 Nb3 21.Nxb3 axb3 22.Qxb3 Nb6 23.Rd2 - Diagram 164

Black sacrificed a pawn for a burst of activity and now had to choose between 23...Na4, winning the Exchange, and 23...Be6, developing and forcing White to deal with the threat against c4. Be it good or bad, he should have given 23...Be6 the nod since his pieces become extremely active (lines like 23...Be6 24.Bf1 d5 25.cxd5 cxd5 26.e5 Nc4 lead to very interesting positions).

> **Explaining the Rating Spread**: 23...Na4 wins material, but that in itself doesn't make it good. I think 23...Na4 would have been very tempting for players under 1800.

In the game, Black couldn't resist **23...Na4 24.Nxa4** (24.e5 Nxc3 25.Qxc3 Qe7 26.Rxd6 Qxd6) **24...Bxa1** when **25.e5** slammed the door shut on black's whole game: **25...Be6 26.Rxd6**

Diagram 164a

It's time to take stock: Black played for the win of the Exchange and ended up getting his wish. Unfortunately, White was granted far too many favorable imbalances in return. Is an overwhelming space advantage in the center and on the queenside worth something? How about the monster Rook on d6? Two laser-beam Bishops? The fact that black's pieces aren't doing anything (Rooks are only worthwhile if they have open files to patrol) seems important. And what about that poor Bishop on a1? Is it ever going to get out alive? Finally, Black isn't even up material since White has two pawns for the Exchange. In other words, it's a complete disaster for the second player.

Moral? Don't play for the win of material unless you've carefully sized up any and all compensating factors the opponent will get in return!

The rest of the game was a slaughter: **26...Qc7 27.Nc5 Rad8 28.Nxe6 Rxe6 29.c5 Rde8 30.Kh2 Qe7 31.Qd1 Bxe5 32.Rd7 Qf6 33.fxe5 Qxe5 34.Qf3 f5 35.Bd4 Qe1 36.Rg7+ Kf8 37.Qf4 R6e7 38.Qh6**, 1-0.

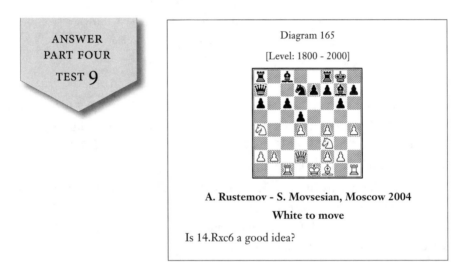

ANSWER PART FOUR

TEST 9

Diagram 165

[Level: 1800 - 2000]

A. Rustemov - S. Movsesian, Moscow 2004

White to move

Is 14.Rxc6 a good idea?

1.d4 d5 2.c4 c6 3.Nc3 Nf6 4.Nf3 a6 5.c5 Nbd7 6.Bf4 Nh5 7.e3 g6 8.h4 Nxf4 9.exf4 Bg7 10.Qd2 b6 11.cxb6 Qxb6 12.Rc1 0–0 13.Na4 Qa7 - Diagram 165

Things are going quite well for White, who has chances of a kingside attack with h4-h5, a bind on the e5-square (Thanks to the doubling of the f-pawns. If white's pawn still stood on the "healthy" e3-square then Black could seek counterplay by ...e7-e5.), more space in every sector of the board, and long-term pressure against the weak pawns on a6 and c6.

Does Black have anything? He has two Bishops, but at the moment white's Knights are dominating them. Black's only other plus is white's central King, but if the center can't be opened then that might not amount to anything since the black pieces won't be able to reach white's monarch on e1.

The question was whether chopping on c6 was a good idea. In this case it gives Black far more play than he deserves after 14.Rxc6?! Nf6 15.Nc5 Ne4 16.Nxe4 dxe4 17.Ne5 Rd8 18.Bc4 e6. Why give your opponent tons of counterplay (White might still be a bit better, but certainly no more than that) when there is more to gain by keeping a solid grip on the position?

Explaining the Rating Spread: White has a lot of advantages, so why give Black counterplay when you're in control of the game? I do appreciate greed, though, and fully understand why 14.Rxc6 would be given a go. However, I suspect that more experienced players would hold off.

In the actual game White wisely avoided the capture on c6 and instead pushed his own agenda by **14.h5 a5 15.hxg6 fxg6** (15...hxg6 was preferable, but still much better for White) when we get yet another chance to chop on c6.

Diagram 165a

In the game White again avoided 16.Rxc6 with the tightening move 16.g3. This was a good practical decision and led to eventual victory. However now, thanks to the newly created weaknesses in black's King position, the circumstances have changed and taking the pawn was best: **16.Rxc6! Nf6 17.Nc5 Ne4** (17...Bd7 18.Ra6) **18.Nxe4 dxe4 19.Bc4+ e6 20.Ng5** with an overwhelming position.

It should be clear that grabbing a material plus isn't always a no-brainer. In fact, if it gives your opponent too many positive imbalances then you should usually beat back the greed-impulse and look for a more controlled way to handle the position. On the other hand, if you were already in trouble, sacrificing material for counterplay (in the case of our last example, 14.Rxc6 allowed 14...Nf6 followed by 15...Ne4 when black's formerly passive pieces spring to life) is something you should get used to doing.

Interestingly, the example in diagram 165 showed many psychological and practical nuances that are related to the giving and taking of material: We saw (on move 14) the defender offer a pawn for counterplay (demonstrating that he's transcended the "I can't ever give away my stuff" syndrome), we saw White wisely refuse it (not allowing the opponent to gain undeserved activity), then (on move 16) we saw White refuse to take a pawn that could have safely been taken. However, this decision is a very human one—when you have a positional lock, why go on tactical adventures (which might easily lead to an oversight) when you can continue to safely "massage" your opponent until he finally cracks and dies?

Part Four / Psychological Meanderings — Mental Breakdown

ANSWER
PART FOUR

TEST 10

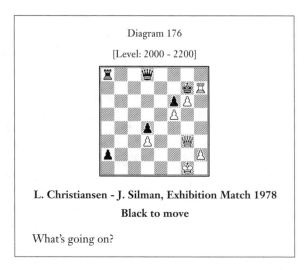

Diagram 176

[Level: 2000 - 2200]

L. Christiansen - J. Silman, Exhibition Match 1978

Black to move

What's going on?

1.e4 c5 2.f4 Nc6 3.Nf3 e6 4.Bb5 Nf6 5.Bxc6 dxc6 6.d3 Be7 7.0–0 0–0 8.a4 a5 9.Na3 Qc7 10.Qe1 b6 11.Bd2 Nd7 12.Nc4 Ba6 13.b3 Bxc4 14.bxc4 e5 15.f5 Rfd8 16.g4 Nb8 17.Qg3 Na6 18.Nxe5 Bd6 19.Bf4 f6 20.d4 cxd4 21.Nd3 Nc5? 22.Rae1 Bxf4 23.Rxf4 Nxd3 24.cxd3 b5 25.axb5 cxb5 26.cxb5 a4 27.g5 Kh8 28.e5 a3

28...fxg5 29.Qxg5 a3 was correct.

29.b6 Qxb6 30.exf6 gxf6 31.Re7

I don't remember why I allowed this to occur, but here I woke up and realized that I was toast. And since I was sure that I would lose (most likely in some grisly fashion), I descended into the self-defeating world of "I can't" (as in "I can't survive this!").

31...Rg8 32.g6??

And here Larry succumbed to an "I have to" moment (as in "I *have* to win after this!"). If he had thought about the position for a moment, he'd have seen that 32.Rh4 wins on the spot (32...Rg7 33.Rxg7 Kxg7 34.gxf6+ mates by force).

32...Rg7 33.Rfe4 Qd8??

More defeatism—"I'm doomed, I'm an idiot, I can't save myself" repeated over and over in my head. If I had shut off the pity spigot, I might have noticed that 33...Qb1+ saves me: 34.Kg2 (34.Re1 a2 35.Rxg7 Kxg7 36.Qc7+ Kh6 37.Qf4+ with a draw, and not 37.Qxh7+?? Kg5 when Black wins) 34...Qa2+! 35.Kf3 Qg8 and the Queen manages to successfully defend its mate.

34.Rxg7??

Larry was having his own problems and he kept playing the "This *has* to win" move instead of settling down and proving it was as crushing as it seemed. If he had done this, then he would surely have changed his mind and played 34.Qe1!, which wins easily.

Unfortunately, he played 34.Rxg7 with such authority (as if saying, "You're dead meat, sucker!") that I completely bought into his delusion. There was no doubt in my mind that the end was near.

34...Kxg7 35.Rh4 a2 36.Rxh7+

Diagram 176

Black to move

Black Resigns! I doubt that this is the move you decided on, but it was indeed my (completely insane) choice during the game. Things *do* look scary, but "resigns" seems a rather extreme "solution" to black's problem!

> **Explaining the Rating Spread**: Of course, you've been alerted to the fact that something's up, but it's still quite difficult. Part of that difficulty lies with the fact that players tend to get a bit freaked out when their King is being kicked about.

There are only two choices for Black in diagram 176, but, as you've already seen, I found a third! I actually took quite a long think here. The first thing I did was reject 36...Kf8 since it gives White the chance to transpose into the same position reached after 36...Kg8 (36...Kf8 37.Rh8+ Kg7 38.Rxd8) while also offering him the extra possibility of 37.g7+ Kg8 38.Rh8+ Kf7, which seemed downright terrifying. As it turns out, the terror was in my head, not on the board: 39.Rf8+ (39.Rxd8 a1=Q+ 40.Kg2 Qa2+ 41.Kf3 Rxd8 42.Qc7+ Ke8 43.Qc6+ is also drawn) 39...Qxf8 40.gxf8=Q+ Kxf8 41.Qd6+ Kg7 42.Qe7+ Kg8, draw.

Since White can force the key line after both 36...Kf8 and 36...Kg8, I concentrated on that particular variation: 36...Kg8 37.Rh8+ Kg7 38.Rxd8 a1=Q+ 39.Kg2 Ra2+ (I didn't trust 39...Qb2+, but it turns out to be fine: 40.Kh3 Rxd8 41.Qc7+ Kh6 42.Qxd8 Qf2, =) 40.Kh3 Qf1+ 41.Kh4

Diagram 176a

Black to move

Pondering this position, I realized it was the end of the road. "I'm doomed, and I've been doomed for a long time. Time to put it to rest."

I reached out (after 36.Rxh7+), said, "I give up" and shook Christiansen's hand. He looked at me in shock and said, "I was about to offer you a draw! It's a perpetual check or stalemate!" He then played out the moves that led to the expected final position (previous diagram that occurred after 41.Kh4) and slammed down 41...Rxh2+!! 42.Qxh2 (42.Kg4 loses) 42...Qf4+! 43.Kh3 (43.Qxf4 stalemate) 43...Qg4+ 44.Kxg4 stalemate.

Fortunately, there were no sharp objects within reach at that moment, and this allowed me to live to fight another day. And, as is so often the case, it proved to be a very important lesson. I realized that my negative frame of mind made it impossible for me to see what was really going on, and I understood that uncontrolled emotion should only be released *after* the game, not during. As a result, I worked hard to eradicate "I can't" from my psyche—in fact, I traded negatives like "I can't" and "I'm doomed" and "It's hopeless" to "There's always a defense!" The belief that one can fight to the bitter end and place serious difficulties in front of your opponent even in the worst of situations served me very well as my career progressed. And, when an opponent would play a dodgy move, I firmly embraced the mentality that it was "Rubbish" or it "Had to be punished."

ANSWER
PART FOUR

TEST 11

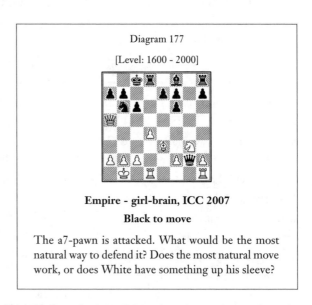

Diagram 177

[Level: 1600 - 2000]

Empire - girl-brain, ICC 2007

Black to move

The a7-pawn is attacked. What would be the most natural way to defend it? Does the most natural move work, or does White have something up his sleeve?

1.e4 c6 2.d4 d5 3.Nc3 dxe4 4.Nxe4 Nf6 5.Nxf6+ gxf6 6.Be3 Bf5 7.Bd3 Nd7 8.Bxf5 Qa5+ 9.Qd2 Qxf5 10.0-0-0 0-0-0 11.Ne2 Nb6 12.Ng3 Qd5 13.Kb1 Qxg2 14.Qa5 - Diagram 177

> **Explaining the Rating Spread**: This example shows us that it's easy to talk ourselves out of even the most logical moves. I suspect that a 1400 player would have played the correct 14...Kb8 right away, but would have missed white's 15.Bf4+ followed by 16.Bc7 idea. If you're 1400 and you saw this line, then accept a round of applause!

White has just attacked a7 and Black (who has an extra pawn and an obvious plus) would like to defend it. The move Black would prefer to play is 14...Kb8, but girl-brain promptly said, "I can't" and chose to return the pawn after 14...Nc4 15.Qxa7 Nxe3 16.fxe3 when the advantage moved to White (though she subsequently outclassed her opponent). What could possibly have spooked her? It turns out that she noticed 14...Kb8 15.Bf4+ Ka8 16.Bc7 and felt she was in trouble. Yes, it looks very threatening—both the Rook and Knight are under attack. But since 14...Kb8 is the dream move, you really need to defend it and do your utmost to prove that the position after 16.Bc7 isn't a problem for Black. Sadly, she didn't make the effort—the threat scared her and that was that. End of story. Time to look for a different 14th move.

Of course, by now you know that a successful player can't afford to be psyched out by mere threats. You need to turn on your "insist that there's something good for you" mindset and look hard for the move that will once again make you master of your domain. One way out would be 16...Nc4 17.Qc3 Rc8 18.Qxc4 Rxc7 but Black certainly can't speak of an edge after 19.Qxf7.

Since girl-brain failed to find the optimal solution, let's try to calmly pose the problem verbally. Since the Rook is hanging (after 14...Kb8 15.Bf4+ Ka8 16.Bc7), ask "How can I get my Rook to safety without giving him time to take my Knight?"

Diagram 177a

Black to move

Put that way, the answer would probably hit you square between the eyes: 16...Rd5! saves the Rook and threatens white's Queen at the same time. In that case, Black retains her extra pawn and with it her control of the position.

ANSWER
PART FOUR
TEST 12

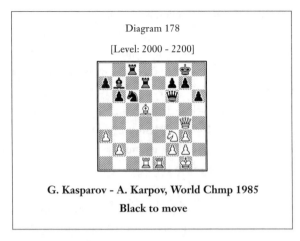

Diagram 178

[Level: 2000 - 2200]

G. Kasparov - A. Karpov, World Chmp 1985
Black to move

1.d4 Nf6 2.c4 e6 3.Nc3 Bb4 4.Nf3 0–0 5.Bg5 c5 6.e3 cxd4 7.exd4 h6 8.Bh4 d5 9.Rc1 dxc4 10.Bxc4 Nc6 11.0–0 Be7 12.Re1 b6 13.a3 Bb7 14.Bg3 Rc8 15.Ba2 Bd6 16.d5 Nxd5 17.Nxd5 Bxg3 18.hxg3 exd5 19.Bxd5 Qf6 20.Qa4 Rfd8 21.Rcd1 Rd7 22.Qg4

White threatens the d7-Rook, but why not end that threat and make a threat of your own at the same time? It's hard to argue with that logic, and 22...Rcd8 is as natural a move as one will ever see. However, it also involves one of our brain melting phrases: "He can't" (as in, "After I defend my Rook he can't take it."). The fact is that personal announcements that stop the thinking process and the process of proving an assertion are one of the main causes of tactical oversights. Yes, 22...Rcd8 makes perfect sense—*if it works*!

Whenever you notice tactical red flags in your position (in this case White has more active pieces, there are some back rank considerations, f7 is under pressure, d7 is hanging, and b7 is undefended) it's critical to prove any move you choose is good not just logically or strategically, but also tactically! These red flags demand that you make a bit more effort than usual in guarding against some hidden unpleasantness.

In the game Karpov decided 22...Rcd8 was not only the most logical move in the position, but that it also held up tactically. For example, 23.Re8+ (trying to make use of black's delicate back rank) 23...Rxe8 24.Qxd7 (attacking b7 and e8 at the same time) fails to 24...Re7. Unfortunately, 22...Rcd8 turned out to be one of the biggest blunders of his career! - Diagram 178

> **Explaining the Rating Spread**: A tricky tactic that even a World Champion missed? Perhaps I'm way off on the rating spread, and a 2000 player can't be expected to spot the danger?

22...Rcd8 23.Qxd7!

A different (this time effective!) way to punish black's back rank weakness and the loose b7-Bishop.

23...Rxd7 24.Re8+ Kh7 25.Be4+, 1-0. The problem isn't just that White has two Rooks for a Queen, but he's also winning a black minor piece by force after 25...g6 26.Rxd7 Ba6 27.Bxc6 since 27...Qxc6 falls victim to 28.Rxf7 mate.

So was Black in trouble in diagram 178? No, he had pretty much equalized. If he had noticed the flaw in his 22...Rcd8, he would surely have found:

22...Rd6!

Battening down the hatches! Now the Queen defends d6, everything seems to be defending c6, and ...Rcd8 is once again "on" (but this time safe).

I should point out that 22...Re7? gets hammered due to the previously mentioned problems with f7 and b7: 23.Rxe7 Qxe7 24.Bxf7+! Qxf7 25.Rd7. This once again illustrates the tactical pitfalls lurking in the position and the care that was needed to avoid them!

23.Ba2

The solidity of black's position can be seen after 23.Re4 (threatening to slice and dice f7 with Rf4) 23...Rf8! 24.Rf4 Qd8 and all is well.

23...Rcd8 24.Rxd6 Rxd6

Diagram 178a

Black's okay

25.Re8+

I give this to illustrate one last try by White to milk the back rank. Quieter moves like 25.Qe4 just lead to equality: 25...g6 26.b4 Kg7 27.Bd5 Qd8, =.

25...Kh7 26.Qe4+ g6 27.Bd5 Kg7 28.b4 Rd7 29.Rg8+

Hoping for 29...Kxg8? 30.Qe8+ followed by 31.Qxd7.

29...Kh7!

Now ...Rxd5 followed by ...Kxg8 is threatened, so the Rook has to admit that its adventure has led to nothing.

30.Rf8

30.Re8 Nd8, =.

30...Kg7 31.Rg8+ Kh7, ½-½.

ANSWER
PART FOUR

TEST 13

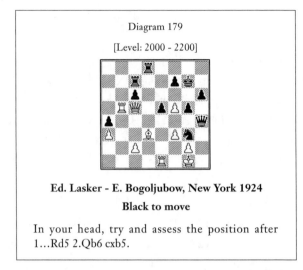

Diagram 179

[Level: 2000 - 2200]

Ed. Lasker - E. Bogoljubow, New York 1924

Black to move

In your head, try and assess the position after
1...Rd5 2.Qb6 cxb5.

1.e4 e5 2.Nf3 d6 3.d4 Nf6 4.Nc3 Nbd7 5.Bc4 Be7 6.O-O O-O 7.Bg5 c6
8.Bb3 h6 9.Bh4 Re8 10.Qd3 Nh5 11.Qc4 Rf8 12.Bxe7 Qxe7 13.Ne2 a5 14.Qc3
a4 15.Bc4 b5 16.Bd3 Bb7 17.dxe5 dxe5 18.Rad1 Rfe8 19.Ng3 Nxg3 20.hxg3
Nf6 21.Nh4 g6 22.Qd2 Kg7 23.Qe3 Ng4 24.Qd2 Qc5 25.Be2 Nf6 26.Bd3 Rad8
27.Qe2 Bc8 28.Kh1 Bg4 29.f3 Be6 30.a3 Re7 31.Rde1 Qd4 32.Qf2 Qxb2 33.Qc5
Rc7 34.Rb1 Qd4 35.Rxb5 g5 36.Nf5+ Bxf5 37.exf5 Nh5 38.Re1 Nxg3+ 39.Kh2
Qh4+ 40.Kg1 - Diagram 179

The move played in the game was 40...f6?, which is a mistake (The finish was
41.Rxe5 fxe5 42.Qxe5+ Kg8 43.Rb4 Qh1+ 44.Kf2 Rf7 45.Rb8?? [45.Kxg3 would
have won.] 45...Rxb8 46.Qxb8+ Kg7 47.Qe5+ Kf8 48.Qb8+ Kg7 49.Qe5+, ½-½.).
Alekhine (who annotated all the games in this event in the classic tournament book)
had this to say: "Here, however, he falters when almost near the goal and in so doing
exposes himself to the danger of losing. With 40...Rd5 41.Qb6 cxb5 42.Qxc7 Qd4+
(not 42...Nxf5 at once, on account of 43.Re4) 43.Kh2 Nxf5 44.Re4 (If 44.Bxf5, mate
follows in four moves) 44...Qc5, the game, thanks to two extra pawns, would have
been easily won for Black."

> **Explaining the Rating Spread**: I think a 1400 can follow those two
> moves in his head, but that's where the fun begins! The illusion that fol-
> lows can easily affect players of all strengths.

Did you, after 40...Rd5 41.Qb6 cxb5, also go on autopilot and snap off the c7-Rook
with 42.Qxc7?

It turns out that Alekhine's analysis is a complete mess. However, let's just concentrate on the position after 40...Rd5 41.Qb6 cxb5?? - see diagram 179a

I think a lot of readers would play 42.Qxc7?? and then try to assess the resulting
position. Both 41...cxb5 and 42.Qxc7 were taken for granted by Alekhine, yet both
are extreme blunders—41...cxb5?? allows a mate in four by 42.f6+ Kf8 43.Qb8+,
and 42.Qxc7?? misses the mate entirely. How could one of the greatest players, and
greatest calculators, of all time have made such mistakes? Well, he did worship the
god Bacchus, so I suppose that inebriation could be given as an excuse. And he was

also known to write a lot of his material without use of a board (he did the analysis in his head and then just wrote it down). But my theory is far simpler: he was a victim of "He has to" or "He must" (as in, "Black has to take on b5 and then White has to take on c7."). Once you get into that mindset, you simply continue with it—thus the first "Black has to take" led effortlessly to the "and White has to recapture" that followed.

Diagram 179a

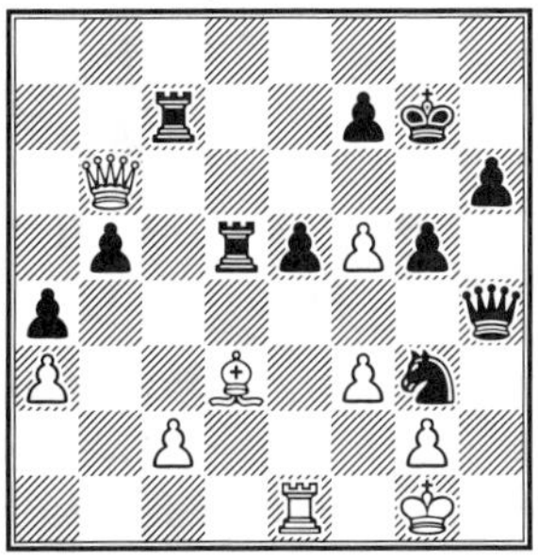

White to move

This brings us to an excellent training recommendation: After playing in an event, sit down and annotate all your games in depth. Don't only input the moves! Also write down why you played them, why you made all your decisions (plus write down why you felt your opponent made his choices). *Don't* use an engine until *after* you finish your analysis! Once your notes are complete, use an engine (or go over them with your chess teacher). You might be surprised to find that you fell victim to "I can't" or "He had to" over and over again. Once you see this happening in your own games, you personalize the problem and can then begin the process of rectifying it.

To finish up, Alekhine was right about 40...Rd5, but after 41.Qb6 Black had to play 41...Rxb5! 42.Bxb5 Qd4+ 43.Qxd4 exd4 44.Bxa4 Nxf5 and White would be in serious trouble.

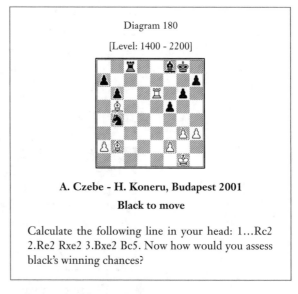

Diagram 180

[Level: 1400 - 2200]

A. Czebe - H. Koneru, Budapest 2001

Black to move

Calculate the following line in your head: 1...Rc2 2.Re2 Rxe2 3.Bxe2 Bc5. Now how would you assess black's winning chances?

1.Nf3 Nf6 2.d4 e6 3.e3 b6 4.Bd3 Bb7 5.0–0 Be7 6.b3 0–0 7.Bb2 c5 8.c4 cxd4 9.exd4 d5 10.Nc3 Nc6 11.Rc1 Rc8 12.Qe2 Nb4 13.Bb1 dxc4 14.bxc4 Bxf3 15.Qxf3 Rxc4 16.d5 Nbxd5 17.Rfd1 Qc8 18.Ne4 Rxc1 19.Rxc1 Qd7 20.Qg3 Rc8 21.Re1 Qb5 22.Qe5 Qd7 23.Bd3 Bf8 24.h3 Nxe4 25.Qxe4 f5 26.Qxe6+ Qxe6 27.Rxe6 g6 28.g3 Nb4 29.Bb5 - Diagram 180

Black was almost certainly winning earlier in the game, but though she gave away a good part of her advantage, she's still in charge and can confidently look forward to either a win or draw. Like you just did, she noticed the forcing 29...Rc2 ("I played 29...Rc2, White defends everything with 30.Re2, I take, she has to take back, I play ...Bc5 and then grind away forever hoping to win.") and decided that it simplified into an endgame that offered some chances of success, though white's two Bishops (and the constant dream of exchanging white's dark-squared Bishop for the Knight, which creates opposite colored Bishops and a likely draw) offered reasonable defensive chances.

Explaining the Rating Spread: More trickery from your evil author. As it turns out, I was setting a trap for you, the poor reader (Don't hate me! Consider it tough love!). Did I catch you in it?

The game continued according to Miss Koneru's plan:

29...Rc2 30.Re2 Rxe2??

Here Black was expecting 31.Bxe2 since White clearly "had to take back." Sadly, something else occurred!

31.Bc4+, 1-0. It's mate after 31...Re6 32.Bxe6. Many players have been put on suicide watch when nightmares like this happen! But *why* did it happen? And, if you fell for the same thing, why did you miss the obvious mate? The answer is simple: once you embrace "He has to" then you see nothing except your own self-imposed lie.

ANSWER
PART FOUR

TEST 15

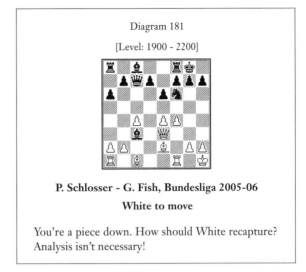

Diagram 181

[Level: 1900 - 2200]

P. Schlosser - G. Fish, Bundesliga 2005-06

White to move

You're a piece down. How should White recapture? Analysis isn't necessary!

1.Nf3 Nf6 2.c4 e6 3.Nc3 c5 4.e4 Nc6 5.Be2 a6 6.0–0 Qc7 7.d4 cxd4 8.Nxd4 Nxd4 9.Qxd4 Bd6 10.Kh1 Be5 11.Qe3 0–0 12.f4 Bxc3 - Diagram 181

> **Explaining the Rating Spread**: The game itself is extremely advanced, but the real purpose of this example is to show how falling into "I have to recapture" mode can blind you to possibilities that deserve at least a bit of exploration.

The only moves that can even be remotely considered are 13.bxc3, 13.Qxc3, and 13.e5. Everything else just loses a piece for nothing. If you noticed all three, then you solved the problem (even if you thought that 13.e5 had to be garbage, the fact that you noticed its existence is important). However, many players will have missed 13.e5 as a result of being in "I have to recapture" mode.

White's down a piece and it's obvious that he "must" get it back. However, it turns out that there are three playable ways to do this:

> ▸ 13.Qxc3 allows 13...Nxe4, but White gets some compensation on the dark squares after 14.Qd4 f5 (14...Nf6!?) 15.Be3.

> ▸ 13.bxc3 is the move that occurred in the actual game: 13...d6? (13...e5 is better) 14.Ba3 Rd8 15.Rad1 Ne8 16.e5 dxe5 17.Qxe5 Rd7 18.Kg1 Qxe5 19.fxe5 Rb8 20.c5 f6 21.c4 Nc7 22.Bf3 fxe5 23.Bb2, 1-0.

Both these moves fall within the confines of the "I have to recapture my piece right away!" mindset. But our third choice, which also regains the piece, is something that's far harder to find.

13.e5!!

So much for "I have to recapture." Of course, this is an extremely advanced example. Don't let it depress you (no, I don't expect you to play moves like 13.e5). Instead, use it as an illustration that shows how a blanket "I have to" can affect players of every level. If "I have to" even torments grandmasters, then you can rest assured that it's a large part of everyone's game—it's a serious disease that few even realize exists!

13...Bxe5?!

Other possibilities:

- ➤ 13...Bxb2? 14.Bxb2 Ne8 and now 15.Ba3 is, of course, both obvious and strong, but 15.c5!? is an interesting choice since it leaves the black army in prison for a long time to come.

- ➤ 13...Bb4? 14.exf6 gxf6 15.Qg3+ Kh8 16.Qh4 Qd8 17.f5 Rg8 18.Rf3 Rg7 19.Rh3 Be7 20.Bh6 Rg8 (20...Qg8 holds out longer, but is also horrible) 21.Bf8! mates.

- ➤ 13...Nd5? 14.cxd5 Bb4 15.d6 and White's advantage (space!) is obvious.

- ➤ 13...d5!? is interesting.

- ➤ 13...Ne4!? might be best: 14.Qxe4 f5 15.Qd3 Bb4 and though White is better, Black is still alive and kicking.

14.fxe5 Ne8 15.Bd2 f6

Also possible is 15...d6, but then White claims a hefty plus with 16.Bb4 a5 17.Ba3 dxe5 (there's nothing better since 17...f6 would be met by 18.Qd3! when either capture on e5 leads to the loss of the h7-pawn—18...fxe5 19.Rxf8+ Kxf8 20.Qxh7 and 18...dxe5 19.Bxf8 Kxf8 20.Qxh7) 18.Bd3! (clearing the e-file with tempo) when both 18...f5 and 18...h6 lose the Exchange *and* the e5-pawn to 19.Bxf8 Kxf8 20.Rae1.

16.Bh5!! and White comes out with at least a large advantage in every line:

- ➤ 16...Qxe5 17.Qxe5 fxe5 18.Rxf8+ Kxf8 19.Bb4+ d6 20.Rf1+ Nf6 21.Bxd6+ Kg8 22.Bf3 when Black's in a serious bind: 22...Nd7 (22...e4 23.Bxe4) 23.Kg1 and it's hard for Black to find useful moves.

- ➤ 16...f5 17.Bb4.

- ➤ 16...g6 17.exf6 Nxf6 (17...gxh5? 18.Qg5+ Kh8 19.f7 is game over, while 17...d6 18.Qg5 Qf7 19.Be2 is also most unpleasant for Black) 18.Bc3!! (Punishing black's dark-square weaknesses) 18...Nxh5 (18...Qd8 19.Bxg6 hxg6 20.Qg5 Kg7 21.Rxf6 and Black has to part with his Queen by 21...Qxf6 since 21...Rxf6 22.Rf1 is even worse.) 19.Qd4 e5 20.Qd5+ and Black can resign.

Part Four / Psychological Meanderings — Macho Chess

ANSWER
PART FOUR
TEST 16

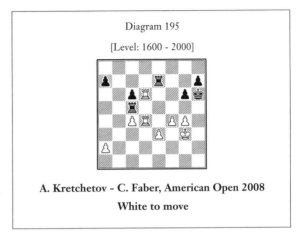

Diagram 195

[Level: 1600 - 2000]

A. Kretchetov - C. Faber, American Open 2008

White to move

1.Nf3 f5 2.g3 Nf6 3.Bg2 d6 4.d4 g6 5.b3 Bg7 6.Bb2 0–0 7.Nbd2 e5 8.dxe5 Ng4 9.Nc4 d5 10.Na3 c6 11.0–0 Qe7 12.c4 Be6 13.h3 Nh6 14.Qc1 Nf7 15.Nd4 dxc4 16.Nxe6 Qxe6 17.Qxc4 Qxc4 18.Nxc4 b5 19.e6 bxc4 20.exf7+ Rxf7 21.Bxg7 Kxg7 22.bxc4 Rc7 23.Rfd1 Na6 24.Rd6 Rac8 25.Rad1 Nc5 26.g4 fxg4 27.hxg4 Kh6 28.Kh2 Re8 29.e3 Ne4 30.Bxe4 Rxe4 31.R1d4 Re5 32.Kg3 Rc5 33.f4 Re7 - Diagram 195

Black has just played 33...Re7, threatening to take the e3-pawn with check. This would convince many players to "obey" and defend the pawn, but Kretchetov refused to give the "threat" any respect and instead went ahead with his own agenda while ignoring black's.

> **Explaining the Rating Spread**: The threat of a capture with check would freak out many players, and it would be perfectly understandable if they decided to keep things safe by any one of a number of solid choices.

34.Rd7!

Moves such as 34.e4 and 34.g5+ Kg7 35.Rd7 Kf7 also win (though in this last line, black's King has been allowed to join in the defense), but 34.Rd7 snuffs out all real resistance.

34...Rxe3+

Suicide, but 34...Rxd7 35.g5+ Kg7 36.Rxd7+ Kg8 37.Rxa7 was also completely hopeless.

35.Kh4 g5+

White threatened to mate by g4-g5. Desperate, Black tries to fend off the inevitable, but it (and every other possible move) turns out to be ineffective.

36.fxg5+ Rxg5 37.R4d6+, 1-0. It's still mate after 37...Rg6 38.g5 mate.

ANSWER
PART FOUR

TEST 17

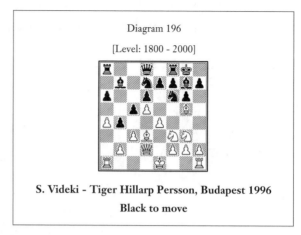

Diagram 196

[Level: 1800 - 2000]

S. Videki - Tiger Hillarp Persson, Budapest 1996

Black to move

1.e4 g6 2.d4 Bg7 3.Nc3 d6 4.Bg5 a6 5.Nf3 b5 6.Qd2 Bb7 7.Bd3 Nd7 8.a4 b4 9.Ne2 c5 10.c3 Ngf6 11.Ng3 0–0 12.d5 - Diagram 196

This is an important moment for Black. White has more central space and, if allowed, will play c3-c4 when the b7-Bishop is a nonentity and hopes of queenside play by Black will be a lot dimmer than they were a moment before. So, how can Black make sure that he obtains active pieces and good overall chances?

One quite reasonable idea is 12...e6 (maintaining queenside options while striking out at the center) when 13.c4 exd5 14.cxd5 (14.exd5? Re8+ 15.Be2 Nb6 16.0-0 h6 17.Bf4 Ne4 gives Black far too much activity, while 17.Bxh6 Rxe2! 18.Nxe2 Nxc4 19.Qc1 Bxh6 20.Qxh6 Bxd5 is in black's favor) is about equal, and 13.dxe6 fxe6 14.0-0 leaves Black with nice center pawns (...d6-d5 would build a large central front) while White hopes to pressure them and prove that the "nice" center pawns are actually targets (moves like Rfd1, Bf4, and or Bc4 will all be possible ways to prove his point).

Tiger, a very aggressive player, felt he should be able to get more than 12...e6 offered, and he immediately strove to push his own agenda in the most dynamic way possible.

> **Explaining the Rating Spread**: A 1400 player might well toss out the excellent 12...e6. But the move I'm really looking for is a much harder proposition.

12...c4!

Taking his fate into his own hands! This move gets his hoped for queenside play under way (After 12...c4 it's no longer "hoped for," it's now a reality!), and frees the c5-square for the d7-Knight. If White retreats the Bishop then Black has gained time, while if White captures on c4 the c-file will be opened and Black gains additional time with ...Rc8.

13.Bxc4

In the actual game White refused to take up the challenge and ended up in some trouble right away: 13.Bc2 b3 14.Bd1 Nc5 15.Bxf6 exf6 16.Be2 He should have gotten his King out of Dodge while the getting was good. Now it's too late: 16...Re8 17.Bxc4 Nxe4 18.Nxe4 Rxe4+ 19.Be2 Qe8 20.Nd4 f5 21.Nc6 Bh6 22.Qd1 a5 23.Kf1 Rxe2 24.Qxe2 Ba6 (The rest can be titled "Death by Bishops!") 25.c4 Qxe2+

26.Kxe2 Bxc4+ 27.Kd1 Kf8 28.Nd4 Bxd5 29.f3 Be3 30.Nb5 Rc8 31.Re1 f4 32.Na3
Bb7 33.Rxe3 fxe3 34.Ke2 Ba6+ 35.Kxe3 Re8+ 36.Kd2 Re2+ 37.Kc3 Rxg2 38.Nb5
Rxh2 39.Rd1 Ke7, 0-1.

After 13.Bxc4 Black has to make a decision: should he play 13...Qc7, 13...Rc8, or
first take on c3? Personally I feel that 13...Rc8 is the most flexible choice since the
immediate 13...bxc3 14.bxc3 Rc8 gives White the additional possibility of 15.Qa2.
Since I'm just trying to show some of black's dynamic possibilities here, we'll settle
for the immediate Rook move.

13...Rc8 14.Bb3

Black has to be happy after 14.b3 bxc3 15.Qc2, when both 15...h6 and 15...Nb6
give him excellent play.

White might consider 14.Ba2!? bxc3 15.bxc3 when Black will have the usual choice
between 15...Nc5!? and 15...Nxd5 (which transposes into 14.Bb3 bxc3 15.bxc3 Nxd5).

14...bxc3 15.bxc3 Nc5!?

This natural move makes use of the square clearing 12...c4 and places the Knight
on an excellent post. The alternative is the complicated 15...Nxd5!? 16.Bxd5! Bxc3
17.Bxb7 Bxd2+ 18.Bxd2 when White has three minor pieces for a Queen. However,
Black is probably still a bit better after 18...Rc2 19.Bxa6 Nc5 20.Bb5 Nb3 21.Rd1
Nxd2 22.Rxd2 Qa5 23.Ke2 Rfc8 because white's minor pieces aren't working together
in any dynamic way and white's King is a bit exposed.

16.Qc2 Rb8 17.Rb1 Bc8 18.0-0 Bd7 19.Nd4 Qc7 20.Ba2 and now 20...Bxa4
can't be bad, while the building move 20...Rfc8 also offers Black nice play.

ANSWER
PART FOUR
TEST **18**

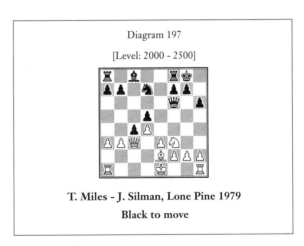

Diagram 197

[Level: 2000 - 2500]

T. Miles - J. Silman, Lone Pine 1979

Black to move

**1.d4 Nf6 2.Nf3 e6 3.c4 d5 4.Nc3 Bb4 5.Bg5 h6 6.Bxf6 Qxf6 7.e3 0-0 8.Qb3
c5 9.cxd5 exd5 10.a3 Bxc3+ 11.Qxc3 Nd7 12.Be2 c4 13.b3** - Diagram 197

> <u>**Explaining the Rating Spread**</u>: This game mixes positional power grabs
> and a striving for controlled dynamics with detailed tactics. For example,
> seeing 13...b5 without understanding what must follow isn't good enough.
> In other words, it's advanced (but highly instructive) stuff.

The late Tony Miles was a far better player than I ever was, but that's no excuse for the horrible psychological dive I made in this game. When entering the position in diagram 197, I had intended to play 13...b5! 14.a4 Nc5!? 15.Nd2 (15.bxc4 bxc4 16.0-0 Ne4 17.Qa5 Qd8 favors Black) 15...Bf5 16.axb5 Nd3+ 17.Bxd3 Bxd3 18.bxc4 dxc4, but then I got spooked by 19.f3 when white's King will sit comfortably on f2 (I wasn't worried about 19.Nxc4 Qg6). I immediately suffered through an emotional crash, thinking that all my calculations were garbage. I suddenly lost faith in myself; after all, I was playing Miles and he had undoubtedly seen and rejected my whole line. Filled with self-loathing, I raised the flag of positional surrender with 13...cxb3? and died like a coward with no play and no hope: 14.Qxb3 (Black has a passive game due to his three pawn islands—b7 and d5 are under pressure, a3-a4-a5 will chase black's Knight if it moves to b6, and 0-0 followed by Rfc1 can easily lead to White penetrating down the c-file.) 14...Qd6 15.Qb4 Qb8 16.0–0 Nf6 17.Rfc1 Bg4 18.Rab1 Bf5 19.Rb3 Rc8 20.Rxc8+ Bxc8 21.Qe7 Bd7 22.Ne5 Qe8 23.Qxe8+ Bxe8 24.Rxb7 Rc8 25.f3 a5 26.Bb5 Rc3 27.a4 Rxe3 28.Ra7 Bxb5 29.axb5 Ra3 30.b6 Rb3 31.b7 Kh7 32.Nc6 Nd7 33.Nxa5 Rb4 34.Ra8 Rb5 35.Rd8 Rxa5 36.Rxd7 Rb5 37.Rxf7 Kg6 38.Rc7 Kf6 39.h4, 1-0. After the game I showed him my intended variation (13...b5 14.a4 Nc5) up to 19.f3. He said, "I didn't see any of that!"

I was guilty of a number of crimes:

- ▶ I bowed to "I can't."

- ▶ I irrationally feared the "all seeing eye" of the superior opponent.

- ▶ Once I noticed something that hadn't occurred to me, I immediately gave up on my variation. Remember: if you don't defend your analysis, who will?

The fact is that the unimaginative (lazy) 13...cxb3 is just a bad move. Rather than accept a passive position with long-term positional woes, it was my job to wave my fist at the "easy way out" and demand more from myself—I needed to make my original intention work since it offered active pieces and a somewhat unstable white King for me to gnaw on.

Such "key" moments occur often, and find you balancing between heroism and doubt. The lines you might look at don't need to be complicated, but they *do* need a confident general to make them work.

As it turned out, my intended variation was fully playable: 13...b5! 14.a4 Nc5!? 15.Nd2 Bf5 16.axb5 Nd3+ 17.Bxd3 Bxd3 18.bxc4 dxc4 19.f3 and now 19...a6! offers Black enough counterplay: 20.b6 (20.bxa6 Rxa6 21.Rxa6 Qxa6 22.Kf2 Ra8 23.Rc1 Qa2 23.Kg3 Ra3 25.Qb4 Ra4 with a draw) 20...Qxb6 21.Kf2 Rfc8, =.

However, let's say that 19.f3 did favor White. Is that the end of the story? Perhaps, perhaps not. The only way to know for sure is to look for earlier improvements after the combative **13...b5 14.a4**. I didn't do this and got what I deserved. But if I had looked at that position with a confident eye, I would have noticed that there was a whole world that I was missing:

Diagram 197a

What's really going on here?

 **14...Nc5!? 15.Nd2 Nd3+** (We've already seen that 15...Bf5 was playable. But 15...Nd3+ is also very interesting!) **16.Bxd3 cxd3 17.0-0** (17.Qxd3 b4! is dangerous for White since 18.Qb5 Qe6 19.Qxb4 Ba6 makes Black ruler of the light-squares) **17...bxa4 18.Rxa4 Qg6** with a complicated game in store.

14...b4! This is far more obvious than 14...Nc5. It's hard to explain how I could have missed it. **15.Qxb4 Rb8 16.Qa5 cxb3** and the powerful passed b-pawn gives Black a good game: **17.0–0 b2 18.Rab1 Qd6** when moves such as ...Qb4 or ...Qa3 will cement the pawn.

ANSWER
PART FOUR

TEST **19**

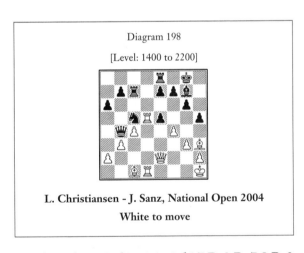

Diagram 198

[Level: 1400 to 2200]

L. Christiansen - J. Sanz, National Open 2004

White to move

1.c4 c5 2.Nf3 Nc6 3.Nc3 Nf6 4.d4 cxd4 5.Nxd4 g6 6.e4 d6 7.Be2 Bg7 8.Be3 O-O 9.O-O Bd7 10.Qd2 Re8 11.Nc2 Rc8 12.f3 Qa5 13.Rfd1 Be6 14.Rac1 h5 15.Qe1 Nd7 16.Na1 Nde5 17.b3 a6 18.Kh1 Nd7 19.Bd2 Qc5 20.Nc2 Nd4 21.Nxd4 Bxd4 22.Bf1 Bf2 23.Qe2 Bh4 24.Be3 Qa5 25.Nd5 Bxd5 26.Rxd5 Qa3 27.Rcd1 Bf6 28.f4 Nc5 29.g3 Bg7 30.Bc1 Qb4 31.Bh3 Rc7 32.e5 dxe5 - Diagram 198

Here Black expected White to recapture the e5-pawn, following the old, "I take you and you take me" paradigm. However, Christiansen (one of the greatest attacking players in U.S. history) is not someone who does anyone's bidding on the chessboard!

Explaining the Rating Spread: A surprising rating spread! How is such a thing possible? Well, the first move, not making the autopilot re-capture, is what I expect from readers of this book in the 1400 class. But Christiansen's lovely tactical follow up is something that might be missed by players of a very high class.

33.Rd8

White will only recapture on e5 if a lull in the action appears that allows him to take without any loss of initiative or momentum.

33...Rxd8 34.Rxd8+ Kh7

34...Bf8 loses right away to 35.Qxe5 when the double threat of 36.Qxc7 and 36.Rxf8+ Kxf8 37.Qh8 mate ends the game.

35.Qxh5+!!

The surprising point of white's play! Now 35...gxh5 leads to the pretty 36.Bf5+ Kh6 37.fxe5+ (*Now* I'll recapture that pawn!) 37...Qd2 38.Bxd2 mate.

35...Bh6 36.Qxe5

A perfect time to recapture the e-pawn—the white Queen not only took a pawn, it also attacks c7, threatens mate on h8, and prevents ...Qe1+.

36...Bg7 37.Qe2

Diagram 198a

Many players get so caught up in their attack that they will want to continue in an aggressive vein even if the situation has changed. Of course, if you can profitably bash the opponent some more, then by all means do so. However, usually a successful raid leaves one's pieces scattered about—they no longer work together for any particular goal. If that occurs, it's best to regroup, make sure your King is safe, and only then push on in an attempt to acquire new gains.

In the position after 36...Bg7 White has a solid extra pawn and two rampaging Bishops. There isn't any reason whatsoever to risk anything here! Yes, a Rook can be captured but that leaves your King to fend for itself. Indeed, after 37.Qxc7? Qe1+ 38.Kg2 Ne6 White loses his iron grip on the position. An example of what might occur: 39.Qb6 Qe4+ 40.Kf1 Nxd8 (Even 40...Bd4!? 41.Rxd4 Nxd4 42.Bg2 Qd3+ 43.Kg1 Ne2+ 44.Kf2 Nxc1 45.Qe3 Qb1 allows Black to battle on) 41.Qxd8 Qh1+ 42.Kf2 Qxc1 43.Qxe7 Bd4+ 44.Kf3 Kg7 and the presence of opposite colored Bishops mixed with the vulnerable white King would have been something best avoided.

White's 37.Qe2 is far more sensible than the madness resulting from 37.Qxc7. White stops all enemy counterplay before it even starts and let's his opponent know that he won't be given any chance to recover from his horrible situation.

37...e6

This move, which seems to tighten up black's position, actually allows another tactical run by White. Better was 37...Qc3, though the position was lost in any case.

38.f5!

Very strong! This move frees the c1-Bishop and threatens to disrupt black's kingside pawn structure.

38...exf5?

Black missed white's reply, which allowed the spectators to get a bit of a thrill!

39.Qh5+!! Sacrificing itself on h5 for the second time! Black resigned since it's mate next move: 39...Bh6 40.Qxh6 mate or 39...gxh5 40.Bxf5 mate. Lovely!

ANSWER
PART FOUR
TEST **20**

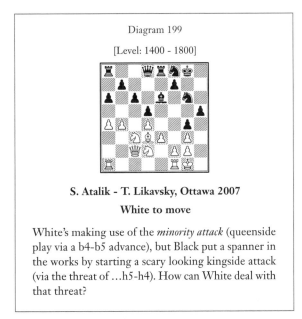

Diagram 199

[Level: 1400 - 1800]

S. Atalik - T. Likavsky, Ottawa 2007

White to move

White's making use of the *minority attack* (queenside play via a b4-b5 advance), but Black put a spanner in the works by starting a scary looking kingside attack (via the threat of ...h5-h4). How can White deal with that threat?

1.d4 d5 2.c4 e6 3.Nc3 a6 4.cxd5 exd5 5.Bf4 c6 6.e3 Bd6 7.Bg3 Ne7 8.Qc2 Bf5 9.Qb3 Ra7 10.Nf3 0-0 11.Be2 Re8 12.0-0 Bxg3 13.hxg3 Nd7 14.Nh4 Be6 15.Qc2 Ra8 16.Bd3 Nf8 17.b4 g5 18.Nf3 Neg6 19.a4 g4 20.Nd2 h5 - Diagram 199

How should White deal with black's not-so-subtle kingside demonstration? Simple—ignore it and send a message that you think your queenside play is more important!

> **Explaining the Rating Spread**: Did you blink and fall to your knees in the face of black's attack, or did you send a message about the superiority of your own plans? Since this section is about pushing your own agenda, I have full confidence that my 1400 rated readers will show Black who's boss!

21.b5!

This move does more than just continuing with your chosen plan (which is important to do), it shows your opponent that you're not worried about his kingside display and it also puts your own brain on track by telling it that fear won't be accepted and you'll only respond to your opponent if there's a real threat to deal with!

For those who aren't familiar with the well-trodden minority attack, here's a quick primer: White uses two pawns (his a- and b-pawns) to attack an enemy pawn majority (since it's 2 pawns vs. 3). The goal is to open lines on the queenside (the files allow white's Rooks to penetrate into the enemy position, while the c5-square can easily become a nice home to one of white's Knights) and, after a mutual capture on c6, to create a permanent pawn weakness that White can attack right into the endgame.

21...h4

Black doesn't blink either. He knows that if he doesn't get something going against white's King, he'll end up defending passively on the queenside forever.

22.gxh4 Qxh4 23.bxc6 bxc6 24.Ne2

A very nice move—the Knight retreat accomplishes two things at once: it allows its Queen to create an immediate threat against c6 (which means that 24.Ne2 was an attacking move) and it also prevents ...g4-g3 (which means that it was a defensive move too).

24...Kg7 25.Rfb1

Diagram 199a

White knows that he will have the game firmly in hand (black's queenside weaknesses aren't going away) if he can prevent the enemy threats from becoming a reality. Of course, he could have chopped on c6, but that would have allowed his opponent to swing a Rook to h8 (after the f8-Knight moves) and pray for a knockout blow. Instead he plays another duel purpose move: 25.Rfb1 places the Rook into attacking position on the queenside while also freeing the f1-square for the other Knight—by setting up a firm defense, Black will be left with no hope at all.

25...Nd7 26.Nf1 Rh8 27.Nfg3

The h1-square is covered and black's attack will run out of steam without ever making White break a sweat.

27...Qh2+ 28.Kf1 Nh4 29.Nf4

And, by defending g2, the attack and the game are over.

29...Rhc8

A sad move—Black renounces his bad intentions on the kingside and switches into pure defensive mode. However, it's a bit too late for that.

30.Ke2!

Suddenly Black wakes up to the fact that his Queen and h4-Knight might have wandered too far into enemy territory! White's threat of 31.Rh1 is a showstopper.

30...Nxg2 31.Ngh5+, 1-0. 32.Rh1 follows, winning the Queen.

ANSWER
PART FOUR
TEST 21

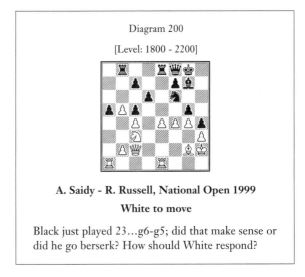

Diagram 200

[Level: 1800 - 2200]

A. Saidy - R. Russell, National Open 1999

White to move

Black just played 23...g6-g5; did that make sense or did he go berserk? How should White respond?

1.d4 Nf6 2.c4 g6 3.g3 Bg7 4.Bg2 d6 5.Nf3 0–0 6.Nc3 Nbd7 7.0–0 e5 8.e4 exd4 9.Nxd4 Re8 10.h3 a6 11.Be3 Rb8 12.a4 Nc5 13.Qc2 a5 14.Rad1 Bd7 15.Ndb5 b6 16.Rfe1 h6 17.f4 Bxb5 18.axb5 Qe7 19.Bf2 Qf8 20.Kh2 h5 21.Bxc5 bxc5 22.Ra1 h4 23.g4 g5 - Diagram 200

After 23.g4 Black, seeing that his a5-pawn was toast, decided to play for a "Hail Mary" and gave 23...g5 a shot. Against best play this move actually hastens his demise (23...Nd7 was more resilient, when the ...g5 idea might come at a better moment), but Mr. Russell deserves credit for it nonetheless—by offering a pawn Black hopes to gain several positional trumps and, ideally, a bit of counterplay.

The move also has some psychological impact. International Master Anthony Saidy, an American chess legend, was feeling very confident—he had completely outplayed his lower rated opponent and expected a trouble free victory. When 23...g5 was played, I can imagine Dr. Saidy refusing to give the move any credit at all. On the other hand, Black had already put his poor opening play behind him and had announced to his opponent that, "I don't intend to go quietly into that dark night!"

So what's good about 23...g5? A glance at the position after 23.g4 will tell you that White has much more space and he's about to eat a free pawn (a5). On the other side of the board, it's hard to see where black's play is coming from—none of his pieces have any advanced squares to call their own. With that in mind, one can begin to understand the point of the 23...g5 pawn sacrifice: after 24.fxg5 Nh7 the Knight will take up residence on g5, the Bishop will rule the board on e5, and the dark-squares around white's King are suddenly severely weakened. In other words, even though Black might be clearly worse after 23...g5 24.fxg5, his pieces will find some activity and he'll have some imbalances that he can be proud of.

> **Explaining the Rating Spread**: If you saw what Black was after, and if you were macho (and wise) enough to deprive him of his hoped for positional/dynamic trumps, then you should feel really good about yourself. Though I started the spread at 1800, if those in the lower rating groups also got on top of this problem, then expect a rapid rise up the rating ladder! Of course, you shouldn't feel any shame if you didn't solve it since Saidy himself failed to do so in the actual game.

So a subtle psychological shift had occurred, and White didn't catch it. In the actual game Saidy chopped on g5, missed several big chances, and ultimately fell victim to his dark-squared weaknesses: 24.fxg5 Nh7 25.Nd5 Be5+ 26.Kh1 Rbc8 27.Rxa5 Nxg5 28.Ra7 Ne6 29.Rf1 Ra8 30.Rxa8 Rxa8 31.Qf2 Bg3 32.Nf6+ Kh8 33.Qf5 Qh6 34.Nh5? (34.e5! was very strong, opening the h1-a8 diagonal for the white's Bishop and also giving white's Knight access to the e4-square) 34...Be5 35.Qf2 Ng5 36.Qxh4 Ra2 37.Rb1 Kg8 38.Qf2 Qg6 39.Qc2 Kf8 40.Qb3 Ra8 41.Re1 Ne6 42.Rf1 Nd4 43.Qe3 Ra2 44.Rb1 Ne6 45.Qb3 Ra8 46.Ng3 Qg5 47.Nf1 Qh4 48.Qe3 Ra2 49.Qe1 Qxe1 50.Rxe1 Rxb2 51.Rd1 Nf4 52.Rd2 Rb1 53.Rc2 Re1 54.Kg1 Bd4+ 55.Kh2 Ne2 56.Bf3 Be5+ 57.Kg2 Nf4+ 58.Kf2 Nd3+ 59.Kg2 Ra1 60.Re2 Nf4+ 61.Kf2 Nxe2 62.Bxe2 Ra2 63.Kf3 Ke7 64.Bd1 Ra3+ 65.Ke2 Bf4, 0-1. So Black was in trouble all the way through, but he had some weapons (the weapons he created with 23...g5) and, after various white mistakes, they came through for him.

Though 24.fxg5 retains a significant plus, White should have asked himself, "Why should I give my opponent anything of worth? Why does he deserve all that dark-square control? Why does he deserve any piece activity? Is there any way I can stomp this guy into jelly?" In fact, throwing in a "Kill!" wouldn't have hurt either!

If Saidy had held this dialogue with himself, he wouldn't have had any trouble finding a far better move:

24.e5!!

Now *this* is a macho move!

24...dxe5

No better is 24...Nd7 25.Bc6 Red8 26.Qf5.

25.fxg5 Nh7 - see diagram 200a

Do you see the difference between this position and the position that occurred in the game (via 24.fxg5 Nh7)? In the game position Black had access to the e5-square, his Bishop was very active, and white's Bishop was a horrible piece. By inserting 24.e5 dxe5 we've changed all that: now black's Bishop is dead, black's pieces don't have access to e5, white's Bishop rules the wide open h1-a8 diagonal, white's Knight has access to e4, and white's Queen is on a fast track to f5. By playing 24.e5 White deprived Black of everything he dreamed of getting while adding to his own already large list of advantages.

Diagram 200a

26.Qf5

Placing the Queen on a powerful square, defending g5, and threatening Be4. Also very strong was 26.g6.

26...Qe7 27.Bc6 Red8 28.Ne4

White has achieved a fairytale position: almost all of his pieces are ideally placed, all of black's pieces are unemployed, and the light-square blockade is a wonder to behold. If we add that black's pawns are weak and his King can easily fall to a mating attack (White can play Rf1 followed by Nf6+), one can see just how hopeless black's cause is.

To sum up: in the actual game White made his opponent happy with 24.fxg5 because it gave him a few stones to throw (meaning, it gave him hope). On the other hand, 24.e5 would have immediately deflated his opponent's dreams and left him with nothing but the misery of a passive, hopeless defense.

ANSWER
PART FOUR

TEST **22**

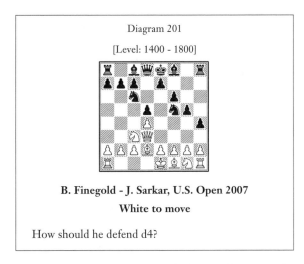

Diagram 201

[Level: 1400 - 1800]

B. Finegold - J. Sarkar, U.S. Open 2007

White to move

How should he defend d4?

1.d4 d5 2.Bg5 f6 3.Bh4 Nh6 4.Nc3 Nf5 5.Bg3 h5 6.Qd3 h4 7.Bf4 g5 8.Bd2 Nc6 - Diagram 201

Black's aggressive opening play has left him with kingside space but also kingside weaknesses. Both sides need to deal with their central King since things can get nasty if one side's monarch gets stuck in the middle while the other castles to safety. Since White can't afford to get too defensive (that would leave Black with an easy development and the aforementioned space), he has to take a stand and ignore black's pseudo-threats to d4.

Explaining the Rating Spread: King in the center, not bowing to enemy threats, pushing one's own agenda. If these things don't spur you into to action, then nothing will. I have full faith that my 1400 rated audience will shine here.

9.0-0-0!

So white's King has found a home and he's remained flexible—White can develop with Nf3, tighten with e3, or smash open the center with e4. The ball is now in black's court; how will he react to all of this?

9...Kf7

Black's King isn't completely happy here and I would think that he should have been able to do better than this. Since it's clear that 9...Nfxd4 10.Qg6+ has to be avoided, and that 9...Ncxd4 10.e3 Nc6 11.Qxd5 gives White a small but bothersome pull, one would deduce that Black should play with more energy—thus 9...Be6 makes a lot of sense (it covers the weakened light-squares and prepares to castle via ...Qd7 and ...0-0-0). In that case some really interesting complications could erupt that would test both sides' imaginations: 10.Nf3 g4 (10...Qd7, simply intending to castle, seems the most sane: 11.e4 dxe4 12.Qxe4 Nd6, =. Also interesting is 10...Nd6!?) 11.e4 and now:

➤ 11...Qd7 12.exd5 Bxd5 13.Nxd5 Qxd5 14.c4 Qd7 15.d5 has to make White happy.

➤ 11...dxe4 12.Qxe4 gxf3 13.Qxe6 Nfxd4 14.Qg4 and White is on top.

➤ 11...Nd6 (locking horns!) 12.exd5 Bf5 13.Qe3 Bh6 14.Qe1 Nb4 15.Bxh6 gxf3 16.g4! Bxc2 17.Bf4 Bxd1 (17...c6!?) 18.Qxd1 c6 (18...Na6 19.Qxf3) 19.Qa4 Nxd5 20.Nxd5 b5 21.Nxf6+ exf6 22.Qb4 Nc8 23.Bd3 and white's two killer Bishops (mixed with black's vulnerable King) leaves him with much the better of it.

10.e3 e5?

As you can see, when you stand up to your opponent's threats and force him to master the position or drown under it, more than a few players will crumble under the pressure! His 9...Kf7 was the first misstep, and 10...e5 is a serious error that loses a pawn. Instead, the sensible 10...Be6 would have been playable (developing and keeping everything firmly defended), though perhaps a bit more comfortable for White.

The rest of the game, though no longer fitting our theme, is quite exciting and well worth checking out: **11.dxe5 Nxe5 12.Qxd5+ Qxd5 13.Nxd5 c6 14.Nc3 Be6 15.Nf3 Nxf3 16.gxf3 h3 17.Ne4 Be7 18.Bc3 b5 19.b3 a5 20.Be2 a4 21.Kb1 axb3 22.cxb3 Rhb8 23.Rhg1 Rd8 24.f4 Rxd1+ 25.Bxd1 gxf4 26.Bh5+ Kf8 27.Nxf6 Bxf6 28.Bxf6 fxe3 29.fxe3 Nxe3 30.Re1?** (One gets the impression that mutual time pressure influenced the following moves. Correct was 30.Bd4 with a firm grip on the position.) **30...Bf5+ 31.Kb2 Nd5 32.Bd4?** (A serious mistake that loses his advantage. 32.Bh4 retained a plus.) **32...Kg8?** (Missing 32...Rxa2+! 33.Kxa2 Nb4+ 34.Kb2 Nd3+ 35.Kc3 Nxe1, =) **33.Re5** (33.Re8+ Rxe8 34.Bxe8) **33...Rf8 34.Bc5**

Nf4 35.Kc3 (35.Bxf8 Nd3+ 36.Kc3 Nxe5 37.Bd6 Ng4 38.Kd4 is winning) **35...Rf6 36.Bf3 Ne6 37.Be3 c5 38.Bc6 b4+ 39.Kc4 Kg7 40.Bd7 Nd4 41.Bxd4**, 1-0.

Part Four / Psychological Meanderings — Various States of Chess Consciousness

ANSWER
PART FOUR

TEST 23

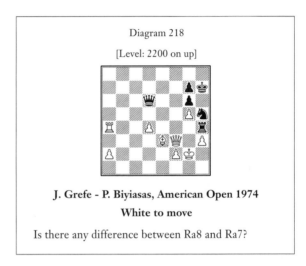

Diagram 218

[Level: 2200 on up]

J. Grefe - P. Biyiasas, American Open 1974

White to move

Is there any difference between Ra8 and Ra7?

1.e4 e5 2.Nf3 Nc6 3.Bb5 a6 4.Ba4 Nf6 5.O-O Be7 6.Qe2 b5 7.Bb3 d6 8.c3 O-O 9.d4 Bg4 10.Rd1 exd4 11.cxd4 d5 12.exd5 Nb4 13.h3 Bh5 14.Nc3 Re8 15.g4 Bg6 16.Ne5 Nbxd5 17.Nxd5 Nxd5 18.Qf3 Nf6 19.Nxg6 hxg6 20.g5 Nh5 21.Bxf7+ Kh7 22.Bxe8 Qxe8 23.Re1 Rd8 24.Qe4 Rd7 25.Be3 Qf7 26.b3 Bb4 27.Red1 Re7 28.Qg4 Qd5 29.Rac1 Re4 30.Qf3 Bd6 31.Kg2 Qe6 32.Rc6 a5 33.Rdc1 a4 34.bxa4 bxa4 35.R6c4 Qe8 36.Rxc7 Bxc7 37.Rxc7 Qe6 38.Ra7 Rh4 39.Rxa4 Qd6 - Diagram 218

This was a battle for first place. John Grefe, who won the U.S. Championship in 1973, was half a point behind his Canadian opponent (who won the Canadian Championship in 1972 and 1975) and needed a win to take the event. And, it seemed he was going to get it! He had outplayed Biyiasas, was three pawns up, and seemed well on his way to the American Open title.

Peter Biyiasas was famous for his defensive powers and his never-say-die attitude—he fought to the bitter end in every game he played. Be that as it may, nothing could have saved him if White had played 40.Ra7. However, how could an obviously strong move like 40.Ra8 be incorrect? The threat of Rf8 (ending all counterplay on f4) followed by Qa8 (creating a nasty mating threat) seems to end the game quickly.

> **Explaining the Rating Spread**: This is an extremely tough one and calls for calculation, inspiration, and a devious mind!

40.Ra8?? Nf4+ 41.Bxf4 Rxf4

Grefe had anticipated all this and had prepared something he thought was a clear winner.

After the game the spectators insisted that 41.Bxf4 was a blunder and that both 41.Kf1 and 41.Kg1 were winning, but it turns out that the game was drawn in any case:

➤ 41.Kf1 Qc7 with the idea of ...Qc4+ gives Black enough counterplay to draw.

➤ 41.Kg1 Nxh3+ 42.Kg2 (42.Kf1 Qb6 and White can't win) 42...Nxf2! draws while 42...Qe6 also suffices to hold the game.

42.Rd8

This is the move Grefe had counted on—surely Black would now resign? The idea is that 42...Qxd8 43.Qxf4 gives White a winning Queen endgame, while 42...Qc7 43.Rd7! also does the job.

White could also have tried 42.Ra6 but Black hangs on: 42...Qxd4 43.Qe3 (43.Qg3 Qd5+ 44.Kh2 Qd2, =) 43...Qd5+ 44.f3 Qxg5+ 45.Kh2 Qf5 46.Ra5 Qxa5 47.Qxf4 Qxa2+ with a draw.

42...Rg4+!

Diagram 218a

Has Black gone berserk? No, it's the point of his earlier play, which White completely missed.

43.Qxg4

And not 43.Kf1?? Qa6+ when Black wins! The only other try is 43.Kh1 but then we see a slightly different version of the same stalemate that occurs in the game: 43...Qh2+ 44.Kxh2 Rg2+ 45.Kh1 Rg1+, =.

43...Qg3+! The final point. The players agreed to a draw since 44.Kxg3 (44.Kf1 Qxf2+ 45.Kxf2 is the same result) leads to immediate stalemate. A stunning save! Our "pay attention" motto is very pertinent here, since White was not paying as much attention to his opponent's defensive chances as he should have. On the other hand, Black was playing close attention indeed to every possible trick the position offered him.

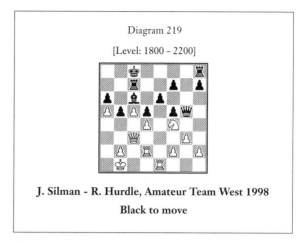

Diagram 219

[Level: 1800 - 2200]

J. Silman - R. Hurdle, Amateur Team West 1998

Black to move

1.d4 Nf6 2.Bg5 d6 3.Bxf6 gxf6 4.e3 c6 5.Bd3 d5 6.Qh5 e6 7.Ne2 Bd6 8.Nd2 Nd7 9.e4 Qc7 10.0-0-0 Bf4 11.g3 Bxd2+ 12.Rxd2 dxe4 13.Bxe4 f5 14.Bf3 Nf6 15.Qh6 Qe7 16.Qe3 Bd7 17.c4 Rc8 18.c5 Nd5 19.Bxd5 cxd5 20.Nf4 Bc6 21.Re1 Kd8 22.Kb1 Rc7 23.Qa3 a6 24.Qb4 Kc8 25.a4 b5!? (Black realized that he was going to die without a whimper, and he leapt at the chance to create a bit of chaos.) **26.a5** (Stronger was 26.axb5 axb5 (not 26...Bxb5?? 27.Nxd5) 27.Rd3 Ra7 28.Ra3, but the shock of his 25...b5 had shaken my equilibrium.) **26...Qg5 27.Qc3?**

Handing Black a chance for counterplay that he never should have been given. - Diagram 219

I sleepwalked through this game feeling (quite rightly) that I had an enormous positional advantage from move 10 onwards. However, I also felt that it was impossible to lose such a position and, as a result, I stopped paying full attention, expecting victory to happen by itself.

In the present position White has a far superior pawn structure, a significant space advantage on the queenside, and a powerful Knight vs. a Tall-Pawn (i.e., black's very bad Bishop). It's hard to find anything that Black can be happy about. As a result of all this "basking in the glory of my position," I got lazy, wrote my opponent off, and forgot that even a badly wounded animal can and will bite. Usually I'm very careful about avoiding enemy counterplay. However, here I just couldn't imagine him creating anything.

> **Explaining the Rating Spread**: The first thing Black has to do is realize that he's on death's door. Once he comes to terms with that, he'll be able to embrace guiltless desperation. Being honest about one's position and then being able to kick any and all soft moves away in favor of going for the gusto is far from easy.

27...b4!

A star move. Computers don't like it, but if black's pawn can't move to b4 then his pieces will be doomed to eternal passivity. In that case Black would have to wait around and pray that White can't find a winning plan in the center or on the kingside.

After the pawn sacrifice, black's Bishop (which had Tall-Pawn status for most of the game) can enter the battle on b5 and his Rooks suddenly get use of the b-file. In other words, Black gets active pieces and a chance to fight!

28.Qxb4 Rb7 29.Qc3 Bb5 30.b4?!

Disappointed by my earlier errors, I do a psychological belly flop and play like a zombie for the rest of the game. On the other hand, my opponent suddenly turns into a shark. Blood in the water has that effect on some players.

Better was 30.b3 (unlike my 30.b4, this move doesn't hand the c4-square to black's Bishop) 30...Kb8 31.Ka1 when White is still better.

30...Kd7 31.Kb2 Rc8 32.Ka3 Bc4 33.Rb2 Rb5 34.Qd2 Qd8 35.Qc3 Rcb8 36.Ka4??

Losing—my King rushes to meet his Queen head on! Simply 36.Re3 protects my Queen and prevents any tactical tricks. White would then still be better, with chances to effect a breakthrough in the center or on the kingside. For example: 36.Re3 Ke7 37.Nd3 (37.h3!?) 37...Bxd3 38.Rxd3 Kf8 39.h3 h5 40.Qd2 Kg7 41.Rbb3 Kh7 42.g4 and White triumphs. Of course, Black could defend far better than this, but the line shows white's general ideas.

Diagram 219a

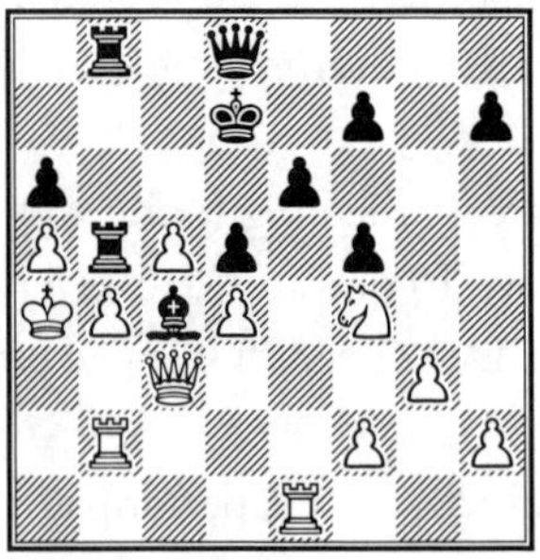

Black to move and win

36...Qxa5+!

Arrgh! I desperately imagined myself teleporting away to a kinder, gentler place. Alas, I remained at the board, with about a dozen people surrounding us intently watching as I got gutted.

37.bxa5 Rxb2 38.Ra1 R8b3 39.Qxb3 Rxb3 40.Re1 Rb2 41.Re3 Rd2, 0-1. A wonderful comeback from my opponent—I was a bit hasty in writing his obituary!

In *Winning With Chess Psychology* (Benko and Hochberg, McKay Chess Library 1991), the authors state: "Lasker was often called lucky by those who failed to appreciate his theory that chess was a fight between two personalities. It was his understanding of human fallibility that led him, in 1926, to make the following remarkable assertion in his *Manual of Chess*: 'He who has a slight disadvantage plays more attentively, inventively and more boldly than his antagonist who either takes it easy or aspires after too much. Thus a slight disadvantage is very frequently seen to convert into a good, solid advantage.'"

As evidenced by my own demise in the game we just saw, there's more than a grain of truth in Lasker's words!

ANSWER
PART FOUR

TEST 25

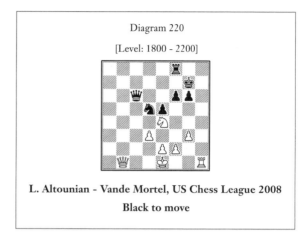

Diagram 220

[Level: 1800 - 2200]

L. Altounian - Vande Mortel, US Chess League 2008

Black to move

This game is a classic example of the need to pay attention. In diagram 220, Black is a pawn down and his King isn't very safe. On the other hand, white's King is still sitting in the middle of the board and tactics are possible based on the h1-Rook being undefended and X-rayed by the enemy Queen on c6.

Naturally, if White is allowed to castle (ending the tactical problems along the h1-a8 diagonal and also getting the King out of harm's way) then his material advantage will give him serious winning chances. Thus, Black must strike right away!

> **Explaining the Rating Spread**: Black has a couple of attractive moves, but the one he chose turns out to be a dead end. I think the correct move is easily missed, while the mistake would prove attractive to a lot of players.

1...f5?

A tempting move that aims to clear the h1-a8 diagonal and drop a tactical bomb on white's position. However, it fails to have the desired effect. Far better (and most likely overlooked) was 1...Rb8! 2.Qa1 (2.Qxb8?? Qc1 mate would be a sudden end to things, while 2.Qd1?? Nc3 3.Qc1 Rb1 wins) 2...Ra8 3.Qb2! (Dodging a bullet: 3.Qb1?? loses to 3...Nc3 4.Qc1 Nxe4! 5. Qh6+ [Avoiding 5.Qxc6?? Ra1+ 6.Qc1 Rxc1 mate] 5...Kf7 6.Qh7+ Ke6 7.0–0 Nc3 and Black has an extra piece) 3...Ra2 (If Black was happy with a draw, then 3...Rb8 4.Qa1 Ra8 is a perpetual on the white Queen. Black could also try 3...Rb8 4.Qa1 Nc3!? 5.0-0 Nxe2+, and though Black now has the better pawn structure, after 6.Kg2 black's own King is so open that he doesn't have any winning chances) 4.Qb1 f5 (4...Nc3 5.Qc1 Nxe4 6.Qh6+ Kf7 7.Qh7+ Ke6 is a draw since black's Rook no longer controls its first rank, which allows checks there: 8.Qg8+ Kd6 9.Qf8+, =) 5. 0–0 Rxe2 (5...fxe4?? 6.Qxa2) 6.Rc1 Qa8 7.Nd6 and black's vulnerable King allows White to hold the balance. For example: 7...Ne3 8.Nb7 Ng4 9.Rc7+ Kf6 10.Qc1 Nxf2 11.Rc6+ Kg7 12.Rc7+, =.

Since the refutation of 1...f5 isn't very subtle, one has to wonder how Black missed the far superior 1...Rb8. Of course, I can't give a definitive answer without asking

Mr. Mortel himself, but the usual "excuse" is something we've all been guilty of: we see a promising move and make it. We fail to follow the old maxim, "When you see a good move, sit on your hands and look for a better one." and, as a result, end up in a ditch—we just play on emotion and fall victim to both a quick move situation and a lack of attention.

2.Ng5 Ne3

2...Rb8 is better, though it doesn't have the same effect as it did a move ago because 3.Qa1 (3.Rh7+?? Kf6 wins for Black) now attacks the undefended e5-pawn: 3...Kf6 4.Nh7+ Ke6 5.0–0 Nc3 6.e4 (Ripping open the center. 6.Re1 is also good) and black's open King leaves him under serious pressure.

3.Rh7+ Kf6 4.fxe3 Kxg5 5.Qb4! f4 6.exf4+ exf4 7.Qxf8 Qc1+ 8.Kf2 Qe3+ 9.Kf1 Qc1+ 10.Kg2 and this move takes us to our next problem:

ANSWER
PART FOUR
TEST **26**

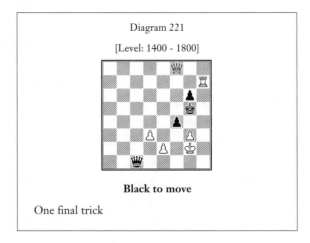

Diagram 221

[Level: 1400 - 1800]

Black to move

One final trick

Explaining the Rating Spread: I would think that "one final trick" would act as a huge hint. The move I'm after doesn't work, but it's far better than resigning since it gives you one final shot at salvation. Would most 1400 players notice this stalemate and set up the trap? Probably not, but I'm hoping that the 1400 players reading this book will!

Black's a Rook and a pawn down, so it's completely hopeless. However, since resignation is an option that will always be available, Black finds one last trap:

1...f3+!

Why not give this a go? If white's not paying attention, he might snap it off with 2.Qxf3?? when 2...Qg1+ 3.Kh3 Qh2+ 4.Kxh2 is a stalemate. Even more unfortunate for White is 2.Kxf3?? Qf1+ winning white's Queen! Finally, 2.exf3?? Qg1+ 3.Kh3?? (3.Kxg1, =) 3...Qh1 mate would, to put it mildly, completely spoil white's day.

2.Kf2, 1-0. It's important that you find tricks like this when things are turning sour (people will fall into them more often than you might imagine), and equally important (if you're the stronger side) to avoid quick moves; instead you should calmly look around and do your best to discover what your opponent is up to.

Part Five / Target Consciousness

ANSWER
PART FIVE

TEST 1

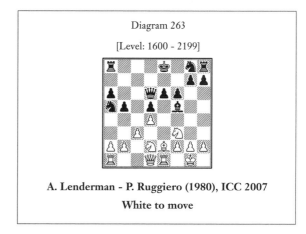

Diagram 263

[Level: 1600 - 2199]

A. Lenderman - P. Ruggiero (1980), ICC 2007

White to move

1.e4 c6 2.d4 d5 3.exd5 cxd5 4.c3 Bf5 5.Qb3 Qd7 6.Nf3 f6 7.Bf4 Nc6 8.Nbd2 e6 9.Be2 a6 10.0-0 b5 11.Rfe1 Na5 12.Qd1 Bd6 13.Bxd6 Qxd6 - Diagram 263

White (who was conducting a clock simultaneous exhibition) has an obvious lead in development and black's King is in the center. The position screams for immediate dynamic play—otherwise Black will consolidate with ...Ne7 and ...0-0 when her queenside play will offer good chances.

> **Explaining the Rating Spread**: The spread is large since different rating groups will show different levels of depth regarding the answer. Players in the 1600 range should notice the central King and white's lead in development. I would be very proud of any 1600 student who noticed these factors and played 14.a4 (trying to open things up). White's best moves, though, are far harder to find and call for players in the "A" and Expert categories. I'm not expecting you to find the tactics that follow (just seeing the logic of moves such as 14.a4, 14.b4, or 14.Nb3 is good enough), but those who did are surely title-strength players.

In the actual game, White didn't show a very good sense of Target Consciousness and played the quiet 14.Nf1? when the following occurred: 14...Ne7 15.Ng3 Bg6 16.Bd3 0-0 17.Qe2 Bf7? (Both 17...Bxd3 18.Qxd3 Ng6 and 17...Rfe8 gave Black an excellent position) 18.Qc2 Bg6 19.Nh4 Bxd3 20.Qxd3 Rae8 21.Nf3 (21.a4! was better for White), ½-½.

It's clear that 14.Nf1 has nothing whatsoever to do with the position. So what should White play? There were actually a few interesting tries, but we'll only look at three (all of them begin an immediate fight!):

▰▶ **14.a4 b4 15.Nh4 Ne7 16.Nxf5 Nxf5 17.Bg4 0-0 18.Qe2 bxc3 19.bxc3 Rfe8 20.Bxf5 exf5 21.Qxe8+ Rxe8 22.Rxe8+ Kf7 23.Rae1 Nb7** and it's not clear if White has anything here since his queenside pawns are easy pickings for the Queen.

After **14.a4 b4**, the insane looking **15.g4** is a great illustration for how a player should strive to make use of his positive imbalances—in this case development and a central enemy King demands quick play and energy, so 15.g4 shows the right spirit, though the move doesn't turn out to be particularly good. Let's take a look at the move's point: **15...Bxg4?** (Simple and sane is 15...Bg6 when I'm not sure what White has gained for the weakening of his kingside) **16.cxb4**

Diagram 263a

Black to move

16...Qxb4 (16...Nb7 17.Nh4 Bxe2 18.Qxe2 Nd8 [18...Kf7 19.Qh5+ Kf8 20.Ng6+ wins the Exchange] 19.Nf5 Qd7 20.Nb3 and black's going to get wiped out. The other Knight retreat, 16...Nc6, also gives White a powerful initiative: 17.b5 Nb4 18.Nh4 Bxe2 19.Qxe2 Kf7 [19...Nc2 20.Nf5 Qd7 21.Nb3 Nxe1 22.Nc5 gives White a winning attack] 20.Nb3) **17.Nh4 Bf5 18.Nxf5 exf5 19.Bf3+ Ne7 20.Rc1** and Black, who is staring Rc7 in the face, is in serious trouble.

▸ **14.b4! Nc4** (14...Nc6 15.a4 Rb8 16.Nb3 Nh6 17.Nc5 is very bad for Black) **15.a4 Rb8** (15...Nb2 16.Qb3 Nxa4 17.c4 dxc4 18.Bxc4 Kf7 19.g4!! Pulling black's Bishop away from the e4-square so that the d2-Knight can safely land there. Black, with his lack of development and vulnerable King, isn't prepared for this kind of brutal assault.

Diagram 263b

White has a monster attack!

19...Bxg4 20.Ne4 Qf4 [20...Qd7 21.Neg5+] 21.Bxe6+ Kf8 22.Qd5 and White has a winning attack: 22...Re8 23.Bxg8 Rxg8 24.Neg5) **16.Nh4 Ne7 17.Nxf5 Nxf5 18.axb5 axb5 19.Nxc4 bxc4 20.Bg4 0–0 21.Qe2** (21.Bxf5 exf5 22.Qa4 is also good)

21...Rfe8 22.Bxf5 exf5 23.Qxe8+ and White, with two Rooks for a Queen and a far superior pawn structure (including the powerful passed b-pawn), should win the game.

14.Nb3! Nc4 (14...Nxb3 15.axb3 Rb8 16.c4 Ne7 17.c5 Qc6 18.Nh4 0–0 [18...Bg6 19.Bg4 f5 20.Bh5 0–0 21.Bxg6 Nxg6 22.Nxg6 hxg6 23.b4 is a bad position for Black, who suffers from a hole on e5 and weak pawns on a6 and e6] 19.Nxf5 Nxf5 20.Bg4 with a clear advantage) **15.Bxc4 bxc4 16.Nc5 Ne7** (16...Nh6 17.Nh4 0–0 18.Nxf5 exf5 19.Re6 is crushing) **17.Nh4** The e6-pawn/square is starting to crack! Black's King will finally be able to castle, but he'll end up with fatal positional woes.

Diagram 263c

Black to move

17...0–0 (17...e5 18.dxe5 fxe5 19.Nb7 Qe6 20.Qa4+ Kf7 21.Nf3 with the double threat of Ng5+ and Nxe5+ wins) **18.Nxf5 exf5 19.Re6** and Black is in serious trouble.

This analysis is not meant to be definitive by any means. It *is* meant to give you a taste of what can happen if you become a Target Consciousness addict and, if the King is the target, play to take maximum advantage of that situation.

Keep in mind that everything starts with recognition—if you don't see what you possess, you won't be able to make use of it.

ANSWER
PART FIVE

TEST 2

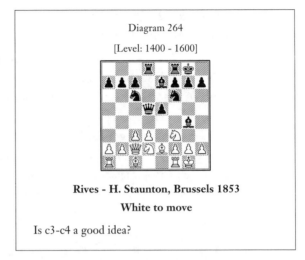

Diagram 264

[Level: 1400 - 1600]

Rives - H. Staunton, Brussels 1853

White to move

Is c3-c4 a good idea?

1.e4 e5 2.c3 d5 3.exd5 Qxd5 4.Nf3 Nc6 5.d3 Bg4 6.Be2 Nf6 7.0–0 Rd8 8.Qc2 Be7 9.Nbd2 0–0 - Diagram 264

> **Explaining the Rating Spread**: I fully expect 1400 players to understand that obvious one move attacks are to be avoided unless there is a deeper point to the threat (other than crossing one's fingers and hoping the opponent won't see it).

10.c4??

A positional blunder. White creates a gaping wound on d4 and gains absolutely nothing for it.

10...Qd7 and Black's advantage is obvious. The rest of the game features more terrible play by White, who quickly gets just what he deserved: **11.a3 Nh5 12.b4 Nf4 13.Ne4 Nxe2+ 14.Qxe2 Nd4 15.Qd1 Bxf3 16.gxf3 f5 17.Ng3 f4 18.Ne4 Qh3 19.Nd2 Rf5**, 0-1. White will be mated in a few moves.

ANSWER
PART FIVE

TEST 3

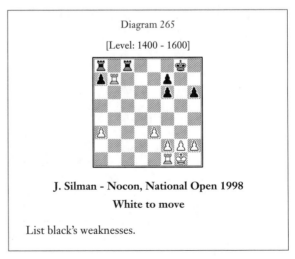

Diagram 265

[Level: 1400 - 1600]

J. Silman - Nocon, National Open 1998

White to move

List black's weaknesses.

White's a pawn up but that's often not enough in Rook endgames. However, white's advantage also lies with black's shattered pawn formation—the pawns on a7, f7, f6, and h6 are all targets! In the play that follows, White heaps attention on every one of these points.

> **Explaining the Rating Spread**: There are weak squares here (thanks to black's bad structure) like f5, f4, h5, and h4, but I would hope that the 1400 player would have embraced his inner greed by this time and, due to this, would have already started drooling in the direction of every one of black's pawns.

1.Rb4

The Rook puts itself in a position where it can hit a7 (Ra4), f6 (Rf4), or h6 (Rh4).

1...Rab8 2.Rg4+ Kh7

2...Kf8 continues the theme of Black going after white's one weakness on a3 while White tickles a host of enemy targets: 3.g3 Rc3 (3...Rb2 4.Rd1 Ra2 5.a4 Rcc2 [5...f5 puts up more resistance, though the position after 6.Rf4 can hardly make Black happy] 6.Rf4 and black's in a bad way) 4.Ra4 Rbb3 5.Ra1 Rb7 (5...Rc2 6.Rd1 Rcc3 7.Rd8+ Kg7 8.Rg4+ Kh7 9.Rd7) 6.Ra6 Kg7 7.Rd1 Rbb3 8.a4 and the threats of 9.Rxa7 and 9.Rdd6 leave Black with a completely lost position.

3.g3

Taking a moment out to stop eventual back rank mate possibilities is always a good idea!

3...Rc3 4.Ra4

Defending a3 and simultaneously tying Black down to the defense of a7.

4...Rb7

4...Rbb3 5.Rxa7 Rxa3 6.Rxf7+.

5.Rd1 Rc6 6.Rd5

Preparing to pound away at a7 by Rda5.

6...Re6 7.Rda5 Ree7

Now Black has been reduced to complete passivity. Next on white's agenda: turn his sights on f6.

8.Ra6

Diagram 265a

Targeting both a7 and f6

8...Kg6

This hastens the end, but the position was already completely lost.

9.Rg4+ Kh5

Of course, Black wasn't enthused by 9...Kh7 10.Rxf6, so he decides to go down in a more picturesque fashion.

10.Rg8

Suddenly black's King finds itself in a mating net.

10...Re6

10...f5 11.Ra5 also mates.

11.Ra4, 1-0.

ANSWER
PART FIVE
TEST 4

Diagram 266

[Level: 1400 - 1800]

A. Grischuk - Ivan Sokolov, Poikovsky 2004

White just played a2-a4. Black won't let White win the b-pawn, so what's the point of a2-a4? Is it any good, or simply a one-move threat?

1.e4 e5 2.Nf3 Nc6 3.Bb5 a6 4.Ba4 Nf6 5.0–0 Be7 6.Re1 b5 7.Bb3 d6 8.c3 0–0 9.h3 Na5 10.Bc2 c5 11.d4 cxd4 12.cxd4 Bb7 13.d5 Rc8 14.b3 Qc7 15.Bd3 Nh5 16.a4 - Diagram 266

After 16...b4, white's 16.a4 will have created three weaknesses in the enemy camp: the b4-pawn is loose, a6 is under pressure, and there's a gaping hole on c4 that, in many lines, will make a great home for a white Knight.

> **Explaining the Rating Spread**: There's a bit of a rating range here because, although 16.a4 creates weaknesses in black's camp, Black gets potential access to holes on c5 and c3. I should also note that b3 is a bit delicate. It would take a player on the higher end of the stated rating range to notice the plusses for both sides after 16.a4 b4.

16...b4 17.Bd2

Instantly targeting the weakness on b4. However, this move takes the d2-square away from white's b1-Knight and also loses time.

17...f5

Black offers up b4 in exchange for some kingside play and potential pressure against d5 (that pawn will be vulnerable once Black plays ...fxe4 and ...Nf4). His main alternative is 17...Qb6 18.Be3 Qd8 19.Nbd2 (taking immediate aim at c4) 19...Nf4 20.Bxf4 exf4 21.Qe2 (giving notice to the a6-pawn) 21... Qb6 22.Nc4 Qc5 (22...Nxc4 23.bxc4! intending a quick e4-e5 also leads to an interesting position) 23.Nfd2 Bf6 24.Rac1 Bc3 25.Red1

Diagram 266a

We've arrived at a very complicated situation filled with mutual weaknesses, targets, and dynamics—White is still eyeing a6, he's making use of c4, at some point e4-e5 will be on the table, black's f4-pawn is a bit far from home, Black has managed to get some use out of the c3-hole, and his b7-Bishop is incarcerated. White is for choice (note that 25...Bxd2 26.Nxd2 Qxc1 27.Rxc1 Rxc1+ 28.Kh2 Ra8 29.e5 favors White).

18.Bxb4 Nf4

White retains a small pull after 18...Qb6 19.Bxa5 Qxa5 20.exf5 Bxd5 21.Na3 Nf4 22.Bc4.

19.Nc3 Nxb3

19...Qb6 appears to be more or less equal.

20.Rb1 Nc5 21.Bxc5 Qxc5 22.Rxb7 and White stands better. Black was quickly brought to his knees after further errors: **22...Qxc3 23.Bxa6 Qa5 24.Rxe7 Qxa6 25.Nh4 fxe4 26.Qg4 Rf7 27.Nf5 h5 28.Qg5 e3 29.Rxf7 exf2+ 30.Kh2**, 1-0.

ANSWER

PART FIVE

TEST 5

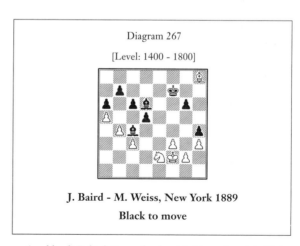

Diagram 267

[Level: 1400 - 1800]

J. Baird - M. Weiss, New York 1889

Black to move

White has just played the strange (and bad) Bd4-h8, no doubt thinking that this Bishop can just go back and forth since it holds the c3-pawn on this diagonal. White most likely also felt that his own King could assure his kingside pawns safety from the hungry eyes of the c4-Bishop, while black's King has no way into white's position. As a result, White must have been confident that his defensive fortress would hold things together.

However, it soon becomes clear that Mr. Baird was oblivious to the strategic subtleties of the position.

<u>Explaining the Rating Spread</u>: At the moment the only vulnerable points in white's position are c3 and g2. However, can Black create a third target? By now, the 1400 players reading this book will be aware of the necessity of creating targets and not just wishing they would appear.

1...c5!

Very strong and also quite annoying. Seeing that the c3-pawn can't be undermined, Black cracks b4, thereby turning a5 into a weakness. Then white's defensive task will be far more difficult since he will have to deal with two weak points on the queenside instead of the lone one on c3.

The ability to not just notice weaknesses, but to also create them, is a major part of Target Consciousness.

2.bxc5 Bxc5+

Simple and good. Black refuses to be sucked into obscure adventures with 2...Bc7 3.Nd4 Bxa5 4.c6, and instead regains his pawn while maintaining safe, long-term advantages like two active Bishops vs. Bishop and Knight, and pressure against both c3 and a5.

3.Bd4 Bd6

Black has no intention of relinquishing his two mighty Bishops!

4.Ke3

White could have put up better resistance by 4.Bb6 (defending a5), but even then his game would have been miserable after 4...Be5 (note the threats against both a5 and c3) 5.Nd4 Bg3+ 6.Ke3 (6.Kg1 Be1) 6...Bf1 7.Ne2 Be1.

4...Bc7. This move is both obvious and effective. Black went out of his way to create a weakness on a5, and now he's targeting it for destruction. Since 5.Bb6 fails to 5...Bxb6 6.axb6 Bxe2! 7.Kxe2 Kf6 8.Kd3 a5 followed by ...Kf5-f4-g3xg2xh3 (which wins easily for Black), White had to accept the loss of the a5-pawn and, eventually, the game.

ANSWER
PART FIVE

TEST **6**

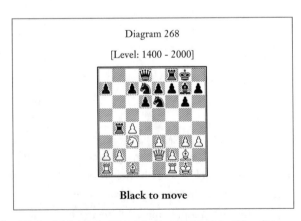

Diagram 268

[Level: 1400 - 2000]

Black to move

Fischer's words (while reviewing Yudovich's book, *King's Indian Defense*) in *Chess Digest*, Vol. 2 1969: "A great disappointment. Perhaps because I had been eagerly awaiting this book when it finally came into my hands in 1968. Most of the references are from the late fifties and early sixties. None from the Havana Olympiad, practically none from

Shakmatny Bulletin or minor Soviet tournaments. There was very little I didn't already know. 229 pages of nothing. I did learn one important thing of value: **1.d4 Nf6 2.c4 g6 3.g3 Bg7 4.Bg2 O-O 5.Nf3 d6 6.O-O Nc6 7.Nc3 Bg4 8.h3 Bxf3 9.Bxf3 Nd7 10.Bg2 Nxd4 11.Bxb7 Rb8 12.Bg2 Rb4 13.e3 Ne6 14.Qe2.**" - Diagram 268

> **Explaining the Rating Spread**: The one thing Fischer learned of value from that book (and the position in diagram 268) has everything to do with the creation of a target. Some will blanch at the solution, but others from 1400 on up will, by this time, have fully embraced moves that give you long-term weaknesses to attack.

Fischer continued: "Now Yudovich gives **14...Bxc3!** I didn't know this move, but judging from the quality of his book, I assume it was copied from another source. Black gets the better of it by destroying white's pawn formation; white's attacking chances are not real. Yudovich does not continue his analysis after 14...Bxc3! but after **15.bxc3 Ra4!** is clearly right."

This actually occurred a couple years later in the game S. Cvetkovic - D. Velimirovic, Yugoslavia 1971. After **14...Bxc3! 15.bxc3 Ra4 16.Rb1 Nec5 17.e4 Qc8 18.Bh6 Re8 19.e5 Qa6 20.Rb5 Rxa2** Black was much better but later blundered and allowed a draw.

ANSWER
PART FIVE

TEST 7

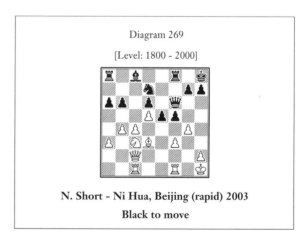

Diagram 269

[Level: 1800 - 2000]

N. Short - Ni Hua, Beijing (rapid) 2003

Black to move

1.e4 c5 2.Nf3 Nc6 3.d4 cxd4 4.Nxd4 Nf6 5.Nc3 e5 6.Ndb5 d6 7.Nd5 Nxd5 8.exd5 Nb8 9.c4 Be7 10.Bd3 a6 11.Nc3 O-O 12.O-O f5 13.f3 Nd7 14.Kh1 Bg5 15.b4 b6 16.a3 Kh8 17.Qc2 Qf6 18.g4 Bxc1 19.Raxc1 - Diagram 269

White's g2-g4 was a bold and greedy move designed to lay claim to the e4-square. Thus, moves such as 19...fxg4 and 19...f4 would give White exactly what he wants. However, Black has no intention of caving to his opponent's demands. So, instead of giving White a square, he lashes out and annexes one for himself!

> **Explaining the Rating Spread**: Another problem, another example of creating a weakness rather than hoping that one will appear. I start the level at 1800 since white's 18.g4 could easily strike fear into the hearts of many players, and the solution seems odd since it opens the f-file so the f1-Rook gets a birds eye view of black's Queen.

19...e4!

White targeted a square and Black does the same thing! As I said earlier, weak squares usually don't just magically appear—a player has to create them. And, if it costs a pawn to do so, it's a small price to pay for winning the strategic battle.

20.fxe4 f4

Black has a clear advantage. Why? Black's Knight will dominate the board from the juicy hole on e5, white's kingside is open and vulnerable, and the f4-pawn will prove to be a very active participant in the coming battle. Note that white's extra pawn (on e4) actually blocks its own pieces—the c3-Knight can't live on e4 anymore, and the d3-Bishop is locked in by the c4 and e4 pawns. The rest of the game was one-sided: **21.Ne2 f3 22.Qd2 Ne5 23.g5 Qg6 24.Ng1 Bg4 25.Bb1 Rf7 26.c5 bxc5 27.bxc5 dxc5 28.h3 Raf8 29.Rf2 Qh5 30.Qc3 Bxh3 31.Nxh3 Ng4 32.Rh2 Nxh2 33.Kxh2 f2 34.Bd3 Rf3 35.Bf1 Rxc3 36.Rxc3 Qd1 37.Kg2 Qg4+ 38.Kh2 Qxe4 39.Rxc5 Qd4 40.Rc6**, 0-1.

ANSWER
PART FIVE

TEST **8**

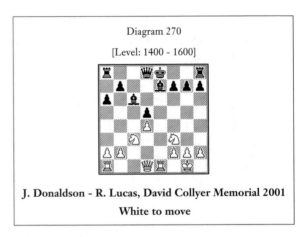

Diagram 270

[Level: 1400 - 1600]

J. Donaldson - R. Lucas, David Collyer Memorial 2001

White to move

1.e4 c6 2.d4 d5 3.exd5 cxd5 4.c4 e6 5.Nf3 Nc6 6.Nc3 Nf6 7.cxd5 exd5 8.Bb5 Bd7 9.0-0 Be7 10.Bg5 a6 11.Bxc6 Bxc6 12.Bxf6 Bxf6 13.Re1+ (Now Black should have seen white's thematic reply and settled for 13...Kf8. Yes, it's ugly, however White doesn't get more than a very slight edge after 14.Qd2 g6 15.Qh6+ Bg7 16.Qf4 Bf6 17.Ne5 Kg7 18.Re3 Re8 19.Rae1 Re6.) **13...Be7** - Diagram 270

> **Explaining the Rating Spread**: If you noticed that black's King is in the middle and if you went out of your way to keep it there, then congratulations on a job well done! I would hope most of my 1400 readers would notice these things, but if they didn't, let's hope that this example will be the catalyst that makes the right decision easy in the future.

14.Qe2!

A common device that keeps the enemy King in the center.

14...Rc8?

Black intends to play ...Rc7 (defending e7) followed by ...0-0, but there turns out to be a price to pay. Instead, 14...f6 should have been tried—it keeps white's Knight out of e5 and plans to follow up with ...Qd7 followed by ...Kf7.

15.Ne5 Rc7

Another miserable option was 15...Kf8 16.Qf3 Bf6 17.Rac1 when Black is under serious pressure. One sample variation: 17...g6? 18.Nxd5! Bxd5 19.Rxc8 Bxf3 20.Rxd8+ Bxd8 21.Nxf3 with an extra pawn in the endgame.

16.Nxc6 bxc6

Even worse is 16...Rxc6 17.Nxd5 Re6 18.Qc4.

17.Qxa6 and though Black finally managed to castle, the damage had been done and White, who is a solid pawn ahead, went on to win a technical game.

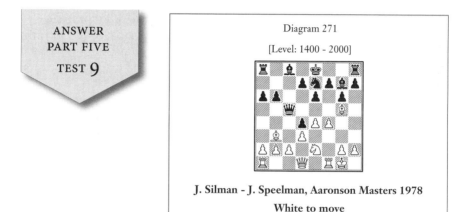

ANSWER PART FIVE TEST 9

Diagram 271

[Level: 1400 - 2000]

J. Silman - J. Speelman, Aaronson Masters 1978

White to move

1.e4 c5 2.Nf3 Nc6 3.Bb5 Qb6 4.Nc3 e6 5.0-0 Nd4 6.Bc4 Ne7 7.d3 a6 8.Nxd4 cxd4 9.Ne2 g6 10.Bg5 Bg7 11.Bb3 Qc5 12.f4 b6 - Diagram 271

White has a lead in development and black's King is still in the center. This screams for immediate action!

> Explaining the Rating Spread: Solving this one called for recognition of the central state of black's King, and of 13.f5, which tries to start a war before the enemy King manages to run to safety. You didn't need to do more than this to solve it.

13.f5!

White had to get the ball rolling since both his advantages (development and black's central King) are temporary (black's King will eventually castle and he'll eventually catch up in development). Thus, I knew that I had to use it or lose it!

Once again, I'm trying to instill in you a primal desire to kill whenever you see a King in the center. First comes recognition of the opponent's possible predicament, then comes the desire to punish it, and finally comes a cool and calm look at what is really going on in that particular position.

13...gxf5 14.Bxe7?!

I can't be sure (it was a lifetime ago), but I think I was moving quite quickly here. That's the only explanation I can give for ignoring the far stronger (and obvious) 14.Ng3! Of course, moving fast in such a rich position is imbecilic, but I probably had worked out (when I explored 13.f5) a line I liked and ran for it as fast as possible. Oh well, my target-loving heart was in the right place, but my aim was off. You can see a proper discussion about quick (lazy) moves in Part Four, Various States of Chess Consciousness.

14...Qxe7 15.exf5 Bb7 16.Ng3 Be5?

Better choices were 16...h5, 16...Qg5, and 16...Qh4.

17.Qh5?

A case of seeing a good move and not looking for a better one. The simple 17.fxe6! dxe6 (17...fxe6 18.Qh5+ and 17...0-0-0 18.exf7 are both unplayable) 18.Qh5 Bxg3 19.hxg3 would have left Black in serious trouble due to the threat of Bxe6. Choices such as 19...0-0-0 20.Rxf7 and 19...0-0 20.Rae1 Rae8 21.Qg4+ Kh8 22.Qxd4+ are extremely grim.

17...Bxg3 18.fxe6!

This good move is what prompted me into tossing out 17.Qh5. Now 18...Bxh2+ 19.Kxh2 dxe6 20.Bxe6 favors White, as does 18...dxe6 19.hxg3 (this transposes into the note to white's 17th move). So Black is forced to sacrifice a pawn, but that also turns out to be nice for me.

18...0-0-0 19.exd7+ Rxd7 20.hxg3 Qe3+ 21.Kh2 Rd6?

The threat of 22...Rh6 is dealt with by a nice maneuver by the White Queen. Far better resistance could have been had by 21...Rg8.

22.Qg4+! Kb8 23.Qf4! Qxf4 24.Rxf4 Re8 25.Raf1 Re2 26.Rf6! Rxg2+ 27.Kh3

Diagram 271a

Black has managed to restore material equality, but this is only temporary—his many pawn weaknesses (which brings up a whole different form of Target Consciousness!) leave him in a hopeless position.

27...Rg1 28.Rxd6 Rxf1 29.Rxb6 Kc7 30.Rb4 Bf3 31.g4 Kd6 32.Rxd4+ Ke5 33.Ra4 h5 34.gxh5 f5 35.Kh4 Bc6 36.Rc4 Bb5 37.Rb4 f4 38.Re4+ Kf6 39.Ba4 Kf5 40.Kh3 Bxa4 41.Rxa4 Rh1+ 42.Kg2 Rc1 43.Rc4 Kg4 44.h6 Rd1 45.h7 Rd2+ 46.Kg1 Rd1+ 47.Kf2 Rd2+ 48.Ke1 Rh2 49.Rc7 f3 50.d4 Kg3 51.Rg7+ Kf4 52.d5, 1-0. The leap from one form of Target Consciousness (Central King) to another (weak pawns) is very common.

Part Six / Statics vs. Dynamics

ANSWER
PART SIX

TEST 1

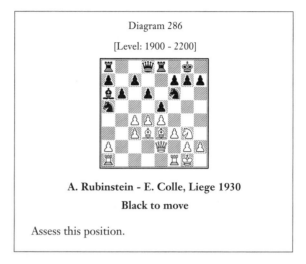

Diagram 286

[Level: 1900 - 2200]

A. Rubinstein - E. Colle, Liege 1930

Black to move

Assess this position.

1.d4 Nf6 2.c4 e6 3.Nc3 Bb4 4.e3 Bxc3+ 5.bxc3 d6 6.Bd3 0–0 7.e4 e5 8.Ne2 Re8 9.f3 b6 10.0–0 Nc6 11.Be3 Ba6 12.Ng3 Na5 13.Qe2 - Diagram 286

Black has managed to create the thematic two-minor-piece setup against the c4-pawn. However, there is no effective way to bring a third attacker to bear on it. The problem is that White has a monstrous pawn center and his pieces are poised for a kingside attack. Since the center and the kingside are white's, Black must break though on the other side of the board or, ultimately, perish.

Other than the ideal …Qd8-d7-a4, which maximizes the pressure against c4 (though this maneuver can be stopped cold by a2-a4), the general way to get play in these positions is to attack c4 with the Queen from c6 or e6 and induce d4-d5, which gives Black use of the c5-square and also allows for …c7-c6, which will open the c-file for black's Rooks. Unfortunately, the only way to do this is by …Qd8-d7-c6 or …Qd8-d7-e6. However, while Black is spending precious time trying to create a subtle shift in the pawn structure, white's kingside attack will wash the black position away.

> **Explaining the Rating Spread**: It takes a pretty sophisticated player to fully appreciate when a known setup is and isn't effective, and when one side's well known plans are overshadowed by the opponent's. On the other hand, most players like to attack and I would guess that white's attacking prospects would prove both obvious and appealing to players 1900 and above.

Some samples:

➤ 13…Qd7 (intending 14…Qa4 or 14…Qc6 or 14…Qe6) 14.Bg5! (Extremely annoying! The Knight has nowhere to run to, the Queen can't comfortably babysit it, and allowing White to double black's kingside pawns is rather horrifying.) 14…Kh8 (14…Qe7 15.Nh5 wouldn't make Black happy, while 14...Qe6 succeeds in getting White to advance the d-pawn, but it leads to kingside ruin after 15.d5 Qd7 16.Bxf6 gxf6 17.f4 with a murderous attack) 15.Bxf6 gxf6 16.f4 Rg8 17.fxe5 fxe5 and now 18.Qf3 (18.Rf5!? is also tempting) 18...Qe6 (and not 18...Bxc4? 19.Qf6+ Rg7 20.Nf5) 19.Qxf7 Qxf7 20.Rxf7 Rac8 21.Raf1 Bxc4 22.Bxc4 Nxc4 23.R1f6 is clearly better for White.

▶ 13...Qe7 14.Bg5 h6 15.Bh4 Bc8 16.f4! exf4 (16...Bg4 17.Qf2) 17.Rxf4 g5 18.Qf3! Nh7 19.e5 gives White a raging attack.

▶ 13...Kh8 14.f4 exd4 (14...exf4 15.Bxf4 Qd7 16.e5 Qc6 17.Bg5 [17.Nh5 is also strong] is winning: 17...dxe5 [other moves fare no better, for example 17...Ng8 18.Qh5 h6 19.Rxf7 and 17...Nd7 18.Rxf7 Bxc4 19.Bxc4 Nxc4 20.Nf5 are both hopeless] 18.Rxf6 [the more pedestrian 18.Bxf6 Bxc4 19.Qg4 also gets the job done] 18...gxf6 19.Be4) 15.cxd4 c5 16.d5 favors White: 16...Qd7 17.Bd2 Qg4 18.Rf3 and Black's in bad shape.

▶ 13...h6 (The idea is to prevent Bg5, but this also wastes time and creates the possibility of various sacrificial explosions on h6) 14.Rad1 and now:

● 14...Nc6 15.a3 (This stops lines like 15.f4 exd4 16.cxd4 Nb4. Since White has a solid center, he doesn't have to be in any hurry.) 15...Qd7 16.h3 (Still taking his time before starting his attack. Now a later f4 can't be met by ...Ng4.) 16... Na5 17.Nf5 (This targets the h6 move. Now explosions on h6 can occur at any moment.) 17...Kh8 (17...Qa4 18.Bxh6 gxh6 [18...g6 though still good for White, was a better defense] 19.Qe3 Bc8 20.Qxh6 Bxf5 21.exf5 and wins) 18.f4 exd4 19.Bxd4 Qe6 20.e5 Nc6 (20...Bxc4 21.Nxg7 wins) 21.Qf2 with advantage for White. For example: 21...dxe5 22.fxe5 Ng8 23.Qg3 g6 24.Nxh6 Nxh6 25.Qg5 Ng8 (25...Kg7 26.Rf6 is painful) 26.Rxf7 and it's the end black's world.

● 14...Qd7 15.f4 exd4 (15...Ng4 16.Bc1 exd4 17.cxd4 Nf6 18.e5 is obviously silly for Black, while 15...Qa4 16.fxe5 dxe5 17.Rxf6 gives a winning attack) 16.Bxd4 (This avoids center destroying tricks like 16.cxd4 d5 17.cxd5 Bxd3 18.Qxd3 Nxe4 19.Nxe4 Qe7) 16...Qe6 17.Bxf6 (Also in white's favor is 17.e5!? c5 18.exf6 cxd4 19.Qxe6 Rxe6 20.cxd4 Bxc4 21.fxg7 Re3 22.Bxc4 Nxc4 23.Rc1 d5 24.Nh5 Rd8 25.f5 b5 26.f6) 17...Qxf6 18.e5 Qe6 19.Qe4 g6 20.f5 Qxe5 21.fxg6 Qc5+ 22.Qd4 (A more imaginative solution is 22.Kh1 Rxe4 23.Nxe4 Qe5 24.Rxf7 Rf8 [or 24...Nxc4 25.Nf6+ Qxf6 26.Rxf6 Nb2 27.Be4 Nxd1 28.Bxa8] 25.Rdf1 Rxf7 26.gxf7+ Kf8 27.Nf6 and wins) 22...fxg6 23.Rf6 Qxd4+ 24.cxd4 Bxc4 25.Rxg6+ Kh7 (25...Kf7 26.Rf1+ Ke7 27.Rg7+ Ke6 28.Re1+ Kd5 29.Be4+ Rxe4 30.Rxe4) 26.Bc2 and White is better.

Of course, Rubinstein didn't need to analyze any of this. He knew from experience that this kind of structure, sans proper counterplay by Black, is in white's favor.

In the game, Black played 13...c5. However, now 14.d5 doesn't have any of the flaws that would exist if the black pawn still stood on c7 (opening the c-file with ...c6 isn't possible, and the c5-square is blocked and unusable). Since ...Qd7 (intending ...Qa4) can be stopped by a2-a4, Black has absolutely no counterplay and has to wait around as White calmly improves his position. Here's the rest of the game: **13...c5 14.d5 Kh8 15.f4 Nd7 16.f5 f6 17.Nh5 Re7 18.g4 Qe8 19.g5?** (There is rarely a need to rush such positions, and there's absolutely no doubt that a prime Rubinstein wouldn't have done so. More in keeping with the position would have been 19.Kh1 Qf7 20.Rf2 Rg8 21.Rg1, etc.) **19...Bxc4! 20.Bxc4 Nxc4 21.gxf6 gxf6?** (Missing 21...Nxe3!) **22.Bh6 Nb2 23.Kh1 Nd3 24.Ng7 Rxg7 25.Bxg7+ Kxg7 26.Rg1+ Kh8 27.Qxd3 Qf7 28.Rg3 Rg8 29.Rag1 Rxg3 30.Rxg3 Nb8 31.Qe2 a6 32.a4 Qe8 33.h4 Qf7 34.Kg2 Qf8 35.h5 h6 36.Qg4 b5 37.axb5 axb5 38.Qg6 Nd7 39.Kf3 Nb6 40.Rg1 Na4 41.c4**, 1-0.

ANSWER
PART SIX

TEST 2

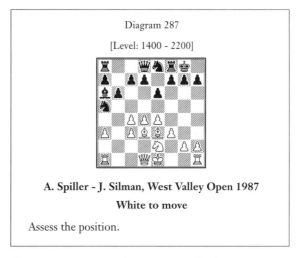

Diagram 287

[Level: 1400 - 2200]

A. Spiller - J. Silman, West Valley Open 1987

White to move

Assess the position.

1.d4 Nf6 2.c4 e6 3.Nc3 Bb4 4.a3 Bxc3+ 5.bxc3 0–0 6.f3 b6 7.e4 Ne8 8.Be3 Ba6 9.Bd3 Nc6 10.Ne2 Na5 - Diagram 287

White didn't play the opening with enough panache and c4 is about to fall. Since 11.0-0 Bxc4 isn't going to offer enough compensation for the pawn, he needs to look elsewhere in an effort to generate some kind of dynamism in exchange for his inferior structure.

> **Explaining the Rating Spread**: I would expect most players to notice that the c4-pawn is hanging. However, some might just shrug their shoulders and give it up (without getting much compensation) while others might vainly try to hold onto it with 11.Qa4, without bothering to see how Black would respond. A solid 1400 player should notice these things and realize that White doesn't really have much choice—it's either 11.c5 or bust! Of course, the prospect of ending up with doubled isolated c-pawns (via 12...bxc5) could easily spook him!

I would considerably raise the rating-bar for black's play—fighting the desire to double white's pawns on move 12 would be tough, and 12...d6 followed by taking away from the center breaks an age-old rule ("always capture towards the center").

11.c5!

Not ideal, but best. Far worse is 11.Qa4? d5 when the c4-pawn is lost and white's Queen move proved to be a waste of time.

11...Bxd3

An important and welcome exchange. Black removes one of white's best attacking pieces, which, after an eventual e4-e5, would exert annoying pressure against black's kingside.

12.Qxd3 d6

Black is trying to saddle White with a structural disadvantage *without* dynamic counter chances. During the game I wasn't sold on 12...bxc5 13.dxc5 d5 14.exd5 (Better than 14.e5 Qh4+ 15.Bf2 Qc4, which favors Black) 14...Nf6 15.Qb5 Nxd5 16.Bf2 c6 17.Qa4 since black's Knights don't have permanent perches and, in some lines, the d6-square can fall into white's hand after Ne2-g3-e4-d6 (also, chasing the d5-Knight off the d-file with c3-c4, and then following with Rd1-d6 is also possible).

13.cxb6 cxb6

13...axb6 was a thought, but by opening the c-file I was intending to make the c4-square my own and to place serious pressure against c3.

Now White has to make an important decision.

Diagram 287a

White to move

14.0–0?

Chess teachers are always imploring their students to castle, yet here's a case where that same teacher would respond—upon seeing a student that expected praise for finally getting his King to safety—"Why did you castle here? It's clearly wrong!"

This natural but lazy move, played by a very experienced master, is an error because it doesn't address the fight over c4. This one loss of tempo assures Black victory in that battle.

Correct was 14.c4, not allowing the c-pawn to be fixed on c3 and thus turning it into both a target and a dynamic force (in the best Static vs. Dynamic tradition). Play might continue: 14...Qc8 15.Rc1 Qa6 16.Bd2 (16.Nf4 Nf6 17.c5 Qxd3 18.Nxd3 bxc5 19.dxc5 d5 20.e5 [20.0–0 dxe4 21.fxe4 Rfc8 22.Ne5 Rc7, =] 20...Nd7 21.c6 Nb6 22.c7 Rfc8 and the pawn has gone too far!) 16...Rc8 17.Bxa5 Qxa5+ 18.Kf2 Nf6 19.Qb3 Rc6, =.

After 14.0-0, the rest of the game saw Black dominate c4, snuff out all enemy counterplay, and infiltrate on the queenside and central light squares: **14...Qc7 15.Bg5 Rc8 16.f4 f6 17.Bh4 Qc4 18.Qe3 d5 19.e5 f5 20.Kh1 Qa4 21.h3 Qc2 22.Rfc1 Qe4 23.Qxe4 dxe4 24.d5** (A desperate bid for activity. The idea of waiting around while the a5-Knight made a home on c4 and the e8-Knight claimed d5 via ...Ne8-c7-d5 couldn't have appealed to him!) **24...exd5 25.Nd4 g6 26.Rab1 Nc7 27.Be7 Rfe8 28.Bb4 Nc4 29.Nc6 Ne6!** (Sacrificing the Exchange for an armada of pawns and total domination of the position.) **30.Ne7+ Rxe7 31.Bxe7 Nxf4 32.Rd1 Kf7 33.Bd6 Nd3** (Knights don't get much better than this!) **34.Kg1 Ke6 35.a4 Ndb2 36.Rd4 Nxa4 37.Rb4 Nxc3 38.Kf2 a5 39.Rdxc4 dxc4 40.Rxb6 Nd5 41.Ra6 c3 42.Ba3+ Kxe5**, 0-1.

ANSWER
PART SIX
TEST **3**

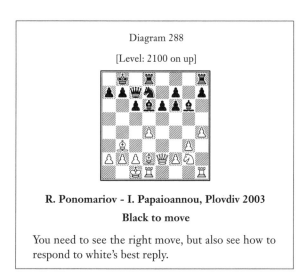

Diagram 288

[Level: 2100 on up]

R. Ponomariov - I. Papaioannou, Plovdiv 2003

Black to move

You need to see the right move, but also see how to respond to white's best reply.

1.e4 d5 2.exd5 Qxd5 3.Nc3 Qa5 4.d4 c6 5.Bc4 Bf5 6.Bd2 Nf6 7.Nf3 e6 8.Nd5 Qd8 9.Nxf6+ gxf6 10.Bb3 Nd7 11.Qe2 Qc7 12.Nh4 Bg6 13.0–0–0 0–0–0 14.g3 Kb8 15.Ng2 Bd6 16.h4 - Diagram 288

The position is actually quite sharp. At the moment we can see that black's pawn structure is inferior to white's, but the very doubled pawns that we label as "potentially weak" also have dynamic plusses: the g-file is opened for a black Rook and the e5- and g5-squares are inaccessible to white's pieces.

Black's thematic break is ...c6-c5, but at the moment he has to deal with the threat of h4-h5. The tactical 16...e5 is possible (though 17.h5 Bf5 18.Nh4 Be6 19.Bxe6 fxe6 20.dxe5 Bxe5 21.Nf3 is in white's favor), but the most obvious replies are 16...h6 and 16...h5.

> **Explaining the Rating Spread**: Many players would notice 16...h5, but few would play it with the express purpose of sacrificing that pawn!

The knowledge needed to fully handle this position (knowing the proper pawn breaks and willfully giving up a pawn for dynamic compensation) requires someone with experience and strength.

16...h5!

Since black's pawn structure is made for dynamics, he needs to "up" the tempo of play by seeking ways to make his pieces as active as possible. On the other hand, White would be happy to slow down the tempo of play, make the important ...c5 advance hard to achieve, and leave Black as passively placed as possible. It turns out that 16...h6 isn't best due to "17.h5 Bh7 18.Ne3 when Black has a weak pawn at h6 and ...c6-c5 is rather hard to carry out"—Ponomariov (*New In Chess* 8, 2003). His point is that 18...c5 is met by 19.d5 when the dual threats of 20.dxe6 and 20.Ng4 (picking up the pawn on h6) are simply good for White.

16...h5, though, is a different animal. Now Ng2-e3-g4 ideas are ruled out because the h-pawn controls g4 (and, of course, there is no pawn on h6 to win), and black's ...c6-c5 push is about to become a reality. Of course, Black paid a price for this: White can play 17.Nf4 and win the h-pawn (giving White another static plus in the form of an extra pawn). However, the Ng2-f4xh5 idea takes time, and Black will use that to maximize the activity of his army.

This will no doubt be very confusing for lower rated readers of this book. But there's really only one lesson you need to absorb here: You can't play a position properly without understanding whether your chances lie with statics or dynamics. Once you know which your (and your opponent's!) position is dedicated to, you can insist on moves that promote it!

17.Nf4 Bf5

Less exciting but playable is 17...e5!? 18.Nxg6 fxg6 19.dxe5 Nxe5 20.Rhe1 Ng4.

18.Nxh5 c5

This is the position Black was aiming for: he's a pawn down but the key ...c6-c5 advance has been realized. Also, white's Knight has been sidelined and needs to be defended by the Queen. The game now becomes very exciting with many tactical tricks popping up all over the place.

19.g4

Other moves:

- ► 19.d5? works well in the position after 16...h6 17.h5 Bh7 18.Ne3 c5 19.d5, but it doesn't hold up here (after 16...h5 17.Nf4 Bf5 18.Nxh5 c5) because the Knight is loose on h5 after 19...c4! 20.Bxc4 Ne5 threatening 21...Nxc4 and 21...Bg4.

- ► 19.dxc5 Nxc5 20.Bc3 Be5 21.Bxe5 fxe5 "when Black still has a dangerous initiative"—Ponomariov (*New In Chess* 8, 2003).

- ► The critical choices are 19.Be3!? and the non-human 19.Ng7. Both are well worth analyzing if you have the time and inclination. However, since this isn't a book of endless analysis (though at times it might seem like it is!), we'll get back to the game and our all-important theme!

19...Rxh5!

Very nice! White keeps trying to put a stopper on black's activity (dynamics) so he can make use of his extra passed h-pawn and better overall structure (statics). Black refuses to bow, and tosses more fuel on the fire in order to keep the dynamics burning!

Having said all that, the more pedestrian 19...Bg6 was also interesting:

Diagram 288a

Leads to a whole new adventure

➤ 20.Bc3 cxd4 21.Bxd4 Bc5 22.Bc3 Bxh5 23.gxh5 Qf4+ 24.Kb1 Qxf2 leads to a crazy endgame where White has two Bishops, a queenside pawn majority, and the passed pawns on the h-file. Black has that central pawn clump on the f- and e-files. White seems better, but I'm not sure by how much.

➤ 20.d5 and now Ponomariov's recommended 20...Ne5 21.Nxf6 c4 (which he claims is fine for Black after 22.Ba4 Nd3+) actually seems to fail to the highly surprising 22.Bc3!! cxb3 23.axb3 when Black is hopelessly placed. The threat is h5 followed by Rhe1 and I can't see how Black can deal with it in a satisfactory manner.

Instead of 20...Ne5, Black can also try 20...exd5 21.Bxd5 Nb6 when 22.Ba5 Be5! is okay for Black, and 22.Be4 Na4! creates some nasty tactical tricks against b2 and seems to solve all black's problems.

Diagram 288b

Position after 22...Na4
White is forced to scramble!

23.Qc4 Nb6 24.Qe2 is a repetition of moves, 23.b3? runs headlong into 23...c4!, and 23.Nxf6 Be5 can't displease Black. Most notably, 23.c3 crashes and burns after 23...Qb6 24.b3 c4! 25.Qxc4 Ba3+ 26.Kb1 (26.Kc2 Nb2) 26...Rxd2! 27.Bxg6 (27.Rxd2 Bxe4+ 28.Ka1 Qd6!! 29.Qxe4 Qxd2 wins) 27...Rb2+ 28.Ka1 Qxf2 29.bxa4 Rb4 30.Qxb4 Bxb4 31.cxb4 fxg6 and Black should win. It's amazing what active pieces can do!

Instead of 22.Ba5 or 22.Be4, White should play 22.Bg2! and I can't see a way for Black to equalize. Of course, pages more on 19...Bg6 can be created, so if you want to find its ultimate truth, you'll have to burn some serious midnight oil.

20.gxf5!

White doesn't bite, and continues his policy of dampening enemy counterplay. Instead, 20.gxh5 cxd4 21.Kb1 Ne5 leaves Black with extremely active pieces and gives him excellent compensation for the sacrificed Exchange.

Hopefully the philosophical Static vs. Dynamic pattern is becoming crystal clear: the side with the static edge tries to impose his static philosophy, while the guy with the dynamics does his best to impose his own brand of play on the board. The first person to cave to the other's desires will most likely lose the game.

20...Rxf5 21.Be3 cxd4 22.Bxd4

Diagram 288c

White has managed to stem the dynamic tide and a purely static (but highly imbalanced) situation is beginning to form. Instead of Statics vs. Dynamics, we've ended up with Strange Statics vs. Strange Statics.

22...Bc5

Ponomariov considered this to be an error and recommended 22...Rh8!, calling the position "unclear". In my view, white's Bishops and passed h-pawn give him a slight advantage, with Black still having to play very accurately before claiming equality. For example, 23.h5 Bh2? 24.h6 Rxh6 seemed okay until I realized that 25.Bxe6!! was possible: 25...fxe6 26.Qxe6 Bf4+ 27.Be3 Rxh1 28.Rxh1 Bxe3+ 29.fxe3 Qe5 30.Qxd7 a6 31.Rh8+ Ka7 32.Qd4+ Qxd4 33.exd4.

A better try (after 22...Rh8 23.h5) is 23...Nc5 24.h6 (24.Kb1!?) 24...Bf4+ 25.Be3 Rg5! (25...Ne4!?) 26.Rh4 (26.Qf3) 26...Bxe3+ 27.Qxe3 Qe5 28.Qxe5+ fxe5 29.Bc4 Rg6 30.h7 Rg7 31.b4 Na4 32.Rdh1 Nb6 33.Bd3 f5 34.f3 Kc7 35.Rh6 Kd7 36.R1h4 Rf7 and Black, who is threatening ...Nb6-d5-f6, is fine. However, 24.Kb1 (instead of 24.h6) seems better.

23.Bxc5 Nxc5 24.Rxd8+ Qxd8 25.h5 and the h-pawn has turned into a world-beater: **25...Nxb3+ 26.axb3 Qd5 27.Qd1 Kc7 28.h6 Qxd1+ 29.Kxd1 Rd5+ 30.Ke2 Rd8 31.b4 a6 32.c4 Rh8 33.Ke3 Rh7 34.Kf4 Rh8 35.Rh3 Rg8 36.h7 Rh8 37.Ke4 Kd6 38.Kd4 Kc6 39.Rh6 Rd8+ 40.Kc3 Rh8 41.Rh5 Kd6 42.c5+ Kc6 43.Kc4 b6 44.cxb6 Kxb6 45.b5**, 1-0. Ponomariov gives 45...a5 46.Kb3 f5 47.Ka4 Kc5 48.f4 f6 (48...Kd4 49.b6 Ke3 50.b7 Kxf4 51.Rh4+ Kg3 52.Rc4) 49.Rh6 e5 50.b6 exf4 51.b7 f3 52.Rxf6 Kd5 53.Rxf5+ Kc6 54.Rxf3 and it's over.

ANSWER
PART SIX

TEST 4

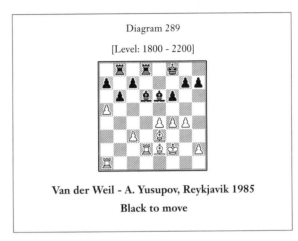

Diagram 289

[Level: 1800 - 2200]

Van der Weil - A. Yusupov, Reykjavik 1985

Black to move

White has an obvious advantage in central and kingside space (a static plus that can turn dynamic at the drop of a hat), and also has some pressure (statics and dynamics) on black's position (he can open the a-file at will and kingside pawn breaks must always be anticipated). Not relishing the prospect of a passive defense, Yusupov finds a surprising way to activate his army.

> **Explaining the Rating Spread**: The ...bxa5 capture, which severely weakens black's pawn structure, goes against most players' training. However, I feel that some class "A" players (1800-1999) might be attracted to the b8-Rook's newfound activity and, as a result, would find the courage to cast their structural fears aside.

1...bxa5!!

This ruptures black's queenside pawn formation (thus giving White a static advantage in space and structure) but turns the formerly dead Rook on b8 into a serious dynamic contender on the open b-file.

2.Rxa5 Rb3 3.Rc2?!

Okay, but a bit passive. The best move is most likely 3.e5 fxe5 4.fxe5 Be7 5.Rxd8+ Bxd8 6.Rxa7 Ke8! (A calm tightening move that defends d8 and takes the sting out of Ra8. The obvious 6...Bh4+ actually forces white's King to a better position after 7.Kf3 when 7...Bd5+ is happily met by 8.Kf4 and 7...Rxc3 allows 8.Ke4 when White is a tiny bit better in both cases. Note that 6...Rxc3?? loses to 7.Ra8) and now:

Diagram 289a

Tricky!

━━▶ 7.Ra8? Bd5 when 8.Ra2?? Bh4+ 9.Kg1 Rb1+ picks up the Rook on
a2, and 8.Rc8?? loses to 8...Kd7. This means that 7.Ra8 Bd5 has to
be met with the slightly embarrassing 8.Ra1 when 8...Bh4+ 9.Kf1
Rxc3 gives Black an initiative (his pieces are far more active than
white's), though White should be able to hold a draw.

━━▶ 7.Bd2?? Rb2 and white's already lost: 8.Ke1 Bh4+ 9.Kd1 Bb3+
10.Kc1 Rc2+ 11.Kd1 (Of course 11.Kb1 Rxd2 is white's best,
but he might as well resign in that case.) 11...Rxc3 mate!

━━▶ 7.Bd4 Rb2 8.Kf1 Rb1+ 9.Kg2 Rb2 10.Kf3?? (Playing for the loss.
Correct was 10.Kf1 Rb1+ with a draw by repetition) 10...Bd5+
11.Ke3 Bg5+ 12.Kd3 (12.Kf2 Bc4 wins a piece and the game)
12...Rd2 mate!

━━▶ 7.Bd3 Rxc3 8.Bf5 Kf7, =.

It's amazing how many tricks and mates there are in the position, a testament to
the power of active pieces!

3...Ra3 4.Rh5

Another trap is 4.Rxa3 Bxa3 5.Bxa7?? (5.c4 a5 6.Ra2 Bb4, =) 5...Bb3 and the Rook
is trapped!

4...Kg8 5.c4 Bb4 6.Rb5 a5 7.c5

No better is 7.Bc5 Rh3 8.Bxb4 axb4 9.Rxb4 Bxg4 10.Kg2 h5, =.

7...Ra2??

7...Rb3 was correct when White has to scramble for equality: 8.c6 a4 9.f5 Bf7
10.Bf4 Rc8 11.Rb7 Ba5 12.Be3 a3 13.Bc4, =.

8.Rxa2 Suddenly Black is in serious trouble! He went down hard and fast: **8...Bxa2
9.Rb7 Rd7 10.Bb5 Re7 11.Bc6 Kf8 12.h4 Bf7 13.Rb8+ Be8 14.Rc8 a4 15.Bxa4
Rxe4 16.Bc2 Re7 17.Bxh7 Kf7 18.h5 Bc6 19.Bg8** mate.

ANSWER
PART SIX

TEST 5

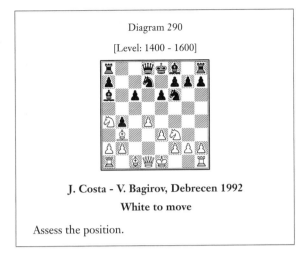

Diagram 290

[Level: 1400 - 1600]

J. Costa - V. Bagirov, Debrecen 1992

White to move

Assess the position.

1.d4 d5 2.c4 c6 3.Nc3 Nf6 4.e3 e6 5.Nf3 Nbd7 6.Bd3 dxc4 7.Bxc4 b5 8.Bb3 b4 9.Na4 Ba6 - Diagram 290

Here White enjoys potential pressure against the backward pawn on c6 (a static advantage). However, his King is stuck in the middle (a dynamic disadvantage).

> **Explaining the Rating Spread**: Yes, I fully expect 1400 players, schooled in the imbalances (and immersed in this chapter!), to notice this Static vs. Dynamic situation. And why shouldn't they? The a6-Bishop would surely make them uncomfortable if they had the white pieces, and being wary of weak pawns like the one on c6 should be autopilot for those that have progressed this far into this book.

Of course, the actual play turns out to be very advanced, but all I was looking for was a basic understanding of the Static vs. Dynamic battle.

10.Bd2

Logical—White hopes to increase his pressure against c6 while simultaneously ending the problems along the f1-a6 diagonal by Rc1 and Bc4.

Since White enjoys a static plus vs. Black's dynamic one, Black should look for a way to meet 10.Bd2 in as dynamic a fashion as possible.

10...c5!

Turning the potentially weak c-pawn into a dynamic trooper! Black has also done okay theoretically with the more restrained 10...Be7 and 10...Rc8.

11.dxc5

Worse is 11.Rc1 cxd4 12.Nxd4? (12.exd4 is better, though Black would have a very comfortable position) 12...Ne5! and white's already in serious trouble!

11...Nxc5 12.Nxc5 Bxc5 13.Bxe6

Winning a pawn since 13...fxe6 14.Qa4+ picks up the a6-Bishop. Other possibilities:

> 13.Ba4+ Kf8 14.Rc1 Qb6 15.Ne5 Rc8 16.Qb3 g6 17.Nc4 Qb8 18.0–0 Kg7 and Black had an excellent position, Z. Ilincic - D. Blagojevic, Podgorica 1996.

13.Rc1 Qb6 14.Bc4 Bb7 15.Qa4+ Bc6 16.Qc2 Bd6 17.Bd3 Bb7 18.Qa4+ Ke7 19.Nd4 Rhc8 20.Ke2? (20.0-0 makes more sense, with approximate equality) 20...Ne4 21.Bxe4 Bxe4 22.f3 Bd5 and Black was better in J. Costa - V. Kramnik, Debrecen 1992.

13...0-0

Diagram 290a

Black has tremendous compensation for the sacrificed pawn since his pieces are very active, and white's King still has to find a way to get castled.

14.Qb3 Bb7 15.Bc4 a5 16.Rd1

Bagirov points out that 16.0-0? fails to 16...Bxf3 17.gxf3 Qxd2 18.Rad1 a4 19.Bxf7+ Kh8.

16...Qc7 17.0-0 Rad8

Perfectly reasonable, though 17...a4 18.Qc2 Ng4 seems to be the more critical way to play: 19.e4 (19.h3 Bxf3 20.hxg4 Bxd1 gives White some, but not quite enough, compensation for the sacrificed Exchange.) 19...Rac8 20.b3 (20.Be1 Rfe8 21.Qxa4 Bc6 22.Bb5 Bxe4 23.Bxe8 Bxf3 24.g3 Ne5 looks grim for White) 20...Rfe8 21.Rde1 Ba6 and Black has more than enough for the sacrificed pawn.

18.h3 Ba7 19.Bc1 Rc8 20.Be2 Bb8 21.Rfe1

21.g3? Ne4 with the idea of ...Nxg3—Bagirov.

21...Ne4

Threatening ...Ng5. However, much stronger was 21...Be4! (threatening ...Bc2) 22. Rd4 Bxf3 23.Bxf3 Qh2+ 24.Kf1 Rxc1! 25.Rxc1 Qh1+ and wins.

After 21...Ne4, I'll give the rest of the game (which had many exciting ups and downs) without notes:

22.h4 Nf6 23.Qa4 h6 24.a3 Bc6 25.Qc2 Qb7 26.Qf5 Qc7 27.axb4 axb4 28.Bd2 Be4 29.Qb5 Bc2 30.Rc1 b3 31.Bb4 Rfe8 32.Bd3 Bxd3 33.Qxd3 Qxc1 34.Rxc1 Rxc1+ 35.Be1 Be5 36.Qxb3 Rb8 37.Qd3 Bxb2 38.Kh2 Ng4+ 39.Kh3 h5 40.Qd7 Nf6 41.Qf5 Rd8 42.Ba5 Rh1+ 43.Kg3 Re8 44.Ng5 Be5+ 45.f4 Bc3 46.e4 Bxa5 47.Qxa5 Rd1 48.Qf5 Rd3+ 49.Kf2 Red8 50.Nf3 Ng4+ 51.Kg3 g6 52.Qg5 Kg7 53.f5 Re8 54.Kf4 Re3 55.f6+ Kg8 56.e5 Re6 57.Nh2 R6xe5 58.Nxg4 R5e4 mate.

ANSWER
PART SIX

TEST 6

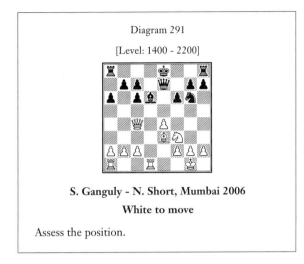

Diagram 291

[Level: 1400 - 2200]

S. Ganguly - N. Short, Mumbai 2006

White to move

Assess the position.

1.e4 e5 2.Nf3 Nc6 3.Bb5 a6 4.Bxc6 dxc6 5.0–0 Bd6 6.d4 exd4 7.Qxd4 f6 8.Be3 Ne7 9.Nbd2 Be6 10.Rfd1 Ng6 11.Nc4 Bxc4 12.Qxc4 Qe7 - Diagram 291

We'll borrow Nigel Short's excellent explanation of this position from his notes in *New In Chess* (issue 1, 2007): "A standard position. Black has been compelled to hand back one of his Bishops and he remains with doubled c-pawns—a losing disadvantage, as we know, if ever we reach a King and pawn endgame. That said, he is not without his prospects: the white e-pawn is particularly vulnerable and can only be protected at some inconvenience. While the statics may favor White, the dynamics are certainly in black's favor and thus an evaluation of approximate equality is in order."

> **Explaining the Rating Spread**: This kind of position mixes ideas that can be easily grasped by players in the 1400 group (i.e., putting pressure on a pawn and making use of one's active pieces) with the subtle—more advanced—nuances we see in the actual game.

Before moving on, let's address Mr. Short's comment about the doubled c-pawns being a losing disadvantage in a King and pawn endgame. One of white's dreams is to exchange all the minor and heavy pieces, which could easily lead to a position like this:

Diagram 291a

White to Move

If it was Black to move, he would actually win by making use of a well-known trick: **1...a3! 2.bxa3 b3!** and the pawn will turn into a Queen.

However, an experienced player would be alert to this possibility and would play **1.a3!** when black's crippled pawn majority is stopped cold. In effect, this means that Black is a solid pawn down in the King and pawn endgame. To win, all White has to do is to create a passed pawn on the kingside, find a way for his King to penetrate into enemy territory, and that will be that. **1...g6** Obviously, moves such as 1...bxa3 2.bxa3 or 1...b3 would leave black's queenside pawns completely immobile. **2.g4** Also possible is 2.h4 h6 3.g4 Kd6 4.h5, but 2.axb4?? cxb4 3.cxb4 c3 loses for White. **2...Kd7** Other moves also lose: 2...g5 3.e5! gxf4 4.exf6 Kxf6 5.Kxf4 h6 6.h4 Kg6 7.Ke4 and White picks off all black's queenside pawns; 2...f5 3.exf5+ gxf5 4.gxf5+ Kxf5 5.h3 Now white's King will reach e4 since any pawns moves can be met by Kf3-e3-f3 until black's King is forced to move—5...h6 6.Ke3 h5 7.Kf3 b3 8.Ke3 Kf6 9.Ke4 Ke6 10.f5+ Kf6 11.Kf4 and it's over. **3.h4 Kd6** 3...h6 4.f5 g5 5.hxg5 hxg5 (threatening to draw with ...Kd6) 6.e5! fxe5 7.Ke4 Kd6 8.f6 Ke6 9.f7 Kxf7 10.Kxe5, 1-0. **4.f5 gxf5 5.gxf5** 5.exf5 Ke5 6.Ke3 also wins. **5...Ke7 6.h5 h6 7.Ke3 Kd6 8.Kf4 b3** Now that Black no longer has tempo moves with his pawns, White can make use of an important idea that assures the decisive penetration of his King into the enemy position. **9.e5+! fxe5+ 10.Ke4 Ke7 11.Kxe5,** 1-0.

Now back to the position in diagram 291 and the Ganguly - Short game:

13.Re1 0-0-0 14.Rad1 Rhe8 15.Bc1 c5

Dominating the white Knight, which no longer has access to d4, e5, g5, or h4. This means that the highly desirable Knight maneuver, Nf3-d4-f5, is (at least for the moment) off the table.

16.b3 Qe6 17.Qxe6+ Rxe6 18.Rd2 b5 19.Kf1 Rde8 20.Rde2 Kb7

20...Ne5!? is also worthy of consideration.

21.g3 h5

Black has a comfortable game, but he will soon feel compelled to do something Short called "ugly and anti-positional" in order to generate winning chances.

22.Nd2 Ne5 23.f4 Nc6 24.c3 b4!?

Diagram 291b

Intensifying the Statics vs. Dynamics battle

Here it is! Nigel didn't want to wait around while White improved his position, but this move further devalues black's queenside pawns and also hands the white Knight the c4-square on a silver platter. However, though it increases white's static advantages, it also gives black's Knight access to d4, thus adding to his dynamics.

25.c4?!

Better was 25.Bb2 bxc3 26.Bxc3 though after 26...Nd4 27.Rf2 g5 it's clear that black's pieces exert a lot of pressure on white's position.

25...Nd4 26.Rf2 g5 27.Bb2 h4 28.Bxd4 cxd4 29.Ke2

White felt that his Knight would dominate black's Bishop, and this might well have been the case if all the Rooks were exchanged. However, the presence of the heavy pieces leaves the white King feeling insecure, and gives Black an annoying initiative.

29...hxg3 30.hxg3 Rh8 31.Rg1??

White folds. If we follow this book's basic tenet, which calls for a player to insist on the creation of favorable imbalances for himself, then 31.e5 gxf4 32.gxf4 fxe5 33.f5 (followed by Ne4) makes good sense. For the sacrificed pawn White has a passed pawn of his own and a vastly superior minor piece—in other words, it's still a battle with each player trying to show why their set of imbalances is better than the opponent's.

31...d3+ 32.Kxd3 Bc5 33.Rff1 Rd6+, 0-1.

Part Seven / Space

ANSWER
PART SEVEN

TEST 1

Diagram 334

[Level: 1600 - 2200]

E. Porper - V. Mikhalevski, Canadian Open 2009

Black to move

In prose, what is this position all about? Also, what kind of moves and themes would be most logical?

1.d4 Nf6 2.c4 g6 3.Nc3 d5 4.cxd5 Nxd5 5.e4 Nxc3 6.bxc3 Bg7 7.Bc4 c5 8.Ne2 Nc6 9.Be3 0-0 10.0-0 Bd7 11.Rb1 Qc7 12.Bd3 Rfd8 13.h3 Be8 14.d5 Ne5 15.c4 a6 16.Nc1 - Diagram 334

White has built a large pawn center and Black has to do his best to tear it down. To accomplish this, he needs to take advantage of the various pawn breaks: ...b5, ...e6, and, in some circumstances, ...f5. In this position he can't afford to play too quietly because White is ready to make even more central gains with f2-f4. Thus, energetic play is required if Black wants to hold the balance!

> **Explaining the Rating Spread**: I think players in the 1600 class will fully understand that Black has to chip away at white's center before it becomes too strong. The analytical details, though, are best tackled by the upper limits of the rating spread.

In the actual game, Black failed to halt white's central ambitions: **16...Rab8 17.f4 Nd7** (He should have tried 17...Nxd3, though White retains the better game after 18.Nxd3) **18.Qc2 Nb6 19.Ne2 Na4 20.e5 b5 21.Nc3 Nxc3 22.Qxc3 e6 23.Be4 exd5 24.cxd5 c4** (White's center trumps black's queenside majority.) **25.Bd4**

Diagram 334a

White's center is too powerful

25...f5? (This loses. 25...Qb7 was possible, hoping to sacrifice the Exchange by ...Rxd5. Of course, White would prevent this by 26.Rfd1 when black's game would be extremely unpleasant.) **26.exf6 e.p. Bf8 27.Be5 Qc5+ 28.Kh1 Rb7 29.f5 Rxd5 30.Bxd5+ Qxd5 31.Rbd1 Qc6 32.Rd8 b4 33.Qg3 c3 34.Bd6** (Good enough, but 34.fxg6 hxg6 35.Bd6 was even stronger since in that case 35...Bxd6 would run into 36.Qxg6+, which is a stone cold killer.) **34...Bxd6 35.Rxd6 Qb5 36.Re1 Rb8 37.Qe3 c2 38.Qe7 Qb7 39.Qxb7 Rxb7 40.Rxe8+ Kf7 41.Rc8**, 1-0.

Since 16...Rab8 did so poorly, let's look at three other possibilities that seem more in tune with the position (from diagram 334):

> ➤ **16...Nxd3** isn't necessary, and it's not as good as our remaining two choices (you cut down on your options by hurrying with this capture). However, if you intended to follow up with **17.Nxd3 b5! 18.Rc1 e6!** (Black's in full Pawn Break mode!), then you get credit for having learned your lessons pretty well!

> ➤ **16...e6** is very logical—he immediately starts chipping away at the enemy center! **17.f4 Nxd3 18.Nxd3 b5**

Diagram 334b

That's the way to go after a center!

19.Bxc5 (19.Nxc5 bxc4 [19...Bf8 is also good] 20.Rb7 [Both 20. Nb7 Rdb8 21.d6 Qc6 22.Nc5 Rxb1 23.Qxb1 Qxd6 and 20.Qf3 exd5 21.exd5 c3 favor Black] 20...Qd6 21.Rb1 and now Black can repeat moves with 21...Qc7, he can go for the gusto with 21...exd5 22.Nb7 Qa3 23.Bc5 Qxa2 24.Nxd8 Rxd8, or he can enter the complications of 21...Qe7 22.Rb7 Qf8, which should be perfectly fine for him) **19...bxc4 20.Bb6 Qd6 21.Bxd8 Rxd8 22.e5 Qxd5 23.Nf2 Bf8!** (Both 23...Bc6 and 23...Qa5 lead to all sorts of interesting complications, but I'm not sure that either of them equalizes. Fortunately for Black, the logical 23...Bf8, getting the dark-squared Bishop into the game, seems to give Black easy play.) **24.Ne4** (24.Ng4?? fails to 24...Qc5+, picking up white's Queen, while 24.Qxd5 exd5 25.Rb6 Bb5 26.a4 Bc5 27.Rf6 Bxa4 28.Rxa6 Be8 can only favor Black) **24...Kg7 25.Qe2 Qd3** (25...Ba4!?) **26.Qxd3 cxd3** and Black is fine since the d-pawn is surprisingly dangerous and the two Bishops are very strong.

16...b5 (Black tries to tear down white's center in as energetic manner as possible.) **17.cxb5 axb5** (Not 17...Nxd3?? 18.b6!) **18.Bxb5 Rdb8 19.a4** (19.Qe2 Ra3 20.Bd3 [20.f4? Ng4 is terrible for White] 20...c4 21.Rxb8 Qxb8 22.Bc2 [22.Bxc4 Nxc4 23.Qxc4 Rc3 24.Qe2 Bb5] 22...Qb5 [22...c3!?] 23.Qd2 [23.f4 Nd3] 23...Qb2 24.Qd1/24.Qe2 [24.Bc5 Rc3] 24...Bb5 with plenty of compensation for the sacrificed pawn) **19...Nc4 20.Qf3 Bxb5 21.axb5** (21.Rxb5 Rxb5 22.axb5 Qb7 23.Nb3 Qxb5 24.Nxc5 transposes) **21...Qa5 22.Nd3 Rxb5 23.Rxb5 Qxb5 24.Nxc5** and now both 24...Ra2 25.Rd1 h5! and 24...Ra5 25.Rc1 Bb2 26.Rb1 Nxe3 27.Qxe3 Be5! 28.Nb3 (28.Rc1 Bb2 is a draw) 28...Ra2 are fine for Black.

These lines are complicated, and even strong masters would have trouble wending their way through it all in an over-the-board game. However, the point of this problem wasn't the analysis, but your ability to understand the general ideas/concepts in our beginning position—including black's need to smack down white's center by using the available pawn breaks. As far as moves are concerned, you can be proud of yourself if you realized that center-destroying pawn breaks like ...e6 and ...b5 were needed.

ANSWER
PART SEVEN

TEST 2

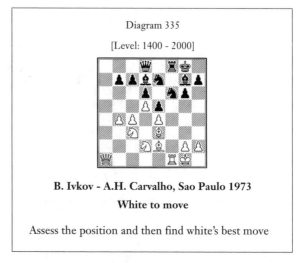

Diagram 335

[Level: 1400 - 2000]

B. Ivkov - A.H. Carvalho, Sao Paulo 1973

White to move

Assess the position and then find white's best move

1.Nf3 Nf6 2.c4 g6 3.Nc3 Bg7 4.d4 0–0 5.e4 d6 6.Be2 e5 7.Be3 Nc6 8.d5 Ne7 9.Nd2 Ne8 10.b4 f5 11.f3 a5 12.a3 Nf6 13.0–0 axb4 14.axb4 Rxa1 15.Qxa1 fxe4 16.fxe4 Bd7 - Diagram 335

Black's position looks solid, but he's actually in terrible trouble.

> **Explaining the Rating Spread**: I would expect a 1400 player that has carefully read all the material in the Space section to appreciate white's enormous space advantage on the queenside. And, I would hope that he would want to expand that spatial plus with the thematic 17.c5. However, it would probably take a higher rated player to realize the true severity of black's situation (after all, black's position doesn't—visually—seem that bad!). Why are things so grim for Black? Because he doesn't have his usual kingside counterplay and, without kingside chances, white's queenside attack will roll him off the board.

17.c5

White marches forward, placing pressure on d6 and preparing to back up that pressure with Nc4.

17...Qa8

Things aren't much better after 17...Ng4 18.Rxf8+ Qxf8 19.Bxg4 Bxg4 20.Nc4.

18.Nc4 Qb8 19.b5

This crushing move was probably played instantly (I'm sure he already considered the game to be over), which explains why a magnificent player like Ivkov missed 19.cxd6 cxd6 20.Nxd6! Qxd6 21.Bc5 Qb8 22.Bxe7.

19...Ne8 20.Rxf8+ Kxf8 21.Qa3 Kf7 22.c6 bxc6 23.bxc6 Bc8 24.Nb5! Black could have resigned here, but he decided to sit back and watch his esteemed foe cut him up a bit more: **24...Kf8 25.Qa5 h6 26.Ba7 Qa8 27.Nxc7 Nxc7 28.Qxc7 Ba6 29.Nb6**, 1-0.

ANSWER
PART SEVEN

TEST 3

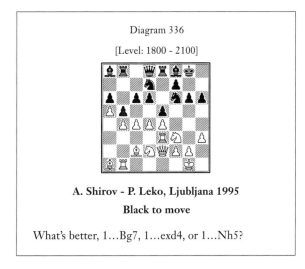

Diagram 336

[Level: 1800 - 2100]

A. Shirov - P. Leko, Ljubljana 1995

Black to move

What's better, 1...Bg7, 1...exd4, or 1...Nh5?

1.e4 e5 2.Nf3 Nc6 3.Bb5 a6 4.Ba4 Nf6 5.0–0 Be7 6.Re1 b5 7.Bb3 d6 8.c3 0–0 9.h3 Nb8 10.d4 Nbd7 11.Nbd2 Bb7 12.Bc2 Re8 13.a4 Bf8 14.b4 Nb6 15.a5 Nbd7 16.Bb2 Rb8 17.Rb1 h6 18.Ba1 Ba8 19.Re3 g6 20.Qe2 c6 21.c4 - Diagram 336

White has been busy grabbing space for some time—he started with a bit more central territory after 10.d4, then he began annexing queenside space with 13.a4, 14.b4, and 15.a5, and the last move, 21.c4, continued the space-gaining trend. Clearly, Black can't afford to let this continue!

> **Explaining the Rating Spread**: Things seem very complicated and it would be easy to miss white's intention to take on e5 followed by c4-c5 with a huge spatial clamp. Thus I gave this problem a high rating spread. Of course, I hope you lower rated players did notice white's threat to envelop the queenside and, by doing so, proved me completely wrong about what the spread should be.

21...Bg7?

Instead of stopping white's plan of world domination, Black quietly developed his Bishop to a reasonable looking square and let White have his way! By now we know that the indignity of suffocation can only be tolerated if some sort of counterplay allows the spatially challenged side to make use of enemy squares weakened by the forward marching pawns, or if we have our own things happening in another sector of the board, or if the space gaining pawns can be viewed as attackable targets. In the position that occurs, Black achieves none of these things and thus ends up with an uncomfortable, passive position.

Though 21...Nh5 is more aggressive than 21...Bg7, White still retains an edge with 22.dxe5 Nf4 23.Qf1 Nxe5 24.Nxe5 dxe5 25.Nf3 Bg7 26.Rd1 Qc7 27.c5.

Clearly best was 21...exd4! 22.Bxd4 Nh5! when both 23.g3 c5! and 23.Ba1 Nf4 24.Qf1 Bg7 25.Bxg7 Kxg7 26.g3 Ne6 give Black his full share of the play.

Note the difference between our three choices: Both 21...Bg7 and 21...Nh5 allow White to consolidate his advantage in space while leaving Black with little or no counterplay. The far more combative 21...exd4! gives Black a fluid position with pieces that are poised to jump to life, and pawn breaks (...c5 or ...d5—often mixed with ...bxc4) that can rip things open at the drop of a hat.

Clearly you don't want to sit around twiddling your thumbs while enemy space envelopes you in its web. Fight back!

22.dxe5 dxe5 23.c5 White's advantage in space is now obvious. Black's pieces are inactive and he doesn't have any targets to strike at. The rest of the game is given without comment: **23...Nh5 24.g3 Qc7 25.Rd3 Rbd8 26.Rd1 Nf8 27.Nf1 Rxd3 28.Qxd3 Nf6 29.Ne3 Bb7 30.Kg2 Qb8 31.Bb2 Qc7 32.Bb3 Re7 33.Qd8 Qxd8 34.Rxd8 Nd7 35.Nh4 Kh7 36.Nhf5 gxf5 37.Nxf5 Bf6 38.Nxe7 Bxe7 39.Re8 Bg5 40.Bxf7 Kg7 41.Bb3 Bf6 42.f4 Ng6 43.f5 Ngf8 44.h4 Kh7 45.Kh3 Kg7 46.g4 Kh7 47.Bc1 Bg7 48.g5 hxg5 49.hxg5 Kh8** and Black resigned without waiting for the reply. 1-0.

ANSWER
PART SEVEN
TEST 4

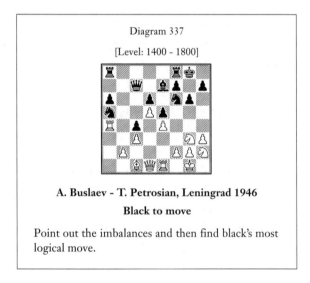

Diagram 337

[Level: 1400 - 1800]

A. Buslaev - T. Petrosian, Leningrad 1946

Black to move

Point out the imbalances and then find black's most logical move.

1.e4 e5 2.Nf3 Nc6 3.Bb5 a6 4.Ba4 Nf6 5.0–0 Be7 6.Re1 b5 7.Bb3 d6 8.c3 0–0 9.h3 Na5 10.Bc2 c5 11.d4 Qc7 12.Nbd2 Bb7 13.d5 Bc8 14.a4 Bd7 15.Nf1 c4 16.Ng3 g6 17.Nh2 bxa4 18.Bxa4 Bxa4 19.Rxa4 - Diagram 337

White has central space and will generally do one of two things: 1) Seek a kingside attack with moves such as Bh6 and Ng4; 2) Place pressure against the potentially weak pawns on a6 and c4 by Qe2, Ng3-f1-e3 (hitting c4), and then swinging the e1-Rook to a1 (smacking the a5-Knight and taking aim at a6).

On a basic level we can say that Black has queenside space, so he will seek play down the b-file against the b2-pawn. However, this is by no means the whole story— there's a lot more going on than that! White's d4-d5 has given him a clear advantage in central space, but he paid a price for it: the c5-square (which was controlled by the white pawn on d4) is now black's, and a Knight on that square leads to control of two other weak squares in the enemy camp: b3 and d3. Once you realize these things (the weakness and connections of the c5, b3, and d3 squares) then black's most logical move should be obvious.

Explaining the Rating Spread: If you noticed the holes on c5, b3, and d3 and saw how to use them (19...Nd7), then take a bow. I trust that the 1400 readers of this book can (or soon will!) be able to find the logical ...Nf6-d7-c5 maneuver with the greatest of ease.

19...Nd7!

It's hard to imagine a more natural move. The Knight wasn't doing much on f6, so it begins a short journey to c5 where it will attack white's Rook and prepare a leap into d3. Compare the Knight on f6, where it's a rather unimposing critter, and c5, where it's a mighty Octopus—its tentacles reaching deep (and in all directions) into the enemy position!

20.f4??

This loses since it not only fails to address the upcoming Knight invasion to d3, but it also creates serious weaknesses along the g1-a7 diagonal—a clear case of a player blindly going about with his own plans without taking anything else into account! White had to play 20.Be3 Nc5 21.Bxc5 Qxc5 22.Qe2 intending to follow up with Ng3-f1-e3 and Rea1 with pressure against black's queenside pawns.

Here's the rest of the game with minimal notes: **20...exf4 21.Bxf4 Nc5 22.Ra1 Nab3 23.Rb1 Nd3 24.Bh6** (24.Rf1 Qa7+ 25.Kh1 Nf2+) **24...Nxe1 25.Qxe1** (25.Bxf8 Qc5+ 26.Kh1 Nd3 27.Ng4 Kxf8 and black's a piece up) **25...Nc5 26.Bxf8 Nd3 27.Qe3 Rxf8 28.Nf3 Rb8 29.Ra1 a5 30.Nd4 Rxb2 31.Nc6 Bd8 32.Nxa5 Qb6 33.Qxb6 Bxb6+ 34.Kh1 Bxa5 35.Rxa5 h5 36.h4 Nf2+ 37.Kh2 Ng4+ 38.Kh3 Rc2 39.Ra8+ Kg7 40.Rd8 Rxc3 41.Rxd6 Nf2+ 42.Kh2 Rxg3**, 0-1.

ANSWER
PART SEVEN

TEST 5

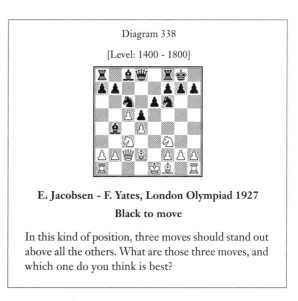

Diagram 338

[Level: 1400 - 1800]

E. Jacobsen - F. Yates, London Olympiad 1927

Black to move

In this kind of position, three moves should stand out above all the others. What are those three moves, and which one do you think is best?

1.d4 e6 2.c4 Nf6 3.Nc3 Bb4 4.Qc2 c5 5.e3 0–0 6.Bd2 cxd4 7.exd4 d5 8.Nf3 Nc6 9.c5 - Diagram 338

White's 9.c5 is a weak move since it doesn't address the fact that his King is still in the center, nor whether or not the advanced c-pawn can be maintained. When this kind of position is reached, the first moves Black should explore are 9...Ne4 (preparing to cement the Knight by ...f5), 9...b6 (tearing down the space-gaining c5-pawn), and 9...e5 (not only nuking white's pawn chain, but also opening up the center in an effort to punish White for leaving his King there).

> **Explaining the Rating Spread**: These ideas were clearly discussed, so an alert 1400 should know them. If you don't (no matter what your rating may be), reread Part Seven, Space until the lessons there fully sink in.

9...e5!

Rending white's pawn chain limb from limb and starting a fight while white's King is still in the middle. The other moves (9...b6 and 9...Ne4) are also fully playable.

10.dxe5 and now **10...Ng4** would have given Black an excellent game: **11.h3 Ngxe5 12.Nxe5 Nxe5 13.0–0–0 Bxc5 14.Bf4 Ng6 15.Nxd5** (15.Rxd5 Qe7 16.Bg3 Be6 and black's lead in development mixed with white's somewhat insecure King give Black a serious initiative.) **15...Nxf4 16.Qxc5 Nxd5 17.Rxd5 Qf6 18.Qd4 Qh6+ 19.Qd2 Qc6+** (19...Qg6!?) **20.Kb1 Be6**.

ANSWER
PART SEVEN

TEST **6**

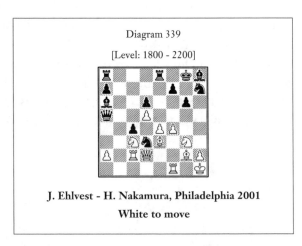

Diagram 339

[Level: 1800 - 2200]

J. Ehlvest - H. Nakamura, Philadelphia 2001
White to move

1.c4 Nf6 2.Nc3 g6 3.e4 d6 4.d4 Bg7 5.f3 0–0 6.Nge2 c5 7.d5 e6 8.Bg5 h6 9.Be3 exd5 10.cxd5 Nbd7 11.Qd2 Ne5 12.Ng3 h5 13.Bg5 h4! 14.Nge2 h3 15.Ng3 hxg2 16.Bxg2 b5 17.0–0 Qb6 18.b3 Re8 19.Kh1 Nh7 20.Bh6 Bh8 21.Be3 Qa5 22.Rac1 Ba6 23.f4 Nd3 24.Rc2 c4 25.bxc4 bxc4 - Diagram 339

As is so common in positions that feature space advantages, a square behind the space-gaining pawns has fallen into the opponent's hands. However, white's central space advantage still exists and black's King seems to be a bit drafty. White decides it's time to use that space advantage to create concrete play on the kingside.

> **Explaining the Rating Spread**: A tough one since it looks like Black achieved something nice by getting his Knight to d3. However, if you saw that White could use his center to strike at the enemy King, then you should consider yourself a very good player.

26.e5!

Black had the initiative for the whole game, but suddenly White cashes in his fine static center for a host of dynamic considerations: 1) 26.e5 blocks black's dark-squared Bishop; 2) It frees the e4-square for white's Knights and Bishop (thus the one pawn move activated three white minor pieces); 3) It intends to crack open the black King with moves such as e5-e6 or f4-f5.

26...f5

I'm not sure what the best defense was, but the change in momentum had to be psychologically difficult for Black to deal with. Other tries:

- 26...dxe5 27.f5 Rad8 28.Be4 seems very dangerous for Black.

- 26...Rad8 27.e6 fxe6 (27...f5 28.h4 Nf6 29.h5) 28.dxe6 Nf6 (28...Rxe6 when both 29.f5 and 29.Bd5 Rde8 30.f5 Bxc3 31.Qg2 are possible) 29.f5 continues the "cracking open" process.

- Perhaps best is 26...Rad8 27.e6 fxe6 28.dxe6 d5! 29.f5 d4

Diagram 339a

A fun position!

One can spend days basking in this position's complexities. I'll give one sample line and leave the rest to interested readers and their faithful army of engines: 30.fxg6 (30.Bxd4 Bxd4 31.Qh6 Bg7 32.Qxg6 Ne5 is a whole other story) 30...Nf6 31.Bxd4 Rxd4 32.Nf5 Qe5 33.Qh6 Rf4 34.g7 Rxf1+ 35.Bxf1 Bb7+ 36.Nd5! Qxd5+ (36...Bxd5+ 37.Kg1 wins for White) 37.Rg2 Nf2+ 38.Kg1 Nh3+ and now White can accept a draw with 39.Kh1 Nf2+ or continue the madness by 39.Qxh3 Qc5+ 40.Rf2 Bxg7 41.Qg3 Re7.

In the actual game, Black was gobbled up and quickly digested: **27.exf6 e.p. Nxf6 28.f5 Nb4 29.Rcc1 Nd3 30.Bd4! Nxc1 31.Qg5! Qc7 32.fxg6 Nd3 33.Nf5 Ng4 34.g7 Nge5 35.Nh6+,** 1-0. Black will be mated after 35...Kh7 36.Be4+ Ng6 37.Bxg6 mate.

ANSWER
PART SEVEN

TEST 7

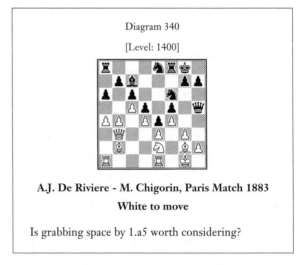

Diagram 340

[Level: 1400]

A.J. De Riviere - M. Chigorin, Paris Match 1883

White to move

Is grabbing space by 1.a5 worth considering?

1.Nf3 d5 2.d4 Nf6 3.e3 Bg4 4.Be2 Nbd7 5.c4 e6 6.Nc3 c6 7.a3 Bd6 8.c5 Bc7 9.b4 0–0 10.0–0 Bxf3 (10...Ne4!? with the idea of ...f5 and kingside play) **11.Bxf3 e5 12.g3 e4 13.Bg2 Ne8 14.a4 f5 15.f4 Qf6 16.Bb2 Qh6 17.Qb3 Nef6 18.Ne2 Qh5 19.Rfe1 a6** - Diagram 340

The respective plans should be pretty well mapped out: White's huge queenside space advantage translates to an eventual b4-b5 advance. Black's only counterplay comes on the kingside (the center is dead, so it's the kingside or bust), and he'll get things going on that wing with ...h6 followed by ...g5.

> **Explaining the Rating Spread**: I expect everyone reading this book to feel revulsion at the sight of 20.a5.

20.a5??

This move should create a scream of horror and agony (it should actually be both psychologically and physically painful to see) by any spectator who happened to pass by. Yes, it gains more space, but what good is space if there's no way to penetrate the enemy position in that sector, or if that space doesn't stop your opponent's play? By playing 20.a5, White has deprived himself of any active plan while giving the green light to Black.

Never accept (let alone willingly create!) a position where you are helpless and have nothing better to do than watch your opponent mass his army in ideal fashion at his leisure.

The rest of the game saw Chigorin set up the ultimate attacking position, only lowering the boom when every piece was in its perfect position: **20...h6 21.Nc3 g5 22.Qd1 Qg6 23.Bc1 Rf7 24.Ra2 Nf8 25.Kh1 Ne6 26.Bh3 Rg7 27.Rf2 g4 28.Bf1 h5 29.Rg2 Kf7 30.Kg1 Rh8 31.Ne2 h4 32.gxh4 Rxh4 33.Ng3 Rgh7 34.Ree2 Nh5 35.Nxh5 Qxh5 36.Ref2 Ng5 37.Kh1 Nf3 38.Qe2 g3, 0-1.**

Part Eight / Passed Pawns

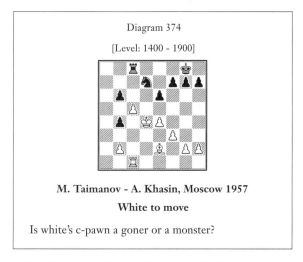

Diagram 374

[Level: 1400 - 1900]

M. Taimanov - A. Khasin, Moscow 1957

White to move

Is white's c-pawn a goner or a monster?

1.d4 d5 2.c4 c6 3.Nf3 Nf6 4.Nc3 dxc4 5.a4 Bf5 6.Ne5 e6 7.f3 Bb4 8.Bg5 c5 9.dxc5 Qxd1+ 10.Rxd1 Bc2 11.Rd4 Nc6 12.Rxc4 a5 13.Nd3 Bxa4 14.Nxb4 axb4 15.Nxa4 Rxa4 16.e4 Ra1+ 17.Rc1 Rxc1+ 18.Bxc1 0–0 19.Be2 Nd4 20.Be3 Nc2+ 21.Kd2 Nxe3 22.Kxe3 Nd7 23.Rc1 Rc8 24.Kd4 b6 - Diagram 374

Black has just played 24...b6 when White pretty much has to push his c-pawn to c6. Black obviously felt (or hoped!) that the pawn would be a goner on c6, but that's not at all the case!

> **Explaining the Rating Spread**: A 1400 player will realize that 25.c6 is forced, but would he be happy about the ensuing Exchange sacrifice? For that particular part of the puzzle, I moved the scale up a bit to Class "B." Whether players in this rating spread notice that they will have to give up an Exchange or not (I pushed the scale up again to 1900 for those that see the Exchange sacrifice coming), they will readily appreciate the follow-up.

25.c6 e5+

25...Nc5 is the critical move, but after 26.Rxc5! bxc5+ 27.Kxc5 the passed c-pawn, supported by its King and Bishop, is much too powerful to resist: 27...Kf8 28.Ba6 Rc7 29.Kb6 Re7 30.c7 and the game is over.

26.Kd5 Nf6+ 27.Kd6 Rd8+ 28.Kc7

That's one powerful King! Black is dead lost due to the 6th rank pawn supported by its dynamic King.

28...Rd2 29.Kxb6

White laughs at the threat to his Bishop since 29...Rxe2 30.c7 creates a new Queen.

29...Ne8

Black's last stand.

30.Rd1!

Breaking black's resistance—trading Rooks leaves him without any counterplay at all, while not trading proves to be no better.

30...Rxe2 31.Rd8 Kf8 32.c7 Rc2 33.c8=Q Rxc8 34.Rxc8. The rest is easy: **34...Ke7 35.Rc4 g6 36.Rxb4 f5 37.Kc6 Ke6 38.Kc5 fxe4 39.fxe4 Nf6 40.Rb6+**, 1-0.

ANSWER
PART EIGHT

TEST 2

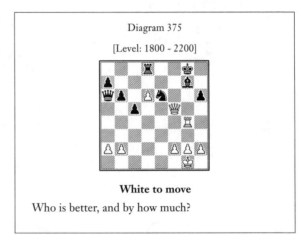

Diagram 375

[Level: 1800 - 2200]

White to move

Who is better, and by how much?

This is a hypothetical position that occurred in an analysis of J. Lautier - M. Sharif, Port Barcares 2005. White's first move is obvious, but then we get into some difficulties. The real answer, which doesn't need much analysis, is based on a concept: White can force a Queen vs. Queen endgame where White possesses a far advanced passed pawn. In the theory section, we already learned how enormously advantageous passed pawns are in this kind of endgame, so playing for that position and simply having faith in a positive outcome would be good enough.

> **Explaining the Rating Spread**: Basic tactics aside, I think seeing past the flash to the resulting Queen endgame would leave serious questions in many players' minds. Things like, "Doesn't Black have chances for perpetual check?" and "Can't black's King waltz over and help its Queen stop the d-pawn?" would nag at most players under "A" class.

1.Qxe6+ Kh8 2.Rxg7

Far worse is 2.Qe7 Rg8 3.Rxg7 Rxg7 4.d7 Rxe7 5.d8=Q+ Kg7 6.Qxe7+ Kg6 7.Qe6+ Kg7 when White is obviously much better, but there's still a long fight ahead. Why settle for this when 2.Rxg7 is gin?

2...Kxg7 3.Qe7+ Kg6 4.Qxd8

You have to acquire faith (this comes from experience, which you're getting now) that this kind of passed pawn plus Queen endgame is usually a slam-dunk win unless the stronger side's King is so vulnerable that he can't avoid perpetual check.

Diagram 375a

White's passed d-pawn is a winner

4...Qa4

Of course, Black has other moves, but all of them end with White winning by the kind of "check, check, check, create luft for the King" sequences that occur after 4...Qa4.

5.Qg8+ Kf6 6.Qf8+ Kg6

Also possible is 6...Ke6 7.Qe7+ Kf5 8.h3 Qd1+ 9.Kh2 Qd4 hoping to draw by 10...Qf4+ 11.Kg1 Qc1+ with a perpetual check. However, White easily deals with this: 10.Qf7+ Ke5 (10...Kg5 11.d7 Qd6+ 12.f4+; 10...Qf6 11.g4+ Ke5 12.f4+; 10...Ke4 11.Qe6+ Kd3 12.Qe3+ and the pawn promotes) 11.d7 Qd6 12.g3 and Black is helpless.

7.h4!

Of course, this isn't the only way to win!

7...Qd7

7...Qd1+ 8.Kh2 Qd4 9.h5+! Kg5 (9...Kxh5 10.Qf5+ Kh4 11.g3 mate; 9...Kh7 10.Qf7+ Kh8 11.d7) 10.f4+ Kg4 (10...Kxh5 11.Qf5+ Kh4 12.g3 mate) 11.Qxh6 Kf5 12.Qg5+ Ke6 13.Qe7+ Kf5 14.Qe5+.

8.h5+ Kxh5 9.Qe7 Qa4 10.d7 Qd1+ 11.Kh2 Qd4 12.Qe8+ Kg4 13.f3+ (Avoiding 13.d8=Q?? Qf4+) **13...Kf4 14.d8=Q**, 1-0.

ANSWER
PART EIGHT
TEST 3

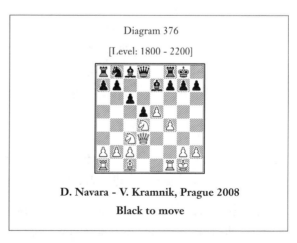

Diagram 376

[Level: 1800 - 2200]

D. Navara - V. Kramnik, Prague 2008

Black to move

1.e4 e5 2.Nf3 Nf6 3.d4 Nxe4 4.Bd3 d5 5.dxe5 Nc5 6.Nc3 c6 7.Nd4 Be7 8.0–0 0–0 9.f4 Nxd3 10.Qxd3 - Diagram 376

White appears to have a very nice position—he's ahead in development, he has more central space, and his kingside pawn majority (which has an eventual f4-f5-f6 expansion programmed into its DNA) in particular seems extremely threatening. Kramnik quickly shows that this is all an illusion.

> **Explaining the Rating Spread**: Though we looked at a very similar situation and answer in Part Eight, Passed Pawns (diagram 358), it tends to psychologically disturb a whole range of players to such an extent that I've given it a very high level of difficulty. Even masters sometimes can't bring themselves to play the right move here!

10...f5!

Handing White a protected passed pawn on a platter! However, it also kills the dynamism of the white pawns. Now Black will: 1) play to increase his control over the blockading e6-square; 2) support his own pawn majority so that he can advance it. Ideally, with white's e-pawn firmly blocked and his own pawns rushing forward in dynamic frenzy, Black will be able to claim an advantage.

11.Nb3 Na6 12.Be3 Nc7

Heading towards e6 while simultaneously giving support to d5 in anticipation of an eventual ...c6-c5 advance.

13.Ne2 b6 14.Nbd4 Ba6

The Bishop shows alarming activity.

15.Qd2 Qe8 16.c3 c5

By taking control over the d4-square, white's Knights are forced back to squares where they can't influence e6. Thus 16...c5 wins the e6-square and allows Black to claim victory in the blockading war!

17.Nf3 Rd8 18.Rfd1 Ne6

Diagram 376a

A dream setup for Black

Black's vision has come together nicely. He has two Bishops, a firm blockade on e6, and a mobile pawn majority. Also note how white's pawns on e5 and f4 are blocking their own pieces! Black eventually won (after various errors and adventures).

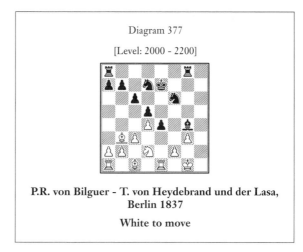

Diagram 377

[Level: 2000 - 2200]

P.R. von Bilguer - T. von Heydebrand und der Lasa, Berlin 1837

White to move

White has an extra pawn. Is it a weakness that can be nipped at and eventually eaten? No, it's a protected passed pawn! White also has two Bishops while all Black can brag about is a lead in development. Surely White must be much better? But, here comes another "no"—Black actually enjoys excellent compensation (note that I'm not stating that Black is better, just that he has real compensation)! The reasons for this are simple:

- Black has all the play while White will be forced to take a defensive stance for a long time to come.

- The passed g-pawn isn't going anywhere.

- The light-squares around white's King are vulnerable.

- Black's play is easy to find—double on the h-file and go after "Fred" on g1.

Of course, most chess engines will leap on white's bandwagon and proclaim black's inferiority to all who will listen. However, don't let yourself become a "Fritz slave"! Don't deprive yourself of instruction just because your computer is clouding your mind with a numeric (soulless) assessment. In his notes to Leko - Kramnik, Linares 2004 (*New In Chess*, issue 3, 2004), Kramnik wrote the following witty and penetrating words about the masses of players who were following his game live: "Black has quite good compensation for the pawn, I considered during the game. 'White is +0.72' thought the numerous online spectators."

> **Explaining the Rating Spread**: Owning an extra protected passed pawn while also having two Bishops and having traded Queens (the usual knockout punch when it comes to kingside attacks) would make most players lean towards white's position. When you add my rather cruel act of giving White the move (usually indicating that white's in charge) to the equation, it would be a rare (and very strong) player who would give Black his due.

19.Nf1

Black also gets plenty of play after 19.c4 (19.Kg2!?) 19...Rg7! since 20.f3? (20.cxd5 cxd5 21.Nf1 Rh8) 20...Bxf3 21.Nxf3?? Rxg3+ wins for Black.

19...Rh8

19...Rg7!? might be more accurate.

20.Ne3

The actual game ended abruptly: 20.Nh2?? Rxh2 21.Kxh2 Rh8+ 22.Kg1 Bf3, 0-1.

20...Rag8

20...Rh5!?

21.Nxg4 Nxg4 22.Bf4

22.c4 Ndf6 23.cxd5 cxd5 24.Bd1 Kd7 also leaves White with no better than equality.

22...Kd8 23.Bd1 Ndf6 and the threat of ...Rh2 ensures Black ample play and full compensation.

ANSWER
PART EIGHT

TEST 5

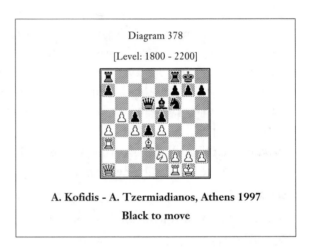

Diagram 378

[Level: 1800 - 2200]

A. Kofidis - A. Tzermiadianos, Athens 1997

Black to move

1.e4 c5 2.Nf3 Nc6 3.d4 cxd4 4.Nxd4 Nf6 5.Nc3 e5 6.Nxc6 bxc6 7.Bd3 Be7 8.0–0 d6 9.b4 0–0 10.a4 d5 11.Ba3 Be6 12.b5 Bxa3 13.Rxa3 Qd6 14.Qa1 d4 15.Ne2 c5 16.c4 - Diagram 378

Black has a protected passed d-pawn, but it's firmly blocked by the d3-Bishop. On the other hand, a Bishop isn't the best of blockaders—note how the d3-Bishop looks more like a Tall-Pawn than a Bishop. Clearly, while a Knight can block a pawn *and* show great activity from the blockading square, a Bishop can easily find itself in a purely defensive posture when holding back an enemy passer.

Though White doesn't have a passed pawn of his own, he does have a very mobile queenside pawn majority. Indeed, after a4-a5 Black will have to constantly worry about the further expansion of white's queenside pawns.

> **Explaining the Rating Spread**: We've looked at this kind of thing in the Passed Pawn section, but that doesn't make black's correct move any less difficult to come to terms with. Quite simply, it's something most players just can't bring themselves to do!

16...a5!

White is handed a protected passed pawn on a silver platter, yet Black is more than glad to do so. Why? Because once he places his Knight on b6, the pawn is going nowhere while the pawns on a4 and c4 will require constant defense. After that Black can (and will) play for the strong break ...f7-f5. Remember that it's not enough to have a firm blockade, you also need active play elsewhere on the board.

17.Ng3 Rfe8 18.Qc1 Nd7 19.Qd2 Nb6

Diagram 378a

Black's Knight is a better blockader than white's Bishop

Black has an excellent position thanks to the fact that his blockading piece stops the pawn and hits a4 and c4. Compare that with white's, which blocks d4 and defends c4, but plays no active role. Black now prepares ...f7-f5, which will give him chances for a kingside attack (if the f-pawn is allowed to continue on to f4) and central domination if White captures on f5.

The rest of the game has some inaccuracies, but it still gives us a clear look into the strength of a mobile pawn majority—in this case Black gets a central pawn majority and shoves it down white's throat: **20.Rc1 Qc7 21.Qe2 f6 22.Nf1 g6 23.Nd2 f5 24.exf5 gxf5 25.f3 Re7 26.Re1 Bd7 27.Qd1 Nc8 28.Qb1 Nd6 29.Nf1 Rf8 30.Ra2 e4 31.fxe4 fxe4 32.Bxe4 Rxe4 33.Rxe4 Bf5 34.Ng3 Nxe4 35.Nxe4 Qf4**, 0-1.

ANSWER
PART EIGHT

TEST **6**

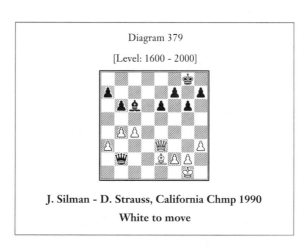

Diagram 379

[Level: 1600 - 2000]

J. Silman - D. Strauss, California Chmp 1990

White to move

1.d4 d5 2.c4 e6 3.Nc3 c6 4.e3 Nf6 5.Nf3 Nbd7 6.Qc2 Be7 7.b3 0–0 8.Be2 b6 9.0–0 Bb7 10.e4 dxe4 11.Nxe4 c5 12.Nxf6+ Bxf6 13.Bb2 Qc7 14.Rad1 Rad8 15.dxc5 Qxc5 16.Rd2 Ne5 17.Nxe5 Bxe5 18.Bxe5 Qxe5 19.Rfd1 Qg5 20.Bf1 Qe7 21.Qc3 g6 22.b4 Rxd2 23.Qxd2 Rc8 24.a3 Bc6 25.Qe3 Rd8 26.Rxd8+ Qxd8 27.Be2 Qf6 28.h3 Qb2 - Diagram 379

White's gotten nothing from the opening, and the short-lived middlegame also offered zero gains. Does White possess anything that would allow him to put a little pressure on his opponent? The answer is yes—the queenside majority.

> **Explaining the Rating Spread**: By remembering the fact that a passed pawn often reaches its peak of strength in a Queen endgame, White can play a move that normally wouldn't occur to most players. In other words, it takes some knowledge about passed pawns to make the following decision. I wouldn't think that a player under 1600 would ever willingly swap Bishops and allow his kingside structure to be crippled. Hopefully, a lot of people reading this book will prove me wrong.

29.Bf3!

29.c5 bxc5 30.bxc5 e5 is very comfortable for Black, e.g. 31.Bf3 e4!

Of course, White isn't winning after 29.Bf3, but it does set Black some problems to solve while White can push a bit without any risk whatsoever.

29...Bxf3 30.gxf3 Qc2 31.c5 bxc5 32.bxc5 Qd1+ 33.Kg2

Diagram 379a

White can safely "massage" his opponent

The doubled pawns form an oddly effective protection of white's King while the passed c-pawn is very annoying.

33...Qd5 34.Qc3 Qc6

Black wanted to avoid 34...Qg5+ 35.Kf1 Qf4 36.c6 Qc7 37.Qc5 when the pawn has become even more menacing than before!

35.Qe5

35.Qa5!?

35...h5??

Black cracks. 35...a6 would hold, though White can continue to probe with 36.Qb8+ Kg7 37.Qb6 Qd5 38.Qb4 Qg5+ 39.Kh2 Qe5+ (not black's only move) 40.f4 Qc7 41.Kg3, etc. Even though the position looks safe for Black, he would have to be careful since "innocent" King and pawn endgames like 41...g5 42.Qd4+ Kf8? (42...f6! had to be tried) 43.Qd6+ Qxd6 44.cxd6 gxf4+ 45.Kxf4 aren't innocent at all! A sample: 45...f6 (even easier for White is 45...Ke8 46.Ke5 Kd7 47.h4 f6+ 48.Kxf6 Kxd6 49.Kg7) 46.Kg4 Ke8 47.Kh5 f5 48.Kh6 f4 49.Kg5 f3 50.Kf4 Kd7 51.Kxf3 Kxd6 52.Kf4 wins for White.

Diagram 379b

Black is Lost

Back to the actual game: After the blunder 35...h5, Black went down quickly:
36.Qb8+ Kg7 37.Qxa7 Qd5 38.Qe7 e5 39.a4 Kh6 40.a5 f5 41.Qd6, 1-0.

ANSWER
PART EIGHT

TEST *7*

Diagram 380

[Level: 1600 - 2200]

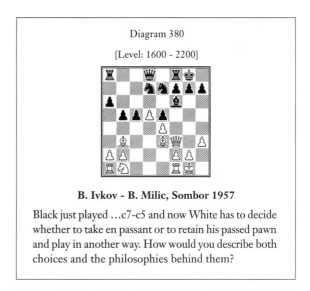

B. Ivkov - B. Milic, Sombor 1957

Black just played ...c7-c5 and now White has to decide
whether to take en passant or to retain his passed pawn
and play in another way. How would you describe both
choices and the philosophies behind them?

**1.e4 e5 2.Nf3 Nc6 3.Bb5 a6 4.Ba4 d6 5.c3 Bd7 6.d4 Be7 7.0–0 Bf6 8.d5 Nb8
9.c4 b5 10.Bb3 Ne7 11.Be3 0–0 12.c5 dxc5 13.Bxc5 Bg4 14.h3 Bxf3 15.Qxf3
Nd7 16.Be3 c5** - Diagram 380

White can't just mindlessly develop and expect his passed pawn to bust up his opponent. For example, 17.Rd1 Nc8 18.Nc3 Nd6 leaves Black with a comfortable blockade
and a perfectly playable position. This means that White has to either take en passant
and go for active piece play or retain his passed d-pawn and strike before Black can
achieve his ideal setup. The second plan would call for moves like 17.Rc1 (hitting c5)
or 17.a4, in both cases trying to create weaknesses in the enemy queenside majority.

> **Explaining the Rating Spread**: I would be happy if a class "B" player
> (1600-1799) appreciated the strength of a d6-blockade and decided to
> go for 17.dxc6 e.p. Some will and some won't, but I also think class "A"
> players will be similarly divided. Would 2200 rated masters find this easy?
> No, I'm sure that quite a few would fail to fully appreciate this position's
> many nuances.

I won't give an analysis of 17.Rc1 or 17.a4, but I highly recommend the student explore both moves in detail! Instead, we'll see how the actual game progressed.

17.dxc6 e.p.

Ripping open the center in an effort to make maximum use of his superior minor pieces. At the moment white's Bishops look great, and his Knight will make a beeline to the d5-hole. White's Rooks can also hit the d-file and add a bit more heat to the proceedings. This is vintage prime Ivkov, who relished situations that allowed him to turn the screws without risking any incoming fire.

17...Nxc6 18.Bd5 Rc8 19.Bxc6!

Else the c6-Knight would hop into d4.

19...Rxc6 20.Rd1 Qc8 21.Nc3 Re8

Avoiding potential Knight forks on e7. Perhaps 21...Nb6 was better, though in that case 22.Bxb6 Rxb6 23.Nd5 ensures White a small but lasting plus thanks to his superior minor piece. An example of the kind of thing White wants to achieve is 23...Rc6 24.b4 h6 25.a4 bxa4 26.Rxa4 Re8 27.Rda1 and Black is under pressure.

22.Rac1 Qb7 23.Qg4

Diagram 380a

Almost all of white's pieces are better than their black counterparts.

23...Ree6 24.Nd5 Rxc1 25.Rxc1 Rc6 26.Rxc6 Qxc6 27.Bh6!

Black has been completely outplayed and must now lose material. After **27...Kf8 28.Nxf6 Qxf6 29.Bxg7+ Qxg7 30.Qxd7.** White, who is a clear pawn up, went on to win.

ANSWER
PART EIGHT

TEST **8**

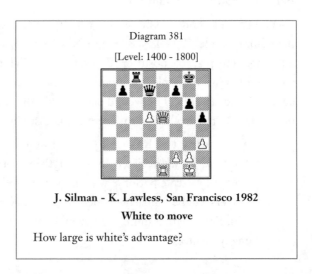

Diagram 381

[Level: 1400 - 1800]

J. Silman - K. Lawless, San Francisco 1982

White to move

How large is white's advantage?

1.d4 Nf6 2.c4 g6 3.Nc3 Bg7 4.e4 d6 5.Be2 0-0 6.Nf3 e5 7.0–0 Nbd7 8.Re1 c5 9.dxc5 Nxc5 10.Qc2 Nh5 11.b4 Ne6 12.Bb2 Nhf4 13.Bf1 Nd4 14.Nxd4 exd4 15.Nd5 Nxd5 16.exd5 a5 17.a3 axb4 18.axb4 Rxa1 19.Rxa1 Bf5 20.Qd2 Qb6 21.Ra5 Rc8 22.h3 h5 23.Ra1 Re8 24.b5 Rc8 25.Rd1 d3 26.Bxg7 Kxg7 27.Bxd3 Bxd3 28.Qxd3 Qc5 29.Qc3+ Kg8 30.Re1!? (30.Rc1) 30...Qxb5 31.Qf6? (31.Re7!) 31...Qxc4 32.Qxd6 Qc7 (32...Qd4) 33.Qf6 Qd8 34.Qe5 Qd7? - Diagram 381

White has a winning advantage thanks to a number of factors:

➤ His passed pawn is much further advanced than black's.

➤ The material mix of Queen + Rook with no minors is ideal.

➤ Black's King is far from safe.

➤ The passed d-pawn can reach d6 (Black failed to create a blockade), where it will prove to be very threatening.

> **Explaining the Rating Spread**: If you appreciated the strength of the passed d-pawn, and if you were aware that the Q + R material mix is an important one in such positions, then you can pat yourself on the back for a job well done.

35.d6 Rd8 36.Qf6!

36.Rd1? (turning the attacking Rook on the open e-file into a defensive piece) would cave to the opponent's fake threat.

36...Rf8 37.Re7 Qd8

Hopeless, but even worse was 37...Qf5 38.Qxf5 gxf5 39.d7 when Black has no answer for the upcoming 40.Re8, which would conquer the final blockade square on d8.

38.d7

First the blockading square on d6 was claimed by White, and now, with the fall of d7, Black finds himself paralyzed and helpless.

38...b5 39.Rxf7

I saw an easy win and I took it, but 39.f4! was much stronger. The unstoppable threat of f4-f5 forces resignation.

39...Qxf6 40.Rxf6 Rd8 41.Rxg6+ Kf7 42.Rb6, 1-0.

ANSWER
PART EIGHT

TEST 9

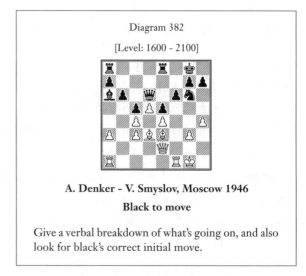

Diagram 382

[Level: 1600 - 2100]

A. Denker - V. Smyslov, Moscow 1946

Black to move

Give a verbal breakdown of what's going on, and also look for black's correct initial move.

1.d4 Nf6 2.c4 e6 3.Nc3 Bb4 4.e3 0–0 5.Bd3 c5 6.a3 Bxc3+ 7.bxc3 Nc6 8.Ne2 d6 9.0–0 e5 10.e4 Re8 11.Qc2 Nd7 12.f4 b6 13.Be3 Ba6 14.fxe5 dxe5 15.d5 Na5 16.Qa2 Nf8 17.Ng3 Ng6 18.Qe2 Nb7 19.Nf5 Nd6 20.g3 f6 21.Nxd6 Qxd6 22.h4 - Diagram 382

If your first impression was, "White has a passed d-pawn and I would love to blockade it with my Knight. How can I accomplish that?" then you did very well. If you also noticed that c4 is weak and that a Knight on d6 would add to the pressure against that point (not to mention e4), then that's even better. And, finally, if you thought that Black has a great game (despite the d-pawn) while also noting that you would love to answer a3-a4 with ...a5, then you're nothing less than a hero!

> **Explaining the Rating Spread**: It's one thing to know you want a horse on d6, but it's quite another to go out of your way to make it happen. That "I insist" mentality is rarely found in players under 1600, though it's also often lacking in players far above that rating too.

22...Ne7

The idea is simple: Black intends to swing his Knight to d6 via c8. Note that the c8-square also allows the Knight to give b6 some support, something the other route (...Ng6-h8-f7) doesn't do.

23.a4 Bc8 24.Kh2 a5!

Nice! Though this leaves b6 weak, it also leaves White with a serious weakness on a4. Note that b6 would have been weakened in any case after a4-a5xb6, but then White wouldn't have that weak a-pawn. Thus, 24...a5 is clearly an excellent move.

25.Qg2 Bg4 26.Be2 Bxe2

26...Bd7 was a logical alternative since it ties the white pieces down to the defense of a4. However, Smyslov understood that exchanging Bishops (even though white's Bishop has that Tall-Pawn look) was the right thing to do since it highlights the weakness of both c4 and e4.

27.Qxe2 Rad8 28.Rab1 Nc8 29.h5 Rf8 30.Rf2 Rf7 31.h6 g6 32.Rbf1 Qe7 33.Qg4 Nd6 Black has achieved his goal and now holds a clear advantage—white's kingside play doesn't fully compensate for the weak pawns on e4, c4, and a4. The rest of the game saw Smyslov continue to outplay his opponent: **34.Qe6 Nxe4 35.Qxb6 f5 36.Rb2 f4 37.Qe6 fxe3 38.Rxf7 Qxf7 39.Qxe5 Nf6 40.Rb8 Ng4+ 41.Kh3 Nxe5 42.Rxd8+ Qf8 43.Rxf8+ Kxf8**, 0-1.

Part Nine / Other Imbalances–Imbalances in the Opening

ANSWER
PART NINE

TEST 1

Diagram 408

[Level: 1900 - 2200]

R. Britton - J. Donaldson, Rhodes International 1980

Black to move

White is threatening to win by Nb6 or Nxe7+, while chopping on f6 is also looming. It's clear that white's Knight has to be taken, but with what? Black usually tries to avoid giving up the two Bishops by ...Bxd5 in analogous positions, but taking with the Knight might hang the e7-pawn (which is often indirectly protected, and this might or might not be the case here). What is the right way to capture on d5?

1.e4 c5 2.Nf3 Nc6 3.d4 cxd4 4.Nxd4 g6 5.c4 Nf6 6.Nc3 d6 7.Be2 Nxd4 8.Qxd4 Bg7 9.Bg5 0–0 10.Qd2 Be6 11.0–0 a6 12.f3 Qa5 (12...Rc8!?) **13.Rfd1 Rfc8 14.Nd5 Qxd2** (14...Qd8!? 15.Nxf6+ [15.Bxf6!?] 15...exf6 16.Bf4 f5! deserves serious consideration) **15.Rxd2** - Diagram 408

Many strong players would give thumb's up to 15...Nxd5, which was the move played in the actual game. However, as we'll soon see, it unexpectedly falls on its face. So, it turns out that 15...Bxd5 is the right move since it avoids black's fate in the game, though after 16.exd5 white's space, two Bishops, and potential pressure down the e-file leaves him a with a little something. One might think it's simply good for White, but Black is solid and has ideas like ...a5 or ...b5 followed by ...b4—both would solidify the c5-square for black's Knight and challenge the supremacy of White's bishops.

Explaining the Rating Spread: I think this is deceptively difficult. Most players under 2000 would avoid 15...Nxd5 since that appears to hang the e7-pawn. On the other hand, many experienced players would want to avoid giving up the two Bishops by 15...Bxd5. In the end, the assessment of this position depends on the tactical and positional ability to see beyond the obvious, and see beyond the usual motifs.

15...Nxd5?

As stated above, Black should have tried 15...Bxd5 16.exd5 when White has a slight advantage. If I was playing this line for Black, I would try one of the earlier suggestions (12...Rc8!? or 14...Qd8!?).

16.exd5 Bd7

This is usually fine for Black because the capture on e7 fails to ...Bh6.

17.Bxe7! Bh6

Winning material since 18.Rc2 Bf5 doesn't help White, and 18.Rdd1 Re8 wins a piece. Did White just fall for a trap?

18.Rad1!

It turns out that Black was the one that fell for a trap!

18...Bxd2 19.Rxd2 Re8 20.Bxd6 and White, with two active Bishops and two pawns for the Exchange (which creates a monster pawn majority) has a winning advantage: **20...f6 21.Kf2 Kf7 22.b3 h5 23.a4 Rad8 24.c5 g5 25.Bc4 Rc8 26.Bc7 Rh8 27.Re2 Rce8 28.d6+ Kg6 29.Rd2 Re5 30.Bd5 a5 31.Bxa5 Rhe8**, 1-0.

Even though you might know a position's basics, you can't go on autopilot and, with "eyes closed," use your usual plans and setups without making sure they work in the exact position in front of you. Even the slightest change can turn all your assessments on their head, so try your best to look at every position with fresh eyes, no matter how much knowledge you possess!

ANSWER
PART NINE

TEST 2

Diagram 409

[Level: 1600 - 2000]

E. Rozentalis - G. Jones, Queenstown 2009

White to move

The Exchange Variation of the Ruy Lopez gives White the superior pawn structure (a healthy pawn majority versus a crippled one), but in return Black gets two Bishops and potential pressure down the e-file against white's e-pawn. In the present situation, Black can also play with the idea of ...f6-f5, opening the position up even further for his Bishops. How should White handle this position?

1.e4 e5 2.Nf3 Nc6 3.Bb5 a6 4.Bxc6 dxc6 5.0–0 Bd6 6.d4 exd4 7.Qxd4 f6 8.b3 Ne7 9.h3 Ng6 10.Ba3 Nh4 11.Qe3 Nxf3+ 12.Qxf3 0–0 - Diagram 409

Though White usually tries to get mileage from his healthy majority, there's just no way to get even a drop of honey from that kind of plan since Black is not only solid, but also has active shots like ...f6-f5. Because of this, White has to eschew his usual ideas and try and create a situation where he will be able to put a bit of pressure on the enemy position. To accomplish this, he needs to change the pawn structure so that Black will have a target that can be reached, and pressured, by white's army.

The answer to these ruminations is 13.Rd1 followed by 14.Bxd6, undoubling black's pawns and also ending any talk of a pawn majority for White! It seems anti-intuitive—in fact, does it even make sense? Yes it does! White's logic, in a nutshell, is that it's better to have a target one can reach and attack than a "someday I'll be able to use it" static plus that doesn't offer active play or a clear plan.

> **Explaining the Rating Spread**: This one's tough because a player often falls in love with whatever positive imbalance he has and fails to notice that it doesn't allow him a way to get anything from it. To make matters worse, the idea of undoubling the opponent's pawns is unthinkable! It's something most players would reject out of hand.

13.Rd1! Qe7 14.Bxd6 cxd6 15.Qd3 Rd8 16.c4

Diagram 409a

Things have drastically changed! Suddenly White has a central space advantage and obvious pressure against the d6-pawn. Now White knows exactly what to do (if Black sits around, then Nc3, Rd2 and Rad1 would increase black's woes), while simultaneously limiting black's active aspirations due to his being tied down to the defense of d6.

The rest of the game sees White clinging to a small edge while he relentlessly strives to increase the pressure against d6: **16...Be6 17.Nc3 b5 18.Ne2 bxc4 19.bxc4 Qf7 20.Rac1 c5 21.Nf4 Rab8 22.Qc3 Rb4 23.Nd5 Bxd5 24.Rxd5 Qb7 25.Qd3 Rb8 26.Rxd6 Rb1 27.Rf1 Rxf1+ 28.Kxf1 Qb1+ 29.Qxb1 Rxb1+ 30.Ke2 Rc1?** (30...Rb2+!) **31.Rxa6 Rxc4 32.Ke3 Rc2 33.a4 Rc3+ 34.Kd2 Ra3 35.f4 h5 36.a5 Ra4 37.Kd3 Ra3+ 38.Kc4 Ra4+ 39.Kxc5 Rxe4 40.Rc6 Rxf4 41.a6 Ra4 42.Kb6 Kh7 43.a7 Kg6 44.Rc5**, 1-0.

ANSWER
PART NINE

TEST 3

Diagram 410

[Level: 1400 - 2000]

P. Leko - T. Radjabov, Morelia 2008

White to move

This is a position from the Sveshnikov Sicilian. Both sides played the opening logically and White has emerged with a small edge. Both sides have active pieces. Black has some pressure against b3 and would love to get his central pawn majority moving by ...d6-d5. Though White has definite designs against a5, his immediate goal is to stop black's dream of ...d6-d5 so that the d-pawn will remain a static weakness instead of a dynamic plus. Once he does that, he can pile up on d6 and place Black permanently on the defensive. What moves best strive to achieve these two goals (i.e., to stop ...d5 and hit d6)?

1.e4 c5 2.Nf3 Nc6 3.d4 cxd4 4.Nxd4 Nf6 5.Nc3 e5 6.Ndb5 d6 7.Bg5 a6 8.Na3 b5 9.Nd5 Be7 10.Bxf6 Bxf6 11.c3 0–0 12.Nc2 Bg5 13.a4 bxa4 14.Rxa4 a5 15.Bc4 Rb8 16.b3 Kh8 17.Nce3 Bxe3 18.Nxe3 Ne7 19.0–0 f5 20.exf5 Bxf5 - Diagram 410

Explaining the Rating Spread: I feel that a 1400 should be able to find at least one of the moves that directly relate to the stated goals. And this is really the whole point of the book—once you learn to read the imbalances, and once you create logical goals that are based on them, then you can find high caliber moves that cater to the position.

White has tried 21.Qa1, 21.Nxf5, 21.Qd2, and 21.Ra2 here. Let's look at each:

➤ 21.Qa1 creates an immediate threat against a5, but has nothing to do with the question that was posed since it actually takes all the pressure off of both d6 and d5. As a result, Black was able to get his d-pawn moving: 21...d5 22.Rd1 Bd7 23.Rxa5 dxc4 24.Ra7 cxb3 25.Rdxd7? (25.Raxd7 Qe8, =) 25...b2 26.Qb1 Qb6 27.Rxe7?? (27.h3) 27...Qg6 28.Qxg6 hxg6 29.Rxg7 b1=Q+ 30.Nf1 g5 31.Rxg5 Rf5 32.Rg4 Qb2 33.Ne3 Qxf2+, 0-1, M. Santo Roman - J. Blaskowski, (U 18) Suedlohn 1981. That's what happens when you let your opponent get undeserved activity.

➤ 21.Nxf5 isn't bad, but it has little to do with the stated goals. In fact, it actually weakens white's control over the d5-square. The game S. Karjakin - A. Khalifman, Amsterdam 2007 ended quickly after 21...Rxf5 22.Bd3 Rf6 23.Bc2 Qb6 24.b4 axb4 25.Rxb4 Qc7 26.Qd3, 1/2-1/2. White doesn't have anything after 26...g6.

 21.Qd2 addresses the question and makes a lot of sense, so you get full credit for making the question and answer match. However, it hasn't proven to be particularly effective: 21...Be4 22.Nd5 (22.Rd1 d5) 22...Bxd5 23.Bxd5 Nxd5 24.Qxd5 Qc7 25.Qxa5 Qxa5 26.Rxa5 Rxb3 27.Rd5 Rf6 28.Rfd1 Rxc3 29.Rxe5 h6, 1/2-1/2, A. Sokolov - I. Nataf, France 2007.

21.Ra2, intending Rd2, is the most interesting move and fits very nicely with the goals I laid out. Though White only has a small plus, he put on a great performance and showed how ironclad adherence to an imbalance-based plan can even drag down a chess superstar:

21.Ra2! Be4 22.Rd2 Rb6 23.Re1 Qb8 24.Qa1!

Having tied Black down to d6, he now adds to his opponent's problems by hitting a5. But the real point is to intensify the heat on d6 by Red1 and Qa3.

24...Qc7 25.Red1 h6 26.h3 Bb7 27.Qa3

Diagram 410a

Logic in motion—White's pieces form a beautiful picture of a team effort. The rest of the game is a lovely display by Hungary's greatest player:

27...Rd8 28.Be6 Qxc3 29.Rxd6 Rbxd6 30.Rxd6 Qe1+ 31.Kh2 Re8 32.Rd7 Nc6 33.Bf7 Ra8 34.Rxb7 Qxf2 35.Bd5 Rc8 36.Rf7 Qxe3 37.Bxc6, 1-0.

ANSWER
PART NINE

TEST 4

Diagram 411

[Level: 1400 - 1600]

J. Bosch - E. Gufeld, Telex Finals 1978

Black to move

White has just played his 7th move and has absolutely nothing. Obviously, it wasn't a very good opening choice. So, what we have here is something White hadn't deeply studied and almost certainly something Black hadn't prepared at all—he was on his own.

What is black's most pronounced favorable imbalance? Once you find that, you'll fully understand and appreciate the moves that follow.

1.Nf3 g6 2.d4 Nf6 3.e3 Bg7 4.Be2 0–0 5.b3 c5 6.Bb2 cxd4 7.Nxd4 - Diagram 411

Though positive black imbalances like a slight lead in development and being castled while White isn't are nice, the real answer concerns black's central pawn majority. Simply put, if you noted the central pawn majority, and if you gave it the respect it deserves (instead of just saying, "Oh, a central pawn majority … who cares?"), then black's play from this position is not only something you would understand and appreciate, but also something you could find yourself if this position appeared in one of your own games.

> Explaining the Rating Spread: I think any player 1400 and up who is conversant with the imbalances should be able to take note of black's central pawn majority. And, once you notice it, you can use that information to find a plan based on that particular imbalance.

Our answer is over and done with, but don't stop here! This game is well worth looking at since it's a command performance by the late grandmaster Eduard Gufeld.

7...d5

Grabbing central space.

8.0–0 Re8

Preparing …e5 with even more central domination.

9.Nd2 e5 10.N4f3 Nc6

Diagram 411a

Only ten moves have been played and Black enjoys a dream position with a big pawn center, a spatial plus, and nicely developed pieces.

11.c4 d4

Gaining more space and threatening to win on the spot with 12...d3.

12.exd4 e4! 13.Ne1 Nxd4 14.Nc2 Nxe2+ 15.Qxe2 Bg4 16.Qe3

Of course, 16.Bxf6?? Bxe2 17.Bxd8 Raxd8 is completely lost for White.

16...Nd5 17.cxd5 Bxb2 18.Rab1 Bg7 19.h3 Bf5 20.Rbd1 Qxd5 21.Nc4 Qd3!!

Diagram 411b

Instead of running from white's Rook, black's Queen gets in its face!

22.Nb4?

White could have still put up resistance with 22.Rxd3 exd3 23.Nd6 Rxe3 24.Nxe3.

22...Qxe3 23.fxe3 Be6 White's busted. The rest of the game doesn't need commentary: **24.Nd6 Re7 25.g4 a5 26.Nc2 h5 27.Nd4 Bxd4 28.Rxd4 hxg4 29.hxg4 Bxg4 30.Nxe4 Bf5 31.Nd6 Bh3 32.Rf3 Be6 33.Rf2 Rc7 34.Kg2 Kg7 35.Kg3 Rh8 36.Rf3 Rc5**, 0-1.

ANSWER
PART NINE

TEST 5

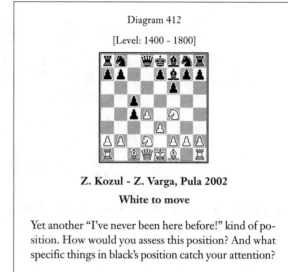

Diagram 412

[Level: 1400 - 1800]

Z. Kozul - Z. Varga, Pula 2002

White to move

Yet another "I've never been here before!" kind of position. How would you assess this position? And what specific things in black's position catch your attention?

1.d4 d5 2.c4 dxc4 3.e3 Be6 4.Ne2 f6? 5.Nd2 c5 6.Nf4 Bf7 - Diagram 412

Two things should stand out with multi-colored clarity: White enjoys a sizable lead in development and the e6-square is severely weakened. These things add up to no less than a winning advantage for White! Since you would like to continue developing your army, and since you want to make the e6-square your own, and (finally!) since you wouldn't mind getting your pawn back, the right move shouldn't be hard to find.

> **Explaining the Rating Spread**: It's not hard to see that one side is ahead in development, and the weakness of e6 should strike your brain as if it were a gong (though this is most likely the one thing that a player under 1400 might miss). Mixing that with the desire to regain your pawn and prepare for castling means that white's best move is something any player would do from 1000 on.

7.Bxc4

Moves don't get more natural than this. Oddly, White played something else in the actual game: 7.d5? Bxd5 8.Nxd5 Qxd5 9.e4 Qd7 10.Bxc4 Nc6 11.Qh5+ g6 12.Qxc5 Nd4 13.0-0 e6 14.Qa5 b5 15.Bb3 Ne7 16.Bd1 Nec6 17.Qc3 Bg7 18.Nb3 0-0 19.Qh3 f5 20.exf5 exf5 21.Be3 Kh8, ½-½.

7...Bxc4

7...Nh6 wasn't much better, since both 8.Ne6 and 8.Bxf7+ leave Black in a bad way.

8.Nxc4 and black's position—faced with ideas like Ne6 and/or d5, or Qh5+ in many positions, or even the quiet 0-0 which allows Black to quietly face his own mortality—is lost.

Part Nine / Other Imbalances — Mixing Imbalances

ANSWER
PART NINE

TEST 6

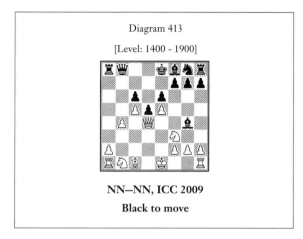

Diagram 413

[Level: 1400 - 1900]

NN—NN, ICC 2009

Black to move

1.e4 c6 2.d4 d5 3.e5 c5 4.dxc5 Nc6 5.Nf3 Bg4 6.Bb5 e6 7.Bxc6+ bxc6 8.b4 a5 9.c3 axb4 10.cxb4 Qb8 11.Qd4 - Diagram 413

Though it looks chaotic, things are actually pretty straightforward. White has an extra pawn (a static plus) while Black enjoys active pieces and pressure against a2, b4, and e5 (his position is driven by dynamics).

White would love to castle, develop his forces, give e5 firm support, and then either go for active queenside play with a2-a4 followed by an eventual b4-b5, or simply solidify his pawn structure with a2-a3.

Black, who is a pawn down, has to turn the game into a fistfight. Time is of the essence, and Black needs to keep White off balance by creating threats against the aforementioned pawn weaknesses on a2, b4, and e5. After he deals with his attacked g4-Bishop, moves such as …Ng8-e7-f5 and/or …Ra8-a4 will follow, increasing the pressure on white's position.

> **Explaining the Rating Spread**: If you noted that Black is down a pawn and needs to play actively, and if you noticed that the g4-Bishop is hanging, and if you saw that 11…Bxf3 not only gains time but also ruins white's pawn structure and gives the black Knight a wonderful hole to leap to on f5, then you've done very well.

In the actual game, Black played the hideous 11…Bh5?, literally handing White a free move. When I asked about this, Black told me, "I retained my Bishop because I wanted it to keep control of the light-squares." Thinking like that can pay dividends in a different kind of position, but when dynamics are your life-blood, a more energetic treatment is called for. Correct was:

11…Bxf3

Obvious and strong. Since the e5-pawn is a target, why not chop off its main defender while simultaneously destroying white's kingside pawn structure?

Less logical is 11. … Ra4 12.Qxg4 Rxb4 13.Qg3 Rxb1 14.Rxb1 Qxb1 15.0–0 Qxa2 16.Nd4 when Black is suddenly the one with the extra pawn, but White's safe King and obvious lead in development gives him good dynamic compensation (complete role reversal!).

12.gxf3 Ne7

The hole on f5 is an ideal home for black's Knight.

13.f4 Nf5 14.Qc3 g5!

I mentioned energy, and this certainly fits the bill! This move strives to tear down e5 and, in many lines, open the g-file for the h8-Rook.

The calmer 14…Be7 15.a3 Qb5 16.Nd2 0-0 offers Black solid compensation for the pawn sacrifice, but 14…g5 is more in the spirit of the position.

15.Nd2 Ra4 16.a3 gxf4 17.Nf3 Rg8 18.Bxf4 Rg4 19.Be3 Qb5 and Black's pieces are all over his beleaguered opponent. One possible variation: **20.Kd2 Rc4 21.Qd3 Nxe3 22.fxe3 Bxc5 23.Rhb1 Be7 24.Nd4 Qb8 25.Qxh7 Qxe5 26.Qg8+ Kd7 27.Qxf7 Ra8!** with a winning attack.

ANSWER
PART NINE

TEST 7

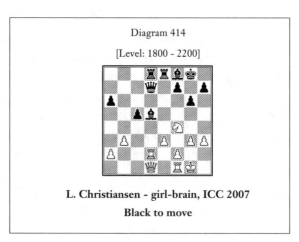

Diagram 414

[Level: 1800 - 2200]

L. Christiansen - girl-brain, ICC 2007

Black to move

1.d4 Nf6 2.c4 g6 3.Nc3 Bg7 4.Nf3 0–0 5.g3 d6 6.Bg2 Nbd7 7.0-0 e5 8.h3 exd4 9.Nxd4 Nb6 10.b3 d5 11.c5 Nbd7 12.c6 Ne5 13.cxb7 Bxb7 14.Ba3 Re8 15.Rc1 a6 16.Na4 Ne4 17.Nc5 Nxc5 18.Bxc5 Nd7 19.e3 Nxc5 20.Rxc5 Bf8 21.Rc2 c5 22.Ne2 Qd7 23.Rd2 Rad8 24.Bxd5 Bxd5 25.Nf4 - Diagram 414

Girl-brain is battling a monster! Christiansen (who was playing a clock simultaneous) is a three time U.S. Champion and is known as the greatest American attacking player since the legendary Frank Marshall. Most players would wilt in the face of such firepower, but girl-brain has managed to hold her own. However, now the heat is on since her Bishop's pinned and, if it falls, she'll be down a pawn for nothing.

> **Explaining the Rating Spread**: If you saw black's correct 25th move, congratulations. However, if you defended the Bishop, thus allowing the curse of "I have to" to tell you what to do, then you should go back and reacquaint yourself with Part Four, Overcoming the Trap of "I Can't" and "I Must".

Here's how the game went with girl-brain's comments:

25...Re5

"I had to defend my Bishop so my move was forced."

26.e4 Bh6

"Trying to mix things up a bit. Of course, I can't play 26...Rxe4 27.Rxd5 Bd6 28.Qd3 Ree8 because 29.Rd1 kills me."

27.Rxd5 Rxd5 28.Nxd5 Qe6 29.Qd3 and White, who is now a safe pawn ahead, went on to win the game.

Did you notice that Black was swimming in the world of "I can't" and "I have to"? First off, take a look at her comment to 26...Bh6 where she states that she can't play 26...Rxe4. Of course, that's the move Black would *like* to play since it would regain her lost pawn. But, instead of staring at it and trying to make it work by dint of pure willpower (since if it doesn't work, you're pretty much going to lose), she simply accepted her fate. What's the truth about 26...Rxe4? Let's give it a closer look:

26...Rxe4 27.Rxd5

27.Nxd5 Kh8 is fine for Black.

27...Bd6 28.Qd3 Rd4

Diagram 414a

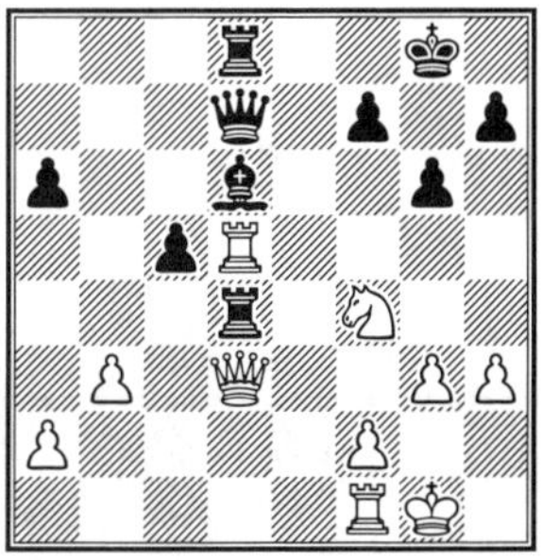

There's a lot going on here!

29.Qxa6

29.Rxd4 cxd4 30.Qxd4 Bxf4 31.Qxf4 (31.Qxd7 Rxd7 32.gxf4 Rd2, =) 31...Qxh3 32.Qf6 Qc8, =.

29...Rxd5 30.Nxd5 Qxh3

30...Kg7!? 31.Kg2 Be5 32.Rd1 h5 is still a fight.

31.Qb6 Bxg3! 32.Qxd8+ Kg7 33.Qf6+ Kh6 is a draw. Sadly, 31.Qa5! is stronger since 31...Bxg3 no longer works: 32.Ne7+ Kg7 33.Qc3+ wins for White. This means that Black has to try something like 31.Qa5 Rc8 32.Nf6+ Kh8 33.Qc3 Bf8! and, though white's still considerably better after 34.Re1, Black can still put up resistance.

Is that the end of the story? No, going back to the position after 26...Rxe4 27.Rxd5 Bd6 28.Qd3 Ree8 29.Rd1 we recall that Black said the Rook move to d1, "kills me," but a better attitude might have helped her notice 29...Qc6!

Diagram 414b

Black's alive after all!

A look with a tactical eye will tell you that the "killing" 30.Rxd6?? (30.Qc4! allows White to retain an edge, but nothing too terrifying) actually loses to 30...Rxd6 31.Qxd6 Re1+! 32.Rxe1 Qxd6.

All this is extremely complicated and, to be honest, beyond most player's analytical ability. However, it shows that there was a whole world hiding behind girl-brain's "I can't" and, if you don't look and insist, you'll never come close to finding that hidden trove of unnoticed possibilities that will turn a certain loss into something a lot more upbeat.

I should add that this whole defensive nightmare began with her comment on the 25th move: "I *had to* defend my Bishop so my move (25...Re5) was forced."

But, this turns out to be completely untrue!

25...Bxb3!

Diagram 414c

Who said Black was worse?

26.Rxd7 Bxd1 27.Rfxd1 Rxd7 28.Rxd7 Rc8 and black's the only one (thanks to the passed c-pawn) who can even consider playing for a win. 25...Bxb3 doesn't seem that complicated or hard to discover, but it's impossible to find if you start out by saying, "I have to defend my Bishop!"

ANSWER
PART NINE

TEST 8

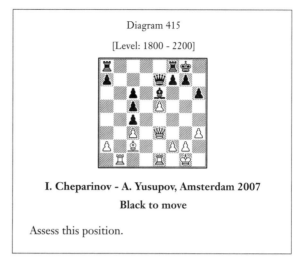

Diagram 415

[Level: 1800 - 2200]

I. Cheparinov - A. Yusupov, Amsterdam 2007

Black to move

Assess this position.

1.e4 e5 2.Nf3 Nf6 3.Nxe5 d6 4.Nf3 Nxe4 5.d4 d5 6.Bd3 Nc6 7.0–0 Be7 8.Nc3 Nxc3 9.bxc3 0–0 10.h3 h6 11.Re1 Bd6 12.Ne5 Qh4 13.Qf3 Be6 14.Rb1 Nxe5 15.dxe5 Bc5 16.Be3 b6 17.Bxc5 bxc5 18.c4 c6 19.Qe3 Qe7 20.c3 dxc4 21.Bc2 - Diagram 415

Black's tripled pawns stand out like a sore thumb, and many players will automatically claim that White has the advantage based on that fact alone. Further "confirmation" of white's superiority appears when one realizes that White has an active pawn majority on the kingside, and the pawn cascade f2-f4-f5 does indeed look threatening.

However, doesn't Black have something to be proud of too? Yes indeed, and you can expect a world of pain in most of your games if you don't take the plusses of *both* sides into account! In the present position, black's trips give him control over quite a few important squares (b5, b4, b3, d5, d4, and d3). The d5-square in particular will prove useful since black's Bishop will find that it's a nice home. Black is also a pawn up, but that doesn't have much impact on the general play (after all, white's one pawn on c3 freezes all three of black's trips).

All in all, black's position is perfectly acceptable!

> **Explaining the Rating Spread**: I think that many masters would automatically give White the nod in this position. If you managed to look past the negative aspects of the tripled pawns and realize that Black has plusses too, then you can be quite proud of yourself.

21...Bd5 22.f4 Rab8 23.f5 Qg5 24.Qf2 Rxb1 25.Rxb1 Rd8 26.Rd1 Rb8 27.Rd2 g6? (Black had a good position, but this is the start of a complete meltdown) **28.h4 Qg4 29.Re2 gxf5 30.Bxf5 Qg7 31.Qf4 Re8 32.Bh3 Kh8 33.Re3 Rg8 34.Rg3 Qh7 35.Qf6+ Rg7 36.Bf5**, 1-0.

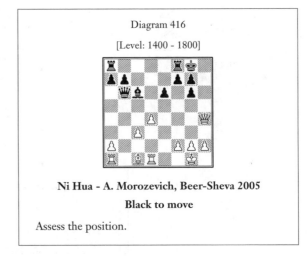

Diagram 416

[Level: 1400 - 1800]

Ni Hua - A. Morozevich, Beer-Sheva 2005

Black to move

Assess the position.

1.e4 c5 2.Nf3 Nc6 3.c3 Nf6 4.e5 Nd5 5.d4 cxd4 6.cxd4 d6 7.Bc4 Nb6 8.Bb5 Bd7 9.exd6 e6 10.0–0 Bxd6 11.Nc3 Ne7 12.Bd3 Bc6 13.Qe2 Nbd5 14.Rd1 0–0 15.Ne5 Bxe5 16.Qxe5 Qb6 17.Qh5 Ng6 18.Bxg6 hxg6 19.Qh4 Nxc3 20.bxc3 - Diagram 416

Let's have grandmaster Alon Greenfeld (from *New In Chess* 8, 2005) assess the position for us:

"Actually, positions with Bishops of opposite colors are very tricky. Whereas the Bishops alone herald a probable draw, the presence of major pieces usually leads to sharp battles, the reason being that nothing can challenge the Bishop, so the control of the respective diagonals may be indisputable. It is often the case therefore that in such positions each side plays on 'his own' diagonals. Thus two elements are highly important: the safety of the King and the pawn structure. In the present game White has two weaknesses (c3 and a2), whereas black's pawn formation is rock-solid."

> **Explaining the Rating Spread**: I would expect everyone who has read this book to notice the inferiority of white's pawn structure. If you got excited by the prospect of total domination of the c4- and d5-squares then all the better. And, if you noticed the Bishops of opposite colors and realized that black's Bishop will enjoy a better diagonal than white's, you can consider your efforts on this problem to be a job well done.

20...Qb5 21.Re1 Rac8 22.Qg3 Rfd8 23.h4 Qf5 24.Bf4 f6

Depriving white's pieces of the use of the e5- and g5-squares.

25.a4 Bd5

It's now clear that White has a passive position that's devoid of counterplay. Of course, he can still hang on (though it won't be fun), but his next move makes things considerably worse. The rest of the game will be given with minimal notes:

26.Bd6? Bxg2! 27.Be7 Rd7 28.Bxf6 Bd5!? (28...gxf6) **29.Be5 Rf7** (White's King is now vulnerable due to the d5-Bishop's unobstructed control of the a8-h1 diagonal.) **30.Re3 a5!** (Freezing the a4-pawn on a light square. This allows black's Rook and

Bishop to attack it.) **31.Rc1 Rc4 32.f4 Rxa4 33.Qg5 b5 34.Qxf5 gxf5 35.Kf2 Ra2+ 36.Re2 Ra3 37.Rb2 Rb3 38.Rxb3 Bxb3 39.Ke3 Rd7 40.Ra1 a4 41.Kd2 Ra7 42.Bd6 Ra6 43.Ba3 Kf7 44.Ke3 Ra8 45.Kf2 Rh8 46.Rh1 Bd5 47.Rh3 Be4 48.Ke3 Rh6 49.h5 Ke8 50.Rg3 Rxh5 51.d5 g5 52.dxe6 g4 53.Kd4 Rh3 54.Rg1 g3 55.Ke5 g2 56.Rd1 Rh1 57.Rd7 g1=Q 58.Bd6 Bc6**, 0-1.

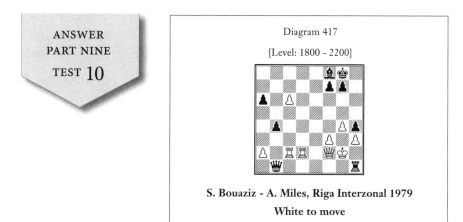

Diagram 417

[Level: 1800 - 2200]

S. Bouaziz - A. Miles, Riga Interzonal 1979
White to move

It's clear that White is winning—he's up an Exchange and his passed c-pawn is about to become a Queen. In such positions (where the game is all but over) it's important to take your time and make sure that the opponent doesn't have any threats or tricks. Sadly, Bouaziz, thinking that Black was about to resign, failed to exercise that last ounce of caution that would have netted him the full point.

> **Explaining the Rating Spread**: This problem is a perfect example of a "pay attention!" moment! It should be clear that you're winning, but by now you should also know that when you think the game is yours you must look long and hard for any potential counterplay so that you don't botch it.

1.c7??

Of course, White should have taken a long think and tried to get a handle on exactly what was going on here. I often tell my students that if you move fast in an interesting position, it shows that you're not enjoying the game. Instead, you should let your clock tick a bit and just absorb the wonder of it all, while also making sure that you're completely in tune with every secret the position might hold. If Bouaziz had done this, he would have noticed black's trick and played **1.g5!** (giving white's King access to g4 after …Rxh3) when Black really would have resigned!

2…Rxh3!

After suffering from a shock like this, it's critical that you sit back for a long think (if you have the time, going out for a breath of fresh air is also a good idea). This allows you to get on top of the position, to calm your nerves and clear your mind, and avoid a hysterical reaction.

3.Kxh3??

I suspect that White was in horrible time pressure. If he wasn't, then this is the kind of hysterical reaction I just mentioned.

White could have drawn by 3.Qf1 Rg3+ 4.Kf2 Rxf3+ 5.Kxf3 Qxf1+ 6.Ke4 when Black would halve the point by perpetual check.

3...Qh1+ 4.Qh2 Qxf3+ 5.Kxh4 Be7+ 6.g5 Bxg5+, 0-1 since 7.Kxg5 f6+ 8.Kh4 (8.Kg6 Qg4 mate) 8...g5 is mate. Poor Bouaziz probably had to be carried out on a stretcher after this horrific debacle!

ANSWER
PART NINE

TEST 11

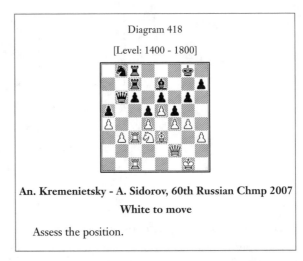

Diagram 418

[Level: 1400 - 1800]

An. Kremenietsky - A. Sidorov, 60th Russian Chmp 2007

White to move

Assess the position.

1.d4 Nf6 2.c4 e6 3.Nf3 b6 4.g3 Ba6 5.b3 b5 6.Bg2 Qc8 7.Ne5 Bb7 8.Bxb7 Qxb7 9.0–0 d6 10.Nd3 Nbd7 11.cxb5 Qxb5 12.Nc3 Qb7 13.f3 Be7 14.e4 Nb6 15.Be3 0–0 16.a4 a5 17.Qd2 Rfc8 18.Rfc1 Nfd7 19.Rab1 c6 20.Qf2 Qa6 21.Qf1 Rab8 22.Bf2 Rb7 23.Rc2 Rd8 24.Rd1 Nb8 25.Na2 N6d7 26.Nac1 d5 27.e5 Qb6 28.f4 Na6 29.Be3 Nb4 30.Nxb4 Bxb4 31.Nd3 Ba3 32.Rc3 g6 33.Qf2 Rc7 34.g4 f5 35.h3 Rdc8 36.Ra1 Be7 37.Rac1 Nb8 - Diagram 418

The center is closed and the queenside is in a perfect state of balance. White has pressure against the backward pawn on c6 while Black has pressure against the backward pawn on b3. On top of that, White is fighting to control the c5-square, which in turn prevents Black from making the …c6-c5 freeing move. And, to continue our tale of balance, Black has a firm grip on b4.

I should stress the enormous importance of the c5-square—if Black is allowed …c6-c5 he'll quite likely have an edge since his main weaknesses will evaporate, while white's weak pawn on b3 will remain.

Since White can't dent Black on the queenside, his last hope for advantage rests on the kingside. Thus, 38.gxf5 suggests itself.

Explaining the Rating Spread: While it's easy to see the good things White has (pressure against c6 and c5 and chances on the kingside), not many players also take their opponent's plusses into account. If you also saw black's highlights, then you should be very pleased with yourself.

38.Nc5

This doesn't lead to anything. The critical move was 38.gxf5 gxf5 39.Kh2 when things aren't so easy for Black: 39...Kh8 40.Rg1 Rg8 41.Rxg8+ Kxg8 42.Qg2+ Kf7 (Worse is 42...Kh8 43.Rc1 Bf8 44.Qg5 Rg7 45.Qf6 Be7 46.Qxe6) 43.Qf3 and black's King is far from comfortable.

In my opinion, Black should meet 38.gxf5 with 38...exf5! 39.h4 when he has the following choices:

Diagram 418a

Position after 39.h4

> 39...Na6 40.Kh2 Ba3 41.Ra1 Bf8 42.Rg1 Rg7 43.h5 Nc7 44.Nc5 Bxc5 45.dxc5 (45.Rxc5 Ne6, =) 45...Qa7 46.Qh4 Ne6 47.Bd2 Rf8 48.hxg6 hxg6 49.Rh3 d4 and Black is fine.

> 39...h5 40.Nc5 (40.Kh1 Nd7 41.Qg3 Nf8, =) 40...Bxc5 41.dxc5 (41.Rxc5 Nd7 42.R5c3 Nf8 with ...Ne6 to follow doesn't worry Black) 41...Qa7 42.Bd4 Nd7 43.Kh1 Nf8 44.Rg3 Rg7 45.Rcg1 Re8! 46.Qf3 (46.e6 Rxe6 47.Bxg7 Kxg7 can only favor Black) 46...Re6 is nothing for White.

In the actual game, White got outplayed: **38...Bxc5 39.Rxc5 Qxb3 40.Rxa5 Nd7 41.Qd2 Nb6 42.Qc3 Qxc3 43.Rxc3 Nc4 44.Ra6 Rb7 45.Kf2 Kf7 46.Bc1 c5 47.dxc5 Rxc5 48.Be3 Rc8 49.Ra7 Rxa7 50.Bxa7 Ra8 51.Bc5 Ra5 52.Bd4 Rxa4 53.Rb3 Na5 54.Rd3 Nc6 55.Be3 g5 56.Kg3 Nxe5 57.fxe5 f4+ 58.Kg2 fxe3 59.Rxe3 Re4**, 0-1 since 60.Rxe4 dxe4 61.Kf2 Ke7 62.Ke3 Kd7 63.Kxe4 Kc6 64.Kd4 Kb5 picks up e5 and wins easily.

ANSWER
PART NINE

TEST **12**

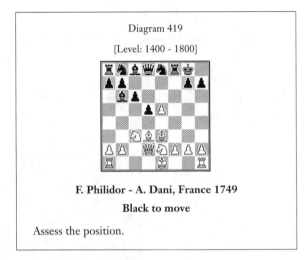

Diagram 419

[Level: 1400 - 1800]

F. Philidor - A. Dani, France 1749

Black to move

Assess the position.

1.e4 e5 2.Bc4 Bc5 3.c3 Nf6 4.d4 exd4 5.cxd4 Bb6 6.Nc3 0–0 7.Nge2 c6 8.Bd3 d5 9.e5 Ne8 10.Be3 f6 11.Qd2 fxe5 12.dxe5 - Diagram 419

Philidor was known for his love of pawns, and he knew how to use them in ways that hadn't been seen up to that time. In this game he demonstrates a plan that he was very fond of: create a pawn majority, turn that majority into a passed pawn, and promote the passed pawn.

In our problem position, I had hoped that you would notice white's four vs. two kingside pawn majority and also note that black has a four vs. two queenside pawn majority. Clearly, both sides need to make use of their majority and prove that what they have is more important than the opponent's.

Explaining the Rating Spread: This problem is all about the respective pawn majorities. If you noticed them, then consider the puzzle solved.

The game itself isn't something that would make a chess computer happy, but Philidor's "full steam ahead" single mindedness of vision is extremely instructive. Just watch how he gets his guys in motion!

12...Be6 13.Nf4

White immediately challenges black's e6 blockade. However, I would have preferred 13.0-0 intending to follow up with f2-f4 and, if allowed, f5.

13...Qe7

13...Bf5 seems more natural, when the Knight on f4 actually blocks its own f-pawn.

14.Bxb6 axb6 15.0–0

The immediate 15.Nxe6 was more accurate.

15...Nd7

Black should have tried the annoying 15...Qg5, though white's position is still slightly preferable after 16.g3.

16.Nxe6 Qxe6

We've already discussed (in Part Eight) how a Queen isn't a very good blockader. This is also the case here.

17.f4 Nc7 18.Rae1 g6 19.h3

Diagram 419a

You have to love this guy! Philidor intends to wash away black's position by g4 and f5 when his snappy pawn majority makes black's look like it's moving in slow motion.

A sharper alternative was 19.f5!? gxf5 20.Qf4 Qe7 (20...Qg6? 21.Bxf5 Ne6 22.Qg3 Rxf5 23.Rxf5 Qxg3 24.hxg3 leaves White with an extra Exchange and a clear advantage) 21.Bxf5 Nc5 when Black intends to block white's passed e-pawn with ...N7e6.

19...d4?

A serious mistake that hands white's Knight the e4-square on a platter.

20.Ne4 h6?

It's clear that Black was worried about Ng5, but this weakening of his kingside pawn structure (and the loss of a critical tempo) is too high a price to pay to stop a move that may or may not have been on white's agenda (this takes us back to the curse of "I must", which we explored in Part Four). He should have played 20...Kh8, though his game would have been very bad in any case.

21.b3

White quietly defends a2 and simultaneously threatens Bc4. However, the more pointed 21.Nd6 (intending a smack-down with 22.f5) was crushing. In this case white's pawn majority isn't trying to make a passed pawn, but is instead being used to smash the enemy King.

21...b5 22.g4?!

22.Nd6 intending f5 was still strong. However, Philidor isn't going to allow anything (including good moves!) to distract him from his original vision (i.e., the creation of connected passed pawns after g2-g4 and f4-f5).

22...Nd5 23.Ng3

Unrelenting! He's finally ready to fulfill his dream of f4-f5.

23...Ne3 24.Rxe3?

As a fan of Exchange sacrifices, I very much wanted this tempting sacrifice to be sound. Sadly, it's not. Instead, the quiet 24.Rf2 intending moves such as 25.Nf1 or 25.Ne2 promises White a large, and safe, advantage.

24...dxe3 25.Qxe3 Rxa2 26.Re1

Philidor is simply amazing. He plays for f4-f5 all through this game, and when his opponent plonks a Knight onto e3 he just sacrificed material by snapping it off and then got right back on track for his longed for f4-f5 push. Quite simply, his pawns want and need that f4-f5 push, and Philidor is, in a way, a pawn whisperer—he hears their desire and does everything possible to make it come true.

26...Qxb3

Not best. Instead, 26...Rb2! is correct, when 27.f5 is met by 27...Qd5.

27.Qe4 Qe6 28.f5

The ChessBase team did their own analysis of this classic game, and it was clear that they are huge fans of Philidor and his contributions to modern chess. For me, seeing chess fans get emotionally invested in a plan's culmination is absolutely delightful! In fact, in their notes they almost gurgled with pleasure as Philidor prepared his f4-f5 advance, and when he finally made his 28th move, they gave a note that will always remain burned into my brain: "YES!! YES!!" I absolutely love this note! That's the kind of rapture I had when I looked over games in my youth, and it's very nice to see others with that same wonderful attitude.

Sadly (in fact, tragically), 28.f5 is a losing blunder! Instead, 28.Qxg6+ was correct, when 28...Qxg6 29.Bxg6 Rxf4 (other moves are possible, but White should be fine thanks to his powerful Philidor pawns) is just a draw after 30.e6 Rf3 31.Ne4 Ne5 32.e7 Rg3+!

Diagram 419b

Forcing an immediate draw

33.Nxg3 Nf3+ 34.Kf1 Nh2+ with a perpetual check.

28...gxf5?

28...Qb3 was a winner. Then 29.f6 is met by 29...Nxe5!, while 29.Qe3 Qd5 threatens both mate and 30...Qc5, exchanging Queens.

The rest of the game, without notes, was an eventual success for our hero: **29.gxf5 Qd5 30.Qxd5+ cxd5 31.Bxb5 Nb6 32.f6 Rb2 33.Bd3 Kf7 34.Bf5 Nc4 35.Nh5 Rg8+ 36.Bg4 Nd2 37.e6+ Kg6 38.f7 Rf8 39.Nf4+ Kg7 40.Bh5**, 1-0. The Philidor pawns had their say after all!

ANSWER
PART NINE

TEST 13

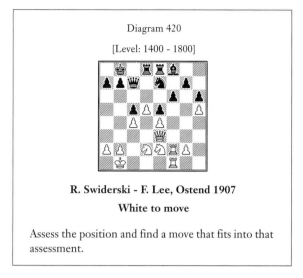

Diagram 420

[Level: 1400 - 1800]

R. Swiderski - F. Lee, Ostend 1907

White to move

Assess the position and find a move that fits into that assessment.

1.e4 c6 2.d4 d5 3.Nc3 dxe4 4.Nxe4 Bf5 5.Ng3 Bg6 6.Nf3 Nd7 7.h4 h6 8.Bd3 Bxd3 9.Qxd3 e6 10.Be3 Ngf6 11.0–0–0 Qc7 12.Kb1 Bd6 13.Ne2 Ng4 14.Rhf1 Nxe3 15.fxe3 0–0–0 16.c4 Nf6 17.e4 e5 18.d5 Rhe8 19.Nd2 c5 20.Rf5 Ng8 21.Rdf1 f6 22.h5 Bf8 23.R5f2 Kb8 24.Qe3 Ne7 - Diagram 420

White has more space and enjoys a protected passed d-pawn. Also, black's position is more or less devoid of counterplay. Other than this, two things stand out:

▶ Black wants to blockade the passed pawn by swinging his Knight to d6.

▶ There's a Bishop vs. Knight battle brewing!

Ideally, White needs to swing a Knight to the permanent support point on f5. This will help challenge the potential blockade on d6. Swapping off a pair of Knights (and then moving the remaining Knight to f5) would be wise, since the resulting Knight vs. Bishop battle is clearly in white's favor.

> **Explaining the Rating Spread**: I know you 1400 players noticed the passed d-pawn and realized that Black will try to block it by placing his Knight on d6. However, if you also realized that White should seek a swap of Knights (which ends black's dream of a comfortable blockade) by placing a Knight on f5 then you did very well. Extra credit if you noticed that trading a pair of Knights would leave White with a superior minor piece!

25.Ng3

Natural and strong—the Knight will set up shop on f5.

25...Nc8 26.Nf5 Qd7 27.Qg3 Qf7 28.Qg4 a6 29.Nf3 Ka7 30.N3h4 Nd6 31.Nxd6 Bxd6 32.Nf5

White is clearly better—his Knight is far stronger than black's Tall-Pawn on d6, g7 is under pressure, and white's space advantage leaves Black facing permanent passivity.

Diagram 420a

Here's the rest of the game: **32...Bf8 33.Rf3 Qc7 34.Rg3 Rd7 35.Qd1 Rb8 36.Rff3 b5 37.cxb5 Rxb5 38.Rc3 Qb8 39.Qe2 Rdb7 40.Rc2 Qd8 41.Rgc3 Qa5 42.Qe3 Rb4 43.d6 Qb6 44.Qxc5 Qxc5 45.Rxc5 Rxe4 46.Rc8 Rf4 47.Rxf8 Rxf5 48.Rc7 Rf1+ 49.Kc2 Rf2+ 50.Kd3 e4+ 51.Ke3 Rxb2 52.d7 Rxc7 53.d8=Q Rc3+ 54.Kxe4**, 1-0.

ANSWER
PART NINE

TEST 14

Diagram 421

[Level: 1600 - 2000]

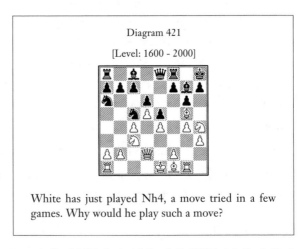

White has just played Nh4, a move tried in a few games. Why would he play such a move?

1.d4 Nf6 2.c4 g6 3.Nc3 Bg7 4.e4 d6 5.Nf3 0–0 6.h3 e5 7.d5 Na6 8.Bg5 Qe8 9.g4 Nd7 10.Rg1 Kh8 11.Qd2 Ndc5 12.Nh4!? - Diagram 421

To understand this move, you need to understand black's usual plans in this kind of position—the answer lies in the pawn structure. Since the center is locked, and since the Rooks aren't doing anything, Black needs to employ pawn breaks to open files for his Rooks and give himself some space for his pieces. The most common King's Indian pawn break is ...f7-f5 (gaining kingside space and instantly activating his Rook on f8), while ...c7-c6 (trying to open some queenside lines) is also a thematic try in quite a few KID systems.

Armed with the knowledge that ...f7-f5 is black's main idea, white's 12.Nh4 makes perfect sense: he's clamping down on f5 and preventing that particular black plan—12...f5? 13.gxf5 gxf5 14.Bh6 (Even 14.exf5 Bxf5 15.Nxf5 Rxf5 16.Be3 is nice for White, since the light-squares inside black's camp are weak due to the absence of his light-squared Bishop) 14...Rg8 15.Bxg7+ Rxg7 16.Rxg7 Kxg7 17.Qg5+ Kh8 18.exf5 is obviously not very attractive for Black!

Explaining the Rating Spread: This problem is all about closed positions and the need for pawn breaks when such structures occur. Once you realize that ...f5 is black's main idea, Nh4 makes perfect sense (whether it's good or not is another matter).

Of course, after 12.Nh4 Black shouldn't panic. Moves such as 12...c6, 12...Na4, and 12...Bd7 have all been tried with reasonable results—black's idea in all these cases is to seek play on the queenside while ignoring the h4-Knight, which is effectively stranded and unable to help when a battle erupts on the other side of the board.

ANSWER
PART NINE

TEST 15

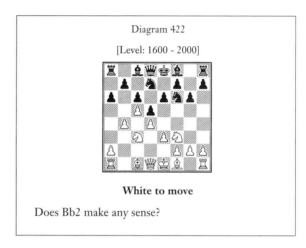

Diagram 422

[Level: 1600 - 2000]

White to move

Does Bb2 make any sense?

1.d4 Nf6 2.c4 e6 3.Nf3 d5 4.Nc3 c6 5.e3 a6 6.c5 Nbd7 7.b4 g6 - Diagram 422

If you said, "No, it doesn't make any sense because the Bishop is nothing more than a Tall-Pawn on b2." then I would applaud you for not wanting to waste a developing move to put a Bishop on a square that you deem to be a dead end street. Your answer isn't correct, but it does show some real chess understanding and I would be happy with any student under 1900 that answered in this way.

Explaining the Rating Spread: The key to this problem is the realization that black's main pawn break is ...e6-e5. If you understood this, then you also understood that Bb2 would prove useful at some point in the game.

The truth is that 8.Bb2 is very sensible (in fact, it's white's most popular move here). Yes, it does look like a Tall-Pawn on that square, and if Bb2 was simply a "let me develop it somewhere" kind of move, then it would be open to serious criticism. However, 8.Bb2 actually demonstrates a deep understanding of not only white's possibilities, but also the opponent's. Remember, you need to know the ideas for both sides. Thus, if Black doesn't want to suffocate due to his lack of space, he'll eventually have to play ...e6-e5. When that happens, White will capture on e5 and turn the "Tall-Pawn" into a very fine piece.

8.Bb2 Bg7 9.Be2 0–0 10.0–0 Qc7 11.Na4 Ne4 12.Ne1 (12.Nd2!?) **12...e5** (12...b5!?) **13.dxe5 Nxe5 14.f3 Nf6 15.Nb6**, V. Bologan - A. Grischuk, Poikovsky 2004, and White, who will follow up with Ne1-c2-d4, has the more pleasant position.

ANSWER
PART NINE

TEST 16

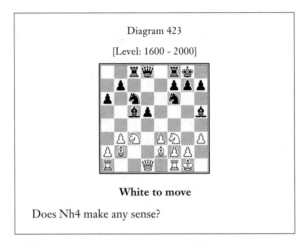

Diagram 423

[Level: 1600 - 2000]

White to move

Does Nh4 make any sense?

1.d4 Nf6 2.c4 e6 3.Nc3 Bb4 4.e3 0–0 5.Bd3 c5 6.Nf3 d5 7.0–0 Nc6 8.cxd5 exd5 9.dxc5 Bxc5 10.b3 Bg4 11.Bb2 a6 12.h3 Bh5 13.Be2 Rc8 - Diagram 423

Black has an isolated d-pawn. As we discussed in Part Five, Weak Pawns, when facing an isolated pawn you ideally want to:

➤ control the square in front of the pawn so it can't move.

➤ swap minor pieces.

➤ end up with a Queen and Rook vs. Queen and Rook, which stamps the isolated pawn as a pure weakness.

All this means that 14.Nh4 does indeed make sense since it forces the exchange of light-squared Bishops. However, just because you follow a basic rule doesn't mean that it will always be effective—rules are simply guidelines that make life easier for you, but they need to be weighed by each position's individual characteristics to determine just how good they really are.

> **Explaining the Rating Spread**: This tests your knowledge of the isolated d-pawn. One of main ways to combat it is to exchange minor pieces, thus depriving the pawn's owner of active minor pieces as compensation. If you understood that Nh4 was making use of this rule, then you did very well.

14.Nh4! Bxe2

14…Bg6 15.Nxg6 hxg6 16.Bf3 favors White, whose two Bishops and threats against d5 leave Black in difficulties since 16…d4 17.Na4 Ba7 18.exd4 Bxd4 19.Bxc6 (Stronger than 19.Bxd4 Nxd4 20.Bxb7 Rc2 21.Bxa6 Rd2! 22.Qc1 Ne4 when black's pieces are extremely active) 19…Bxb2 20.Bxb7 Bxa1 21.Bxc8 Qxd1 22.Rxd1 Rxc8 23.Rxa1 Rc2 24.b4 Ne4 25.a3 leaves Black struggling in the endgame.

15.Nxe2 Re8 16.Nf5

16.Rc1!?

16…Bf8 17.Rc1 g6

17…Qd7 18.Nh6+!

18.Nfd4 and White enjoys a small but lasting edge.

ANSWER
PART NINE

TEST **17**

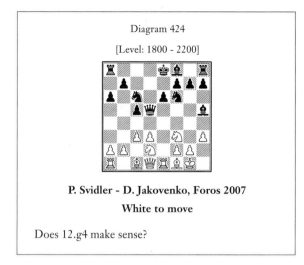

Diagram 424

[Level: 1800 - 2200]

P. Svidler - D. Jakovenko, Foros 2007

White to move

Does 12.g4 make sense?

1.e4 c5 2.Nf3 Nc6 3.Bb5 d6 4.0–0 Bd7 5.Re1 Nf6 6.c3 a6 7.Bf1 Bg4 8.d3 e6 9.Nbd2 d5 10.exd5 Qxd5 11.h3 Bh5 - Diagram 424

Black, whose pieces seem active and who can hope to eventually place some serious pressure against white's d3-pawn, appears to stand well. This would be true if he was allowed the time to play ...Be7 followed by ...0-0.

On the other hand, black's King is still in the center. This, combined with the weakness of the b6 and c4 squares (Nc4 would immediately threaten Nb6), means that dynamic play is called for so he can make maximum use of these factors.

Since Nc4 begs to be played, 12.g4 is necessary since the immediate leap with the Knight (12.Nc4) allows 12...Bxf3 13.gxf3 Qf5 and Black is fine.

> **Explaining the Rating Spread**: If weakening your King by g4 made you a bit uncomfortable, good for you! You should feel a tad spooked when you play a move like that. On the other hand, g4 only makes sense if you realized that White was going to embrace dynamics (thanks to black's central King) and g4 was an important part of the dynamic philosophy (which called for a follow up of Nc4).

Though 12.g4 weakens white's kingside a bit (the f4-square in particular has "hole-like" qualities), the advance of the g-pawn is the only way to allow his forces to leap into action and begin a fight while black's King still resides in the center.

As always, it's important to decide if your position is dynamically or statically inclined. If the answer is dynamic, then you have to play with all the energy you can muster, often sacrificing material and/or allowing weaknesses for fluid, active possibilities.

12.g4! Bg6 13.Nc4

White's constantly dishing out threats (in this case the fork by Nb6), which means that black's hoped for ...Be7 and ...0-0 isn't going to happen anytime soon.

13...Qd8

Best. 13...Rd8 14.Bf4, threatening to trap black's Queen with Nb6, is very strong.

13...Ra7 doesn't inspire confidence either: 14.Nfe5 Nxe5 15.Nxe5 Nd7 16.Bg2 Qd6 17.Bf4 Nxe5 18.Bxe5 Qxd3 19.Qa4+ Qd7 (19...Qb5 20.Qf4) 20.Qa5 Qd8 21.Bc7 Qc8 22.Qb6 is hideous for Black.

14.Bg2

Diagram 424a

Note that, over the course of the last few moves, white's pieces have taken up very active positions while black's forces have actually lost ground.

14...Qc7?

Black gets run over after this. Other tries:

▸ 14...Bd6, striving to castle as quickly as possible, makes sense. However, then 15.d4 0–0 16.Be3 leaves Black under serious pressure.

▸ 14...Qxd3 15.Qb3 is too strong.

▸ 14...Bxd3 is best: 15.Nce5 Be4 16.Qxd8+ Nxd8 (16...Rxd8 17.Nxf7! Bxf3 18.Nxd8 Bxg2 19.Nxe6 and Black's in serious trouble) 17.g5 Bxf3 18.Bxf3 Nd7 19.Nc4 and though Black's a pawn up, the position is unpleasant for him due to white's lead in development and two raging Bishops. One sample: 19...Rc8 20.Rd1 (20.a4!?) 20...b5 21.Nd6+ Bxd6 22.Rxd6 and the two Bishops plus white's strong initiative are far more important than black's extra pawn.

15.Nfe5 Nxe5 16.Bf4! Rd8

16...Nfd7 gets smacked down by 17.Rxe5! Nxe5 18.Bxe5 Qd8 19.Bxb7 f6 20.Qa4+.

17.Bxe5 Qd7 18.d4

18.Nb6!? is also good

18...cxd4 19.Qxd4 Qb5

19...Qxd4 20.Bxd4 Nd5 21.Rad1 highlights white's huge lead in development.

20. Nd6+ Bxd6 21.Bxd6 Qd3 22.Rad1 Qxd4 23.Rxd4

Diagram 424b

Black, whose King never did get castled, is dead lost. The rest of the game doesn't need commentary: **23...Rd7 24.Red1 Nd5 25.Ba3 b5 26.b3 Kd8 27.c4 Nf6 28.Rxd7+ Nxd7 29.cxb5 axb5 30.Bb4 f6 31.Bc6 Be8 32.Bxb5 h5 33.a4 hxg4 34.hxg4 Rh3 35.Bc4 f5 36.a5 Kc7 37.Bxe6 Nf6 38.g5 Bc6 39.Bd6+ Kb7 40.f3 Ne8 41.Be5 Nc7 42.Bd7 Bxf3 43.Rd6 Na6 44.Rb6+ Ka7 45.Bxf5 Rh4 46.Kf2 Bb7 47.Kg3**, 1-0.

**ANSWER
PART NINE
TEST 18**

Diagram 425

[Level: 1600 - 2000]

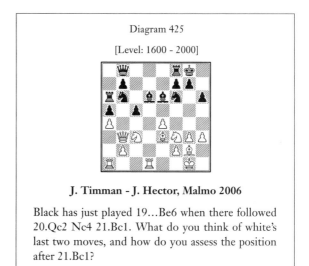

J. Timman - J. Hector, Malmo 2006

Black has just played 19...Be6 when there followed 20.Qc2 Nc4 21.Bc1. What do you think of white's last two moves, and how do you assess the position after 21.Bc1?

1.Nf3 d5 2.g3 Bg4 3.Bg2 Nd7 4.c4 e6 5.cxd5 exd5 6.0–0 Bd6 7.Qb3 Nb6 8.Nc3 Nf6 9.h3 Bd7 10.d3 0–0 11.a4 a5 12.Be3 Ra6 13.Bd4 Re8 14.e4 dxe4 15.Ng5 Rf8 16.dxe4 c5 17.Be3 h6 18.Rfd1 Qb8 19.Nf3 Be6 - Diagram 425

20.Qc2 Nc4 21.Bc1

Timman now wrote (in *New In Chess* 4, 2006): "For the moment, White has had to withdraw his pieces, but he keeps holding all the strategic trumps. The black initiative is short-lived."

Timman is telling us that White has a clear static advantage while black's dynamics are nothing more than temporary shots in the dark. The strategic trumps Timman is referring to are:

➤ A hole on b5 that is beckoning the c3-Knight.

➤ A hole on d5 that might come in handy for White at some point.

 Black's queenside pawn majority is devalued since it can't advance as a single unit due to the fact that one white pawn (on a4) is holding back two black pawns (on a5 and b7).

 White's central pawn majority will be a real force after an eventual f2-f4. Of course, in some lines, if e4-e5 can be played without help, then f2-f4 won't even be necessary.

Explaining the Rating Spread: This sounds like a very hard problem but, if you noticed the holes on b5 and d5 and the potential strength of white's central pawn majority, then consider it solved.

The remainder of the game shows white's positive imbalances (strategic trumps) taking over the game in seemingly effortless fashion: **21...Ne5 22.Nxe5 Bxe5 23.Be3 Qc8 24.Kh2 Re8 25.Nb5 Bb8 26.Qxc5 Qxc5 27.Bxc5 Rc6 28.Bd4 Bb3 29.Re1 Rc4 30.e5 Nd7 31.Ra3 Bc2 32.Bd5 Rxa4 33.e6 fxe6 34.Rxe6**, 1-0.

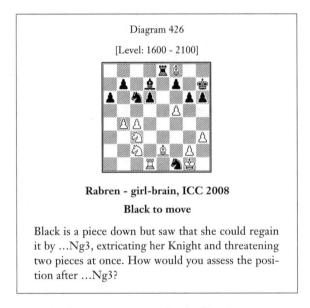

ANSWER
PART NINE

TEST **19**

Diagram 426

[Level: 1600 - 2100]

Rabren - girl-brain, ICC 2008

Black to move

Black is a piece down but saw that she could regain it by ...Ng3, extricating her Knight and threatening two pieces at once. How would you assess the position after ...Ng3?

1.d4 Nf6 2.c4 g6 3.Nc3 Bg7 4.e4 d6 5.Bd3 0–0 6.Nge2 Nc6 7.h3 e5 8.Be3 exd4 9.Nxd4 Ne5 10.Be2 a6 11.0–0 c5 12.Nc2 Be6 13.b3 h6 14.Qd2 Kh7 15.f4 Nc6 16.Rad1 Qa5 17.f5 Bd7 18.a3 Rae8 19.b4 cxb4 20.axb4 Qe5 21.Bf4 Nxe4 22.Bxe5 Nxd2 23.Bxg7 Nxf1 24.Bxf8 - Diagram 426

In the actual game White (after 24...Ng3) played 25.fxg6+ fxg6 26.Bf3, retaining an advantage, though Black ultimately drew. However, just because I appeared to accept black's view that she would regain the piece (and White also accepted it) doesn't mean that you have to! Don't buy into your opponent's (or anyone else's!) delusion. In this kind of position, you should say, "I *must* have a way to win material! I *must*!"

Naturally, at times you'll discover that you don't have a winner, but at the very least you'll find that you have a deeper understanding of the position than if you merely went along for the ride. However, in many cases you'll find something worthwhile or even winning. But without that combative "I must!" such discoveries just won't happen.

Explaining the Rating Spread: This turns out to be an "I must" problem! I hope you refused to buy into my "Black will regain the piece" smokescreen—in real games, your opponent will constantly try to feed you lies and you have to learn to ignore everything he says and seek your own truth in each and every position.

The refutation of black's concept (after **24...Ng3**) was:

25.Bg4! when black's busted:

 25...Rxf8 26.fxg6+ fxg6 27.Bxd7.

25...Nxf5 26.Bxd6!

25...gxf5 26.Bxd6, hitting the Knight on g3.

ANSWER PART NINE TEST 20

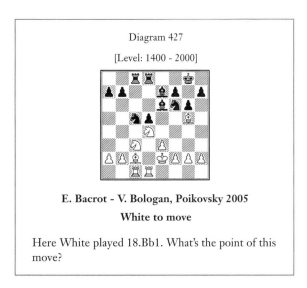

Diagram 427

[Level: 1400 - 2000]

E. Bacrot - V. Bologan, Poikovsky 2005

White to move

Here White played 18.Bb1. What's the point of this move?

1.d4 Nf6 2.c4 e6 3.Nf3 d5 4.Nc3 Be7 5.Qc2 0–0 6.cxd5 exd5 7.Bg5 c5 8.dxc5 Qa5 9.e3 Nc6 10.Bb5 Nb4 11.Qa4 Qxa4 12.Bxa4 Nd3+ 13.Ke2 Nxc5 14.Bc2 Be6 15.Nd4 Rac8 16.Rac1 g6 17.Rhd1 Rfd8 - Diagram 427

This problem is all about Target Consciousness. The target is the isolated pawn on d5 and, logically, White wants to bring more pieces to bear on it.

> **Explaining the Rating Spread**: If you didn't notice that d5 was white's long-term target then you would have no chance in solving the problem.

18.Bb1!

I like this move! White wants to have his light-squared Bishop join in the battle against d5, but right now it's not able to do so since 18.Bb3 allows 18...Nxb3 and 18.b4 weakens all sorts of squares along the c-file after 18...Na6. 18.Bb1 intends to follow up with a3 and Ba2 when the goal has been reached.

Here's the rest of the game with minimal notes:

18...a6 19.a3 Kg7 20.Ba2 h6 21.Bh4 g5? (21...Ncd7 followed by ...Nb6 would have kept white's edge to a bare minimum.) **22.Bg3 Nce4 23.Nxe4 Nxe4 24.Bc7 Re8**

25.Rc2! Bf6 26.Nxe6+ fxe6 27.Rdc1 g4 28.f3 gxf3+ 29.gxf3 Ng5 30.f4 Nf7 31.f5 exf5 32.Bxd5 (White's two Bishops are extremely strong.) 32...Bg5 33.Bb6 Rxc2+ 34.Rxc2 Nd6 35.Kf3 Bf6 36.Bc5 Ne4 37.Bb4 Ng5+ 38.Kf2 b6 39.Rc7+ Kg6 40.h4 Ne6 41.Rc6 a5 42.Bc3 Bxh4+ 43.Kf3 Kf7 44.e4!, 1-0. After 44...fxe4+ 45.Kxe4 White picks up the horse by Kf5.

ANSWER
PART NINE

TEST 21

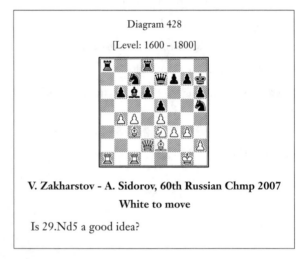

Diagram 428

[Level: 1600 - 1800]

V. Zakharstov - A. Sidorov, 60th Russian Chmp 2007

White to move

Is 29.Nd5 a good idea?

1.d4 Nf6 2.c4 e6 3.Nf3 b6 4.Nc3 Bb4 5.Qc2 Bb7 6.a3 Bxc3+ 7.Qxc3 d6 8.e3 0–0 9.Be2 Re8 10.0–0 Nbd7 11.b4 Qe7 12.Bb2 e5 13.Rfd1 a5 14.Qb3 Qe6 15.Qc2 h6 16.d5 Qe7 17.Nd2 Rec8 18.e4 c6 19.dxc6 Bxc6 20.Qd3 Nf8 21.g3 Ne6 22.f3 Ba4 23.Rdc1 Bc6 24.Nf1 Nh5 25.Qd2 Rd8 26.Bc3 Kh7 27.Ne3 axb4 28.axb4 Nc7 - Diagram 428

One might think it is, since after 29.Nd5 Nxd5 30.cxd5 the c-file is opened for white's Rook and the c6-square might make a nice home for a white piece someday. However, this isn't the case and 29.Nd5 would be a serious mistake.

> **Explaining the Rating Spread**: If you noted the weakness of d6 and also saw that Nd5 led to a hole on c6 but one that wasn't useable, then you've passed this problem with flying colors!

Problems with the black position: the weakness of the d5-square, the vulnerability of the f5-square, and the offside black Knight on h5. However, even more important than these things are the targets on b6 and d6. 29.Nd5 Nxd5 30.cxd5, though still better for White, covers up the weakness on d6. Simply put, when you see an enemy weakness, don't go out of your way to make it inaccessible!

In the game, White went right after d6:

29.Nf5 Qf8 30.Qe3 Rdb8 31.Rxa8 Bxa8 32.Rd1 Ne8 33.Qd2 Nhf6 (33...Rd8 34.Bxe5) 34.Nxd6 Qe7 35.Nxe8 Rxe8 36.Qd6, 1-0.

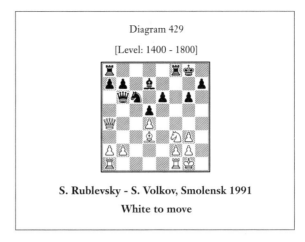

Diagram 429

[Level: 1400 - 1800]

S. Rublevsky - S. Volkov, Smolensk 1991

White to move

If the hole on e5 hit you in the face and made you long for complete domination of that square, then you possess a keen positional eye.

> **Explaining the Rating Spread**: You could only solve this if you noticed the hole on e5 and you wanted to make it your own.

Since domination of e5 is your main goal (to be followed by pressure against the backward pawn on e6), you need to find a move that increases your control over that point. Furthermore, since black's Knight is the main defender of e5, it stands to reason that getting rid of that Knight will vastly increase your claim to the desired square.

1.Bb5

Getting rid of this Knight takes the pressure off of d4, leaves e6 weak, and also permanently claims possession of the critical e5-square. Once the Knight gets to live there, the superiority of the horse over the Bishop will be clear.

1...Rac8 2.Rac1

The immediate 3.Bxc6 might have been a bit more accurate.

2...a6 3.Bxc6 Bxc6 4.Qa3 and white's advantage is beyond dispute. The rest of the game led to a surprisingly easy win: **4...Bb5 5.Rfe1 Rxc1 6.Rxc1 Be2 7.Ng5!
Re8** (7...Qxd4 8.Qxf8+ Kxf8 9.Nxe6+) **8.Qe3 Qxb2 9.Rc8 Rxc8 10.Qxe6+ Kg7
11.Qe7+ Kh6 12.Nf7+ Kg7 13.Ng5+ Kh6 14.Ne6! Qc1+ 15.Kh2 Rc6 16.Qg7+
Kh5 17.f4 h6 18.Qf6 g5 19.Ng7+**, 1-0.

ANSWER
PART NINE

TEST 23

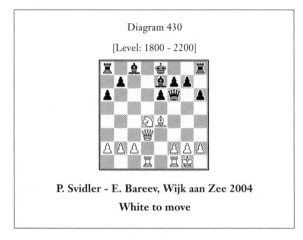

Diagram 430

[Level: 1800 - 2200]

P. Svidler - E. Bareev, Wijk aan Zee 2004

White to move

1.e4 e6 2.d4 d5 3.Nc3 dxe4 4.Nxe4 Nd7 5.Nf3 Ngf6 6.Bd3 c5 7.0–0 Nxe4 8.Bxe4 Nf6 9.Bg5 cxd4 10.Nxd4 h6 11.Bxf6 Qxf6 12.Qd3 a6 13.Rad1 Be7 - Diagram 430

White has a queenside pawn majority, a lead in development, and more active pieces. Black has a central pawn majority and two Bishops, but his King is still in the center. Of course, Black will have a playable position if he's able to castle, so White has to either prevent castling altogether or make Black pay a price to get his King to safety.

> **Explaining the Rating Spread**: Black's King is still in the center and you should demand something lasting if he manages to castle. In other words, you should have looked long and hard for a dynamic solution.

White is able to make tactical use of his lead in development and black's vulnerable King. However, whether you noticed white's move or not, consider the problem solved if you came up with a similar breakdown to the one above.

14.Nc6! e5?

Not a good idea. He had to get his King out of the danger zone as quickly as possible, though the position after 14...0–0 15.Nxe7+ Qxe7 16.Qd6 Qxd6 17.Rxd6 is far from comfortable for Black.

15.Nxe7

There goes black's two Bishops! A serious alternative was 15.Qc3, netting a free pawn.

15...Qxe7 16.f4

Continuing to try to open the position, threatening both fxe5 and f4-f5, and also setting a deadly trap.

16...exf4??

Alternatives such as 16...0–0 17.f5—when Black is bound hand and foot—and 16...Bg4 17.Rde1 0-0 18.Qg3—winning a pawn—were not very attractive, but after 16...exf4 the game comes to a stunning end.

17.Bxb7!, 1-0. The threats of 18.Bxa8 and 18.Rfe1 force Black to tip over his King.

ANSWER
PART NINE

TEST 24

Diagram 431

[Level: 1400 - 2000]

A. Gupta - V. Bhat, Spain 2007

White to move

There's a lot going on here. Instead of drowning you in the complications, let's have you search for a single shred of clarity: what is the most important square on the board in this position?

1.d4 d5 2.c4 c6 3.Nc3 Nf6 4.Nf3 e6 5.Bg5 h6 6.Bh4 dxc4 7.e4 g5 8.Bg3 b5 9.Be2 Bb7 10.0–0 Nbd7 11.Ne5 Bg7 12.f4 Nxe5 13.dxe5 Qxd1 14.Raxd1 Nd7 15.f5 0–0–0 16.Bh5 Nc5 17.Bxf7 Bf8 18.Rd6 b4 19.Rxd8+ Kxd8 20.Rd1+ Kc7 21.Ne2 Rh7 22.fxe6 Bc8 - Diagram 431

One could argue about the vast importance of a number of squares—the e-pawn dreams of promoting on e8, black's Knight longs to leap into d3, etc. However, I'm hoping the pawn structure (as odd as it seems to be) brought to mind a lesson we learned in Part Eight, Passed Pawns—when you have a passed pawn, the most important square is the one directly in front of it. In this case the passed pawn is on e6, which means the answer to our problem is e7!

> **Explaining the Rating Spread**: If you understood that white's e6-pawn was passed, then you should have also understood that laying claim to the square in front of it is often critical in such situations.

The tripled pawns are almost a distraction from what's really going on: White has a passed e6-pawn and would love to push it. His light-squared Bishop is containing black's Rook, and it also controls the promotion square on e8. Thus it's up to White to make his passer count. To accomplish this, he needs to take control of the e7-square so the pawn can advance.

23.Nd4

This not only protects e6, but it also prepares to fight for the e7-square with a well-timed Nf5.

23...Rh8?

Black cracks and goes down without much of a fight. He had to try 23...Nd3 (this not only brings the Knight into the thick of things, but also frees c5 for the f8-Bishop), when 24.b3!? Nb2 25.Rf1 c3 leads to some very interesting positions. One possible line: 26.Bg6 Bc5 27.Bxh7 Bxd4+ 28.Bf2 Bxf2+ 29.Kxf2 Ba6 30.Ra1 Nd3+ 31.Ke2 c2.

24.e7!

The prized e6-pawn sacrifices itself, knowing that it will immediately be reincarnated via e5-e6. The point of the sacrifice is that it allows white's dark-squared Bishop to enter the battle, it leads to the black King being forced away from the embattled area, and it also forces black's dark-squared Bishop to the vulnerable e7-square.

24...Bxe7 25.e6+ Kb7 26.Nf5

Diagram 431a

White "wins" the e7-square, and with it comes decisive material gain.

26...Bf6 27.e5 Bd8 28.e7 Bb6 29.Nd6+ Ka8 30.Nxc4, 1-0.

ANSWER
PART NINE

TEST 25

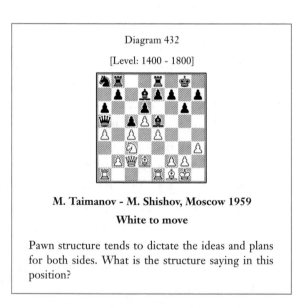

Diagram 432

[Level: 1400 - 1800]

M. Taimanov - M. Shishov, Moscow 1959

White to move

Pawn structure tends to dictate the ideas and plans for both sides. What is the structure saying in this position?

1.d4 Nf6 2.c4 g6 3.Nc3 Bg7 4.e4 d6 5.Be2 0–0 6.Nf3 c5 7.0–0 a6 8.Re1 Nfd7 9.d5 Ne5 10.Nxe5 Bxe5 11.Bh6 Re8 12.Qd2 Nd7 13.Bf1 Rb8 14.h3 Qa5 15.a4 Nb6 16.Qc2 Bd7 17.Bd2 Na8 - Diagram 432

White has an advantage in central space and his natural plan is to play for e4-e5, which gains even more central space and also gives the e1-Rook lots of leverage down the e-file. Black's pawn structure is aiming at the queenside (e7-d6-c5), and his most natural move is ...b7-b5. However, White has prevented that move. Other typical ideas for Black are ...e7-e6 (trying to kick-start the e8-Rook) and ...f7-f5 (though this move would weaken black's King position and also open the e-file for white's Rook).

> **Explaining the Rating Spread**: Moves aren't important here, but knowing what the structure expects from you is! If you were aware of all three major pawn breaks (...b7-b5 and/or ...e7-e6 for Black and e4-e5 for White) then you've passed this test with flying colors.

Since White wants to play e4-e5, Taimanov's 18th move is easy to understand. Note how the whole game (given without notes) revolves around white's ever-growing central space.

18.f4 Bd4+ 19.Kh1 Qc7 20.Be3 Bg7 21.Bf2 Qc8 22.e5 Nc7 23.Ne4 Bf5 24.g4 Bxe4+ 25.Qxe4 a5 26.Rad1 Qd7 27.b3 Rf8 28.Bg3 f5 29.Qe2 b6 30.Bg2 Kh8 31.Rd3 Rbe8 32.Bh2 Na6 33.Re3 Nc7 34.Bf3 fxg4 35.e6 Qd8 36.hxg4 Bd4 37.Rd3 Rf6 38.g5 Rf5 39.Be4 Ref8 40.Qg4 Ne8 41.Rh3 Ng7 42.Rh6, 1-0.

Appendix / Instructive Articles

Contents

Instructive Articles

Introduction

In 2009 I was asked by the website chess.com to write a question-and-answer column for players ranging from complete beginners to titled players. Naturally, everything one could imagine was asked, ranging from opening theory to study habits to diet to whether or not a person was qualified to teach chess to children. Later, it occurred to me that some of my answers would nicely complement the chapters in this book, while others would embrace completely new (but highly useful) subjects.

As a result, often-asked topics like "How to create an opening repertoire" will please those interested in opening study, while practical but rarely voiced questions like "what to eat during a tournament" and "how to offer a draw" should prove extremely interesting to a myriad of readers who often wondered about such things, but didn't know where to look for an answer.

*   *   *   *   *

Imbalances

Tom asked:

If I'm doing a tactical puzzle, should I be looking at the imbalances before I start calculating? Or does this not apply when you know there's a tactical shot in the position?

Dear Tom,

Imbalances (space, material, pawn structure, weak squares, superior/inferior minor pieces, etc.) offer a player a firm grasp of what's happening in any given position. Instead of looking at a position and not knowing what in the world is going on, you can train yourself to quickly recognize any and all imbalances for both sides. Then, any move you consider will have something to do with the positive/negative features on the board.

Most players simply calculate. For example, when looking at their position (as the clock ticks) they internally say, "I go there and he goes there and I go there, etc." However, if I were to ask them at that exact moment to lecture me on the ins and outs of the position, they will usually be way off, or in many cases even clueless. How can you find a move that conforms to the needs of a position if you don't know what those needs are?

Tactics are another matter. Having the ability to calculate deeply is a huge plus, but few can do it. In fact, though you can work on and improve your ability to calculate to some degree, possessing the ability to calculate deeply, quickly, and accurately (at a GM level) is a god given gift (don't mix this up with learning tactical patterns—it's relatively easy to vastly improve your tactical IQ by the study of each mating pattern, each basic tactical pattern [forks, pins, etc.], and going over all sorts of tactical puzzles).

I tend to place very high-level calculation under the umbrella of "talent," while positional skills are something everyone can learn and excel at. Oddly, few players hone their positional skills, preferring to muddle through with a good tactical IQ and poor calculation. Sadly, many players that do have serious calculation mojo rely on that skill set while ignoring all the others (I've known several IMs that have grandmaster level tactical ability but 2300 positional skills).

When looking over a "find the tactic" type problem, you can indeed just look for the tactical solution (since it's been announced that there is one). Be aware that almost all tactics are based on double attacks, undefended (or inadequately defended) pieces, and/or a vulnerable King—that will make it easier to find.

However, in actual play no voice of authority says, "Tom, there is a tactic here. Find the tactic Tom!" Thus (in a real game), it's important to do that imbalance rundown so you know exactly what's going on in every position you reach, while also asking (after you do the imbalance thing) if there are any double attacks and/or undefended/inadequately defended pieces, and if the enemy King appears vulnerable to a karate chop to the throat.

In some situations you'll find that there is a tactic, but it gives you less than the correct positional move. Here's an example:

Here's a line in the Semi-Slav that used to be fairly popular: 1.d4 d5 2.c4 c6 3.Nc3 e6 4.e3 Nf6 5.Nf3 Nbd7 6.Bd3 Bd6 7.0–0 0–0 8.e4 and now 8...dxc4 is black's best move since 8...dxe4 9.Nxe4 Nxe4 10.Bxe4 e5?? (10...h6, intending 11...e5, is a better try) 11.dxe5 Nxe5 12.Nxe5 Bxe5 (Black has an undefended piece, so White finds a tactic based on that and a double attack) 13.Bxh7+! Kxh7 14.Qh5+ Kg8 15.Qxe5 leaves White with a solid extra pawn and a huge plus.

An almost identical position was often reached by 1.d4 d5 2.c4 c6 3.Nc3 e6 4.e3 Nf6 5.Nf3 Nbd7 6.Bd3 Bb4 7.0–0 0–0 8.a3 Bd6 (it seems that White got a2-a3 in for free, why would Black allow this?) 9.e4 dxe4 10.Nxe4 Nxe4 11.Bxe4 e5 and here, in the game G. Kasparov - R. Huebner, Brussels 1986, the great K played 12.Bc2 Re8

13.Re1 exd4 14.Rxe8+ Qxe8 15.Qxd4 Be7 16.Bg5 Bxg5 17.Nxg5 Nf6 18.Rd1 Be6
19.Re1 Qd8 20.Nxe6 fxe6 21.Qe3 Kh8 22.h3 Qd7 23.g4 Re8 24.Qe5 Qd8 25.Kg2
Qb6 26.Rd1 c5 27.Ba4 Rf8 28.Rd6 Qc7 29.Rxe6 Qf7 30.Qxc5 Nxg4 31.Qxf8+ Qxf8
32.hxg4, 1-0. White regains the Queen with Re8 and ends up with an extra piece.

At this point, astute readers will be asking, "Wait a second! Did Kasparov really miss the same tactic from the previous example?" Let's see if it still works: 12.dxe5 Nxe5 13.Nxe5 Bxe5 14.Bxh7+ Kxh7 15.Qh5+ Kg8 16.Qxe5 with an extra pawn. Yep, the tactic does indeed work. Of course, Kasparov saw that he could do this, but was also aware that this position (after 16.Qxe5), though a bit better for White, is basically drawn!!!

I can imagine that many of you are now shaking your head with pity. "Silman must have hit his head again! The poor fool doesn't realize it's the same position."

But, is it really the same position? There's one "small" difference: White's a-pawn is on a3 in the Kasparov game, and on a2 in the earlier position with 6...Bd6. In fact, players with Black often chose 6...Bb4 7.a3 Bd6 hoping to get this very same pawn down (drawn) position, while the pawn down position with the a-pawn on a2 is more or less lost.

This still sounds like gibberish (thereby strengthening the concussion theory), but here's the rub: All the tactical skill in the world won't give you the answer, but a positionally trained eye will tell you that, with a2-a3 in, the b3-square is weakened and, after 16...Qd3, White is forced to push his c-pawn (in the position with 6...Bd6 White would simply play 17.b3), thereby giving black's light-squared Bishop access to d5 (that, combined with the Bishops of opposite colors, makes it more or less impossible for White to win). Many games were drawn from this position. Here's one example: 17.c5 Be6 18.Bf4 Bd5 19.Rfe1 f6 20.Qh5 Bf7 21.Qg4 Rfe8 22.h3 Qc4 and Black drew without too much difficulty in B. Larsen - A. Bisguier, San Juan 1969.

You may see a number of tactics in various games, but is the pretty combination really the best way to play the position? If you don't have a grasp of the imbalances, you'll have no way to answer that question. Ultimately, high-level chess is a game that demands balance. Tactics without positional skills just won't hold up, while positional skills without tactics will also fall on its face.

★　　★　　★　　★　　★

Help! I Need a Plan!

IM David Pruess asked:

I do know a few things about planning—I even teach "how to plan" to my own students sometimes. But I still come across positions fairly often, maybe one in ten games, where I feel I should have a plan, but can't come up with anything. Typically I get into time trouble in such games. Now, I believe there are games where you don't need a long-term plan, just a series of 2-3 move operations; but I have the distinct feeling that in these games I am thinking of there was a good plan to be had.

I'm going to include the opening moves of this game, because they are kind of interesting, and might help a tiny bit in orienting yourself to the position I am interested in:

1.c4 e6 2.Nc3 d5 3.d4 c6 4.cxd5 exd5 5.Qc2 Bd6 6.Nf3 Ne7 7.Bg5 f6 8.Bh4 Bf5 9.Qd2 0-0 10.Bg3 Be4 11.e3 Bxf3 12.gxf3 f5 13.Bxd6 Qxd6 14.f4

So first of all, my state of mind at this point: I was quite selbst-zufrieden, a little bit self-congratulatory about the success of my "interesting idea" of ...f6, ...Bf5-e4. I evaluated the position fairly optimistically based on these factors: I felt my position had enough space, my pieces could all find decent squares, f5 and g7 could be defended by pieces so I would not have to push g6, and I had even inflicted a slight structural weakness on white that might eventually tell.

I also thought that White had a little question to figure out with his King. If he castled queenside, I thought I might have the stronger attack when I advanced my pawns there, as the kingside seemed pretty static. If he castled kingside, maybe his pawn weaknesses there would allow me to lift my rooks via the third rank and generate some attack there too.

However, over the next few moves, the psychological initiative swung back my opponent's way, as he made several pretty quick moves, and I began to burn up time, unable to come up with any plan. He left his king in the center, so I could not go for any direct attack.

Now, often, I make a plan by picking a part of the board where I think I am stronger (or potentially stronger) than the opponent. This was not helpful here. Other times, I look at some piece of mine and ask: where would I put it ideally—in this position I had trouble doing that for my knights.

Thanks in advance for any light you can shed on this for me!

Dear Mr. Pruess,

I think the vast majority of positions call for 2-3 move operations. Of course, this comes after you decide whether the position is static or dynamic in nature, and what the various imbalances for both sides are (a trained player does all that in seconds). Then you quickly decide what move(s) fit the needs of the position and analyze them and all tactics that arise from them.

This is why, in my 4th Edition of *How to Reassess Your Chess*, I stress the need for every player to master the necessary (but simple) skill of recognizing imbalances over any particular thinking technique since that one thing gives you a firm handle on a position's nature and its needs.

Having said that, there are times when a position calls for a far deeper plan or, on very rare occasions, even a "grand plan." For example, in the following game (I'll use examples from my own practice since it saves me the trouble of looking up other sources and I also know what I was thinking, which is very important in the context of this article.) I used a grand plan, which enabled me to pretty much "see" the way the game would go from move 18 to 38.

D. Gliksman - J. Silman, Software Toolworks 1988

1.d4 Nf6 2.c4 e6 3.Nf3 Bb4+ 4.Nc3 c5 5.e3 Nc6 6.Bd3 Bxc3+

This is the Huebner Variation of the Nimzo-Indian, a line that instantly creates a Bishop versus Knight imbalance in the hope of proving that the upcoming pawn structure (made possible by the lack of flexibility of white's doubled pawns) will prove conducive to Knights.

As you play through the game, you'll see just how important that Knight vs. Bishop battle was—it raged from the opening to the endgame. This in itself can be considered a rather basic plan, though others might think of it as a means of creating a long-term static plus. If the student learns to create this kind of logical plan (which conforms to the dictates of the position), then he'll do very well for himself.

7.bxc3 d6 8.0-0 e5

A major part of Black's strategy—by closing the position he keeps the Bishops at bay.

9.Nd2 0-0

Black refuses to win a pawn by 9...cxd4 10.cxd4 exd4 11.exd4 Nxd4 since after 12.Bb2 white's Bishops would be very strong on their wide open diagonals.

10.d5 Ne7 11.f4

White is still trying to open up lines for his Bishops. In addition, Black must take the threat of 12.f5 (gaining a crushing advantage in space) very seriously.

11...exf4 12.exf4

Again threatening 13.f5, which would activate his dark-squared Bishop and squeeze Black to death due to his lack of territory.

12...Bf5!

A tremendously important move! This simultaneously exchanges a pair of Bishops (depriving White of his Bishop pair) and stops the advance of White's f-pawn in its tracks.

13.Qc2

Beginning a battle for the f5-square. Less good is 13.Bxf5 Nxf5 14.Nf3 h5! preventing a g2-g4 push and ensuring that f5 will remain in Black's hands.

13...Qd7

And not 13...Bxd3? 14.Qxd3 g6 (14...Qd7 15.f5 is horrible for Black) 15.f5! Nxf5 16.Rxf5 gxf5 17.Qxf5 when the dormant Bishop is suddenly a major player: 17...Re8 18.Nf3 (Threatening 19.Bg5 with a crushing pin.) 18...Ne4 19.Ng5. Obviously, Black can't lose the fight for the f5-square since that would also lose the battle of the minor pieces!

14.Ne4

This leads to a strategically lost position. However, White would also feel no joy after 14.Nf3 g6 15.Nh4 Bxd3 16.Qxd3 Qg4 (Forcing White to further damage his Bishop by bringing another pawn to a dark square.) 17.g3 Nf5 18.Nxf5 Qxf5 19.Qxf5 gxf5 when White's Bishop is absolutely horrible.

14...Nxe4 15.Bxe4 Rae8 16.Bd2 Bxe4 17.Qxe4 f5

Permanently blocking the position and creating a nice support point on e4 for the Black Knight and/or Rooks.

18.Qd3 Nc8

And here we come to the "grand plan." After this, I had worked everything out and, incredibly, it all actually occurred!

My old note: A move with an obvious threat and a much deeper, hidden, purpose. If left alone, Black will surround White's c4-pawn by ...Nb6 followed by ...Qa4. White can prevent this and chase the Knight back by a2-a4-a5, but that brings White's a-pawn into striking distance of Black's b-pawn, allowing an eventual ...b7-b6 advance which will lead to the creation of a winning passed a-pawn for Black.

The rest of the game was already clear to me, I only had to work out individual tactics, never allowing White to veer the game off the positional path I had foreseen.

19.Rfe1 Nb6

The threat of ...Qa4 is very annoying for White, so he stops it in the only way possible.

20.a4 Rxe1+ 21.Bxe1 Re8

Also possible is 21...Nxa4 22.Qd1 Nb6 23.Rxa7 Nxc4, but I didn't see a need to give White any possible counterplay. I was much happier simply keeping his pieces contained and helpless.

22.a5 Nc8 23.Bh4 g6 24.Re1 Rxe1+ 25.Bxe1 Qe7 26.Bf2 Kf7 27.Qb1 a6

The game is now over. Black's plan (prepared on move 18) is now simplicity itself: he will march his King over to c7 and play ...b7-b6. The passed a-pawn that results will prove decisive.

28.h3 h5 29.Qc2 Ke8 30.Qb1 Kd8 31.g4 hxg4 32.hxg4 Qf7 33.gxf5 gxf5 34.Bh4+ Kc7 35.Bg5 Qd7 36.Kg2 b6 37.Qa2 Kb7 38.axb6 Nxb6

This was more or less what I had played for from move 18—the grand plan is over and it's been extremely successful!

39.Qe2 a5 40.Kg3 a4 41.Kf2 a3 42.Qa2 Qa4 43.Bd8 Nxc4 44.Qe2 a2 45.Qe7+ Ka6 46.Qc7

Threatening perpetual check. Black's next move prevents this.

46...Qb5, 0-1. So how did I see so far? Actually there was very little calculation. To me, the position seemed to "absorb" these ideas in a natural way and it seems all too natural for the path I created to be followed (that's not to say that a stronger opponent wouldn't have veered off course!).

When a "grand plan" is used, it usually means that:

• The stronger side has a huge advantage and the defender is hard pressed to stop his opponent's intentions.

• The strategic elements are so clearly defined that it would take a blind man not to see the potential long-term continuation right through to the end. When this occurs, it's up to the defending side to notice his opponent's intention and do everything he can to prevent it from going "according to script."

I got to play another grand plan against a very strong IM. This time the plan was more general, but just as effective.

J. Silman - C. Lakdawala, California Chmp 1989

1.d4 g6 2.c4 Bg7 3.Nc3 d6 4.e4 Nc6 5.Be3 e5 6.d5 Nce7 7.c5 f5 8.cxd6 cxd6 9.Bb5+ Kf8

Usually White is delighted to exchange light-squared Bishops in KID structures. The text isn't as bad as it looks: Black's King is quite safe on f8 and his kingside pawn storm can become very threatening.

10.Nf3 f4 11.Bd2 h6 12.a4

And here I mapped out a "grand plan." However, it was based on simple concepts—I knew the moves to support those concepts would be found as the game went on since I already deemed my position (whether it's true or not!) strategically won.

The PLAN:

- First I map out huge territorial gains on the queenside.

- Then I deprive my opponent of any real play on the kingside.

- Then I target d6.

- Eventually I effect a decisive penetration on the queenside—most likely on the c-file.

12...g5 13.a5 g4 14.Ng1 Nf6 15.Nge2 Ng6 16.g3

Killing my opponent's counterattack on the kingside. Quite honestly, after playing 16.g3 I felt that the point was already mine!

16...f3 17.Nc1 h5 18.Qa4 h4 19.Rf1

Getting off the h-file and defending the potentially vulnerable pawn on f2.

19...hxg3 20.hxg3 Bh6 21.Nb3 Rb8 22.Qb4

Targeting d6.

22...Kg7 23.Bxh6+ Rxh6 24.Nd2

The Knight heads for c4 where, at first glance, it will work with my Queen against Black's d-pawn. However, there is an even more nefarious purpose to this Knight maneuver.

24...Nh8 25.Nc4 Nf7 26.Ne3

My only weakness (on f2) is solidly defended, while Black is going to have to worry about g4, f5, d6, b7, and possible intrusions along the c-file for a long time to come.

26...Qh8 27.0-0-0 Rh2 28.Kb1 Qh6

Hoping to gain counterplay by sacrificing the Exchange, i.e., 29...Rxf2 30.Rxf2 Qxe3. Of course, I don't allow this to happen.

29.Rde1

As usual, patience is required. My plusses are not going away, so there is certainly no reason to rush.

29...Nh7

Desperate, Black hopes to put more heat on f2 by ...Nh7-g5-h3. Unfortunately, the fact that most of his army is on the kingside allows me to stomp him on the other side of the board.

30.Qc4

A decisive penetration into c7 is assured. The grand plan has worked to perfection!

30...a6 31.Qc7 Ra8 32.Bd7

By getting rid of Black's light-squared Bishop, Black's weaknesses on b7, f5, and g4 all fall into my hands. Also very strong was 32.Be8.

32...Bxd7 33.Qxd7 Nf6 34.Qxb7 Qh8 35.Nf5+ Kg6 36.Nh4+ Kg7 37.Nf5+ Kg6 38.Nh4+

My last few moves gained a bit of time on the clock. Now I'm ready to proceed with the mopping up process.

38...Kg7 39.Rh1

It's ironic that Black's final demise will occur on the very file that he coveted so highly.

39...Rxh1 40.Rxh1 Qd8 41.Nf5+ Kg6 42.Rh6+, 1-0. He didn't need to see 42...Nxh6 43.Qg7+ Kh5 44.Qxh6 mate.

As you can see, a "grand plan" doesn't mean you have to calculate 30 moves ahead. In fact, often such a plan is almost devoid of calculation—it's completely made up of concepts based on the correct reading of the imbalances and the plusses and minuses in each respective position.

As I said earlier, "grand plans" are rare, and usually one simply plays moves (Pruess' 2 to 3 move operations) that suit the particular position (again, based on the specific imbalances and on the position's dynamic or static needs). Here's a case of a dynamic, tactical situation:

J. Polgar - J. Silman, New York 1988

1.e4 c5 2.Nf3 Nc6 3.d4 cxd4 4.Nxd4 Nf6 5.Nc3 d6 6.Bc4 Qb6 7.Nb3 e6 8.Be3 Qc7 9.f4 Be7 10.Qe2 0-0 11.0-0-0 a6

No deep plans here! It's all about tactics and me getting her on the queenside while she gets me on the kingside! The "script" is clear, and the winner is the one who sticks to it with the most imagination, energy, and tactical acumen.

12.g4 b5 13.Bd3 Nb4 14.g5 Nxd3+ 15.Rxd3 Nd7 16.Bd4 Re8 17.Qh5 Bb7 18.Rh3 Nf8 19.f5 e5 20.Be3 b4 21.g6

Nothing subtle here!

21...fxg6 22.fxg6 hxg6 23.Qh8+ Kf7 24.Rf1+ Ke6 25.Nd5 Bxd5 26.Qg8+ Kd7 27.Qxd5 Qc6 28.Rf7 Ne6, ½-½. I could have played on, but the little girl (Judit was only two or three years old at this time) had attacked me with such ferocity that I was happy to have the whole thing over and done.

And here's another example of a "2 to 3 move operations" plan—this time we'll look at a game that's completely positional:

J. Silman - C. Lakdawala, Los Angeles 1987

1.d4 Nf6 2.c4 g6 3.Nc3 Bg7 4.e4 d6 5.Be2 0-0 6.Bg5 h6 7.Be3 e5 8.d5 Nbd7 9.Qd2 Nc5 10.f3 a5 11.Bd1 c6 12.Nge2 cxd5 13.cxd5 b6 14.0-0 h5

And now, after some typical KID moves that I've used a million times before, a plan needs to be created. As is so often the case, no calculation is necessary at this time (though you do calculate before playing every move to ensure that your artistic designs hold up to the cold truth of tactics).

PLAN: Grab the b5-square with two hands, then chase away his best piece (the c5-Knight) by b4 (prep like b3, a3, and only then b4 might be necessary), then penetrate down the open c-file. Due to white's obvious advantage in space on the queenside, this should prove decisive.

15.Nb5 Ne8 16.Nec3 a4 17.Bc2 Ba6 18.b4 (Black is strategically lost) **18...axb3 19.axb3 Nc7 20.Nxc7 Qxc7 21.Rfc1 Rfc8 22.b4 Ne6** (Realizing that he would be toast after 22...Nd7 23.Ba4, he gives this a try, hoping that tactics might confuse his opponent. However, this merely speeds up the end. Now we leave planning behind and enter a world of pure, though simple, calculation!) **23.dxe6 Qxc3 24.Qxc3 Rxc3 25.Bd2 Rcc8 26.exf7+ Kf8 27.Bb3 Bb7 28.Rxa8**, 1-0.

Now (finally!) it's time to address E. Tangborn - D. Pruess, USCL 2009: **1.c4 e6 2.Nc3 d5 3.d4 c6 4.cxd5 exd5 5.Qc2 Bd6 6.Nf3 Ne7 7.Bg5 f6 8.Bh4 Bf5 9.Qd2 0-0 10.Bg3 Be4 11.e3 Bxf3 12.gxf3 f5 13.Bxd6** (13.Be5 Bxe5 14.dxe5 f4 15.exf4 entranced me—I'm a sucker for odd pawn formations!) **13...Qxd6 14.f4**

Though many positions call for a quick set of moves, this isn't one of them! The basic details are easy to map out:

- Black only has two pawn breaks: ...c6-c5 (a dynamic move that makes d4 and d5 very weak ... however, it's his main break and is thus very important!) and ...g7-g5 (which won't be happening any time soon, but remains a very real possibility down the line a bit!). Black can also preface ...c5 with ...b6 so that a capture on c5 would allow ...bxc5.

- Pawn advances for Black are ...a7-a5-a4-a3 and/or the advance of the b-pawn. But ...b7-b5 leaves c5 and c6 weak—this might not matter, or it might have profound long-term static ramifications.

- White's breaks are: b2-b4-b5 (minority attack, which I don't see happening in this exact position) and f2-f3 followed by e3-e4, which leads to all sorts of potentially catastrophic pawn weaknesses. Of course, f2-f3 without e3-e4 is also important since, though it weakens e3, it also deprives the enemy Knights of e4 and g4.

- Other factors: White has the half open g-file and can try and make his potentially weak h-pawn into a dynamic asset by h2-h4-h5-h6.

- One other key question is: where to put the white King?

ALL of this zips through my mind quickly as a result of training and retained patterns from millions of games/structures. But in this case, it doesn't give me a clear answer! It seems simple, but it's actually a very tough position, and (in a real game situation) I would sit there and stare for ages, balancing all these considerations and trying to form a logical continuation/plan.

Again: If you aren't armed with these elementary details, then it's impossible to play the position with any intelligence!

If I was sitting at the board actually playing this position, other ideas would—in haphazard fashion—flit through my aged and rapidly decomposing brain:

- If Black goes for queenside pawns on a4 and b5, then a2-a3 followed by Nc3-a2-b4 hits c6 and d5 and prepares Nd3 with control over c5 and e5.

This isn't necessarily bad for Black, but it's something he has to take into consideration.

- If Black plays ...a5 and ...b5, I can respond with a2-a4 ...b4 Ne2 hoping to bring my Knight to d3 or b3 and Rooks to the c-file so I can play whack-a-mole against c6 while also pressuring a5 and c5.

- If White pushes his h-pawn down the board, Black will let it go to h6 (playing ...h6 himself leaves a hole on g6 that White might be able to utilize, it also makes defending f5 harder since ...g7-g6 is no longer "on") and then close up the g-file with ...g6—the pawn on h6 might really bother black's King later in the game, but also closes off the g-file and, in endgames, might become weak (or it might fix h7 and turn into a tower of strength!).

- Black will likely try to push his a-pawn all the way down to a3.

- If black's pawns get to a4 and b5 (with my pawn on a3), he will likely swing a Knight to c4.

- Black might wish to leave his b-pawn on b7, when there aren't any serious weaknesses in black's camp (the e5-square and placing a bit of pressure against f5 by Bd3 and Nc3-e2-g3 stand out). In that case, it will be hard for White to find an active plan. On the other hand, Black can only get active if he loosens his own position up.

- If Black does leave his b-pawn on b7, White has to be wary about the following scenario: (one with white's pawn on h6) Black plays ...Nf6 and ...Ne4. White trades, Black takes back with ...fxe4 and then swings his remaining Knight to f5. If White chops that Knight by Bg4xf5, Black will recapture with his Rook, perhaps double on the f-file, play ...Kh8, and then smash through with ...g6-g5. This series of moves, more than any other, strikes me (from white's point of view) as disturbing. This might compel me to take measures to avoid it by playing f2-f3, stopping the whole ...Ne4 thing from ever happening.

Again, I didn't do any actual calculation—instead I explored various pawn and piece configurations in an effort to deem what ones were most dangerous for both sides. It seems that Black has a slightly easier time leading the dance, though I consider things to be more or less equal.

Anything could happen in this game! Here's a hypothetical series of moves: Black would most likely play 14...Nd7 when I (as White) would temporize a bit and push my h-pawn (since it's something I know I need to do): 15.h4 a5 16.h5 Nf6 17.f3 (Perhaps not necessary since the ...Ne4 plan, with an eye to a later ...g5 push, isn't effective if white's pawn hasn't gone to h6. On the other hand, I don't like Black dictating things, so I might go with 17.f3 since it dominates his Knights) 17...a4 18.Bd3 when I would follow up with Rc1, Kf2 and ... it's just a game that offers mutual chances.

✳   ✳   ✳   ✳   ✳

Two Questions on Planning

E. J. asked:

I have a question that can get rid of some thorns in my mind if answered. What is a plan? I mean, how do I plan? Also, how do I know what plan is right for me? This whole "plan thing" among grandmasters is getting really confusing.

Dear Mr. E. J.,

Eliot, you're not alone! Many players haven't grasped the concept of planning. Quite simply, a plan is a way of taking advantage of the positive features (imbalances) in your position and the negative imbalances in the opponent's. For example, if the opponent has an isolated pawn on an open file, a logical plan would be to bring as many pieces as possible to bear on it. Double or even triple your heavy pieces on the open file. Let a Knight and Bishop join in on the destruction of that poor pawn. Remember: chess is a team effort and you want your whole army to work together towards a particular goal.

You said something very interesting: "How do I know what plan is right for me?" The fact is, in most cases a plan isn't based on what's right for you. It's not a personal decision. A plan is something the board wants (even needs!) you to do. And it's up to you to learn to read the body language of the board and ascertain what the proper plan is. Thus, you might be the greatest tactical genius the world has ever seen, but if the right plan is to quietly take more space and squeeze him to death, then that's what you have to do.

Abhilash_007 asked:

How do you decide it's time to map a grand plan?

Dear Abhilash_007,

Grand plans are rare, even in grandmaster chess. To create them, you need to have a deep understanding of the given position's inherent tactics, structural needs, and the way both sides pieces can help/inhibit those needs. And you would only create one if you are positive that the basics of the position will remain unchanged for many, many moves. This tends to be very advanced, and I don't think that any amateur of any rating should be looking for grand plans. Appreciating them while going over an annotated game is one thing, but actually beating your head against a brick wall in the hope of creating one is quite another.

One reason that a grand plan is rare is that the opponent can always do something that alters the trajectory of even the most logical train of thought. A chess position is always changing, and thus a grand plan rarely stays valid for too long (which means it was never a proper grand plan in the first place). In fact, some strong players don't believe that grand plans even exist—they view them as the creation of after-the-fact artistic license.

Nevertheless, whether one believes in grand plans or not, long plans do appear from time to time, though the extent of what the player actually saw during the game and said he saw afterward the game was over will never be known! Here's a classic example of such a plan, by none other than the 4th World Chess Champion:

E. Znosko-Borovsky - A. Alekhine, Paris 1933

1.e4 e5 2.Nf3 Nc6 3.Bb5 a6 4.Ba4 Nf6 5.0–0 d6 6.c3 Bd7 7.Re1 Be7 8.d4 0–0 9.Nbd2 Be8 10.Bxc6 Bxc6 11.dxe5 dxe5 12.Nxe5 Bxe4 13.Nxe4 Qxd1 14.Nxf6+ gxf6 15.Rxd1 fxe5

The following is what Alekhine had to say about this position (from the second book of his best games):

"The endgame position thus reached is by no means as easy to conduct—especially for the first player—as it looks. Black's plan of campaign—which will prove a complete success—is divided into the following parts:

1) Exchange of one pair of Rooks.

2) Bringing the King to e6 where he will be protected from a frontal attack by the e-pawn and be used to prevent the entrance of the remaining White Rook at d7.

3) By operating with the Rook on the open g-file and advancing the h-pawn, force the opening of the h-file.

4) After this the White King—and eventually also the Bishop—will be kept busy in order to prevent the intrusion of the Black Rook at h1 or h2.

5) In the meantime Black, by advancing his a- and b-pawns will sooner or later succeed in opening one file on the queenside.

6) At that moment the White King will still be on the other wing, the first player will not dispose of sufficient forces to prevent the final intrusion of the enemy's Rook on his first or second rank.

Granted that if White had, from the beginning, realized that there actually existed a danger of losing this endgame, he probably would by extremely careful defense have saved it. But as it happened, Black played with a definite plan, and White only with the conviction that the game must be a draw. And the result was a very instructive series of typical stratagems much more useful for inexperienced players than the so-called 'brilliances.'"

The rest of the game seems a picture perfect replication of the plans Alekhine listed, but it must be admitted that White was most helpful in going along with the program: **16.Bh6 Rfd8 17.Kf1 f5 18.Rxd8+ Rxd8 19.g3 Kf7 20.Be3 h5 21.Ke2**

Ke6 22.Rd1 Rg8 23.f3 h4 24.Bf2 hxg3 25.hxg3 Rh8 26.Bg1 Bd6 27.Kf1 Rg8 28.Bf2 b5 29.b3 a5 30.Kg2 a4 31.Rd2 axb3 32.axb3 Ra8 33.c4 Ra3 34.c5 Be7 35.Rb2 b4 36.g4 f4 37.Kf1 Ra1+ 38.Ke2 Rc1 39.Ra2 Rc3 40.Ra7 Kd7 41.Rb7 Rxb3 42.Rb8 Rb2+ 43.Kf1 b3 44.Kg1 Kc6 45.Kf1 Kd5 46.Rb7 e4 47.fxe4+ Kxe4 48.Rxc7 Kf3 49.Rxe7 Rxf2+ 50.Ke1 b2 51.Rb7 Rc2 52.c6 Kg3 (And not 52…Rc1+ 53.Kd2 b1=Q 54.Rxb1 Rxb1 55.c7) **53.c7 f3 54.Kd1 Rxc7 55.Rxb2 f2,** 0-1.

Ironically, this same Znosko-Borovsky is quoted as saying: "It is not a move, even the best move, that you must seek, but a realizable plan."

✷   ✷   ✷   ✷   ✷

The Art and Science of the Isolated d-Pawn

Madhacker asked:

I'd like to ask about the correct handling of positions where White has an isolated queen's pawn. The question was raised in my head by the following game I played in a local league match, against a significantly stronger opponent.

Madhacker (1950) - Maria Ignacz (2200), Cardiff vs. Caerphilly

1.d4 Nf6 2.c4 e6 3.Nc3 Bb4 4.e3 b6 5.Bd3 Bb7 6.f3 (Is this okay?) **6…c5 7.Ne2 0-0 8.0-0 d5 9.Qc2 cxd4 10.exd4 dxc4 11.Bxc4 Nc6 12.Rd1 h6 13.d5 Bc5+ 14.Kh1 exd5 15.a3 Ne5 16.Bxd5 Nxd5 17.Nxd5 Bxd5 18.Nc3 Qh4 19.Nxd5 Rfd8 20.Ne3 Rxd1+ 21.Qxd1 Rd8 22.Qe2 Nd3 23.b4 Nf2+ 24.Kg1 Rd1+ 25.Nxd1 Ng4+ 26.Kf1 Nxh2** mate.

My conclusion after the game was something like, "I played d5 too early, if I had played a3 first and kicked the bishop away from b4, then played d5, it would have been much stronger because all her tactics involving …Nb4 would have been taken away, and I would have had a good game."

However, on examination by Fritz it turns out that this was not the case and I would have been at least slightly worse anyway. I understand that White should try to liquidate the IQP by playing d5, but I never seem to get it quite right. I'd like to be able to play these positions better, so is there any advice you could give me?

Dear Madhacker,

A very good question. Your problem is that you view the isolated d-pawn as a weakness that needs to be swapped off by a quick d4-d5. However, though this pawn is a potential static weakness, it's also a dynamic tower of strength. If you are going to enter these kinds of positions, you need to adjust your mindset to the "It's strong!" view rather than your negative "I have to trade the sucker off fast!" association.

In your game, 6.Nf3 is the main line, but 6.f3 (played way back in 1914) and even 6.Nge2!? Bxg2 7.Rg1 are also fairly common.

White (from a number of different openings!) usually gets the isolated d-pawn with a Knight on f3. In that case, the d-pawn gives White control over the e5-square (his f3-Knight will eventually hop there) and also gives White a central space advantage. These things, combined with moves such as Rfe1 and Bc2 followed by Qd3 give White serious chances of a kingside attack. And yes, the move d4-d5 is always on the table, but it tends to be part of white's attacking scheme and not, as you seem to imply, a try at trading and fighting for equality.

Strategy for Both Sides

In general, White wants to retain as much tension as possible, avoid minor piece exchanges, and either make use of his space or go directly for a kingside wipeout.

Black needs to fix the d-pawn on d4 by controlling and occupying the d5-square. He has two basic ways to handle the position after this:

- He can bring pressure to bear against d4 in an effort to tie White down to its defense.

- He can seek soothing minor piece exchanges. This gets rid of all white's dynamic compensation and turns the pawn into a long-term static weakness.

Black's ideal position is a Rook and Queen vs. a Rook and Queen (retaining the Queens prevents White from using his King to defend the pawn). Black will place a Rook on d5 (blocking the pawn) and put his Queen behind it—this leaves the d-pawn under enormous pressure, and often a pawn advance like ...c5 or ...e5 (whichever pawn he has) wins the pawn since the mutually doubled heavy pieces on either side of the d-pawn creates a pin. See the Silman - Filguth game (page 630) for an example of this.

If things go bad for White (i.e., all the minor pieces are gone), he does best to exchange all the Rooks. Then the lone Queen vs. Queen situation will be drawable since a defending Queen on c3 or e3 won't be susceptible to pins on the d-file.

First, let's look at a game with a structure that was similar to the one you got in your game:

V. Korchnoi - A. Karpov, Baguio City World Chmp Match 1978

1.c4 Nf6 2.d4 e6 3.Nc3 Bb4 4.e3 c5 5.Ne2 d5 6.a3 Bxc3+ 7.Nxc3 cxd4 8.exd4 dxc4 9.Bxc4 Nc6 10.Be3 0–0 11.0–0 b6 12.Qd3 Bb7 13.Rad1 h6 14.f3 Ne7 15.Bf2

Though White can't get a Knight to e5 like he does in most isolated d-pawn positions, he can still keep Black under pressure by retaining tension, avoiding minor piece exchanges, and aiming his guys at black's King.

15...Nfd5 16.Ba2 Nf4 17.Qd2 Nfg6 18.Bb1 Qd7 19.h4 Rfd8 20.h5 Nf8 21.Bh4 f6 22.Ne4 Nd5 23.g4 Rac8 24.Bg3 Ba6 25.Rfe1 Rc6 26.Rc1 Ne7 27.Rxc6 Qxc6

28.Ba2 Qd7 29.Nd6 Bb7 30.Nxb7 Qxb7 31.Qe3 and the two Bishop vs. two Knights battle is obviously good for White, but (after White missed a forced win) the game was eventually drawn in an exhausting 124 moves (and Black suffered every bit of the way)!

As mentioned earlier, usually White has a Knight on f3, which allows Ne5 and serious chances against the enemy King. This kingside attack has left countless victims laying in their own entrails over the years. Here are a few examples:

M. Hebden - John Littlewood, England 1981

1.e4 c6 2.d4 d5 3.exd5 cxd5 4.c4 Nf6 5.Nc3 e6 6.Nf3 Be7 7.cxd5 Nxd5 8.Bd3 Nc6 9.0-0 0-0 10.Re1 Bf6

10...Nf6 11.Be3 b6 12.Rc1 Nb4 13.Bb1 Nbd5 14.Bg5 Bb7 15.Ne5 Rc8 16.Qd3 g6 17.Bh6 Re8 18.Qh3 Bf8 19.Bg5 Qd6 20.Nxd5 Nxd5 21.Nxf7 Kxf7 22.Qxh7+ Bg7 23.Bxg6+ Kf8 24.Bh6, 1-0, Jacobo Bolbochan - R. Garcia Vera, Mar del Plata 1952;

10...Ncb4 11.Bb1 Nf6 12.a3 Nbd5 13.Qd3 g6 14.Ba2 b6 15.Ne5 Bb7 16.Bh6 Re8 17.Qh3 Bf8 18.Bg5 Be7 19.Rad1 (19.Nxf7! Kxf7 20.Rxe6 Kg7 21.Rae1 gives White a crushing attack) 19...a6 20.Rd3 Rc8 21.Rf3 Nxc3, J. Mason - A. Burn, Hastings 1895, and now White could have shredded his opponent by 22.Nxf7! Kxf7 23.Qxh7+ Kf8 24.Bh6 mate.

11.Be4 Nce7 12.Ne5 Bd7

12...g6 13.Bh6 Bg7 14.Bxg7 Kxg7 15.Qf3 Rb8 16.Qg3 Qd6 17.Bxd5 exd5 18.Rad1 Nf5 19.Qf4 Be6 20.g4 Nh4 21.Rd3 Qd8 22.g5 Nf5 23.Ng4 Qd6 24.Re5 Rbd8 25.Ne2 Bd7 26.Nf6 h6 27.Ng3 hxg5 28.Ngh5+ Kh6 29.Ng4+ Kh7 30.Qxg5 gxh5 31.Nf6+ Qxf6 32.Qxf6 Rg8+ 33.Kf1 Ng7 34.Rg3, 1-0, D. King - S. Conquest, England 1985.

13.Qd3 g6 14.Bh6 Re8 15.Qf3

White's pressure is obvious

15...Bc6 16.Bxd5 Nxd5 17.Ne4 Rc8 18.Rac1 Qe7 19.Rc5 Bg7 20.Bxg7 Kxg7 21.Nd6 Qxd6 22.Qxf7+ Kh6

Better was 22...Kh8 23.Rxc6 bxc6 24.Qxe8+ Rxe8 25.Nf7+ when White's a pawn up.

23.Ng4+, 1-0.

The isolated d-pawn is a common visitor for both White and Black. Here's an example of Black accepting the isolated d-pawn for active piece play, only to fall victim to the anti-isolated pawn "trade the minor pieces" strategy.

J. Silman - R. Filguth, San Francisco 1977

1.e4 e6 2.d4 d5 3.Nd2 c5 4.exd5 exd5 5.Ngf3 Nc6 6.Bb5 Bd6 7.0-0 Nge7 8.dxc5 Bxc5 9.Nb3 Bd6 10.c3 0-0 11.Nbd4 Bg4 12.Be2 Qd7 13.Be3 Rad8 14.Re1 Bb8 15.Ng5

I begin to exchange as many minor pieces as possible. The main form of compensation for the isolated d-pawn is active minor pieces. To put it simplistically, if you trade the minor pieces, they can't be active! In that case, the isolated d-pawn can easily turn out to be a pure weakness.

15...Bxe2 16.Qxe2 Nxd4

Apparently my opponent wasn't aware of my "boring" but highly effective plan!

17.Bxd4 Nf5 18.Qd3 h6 19.Nf3 Rfe8 20.Rad1 Rxe1+ 21.Rxe1 Ne7 22.g3 Nc6 23.Kg2

Black's game is uncomfortable and he has very little counterplay. As a result, I take my time and make tiny improvements in my position.

23...Re8 24.Rd1

The ideal position for White is Queen and Rook versus Queen and Rook. An exchange of the final pair of Rooks would result in a draw since White would not be able to bring sufficient pressure to bear against the d-pawn.

24...Qe6 25.Re1 Qd7 26.Be3

Once again I prevent the exchange of Rooks while simultaneously preparing to get rid of more minor pieces by Nd4.

26...Rd8 27.Rd1 Qe7 28.Nd4 Nxd4

Black is much too kind. He should try for as much activity as possible by 28...Ne5. At the time I intended to answer 28...Qe4+ with 29.Qxe4 dxe4 30.Nxc6 Rxd1 31.Nxb8. Today I would be highly doubtful about this line, and would instead go for a slight but lasting edge in the Rook endgame after 29.f3 Qxd3 30.Rxd3.

29.Qxd4 a6 30.Bf4

The final nail in his coffin! Black's position now becomes extremely depressing.

30...Bxf4 31.Qxf4 Qc5 32.Rd4

Now that the minor pieces are gone, I want to lead with my Rook on d4 (which also fixes his pawn in the case of a later c3-c4) as I double against his d-pawn.

32...Qc6 33.Qd2

White's dream position

33...b5 34.Kg1 Qg6 35.a3

A bit of cat and mouse. I intend to eventually play a3-a4 (creating a second weakness), but first I want to make a few minor improvements in my position.

35...Kf8 36.h4

Giving my King some breathing room and avoiding 36.Rxd5?? Qb1+ 37.Kg2 Qe4+.

36...Qb1+ 37.Kg2 Qf5 38.a4

Forcing the creation of a second weakness.

38...Qe6 39.axb5 axb5 40.Qd3 Kg8

An overreaction, but 40...Qc6 41.Qh7 (41.Rb4 is probably even stronger) 41...Qg6 42.Qxg6 led to a thoroughly miserable Rook endgame.

41.Qxb5 Rd6 42.Qd3 g6 43.c4

This key break, taking advantage of the pin along the d-file, is a major part of white's long-term strategy. The fact that he already has a material advantage makes black's cause completely hopeless.

43...dxc4 44.Rxd6 cxd3 45.Rxe6 fxe6 46.Kf3 e5 47.Ke3 e4 48.f3 exf3 49.Kxd3 g5 50.hxg5 hxg5 51.g4, 1-0.

Mr. Madhacker, in future treat the isolated d-pawn as a hero (and avoid the trade of minor pieces!) and you'll be rewarded with many nice victories.

✳   ✳   ✳   ✳   ✳

The Art of Stealing Opening Ideas

A chess professional has to do many forms of chess preparation: If he's having trouble in endgames and technical positions, he has to do a detailed study of that phase of the game. If he finds that he often fails in sharp positions, he needs to do everything possible to iron out this flaw. And, of course, he also needs to go over all his games (especially losses) to see what he did well, and what he did poorly—once he figures out the poor part, it's back to the grindstone in an effort to fix all his chessic ills!

Preparation is a never-ending part of a chess professional's life, but one area that always seems to be riddled with holes is a player's opening repertoire. No matter how hard you work on it, new moves constantly crop up from all corners of the globe that challenge your favorite lines. Thus databases and magazines need to be carefully scrutinized so that you'll be forewarned about some hidden "bomb", thereby preventing it from crashing down on the board and turning your favorite opening system into mush.

Since theory changes minute by minute on the world stage, a player's openings can never be as safe or as effective as he would like them to be. And, because memorizing a bunch of book lines just doesn't cut it, a real pro needs to fortify his systems with new moves and ideas, and new interpretations of old ideas.

Since staying on top of the game is a 24/7 process, a true chess professional doesn't have much of a life outside the game. In fact, even if the hunky chess god manages to somehow score the attentions of a young lady for an evening, he'll be so obsessed with the millions of variations swirling around in his brain that, as her lips draw close to his, he'll be thinking, "Damn, how do I answer Kasparov's new idea in the Sicilian? This is a nightmare! I must come up with something or I'm toast! And what about Anand's bust to my Philidor's Defense? I think Vishy did this to me on purpose! He's out to get me! But what can I do about it? *What am I going to do?*"

Yes, all chess professionals live in a permanent state of hysteria. And, while our dates might take that far away look in our eyes and the drool that's pouring from the side of our mouth as the first sign of infatuation or even love, they never guess that it is indeed love/devotion/passion—but for the game, not them.

Since the opening workload is so enormous, and since the cutthroat world of chess is so overwhelming, every player (without exception!) has to fully embrace one of the most important and useful preparation strategies available: The art of stealing other player's ideas!

This "stealing" comes in a few forms:

- You pay other players to come up with new stuff, and they give it to you (with a signed statement that they will never use it—it's yours and only yours!).

- You take other player's recommendations and make them your own.

- You work with other players and, hopefully, they'll come up with some neat ideas that you can use before they do!

I remember a situation in Toronto thirty-five years ago—a famous grandmaster was playing for first place in the final round but didn't know how to meet his opponent's ultra sharp system in the Sicilian. Since I was known to be an opening expert in those days, he asked if I had anything interesting against this system and, when I said yes, he offered to buy it from me. So, like a drug addict and his pusher doing their business away from judgmental eyes, we consummated our unholy deal in the privacy of his room—I handed him several pages of analysis and he handed me cold, hard cash. Months later, thanks to the game he played, the line I sold him became all the rage and the pundits sang songs of praise about the grandmaster's creative genius.

The most common way of finding a new scheme, system, or analysis is by looking for games with a strange new move—the stranger the better since most players will discount it as garbage. A serious look might convince you that it's actually quite good, and after some work you'll be ready to unleash it against an unsuspecting opponent. The same holds true for game annotations like, "Also interesting is 23.Nb5!?" The word *interesting* translates to, "I just thought of this so I'll offer it as filler. Of course, I'm too lazy to see if it's actually any good, or even if it's playable."

The well-trained chess pro's eye leaps at every "also interesting" note, and tries hard to ascertain whether or not it's legitimate.

And finally we come to my favorite opening prep technique: working with another player and, if they show me some amazing new idea, playing it as quickly as possible and claiming it as my own! There's nothing like the look of fury on my analyst partner's face when I use an idea he's worked on for two years to beat a world class player in the last round for first place! After I collect my huge check, I always make a point of avoiding him for a few months until the memory of my "crime" fades. Then I'll call him from out of the blue and see what other ideas I can wring from his fertile mind.

Here are a few examples of the "stealing process" from my own games:

While sifting through a *Chess Informant* in 1980, I noticed the following game:

E. Kuuskmaa - V. Salceanu, correspondence 1978

1.d4 Nf6 2.c4 c5 3.d5 e6 4.Nc3 exd5 5.cxd5 d6 6.e4 g6 7.Bf4 a6 8.Nf3 b5 9.Qe2 Ra7 10.e5 Re7 11.Be3 Ng4 12.Ne4 dxe5 13.d6 Rd7 14.Bg5 f6 15.Nxf6+ Nxf6 16.Nxe5 Qa5+ 17.Bd2 Qa4 18.Nc4+ Re7 19.dxe7, 1-0.

Is 9.Qe2 for real?

My first thought was, "9.Qe2 can't be good!" Indeed, nobody else had played it after the Kuuskmaa game. Apparently everyone had the same impression I did—that 9.Qe2 was too primitive to work. Nevertheless, I began to analyze it and, to my amazement, I decided that 9.Qe2 was not only fully playable, it was extremely strong! So, after putting many weeks of analysis into this line of the Benoni, I decided to give it a go:

J. Silman - G. Sanchez, San Jose 1981 .

This game was a last round contest for first place. A lot of money was at stake (at least, it was a lot of money for me at that time). My opponent was a very strong, solid master, so I decided to "gift" him with my little opening surprise.

1.d4 Nf6 2.c4 e6 3.Nf3 c5 4.d5 exd5 5.cxd5 d6 6.Nc3 g6 7.Bf4 a6 8.e4 b5 9.Qe2 Bg4?? (Believe it or not, the game is now over!) **10.e5** (Black can resign, but he didn't realize that he was in trouble!) **10...Bxf3 11.gxf3! Nh5 12.exd6+ Kd7 13.Bh3+ f5 14.Qe6** mate. Wow! He didn't see it coming!

I continued to play Kuuskmaa's 9.Qe2, though it seems I was the only player in the world to do so! Good news for me since it remained a surprise for a long time to come (information moved slowly in those days) and that meant lots of juicy points against a variety of grandmasters and international masters!

J. Silman - V. McCambridge, San Francisco 1982

1.d4 Nf6 2.c4 e6 3.Nf3 c5 4.d5 exd5 5.cxd5 d6 6.Nc3 g6 7.Bf4 a6 8.e4 b5 9.Qe2 Nh5 10.Bg5 f6 11.Be3 Bg4 12.h3 Bxf3 13.Qxf3 Nd7 14.g4 Ng7 15.Qg3 Qe7 16.Bg2 0-0-0 17.0-0 h5 18.b4! h4 19.Qf3 cxb4 20.Nb1 Ne5 21.Qe2 Ne8 22.Bb6 Rd7 23.Nd2 f5 24.f4 Nf7 25.Nb3 Bg7 26.e5 dxe5 27.Rac1+ Nc7 28.Nc5 exf4 29.Qf2 Rxd5 30.Nxa6 Bc3 31.Nxc7 Rd2 32.Qxd2 Bxd2 33.Nd5+ Bxc1 34.Nxe7+, 1-0.

J. Silman - N. De Firmian, San Jose 1982

1.d4 Nf6 2.c4 c5 3.d5 e6 4.Nc3 exd5 5.cxd5 d6 6.Nf3 g6 7.Bf4 Bg7 (Nick avoids 7...a6, but he still gets squashed in the opening.) **8.Qa4+ Bd7 9.Qb3 Qc7 10.e4 0-0 11.Be2 Nh5 12.Be3 a6 13.Nd2 b5 14.a4 bxa4 15.Nxa4 Bb5 16.Bxb5 axb5 17.Qxb5 Ra5 18.Qb3 Nd7 19.Nc4 Ra7 20.0-0 Rb7 21.Qc2 f5 22.exf5 gxf5 23.f4** (The opening is a complete fiasco for Black, who is already dead lost.) **23...Kh8 24.Rf3 h6 25.Re1** (Making life difficult for myself.) **25...Nhf6 26.Qxf5 Rb4 27.Qc2 Nxd5 28.Bd2 Rbb8 29.Re6 Rf6 30.Qe4 Nf8 31.Rxf6 Nxf6 32.Qf5 d5 33.Ne5 c4 34.Be3 Qa5 35.Nc3 Rxb2 36.Bd4 Rb7 37.h3 Ne4 38.Qxf8+ Bxf8 39.Nxc4+,** 1-0.

Looking in my database of several million games, I noticed that (other than the Kuuskmaa contest) the earliest game mentioned was V. McCambridge - E. Lobron, Dortmund 1982! That's right, Vince was so impressed by "my" 9.Qe2 that he stole it himself against grandmaster Lobron and scored a win! I'm sure people in Europe were saying, "McCambridge's 9.Qe2 is pretty interesting!" Indeed, after that game the move finally became popular.

1982 was a busy year for me, and I often analyzed with former U.S. Champion John Grefe. During one of our sessions, he showed me a new idea he had for White in the 4.f3 Nimzo-Indian. A few days later I found myself facing the very strong George Kane, and after 1.d4 Nf6 2.c4 e6 3.Nc3 Bb4 decided to "steal" Grefe's idea there and then!

J. Silman - G. Kane, San Francisco 1982

1.d4 Nf6 2.c4 e6 3.Nc3 Bb4 4.f3

Poor Mr. Kane was the unlucky recipient of a couple of my novelties. The first occurred after 4.e3 d5 5.Bd3 0-0 6.Nf3 b6 7.0-0 Bb7 8.cxd5 exd5 9.a3 Bd6 10.b4 a6 11.Qb3 Re8 12.a4 Nc6 13.Ba3 a5. At the time, this position was thought to be comfortable for Black, but I showed this assessment to be false after 14.Bb5! axb4 15.Bxc6 Bxc6 16.Bxb4 Ne4 17.Rfc1 Bxb4 18.Qxb4 when I had a clear advantage and scored a smooth win (part of that game appeared in *Chess Informant*).

4...c5 5.d5 Bxc3+ 6.bxc3 Nh5 7.g3 f5 8.e4 f4

This well-known position was considered to be quite nice for Black at that time, but Grefe's idea completely turned this assessment around.

9.dxe6 Qf6

Of course, 9...0-0 loses right away to 10.Qd5 with the double threat of 11.Qxh5 and 11.e7+.

10.Ne2 fxg3 11.Bg2 Qxe6 12.hxg3 Nf6 13.g4

White now has a clear advantage, though I can't say my technique was all it could have been. Here's the rest without comment: **13...0-0 14.g5 Ne8 15.Nf4 Qe5 16.Nd5 Qg3+ 17.Kf1 Nc6 18.Rh3 Qe5 19.Kg1 g6 20.f4 Qg7 21.e5 d6 22.Nf6+ Nxf6 23.exf6 Qf7 24.Re3 Qc7 25.Bd5+ Kh8 26.Qe2 Bf5 27.Bd2 Rad8 28.Re1 h5 29.Re7 Rd7 30.Re8 Rd8 31.Rxf8+ Rxf8 32.Qe8 Qd8 33.Bxc6 bxc6 34.Qxc6 Qd7 35.Qxd7 Bxd7 36.Re7 Bf5 37.Rxa7 Rb8 38.Ra6 Kg8 39.Rxd6 Ra8 40.Be3**, 1-0.

Imagine my surprise when I was reading the excellent *Play The 4.f3 Nimzo-Indian* by Yakovich (2004) and noticed this same line (they hold off on ...Bxc3+ for an extra move, meaning ...f4 comes on move 7 instead of move 8—of course, it all transposes back into the exact same position) with this comment: "Up to the end of the 1980s it was generally thought that 7...f4 promised Black a good game. However, Moskalenko's discovery 8.dxe6! gives White the advantage."

What the hell? I go to the trouble of stealing this from Grefe only to have it stolen from me? Do the Russians have no shame? Even worse, they then give the following "analysis": 8...Bxc3+ 9.bxc3 Qf6 10.Ne2 fxg3 11.Bg2! Qxe6 12.hxg3 Nf6 13.g4 0-0 14.g5 Ne8 15.Nf4 Qe5 16.Nd5 with a winning game for White. They didn't just steal 8.dxe6, they also stole my entire game! Oh chess, at times you just break my heart.

In 1994 I was flitting around Eastern Europe playing in various events. While in Budapest, I spent time with English grandmaster (and chess writer extraordinaire) Peter Wells. Somehow we began talking about Kasparov and I brought up a little mystery: Why did Kasparov go into this line? Did he have something special prepared?

Z. Ribli - G. Kasparov, Belfort 1988

1.Nf3 g6 2.e4 c5 3.c4 Bg7 4.d4 cxd4 5.Nxd4 Nc6 6.Be3 Nf6 7.Nc3 Ng4 8.Qxg4 Nxd4 9.Qd1 e5 10.Nb5 0-0 11.Qd2 Qe7 12.0-0-0 Nxb5 13.cxb5, ½-½.

It turns out that Wells had pondered the same thing and set out to discover what Kasparov's improvement was (Much later we discovered that Kasparov didn't have an improvement and entered the whole line more or less by mistake). Wells showed me a very inventive idea for Black, but for some reason he didn't seem to have that much faith in it. On the other hand, I continued to look at it and thought the whole line was extremely interesting. Again, luck was on my side since I arrived at Kasparov's final position a few days later in a game against E. Anka (now a grandmaster).

E. Anka - J. Silman, Budapest 1994

1.e4 c5 2.Nf3 Nc6 3.d4 cxd4 4.Nxd4 g6 5.c4 Bg7 6.Be3 Nf6 7.Nc3 Ng4 8.Qxg4 Nxd4 9.Qd1 e5 10.Nb5 0-0 11.Qd2 Qe7 12.0-0-0 Nxb5 13.cxb5 d5! (theory) 14.exd5 Rd8!!

A new move, courtesy of Mr. Wells

15.d6 Qe6 16.Kb1 Bf8 17.Bc5 b6 18.Bb4 Bb7 19.h4 Rac8 20.h5 Bxd6 21.Bc3 Be7 22.Qe1 Qf5+ 23.Ka1 Rxd1+ 24.Qxd1 Rd8 25.Qb3 Bd5 26.Bc4 Bxc4 27.Qxc4 Qxh5! and I went on to win a tough technical grind: 28.Qf1 Qf5 29.a3 Bc5 30.f3 Bd4 31.Qe1 Qd3 32.Bxd4 Qxd4 33.g4 Rd5 34.Qh4 Rxb5 35.Qxh7+ Kf8 36.Qh2 Rb3 37.Qc2 Rxa3+ 38.Kb1 Rd3 39.Qc8+ Ke7 40.Qc7+ Ke6 41.Qxa7 Rd1+ 42.Rxd1 Qxd1+ 43.Ka2 Qd5+ 44.Kb1 Qd6 45.g5 Qc5 46.Qb7 b5 47.Qa6+ Ke7 48.Qf6+ Ke8 49.Qh8+ Kd7 50.Qb8 Ke7 51.Qb7+ Kf8 52.Qb8+ Kg7 53.Qd8 b4 54.Qf6+ Kg8 55.b3 Qg1+ 56.Kc2 Qf2+ 57.Kd3 Qd4+ 58.Ke2 Qb2+ 59.Ke1 Qxb3 60.Qxe5 Qe6 61.Qxe6 fxe6 62.Kd2 Kf7 63.Kc2 e5 64.Kb3 Ke6 65.Kxb4 Kf5 66.Kc4 Kxg5 67.Kd3 Kf4 68.Ke2 e4 69.fxe4 Kxe4 70.Kf2 Kf4 71.Kg2 Kg4 72.Kh2 Kf3 73.Kg1 Kg3 74.Kh1 g5 75.Kg1 g4, 0-1.

I published an article on this opening variation in *New In Chess Yearbook 33* and, in an effort to make poor Wells feel a bit better about me stealing his analysis, I made sure to give him full credit for its creation! Using other people's ideas is one thing, but claiming that you were the one that came up with them is quite another!

✶   ✶   ✶   ✶   ✶

Creating a Study Program

Mr. Svorcan asked:

I am self-taught chess player. I have read a few books and have some chess software (Fritz, Chessmaster, etc). I play chess regularly on the net but my "real" rating is unknown, however on some websites I'm in the 1700 range. I play well against ordinary people that play for fun but have never studied chess. Anyhow, I can see that my game needs lots of improvement. Mastering the opening, planning, endgame, strategy, tactics, etc. I just don't know how to go about this—I feel that I'm jumping from one topic to another and leaping from one book to another without ever finishing anything. In other words there is no real order to my study and no real plan of study. What should I study first, and how long should I study it? At the moment I have the time and dedication to study chess, so I was hoping you could give me some advice.

Dear Mr. Svorcan,

I'm sure a lot of readers will identify with your question. And yes, it can easily be overwhelming! Some old time players (like Capablanca) recommended that you study the endgame first, but many are bored by endgames and he failed to tell the masses just what endgames should be studied. Others say tactics, tactics, tactics. Personally, I believe in balance (a bit of everything).

In general, I would recommend that you keep things simple and only get one book for each area of study. For example, here's a possible program:

Learn Basic Tactical Patterns

There are quite a few great books on beginning tactics, but I would recommend that you get one that teaches the most basic themes. Here are two good choices (of course, every teacher will most likely have their favorites!):

Winning Chess Tactics by Seirawan and Silman

The Art of Attack in Chess by Vukovic (a classic!)

Both books are great for anyone under 1400 (lots of very basic but critically important material), while also being useful for players up to 2000 (both books also offer more challenging chapters as you work through them).

There are at least a trillion books that feature tactical puzzles. Get a basic one and try to solve a problem or two (solve it from the book diagram) whenever you have a spare moment. This would be a nice complement to the two tactical theme books mentioned.

Create a Basic Opening Repertoire

FCO: Fundamental Chess Openings by Paul van der Sterren

Modern Chess Openings (MCO) by Nick de Firmian

I highly recommend *FCO* as your only opening book for anyone under 1400. It gives you the plans and ideas for every opening so you can decide which ones are to your taste. Once you're past 1400 (or ready to memorize some variations), another "everything in one volume" tome allows you to continue our "keep it simple" theme. Thus *MCO* is a good choice.

Deeper opening study should occur once you have ironed out the deficiencies in the other phases of your game. When you reach that more advanced phase, you'll find a mindboggling amount of opening books which offer many hundreds of pages on every possible line.

Positional Play

I'll be shamelessly self-serving here:

The Amateur's Mind by Silman (for players 1000 to 1600)

How to Reassess Your Chess 4th Edition by Silman (for players 1400 to 2100)

It's extremely important that the chess student creates a solid base of positional understanding that will work side by side with his tactical skills. So don't let anyone put down this critical phase of the game!

The Endgame

Okay, here I go again (forgive me!):

Silman's Complete Endgame Course

If you're a beginner to 1900, that's all you will need. Chapters are based on rating groups. The nice thing about this book is that you should only read up to your group, or one past it. Then you can concentrate on the other areas of study (opening, tactic, positional chess).

There are many fine endgame books that offer more advanced material. If you find that you love the endgame, don't hesitate to pick up more books on this subject—*after* you become fairly well rounded in all areas of chess study.

In Search of a Chess Hero

Looking over master games is always useful since one full game can give you insights into openings, the middlegame, and the endgame (the whole package!). By going over lots of games, you begin to pick up patterns that, over time, become engrained in your brain. The acquisition of chess patterns is *the* main ingredient for chess mastery.

To make this fun, pick one player (Alekhine, Capablanca, Tal, Fischer, Kasparov, Karpov, Anand, etc.) and slowly go over their (annotated) games. Another possibility is a tournament book like *New York 1924* (annotations by Alekhine). I love these things! You learn about chess history, you follow the event as if it was happening live, and you come to terms with which players bore you, and which ones really excite you—for example, Em. Lasker won NY 1924 and you might decide that he's the ultimate chess god.

It's also possible to use a database to collect all the games of your chess hero. However, a database might not give you the quality annotations that you'd find in that *New York 1924* tournament book or in a player's "My best games of chess" collection.

Time Frames

I would recommend that you start with basic tactical themes. Master pins, forks, various mating patterns and whatnot (you can do this in a couple weeks, but keep it up until you really feel you are familiar with that material) and then . . . stop.

Move on to the creation of an opening repertoire. Why change from opening to opening when you can put together a repertoire and learn from every disaster, every loss, and even every victory? Make sure you choose openings that suit your tastes. Thus, an all-gambit repertoire is great fun, while a positional repertoire would offer "good times" for another kind of player. *FCO* will make this "what should I play" process easy, fun, and quick.

Once you have your tactical basics down and your opening repertoire primed and ready to launch, it's time to leap into a study of positional chess. This might take a few months, but it will prove invaluable. Don't hesitate to relax and solve various tactical puzzles during that time!

Finally, make sure your endgame IQ matches your rating. And, whenever you find yourself moving up the rating ladder, read more of that endgame book so your endgame skills are in accord with your overall strength.

After you do all this (it could take anywhere from two months to three years, depending on the amount of study time that's available for chess), start to look at master games and/or go deeper into the topics you already studied.

✻　✻　✻　✻　✻

The Study of Master Games

Ali K. asked:

I followed your advice about studying master games and I already can see that my planning and transition from opening to middle game is much better now, and I can actually understand the reasons behind the opening moves I had previously played just by memorization. May I ask a few more questions about the study of master games?

1. Should I only study master games in the openings I usually play, or should I study other games too?

2. What's the best way to go over a game? I usually play the game on an actual board and try to understand the plan behind the moves, but I've seen others doing different things, like trying to guess the next move, or annotating the games, etc.

3. Which games do you think are the best to study? Those that are annotated move-by-move (like Neil McDonald's *Art of Logical Thinking*) or just important moves annotated (like normal games found in Magazines) or not annotated at all?

4. I've got *ChessBase Mega Database 2007*, and it contains many 2200 - 2300 games along with 2700-2800 games. Considering that I'm a 1700 player, should I study those lower rated games or should I only study the super grandmasters' games?

Dear Mr. Ali K.,

Good questions! Actually, there's no correct way to go over master games. Looking at (and thus absorbing) patterns is instructive no matter how you look at the moves. However, lets discuss your queries in the order they were given:

1. "Should I only study master games in the openings I usually play, or should I study other games too?"

When I was starting out, I would go over master games that featured my favorite openings if I was doing a study of a specific opening(s). On other occasions, I would look at all the games of a favorite player, or look at all the games from a specific tournament (which would feature all sorts of openings), or just start on page one of *Chess Informant* and go through everything in the book. In other words, no matter how you do it, it's good.

One reason that you don't want to stick with games that only feature your openings is that you'll miss out on ideas and structures that usually don't occur in your chosen systems, thus limiting your ultimate growth. On the other hand, if you are making a detailed study of some opening (let's say the Caro-Kann), then looking at 1,000 games that featured 1.e4 c6 is extremely useful since you'll see all the best setups, setups that don't work, correct middlegame plans, typical tactics, and also common endgames.

2. "What's the best way to go over a game? I usually play the game on an actual board and try to understand the plan behind the moves, but I've seen others doing different things, like trying to guess the next move, or annotating the games, etc."

If I want to absorb as much information as possible, as quickly as possible, from a large number of games (like the 1,000 games I mentioned in my answer to question one), I'll use a computer board in ChessBase so I can zip through a game in five to twenty seconds. Five seconds if I realize it's complete rubbish, and twenty seconds if I decide that it's worth going over every move. If I find a game that I deem worthy of serious study (a new plan or move), I'll stick it in a special database reserved for games that need independent analysis.

On the other hand, when IM John Donaldson drops by for a couple days to do some opening research, he's already picked out the key games from ChessBase. That leaves us free to do in-depth independent analysis, which we do on a nice board and set (with Fritz and/or Rybka humming away on a laptop next to us).

Many younger players will only use a computer screen, but I prefer a real board and a nice wood set. It's strictly a matter of taste.

If you wish to improve your powers of calculation (or see how positionally adept you are), then you should go over a game (with no notes showing) and do your best to figure out what's going on. Write down your thoughts for each move and also write down any variations that come to mind. Afterward, look at an annotated version of that game and see how close your own impressions were to reality.

There are many reasons to go over master games, ranging from the assimilation of patterns to opening study to various forms of instruction to pure enjoyment. Each is valuable in its own way.

3. "Which games do you think are the best to study? Those that are annotated move-by-move (such as Neil McDonald's *Art of Logical Thinking*) or just important moves annotated (like normal games found in magazines) or not annotated at all?"

It depends! If I'm simply trying to absorb patterns, I go with huge numbers of games with no notes. If I'm doing a deep exploration into a specific player's games, I much prefer to look at games annotated by that player (the more prose the better) so I can see what he was thinking about during each phase of the game.

By the way, Neil's *The Art of Logical Thinking* is an excellent book!

4. "I've got *ChessBase Mega Database 2007*, and it contains many 2200 - 2300 games along with 2700-2800 games. Considering that I'm a 1700 player, should I study those lower rated games or should I only study the super grandmasters' games?"

When researching openings, I don't consider games by players who are below 2300 (FIDE) to be very valuable. And if I'm looking at games for enjoyment, or games that are theoretically interesting, I'll only go over grandmaster games or games by past greats (from 1800 to the present). However, when writing a book, I absolutely love using extremely old games, games played by beginners, on-line blitz games, and anything else that contains instructive content. In fact, games by lower rated players are often far more instructive than games by grandmasters. Why? Because the mistakes weak players make are the same mistakes my students (and most amateurs) make. Thus, these become a mirror into the student's soul, and the games and their lessons are simply more personal than any grandmaster game.

In *How to Reassess Your Chess, 4th Edition*, I use lots of games from the 17th century to the present. And I also use copious amounts of games by players from 1100 on up. It's not unusual to see one example showing a battle between two 1400 players, the next a 400 year old struggle, and the next example a war between two 2700s played in 2009. If two earthworms played an instructive chess game, I'd make use of it! My goal is to teach, not to stick my nose in the air and proclaim that my upper-crust brain can only be fed moves blessed by grandmasters.

Sadly, many players make the huge mistake of thinking that only top grandmaster games can teach them anything. While I agree that going over lower rated games in ChessBase is a waste of time, these same games (between low rated players) can turn into gold if a caring author deconstructs them into their highly instructive components. And let's be honest: though you might stare in wonder at a 20-move long grandmaster maneuver that leads to some obscure winning endgame, you won't really understand it because it's simply too advanced. But a 1200 player who misses a big chance to turn his Knight into a force of nature is something that can be readily understood, and it's something that will help make you a far stronger player.

✶　✶　✶　✶　✶

Offering a Draw

Doomclaw asked:

When do you think is the right time to offer a draw? I have been confused by this question since I started learning about chess.

Dear Doomclaw,

An interesting question! There is actually a bit of etiquette related to draw offers. For example, one should only offer a draw when it's your move. Don't offer it when the opponent is thinking since that could distract him and thus be construed as a deliberate shady attempt. The proper way is to make your move and then offer the draw *before* pressing your clock. Once you offer the draw, *then* press the clock. At that point the opponent can accept it at any time before he makes his move and presses his own clock. Thus: 1) Make a move; 2) Offer a draw; 3) Punch your clock.

Of course, you can offer a draw before you move (while your clock is running), but that puts you in a strange situation since a street-smart opponent will (or should) say, "Make your move and I'll consider it." This means that if you make a move that forces mate in two, he can shake your hand and accept a draw. However, if you hang your face, he'll say no and beat you. So for your own protection, think hard about your move, play what you feel is the best in the position, and only then make your offer, after which you can press your clock.

It's also considered to be "bad form" if you offer a draw to a far stronger player. The idea is that if the superior player wanted a draw, he would ask you for it. So, if you are rated 1800 and are paired with a grandmaster, you really shouldn't make any offer—if you're winning, why chicken out and offer a draw? If it's equal, play chess and if the chess god you're facing wants a draw he'll offer it to you (trust me, he knows you want a draw—it's not a secret!). If you're worse and offer a draw to a far superior opponent, it amounts to an insult and a deliberate attempt to bother him. Perhaps you were hoping to go over the game with him afterwards. Making an insult offer like that will only ensure that he will refuse any attempts at a postmortem.

In general, I tell my students to never offer a draw unless there's simply nothing left in the position, and to never accept a draw unless the board is devoid of play or if they are seriously worse. It doesn't matter if they are playing Kasparov, accepting a draw means they will miss out on an important learning experience. The fact is, a player that fights to the bitter end becomes feared, with even higher rated players knowing such an opponent has no respect for anyone and will take you to the brink each and every time he sits down.

I remember hearing about a simultaneous exhibition given by Spassky (I think he was playing somewhere in the area of forty to fifty people). After about ten moves, one of Spassky's opponents offered a draw. Spassky, who was delighted, happily shook the guy's hand and said, "Good game!"

Suddenly hysteria broke out! Everyone started offering draws and Spassky happily accepted—he was being paid, and if these misguided individuals wanted to throw away a rare chance to play the World Champion (ten book moves isn't playing), then why should he care? He was just happy to have a quick night.

Something similar occurred with Kasparov, who was giving a small clock simultaneous against a handful of the most talented young players in the U.S. One guy pounded out a few books moves and then forced a well-known repetition, thus getting a quick draw. Afterwards Kasparov criticized his opponent, telling him that this wasn't even a game, and that he might never get the chance to play Kasparov again. In other words, the guy threw away a huge learning experience (nobody will care when you say, "Look, I played eight book moves and then shook hands with Karparov.").

There are also quite a few draw-offer oddities. Here are three typical cases:

- I saw one game where White offered Black a draw. Black thought about it for fifty minutes, leaving himself only twenty seconds on the clock. He then said, "Okay, I accept!" and reached out to shake hands. White replied, "You accept what?" Black: "You offered a draw!" White: "I never offered a draw!" Fortunately for the guy playing Black, I witnessed the very clear draw offer, and told the director that White was a scumbag. Black, of course, got his draw.

- Decades ago, one famous grandmaster would often ask his opponents, "Are you playing for a draw?" If they replied, "Yes, I accept your offer!" he would say, "Oh no! I didn't offer a draw, I just wanted to know if you were playing for one!"

- I've had many games where a far weaker opponent offered me several draws during a game. In one sense I don't mind this, since he's (in effect) offering me draw odds on top of the fact that I'm a higher rated player. In some cases I would push too hard to win against such an opponent, and, when I realized that I had committed suicide, I'd offer the draw. Then, without any thought, his hand would leap out and shake mine. Don't let this happen to you! Don't offer draws, and always play to beat anyone of any rating!

✶   ✶   ✶   ✶   ✶

Proper Tournament Diet

Unknown asked:
What do you think is the best food to be eaten during a big tournament?

Dear Unknown,
Actually, this is quite an interesting question! Of course, people eat all sorts of garbage before an event, but should that change during it? I think the answer depends on the individual. Do you have blood sugar problems? Do you find that you can't think as well after a large meal? Or, are you more or less the same no matter what you consume?

Long ago, grandmaster Walter Browne used to insist that he would happily buy his opponent a huge steak dinner right before their game. Why? Because he felt all the blood would leave the brain and go to the stomach, making it impossible for the other guy to think clearly.

Grandmaster Gligoric would eat chocolate throughout his games, while Fischer would sip apple juice. In the 1800s, top players would often bring a bottle of booze with them to the board and empty it during play. That doesn't happen anymore, but many grandmasters and international masters get completely drunk after a game—often staying out all night at the local bar and somehow appearing the next day fresh and strong. Of course, not all alcohol-loving players would drink after the game—there are many cases of titled players drinking before the game and appearing at the board in a state of near coma.

In the 60s and early 70s, some players gave drugs a try during tournament games. In general, LSD didn't work out too well for them (an unnamed IM wasn't able to make even one move, sitting there watching dinosaurs fly through the air until his flag fell on move one). Others gave pot a try (in fact, many players used it before, during, and after play!), others speed, and others opium. Times were quite different then, especially when you consider that too much caffeine is now a FIDE offense, and if you're caught a couple times imbibing too many cups, you can be banned for a few years. That's quite a huge leap from the "Exploration Uber Alles" mentality of the 60s!

Personally, I always had a serious sensitivity to sugar, and this more or less destroyed my career since I never made proper adjustments to the problem. In my youth, I would toss down chocolate bars during play, but would start falling asleep as the game progressed. I actually found myself waking up in several games with twenty to forty minutes having ticked off my clock! Later I would try juice, but even that level of sugar wiped me out and led to endless blunders as my brain melted and vision blurred. I only cured the problem in my final couple of tournament years—I brought a high-grade ginseng root to the board and sucked on it all through the game.

Ultimately, you have to figure out what's right for your body. Knowing which foods and beverages work for you is extremely important. And, if you find coffee wakes you up and allows you to play at your usual level, or if cough syrup (banned by FIDE) is needed so you don't cough and disturb your opponent—go for it. Last I heard, coffee and over the counter cough syrup are legal in the real world—and personally, I would love it if my opponent glugged down forty cups of java. I can't understand why any chess organization has a say in such things.

* * * * *

Is Chess a Gentleman's Game?

Anonymous asked:

I thought chess was supposed to be a gentleman's game, but at times my opponents act rudely during tournament play. What can I do about this?

Dear Anonymous,

During a tournament in Los Angeles, two players got into a fight while playing and began stabbing each other with their pens. This is probably not a good way to deal with a rude opponent. In fact, the only correct thing to do when an unruly imbecile is sitting opposite you is to find the tournament director and ask him to put an end to your opponent's deplorable behavior before it escalates into something like the aforementioned duel.

Rude and/or crazy behavior is a time-honored part of the game. The 16th Century Spanish priest and chess player Ruy Lopez de Segura recommended that, when playing outside, you should always face your opponent toward the sun so he will be unable to see the whole board through his permanent squint.

I've personally faced players who covered the whole spectrum of bizarre behavior: one guy would whistle a song (his tone would get more dominating if he felt he was doing well, and it would taper off into a beaten, pathetic drone if he was losing), another would mumble, an old man made disgusting gagging sounds from the first move to the last, another old man kept saying, "Go get the body! Go get the body!" over and over, and one guy who appeared to have a bird's nest on his head kept picking at it, popping whatever he had gotten from the nest into his mouth.

Here are a few more that I've faced, all of which are 100% true:

- A famous IM used to empty one of those huge plastic coke bottles and fill it with tequila. He'd keep it on the table, ready for use in case of an "emergency." His philosophy was, if something unpleasant happens on the board, take several deep glugs directly from the bottle and drink your worries away. He tried this on me once, emptied the bottle, and ended up with his face literally lying flat on the table. When it was his turn to move, his hand would rise up blindly, grope for a piece to move, and then (after pushing some piece somewhere) fall limply back to the ground. After he hung all his pieces, he quietly resigned and stumbled out of the hall.

- I first experienced this one while playing a well-known chess politician. After I made a move that my esteemed opponent felt was annoying, he slowly took a sandwich out of his backpack, carefully unwrapped it, and then took huge, loud bites—chomping sickeningly as if he was a lion eating human flesh. Once the sandwich was consumed, he then made eye contact with me, smiled, calmly reached into his pocket, and took out some dental floss. Then he flossed away, bits of sandwich flying all over the board.

- Many decades ago, I was teaching a fourteen-year-old girl who was all the rage. She did TV interviews, was big with celebrities, and was considered to be the next big chess thing by many pundits. While watching her play a tournament game, she hung a piece and, shockingly, quickly wrote a letter and handed it to her opponent under the table. It said, "Please don't take my piece. My father will beat me if you do!"

- When things have gone badly and it's time to resign, some players have a final bit of fun by making use of creative ways to give up. Alekhine once threw his King across the room in disgust, while Nimzovich (against Saemisch) stood on the table (and by some accounts got down on his knees) and shouted, "Gegen diesen Idioten muss ich verlieren!"—"Must I lose against these idiots!"

- Finally, while playing an event in London, an opponent of mine found a far calmer way to end the game—he simply pushed all the pieces off the board and onto my lap, and then got up and walked out of the tournament hall.

✶   ✶   ✶   ✶   ✶

Teaching Chess to Children

Rambaldi23 asked:

I have a question regarding teaching chess. I'm very interested in giving students/beginners private lessons and originally felt it most appropriate to wait until I achieve an expert rating, but I really have the urge to teach now. Right now I'm in the 1700s USCF and my rating is on an upward spiral. I feel I can certainly help beginners/young kids with the basics, develop an opening repertoire, tactics, etc. In addition, I am a public school teacher by day so I have plenty of experience working with kids. My thinking is that once the student achieves a class C rating, the parent can decide if he/she should then study with someone higher rated.

Do you feel it's appropriate for me to take on young students/beginners interested in entering tournament chess (or hobbyists), or am I correct that it's really not appropriate until I'm an expert? I value your input very much. There seems to be conflicting opinions on this.

Dear Rambaldi23,

Conflicting opinions? Well, there are always conflicting opinions among people that don't have a clue, so try to discount those that couldn't teach a dog to bark but love to speak, and strong players who love to put themselves on a pedestal.

If you look at the various scholastic programs, you'll find that the vast majority of teachers are in the 1400 - 1700 range. And, that's perfect for kids (rating wise).

When you want to teach children, there are a couple things that are far more important than a player's rating:

- Do you have the patience to teach young children?
- Are you a natural born teacher, able to communicate in a simple, clear, and entertaining fashion?
- Do children feel comfortable around you?

It's also important to understand one great truth: a high rating (expert, master, or even grandmaster) doesn't mean a person can successfully share his knowledge. It doesn't mean he can write. And it doesn't mean he can teach. Teaching calls for a specific skill-set, and teaching children calls for a skill-set all its own!

I remember a gentleman in the San Francisco Bay Area who was "only" rated 1500, yet he taught chess for years at a junior college (he might still be at it!) and was widely respected as a very, very good teacher. Even players who were considerably higher rated than he was attended his classes. In fact, I attended one of his classes and was very impressed!

So, your thought about having to be an Expert before you teach is simply wrong. Trust me when I say that you already have the goods: experience with children, experience with teaching, and a solid 1700 rating. And lest I forget, it also seems that you have a passion for it—a real desire to share your love of chess with young people. Sounds to me like you're a natural.

Get out there and teach! And don't let anyone tell you differently!

Bibliography

Books

Best Games

Alekhine, Alexander, *My Best Games of Chess 1908 – 1937*. New York: Dover Publications, Inc., 1985.

Averbakh, Yuri, *Averbakh's Selected Games*. London: Cadogan Books, 1998.

Benjamin, Joel, *American Grandmaster*. London: Everyman Chess, 2008.

Benko, Pal and Jeremy Silman, *Pal Benko: My Life, Games, and Compositions*. Los Angeles: Siles Press, 2003.

Bisguier, Arthur and Newton Berry, *The Art of Bisguier, Volume 1 The Early Years 1945-1960*. Hazel Crest, Il: 3rd Millennium Press, 2003.

Bisguier, Arthur and Newton Berry, *The Art of Bisguier, Selected Games 1961-2003*. Milford, CT: Russell Enterprises, Inc., 2008.

Clarke, P.H., *Petrosian's Best Games of Chess*. London: G.Bell and Sons Ltd, 1964.

Donaldson, John and Nikolay Minev, *Akiba Rubinstein: Uncrowned King*. Seattle: International Chess Enterprises, 1994.

Donaldson, John and Nikolay Minev, *Akiba Rubinstein: The Later Years*. Seattle: International Chess Enterprises, 1995.

Golombek, Harry, *Capablanca's 100 Best Games of Chess*. With a Memoir by J. du Mont. New York: Harcourt, Brace and Company, 1947.

Karpov, Anatoly, *My Best Games*. Great Neck, NY: R.H.M Press, 1978.

Larsen, Bent, *Larsen's Selected Games of Chess*. London: G.Bell and Sons, Ltd, 1970.

Marshall, Frank J., *Marshall's Best Games of Chess*. New York: Dover Publications, Inc., 1960.

Shekhtman, Eduard, *The Games of Tigran Petrosian Volume 1, 1942-1965*. Trans. and ed. by Kenneth P. Neat. Oxford: Pergamon Chess, 1991.

Shekhtman, Eduard, *The Games of Tigran Petrosian Volume 2, 1966-1983*. Trans. and ed. by Kenneth P. Neat. Oxford: Pergamon Chess, 1991.

Smyslov, V.V., *My Best Games of Chess 1935-1957*. New York: Dover Publications, Inc., 1958.

Soltis, Andrew, *Bobby Fischer Rediscovered*. London: B.T.Batsford Ltd, 2003.

Soltis, Andrew, *Why Lasker Matters*. London: B.T.Batsford Ltd, 2005.

Taimanov, Mark, *Taimanov's Selected Games*. London: Cadogan Books, 1995.

Tal, Mikhail, *The Life and Games of Mikhail Tal*. London: Cadogan Books, 1997.

History

Golombek, Harry, *The Encyclopedia of Chess*. London: B.T.Batsford Ltd, 1977.

Hooper, David and Kenneth Whyld, *The Oxford Companion to Chess*. Oxford: Oxford University Press, 1992.

Kasparov, Garry, and Dmitry Plisetsky, *Garry Kasparov on My Great Predecessors*, books 1–5. London: Everyman Chess, 2003 – 2006.

Winter, Edward, *Capablanca*. Jefferson, NC: McFarland & Company, Inc., 1989.

Instruction

Crouch, Colin, *How to Defend in Chess*. London: Everyman Chess, 2000.

Dvoretsky, Mark, and Artur Yusupov, *Opening Preparation*. London: B.T.Batsford Ltd, 1994.

Kotov, Alexander, *Think Like a Grandmaster*. London: B.T.Batsford Ltd, 1971.

Reshevsky, Samuel, *The Art of Positional Play*. Philadelphia: David McKay Company, Inc., 1976.

Silman, Jeremy, *How to Reassess Your Chess, 3rd Edition*. Los Angeles: Siles Press, 1993.

Openings

Davies, Nigel, *Starting Out: The Modern*. London: Everyman Chess, 2008.

Marin, Mihail, *A Spanish Repertoire for Black*. Glasgow: Quality Chess, 2007.

Ward, Chris, *The Controversial Samisch King's Indian*. London: B.T.Batsford Ltd, 2004.

Ward, Chris, *Nimzo-Indian Kasparov Variation*. London: Everyman Chess, 2003.

Ward, Chris, *Starting Out: The Nimzo-Indian*. London: Everyman Chess, 2002.

Watson, John, *Mastering the Chess Openings Volume 1*. London: Gambit, 2006.

Watson, John, *Mastering the Chess Openings Volume 2*. London: Gambit, 2007.

Watson, John, *Mastering the Chess Openings Volume 3*. London: Gambit, 2008.

Yakovich, Yuri, *Play the 4.f3 Nimzo-Indian*. London: Gambit, 2004.

Psychology

Benko, Pal and Burt Hochberg, *Winning With Chess Psychology*. New York: David McKay Company, 1991.

Dunnington, Angus, *Chess Psychology*. London: Everyman Chess, 2003.

Hartston, W. R. and P. C. Wason, *The Psychology of Chess*. London: B.T.Batsford, 1983.

Holding, Denis H., *The Psychology of Chess Skill*. Hillsdale, NJ: Lawrence Erlbaum Associates, 1985.

Pfleger, Helmut and Gerd Treppner, *Chess: The Mechanics of the Mind*. Marlborough: The Crowood Press, 1987.

Rowson, Jonathan, *The Seven Deadly Chess Sins*. London: Gambit, 2000.

Tournament and Match

Bronstein, David, *Zurich 1953*. New York: Dover Publications, Inc., 1979.

Kashdan, Isaac, *First Piatigorsky Cup*. Los Angeles: The Ward Ritchie Press, 1965.

Kashdan, Isaac, *Second Piatigorsky Cup*. Los Angeles: The Ward Ritchie Press 1968.

Kasparov, Garry, and Dmitry Plisetsky, *Garry Kasparov on Modern Chess, Part Two Kasparov vs. Karpov 1975-1985*. London: Everyman Chess, 2008.

Kasparov, Garry, and Dmitry Plisetsky, *Garry Kasparov on Modern Chess, Part Three Kasparov vs. Karpov 1986-1987*. London: Everyman Chess, 2009.

Utterberg, Cary, *De la Bourdonnais versus McDonnell, 1834*. Jefferson, NC: McFarland & Company, Inc., 2005.

Periodicals

Chess Informant, 1-103. Belgrade, Serbia

New In Chess Yearbook, 1-92. Alkmaar, The Netherlands: New In Chess.

New In Chess magazine, 1995 – 2009. Alkmaar, The Netherlands: New In Chess.

Software

ChessBase 9: MegaBase 2008

Deep Rybka 3

Fritz 11 & 12

Index of Concepts

Material

Exchange (Rook for Minor Piece), 11, 22, 58, 61, 65, 135, 137, 141, 146, 148, 149, 153, 179, 200, 215, 219, 296, 343, 347, 367, 405, 444, 450, 495, 496, 508, 528, 543, 546, 550, 554, 563, 576, 589, 593, 620

Material vs. Other Imbalances, Material Sacrifice, 4, 7, 9, 18, 19, 28, 57, 119, 129, 135, 136, 137, 138, 139, 140, 141, 142, 143, 144, 145, 146, 147, 148, 149, 151, 153, 154, 155, 158, 159, 182, 185, 197, 198, 200, 225, 245, 256, 257, 295, 296, 303, 343, 347, 419, 464, 479, 486, 489, 491, 492, 495, 496, 497, 517, 524, 538, 554, 563, 584, 593, 608

Minor Pieces

Bishops

Active Bishop, 40, 43, 54, 55, 56, 57, 58, 60, 74, 82, 137, 283, 320, 415, 431, 471, 494, 534, 576

Entombed Bishop, 62, 63, 444

Get the Bishop Outside the Pawn Chain, 44, 54, 61, 65, 66, 67, 68, 74, 304, 324, 450

Good Bishop, 54, 60, 74, 138, 323

Inactive Bishop, 14, 54, 56, 61, 62, 68, 74, 79, 185, 253, 323, 434, 471

Tall Pawn, Bad Bishop, 44, 54, 55, 62, 63, 64, 65, 66, 68, 74, 75, 88, 96, 99, 193, 251, 304, 309, 323, 394, 414, 433, 447, 450, 452, 461, 463, 471, 478, 523, 524, 568, 574, 595, 597

Two Bishops, Bishop Pair, 37, 54, 78, 79, 83, 84, 86, 87, 93, 102, 103, 104, 153, 180, 188, 189, 190, 257, 283, 286, 294, 313, 410, 411, 414, 421, 422, 432, 434, 438, 442, 455, 457, 462, 464, 467, 469, 480, 484, 486, 496, 506, 545, 555, 566, 567, 575, 576, 598, 600, 604, 606, 617

Useful Bishop, 54, 58, 59, 60, 62, 65, 74, 90, 102, 471

Knights

Anti-Knight Strategy, 43, 90, 93, 102, 314, 464, 472

Entombed Knight, Dominated Knight, Trapped Knight, 45, 46, 47, 90, 91, 92, 102, 431, 432

Octopus, 31, 35, 50, 88, 97, 98, 99, 437, 438, 559

Mixed Minor Pieces

Bishop vs. Knight, 4, 25, 68, 77, 78, 79, 81, 83, 87, 88, 90, 91, 102, 164, 185, 188, 253, 295, 304, 394, 397, 414, 432, 455, 458, 459, 460, 461, 467, 471, 523, 595, 617, 629

Exchanging Pieces, Trading Pieces, Trading Bad Pieces for Good Ones, 13, 14, 66, 74, 80, 83, 90, 95, 102, 193, 229, 231, 234, 323, 324, 348, 370, 432, 452, 460, 462, 471, 475, 477, 480, 484, 485, 506, 564, 574, 594, 595, 626, 628

Miscellaneous

Cat and Mouse, 204, 205, 206, 207, 220, 307, 309, 315, 349, 365, 478, 631

Catapult, 57, 58

Development, 4, 9, 12, 19, 20, 21, 25, 28, 37, 59, 120, 142, 146, 151, 152, 190, 191, 197, 210, 213, 214, 262, 264, 283, 292, 327, 368, 400, 401, 415, 418, 434, 449, 457, 488, 490, 494, 519, 527, 528, 537, 560, 566, 567, 580, 582, 584, 600, 606

Pawns and Their Effect on the Game

Open and Closed Formations

Passed Pawns

Pawns as Fences

Pointing and Cascades

Psychology

Attention to Detail

Man or Mouse

Rooks Need Files and Ranks

Files

Ranks

Weaknesses

General Structure

Pawn Weaknesses

Squares

Targets

Index of Players / Games